The Shaping of German

CW01495019

German identity began to take shape in the late Middle Ages during a period of political weakness and fragmentation for the Holy Roman Empire, the monarchy under which most Germans lived. Between the thirteenth and fifteenth centuries, the idea that there existed a single German people, with its own lands, language and character, became increasingly widespread. This book – the first on its subject in any language – poses a challenge to some dominant assumptions of current historical scholarship: that early European nation-making inevitably took place within the developing structures of the institutional state; and that, in the absence of such structural growth, the idea of a German nation was uniquely, radically and fatally retarded. In recounting the formation of German identity in the late Middle Ages, this book offers an important new perspective both on German history and on European nation-making.

LEN SCALES is a lecturer in the Department of History at Durham University. He has published widely both on late medieval German history and on the history of peoples and nations in medieval Europe. He is the editor (with Oliver Zimmer) of *Power and the Nation in European History* (Cambridge, 2005).

The Shaping of
German Identity

Authority and Crisis, 1245–1414

Len Scales

CAMBRIDGE
UNIVERSITY PRESS

CAMBRIDGE
UNIVERSITY PRESS

University Printing House, Cambridge CB2 8BS, United Kingdom

Cambridge University Press is part of the University of Cambridge.

It furthers the University's mission by disseminating knowledge in the pursuit of education, learning and research at the highest international levels of excellence.

www.cambridge.org
Information on this title: www.cambridge.org/9781107460348

© Len Scales 2012

First published 2012
First paperback edition 2015

A catalogue record for this publication is available from the British Library

Library of Congress Cataloguing in Publication data
Scales, Len, 1961–
    The shaping of German identity : authority and crisis,
    1245–1414 / Len Scales.
        p.   cm.
    Includes bibliographical references and index.
    ISBN 978-0-521-57333-7 (hardback)
    1. National characteristics, German–History–To 1500.
    2. Nationalism–Germany–History–To 1500.   3. Political culture–
    Germany–History–To 1500.   4. Monarchy–Germany–History–
    To 1500.   5. Crises–Germany–History–To 1500.
    6. Germany–Politics and government–1273–1517.
    7. Germany–History–1273–1517.   8. Germany–Relations–
    Holy Roman Empire.   9. Holy Roman Empire–Relations–Germany.
    I. Title.
    DD76.S33 2012
    943′.02–dc23
    2012000309

ISBN 978-0-521-57333-7 Hardback
ISBN 978-1-107-46034-8 Paperback

To Dorothea, Millie and Julian
For so much

Contents

Maps

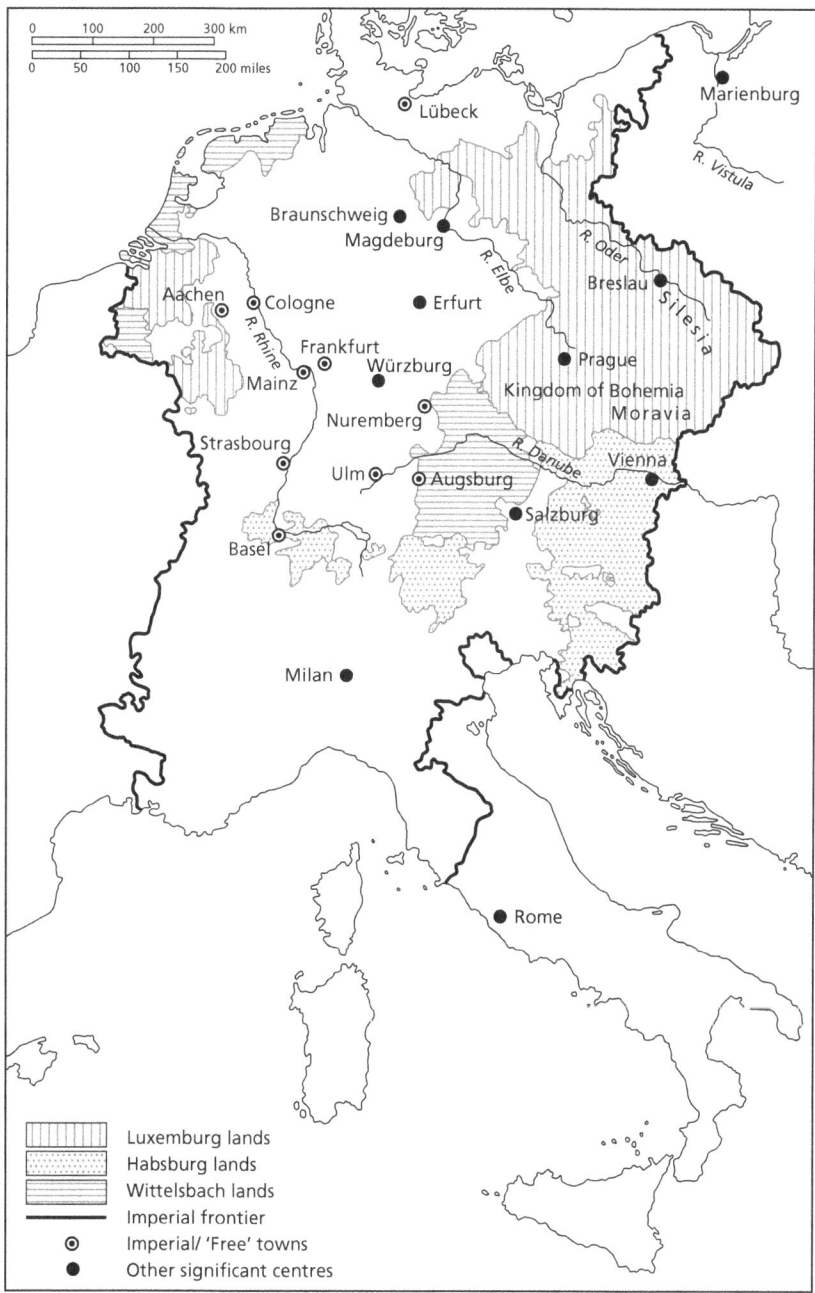

Map 1 The Empire in the time of Charles IV (*c.* 1378).

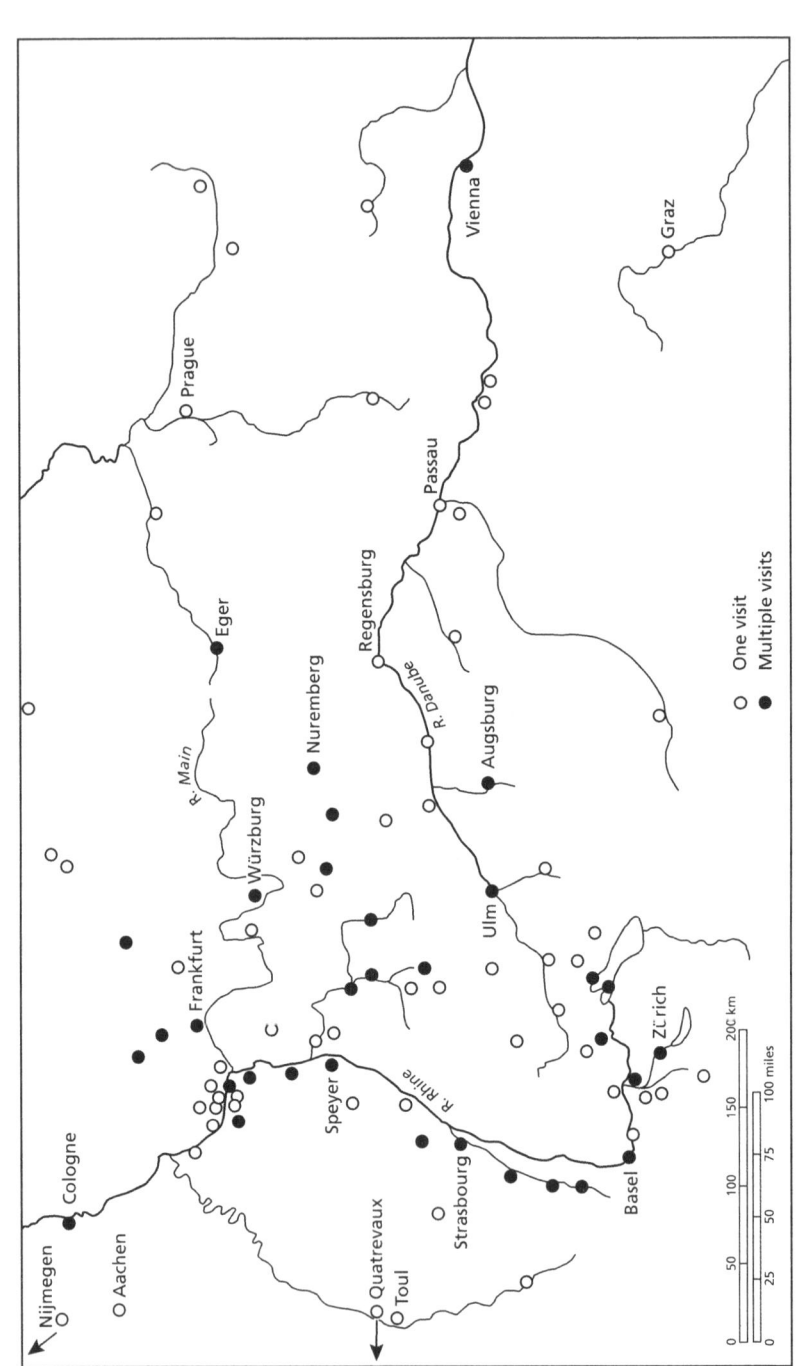

Map 2 Albert I (1298–1308): places of stay.

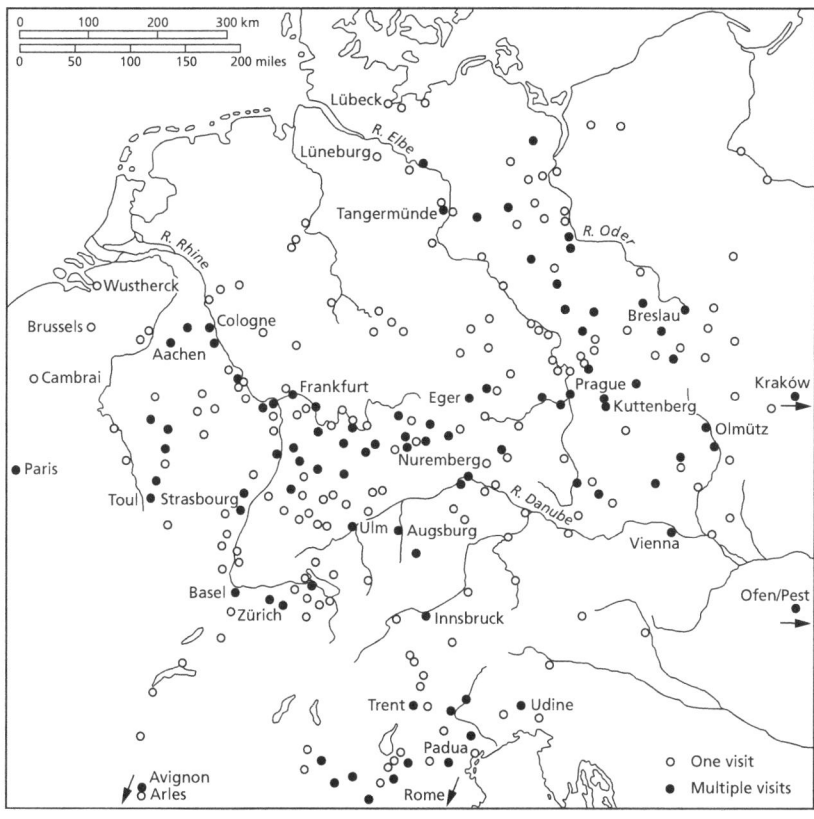

Map 3 Charles IV (1346–78): places of stay.

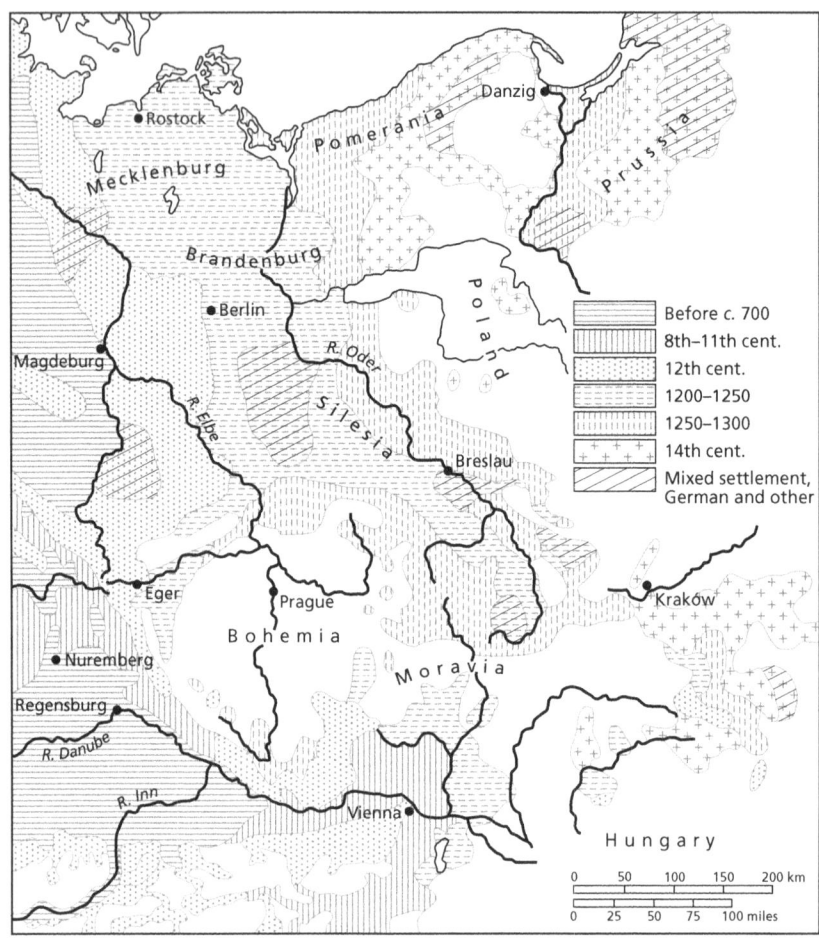

Map 4 German rural settlement in east-central Europe.

Acknowledgements

This book goes back a long way, and so do its debts. In my parents, Leonard and Edna Scales, I had the best of friends and allies, unwavering in their loyalty and support. Chris Young cannot evade a share of responsibility for turning me away from gainful employment and towards the pursuit of remote periods of history. Without my teachers at the University of Manchester the present book would have been literally unthinkable. My greatest Manchester debts are to Jeff Denton and John Breuilly, both of whom in their different ways challenged me to think seriously about the questions which the following chapters attempt to explore. Jeff also guided to completion the undergraduate and doctoral dissertations which gave me my first grounding in late medieval German history.

In Sheffield, the Friday Seminar proved seminal, particularly for the all-important broader contexts: thanks, therefore, to Bill Aird, Tim Cooper, David Roffe, Vanessa Toulmin and Alex Woolf. Colleagues and students, past and present, have made the Durham University History Department an enormously fruitful and stimulating place to be. The Department as a whole has been unfailingly supportive, not least in allowing me to take leave from teaching and in helping to fund repeated research visits to Germany. For advice and encouragement I am particularly grateful to Jo Fox, Ranald Michie, Philip Williamson and Justin Willis. I have learned a great deal from Durham conversations with Geoff Carter, Robin Frame, Giles Gasper, Chris Jones, Andy King, Sarah Layfield, Christian Liddy, Margaret Harvey, Ben Pope, Michael Prestwich, David Rollason and Oliver Zimmer. In addition Robin, Michael and Oliver each commented on portions of the book in draft. Special thanks must go to the Durham undergraduates who took my second-year course on 'Gothic Germany 1250–1520', for encouraging me to take a broad view of late medieval German history and to attempt to explain why the subject might matter at all.

Robert Lerner, Jürgen Miethke, Robert Swanson and Michael Wilks have all, at various times, generously shared their expertise on matters specific or more general. For advice on cartographic representations of medieval Germany I am indebted to Paul Harvey. Martin Kaufhold allowed me to test out my ideas in the very stimulating atmosphere of his research colloquium in Augsburg. For sharing with me their own work, as well as for ideas and stimulus more generally, I am grateful to Michail Bojcov, Erik Spindler, John Watts and Björn Weiler. I owe a particular debt to Andrea Ruddick for generously allowing me to read portions of her forthcoming work on late medieval English identity.

At an earlier stage in this project, I benefited from research leave funded by the Arts and Humanities Research Board. At Cambridge, Liz Friend-Smith has been an ideal editor, whose patience, seemingly inexhaustible, has at times been sorely tested. Jonathan Shepard has been not only an insightful reader of the developing manuscript but an unflagging source of encouragement and judicious advice and a staunch ally throughout. Among the many libraries from whose resources and support I have benefited, special mention should go to that of the Historisches Seminar of the University of Cologne, a familiar and congenial workplace during research stays in Germany. The present book was originally intended as a contribution to the 'Cambridge Studies in Medieval Life and Thought' series. However, during the course of research and writing, it expanded well beyond its original thematic focus, which was solely concerned with late medieval Germany. I am therefore especially grateful to the 'Life and Thought' series editors for their understanding and generosity in agreeing to release the book for stand-alone publication.

Members of the Scheibe family have been unfailing in their kindness and hospitality to a wandering scholar with a perpetually unfinished book in his rucksack. Friedrich Carl and Christa in Engelskirchen, Katharina and Tina have offered much more than just a place to stay. At home, Seren has provided broader perspectives of her own. My greatest debt is to the book's dedicatees. 'Couldn't have done it without you' doesn't say the half of it.

Abbreviations

ADB	*Allgemeine Deutsche Biographie* (Leipzig: Duncker & Humblot, 1875–1912)
AHR	*American Historical Review*
AKuG	*Archiv für Kulturgeschichte*
BdtLg	*Blätter für deutsche Landesgeschichte*
CdtS	*Die Chroniken der deutschen Städte*
DA	*Deutsches Archiv für Erforschung des Mittelalters*
DGOE	Deutsche Geschichte im Osten Europas
EHR	*English Historical Review*
EMC	*The Encyclopedia of the Medieval Chronicle*, ed. G. Dunphy, 2 vols. (Leiden and Boston: Brill, 2010)
Ergbd	Ergänzungsband
Fs	Festschrift
GWU	*Geschichte in Wissenschaft und Unterricht*
HJb	*Historisches Jahrbuch der Görres-Gesellschaft*
HUB	*Hansisches Urkundenbuch*
HZ	*Historische Zeitschrift*
JbfL	*Jahrbuch für fränkische Landesforschung*
JbwdLg	*Jahrbuch für westdeutsche Landesgeschichte*
LMA	*Lexikon des Mittelalters* (Munich and Zurich: Artemis, 1980 1999)
MGC	*MGH Constitutiones et Acta Publica Imperatorum et Regum*
MGDip	*MGH Diplomata regum et imperatorum Germaniae*
MGDtChron	*MGH Deutsche Chroniken*
MGFiGa	*MGH Fontes iuris Germanici antiqui*
MGH	*Monumenta Germaniae Historica*
MGS	*MGH Scriptores*
MGSrG	*MGH Scriptores rerum Germanicarum*
MG Staatsschriften	*MGH Staatsschriften des späteren Mittelalters*

MIöG	*Mitteilungen des Instituts für österreichische Geschichtsforschung*
NCMH	*The New Cambridge Medieval History*
NDB	*Neue Deutsche Biographie* (Berlin: Duncker & Humblot, 1953–)
NF	Neue Folge
NS	Nova Series, New Series
Originalurkunden	*Corpus der altdeutschen Originalurkunden bis zum Jahr 1300*
P&P	*Past & Present*
RGA	*Reallexikon der Germanischen Altertumskunde*, ed. J. Hoops (Berlin and New York: De Gruyter, 1978–2008)
Rh	*Revue historique*
RhVjbl	*Rheinische Vierteljahresblätter*
RS	*Rolls Series*
RTA	*Deutsche Reichstagsakten*
Strassburg UB	*Urkundenbuch der Stadt Strassburg*
TRHS	*Transactions of the Royal Historical Society*
VL	*Die deutsche Literatur des Mittelalters: Verfasserlexikon*, 2nd edn, ed. K. Ruh (Berlin and New York: De Gruyter, 1978–2008)
VuF	Vorträge und Forschungen
ZbLg	*Zeitschrift für bayerische Landesgeschichte*
ZGORh	*Zeitschrift für die Geschichte des Oberrheins*
ZhF	*Zeitschrift für historische Forschung*
ZSSRg (GA)	*Zeitschrift der Savigny-Stiftung für Rechtsgeschichte: Germanische Abteilung*

Introduction: German questions

Long journey

When Heinrich August Winkler celebrated his seventieth birthday in December 2008, the occasion was prominently marked in the German quality press. Public honours seemed only fitting. Had not the distinguished chronicler of modern Germany (the Treitschke of the Berlin Republic, teased *Die Welt*) traced the final and wholesome resolution of the German question itself? Winkler's epic German history, *Der lange Weg nach Westen*, which had appeared in two volumes eight years before, was a 'Geschichte mit Happy End': in consequence of the events of 1989–90 'the specifically German element' in history had receded.[1] Since that epochal moment, the problems facing Germany had become merely those which faced all advanced democracies. The time seemed ripe for bold historical judgements. The normalisation of Germany, and specifically German nationhood, stood out as one of the principal European attainments of the early twenty-first century. Winkler's message appeared to find warm popular affirmation in the black-red-gold *Partyotismus* of the 2006 football World Cup on German soil. Germans, secure within their reassuringly 'post-classical' nation state, could now at last enjoy being German without any need for their neighbours to quake in their boots.[2] Or as an English commentator would put it, in a darker mood for more uncertain times at the decade's end, Europe's erstwhile scourges had settled down to become citizens of Greater Switzerland.[3] The German *Sonderweg*, as Winkler had argued, was at an end.[4]

---

[1] *Die Welt*, 8 December 2008; *Die Zeit*, 19 December 2008. Winkler, *Der lange Weg*, 2 vols.
[2] For post-1990 Germany as a 'post-classical' nation state, see Winkler, *Germany*, vol. I, p. 2.
[3] T. Garton Ash in *The Guardian*, 30 September 2009.
[4] Winkler, *Germany*, vol. II, p. 588.

1

The closing of historical questions calls attention to their purported origins. Winkler, like so many before him, embarked on his long German journey in the Middle Ages. Likewise hallowed by long tradition was his identification of the Holy Roman Empire as the factor which in Germany had thwarted the nation-state-making processes traceable in the western kingdoms of England and France.[5] One of Winkler's missing components – a 'state' to compare with the western monarchies – does indeed seem lacking in Germany, where the processes of institutionalisation and centralisation already visible in the western realms by the thirteenth century had made little comparable progress.[6] What, though, of the German 'nation'?

According to some influential views, looking for nations anywhere in Europe in the Middle Ages, or for a long time thereafter, is a fool's errand. Nations as they are known to the modern world, nations justified by systematic and hegemonic ideology (national*ism*), nations as platforms for mass mobilisation and motors of political change: these are rarely or never to be found in Europe before the onset of industrialisation.[7] But modern nations, others would insist, are not the only nations. Medievalists have long pointed to abundant evidence to show that medieval Europeans were already conceiving of their world as divided into ethnic groups which were also units of politics – and investing their own with sentiments of affection and loyalty. That the social base of these medieval nations was markedly smaller than their modern successors is undeniably true, but, many would contend, that fact need not invalidate their study. The beliefs of relatively small groups can matter too.[8] And in any case, particularly by the later Middle Ages, the public for ideas invoking common allegiance and ethnicity may well have been larger and more socially diverse than often supposed.[9] From Ireland to Poland, from Iceland to Iberia, therefore, medievalists continue to study peoples and nations and to insist on their historical importance. Indeed, by the start of the twenty-first century the study

---

[5] Ibid., vol. I, p. 4. The argument has a distinguished pedigree, rooted in the patriotic medievalism of the nineteenth century (below, Ch. 1, pp. 19–25). Modern scholars who have sought to revive it include Pleßner, *Die verspätete Nation*, pp. 52–64, and Elias, *The Germans*, esp. pp. 317–21. Winkler's ascription of such a central explanatory role to the *Reichsidee* has not escaped criticism: see the review by J.J. Sheehan in *German History* 19 (2001), pp. 619–21.

[6] Medieval 'state-building' and its modern historiography are discussed below, Ch. 2.

[7] For the contending historiographies of the nation, see below, Ch. 1, pp. 40–50; for the eighteenth century as turning point, Smith, 'National identities', p. 37.

[8] Argued in H. Münkler, 'Einleitung', in Münkler, Grünberger and Mayer, *Nationenbildung*, p. 27.

[9] For the communicating of nations, medieval and post-medieval, and the extent of their publics, see below, Ch. 3, pp. 98–9.

of pre-modern nationhood had attained an unprecedented scholarly vogue.[10]

German medievalists were once avid in pursuit of the origins of their own people; indeed, in the study of medieval peoples and nations, Germans were pioneers.[11] Much more commonly, however, German scholars of the nineteenth and early twentieth centuries simply took as axiomatic the existence of a 'national' spirit infusing the thought and feelings and motivating the actions of their remote forebears. A nationalistic *Deutsches Mittelalter* was conjured into being, to serve contemporary national ends. At its heart was placed the ('German') *Kaiserzeit*: the long age of imperial glory and intermittent and mounting tragedy which began with the accession of the Ottonian dynasty in the tenth century and ended in the thirteenth with the downfall of the Hohenstaufen. This deeply politicised vision of a German past at once glorious and portentous was swept away by the cataclysm of 1945.[12] A further consequence of that event, however, was to cast a lingering shadow of unease over the study of pre-modern German nationhood as such.[13] While never altogether abandoned, the subject became increasingly unfashionable in the post-war era. On one central issue, moreover, a consensus now emerged: any medieval 'German nation' which may have existed was of an altogether more limited, precarious and problematic character than those to be found among the Germans' neighbours, particularly in the west. Here, it now seemed clear, was no space for ethnocentric boasting, medieval or contemporary, but for a sober recognition of things unachieved. German nationhood was set back in the Middle Ages; hence Winkler's long road to its ultimate attainment.

This book adopts a perspective different both from the German-nationalist scholarship of the nineteenth and twentieth centuries and from the generally negative visions of more recent studies. It argues that the evidence for the emergence of ideas of common German identity in the Middle Ages, while in some respects different in character from what is found in other European realms, is not obviously less substantial. It also contends, however, that references to the existence of a single German people, to its purported character and defining features, its

---

[10] The range of themes and approaches is surveyed in Hoppenbrouwers, *Medieval Peoples*.

[11] Fully discussed below, Ch. 1, pp. 16–25.

[12] Its character and obliteration are traced by Althoff, 'Das Mittelalterbild'. A language of celebratory and unreflective *Deutschtum* nevertheless long outlasted the war among survivors of the older generation: Moraw, 'Kontinuität', pp. 131–2.

[13] Discernible, e.g., in the comments of Johanek, 'Zu neuen Ufern?', pp. 146–8, 152, discussing the Marburg *Nationes* project, and its links with earlier German themes and approaches.

history, political affairs and relationships with other peoples, all multiply in the period after the *ending* of the medieval *Kaiserzeit*. It was in the troubled period which commenced with the fall of the Hohenstaufen that inhabitants of the broad territories of German speech in northern continental Europe began, in growing numbers and with growing conviction, to perceive themselves *as* German. Now, when some (if still only a small minority) contemplated the state of the imperial monarchy, the events of their time, or their own environment or experiences, their conceptual vocabulary and standards of judgement were increasingly ethnic ones. Between the thirteenth and the fifteenth centuries Germans – or rather, we must keep on saying, some Germans, under some circumstances – discovered increasingly complex, varied and meaningful ways of *being* German. What they came to believe about themselves (and about their neighbours) and the conclusions which they drew from such beliefs were to become matters of much significance and controversy in the age of humanism and reform at the end of the Middle Ages.

The bounds of the present book are set by the deposition of the Hohenstaufen emperor Frederick II by an ecclesiastical assembly at Lyon in 1245 and by the opening of the Council of Constance in 1414, under imperial auspices, to heal a schismatic Church. Much of the thematic unity of the intervening period comes from the troubles and periodic crises which faced the imperial monarchy: its divisions, its precipitate changes of ruler and shifts in geographical focus, its dwindling revenues and resources, and its failure to develop durable institutions. Not least among the apparent paradoxes of the period is therefore that, while it begins with an emperor's condemnation at an ecclesiastical council under the pope, it ends with the ruler of the Empire sitting enthroned in church as arrangements are made to set aside contending pontiffs.[14] As we shall see, even (or especially) in crisis, the imperial monarchy is rich in seeming paradoxes. However, it will also be necessary fairly regularly to step beyond the book's terminal dates, looking both forward and, particularly, backward. Assessing the role of an institution which claimed the heritage of the Roman Caesars cannot set off from a standing start in the time of the last Staufer. Examining social and cultural developments in and beyond the German lands will also demand at times a wider chronological stage.

---

[14] For the role of Sigismund of Luxemburg at Constance, see below, Ch. 5, p. 228. In what follows, 'Empire', when capitalised and without a proper adjective, refers always to the medieval western Empire.

Very seldom has German scholarship looked closely at the development of German identity between the end of the Staufer and the time of the Councils. The most salient studies in the field date from the 1930s.[15] Even the great upsurge of interest in the late Middle Ages which took place in the German universities in the closing decades of the twentieth century was directed overwhelmingly at different themes and questions.[16] This is the first book-length study of its subject in any language. Yet the proliferation of a sense of shared Germanness in a period thus marked by crises of monarchy and political decentralisation is a phenomenon which calls out for explanation. The course of medieval European nation-making, after all, continues to be understood as marching in step with the growth of royal bureaucracies and the extension of the theoretical claims and material powers of their monarchical heads: with early 'states' come the first 'nations'. To trace the development of ideas of common peoplehood in lands where monarchical power was small, and its institutionalised rule limited or even contracting, is thus to place in question a key element in dominant accounts of European modernisation. Other studies have already proposed a partial decoupling of the pre-modern nation from emergent state structures.[17] The present book, however, goes further, arguing for the formative role of crisis, doubt, insecurity and perceived decline as early nation-making elements.[18]

It will therefore be important above all to determine how much substance ideas of common German identity actually possessed. Here, a broad perspective is required: one which pays regard to the great extent and variety and the poly-centric political character of the German lands themselves. For Germany, it will not be possible to limit investigation to images and symbols disseminated from just a single dominant ideological centre, as no such centre existed.[19] Speaking of notions or images of German identity, moreover, raises many further questions. Of what did these consist? Who made, propagated and received them? How were they spread? On what sources, what authorities, did they

---

[15] Notably, the work of Hermann Heimpel: see below, Ch. 1, pp. 33–6.

[16] For these developments, see Moraw, 'Kontinuität', pp. 134–7.

[17] Thus H. Münkler, 'Einleitung', in Münkler, Grünberger and Mayer, *Nationenbildung*, esp. pp. 13–14.

[18] The role of crisis in identity-formation has been relatively little studied by historians of pre-modern Europe. Problems and approaches are discussed in Meyer and Dartmann, 'Einleitung'. The ethnogenetic effects of political crisis and failure in one very particular medieval context are considered by Page, *Being Byzantine*, esp. pp. 6–7, 17–18, and Ch. 8.

[19] Essentially the approach taken to late medieval French identity in the influential study by Beaune, *The Birth*.

draw? What modes of thinking did they legitimise, what (if any) obligations did they enjoin, and how clearly and accessibly were their messages conveyed? What constitutional principles did they invoke and what political claims did they stake? Did a general consensus prevail, or were different, or even contradictory, constructions of Germanness available? And if the latter, how did people choose between contending versions? How were Germans' assessments of themselves affected by the ways in which they were described and judged by others? How did their self-identifications relate to their own characterisations of their neighbours? How did late medieval people reconcile being 'German' with being Bavarian, or Saxon, or Frankish – or with being a cleric from Cologne, a merchant resident in Stockholm, or a courtier serving the king of Bohemia?

In particular, it will be necessary to ask – why then? Why is such abundant and varied evidence for German identity – or better, identities – encountered in the late Middle Ages, a time of the Empire's relative weakness, when comparatively so much less survives from the high medieval *Kaiserzeit*, when emperors appeared at times to bestride the European stage? Answering this question means examining the working in Germany of those political and governmental structures, focused on the monarchy, which are so often deemed central to medieval nation-making, and assessing the place of the Empire in the late medieval German lands. But it also demands that account be taken of a much wider range of developments in social, economic and cultural life within (and indeed, particularly at the eastern margins, beyond) the German lands, in a period which in many spheres witnessed hitherto-unknown forms and levels of dynamism and creativity.

To investigate these matters, a wide and diverse range of evidence has been drawn upon, from a period which brought both a rich proliferation of genres and a remarkable growth in the sheer quantity of texts and artefacts produced. For the first time in Germany, tracts and treatises were now composed, which were concerned not only with the character and condition of the imperial monarchy itself but with its relationship with the Germans and their lands. These require close attention, but so too do the numerous and diverse chronicles and annals, by now being compiled both in Latin and in the vernacular, from the German lands. Vernacular legal manuals, assembled particularly in the thirteenth century, but very widely copied and disseminated throughout the period, are another characteristic genre, from which much is to be gleaned. Governmental and administrative documents expanded massively in number, with even the imperial chancery showing a significant absolute increase in output, and with the German vernacular once again becoming entrenched alongside Latin. Something of this profusion must also be sampled, and attention given to the content not only of imperial documents but also of an array of pragmatic writings, both more and less formal in character, produced by princes, towns, nobles and others. Yet the net must be cast wider still if justice is to be done to a period notably prolific in vernacular writings, within a remarkable range of genres. Invocations of varied facets of Germanness are thus to be encountered, fleetingly or more fully, in courtly romances and epics, in political songs and popular rhymes, and in encyclopaedic, didactic, moralising and devotional works. Writings of all these types therefore also find a place in what follows. So too does a diverse assortment of artefacts and visual representations, ranging from buildings and monuments to drawn and painted images, coins and seals. Taking some account of non-textual media (which also include rituals and public spectacles) is particularly important when surveying the mental landscapes of an era so much preoccupied – in Germany, no less than elsewhere – with image-making and political communication.

Yet the present book is also, on a subsidiary level, inescapably concerned throughout with *modern* German identities, and with the shifting self-images which modern Germans have sought – and more lately chosen not to seek – in the Middle Ages. Only by understanding why some nineteenth- and twentieth-century Germans read the early evidence for German identity as they did does it become possible to judge it afresh. The author is untypical among writers in the field in not himself being German; and most of what follows was written from a vantage point in the north-east of England. None of that, of course, renders him an objective witness, or constitutes assurance that he has not merely fashioned a new distorting mirror with its own, different, distortions. Whether he has or not, and if so what corrections should apply, others must judge.

Our route therefore proceeds broadly from modernity to the late Middle Ages, and to an ever-closer engagement with the medieval evidence – though rarely will we be able to leave modernity behind us altogether. Chapter 1 is concerned with what modern Germans made of the medieval German nation, what it has meant to them, and how and why its importance has changed. Chapter 2 examines the state-centred paradigm of nation-making which has proved so influential among medievalists generally, and assesses the extent and character of formal political structures in Germany. In Chapter 3 an attempt is made to rethink the role of power and government in the formation of collective identities by investigating the capacity of the German lands to function as a stage for political communications. With the next three chapters, the focus moves from structures and paradigms to late medieval concepts and ideas. Chapter 4 considers how far Germany was understood in this period as a discrete political community, while Chapter 5 reviews the significance of the imperial idea itself as a source for late medieval identities. In Chapter 6, the relationship between imperial doctrines and ideas of a specifically German political role is scrutinised. The last five chapters look more closely at the content of late medieval German identity. Chapter 7 asks whether notions of a common past were really as insubstantial in Germany as is often alleged. Chapters 8 and 9 examine the construction of the Germans as a people in relation to other, neighbouring peoples, respectively in the south and west and in the north and east. Chapters 10 and 11 look more closely at some of the components of late medieval Germanness: the spatial construction of 'Germany', the names and concepts available to describe a German community, and the idea of the Germans as a people defined by law and by common language. Finally, consideration is given to the relationship between German identity and other, more geographically limited affinities within a strongly regionalised, late medieval landscape.

Concepts, terms, names

'See, I have this day set thee over the nations [*gentes*] and over the kingdoms [*regna*]', God tells the prophet Jeremiah.[20] Literate people in the Middle Ages – and the non-literate too, when they listened or looked – found a rich and insistent language of peoplehood enshrined within the Bible itself.[21] Thinking of an ethnically ordered world came naturally to them. Peoples were fundamental: there were *gentes* before ever there were social ranks, explained the treatise-writer Alexander von Roes.[22] No less natural was to distinguish (indeed, discriminate) between different peoples, because that was what God himself was seen to do. A modest degree of Latin learning granted access to the ethnographic lore of Graeco-Roman antiquity. Fortified with this, the medieval reader was able to explain even more cogently what set different peoples apart from one another, why they looked and acted as they did and why some would conquer and others be subjugated.[23]

---

[20] Jeremiah 1:10.
[21] For a biblically derived language of nationhood in late medieval England, see Ruddick, 'National sentiment'.
[22] Alexander von Roes, *Noticia seculi*, cap. 15, ed. Grundmann and Heimpel, p. 161.
[23] See below, Ch. 8, esp. pp. 356–60.

Nor was it only the Latinate whose cultural world was marked out in ethnic colours. Anyone experiencing, as text or oral performance, vernacular epic poetry (and, by the late Middle Ages, prose) might find themselves drawn into landscapes of contending peoples. The colourful multi-ethnic throng, of knights *von vil maniger sprâche*, which rides out to greet Kriemhild when she comes to Etzel's court in the *Nibelungenlied* is just one vivid encapsulation of a characteristic mode of thought.[24] Medieval people similarly encountered a world of ethnic divisions when they read chronicles of the past, or of their own times, or listened to such chronicles being read to them. The same vision of a richly and diversely peopled world was also to be discovered in devotional writings. A princely court thronged with 'Hungarians and Russians, Saxons and Prussians' (not to mention knights 'from all the German lands') thus furnishes a natural backdrop for the life of St Elizabeth of Thuringia (d. 1231), in a hagiographic account in German verse.[25] Ethnic divisions, it was widely maintained, were both fundamental and immediately recognisable.

They were not, of course, the only distinctions that mattered. Indeed, they would certainly not have been the ones that mattered most to the majority of people in their daily lives. Nevertheless, the idea of belonging to an extended community of history, culture and descent was a significant co-ordinate, alongside others, on many people's maps of selfhood. Such notions were, of course, constructs – fictions, if we will – supplying no objective explanation for the affinities and divisions which medieval people imagined and experienced. But they could prove to be powerfully compelling constructs nevertheless, resting upon venerable authorities and often drawing additional force from the way in which they appeared to underlie and explain contemporary political configurations.[26] Between the twelfth century and the end of the Middle Ages in Europe, peoples and nations became the subject of increasingly widespread and articulate reference within a growing range of genres.[27]

---

[24] *Der Nibelunge Nôt*, ed. Bartsch, vol. I, p. xxii. âventiure, pp. 219–20, str. 1338–40. The *Nibelungenlied* remained influential throughout the late Middle Ages: when fragments are also counted, significantly more manuscripts are known from the fourteenth than the thirteenth century: M. Curschmann, '"Nibelungenlied" und "Klage"', in *VL* 6, cols. 926–69 (here cols. 928, 959–60).

[25] *Das Leben der Heiligen Elisabeth*, ed. Rieger, p. 67, vv. 153–62: 'Man suochte den wiganden / uz allen tuschen landen. / Ungere unde Ruzen, / Sassen unde Pruzen, / Denen mit den Winden / sich liezen ouch da vinden. / Beheime unde Polane, / mit graven di sopane, / dinstherren unde frien vil, / di alle suochten ritter spil.'

[26] For the idea of political communities as the frameworks for peoples, see below, Ch. 2, pp. 56–65.

[27] See the survey by Hoppenbrouwers, *Medieval Peoples* (pp. 26–7, 32, 39–40) for some of the evidence for a growing ethnocentrism in the late Middle Ages.

There was nothing rare or anomalous about their invocation. The lapidary assurance proffered by one authoritative-looking modern handbook, that 'the nation' was a foreign concept to 'the medieval mind', is invalidated by the briefest inspection of the evidence.[28]

To give such ideas expression, there existed a rich and flexible vocabulary in Latin and the vernaculars. Fundamental Latin terms were *gens*, *populus* and *natio*.[29] In German, aspects of the same ideas were captured in *diet*, *liut* and (although with different and more limited significance than later) *volc*, as well as, perhaps most characteristically, *zunge*.[30] The objection is sometimes raised that the medieval vocabulary of peoplehood is not directly translatable into a modern language of race and nation. There were no medieval words for ethnic groups or nations that could not also stand for other kinds of affinity; and there was no such term which has cognates of identical meaning in modern European languages. Yet none of this is either surprising or especially troubling. Medieval writers were generally capable of making their own meanings fairly plain. To do so, they were able to draw upon a rich array of auxiliary terms, which proved suitable for defining, distinguishing and judging ethnic groups and for explaining their relationships with political power and with one another. Of course, they applied and adapted their vocabulary with the same pragmatic and easy-going inconsistency with which most people have employed ethnic terms in most ages and societies.

Historians can claim no such latitude, however. They expect to have to justify their choices of terminology, and understand the importance of clarity in analysis and exposition. Unfortunately, among medievalists in pursuit of the nation, the quest for terminological orderliness has often tended to have an opposite outcome. While a bold minority have felt able to discover even full-blown nationalism in their sources, most have urged more cautious approaches, with some ruling 'nation' itself off-limits for the pre-modern world, and many recoiling from the

---

[28] 'The medieval mind did not think in terms of *nation* and *nationalism*.' Thus the unattributed entry under the heading 'Medieval Nationalism', in Motyl (ed.), *Encyclopedia*, p. 331. The second part of the proposition is defensible; the first is not.

[29] For the broad semantic fields covered by these terms, compare *Mediae Latinitatis Lexicon Minus*, ed. Niermeyer and van de Kieft, pp. 610, 930, 1060–1, with *Dictionary of Medieval Latin*, ed. Latham, pp. 1065–6, 1888, 2348. Their use and interrelationship are explored in Görlich, *Zur Frage*, pp. 75–6, 89, 106–7; Bartlett, 'Medieval and modern concepts'. For *natio*, see also Kahl, 'Einige Beobachtungen'; Nonn, 'Heiliges Römisches Reich', esp. pp. 130–7.

[30] *Mittelhochdeutsches Handwörterbuch*, ed. Lexer, vol. I, pp. 430, 1942–3, vol. III, p. 437. For *zunge*, see below, Ch. 10, p. 481.

historically burdened 'race'.[31] 'Ethnicity' has been variously valued and applied.[32] Yet the pursuit of terminological purism, although driven by a desire for greater clarity, often results in further clouding the issue. The problem here is that sharp distinctions are often demanded between things that were – and are – not in fact sharply distinct at all. That categories such as 'nation', 'people' and 'ethnic group' tend to bleed into one another is a reflection not of our imprecise thinking but of the fluid boundaries of the concepts themselves, particularly in relation to the loosely structured and unevenly documented world of medieval Europe.[33]

In what follows, reference is made to the Germans both as a nation and as an ethnic group – as well as simply a people.[34] The last of these terms matches comfortably a wide range of forms of reference to be encountered in the sources. However, the other two – 'nation' and 'ethnic group' – are each treated here as having a somewhat different centre of gravity, suited to particular applications. 'Nation' is deployed as especially suited to those writings which invoke large imagined communities, and which associate notions of common belonging with political institutions and titles and with the deeds of political actors. It is also particularly applicable where we encounter elements of explicit reflection on the social and political organisation of peoples and when general principles are being invoked. Some constructions of Germanness in the late Middle Ages had a more overtly political character than others, and it is helpful to have available a means of designating these (although, it might be noted, the Latin *natio* itself was not systematically applied with a more political meaning than were its cognates).[35] 'Ethnicity', by contrast, is preferred when discussing those manifestations of collective identity which made less appeal to large, formally

---

[31] For 'nationalism', see: Huizinga, 'Patriotism', p. 117; Post, *Studies*, p. 435; Graus, *Nationenbildung*, p. 16; and for terminology and its problems more broadly: Thomas, *The English*, pp. 8–9; Beaune, *The Birth*, pp. 4–5; Guenée, *States*, pp. 218–19.

[32] For its value (and the non-applicability of 'nation') in an East Roman context – applying the model of Fredrik Barth, but also reacting against the distortions of modern Greek nationalism – see Page, *Being Byzantine*, esp. pp. 11–26. Terms are usefully defined in Amory, *People*, p. xiv.

[33] For the problem of terminology and an attempt to establish general principles, see Connor, 'A nation', esp. pp. 90–1. His distinctions, however, are mainly conceived in order to account for the functioning of modern nationalist movements. Medieval conceptions of nation hardly ever worked in direct opposition to political structures in the way Connor describes.

[34] For some cogent distinctions, see the wide-ranging and very useful survey by Eriksen, *Ethnicity*, esp. Chs. 1–6.

[35] *Natio* was certainly used on occasion to denote a political conception of peoplehood: thus Bartlett, 'Medieval and modern concepts', p. 50. There was no regularity of usage, however.

defined structures, whether material or conceptual.[36] Ethnicity, as we encounter it in our sources, need not be fully articulated, and may be manifested mainly in social practices and rooted primarily in local institutions and privileges.

There have thus been occasions when it has seemed preferable to favour one term over the other. A university-trained pamphleteer, arguing systematically for a political role for the German people, under the imperial monarchy, within a world of peoples is deploying a concept of nation. A German-speaking guild master in a Baltic town, establishing before his peers his entitlement, as a German, to enjoy corporate privileges, is acting as a member of an ethnic group. However, by far the majority of the references to aspects of German selfhood which we will encounter fall between these two poles, and can thus be more flexibly handled. Accurately describing and analysing their content, and establishing their social and political contexts, will generally matter more than particular choices of label.

Several other, related, words are also made use of in what follows. There will be occasional reference to 'race', to denote groups which medieval people conceived of as units of common blood and descent.[37] (That such notions were just as much cultural constructs as were any other medieval 'imagined communities' should be taken as axiomatic.) 'Patriotism' finds occasional application. 'Nationalism', by contrast, as a systematic ideology which, rather than merely naming or describing nations, demands and sanctions their propagation is not used here for the medieval period.[38] However, one term used throughout requires some clarification at the outset, since it is widely and variously employed in recent and current scholarship, often with a weighty appendage of theory: 'identity'.[39] Here its application is fairly straightforward, referring to the idea of belonging to a community, along with the large penumbra of questions and implications which such belonging necessarily invoked.

I have therefore favoured flexibility in choice of terminology and its application, and have not treated the array of terms deployed as being to any special degree problematic. If 'people' or 'nation', for medieval writers and readers, possessed imaginative force fields somewhat differently

---

[36] For its application, see particularly Ch. 9, pp. 424–30.
[37] For a defence of the use of 'race', see Bartlett, 'Medieval and modern concepts', pp. 41–2.
[38] A classic account of its intellectual lineaments is Kedourie, *Nationalism*.
[39] For the application of 'identity' to the Middle Ages, and the problems which this raises, see: Bedos-Rezak, 'Medieval identity'; Meyer and Dartmann, 'Einleitung', esp. pp. 15–17.

configured than their modern counterparts, the same is no less true of 'town', 'law', 'reform' or a host of other terms without which we could say little of substance about the Middle Ages at all. A twenty-first-century, English-language vocabulary perfectly adapted to the present book's subject matter is not available to us. I have endeavoured to make clear from the context what are my own meanings and intentions.

A further question arises: what to call the subjects of the present book? Naturally, in certain respects they were 'Germans'. In precisely what respects, and with what significance, it is the purpose of the following chapters to discover, and the matter must not be prejudged. I have accordingly sought to avoid reifying 'the Germans' unduly through too much unqualified direct reference.[40] With this in mind, I also have recourse to the more tentative 'German-speakers', and similar forms. This should not, however, be taken as implying that common speech was the key defining element in late medieval German identity. Matters were more complex than that, although language (despite the problems with even speaking of a single 'German' tongue at this time) was certainly a strong external identifier of all the people with whom this book is concerned. How far they were 'German' in ways which went beyond language, and how (much) that mattered, remains to be seen. The regions of their habitation I refer to both as 'Germany' and 'the German lands'. To late medieval people – those, at least, with sufficient learning or experience to form a judgement on the matter – the German-speaking centre of northern continental Europe represented *both* a plurality of landscapes and populations *and* (although often nebulously and inconsistently) a unity. I have sought in my own use of language to capture something of that tension.

It should be emphasised that when I state here that 'Germans' thought or believed this or that, all that can usually be said with confidence is that particular writers and, probably although less certainly, their circles of readers (and possibly also hearers) appear to have thought or believed it.[41] Far beyond that it is rarely possible to go with confidence. About the size of such textual and aural communities we can speculate only tentatively. And about the further reach of notions of shared identity, beyond these groups, to encompass larger, more diffuse or obscure audiences, for much of the time we can scarcely do that. In part, my

---

[40] In particular, I have avoided referring to 'German' kings or emperors, although this usage remains common in both German- and English-language historical works. If we are concerned with contemporary mentalities we must recognise that, in official writings but also mostly in more general usage, these were *Roman* monarchs.
[41] For the reception of German vernacular literature, including the importance of aural reception, see Green, *Medieval Listening*, esp. Chs. 4, 8.

argument proceeds by addition, through the sheer accumulation of evidence. Taking account of a more diverse range of sources than has been customary in studies of this kind, including non-textual sources, will also help us here, though it still offers no definitive solution. Much will be gained from examining how ideas worked within society, how they were disseminated and received, and how they functioned within cultures of debate. Nevertheless, establishing the extent and the composition of the late medieval public (or rather, multiple publics) for conceptions of Germanness remains not only one of the most important but also one of the most difficult questions confronted in the pages that follow.

In selecting names for persons and places, I have aimed for a balance between authenticity and accessibility, rather than striving after complete consistency. Personal names for figures of international importance are anglicised. However, I have preferred German forms for the majority of lesser individuals whose cultural milieu and self-conception were predominantly Germanophone. Place names are anglicised where there is a well-established modern form. For regions of ethnically mixed settlement, I have generally adopted the German version (with the modern place name bracketed upon first mention) where German-speakers were predominant in the period with which the book is concerned: Breslau (Wrocław). Where Germans were in a minority, the principle is reversed: Zagreb (Agram). 'Lotharingia' is employed to designate the large historical region of the Empire west of the Rhine, while 'Lorraine' is used for the more limited, mainly French-speaking imperial duchy, centred on Metz and Nancy. German and Latin terms and names are reproduced as they appear in the (mostly published) sources, with no attempt at standardisation.

Even to write of nations and peoples in the Middle Ages is to risk overstating their importance – relative to other medieval bonds and affinities, and relative also to their role in more recent societies. When they appear in medieval sources, it is mostly as ideas and assumptions, only very seldom in the context of calls to social action (which were still more rarely answered), and virtually never as party programmes or systematic, public doctrines of state.[42] The late medieval German nation is in these respects no exception. Nevertheless, its re-evaluation is timely. Its reification and ideological manipulation by earlier scholars and its more recent elision each reflect above all the longings and anxieties of

[42] For a classificatory scheme which attempts to order different kinds of 'nationalism' according to their intensity, see Gorski, 'The mosaic moment', p. 1459. Medieval expressions of national identification would all fall within the lowest of his four categories ('discourses that invoke "the nation"').

modern Germans. But the question of the medieval German nation is not, and cannot be allowed to remain, only a German question, its formulation or neglect reflecting modern national teleologies and susceptibilities. To address it is to engage with the problem of European nation-making as a whole. Late medieval people already had a good deal of their own to say on the subject, and it remains the historian's job to attempt to determine what they might have meant.

1 Modern history: inventing the medieval German nation

Wilhelmine Gothic

2 August 1914 was a fine day for an excursion. But more than the weather had drawn the burghers of the Bavarian capital from their homes. A fateful turn in world events had brought the crowds together on the Odeonplatz, to sing *Die Wacht am Rhein* and *Deutschland über Alles*. A photograph, scrupulously enlarged in a later time, would disclose amid the press the agitated features of a young Adolf Hitler.[1] Meanwhile, a distinguished fellow resident of the future Führer was experiencing the coming of the World War in different, though as it turned out hardly less memorable, surroundings. Family misfortune had cheated Paul Joachimsen, eminent German-Jewish scholar of Renaissance humanism, of the university professorship for which he had seemed destined, casting him up instead in a teaching post at Munich's Wilhelmsgymnasium.[2] That early August Sunday found him in the Alps. This we know, because Joachimsen's experiences on that day inspired a book. *Vom deutschen Volk zum deutschen Staat* was a modest, paper-covered volume, retailing at 1,20 Reichsmarks.[3] It appeared in 1916, in a series published by B.G. Teubner, aimed at presenting the latest advances in learning to the lay reader. It would have fitted neatly into the kit bag of a young recruit, on his way to the Kaiser's war. Perhaps that was the intention: the endpapers advertised further volumes from the same press, with exciting titles like *A Visit to the Saxons at the Front*. Joachimsen's book was more soberly subtitled *A History of German National Consciousness*. But it too was unmistakably a product of its time, aimed at a specifically German public: it was *'our* national consciousness' that the author would trace to its origins.

---

[1] Kershaw, *Hitler*, p. 89.
[2] O. Schottenloher, 'Joachimsen (Joachimsohn), Paul', in *NDB* 10, pp. 441–2 (here p. 441).
[3] Joachimsen, *Vom deutschen Volk*.

His reflections start with a Sunday assembly in an Alpine village square. What Joachimsen claimed he saw in the villagers who gathered there in the shadow of the church was neither wild enthusiasm nor mute passivity, but quiet acceptance that the coming war – on distant frontiers, which few if any among them could have seen – was a war for *Volk* and *Staat* and, for that reason, their war also.[4] Joachimsen's own love of Fatherland was stirred, but also, he recalled, his historical curiosity. How had such durable and widespread bonds to nation and state come to be? His slim book would provide answers. A scrupulous historian, he took care not to suggest that the nation-forming process had been straightforward, or a tale of unmixed glory. But it was certainly lengthy. True, he cautioned the reader, 'in the year 919, and for long thereafter, there was [still] nothing that one could call a political German national consciousness'.[5] Nevertheless, as early as 842, with the swearing (in separate 'German' and 'Romance' versions) of the Strasbourg Oaths, the historian might discern 'the German and French nations beginning to separate'.[6] Here and there the book invoked directly the nationalistic slogans of the day: the ancient Franks, readers were assured, were a *Herrenvolk* who, when they subjected other Germanic peoples to their rule, had 'prevented the land between Rhine and Elbe from becoming Slavic, that is to say, Asiatic'.[7]

Joachimsen was not alone in turning, under the impulse of the World War, to ponder the earliest history of Europe's nations. In 1916 the Catholic medievalist Heinrich Finke took time off from his labours in the records of the late medieval Church to address the anniversary gathering of Freiburg's Wissenschaftliche Gesellschaft on the theme of 'World Imperialism and National Movements in the later Middle Ages'.[8] Germany, Finke remarked indignantly, was currently being traduced by her neighbours as the rejuvenator of a baleful historical legacy of world domination. It was partly to rebuff this calumny that Finke surveyed the history of the European Middle Ages. Far from seeking world rule, he pointed out, the Germans could claim as their epochal achievement (*Großtat*) the liberation of Europe's peoples from its yoke: it was 'the racial energy [*Rassenkraft*] of fresh and youthful Germanic peoples' that once overthrew the dominion of imperial Rome. Consequently, 'the western world has the Germans to thank for its division into nations'.[9] Not, of course, that the western world

---

[4] Ibid., pp. 1–2.   [5] Ibid., p. 17.
[6] Ibid., p. 14.   [7] Ibid., p. 9.
[8] Finke, *Weltimperialismus*. On Finke himself, see J. Spörl, 'Finke, Heinrich', in *NDB* 5, p. 162.
[9] Finke, *Weltimperialismus*, p. 9.

was thankful. Among the evidence which he adduced for the growth of medieval national consciousness was the catalogue of mutual denigration which Europe's peoples had once heaped on each other. It is at this point that Finke's own pressing concerns come into view. Other scholars, among them the distinguished Louvain medievalist Maurice de Wulf, were, we learn, already busy ransacking this ancient storehouse of abuse for propaganda weapons to hurl at contemporary Germany.[10] Despite spinsterishly professing his own inability to match his adversaries in the language of the street, Finke gave as good as he got. Were such persons not aware of what Salimbene or Arnald de Villanova once had to say about the notorious drunkenness of the French? Not that the English were in medieval report any better. And the mere thought of the pomposity (*Aufgeblasenheit*) of Renaissance Italians, who had disdained as barbarians their neighbours in the north, roused the Freiburg professor to a furious barrage of exclamation marks.[11]

The modern reader of Joachimsen's booklet or Finke's address is struck at once by two things. The first is, for their time, the breadth and ambition of their inquiries into the early history of European nationalities, and the solid learning on which they rested. Nowhere else in Europe was work on this subject being undertaken comparable in volume, substance or scope to that which flowed from German pens around the beginning of the twentieth century. In the study of the nation in pre-modern history, German scholarship unquestionably led the field. Indeed, there scarcely yet *was* a field outside the German universities, which had made the investigation of the nation, as a distinct and deep-rooted historical phenomenon, peculiarly their own. But equally inescapable is the truculent partisanship of both pieces. In this respect, too, they indicate a larger phenomenon. Over the course of the nineteenth and the early twentieth century, German scholarship on the pre-modern nation was usually committed, sometimes openly agitational, not uncommonly myopic and wilfully Germanocentric, and at worst a platform for coarse boasting and denigration and the trumpeting of aggressive political claims. For a handful of supposedly serious historians, a path led via the medieval German nation to unapologetic racial supremacism and to modes of argument geared to sustaining policies of genocidal imperialism. If the study of early German nationalities for most of its course kept clear of such nightmare extremes, it less often evaded the snares of heavy-handed instrumentalism, the impulse to yoke complex pasts to specific present ends. Precociousness and intellectual ambition on the one hand; narrowness of vision and

[10] Ibid., pp. 3–4, 37.   [11] Ibid., pp. 37–8, 41.

transparent bias on the other; these were but two sides of the self-same pursuit. Polemic was no mere regrettable pollutant in an otherwise pure stream of learning, but its fountainhead and not infrequently its end. None of this is cause for surprise. The medieval nation was confected, in various forms, to serve the ambitions and assuage the anxieties of modern Germans. Anxieties and ambitions alike centred on the modern German nation and its relationship with political power. The medieval nation belongs squarely to modern German history: such authentically Romanesque or Gothic fragments as its makers found quickly became part of a now crumbling and blackened monument to the political medievalism of the nineteenth and twentieth centuries. To discover whether it was *more* than that, whether, stripped of the sinister Gothick accretions, what remains possesses enough substance to justify serious study, is the objective of this book.

Sonderweg

The medieval German nation, as a subject for learned inquiry and reflection, entered the world with the harbingers of a modern nation already in attendance. 'It was only by embracing the national principle with all its energy, and being embraced by it' that, according to Wilhelm von Giesebrecht, historical scholarship in Germany had 'attained complete liberation as an autonomous field of study.' Giesebrecht, prolific chronicler of the medieval *Kaiserzeit*, was writing in 1859, in the inaugural volume of *Historische Zeitschrift*.[12] Dietrich Schäfer, in a lecture at Jena two decades later, offered a kindred reflection: safeguarding and nourishing the national consciousness was the highest task facing German historians.[13] For some, he added sharply, it was the *only* task. Schäfer did not shirk his own share of the common burden: Germany's medieval rulers had headed 'the bravest and most excellent of the western peoples'.[14] The first half of the nineteenth century brought in Germany the conjunction of three significant movements. The first was the clamour of certain social elements, particularly the educated bourgeoisie, to see their burgeoning sense of nationhood embodied in all-German political institutions. The study of Germany's medieval past was itself given institutional foundations, with the establishment in 1819 of Freiherr

---

[12] Wilhelm von Giesebrecht, 'Die Entwicklung der modernen deutschen Geschichtswissenschaft', *HZ* 1 (1859), quoted in Schulin, *Hermann Heimpel*, p. 18. For the role of nation in German historical writing, see generally Berger, *The Search for Normality*, Ch. 2.
[13] Schäfer, *Deutsches Nationalbewußtsein*, p. 31.
[14] Ibid., p. 10.

vom Stein's Gesellschaft für Deutschlands ältere Geschichtskunde, reinforced by the growing importance of history in the universities. At the same time, German historians started to examine the historical roots of that principle which was laying such visible hold upon the world of their day: the principle of nationality.

It was a significant conjunction, detectable from an early date. Stein's *Monumenta Germaniae Historica* (*MGH*), with its oak-wreathed injunction to 'sacred love of Fatherland', had been founded to gather and safeguard the historical deposit, the dark subsoil of Germanic antiquities from which it was hoped a sense of nationhood might spring anew.[15] Historians received a spur from the poets and dramatists, who had enshrined the Middle Ages at the heart of Romantic myth-making.[16] The process gained urgency from fresh and recent memories of the Napoleonic occupation of Germany, and of the heroic struggle which had driven the foreigner from the native soil. The two decades following the 'Wars of Liberation' brought the publication of a succession of monumental, multi-volume medieval German histories. Friedrich von Raumer's *History of the Hohenstaufen and Their Times* (six volumes, published between 1823 and 1825) was followed in quick order by Stenzel's *History of Germany Under the Franconian Kaisers* (a mere two volumes, in 1827 and 1828), and Luden's *History of the German People*, which attained the year 1237 via twelve volumes.[17] The literate public, its appetite for medieval glories already whetted by the poets, turned out in numbers to buy these monumental slabs of history. Their authors, for their part, were unapologetic about their own patriotic motives, and did not conceal the roots of their histories in the turbulent recent past. Stenzel explained how he had first conceived his work in the time of the French occupation, in order to 'tell the subjugated [German] people how bold and free were [their] forefathers, how they upheld their independence'.[18] What seemed to make the study of the medieval Reich so worthwhile was the proud national spirit on which its glories had manifestly rested: a spirit whose revival was adjudged a prime contemporary desideratum.

These Biedermeier antiquarians did not doubt that their medieval forebears were warmed by the same patriotic flame that burned in their own breasts. Luden recounted vividly how the German princes,

---

[15] For the early history, see Bresslau, *Geschichte*.

[16] For the Romantic tradition of historiography on the medieval Empire, see Leerhoff, ' "Des Reiches Herrlichkeit" '.

[17] Raumer, *Geschichte der Hohenstaufen*; Stenzel, *Geschichte Deutschlands*; Luden, *Geschichte des Teutschen Volkes*.

[18] Stenzel, *Geschichte Deutschlands*, vol. I, p. vii.

returning north from imperial campaigns in Italy, 'shouted loudly for joy, as they set foot on German soil ... and heard the language of their people'.[19] To historians of his generation, it was axiomatic to tell of the achievements of 'German' kings and emperors, who had once reigned over 'Germany', for the sake of the 'Fatherland' and the German *Volk* – all regardless of the mantle of Roman and Christian universalism in which those far-off rulers had by custom enfolded themselves. In truth, how medieval people had actually identified themselves, and what part conceptions of national allegiance might have had in their identification, troubled this generation hardly at all: their spacious volumes certainly found little room to ponder such matters. The medieval German nation was a datum: a basis for historical inquiry, not its object. The root of their thinking is best revealed by the striking chronological concurrence of their histories, which invariably focused on the period between the tenth and thirteenth centuries, when the imperial monarchy had attained the zenith of its powers: no mere *Kaiserzeit*, but a *deutsche Kaiserzeit*. If a nation was a people's collective soul, its natural embodiment the sovereign state, then the nation surely existed most fully in those epochs when the power of rule was most substantial.[20] Giesebrecht, whose work marked the culmination of the Romantic tradition, explained in 1858 that the medieval *Kaiserzeit* was the time 'in which our people, strong in its unity, attained the fullest extent of its powers, not only having mastery over its own destiny, but commanding other peoples also; [a time] in which the German man counted for most in the world, and the German name enjoyed its fullest resonance'.[21] What more was there to say?

The new political climate after mid-century brought changes in the approach taken by some historians to their nation's medieval past.[22] The German nation, as concept and historical phenomenon, now became for the first time a matter for deliberate study. The political upheavals in central Europe during the 1850s and 1860s – Habsburg Austria's humiliation and the relentless rise of Prussia – rendered the destructive and formative power of national sentiment visible as never before. The nation, it now seemed obvious, was more than just an immanent principle infusing human experience; it was a historical force, which might be unlocked and harnessed in specific circumstances by historical actors,

---

[19] Luden, *Geschichte des Teutschen Volkes*, vol. X, p. 119.
[20] For the problem of 'state' in studies of medieval Germany, see below, Ch. 2, pp. 65–8.
[21] Giesebrecht, *Geschichte der deutschen Kaiserzeit*, vol. I, pp. vii–viii.
[22] For new directions in this period, see Leerhoff, ' "Des Reiches Herrlichkeit" ', esp. pp. 281–3.

to bring material, quantifiable change.[23] The scholars who turned their attention to the medieval nation now usually invoked as justification the upheavals being wrought before their eyes by its contemporary counterpart. Giesebrecht, in an early attempt at surveying the history of German collective consciousness, reflected in 1861 that his theme touched 'a burning question in day-to-day politics: the nationalities question'.[24] Not everyone contemplated the changes with enthusiasm: Giesebrecht himself claimed to fear them. Nevertheless, the urgent contemporary importance of the national idea now seemed on its own sufficient to justify exploring its earlier history.[25] It was surely naive to think that a force which manifested itself so dramatically in the present could have had only shallow historical roots.[26]

For many educated Germans, the new political landscape seemed now to clear a way for the longed-for national state. The urgent questions were therefore how the force of history might be harnessed to attain that happy outcome, and what the extent and character of the Germans' new political home should be. In this climate, the national past became a resource to seize: a blueprint for the rival solutions of different parties, a charter for spacious new national claims, and a road map marked with fateful wrong turnings to evade. By 1871, the policies pursued by twelfth-century German emperors had come to seem an appropriate topic for debate in the new Reichstag.[27] It was therefore only natural that the historiographical *cause célèbre* of the age should have centred on the *Kaiserzeit*. The harmful results which, according to the Prussian publicist Heinrich von Sybel, had flown from the entanglements of medieval emperors south of the Alps were contested by the Catholic medievalist Julius Ficker.[28] Inevitably, their divergent readings of Germany's medieval past sustained rival, *kleindeutsch* and *großdeutsch*, conceptions of a national future. The Sybel–Ficker quarrel was mainly concerned with imperial grand policy, and only implicitly and indirectly with medieval nationalities. Nevertheless, the attention which the protagonists gave to the actions and motives of medieval German rulers did now seem to invite a more robust and concrete

---

[23] For the growing importance after mid-century of the theme of power in accounts of Germany's medieval past, see Althoff, 'Die Rezeption', pp. 482–4. It was Ranke and his pupils, who included Giesebrecht, who were instrumental to this change.

[24] Giesebrecht, 'Die Entwicklung', p. 57. The essay originated as a lecture given at Königsberg on 21 March 1861 as part of the birthday celebrations for King Wilhelm I of Prussia.

[25] Schäfer, *Deutsches Nationalbewußtsein*, p. 5.

[26] Schultheiß, *Geschichte des deutschen Nationalgefühles*, p. 4.

[27] Gollwitzer, 'Zur Auffassung', pp. 486–92.

[28] See: Schneider (ed.), *Universalstaat*; Below, *Der deutsche Staat*, vol. I, pp. 353–6.

view of medieval nations, as communities fashioned by human beings, reflecting their decisions and outlooks. The instrumentalisation of the German past for power-political ends only reinforced the growing perception of the German nation as a phenomenon made within and through the historical process, rather than floating above it. It was a historical artefact, with origins and a course of development that could and should be traced. In tracing them, medievalists were at the forefront.[29]

But the multiplication after 1850 of writings about the medieval German nation is not the whole story. Often they were short pieces, written to be heard, particularly on those occasions when the professor was called on to put away his editions and monographs and to tailor his erudition to the tastes of a broader patriotic public. The subject seemed an ideal one for orations on the Kaiser's birthday or the Bismarck celebrations, or for inaugural lectures. Content tended to reflect the occasion, with flatulent, self-congratulatory generalities taking the place of serious engagement with the evidence. Professorial bombast attained new heights in the years after the foundation of the Bismarckian Reich, when audiences were able to learn (had they not suspected already) that the Germans, in their medieval heyday, had rejoiced in 'the proud consciousness of being superior to all other peoples'.[30]

With time, however, the subject attained more substantial foundations. In 1893 Franz Guntram Schultheiß published his *History of German National Sentiment*. Nearly 300 pages long, resting on a thorough scrutiny of the printed sources, it extended from Germanic prehistory to the middle of the thirteenth century.[31] Its author intended it as the first of three volumes, covering the subject exhaustively from the earliest times to his own day. Comprehensive scope was joined to intellectual ambition, announced in his choice of subtitle: *A Historical-Psychological Study*. The work remained a torso, the second and third volumes never appearing. But the monumental design proclaims its own message: here was a subject both free-standing and of prime importance. By the turn of the new century, nationality had established itself as a distinct and, for some, indispensable element in the grand sweep of the German past. Karl Lamprecht's vast,

---

[29] For the centrality of the Middle Ages – and specifically, the *Kaiserzeit* – to programmes and charters for a modern German nation, see Althoff, 'Das Mittelalterbild', pp. 731–2.

[30] Schäfer, *Deutsches Nationalbewußtsein*, p. 12. For German medievalists in the period, see generally Schieffer, 'Weltgeltung'.

[31] Schultheiß, *Geschichte des deutschen Nationalgefühles*.

idiosyncratic *German History*, published in eleven volumes between 1891 and 1902, thus made space for a long prefatory essay on medieval German national consciousness.[32]

The preceding decades had seen perceptions of the subject grow broader, but also more complex and in some ways more troubled. The refashioning of the contemporary German nation around an ascendant Prussia inevitably brought the German east into the medieval frame, offsetting the older focus on the southern and western heartlands of the Reich. At the same time, the overt politicisation of the medieval nation highlighted new topics for discussion: the relations of the Germans with neighbouring peoples in the medieval period; the role of inter-ethnic antipathies and stereotypes in forming identities; and the distinctiveness, capabilities and relative worth of different medieval nations. The stern martial virtues of the Germans, it was now proclaimed, were well attested in the reports of their medieval neighbours.[33] Both the harsh, bellicose public tone of the time and the shifting political horizon were captured in the best-selling history of the Teutonic Order published in 1862 by the Prussian historian and propagandist Heinrich von Treitschke.[34] The 'aggressive strength and haughty, pitiless hardness' which, for Treitschke, the German knights brought to their rule, were recommended as a pattern for Germany's future dealings with the 'anarchic' eastern peoples.[35]

At the same time, new insecurities were clouding the view. Economic pessimism and social tensions in the new Reich fed in some quarters a mood of scepticism about the benefits of modern life itself.[36] In 1887, the sociologist Ferdinand Tönnies contrasted the artificiality and individualism which he thought characteristic of modern societies with the wholesome, organic bonds of community and order to be found in the pre-industrial past.[37] His work was a straw in a wind that was stirring historians too. The remote past became a measure, against which the present might be judged and found wanting. The Middle Ages became, for some, a social ideal, and the nation a repository of anti-modernist virtues. The essence of that 'Germanic superiority' which brought low the Roman Empire lay in the mutual love of the true communities in which the ancient Germans had lived, prevailing over the heartless reciprocity

---

[32] Lamprecht, *Deutsche Geschichte*, vol. I.
[33] Schultheiß, *Geschichte des deutschen Nationalgefühles*, pp. 215–26.
[34] Treitschke, *Ordensland*.
[35] Quoted in Burleigh, 'The knights', pp. 41–2.
[36] For what follows, see: Oexle, 'The Middle Ages', esp. pp. 130–5; Oexle, 'German malaise', esp. pp. 37–8.
[37] Tönnies, *Gemeinschaft*.

of mere citizens in a world empire.[38] Contemporary pressures perhaps also helped to shape the periodisation of the pre-modern nation, in an age in which the social breadth of the public for the national idea was expanding. More often than before, consideration was now extended to the later Middle Ages, as the time when the 'national spirit' first penetrated middling and lower social groups, particularly in the growing towns.[39]

Most attention continued, however, to fall on those earlier periods where the case for German national greatness was most easily made. Some now proclaimed the historic precocity of the Germans among Europe's peoples in attaining 'the sentiment of a unified nationality'.[40] Even the fashion for dyed hair among the ancient Germans seemed to indicate the presence among them of 'a barbarian stage of the national sentiment'.[41] Most writers on the subject felt obliged to begin with at least a gesture towards the ancient *Germani*, even if their common nationhood turned out on closer inspection to be disappointingly 'fragmented'.[42] All evidence was welcome which seemed to lengthen the national pedigree. The *Kaiserzeit*, however, retained its title as the apotheosis of the medieval German nation. The age of 'Barbablanca' and the new Reich turned for inspiration to that of Barbarossa and his *imperium* of implacable Teutonic iron.[43] Their own experience of Bismarckian nation-making, and its triumphal martial accompaniment, had for many educated Germans reinforced a lesson that they had already imbibed from histories of their people's medieval past: that 'the indispensable precondition for a strong national consciousness is national pride'.[44] If a self-conscious German nation was to be found anywhere in the Middle Ages, then surely it was in those centuries when militant pride was most justifiable – and thus, it was assumed, most warmly felt.

Different times, different needs – and a medieval nation (and *Volk*) to match them.[45] After World War I, it was not 'national pride' but national humiliation, resentment and anxieties that provided the spur

---

[38] Dove, *Der Wiedereintritt*, p. 12.
[39] Giesebrecht, 'Die Entwicklung', p. 78; Schäfer, *Deutsche Nationalbewußtsein*, p. 19.
[40] Schäfer, *Deutsches Nationalbewußtsein*, p. 17.
[41] Schultheiß, *Geschichte des deutschen Nationalgefühles*, p. 17.
[42] Giesebrecht, 'Die Entwicklung', p. 61.
[43] See: Seeber, 'Von Barbarossa'; and for nineteenth-century uses of *Reich*, Stolleis, *Heiliges Römisches Reich*, pp. 10–14.
[44] Schäfer, *Deutsches Nationalbewußtsein*, p. 12.
[45] For German medievalists in the interwar years, see generally Oexle, ' "Staat" – "Kultur" – "Volk" '.

for studying pre-modern collective selfhood. As Germany's frontiers contracted, following the debacle of 1918, the geographical limits, methodological bounds and contemporary utility of the medieval
German nation were all extended. Established themes and preoccupa-
tions did not wither, but received a new colouring. Looking back from
1933, the medievalist Erich Maschke reflected, 'perhaps our people was
never so conscious of itself as in recent decades, since the outbreak
of the Great War'.[46] A keener sensitivity to the qualities and consequences of national feeling is certainly detectable in German writings
on the Middle Ages. Studies of the pre-modern nation, hitherto often
materially and intellectually somewhat flimsy, put on weight. Festive
addresses were eclipsed by research monographs and edited volumes of
specialised papers. Raucous partisanship could now rest on deep foundations of learned footnotes.

Two obvious problems confronted historians schooled in the patriotic traditions of the Wilhelmine Reich. First, how should an abased,
disarmed and republican Germany engage with a medieval *Kaiserzeit*
made glorious through the feats of German swords? The honouring
of a medieval emperor in a Kaiser-less age was to form the dramatic
curtain-raiser to Ernst Kantorowicz's sensational biography of the
Hohenstaufen Frederick II.[47] Secondly, how might the Middle Ages
illuminate a Europe in which, as a result of the post-war treaties, substantial groups of Germans dwelt outside the 'bleeding frontiers' of
Germany altogether, within states self-consciously national but not
German?[48] And, most urgently – what resources could the Middle Ages
furnish towards redressing the unhappy plight of the contemporary
German nation? For a conservative, nationalistic professoriate in the
Weimar era, the German Middle Ages became more than just a field for
study, or even a legitimising charter; they were a 'weapon'.[49]

Post-war Germany was a landscape fraught with maps: a place where
political divisions, worlds lost and remade, were laid out on paper to the
public view.[50] Weimar-era school atlases coloured the Hohenstaufen

---

[46] Maschke, *Das Erwachen*, p. 3.
[47] Kantorowicz, *Kaiser Friedrich der Zweite*, 'Vorbemerkung', for the wreath marked 'das
geheime Deutschland' which was to be seen in 1924 adorning Frederick II's tomb in
Palermo. For what is known about this shadowy event, see Ruehl, ' "In this time" ',
p. 187.
[48] The phrase was that of the medievalist Hermann Aubin, writing in 1939: Althoff,
'Die Beurteilung', p. 153.
[49] Oexle, 'German malaise', p. 34.
[50] For World War I as a stimulus to map-making in Germany, see Herb, *Under the
Map*.

Reich boldly in unvaried imperial pink.[51] Contemporary German maps, by contrast, told the stark tale of a Reich fragmented and truncated. For the German-speaking communities who now found themselves citizens of such national states as France, Hungary, Romania, Czechoslovakia and Poland, and for their advocates in Germany and Austria, changed times brought new perspectives: on the relationship between nationality and state power, and on the relations of different nationalities one with another. Meanwhile, the threat which the new political arrangements were felt to pose to the German culture of the minority populations encouraged the systematic study of that culture, with the aim of saving those communities from *Volkstod*.

The 1920s saw the study of pre-modern nationalities set upon new, institutional, foundations. The impulse was not only narrowly political. The founding of historical research institutes was a general feature of the time, and, particularly in Germany, regional or area studies (*Landeskunde, Raumforschung*) were a scholarly vogue.[52] But a sense of urgent cultural threat certainly underlay the new, more collaborative and interdisciplinary approach, which set historians to work beside archaeologists, folklorists, scholars of language and dialect, and specialists in the history of place- and personal names. Official objectives played an unmistakable part: research institutes like the Stiftung für deutsche Volks- und Kulturbodenforschung, established at Leipzig in 1926, enjoyed state funding.[53] By studying the post-Versailles map of power and nationalities in Europe in long-term perspective, researchers aimed ultimately to supply raw materials for its revision. Attention focused on tracing medieval settlement patterns, and the diffusion of social, economic and cultural forms held to be characteristically German, in regions lying outside the contemporary German and Austrian states. Since one aim was to demonstrate the centuries-old habitation and cultural dominance of Germans in these contested zones, medievalists found their expertise in particular demand. The main focus was on the lands of east-central Europe, extending in a broad arc from the Baltic to the Carpathians and the Adriatic: lands which German-speakers had settled in significant though variable numbers during the central and later Middle Ages. A new discipline was born: *Ostforschung*.[54] Its weapons

---

[51] See, e.g., Baldamus, Schwabe and Ambrosius (eds.), *F.W. Putzgers Historischer Schul-Atlas*, pp. 66–7 ('Mittel- und Westeuropa zur Zeit der Staufer'). The map can be contrasted with that of 'Europa nach dem Weltkriege', towards the end of the volume (pp. 142–3).

[52] Oberkrome, *Volksgeschichte*, pp. 28–41; Gerlich, *Geschichtliche Landeskunde*, p. 80.

[53] Burleigh, *Germany Turns Eastwards*, p. 25.

[54] For *Ostforschung*, see: Burleigh, *Germany Turns Eastwards*; Althoff, 'Die Beurteilung'; Schönwälder, *Historiker*, esp. pp. 35–50.

were the card index and historical atlas, its battlegrounds conferences, journals and essay collections. In the Third Reich, its resources were drawn on to plan the resettlement of eastern Europe with Germans, and the eviction, enslavement or mass murder of non-German native populations.

The post-war German minorities, and the institutions established for their study, influenced in several ways approaches to the medieval German nation. They encouraged a concentration on frontier regions, as against the old imperial heartlands, as places where collective selfhood was forged. They focused attention on the formative power of conflict and competition between different nationalities, and on the polemical utterances and ethnic stereotypes through which this conflict was expressed in medieval writings. And they encouraged the study of the ethnic community – the *Volk* – as an autonomous, multi-faceted, cultural and social (and racial) formation, rooted in the soil which it had settled (*Volksboden*).[55]

For proponents of the new *Volksgeschichte*, the people had no necessary or immutable relationship with specific constitutional or political forms: what mattered was its integrity, its survival, and its power and standing relative to other peoples. Discussing German colonial institutions east of the Elbe, Karl Gottfried Hugelmann declared that 'the advance of Germandom [*Deutschtum*] in this region [in the Middle Ages] was far less the result of state power than of higher culture, greater inner strength and superior achievement'.[56] Not the state but the *Volk* was what counted historically.[57] Such perspectives were far from being wholly new. We have observed already how medieval literary clichés on the subject of ethnicity were compiled and recycled during World War I: indeed, their study in Germany was older than that.[58] A violently nationalistic view of the early history of the 'German east' went back to Treitschke. And the danger allegedly facing frontier populations from aggressive neighbours already underlay Fritz Kern's 1910 study of the medieval 'beginnings' of France's historical, anti-German 'expansionist policy'.[59]

The establishment of a firm institutional basis did, however, lend the subject solidity and permanence, as well as binding it more directly to the pursuit of material political goals. The *Ostforscher* who examined

---

[55] See generally Oberkrome, *Volksgeschichte*, esp. pp. 22–5.
[56] Hugelmann, 'Die Rechtsstellung', p. 256.
[57] Melton, 'From folk history', pp. 282–8.
[58] See, e.g., Zimmermann, 'Die Beurteilung'; Remppis, *Die Vorstellungen*.
[59] Kern, *Die Anfänge*.

medieval nationalities brought to their inquiries the spirit of the political activist. They were desk-bound warriors in a centuries-old struggle for survival, which in their own time, they claimed, had entered a critical new phase. In this spirit, the Prague medievalist Heinz Zatschek in 1936 urged the need for historians to determine which nations medieval Germans had viewed as their natural enemies, 'because for the present too this is not without importance'.[60] Erich Maschke insisted that his study of national consciousness on the medieval German–Slav frontier dealt with matters 'that over the centuries have by no means lost their relevance': his chosen topic reflected the historian's responsibility 'towards the fate of our people'.[61] His book was not aimed only at the specialist, but it was exclusively for Germans, and wilfully turned its back on an international learned public.[62] Both scholars actively promoted the nationalist and racist ends of Hitler's Germany: Maschke was a National Socialist and SA man, Zatschek part of the directorate of the shadowy and sinister Reinhard Heydrich Foundation in Nazi-occupied Czechoslovakia.[63]

Medieval Germans were summoned to be activists too. National consciousness was 'awakened' (the term has clear echoes of contemporary agitation) on the frontier, and accolades went to the most wakeful – to those medieval writers displaying what the appointment criteria for academic staff at the new Nazi university in Strasbourg called 'a combative German character'.[64] Commenting on the anti-French theme in late medieval polemical writings, Zatschek noted approvingly that 'what was here said and written to rebuff French distortions of history shows

---

[60] Zatschek, *Das Volksbewußtsein*, p. 52. As late as 1945, Zatschek was offering in Prague a course on 'Reich und Reichsfeinde im frühen und hohen Mittelalter': Hruza, 'Heinz Zatschek', p. 771.

[61] Maschke, *Das Erwachen*, p. 51. For the growth of Maschke's interest in *Volksgeschichte*, and for his view of 'the function of history as a weapon', see Schneider, 'Geschichtswissenschaft', esp. pp. 94–8.

[62] Maschke, *Das Erwachen*, p. 51. The book's opening sentence (p. 3) invokes 'unser Volk'.

[63] For Maschke, see: Schneider, 'Geschichtswissenschaft'; Burleigh, *Germany Turns Eastwards*, pp. 57–8; Schönwälder, *Historiker*, pp. 103–4, 110, 148, 242, 245; for Zatschek and the Reinhard Heydrich Foundation, Hruza, 'Heinz Zatschek', pp. 722–7. Both paid a price for their political engagement – Maschke's, who spent 8 years in a Soviet labour camp following his capture in October 1945, by far the more exacting. Zatschek was barred from returning to a university career after the war, but was able to gain a curatorial post in a Vienna museum, until becoming the subject of anonymous denunciation in 1962. See: Schulze, *Deutsche Geschichtswissenschaft*, p. 26; Hruza, 'Heinz Zatschek', esp. pp. 677–9; Wolf, *Litteris*, p. 418.

[64] Thus the title of Maschke's 1933 book. For Strasbourg, see Schulin, *Hermann Heimpel*, p. 38.

the greatest clarity and the fullest determination'.[65] Medieval writers were praised when they stood up for 'the true, German, past' or bore witness to 'the superiority of the Germans over the other peoples'.[66] Yet the same historians who judged such remarks appropriate in a learned monograph esteemed themselves as pioneers in their discipline.[67] And in a way, that is indeed what they were. The novelty of their approach lay in its detailed attempts at tracing the historical roots of a *self-conscious* sense of Germanness, and supplying a general theory (however crude and self-serving) capable of explaining its origins. Inter-ethnic frontiers were, they argued, the crucial locations, conflict and rivalry the main motors of early collective selfhood. Germans first became aware of their own common identity where they came into regular contact and competition with other peoples, of different collective character. Medieval people knew their neighbours before they knew themselves.[68] It was the 'fanatically exaggerated self-consciousness' of thirteenth-century Poles, their 'hatred' of their culturally more advanced German neighbours, that had rallied these latter in common 'defence'.[69] The first evidence of these fateful processes at work was from the central and later Middle Ages.

The interaction of the personal and the political with new currents in the study of medieval nationalities stands out sharply in the long career of the Austrian legal historian Karl Gottfried Hugelmann, a prolific writer on the medieval German nation during the interwar period. Born in 1879, the son of a high-ranking Habsburg official, Hugelmann witnessed as a mature man the Great War, the peace settlements and the breaking up of the Habsburg empire, in whose nationality laws he was an expert.[70] His historical writings were the work of such time as remained amid a busy career in the law and in the nationalist politics of interwar Austria. Something of the demagogue's tone surfaces in his learned papers, with their taste for bellowing at readers through extended passages of *Sperrdruck*. A champion of *Anschluß*

---

[65] Zatschek, *Das Volksbewußtsein*, p. 80. Among the reviews arguing for the importance of Zatschek's 1936 book was one in the *Völkischer Beobachter*: Hruza, 'Heinz Zatschek', pp. 741–2.

[66] Zatschek, *Das Volksbewußtsein*, pp. 53, 67.

[67] Ibid., p. 1. Zatschek argued that German medievalists were still largely following an agenda established by Giesebrecht. He identified the emergence of a *Volksbewußtsein* as a key historical question which scholars were still unprepared to answer.

[68] Maschke, *Das Erwachen*, p. 49.

[69] Ibid., p. 30.

[70] W. Wegener, 'Hugelmann, Karl', in *NDB* 10, pp. 9–10; Leuschner, 'Karl Gottfried Hugelmann', pp. 483–4. It is perhaps a mark of how far Hugelmann's intellectual stock had fallen by his death that *MIöG*, the principal Austrian medieval history journal, did not accord him an obituary.

with Germany, whose suspected Nazi sympathies earned him a spell in an Austrian concentration camp, his Greater German enthusiasm and admiration for the medieval Empire are no surprise.[71] To his death in 1959 Hugelmann argued, from an increasingly isolated position, that the Reich of the Salians and Staufer had constituted a fully fledged 'German national state'.

Hugelmann's political activism also embraced the nationalities question: matters to which he devoted his professional expertise included the protection of the Transylvanian Germans and the exclusion of Jews from national life.[72] It is therefore unsurprising that medieval interethnic relations, viewed in their legal aspect, formed the subject of his most characteristic scholarly writings.[73] As was usual at the time in studies of this sort, no attempt was made to hide the impulse of contemporary parallels. In an essay of 1927, he began by observing how the 'coerced peace' (*Zwangsfrieden*) of 1918 had manifestly failed to resolve Europe's nationalities conflicts, before moving on to recount how the coexistence of different ethnic groups was (better) managed in medieval law.[74] But to argue his case against the iniquities of his day Hugelmann needed to show that ethnic groups in the Middle Ages were, like contemporary ones, self-conscious communities, capable of being ascribed rights and afforded protection in law. A hurdle in his way, he recognised, was the refusal of some social scientists to acknowledge the existence of self-conscious nations in the medieval world. Friedrich Meinecke had written that the nation had only in modern times developed a 'conscious will to self-determination'.[75] This view was 'surely wrong'. Echoing Meinecke, Hugelmann insisted that 'this people, the German people, claimed already in the Middle Ages the right to self-determination'.[76] He proceeded to contrast a wise and just medieval order, under German direction, in which all nationalities lived secure in their legal rights, with a pernicious present-day Europe in which states meddled in the social and cultural life of their populations to the grave harm of (German) minority groups. His case rested on racist

---

[71] For pan-German enthusiasm among Austrian medievalists in the interwar period, see Melton, 'From folk history', pp. 268–9.

[72] On these matters, see Fahlbusch, 'Die "Südostdeutsche Forschungsgemeinschaft"', pp. 251, 254, 261 n. 3.

[73] Hugelmann, 'Studien zum Recht'; Hugelmann, 'Mittelalterliches und modernes Nationalitätenproblem'; Hugelmann, 'Die Rechtsstellung der Wenden'.

[74] Hugelmann, 'Studien zum Recht', p. 275 n. 1.

[75] Meinecke, *Weltbürgertum und Nationalstaat: Studien zur Genesis des deutschen Nationalstaates* (1908), quoted in Hugelmann, 'Mittelalterliches und modernes Nationalitätenproblem', p. 734.

[76] Ibid., p. 735.

assumptions similar to those articulated by *Ostforscher* like Maschke:
that Germans had historically shown an innate capacity for fair and
moderate rule over other nationalities that non-German (particularly
Slav and Romance-speaking) peoples manifestly lacked.[77] Driven by
the imperatives of contemporary nationalist politics, Hugelmann did,
however, develop quite a thorough, closely argued comparative analysis
of the treatment of ethnic minorities by medieval and modern governments. To support his argument, that medieval people viewed ethnic
groups as primal components of social life, he marshalled an array of
authorities.[78] Against modernist theorising was pitted the unanswerable
voice of the sources. The unsavoury Hugelmann had struck up what
was destined to become a popular refrain among subsequent generations of medievalists, within Germany and outside.

Among Germans of the Weimar era there were those who longed for
their imperial past to speak to them in the same rousing tones in which
it had addressed their nineteenth-century forebears. Imperialist nostal-
gia was never more fervent than in the years after Versailles.[79] Yet that
past seemed dumb. The Reich was broken; the slumbering Barbarossa
had failed his people in its hour of need. It was while searching for
the elusive voice of that past, for guidance and justification in a dismal
present, that a handful of German medievalists now discovered routes
to a more empathetic, if also more subjective, vision of medieval political sensibilities than had hitherto been known. In a troubled and dis-
contented age, a fresh spirit of patriotic radicalism was abroad among
an emergent, youthful generation of German medievalists.[80] Some were
now ready to denounce as musty irrelevance the source-grubbing posi-
tivism of university professors and demand a new kind of history.[81] The
call was answered in 1927, with the publication of Kantorowicz's life of
the last Hohenstaufen Kaiser. If *Friedrich der Zweite* provoked a storm, it
also fed a hungry public, thus helping to rejuvenate the medieval Reich
as a proper subject for national pride.[82] Kantorowicz sought inspiration
where his patriotic forebears had habitually looked, in the *Kaiserzeit*,

[77] Another scholar of medieval nationalities who took this view was Hermann Heimpel:
Wolf, *Litteris*, p. 254.
[78] Hugelmann, 'Mittelalterliches und modernes Nationalitätenproblem', p. 735.
[79] For the Reich as rallying point for antiliberal, antidemocratic and extreme nationalist
longings in Weimar Germany, see Stolleis, *Heiliges Römisches Reich*, pp. 15–16; for the
Reich as consolation and promise, Goebel, *The Great War*, pp. 262–7.
[80] For the new spirit, see Rexroth, 'Geschichte erforschen?', pp. 126–7 (and, for the
'breakdown of the fathers' world' in the eyes of the post-1918 academic generation,
p. 128).
[81] Oexle, 'German malaise', p. 40; Wolf, *Litteris*, pp. 38–9.
[82] For the book's reception, see Abulafia, 'Kantorowicz', esp. p. 201.

although his hero, the enigmatic and apparently un-German Frederick
II, was far from a customary choice. But what set his book apart from
earlier German scholarship (which, for Kantorowicz, had 'completely
ignored the national tasks and duties') was its empathetic identification with medieval political mentalities, which Kantorowicz sought to
recapture on their own terms.[83] Empathy had its price, however, in a
narrow ethnocentrism which denounced 'cosmopolitanism', set its face
against international scholarly exchange, and demanded the 'nationali-
sation' of historical writing: attitudes, for Marc Bloch, all too typical of
German medievalists of the day.[84]

If Kantorowicz set a new precedent for exploring medieval political
sensibilities, a younger contemporary would extend it to the German
nation. Hermann Heimpel's enthusiasm for the glory days of high
medieval emperorship had received a boost when the era of Weimar
gave way – unlamented by him, or by most of his fellow medievalists – to a new Reich.[85] The Nazi seizure of power gave fresh wind to
studies of Germany's first Reich: for one of Heimpel's contemporaries, the emperors were 'educators' of the Germanic peoples in their
Germanness, their age the 'Medieval Stretch of the Road to German
Unity'.[86] Heimpel himself would hardly have dissented from the
assertion, made in 1940 by Theodor Mayer, pro-Nazi director of the
Reichsinstitut that had absorbed the *MGH*, that 'the Greater German
Reich takes up the course of historical development where it lapsed
under the Staufer'.[87] *Deutschlands Mittelalter* continued to hold the
key to *Deutschlands Schicksal*, furnishing 'primal images of German

---

[83] For Kantorowicz's denunciation of the shortcomings of contemporary German scholarship (in a paper to German historians at Halle in 1930), see Oexle, 'German malaise', p. 49.
[84] Ibid. The elements of German nationalism in Kantorowicz's account, and its place
within the broad German-nationalist (or 'Ghibelline') tradition of interpreting the
Kaiserzeit, are emphasised (against the traditional stress on the book's cosmopolitanism) by Ruehl, '"In this time"'. For Bloch, see Schlötter, 'Marc Bloch', esp. pp.
129–31.
[85] On Heimpel, see: Boockmann, *Der Historiker*; Schulin, *Hermann Heimpel*; Wolf, *Litteris*,
pp. 248–64; and, for the controversy which has blown up around his reputation since
the 1990s, Sommer, 'Eine Frage?'. Sommer depicts Heimpel's German-nationalist
reading of the Middle Ages as reflecting a late intellectual reorientation, coinciding
with the Nazi seizure of power and motivated largely by careerist considerations.
However, Sommer entirely overlooks Heimpel's interest in questions of medieval
'national consciousness', an interest which antedated 1933: pp. 209–14.
[86] Kirn, *Aus der Frühzeit*, p. 73, and the heading to Ch. 5.
[87] Quoted in Thamer, 'Mittelalterliche Reichs- und Königstraditionen', p. 830. For
Reich in the Nazi era, see Stolleis, *Heiliges Römisches Reich*, p. 17; for Mayer, an
NSDAP member since 1937, Maurer, 'Theodor Mayer', esp. pp. 503–23.

being ... according to which today once again youth fashions itself and men act'.[88]

Heimpel himself was a complex and contradictory figure, never a two-dimensional NS-man; but some salient traits and attitudes he certainly shared with medievalist friends of the regime.[89] His interests in the Franco-German frontier and in medieval inter-ethnic strife were underpinned by deep xenophobia.[90] For Heimpel, as for contemporary *Ostforscher*, the ancient struggle for survival and self-assertion went on, and it was in some ways a natural step when in 1941 he took up a chair at the newly established Reichsuniversität at Strasbourg in German-occupied Alsace. Heimpel was clearly ready to do his bit for the triumph of Germandom in this long-contested zone, drafting a research programme for 'The Study of the German Middle Ages in German Alsace'.[91] His approach gave substance to Kantorowicz's clarion call, uttered in earlier, less happy times, for a usable German past. 'The Present', declared Heimpel in 1941, 'is History's most noble task.'[92]

Among the projects envisaged in his Strasbourg scheme were a 'history of German self-consciousness' and a plan to edit the late medieval publicist texts in which Heimpel detected its first stirrings.[93] His identification of the late Middle Ages – not the golden centuries of the *Kaiserzeit* – as the time when Germans first discovered themselves as 'indigenae, sui generis' sets him apart from most earlier seekers after a medieval German nation.[94] The early history of German collective selfhood was a theme to which Heimpel returned repeatedly, and one which inspired some of his principal writings – writings which still number among the most substantial studies in the subject. The origins

---

[88] Heimpel, *Deutsches Mittelalter*, p. 9. These are among the opening words of a lecture which Heimpel delivered at the University of Freiburg in 1933, in the presence of the rector, Martin Heidegger, under the title 'Deutschlands Mittelalter – Deutschlands Schicksal'. See also Althoff, 'Das Mittelalterbild', p. 734.

[89] My reading of Heimpel here differs from the reductionist verdict of Sommer, 'Eine Frage?', esp. pp. 214–23.

[90] For Heimpel's attitude to the French, see Schulin, *Hermann Heimpel*, pp. 37–8. A lecture on the subject of 'Frankreich und das Reich' (Heimpel, *Deutsches Mittelalter*, pp. 160–75) depicted a centuries-long struggle between the German and French heirs of the Franks, in which the former had always stood at a disadvantage – a situation only redressed by the historically new (i.e., post-1933) 'Verbindung von Geist und Macht ... im Deutschland Karls des Großen' (ibid., p. 175).

[91] Boockmann, *Der Historiker*, pp. 19–20.

[92] Quoted in ibid., p. 24.

[93] Ibid., p. 21; Wolf, *Litteris*, pp. 260–2.

[94] Heimpel, *Deutsches Mittelalter*, p. 125. The phrase occurs in a lecture which Heimpel delivered in 1937, entitled 'The German Late Middle Ages: Character of an Era'. For Heimpel's 'German' late Middle Ages, see also: Wolf, *Litteris*, p. 258; Rexroth, 'Geschichte erforschen?', pp. 128–9.

of his approach deserve consideration. Early stimulus came from his mentor, Finke, who guided his pupil towards the later Middle Ages and the treatise literature surrounding the Church councils.[95] There, Heimpel discovered writers whose articulate delineations of a German political identity were without parallel in earlier times. His most substantial publications in the field were on figures of this sort, the publicist Dietrich von Niem (d. 1418), and his thirteenth-century forebear Alexander von Roes.[96] But it is probable that Heimpel's own early life also had a share in nurturing his sympathy for the crisis-torn epoch that followed the end of the Staufer.[97] Like several other students of medieval German identities, Heimpel was born at the beginning of the twentieth century; the Great War coincided with his adolescence.[98] He witnessed as a young man the turbulence and shame of the war's end, serving for a time in the anticommunist Bavarian *Freikorps*. A native of Munich, he observed Hitler's 1923 coup attempt.[99] Such experiences can hardly have failed to sharpen his eye for the often complex historical interactions between constitutional crisis, national self-esteem and common political identity.[100]

The old Reich, with its Christian and neo-Roman official trappings, had traditionally posed an obstacle to scholars in pursuit of a pre-modern German nation. The problem was heightened by the long-standing fidelity of German medievalists to their core premise, that the collective selfhood of their medieval forebears necessarily found most eloquent expression in that epoch when German power was at its height: the central Middle Ages, the heyday of Christian-Roman universalism. Kantorowicz had been forced to settle for weaving a purely mystical German national destiny around his unshakably neo-Roman hero. Not all were blind to the paradox: Paul Kirn observed that only in

---

[95] Schulin, *Hermann Heimpel*, pp. 27–8; Boockmann, *Der Historiker*, pp. 10–12.

[96] Heimpel, *Dietrich*; Heimpel, 'Alexander von Roes'.

[97] For the appeal of this era to the sensibilities of Heimpel's generation, see Rexroth, 'Geschichte erforschen?', pp. 126–7.

[98] In his memoir of his childhood and youth, *Die halbe Violine*, first published in 1949, Heimpel vividly evoked episodes from his own early scholarly formation and enthusiasms against the backdrop of the hardships of the closing months of the war: e.g., pp. 251–3. Medievalist contemporaries who studied identities and *Volksgeschichte* include Erich Maschke (b. 1900), Heinz Zatschek (b. 1901), Herbert Grundmann (b. 1902). Heimpel himself was born in 1901.

[99] Schulin, *Hermann Heimpel*, pp. 26–7; Boockmann, *Der Historiker*, p. 10; and, for (uncertain) evidence indicating sympathy on Heimpel's part for the *Putsch* attempt, Sommer, 'Eine Frage?', p. 204.

[100] Thus Heimpel, *Deutsches Mittelalter*, p. 126: the emergence of a patriotic treatise literature in the time of the Empire's late medieval weakness demonstrated that an unshakable 'Bund von Volk und Reichsidee' would live on 'auch in den Tiefzeiten unserer Geschichte'.

the late Middle Ages did German unity receive written expression; for the *Kaiserzeit*, it must be read off from the facts.[101] Heimpel's achievement was to see beyond the dazzling tokens of high medieval Teutonic glory, to a later period, where perceiving a German political identity no longer required the eye of faith. That did not mean that German greatness, medieval or modern, moved Heimpel less than his peers. His excavation of late medieval German selfhood was no exercise in detached scholarship, but a task with urgent contemporary utility. The National Socialist government, wrote Heimpel in 1938, was fulfilling the same historic role as had the medieval Reich: safeguarding 'the peace of the peoples [of Europe] from the strength of their [geographical, i.e., German] centre'.[102] It was a role which drew the legitimacy of remote precedent from an outlook (which he thought timelessly German) which Heimpel discerned among his late medieval treatise-writers, who had ascribed to the German people hegemonic power, which they understood as 'service' for the general good.[103]

Opportunities to supply this traditional brand of German service contracted sharply after 1945. Henceforth, the Reich would be banished from respectable political discourse: as late as the year 2000, a German government minister was moved to declare that 'no country is as little *reichsorientiert* as the German Federal Republic'.[104] What was still unclear at the war's end was whether, with the golden thread of neo-medieval political fantasy broken, German medievalists would feel able or willing to continue with their accustomed search for early signs of German collective selfhood. Both the utility and the political acceptability of such a quest seemed in doubt. The public mood of the 1950s and 1960s did not favour spacious reflections on the German past.[105] Contemporary debate about what it meant to be German and about the proper shape of a German political order was more urgent and agitated than ever; but few people any longer thought that such matters could be illuminated by turning to Germany's medieval past.[106] When the aged Hugelmann published in 1955 a doggedly

---

[101] Kirn, *Aus der Frühzeit*, p. 124.
[102] Quoted in Schulin, *Hermann Heimpel*, p. 38.
[103] Heimpel, 'Alexander von Roes', p. 41.
[104] Quoted in *Die Zeit*, 21 June 2000. Foreign Minister Joschka Fischer was responding to some mild teasing from Jean-Pierre Chevènement, aimed at allegedly neo-imperial elements in Fischer's proposals for the development of the European Union.
[105] For Heimpel's attempts in the 1950s to frame an ambitious German history, and the reasons for their failure, see Schulin, *Hermann Heimpel*, esp. pp. 9–15.
[106] For the contemporary mood, see Fulbrook, *German National Identity*, p. 2. The incapacity of the ('German') Middle Ages to furnish national myths after 1945 is emphasised by Althoff, 'Das Mittelalterbild', pp. 748–9.

Germanocentric summation of his life's work on the medieval German 'national state', it was received frostily where it was noticed at all.[107] Only in the German Democratic Republic (DDR), where Marxist-Leninist teleology drove an official quest for the medieval origins of a German 'feudal state', did the traditional study of early political identities retain some vigour.[108] In the West, historians had mostly found new goals.

'Out of German, into European history!', Peter Rassow urged in 1946.[109] Medievalists in the Federal Republic took up his call with enthusiasm in the years that followed.[110] By the time of the landmark Charlemagne exhibition at Aachen in 1965 (mounted with the backing of the Council of Europe), the Frankish warlord was no longer a fighter for his German (or French) nation, but a good European. Among his central achievements, it now transpired, was to enable later generations to speak of a 'Community' of 'European peoples and nations'.[111] The gallery of historic dates and keynote exhibitions underwent European refurbishment, and the pantheon of medieval heroes was reorganised to suit. Charles the Great's fourteenth-century namesake, Charles IV, was one notable beneficiary, in his anniversary year of 1978. The sickly and devious Luxemburger, who had found little favour in the muscular German historiography of times past, was able now, in a climate of *détente*, to emerge as (in one biographer's phrase) 'a *Kaiser* in Europe', a wise sponsor of *Ostpolitik* – even a 'European Prince of Peace'.[112]

Some of the more supple medievalists of an older generation managed to repackage their favourite subjects, just as they had repackaged themselves, in terms more acceptable to new political masters. Putative racial warriors from the Middle Ages learned to recognise the value of becoming responsible and peace-loving European citizens. The thirteenth-century treatise-writer Alexander von Roes was one who in

---

[107] Hugelmann, *Stämme*. For a detailed critique, see Sproemberg, 'La naissance'.
[108] See esp. Müller-Mertens, *Regnum Teutonicum*. For the context, see Borgolte, 'Anfänge?', pp. 42–3.
[109] Quoted in Schulze, *Deutsche Geschichtswissenschaft*, p. 160.
[110] Borgolte, 'Anfänge?', pp. 43–4; Borgolte, 'Vor dem Ende?', pp. 573–4.
[111] Helmut Beumann's words in W. Braunfels (ed.), *Karl der Große: Lebenswerk und Nachleben*, vol. I (Düsseldorf: Schwann, 1965), p. 7.
[112] Seibt, *Karl IV*. For Otto Habsburg, *Karl IV.: ein Europäischer Friedensfürst*, and other publications from the jubilee year, see Graus, 'Kaiser Karl IV.', esp. p. 78. For the media excitement generated by the commemorations, see E. Straub, 'Viel Lärm um Karl: Die Rückkehr Karls IV. auf die Nürnberger Burg', *Frankfurter Allgemeine Zeitung*, 19 June 1978. Charles' previous place in the German academic tradition is reviewed in Frey, 'Karl IV. in der älteren Historiographie'.

the 1930s had stood out for his 'strong *völkisch* sensibility'.[113] Herbert Grundmann wrote in 1936 of the 'national profession of truly German character' that his works comprised.[114] But returning to the theme in 1951, Grundmann discerned a morally re-educated Alexander, who 'seeks for a way … whereby his own people can coexist with other peoples [and], complementing one another without rivalry, work together with them'.[115] By the century's end, Alexander had become the author of a concrete 'programme', designed to reconcile divisions within a union of European powers.[116] The fruits of an age of crisis, his works aspired to nurture a new, more harmonious European order, out of the ruins of the old.

Only rarely after 1945 did contemporary events cause medievalists to summon up images of a German nation, medieval or modern. The turbulent German politics of the late 1960s and 1970s stirred occasional ripples in the West and, more obscurely, the East. Early in 1969, in a necessarily low-key coda to the Year of Revolutions, East Berlin Monumentists had marked the 150th anniversary of the establishment of the *MGH* by laying flowers at Stein's memorial – a 'demonstrative', even a 'daring' act under the circumstances and, in the recollection of their director, a public profession of that *sanctus amor patriae* which the *MGH* logo still enjoins.[117] In the Federal Republic, student radicalism combined with changing relations between the two Germanies to stir in some older medievalists anxious musings about the future of the German nation itself. Taking his text from Ernest Renan, Walter Schlesinger reflected that, just as the nation is born within history, so it can expire, should it lose the common will to endure.[118] Just such a loss of will was manifest in a Federal Republic in which some political elements 'regard their real Fatherland as the Soviet Union or China, although without showing any intention of settling there'.[119] The fact that an essay ostensibly addressing the origins of the medieval nation found space to polemicise at length against recent constitutional

---

[113] Kirn, *Aus der Frühzeit*, p. 103.
[114] Grundmann, 'Das deutsche Nationalbewußtsein', p. 55.
[115] Grundmann, 'Sacerdotium', p. 20.
[116] Fuhrmann, *Alexander von Roes*.
[117] Müller-Mertens, 'Constitutiones', p. 2. Their action was noted in the annual report on the *Monumenta*: H. Grundmann, 'Bericht für das Jahr 1968/69', *DA* 25 (1969), i. Although a member of the East German Communist Party, Müller-Mertens became during the later DDR period increasingly unorthodox in his approach to the Middle Ages: see Borgolte, 'Anfänge?', pp. 42–4.
[118] Schlesinger, 'Die Entstehung', p. 12.
[119] Ibid., pp. 34–5.

changes in the DDR underlines that, for some at least, national past and present remained one.[120] It even seemed likely for a time that the German nation itself would resurface as a historical theme.[121]

But while the turn of the new Millennium brought a fresh wave of reflections on what it meant to be German, these tended not to draw upon any but the most recent history. By the twentieth century's close, indeed, German medievalists were to be found warning their peers off a subject whose currency and utility were fading fast. Had not two World Wars discredited the entire *nationalstaatliches Prinzip* among scholars?[122] But that unhappy epoch had in any case mercifully run its course; it was a plain fact, declared one study of pre-modern nation-making, that 'in western Europe, the two-hundred-year long dominance of the national state and of an order of states formed by nations is moving towards its end'.[123] It was therefore high time that medievalists also moved on. An audience of schoolteachers assembled in the Ottonian abbey church at Quedlinburg in October 1999 was able to learn that 'the needs of the present, in Germany as in Europe as a whole', demanded that historians now lend a hand to building 'the edifice Europe'. 'National' histories, though not definitively banned, were best left to those 'despondent traditionalists' who lacked the creativity and courage for the greater task.[124]

Although the closing years of the twentieth century yielded a crop of new German histories, not everyone judged them timely. Michael Borgolte, surveying the political landscape after the events of 1989–90, stipulated that what the challenges facing the new Germany required from the medievalist were studies of neither the old Reich nor the German principalities but of the settlement and integration of medieval east-central Europe – a movement which had, after all, embraced most of the former DDR.[125] The approach taken to this subject by scholars and teachers in the future would reveal the state of health of the unified Germany. But while the place of the medieval German nation in post-war German historiography was a transformed and greatly shrunken one, its function (and the function of Germany's medieval centuries more broadly) still attested to remarkable continuities. As so

---

[120] For the context, see Borgolte, 'Anfänge?', pp. 47–8.
[121] On the 'worrying trend' of the 1970s towards demands for inclusive German national histories, see Berger, *The Search*, pp. 86–7; for its manifestation among German medievalists, Johanek, 'Zu neuen Ufern?', pp. 147–8.
[122] Fuhrmann, *Alexander von Roes*, p. 5.
[123] H. Münkler, 'Einleitung', in Münkler, Grünberger and Mayer, *Nationenbildung*, p. 13.
[124] Borgolte, 'Vor dem Ende?', pp. 580, 583–4, 589.
[125] Borgolte, 'Vom Sacrum Imperium', esp. pp. 71–2.

often before, the medieval past was summoned to explain and legitimise the political present, to assuage contemporary traumas and anxieties, to elucidate (and occasionally denounce) change, and to justify and underpin forecasts, agendas and programmes for Germany's future. Polemic, and the heat of contemporary political frictions, continued occasionally to accompany the debate. As in times past, identifying the aspects of the German Middle Ages most appropriate and fruitful for present German needs remained for some a key priority.

The medieval nation: roots and routes

In February 1940 the great Dutch medievalist Johan Huizinga delivered a series of lectures at the University of Leiden on the subject of 'Patriotism and Nationalism in European History'.[126] His pessimistic message, delivered, he insisted, against the prevailing view among social scientists in his day, was that national divisions and hatreds had an unbroken history in Europe, traceable back to the twelfth century, if not before. Within three months, German bombs would reduce to rubble the city of Rotterdam, a mere 30 kilometres from Leiden's lecture halls. The world crisis of the 1930s and 1940s was accompanied by a visible surge of interest in the medieval nation as a matter for historical study in western Europe and north America.[127] Marc Bloch, whose own life was soon to be consumed in the cataclysm wrought by Nazi Germany, sounded an early clarion for the subject.[128] Interest grew in the period after 1945, but intensified during the closing decades of the twentieth century – a time when movements for regional devolution, the re-emergence in Europe of violent nationalist politics, the consolidation of a European political union, and the shifting forces of global politics and economics were all raising new questions around the nature and future of European nationalities.[129]

A striking feature of the studies which medievalists now offered on the subject – apart from the visible impetus of contemporary affairs[130] – was their combative note: a concern to champion the importance of

---

[126] Huizinga, 'Patriotism'.
[127] Examples: Galbraith, 'Nationality'; Koht, 'The dawn'; Keeney, 'Military service'.
[128] Bloch, *Feudal Society*, vol. II, pp. 431–7.
[129] For some of these factors, and their reflection in historical scholarship, see Applegate, 'A Europe'.
[130] For the CIA career of Joseph R. Strayer, an important American historian of the medieval (French) nation during the Cold War era, see Cantor, *Inventing*, pp. 261–2, 279, 406–7; Strayer's essays are collected in his *Medieval Statecraft and the Perspectives of History* (Princeton University Press, 1971).

peoples and nations in the Middle Ages against the benighted views of modern historians, and 'social scientists' more broadly, who insisted on the nation's quintessential modernity.[131] The argument itself was scarcely novel: for much of the twentieth century, succeeding generations of medievalists believed themselves to be making, in the teeth of received wisdom, a pioneering case for the medieval nation.[132] What distinguished the best studies from the post-war epoch, however, was their intellectual ambition and methodological rigour. Some now unfolded large comparative schemes for explaining and classifying the development of European nationalities over the centuries between the end of the western Roman Empire and the French Revolution.[133] If the late twentieth-century picture remained marked by much eclecticism and not a little myopia, it also disclosed stronger ties of international co-operation, particularly within western continental Europe, around ambitious comparative projects addressing the medieval nation. The prominent participation of German-speaking medievalists in these European joint ventures is revealing.

Academic collaboration was not the only thing that gained a European frame. The projects themselves often took a pan-European perspective, approaching medieval nations in their plurality, as comparable and interdependent social formations.[134] The view for the whole was now lent durability by a tendency to find Europe's early realms and peoples taking shape in the shadow of pan-European empires, Roman and Carolingian, and their formative, unifying cultures.[135] But the Europe of nations now conjured into being often had a distinctly Frankish flavour. The Marburg-based *Nationes* project, dedicated to investigating 'The Emergence of European Nations in the Middle Ages', which published a series of important volumes in the 1970s and 1980s, was a venture with its heart unmistakably in Carolingia.[136] It was not only at the level

---

[131] As an example, see Stringer, 'Social and political communities'.

[132] See thus the arguments advanced by Hugelmann, above p. 32.

[133] Examples: Werner, 'Les nations'; Reynolds, 'Our forefathers?'; Geary, *The Myth*.

[134] In addition to the *Nationes* project discussed below, note, e.g., the European Science Foundation programme on 'The Transformation of the Roman World', active during the 1990s.

[135] For the Roman legacy, see the essays in Goetz, Jarnut and Pohl (eds.), *Regna and Gentes*; for the Carolingians: Werner, 'Völker', p. 43; Ehlers, 'Nation und Geschichte', p. 205.

[136] For its foundation and ethos, see: Borgolte, 'Anfänge?', p. 47; Johanek, 'Zu neuen Ufern?', pp. 146–8. Schlesinger, 'Die Entstehung', p. 61, argued for the primacy of a European 'heartland' co-terminous with Charlemagne's empire, over the European 'periphery' for the student of medieval nation-making. For a defence of the project by one of its leading lights, reflecting criticisms which had been voiced after its launch, see Beumann, 'Zur Nationenbildung', esp. pp. 21–4, 33.

of the grand project that the post-war era saw Franco-German barriers torn down and that most troubled and fought-over historiographical frontier thrown open to cordial two-way traffic. Individual conferences likewise assembled impressive lists of French and German scholars, to address in dialogue medieval political identities.[137] A key sponsor was the German Historical Institute in Paris, whose journal *Francia*, subtitled *Studies in Western European History*, captured neatly the merging of Franco-German into European perspectives characteristic of the time. Among the medievalists who in the later twentieth century turned their minds to European nation-making were Germans whose principal work was in medieval French history, and French scholars who published on Germany. Something of a landmark in the conjoining of French and German traditions of medieval nation-making was reached in 1990, with the publication of Carlrichard Brühl's monumental study of *Deutschland–Frankreich: Die Geburt zweier Völker*, a work commissioned by the then mayor of Paris, Jacques Chirac, and subsequently translated into French.[138] Brühl's pugnacious book sought to show that the Carolingian Empire had exercised a longer-lasting influence than previously thought over the formation of both the German and French peoples, extending well into the eleventh century. The 'two peoples' of his title had grown together, from a common root: not differences but things shared, not Darwinian struggle but peaceful exchange had attended their birth.[139] The starkness of Brühl's position only fuelled further debate;[140] but it also illuminated sharply some salient themes in the study of nationalities among German-speaking medievalists at the end of the twentieth century.

Brühl's book is but one prominent example of the leading place taken after 1945 in Germanophone scholarship on the nation by early medievalists: students of those centuries in which the shaping influence of pan-European empires, cultures and elite traditions was particularly detectable. The picture of European nation-making which resulted was

---

[137] Examples of the fruits of such dialogue: Babel and Moeglin (eds.), *Identité régionale*; Ehlers (ed.), *Deutschland und der Westen Europas*; Weiß (ed.), *Regnum et Imperium*.

[138] Brühl, *Deutschland–Frankreich*. For Brühl's view of Franco-German relations, and of the place of the two peoples within Europe, see Borgolte, 'Anfänge?', pp. 48–50; for the book's style and reception, Scales, 'Identifying "France"'.

[139] Brühl, *Deutschland–Frankreich*, p. 181. For a subsequent attempt at tracing back to its Carolingian roots the 'truly common history' of France and Germany, see Kintzinger, *Die Erben*, esp. p. 7. Significantly, Kintzinger likewise began with the contemporary EU and with the 'dominant role' of Paris and Berlin within a 'core Europe'.

[140] Several contributions to this debate are published in Brühl and Schneidmüller (eds.), *Reichs- und Nationsbildung*.

very much an early medievalist's vision. The medieval political community was, from this perspective, cohesive and socially limited, a 'nation of nobles and clerics' gathered around a ruling dynasty, centred on its court.[141] It was in this milieu that ancestry legends and mythologised common histories were fashioned, which, acting as repositories of illustrious shared memories, became the foundations of unifying collective identities for the elites of tradition-bearers (*Traditionskerne*, *Trägerschichten*) who were their custodians.[142] No less striking is the importance which post-war German medievalists ascribed to rulership and power in shaping collective selfhood.[143] The medieval nation was demysticised, de-Romanticised, and unmasked as a tool of high politics. Most importantly, it was now held to be a construct, a fiction confected by tiny educated elites, drawing on the resources and templates of that ancient common Latinate culture on whose ruins their own realms were raised up.[144] One source of this view lies in a seminal book by Reinhard Wenskus, published in 1961, tracing the formation of barbarian peoples in late antiquity.[145] Its pioneering approach, to which the term 'ethnogenesis' later became attached, was extended and adapted by other early medievalists in Austria, Germany and elsewhere, eventually hardening into an orthodoxy.[146] Just as *Volksgeist*, from this perspective, gave way to ideology, immanence to instrumentalism, so the medieval communities of blood and descent conjured up by nationalist scholarship in the nineteenth and earlier twentieth centuries were likewise replaced by heterogeneous bands of soldiers and courtiers, clustered around the successful warlord and his kin.[147] It was these groups that came over time to believe and reproduce the official fictions of their own common descent, as identification with the 'people' became a title to share in power. Far from manifesting a natural order beyond history, European nations, it was now argued, were historical artefacts of a highly unnatural and unpredictable kind.[148]

---

[141] The phrase is from J. Ehlers, 'Natio. 1. N. (Nation)', in *LMA* 6, cols. 1035–6 – a convenient summary of the approach described below.

[142] Ibid., col. 1036; and see also Ehlers, 'Die deutsche Nation', pp. 23–4.

[143] Ehlers, *Die Entstehung*; and see the works by Ehlers cited above. Also: Werner, 'Völker', p. 43; Fried, *Der Weg*, pp. 24–5.

[144] Ehlers, 'Methodische Überlegungen', p. 6.

[145] Wenskus, *Stammesbildung*.

[146] Another seminal work developing Wenskus' approach is Wolfram, *History of the Goths*. For criticism, see Bowlus, 'Ethnogenesis models'.

[147] See the essays in Pohl and Reimitz (eds.), *Strategies*.

[148] W. Pohl, 'Introduction: strategies of distinction', in Pohl and Reimitz (eds.), *Strategies*, p. 4: 'What we have to understand is that the large ethnic communities that late Romans called Franks, or Goths, are in no way natural facts. They are highly abstract, culturally constructed ways of categorising people...'

Grasping the full significance of this approach also means noting those aspects of the pre-modern nation – problems, interpretations, assumptions, whole categories of evidence – which it could not accommodate, or which its advocates deliberately minimised or rejected altogether. The patterns of emphasis and exclusion characteristic of late twentieth-century German models of medieval nationhood reflect in part the leading role taken by early medievalists in fashioning the dominant framework of analysis. This ensured that only modest attention was paid to the composition of the 'public' for the idea of nation and to the media for its propagation – matters of foremost concern to students of modern national identities. Such questions seemed for the (early) Middle Ages capable of fairly straightforward resolution by emphasising the primacy of the self-contained world of the court, its face-to-face relationships and exclusive high culture. Relatively little attention was given to questions of the nation's capacity to infuse diverse social and political interest groups, to sustain plural interpretations, or to become the focus of argument or controversy. These, too, are fundamental aspects of the nation's role in modern political discourse. Here again, adequate answers seemed to lie in the highly group-specific character of the (early) medieval nation, and in the court's capacity to sustain a uniform political culture among the elites around the ruler. Such a univocal model of nation was doubtless well adapted to explain the formation of collective identities in the sub-Roman and Carolingian successor-kingdoms. But it is less well suited to analysing the more complex, fractured, polycentric and contested political landscapes of later times, with their more numerous, varied and socially penetrative channels for articulating and disseminating common bonds.[149]

Other conspicuous absences from post-war (West) German visions of the medieval nation appear more directly rooted in the cultural changes and political imperatives of the day. Not only was the nation an essentially political formation, of narrow social composition; it was also a community founded, validated and held together from within.[150] Now marginalised or abandoned, therefore, were precisely those elements which for an earlier scholarly tradition had attested to the nation's individuality – its living collective soul, its *Volksgeist* – and which embodied the supposedly formative role of conflict with other peoples. Common language and law, it was now insisted, were of merely secondary importance in

---

[149] For a more complex conception of the workings of the idea of nation in various spheres of German society in the *late* Middle Ages, see Moraw, 'Bestehende'.
[150] Ehlers, 'Natio. 1. N. (Nation)', in *LMA* 6, col. 1035: the nation was primarily the expression of a political will to common belonging. See also Ehlers, 'Nationsbildung in Frankreich', p. 587. Fried, *Der Weg*, pp. 26–7, gives more emphasis to the formative role of interactions with neighbours.

the nation-making process, capable at most of reinforcing established solidarities, not of forming communities on their own.[151] References in medieval writings to common styles of dress, customs, weapons or other cultural measures of belonging were significant above all for their constructed, and thus fictitious, self-deceiving, character. The medieval frontier, so central to some older accounts of early nation-making, was dismissed as an untypical place, and warnings sounded about the dangers of generalising from the evidence found there.[152]

In particular, expressions of inter-ethnic hostility, with their attendant stereotypes of self-glorification and calumny for neighbours and rivals, so significant for nationalist historians in times past, were cast aside as historically worthless: the mere predictable, primitive accompaniments to even the crudest forms of group consciousness, with nothing to reveal specifically about the dynamics of pre-modern nation-making.[153] The medieval community of European nations, it now transpired, had come into being without any need for those rivalries and outbursts of ill-mannered abuse and mud-slinging which Germans had in former, more bellicose times judged so crucial to the transhistorical, inter-ethnic struggle for survival.

Little wonder, then, that in the second half of the twentieth century the history of the medieval German nation was written in Germany in such a minor key. The model of pre-modern nation-making now in widespread vogue could hardly have obscured or diminished more fully the lineaments of German identity, had it been designed with that end in view.[154] It gathered its evidence above all in the early Middle Ages; but 'German' political identity was, in European comparison, a late formation – fashioned in the cold light of history, long after the pan-European movements of migration and acculturation that now so excited medievalists had subsided.[155] The bewildered reader was confronted with studies in medieval German 'nation-formation' which barely reached even into the eleventh century – the time of the earliest tentative invocations of a 'German' people or political community to survive from German pens.[156] Emphasis was placed upon the formative

---

[151] Ehlers, 'Die deutsche Nation', p. 56; Ehlers, 'Nationsbildung in Frankreich', pp. 584–5.
[152] Ehlers, 'Die deutsche Nation', pp. 24–5.
[153] Ehlers, 'Nation und Geschichte', p. 208; Ehlers, 'Die deutsche Nation', p. 24.
[154] Some of the shortcomings of medieval German nation-making are thus emphasised in Ehlers, 'Die deutsche Nation', pp. 45–6.
[155] See esp. Fried, *Der Weg*, p. 22.
[156] Hlawitschka, 'Vom Ausklingen', pp. 55–6, goes so far as to suggest that the lack of a specific terminology was largely immaterial to German nation-formation in the tenth century. For the vocabulary of 'German' peoplehood and its origins, see below, Ch. 10, pp. 470–5.

power of central institutions of rule; but such institutions were always weak in Germany. The prevailing viewpoint sought in the medieval sources a single, strong and unifying language of common identity; but German identities were diffuse and multiple, overlying and interacting with a diversity of local and regional perspectives.[157] It judged internal coherence to be a principal motor of shared belonging; but vital components of German identity were from the earliest days constructed from without, and received by Germans, ready-fashioned, from their neighbours.[158] 'The Germans', Johannes Fried has written, 'stumbled into their national existence without noticing it and without striving for it' (though what medieval nation *did* arise through its own 'striving'?).[159] The dominant perspective viewed historiography and unifying myth as the prime cultural expressions of collective selfhood; but the formation of anything describable as a 'German' origin story was late and problematical.[160] On the other hand, some of the main types of evidence which German medievalists had traditionally piled up – writings from the frontier, utterances of a xenophobic kind, or statements invoking 'German' language, culture, or purported character traits – were now widely dismissed as uninteresting or inadmissible.

It is easy to see why, by the late twentieth century, the German example loomed so large for those social scientists, within Germany and outside, who sought to demonstrate the modernity of nations as such, and to locate their construction in the age of European nationalism and industrialisation. Whether they rested their case on the growth of state power, the emergence of new intellectual movements, the modernisation of national economies, or 'the print and communications revolution', they were able to argue that in Germany the national community was forged largely from scratch in the period between the later eighteenth and the end of the nineteenth centuries.[161] Some, it is true, did make out flickering harbingers of a German nation in much earlier epochs; but in the absence of clearly discernible or continuous links to structures of power or government, it was hard to credit these with much importance.[162] Even historians otherwise convinced of the

---

[157] Schubert, *Einführung*, p. 45: 'Deutsche Geschichte im Spätmittelalter ist die Geschichte regionaler Vielfalt'.

[158] Fried, *Der Weg*, p. 18; Thomas, 'Sur l'histoire', p. 29. For the image of 'the German' and its sources, see below, Ch. 8, pp. 359–60.

[159] Fried, *Der Weg*, p. 15.

[160] See below, Ch. 7, pp. 310–24; and Thomas, 'Julius Caesar'.

[161] Examples: Kedourie, *Nationalism*; Hobsbawm, *Nations*, pp. 37–8, 98–9; Schulze, *The Course of German Nationalism*, esp. p. 47; Breuilly, *The Formation*, esp. pp. 8–10; Blackbourn, *The Long Nineteenth Century*, esp. p. 129.

[162] Thus Hughes, *Nationalism*, p. 2; Vick, *Defining Germany*, p. 15.

existence of significant national bonds in pre-modern Europe deemed Germany an exception.[163] The determined efforts to which such studies customarily attest, to locate the formation of 'nations' in the earliest possible era in the European past, were frustrated by the shortcomings of the German evidence. Some attempts were admittedly made to undermine the deeply ingrained account of Germany's supposedly calamitous medieval *Sonderweg*, and to identify ways in which German forms of political life resembled those found elsewhere in Europe.[164] But such scepticism has yet to be applied in any detail to medieval German political culture or to the evidence bearing upon collective identities.

But not every study of German nation-making by the beginning of the twenty-first century concentrated either on the sub-Carolingian world or on the post-Napoleonic period. Re-evaluations of the Holy Roman Empire in the seventeenth and eighteenth centuries now struck more positive notes than had once been the norm, arguing both for the effectiveness of the old Reich as a polity and for its importance in fostering German nationhood.[165] Some German medievalists took a long view of the nation-making process, or gave weight to the importance within it of the later medieval centuries.[166] Heinz Thomas portrayed the formation of a German identity as a protracted and intermittent process, within which some elements are detectable already in the tenth century, while others develop only in the central or later Middle Ages or thereafter.[167] Others concentrated on the consolidation (*Verdichtung*, as Peter Moraw termed it) of politics, culture and social life in Germany at the end of the Middle Ages, in the time of imperial reform and the patriotism of the humanists and Maximilian I.[168] Particularly in the more integrated character of its political life, within a more limited,

---

[163] Greenfeld, *Nationalism*, Ch. 4.

[164] Gillingham, *The Kingdom of Germany*; Reynolds, *Kingdoms and Communities*, pp. 289–97.

[165] For the relevant literature, see Green, 'Political institutions'. For a different view of the importance of the early modern period, concentrating on the growth of voluntaristic cultural associations, see Hardtwig, *Nationalismus*, Ch. 2.

[166] Rare instances of major studies concentrating on the late medieval period are Ritscher, *Literatur*; Hoen, *Eigenbewußtsein*.

[167] His approach is summarised in Thomas, 'Das Identitätsproblem'. In fact, postwar German medievalists often readily acknowledged that the course of German 'ethnogenesis' was gradual, extending over several centuries; the problem lay rather with the failure of their models of medieval nation-making actually to illuminate its full scope. For the difficulty of setting clear dates for its emergence, see Schnell, 'Deutsche Literatur', esp. pp. 292–3.

[168] Moraw, 'Voraussetzungen', pp. 100, 110–11; Hirschi, *Wettkampf*. For the importance of Maximilian, see Schubert, *Einführung*, p. 32.

Germanised Reich, the final medieval century in Germany seemed for some to mark a new epoch.[169]

But the turbulent decades between the end of the high medieval *Kaiserzeit* and the start of the Habsburg age in the fifteenth century have since 1945 largely been ignored by studies of pre-modern German nation-making.[170] In many ways, this lacuna appears strange. From the period between the mid-thirteenth and mid-fifteenth centuries comes an array of invocations of the German lands, people and political institutions which, in their quantity, variety, detail, reflectiveness and likely social reach, surpass what survives from earlier epochs. Yet the continuing neglect of the post-Staufer era is only initially surprising. Earlier convictions, that national self-consciousness was forged in periods of power and political self-assertion, yielded during the later twentieth century to an insistence that pre-modern ethnic identities were nourished by the existence of powerful ruling dynasties, tight, cohesive elites and prestigious courts as a setting for cultural activities. Moreover, German historians, having renounced the blood-and-soil bellicosity of their forebears, now approached the pre-modern nation (particularly the German nation) only with caution, treading warily around aspects which seemed hard to reconcile with the imperatives of European good neighbourliness. The voices of Germany's (and Europe's) fractured and troubled later medieval centuries, with their occasionally shrill and truculent outbursts of wounded pride, resentment and paranoia, were hard to attune to a late twentieth-century taste for harmony and commonality. Shared origins and common cultures, not divided landscapes, friction and recrimination, were the images of the medieval past that the prevailing political mood demanded – though it is true that the new century brought signs of a widening of approaches.[171]

Different national historiographies, different historical legacies and different contemporary goals had together resulted by the century's close in divergent visions of the medieval nation and its importance. If the German tradition tended after 1945 towards a wary and limited approach, academic cultures elsewhere in Europe and in North America acknowledged fewer (or different) traumas and taboos. At a variety of centres, the study of medieval identities was now extended to fill increasingly ambitious explanatory frames, linking them with major processes of long-term social, political, cultural and religious change. The consolidation of secular 'kingdoms and communities', the formation of a

[169] For the older literature, see Isenmann, 'Kaiser'.
[170] For the period's place within pre-modern German history, see Moraw, 'Gedanken'.
[171] Thus, particularly the works listed below, n. 181.

European 'persecuting society', even the 'making of Europe' itself: each was claimed to rest upon interactions of power and culture in which the fabrication of imagined common selfhoods and the establishment of divisions and boundaries had a central part.[172] Among Anglophone medievalists in particular, peoples and political communities had by the early twenty-first century become the subject of a startling variety of approaches and chronologies. The idea of the nation itself and the origins of its power over European imaginations were subjected to close scrutiny.[173] No holds were barred: law, language, customs, modes of life and styles of economic activity, as well as common histories and myths: all were credited with a part in individual processes of nation-making.[174] Studies of the changing patterns of control, allegiance and subjection in Latin Europe over the course of the Middle Ages ascribed central importance to the frontier, as a place where collective identities were forged and manipulated as tools of power.[175]

Approached in this way, nation-making looked like anything but a harmonious or internally self-sustaining process. Peoples and nations were fashioned in proximity, and often in violent competition, with other peoples and communities. 'Defining a nation', it was insisted, 'necessarily involves exclusion.'[176] The shaping of common selfhood was inextricably bound up with the construction of an alien Other, through which shared identities were authenticated and claims to power legitimised.[177] 'In other words,' as a historian of early-modern Britain observed, 'men and women decide who they are by reference to who and what they are not.'[178] The medieval language of collective stereotype, far from representing merely dull abuse, was a flexible and sophisticated weapon, forged anew during the central Middle Ages at the interface of ascendant princely power and rejuvenated Classical culture.[179] With its aid, self-confident regimes and elites from western Europe's ancient, expanding heartlands staked their claims to colonial

---

[172] Reynolds, *Kingdoms and Communities*; Moore, *The Formation*; Bartlett, *The Making of Europe*.
[173] Thus Reynolds, 'Medieval *origines gentium*'. For an important German-language study in the field, see Kersken, *Geschichtsschreibung*.
[174] For abundant examples, see Davies, 'The peoples of Britain and Ireland', parts I–IV.
[175] See: Bartlett and MacKay (eds.), *Medieval Frontier Societies*; Power and Standen (eds.), *Frontiers in Question*.
[176] Turville-Petre, *England*, p. 1.
[177] For stereotyping and power in the Middle Ages generally, see: Richards, *Sex*; Boswell, *Christianity*; Moore, *The Formation*.
[178] Colley, *Britons*, p. 6.
[179] Meyvaert, ' "Rainaldus" '; Jones, 'The image of the barbarian'.

rule over the 'barbarians' at the continent's margins.[180] Other factors shaping the development of collective identities lay in the growth of secular government, with its intrusive demands for human and material resources, 'national' wars and an increasingly wide-ranging command of communications and propaganda resources. By the early twenty-first century, collective identities, the Other and images of the foreign had also become the subject of increasingly widespread study among a new generation of German medievalists.[181] Their work, which now drew heavily upon cultural theory and on the fruits of non-German scholarship, displayed much methodological sophistication and a new interest in themes such as division and exclusion. Yet it devoted comparatively only modest attention to medieval German identity, and less to the late Middle Ages.[182]

Reframing the nation: the late Middle Ages

What, then, if perspectives and approaches such as these were to be applied to later medieval Germany? Whatever might be the result, the uncertainty surrounding the subject of early German nation-making could scarcely be greater than it had become at the start of the twenty-first century. As will by now be clear, the very existence of anything meriting the title of a German nation before the nineteenth century had been sharply contested; and the nature, the significance and the periodisation of any common German identity discernible in pre-modern times were all matters likewise still awaiting resolution. The potential interest of the late medieval period for a study of this kind is considerable. The series of profound social, economic and cultural changes which had reshaped life in much of western Europe between the tenth and thirteenth centuries penetrated Germany relatively late.[183] The thirteenth century had witnessed a tenfold growth in the number of German towns; not until the fourteenth would the tide of German migration into the lands of east-central Europe gradually abate. It was in the later Middle Ages that in much of German-speaking Europe the old-established duality of nobles and peasants – a type of society which has been judged particularly ill-suited to sustaining large, impersonal

---

[180] Bartlett, *Gerald*, Ch. 6; Bartlett, *The Making of Europe*, Ch. 4; Gillingham, 'The beginnings'; Davies, *The First English Empire*, Ch. 5.

[181] As examples: Scior, *Das Eigene*; Mohr, *Das Wissen*; Plassmann, *Origo gentis*; Fraesdorff, *Der barbarische Norden*; Jostkleigrewe, *Das Bild*; Borgolte, Schiel, Schneidmüller and Seitz (eds.), *Mittelalter im Labor*, esp. part II.3; Foester, *Vergleich*.

[182] The main exception was Jostkleigrewe, *Das Bild*.

[183] Moraw, *Von offener Verfassung*; Schubert, *Einführung*.

'imagined communities' – began to give way to more complex social formations.[184] Some of the changes observable in the life and thought of the period merit special attention in the case of Germany, where royal government, which had long commanded only meagre institutional resources, did not consolidate and intensify in the fashion observable elsewhere in late medieval Europe. Particular interest therefore attaches to those social and cultural formations which were capable of nurturing, supporting and propagating notions of common 'German' belonging even in the comparative absence of intrusive royal rule. Some of these came during the later Middle Ages to attain in certain regions of Germany a degree of sophistication comparable to that found in the most economically and culturally advanced European regions of the time.

Successive waves of settlement by German-speakers in the lands bordering Germany's ancient heartlands in the east and south-east had by the fourteenth century greatly extended the geographical reach of German language and culture. A process of such magnitude (in which the imperial monarchy played after the twelfth century only a very limited part) seems likely also to have found some reflection in the articulation of German identities. Continuing urbanisation in late medieval Germany was accompanied by the extension of trade and monetarisation, which in turn stimulated the mobility of people, ideas and cultural forms, as well as goods. Literacy and the education of the laity also advanced, with the growing towns providing both a setting for schools and a buoyant demand for literate skills. After the mid-thirteenth century, the use of the vernacular for pragmatic written communication in diverse spheres of German life expanded rapidly.[185] The process of *Verdichtung*, which Peter Moraw judged characteristic of the closing decades of the Middle Ages, was in significant parts of Germany already well advanced by the beginning of the fifteenth century. The climate of culture, thought and controversy characteristic of the later Middle Ages likewise favoured the dissemination in Germany of texts and ideas. The quantity of manuscripts in circulation rose sharply, and by the end of the fourteenth century a number of universities had already been established in German-speaking Europe; others would quickly follow. The great Church councils which met on German soil during the first half of the fifteenth century, and the lively manuscript trade which accompanied them, reflected and reaffirmed the cultural

---

[184] For the weakness of national ties in societies of peasants and nobles, see Hastings, *Construction of Nationhood*, p. 27.

[185] See below, Ch. 11, pp. 487–90.

vibrancy of the old heartlands of the south-west. The towns provided in the late Middle Ages a new public forum for ideas. The rapid spread of the mendicant orders in Germany during the thirteenth century underlines the growing integration of an urban public into the world of words, texts and controversies.[186] In an age of increasingly fundamental challenge to the authorities, secular and spiritual, words were weapons for which growing numbers of people were moved to reach. Above all, in Germany, where the imperial monarchy had from the earliest times been enmeshed in debates about the proper order and future course of Christian society, the crises which shook the Church, as well as the continuing periodic clashes between the Empire's ruler and the pope, stimulated debate about the character and political destiny of the German people. The significant corpus of imperialist tracts from German pens, which saw the light of day in the decades between Lyon and Constance, with their thoroughgoing reflections on German political selfhood, would on their own attest clearly to the capacity of periods of crisis, discontinuity and perceived decline to nourish common identities at least as effectively as can epochs of ascendant power.[187] They do not stand on their own: writings of widely varying kinds are to be found telling a comparable tale. Establishing what they meant and whether and how, for the history of European nation-making, they might matter requires first some scrutiny of the relationship between medieval nations and their familiar historiographical counterpart, the medieval 'state'.

---

[186] Freed, *The Friars*; Schubert, *Einführung*, p. 39.
[187] For this view of the evidence, see Schubert, *Einführung*, pp. 23–4.

2 Ruled out: monarchy, government and 'state' in Germany

At the tomb of Archbishop Siegfried

The modern visitor to the cathedral church at Mainz can hardly fail to notice the mighty, polychromed figure of a medieval archbishop at the eastern end of the nave. Now mounted on a pier, the effigy originally lay in the eastern choir, probably above a tomb chest. Its subject, Siegfried III von Eppenstein (d. 1249), imperiously meets the visitor's gaze, resplendent with mitre and crosier, triumphantly trampling underfoot lion and basilisk.[1] Arresting in a different way are the two miniaturised figures over which the archbishop towers to left and right, his gloved, bejewelled hands resting upon crowns on their heads. Inscriptions reveal them to be Landgrave Henry Raspe of Thuringia (1246–7) and Count William of Holland (1247–56), both installed by the Rhineland princes, backed by the pope, as rulers of the Empire in opposition to Frederick II and his son. But what are these two dwarf-kings doing in Mainz? Neither of them (nor, for that matter, any other medieval monarch) is buried there. William was not even crowned by the archbishop – though the shadowy Henry may have been.[2] In fact, the medieval cathedral turns out to have been thronged with petrified kings and emperors. The monument to Archbishop Peter von Aspelt (d. 1320), set up around a century after Siegfried's, yields two more: Henry VII and Ludwig IV, as well as King John of Bohemia (d. 1346); and there were once others besides.[3] Of Peter's three kings, Ludwig alone received an imperial crown from the archbishop's hands – though not in his cathedral, but at far-off Aachen. (While Mainz had hosted the installation of imperial monarchs in the eleventh century,

---

[1] For the Mainz tombs generally, see Kessel, 'Sepulkralpolitik'; and also, for Siegfried's effigy, Williamson, *Gothic Sculpture*, pp. 188–9.

[2] Hehl, 'Die Erzbischöfe', p. 101.

[3] For Peter, and for the largely lost monument to Archbishop Gerhard II von Eppenstein, see: ibid., pp. 101–2; Kessel, 'Sepulkralpolitik', esp. pp. 15–18.

Charlemagne's minster was subsequently established as the customary coronation seat.)[4]

Why start in Mainz? Then again, why not? One of the distinguishing characteristics of late medieval German identity is that there is no single, natural geographic centre, comparable to Paris or Saint-Denis for the French, whence the quest for it might be embarked upon. But one inescapable focus of attention, as will soon become clear, is supplied by the neo-Roman, German, imperial monarchy, which in the late Middle Ages claimed the rule of the greater part of German-speaking Europe. With this in mind, Roman Mogontiacum, seat in the Middle Ages of the Empire's archchancellor *per Germaniam*, appears as fitting a starting point as any.[5] And if problems and paradoxes seem, as they do, at once to crowd in around our place of departure, and around Archbishop Siegfried and his diminutive royal protégés, that will at least set the tone for what is to follow. For what, we must surely ask ourselves, is the impression more forcefully conveyed by the archbishop's monument: of the feebleness of monarchy in Germany at the traumatic close of its 'high' medieval centuries – of its fractures, absences, and painfully public abasement; or of its unexpected presence, paradoxical visibility and patent indispensability – not least, as a source of prestige to those powerful men who, like the archbishop, aspired to control it? What lesson should we read from the stones: of fissure and disharmony – between a shrunken monarchy and ascendant, increasingly sovereign ('German') princes; or of the natural unity of head and members, within a uniquely illustrious, still indispensable political order?

Mainz itself must seem to the historian in quest of a medieval 'German' identity a city enfolded in paradox: simultaneously central and somewhat peripheral to imagined maps of 'Germany'. The Carolingian metropolis dominated one of the ancient heartlands of the medieval Reich, and was an old-established staging post on the travels of its rulers. The so-called *Book of Kings of the New Law*, composed in late thirteenth-century Augsburg, still recorded diligently the visits that Charlemagne himself had made to the city, and his meetings there with his 'German' princes.[6] 'Kings of the New Law' continued to

---

[4] Mainz was the site of the *un*making of a king: Adolf of Nassau, in June 1298, though this did not take place in the cathedral: *MGC* 3, no. 589, pp. 549–52; Trautz, 'Studien', esp. pp. 30; Wolf, *Die Entstehung*, pp. 64–6.

[5] For this title, see below, Ch. 4, pp. 182–4; for the Roman settlement, J. Oldenstein, 'Mogontiacum', in *RGA* 20, pp. 144–53.

[6] *Der kunige buoch*, ed. Massmann, e.g., pp. clxxiii, clxxvii, clxxviii–ix. For the character and dating (probably late 1270s) of the work, see: H. Herkomer, 'Das Buch der Könige alter ê und niuwer ê', in *VL* 2, cols. 1089–92; F. Shaw, 'Buch der Könige alter ê und niuwer ê', in *EMC*, vol. I, p. 221. Also known as the 'prose *Kaiserchronik*', it was

come in the fourteenth century, when Mainz's merchants' hall gained its magnificent stone frieze, displaying monarch and electors in perfect harmony.[7] Yet the town lay towards the western rim of German-speaking Europe, to the left of the Rhine. Indeed, on the weighty and oft-repeated authority of Roman geography, the seat of the Empire's archchancellor 'throughout Germany' did not lie within *Germania*, but in Gaul.[8] What is more, its ecclesiastical lords had in the thirteenth century done as much as any prince in Germany to stoke the fires of conflict with the Empire's ruler, to undermine his position in his ancient power base around the Rhine, to foster divisions and to contrive constitutional crises.

City and cathedral church therefore encapsulate, as if in microcosm, some of the defining qualities of the imperial monarchy and its culture in Germany at the time of Frederick II's downfall, when Archbishop Siegfried's monument was made – and when this book begins. First impressions are of ambiguity, contradictions, multiple meanings, a penumbra of crisis and contention, and the partial, off-centred character of royal rule in Germany. Yet, alongside these, the observer is struck by the evident continuing significance – indeed, unexpected visibility – of rulership, and the distinctive scope and grandeur of its titles and claims. The complex and troubled relationship between authority, power of rule and the articulation of notions of common 'German' belonging will be the concern of this and of the next four chapters.

Monarchy, government and nation: a European paradigm

There are several justifications for commencing a study of medieval German identity with monarchy, and with the government through which it found expression. A subsidiary one might be mentioned first: practical convenience. Examining the evidence for a specifically German self-consciousness will entail frequent encounters with the imperial monarchy and with the persons, deeds and reputations of its

evidently produced in connection with the vernacular law codes compiled in the city, the *Deutschenspiegel* and *Schwabenspiegel*.

[7] For the town's continuing importance to the ruler's itinerary, see Eberhard, 'Herrschaft', esp. p. 103; for the frieze, Thomas, *Ludwig der Bayer*, p. 252.

[8] The construction of the Rhine as an ethnic and cultural frontier originated with Caesar. The idea prevailed despite the subsequent establishment of the Roman provinces of Germania Superior and Germania Inferior to the left of the river, with Mainz as the administrative seat for Germania Superior: B. Scardigli, 'Germania (Provinzname) – Germania Magna', in *RGA* 11, pp. 245–59 (esp. p. 251). For the place of the Rhine in geographical conceptions of Germany, see below, Ch. 10, pp. 455–61.

late medieval custodians. It therefore makes some sense to adopt an approach route that will enable those monarchs to be introduced early on and allow something of the nature and scope of their rule and of the lineaments of German government and institutions quickly to be established.

Other reasons go deeper. For one thing, medieval people were themselves often disposed to regard the rule of kings both as an archetypal form of dominion and as a natural mould and measure for common identities. There was 'no public authority among the Irish', concluded the English chronicler Ralph of Diss, gazing in vain beyond the Irish Sea for the kind of substantial royal rule to which the English king's subjects had by the thirteenth century long grown accustomed.[9] Realms and peoples, moreover, naturally went together. 'There are three things', argued Fulbert of Chartres, 'without which there can be no kingdom (*regnum*), namely a land (*terra*), within which the kingdom exists, a people (*populus*), which inhabits the land, and the person of the chosen king, who lays claim to the land and governs the people.'[10] The making and imagining of national – or, as she prefers, 'regnal' – communities within a form supplied by the realm has been proposed with much lucidity by Susan Reynolds. Her approach to the subject has lent new explanatory force to a conviction long harboured by medievalists, namely that Europe's nations emerged out of the downfall of the western Roman and (especially) Carolingian empires, within broadly political processes which also saw the establishment of a plurality of new realms.[11] It was 'the fact of being a kingdom ... and of sharing a single law and government which promoted a sense of solidarity among its subjects and made them describe themselves as a people'.[12] Establishing what, and how much, it meant to be 'German' must therefore, from this (in origin, medieval) perspective, mean above all investigating how, and how intensively, inhabitants of the German lands related to the monarchy set over them.

But this is not the only motivation for starting with kings and their rule. Reynolds' concern is above all with the kingdom's role as an *imaginative* framework for constructing shared peoplehood; and she is at pains to evade the snares of teleology, insisting that the study of medieval 'states' and 'nations' ought not to be limited to those

[9] Quoted in Davies, 'The medieval state', p. 285. Only those 'seized by the madness of evil', according to the twelfth-century English chronicler Henry of Huntingdon, would choose to live without the rule of a king: Given-Wilson, *Chronicles*, p. 269.

[10] Quoted in Moeglin, 'Die historiographische Konstruktion', p. 354.

[11] See above, pp. 41–3.

[12] Reynolds, *Kingdoms and Communities*, p. 253.

with direct modern successors.[13] Furthermore, Reynolds, despite her insistence on the formative role of law and government, is prepared to envisage the emergence of 'regnal' communities within medieval realms of varied configuration and institutional development – including Germany.[14] Yet there exists another, influential, approach to rulership and nation-making, apparently similar to hers, but in fact rather different in assumptions and focus. This perspective concentrates upon royal power and the 'machinery of government' as the key factors in 'welding' a people together, and 'forging' from it a national community. (We should perhaps regard as an unconscious nod to the modern Europe on which their gaze is usually half-set the habit common among proponents of this approach of invoking medieval political relationships through the imagery of the Industrial Revolution.) Not merely the existence of monarchical regimes possessing continuity and legitimacy, but the development of governmental institutions and techniques, and sometimes also the elaboration of specific supporting doctrines, are ascribed much importance in the early history of European nations. Studies applying this perspective are often disposed, and sometimes positively anxious, to see medieval realms and peoples in terms of their relation to, and contribution to forming, the contemporary political order.

Government-centred accounts of nation-making tend – as also do Reynolds' and other influential approaches – to identify a major new historical phase, commencing around the Millennium and broadening and deepening in the centuries that followed.[15] It was in this period that, on a widely held view, there was established in Europe a plurality of discrete (if not yet fully 'sovereign') political communities, under monarchical headship, characterised by a new level and kind of durability.[16] In place of war-bands clustered around charismatic leaders and their kin, stable royal regimes are now to be observed, presiding over definite, consolidating territories, some of which were subjected to increasingly elaborate and ambitious institutional government. What distinguished the 'nations' which emerged in the course of these developments was not so much their patently imagined, fictive and ideological qualities, or their links with power as such – much of which, it is now clear, could equally be said of their dark-age forebears – as

[13] Ibid., pp. 252–3.   [14] Ibid., esp. p. 289.
[15] Examples: Koht, 'The dawn', p. 266; Huizinga, 'Patriotism', pp. 104–5; Reynolds, *Kingdoms and Communities*, Ch. 8.
[16] Reuter, 'Introduction', p. 10; Strayer, *On the Medieval Origins*, p. 17.

their formation, in the view of many historians, within the nascent structures of the 'state'.[17]

The view that a new political form, with a long and influential career ahead of it, first arose in Europe during the central Middle Ages has garnered substantial and wide-ranging scholarly acceptance.[18] Charles Tilly, taking a long view of the European state, traced its origins to the end of the tenth century, while Joseph Strayer argued that 'in the centuries between 1000 and 1300 some of the essential elements of the modern state began to appear', above all in England and France.[19] Others prefer a somewhat later chronology. One international research project of the 1990s chose to commence its quest for 'the modern state in Europe' in the thirteenth century (concluding in the eighteenth).[20] Bernard Guenée identified the period around 1300 as marking in France a watershed in the formation of state and nation alike.[21] Jean-Philippe Genet contends that *l'État moderne* was 'born' in western Europe (specifically, in France, England, Scotland and the Iberian kingdoms) – or, more precisely, it crystallised out of a series of more ancient elements – in the decades between 1280 and 1360.[22] Studies such as these tend to rest upon two clear convictions, explicit in some, implicit in others: that the connection between state-building and nation-formation in medieval Europe went beyond mere chronological congruence; and that

---

[17] Thus, e.g., Black, *Political Thought*, p. 111; Post, *Studies*, p. 435: 'Like representation in assemblies, early modern nationalism arose, in the 12th and 13th centuries, at the king's command... Ideas of the public law and the State supported the rise of the national State, and early nationalism at the same time strengthened the public authority of the king.' A similar view, though concentrating on the early modern period, is advanced in Kiernan, 'State and nation', pp. 20–1. The literature is surveyed in Reynolds, 'The historiography'.

[18] Strayer, *On the Medieval Origins*, p. 12: 'The modern state, wherever we find it today, is based on the pattern which emerged in Europe in the period 1100 to 1600.'

[19] Tilly, *Coercion*; Strayer, *On the Medieval Origins*, p. 34. For Michael Mann, the 'European dynamic' entered a new 'intensive phase' after the year 800, and found expression in a 'rise of coordinating states' from the mid-twelfth century: Mann, *The Sources*, vol. I, Chs. 12, 13. For a comparable chronology, see Given, *State*, p. 8.

[20] European Science Foundation: 'The Origins of the Modern State in Europe, 13th–18th Centuries'. For a recent attempt at tracing European state-making 'from below' across the same broad period, see Blockmans, Holenstein and Mathieu (eds.), *Empowering Interactions*.

[21] Guenée, 'État et nation', p. 29. As early as 1951, the Swiss historian Werner Näf, in seeking the origins of the 'modern state' in western Europe, had reached a similar conclusion. In France, there took place a 'sichtbare Wandlung des Staatscharakters um und seit etwa 1300': Näf, 'Frühformen', p. 226.

[22] Genet, 'La typologie', p. 10. For other comparative studies concentrating on the central-later Middle Ages and on France and England, see: Seton-Watson, *Nations*, esp. p. 17; Schulze, *States*, esp. p. 17.

the two interlinked processes took much larger steps forward in some realms than in others.[23]

Often, the nations which took shape during this period were formed within kingdoms which had been enlarged and stabilised through the conquest or absorption of neighbouring, once-independent, territories and their populations. The geographical extension of the Capetian dynasty's rule within western Frankia during the central Middle Ages is just one startling instance of developments which were being repeated across much of western Europe.[24] One striking element in many expanding realms of the eleventh, twelfth and thirteenth centuries was their clearly composite character. Consisting as they often did of a plurality of distinct peoples, brought together under a single ruler, the key nation-forming role in kingdoms like France, England or the Iberian realms, or even in a smaller polity like Scotland or looser ones like the Scandinavian kingdoms, was taken by monarchy and its apparatus of rule.[25] If the pattern was not in itself wholly new, more novel was the intensity and insistence with which it revealed itself, within clearly visible bounds and structures. It was institutionalised royal power, so the argument goes, that proved able over time to weave around the disparate, even antagonistic, ethnic groups enclosed by the growing realms the idea of a single, all-embracing political 'nation' under the crown.[26] Normans, Bretons and Burgundians gradually grew accustomed to viewing themselves simultaneously (and being represented in official utterances primarily) as French, while Scottish royal charters, which in the early 1100s had addressed the 'Frenchmen and Englishmen, Scots and Gallowegians' under the king, were by the century's close being directed simply at 'all the men of the land'.[27] In a kindred process, conquering elites were induced to reimagine themselves in the image of their recently acquired realms, with the descendants of William the Conqueror's French-speaking barons, for example, coming within a

---

[23] Schulze, *States*, p. 15: 'The first modern state to come into permanent existence in Europe [from the twelfth/thirteenth centuries onward] was France.' For the link between French royal power and nation-making, see Waley and Denley, *Later Medieval Europe*, p. 58: 'It is extremely difficult to know what the "average" Frenchman thought, yet there are some signs among the more articulate that the monarchy's increasing strength was reflected in a growing awareness of nationality and a new sense of being bound by French loyalties.'

[24] For a convenient overview, see Hallam and Everard, *Capetian France*.

[25] Guenée, 'État et nation'; Carpenter, *The Struggle*, Ch. 1; Grant, 'Aspects', esp. pp. 12, 16.

[26] For this argument applied to France, see Waley and Denley, *Later Medieval Europe*, p. 59; for a dissenting voice, Given, *State*, esp. p. 248.

[27] Grant, 'Aspects of national consciousness', p. 79.

relatively short span of generations to conceive and describe themselves as English.[28]

Governmentality, it seems, increasingly overlaid, out-trumped and redefined ethnicity, submerging older collective loyalties beneath new, officially sanctioned common identities. It was the sophistication and intrusiveness of late Anglo-Saxon royal government that led one historian to declare a 'certainty' the precocious existence of a fully formed 'nation state' in pre-Conquest England.[29] The resources of power in the ruler's hands were destined nevertheless to take startling leaps forward in the centuries that followed. Some of these reflected the opportunities opened up, for those kings with the means to grasp them, by the growing confidence of Europeans in making use of writing.[30] In England, to cite one resonant statistic, the royal chancery's weekly consumption of sealing wax had grown from under 4 pounds in the late 1220s to nearly 32 pounds by 1271.[31] In France meanwhile, the *c.* 15,000 royal letters surviving from the 29-year reign of Philip IV (1285–1314) contrast starkly with the *c.* 2,500 which exist from the longer reign of Philip Augustus, less than a century before (1180–1223).[32] Where royal government was already strong, the transformations under way in society and economy tended to strengthen it further. Demographic boom helped to refashion seats of rule into great cities, with the population of Paris probably doubling in the time of Philip Augustus alone.[33] The kind of pulpit propaganda which accompanied the pan-European wars of the later Middle Ages would have been impossible without the establishment of a dense network of local churches, and the expectation that people should attend them.[34] The growing use of money in western Europe represented an opportunity for those rulers with the institutional and ideological means to invade their subjects' purses; burgeoning royal incomes, in their turn, sustained the further mushrooming of bureaucracies, war machines, building projects and other conspicuous manifestations and instruments of power.

Not, of course, that the story was one of uninterrupted plain sailing, even in the most advanced or best regulated of realms. On the contrary, the flexing of royal muscles at home and abroad provoked

---

[28] See generally Thomas, *The English*. A number of essays dealing with the formation of an overarching English political identity in the period are collected in Gillingham, *The English*.
[29] Campbell, 'The late Anglo-Saxon state', p. 10.
[30] Strayer, *On the Medieval Origins*, p. 24.
[31] Clanchy, *From Memory*, p. 43.   [32] Ibid., p. 45.
[33] Ehlers, *Die Kapetinger*, p. 132.
[34] See McHardy, 'Liturgy'.

widespread tensions, resentments and periodic full-blown crises, which
during the late Middle Ages sometimes attained epic proportions. Yet
such frictions are often viewed as, in the long run at least, a further
element in the European nation-making scheme: at once a measure of
the road already travelled, and in themselves a further boost to progress
along the way.[35] Much of the time, there is little doubt, taxes and dues
were paid, military service performed, the king's mandates heard and
the interfering hand of royal government borne, with gritted teeth or
conscious ill-will.[36] There are indications that the great, in later memory patriotic, wars of the fourteenth and fifteenth centuries inspired at
times rather less popular fervour than has sometimes been supposed.[37]
While the period certainly abounds in strident expressions of collective
'self-glorification at the king's command', it is not always easy to judge
how widely such sentiments were echoed beyond the circles, close to the
court or royal administration, from which their authors often hailed.[38]
Yet, if the burdens of war were unpopular, that fact itself serves in a
way to underline the formative power at the disposal of regimes capable
of enforcing them, and of compelling from entire populations a measure of identification, however grudging and qualified, with the cause
of king and kingdom. Late medieval patriotism was to some degree
imposed by act of government.[39]

Possessed of such substantial underlying strengths, royal government was, it appears, capable of stimulating the growth of a national
community even when faced with incapable kings, domestic challenges to its legitimacy, or even outright collapse. In thirteenth- and
fourteenth-century England, sentiments of political nationhood were
probably instilled and articulated as much through periodic opposition
to the crown, its friends and agents, and its acts, as through any rise in
popular attachment to the monarchy itself.[40] Constitutional and military disasters such as overwhelmed France in the fourteenth and early
fifteenth centuries tended in the end, it has been argued, to thrust the
king's far-flung subjects together, extend the shared burdens upon their
backs, and thus confront them starkly with a common fate defined in
terms of the regnal community and its head.[41] The fact that an obscure

---

[35] The importance of the fourteenth and fifteenth centuries in the formation of political
   communities in Europe is powerfully argued by Watts, *The Making*, esp. pp. 420–5.
[36] Keeney, 'Military service', esp. pp. 547–8.
[37] Examples in: McHardy, 'Liturgy', p. 223; Ruddick, 'National sentiment', pp. 16–17.
[38] For some of the English evidence, see Scattergood, *Politics*, Ch. 3.
[39] Post, *Studies*, p. 434.
[40] Clanchy, *England*, Ch. 10; Turville-Petre, *England*, pp. 130–4.
[41] Thus Allmand, *The Hundred Years War*, p. 148.

teenage girl from the kingdom's eastern marches was eventually able to emerge as the champion of monarch and nation alike is striking testimony to the social and geographical scope which the identification of people and 'state' had attained in France by the fifteenth century.[42] Behind such eye-catching individual events lay long-term processes, in the course of which the number and intensity of the channels, both formal and less formal, connecting rulers with the populations subject to their rule increased.[43] Some of these had originated as devices for royal administration and control, which, however, proved capable of adaptation in practice to allow local communities to place their own concerns, perspectives and grievances before the crown.[44] The consolidation throughout western Europe in the later Middle Ages of a whole plethora of representative assemblies of varying size, scope, composition and powers is just one visible expression of the processes of interaction – generally unequal, yet real, and in much of Europe increasingly intensive – between rulers and ruled which the growing burdens of government both demanded and made possible.[45] If the community of the realm became during the later Middle Ages in some ways more fractured, and fractious, it also increased in size and social diversity. Relations between crown and people grew more ramified and urgent, as well as more troubled. And with them, historians have often argued, grew the political nation itself.[46]

In the end, much came down to persuasion, which in its turn implied the ability of regimes and their servants (and in times of crisis, their rivals and opponents too) to communicate effectively with the expanding groups of people whose lives were touched by royal politics. By the late Middle Ages, some European governments were deploying with conscious intent a growing array of media and techniques to reach their subjects with what it often seems quite appropriate to call propaganda messages.[47] Political communication was one natural use to which ancient and more recent institutions might be put: the English Parliament and the general assembly of the French Estates each provided venues in which, particularly in times of crisis, support for the Crown's position could be mobilised among a wide-ranging political

---

[42] See Warner, *Joan of Arc*, esp. Ch. 2.
[43] Illustrated in Strayer, 'The laicization'.
[44] For an English example of this, see Scales, 'The Cambridgeshire Ragman Rolls'.
[45] Myers, *Parliaments*; Blockmans, 'A typology'; Watts, *The Making*, pp. 233–8. The nation-making role of the English Parliament is argued in Hastings, *The Construction*, pp. 50–1.
[46] See, e.g., Allmand, *The Hundred Years War*, Ch. 6.
[47] Menache, 'Symbols'; Guenée, *States*, Ch. 1.

public. In England during the war-torn fourteenth century, the regular, well-attended meetings of the county court were subjected to a barrage of royal proclamations.[48] The power of administrative kingship in France and England to mount startling public gestures was displayed to sinister effect in carefully orchestrated police actions against unpopular minorities: Jews, Templars and even the clergy of the realm.[49] During the wars of the fourteenth and fifteenth centuries, kings and their ministers had recourse to a wide range of communications forms – from prayers, proclamations and the public display of texts and images to solemn entries and processions, theatricals, pageants and festivities – in order to convince as many of their subjects as possible of the justice of their own, and thus (it was argued) their people's, cause.[50]

Many of the ideas and doctrines that had over the course of the Middle Ages been drawn down around European kings, their families and their rule tended to encourage the formation of ties, concrete and imagined, with the populations subject to them. The process received further stimulus from social and cultural processes at work in Europe in the centuries after the Millennium. The results were especially potent in those kingdoms in which the throne descended over the course of successive generations within a single dynasty. Within such realms, from Hungary to Norway, Bohemia to Scotland, the cults of royal saints supplied a focus for glorification of the ruling house, and a channel between familial *memoria* and devout inhabitants of the realm.[51] On occasion, as in Bohemia, a holy ruler's cult came to transcend dynasty altogether and become symbolic of the political community as a whole.[52] In the most prestigious ruling families, the aura of holiness embraced not only saintly ancestors, but the living king himself, who was credited with miraculous healing powers. The most prominent embodiments of this doctrine were the kings of France, whose court drew in supplicants from far and wide, hoping to benefit from the royal touch.[53] However, by the twelfth century, there is already evidence that their rivals, the English kings, were claiming comparable powers, just as they would go on in the centuries that followed to appropriate further trappings of sacral monarchy.[54] Settled urban residences like Paris and Westminster developed into royal cult and memorial sites, where pilgrims and other

---

[48] Maddicott, 'The county community'.
[49] Prestwich, *Edward I*, pp. 343–6, 415–18; Strayer, *The Reign*, Ch. 4.
[50] See, e.g., Allmand, *Henry V*, Ch. 19; Allmand, *The Hundred Years War*, Ch. 6.
[51] Klaniczay, *Holy Rulers*. For France, see Beaune, *The Birth of an Ideology*, Chs. 1–3.
[52] Prochno, 'Terra Bohemiae'.
[53] Bloch, *The Royal Touch*, esp. p. 62.
[54] McKenna, 'Englishman'.

visitors were exposed to the full splendour of the religion of royalty.[55] By the late Middle Ages, the fruits of dynastic memory-keeping, long cultivated behind the walls of favoured royal monasteries, had begun to reach eyes beyond the cloister. Among the most influential examples of this trend must be numbered the *Grandes Chroniques de France*, a vernacular translation made in 1274 (and subsequently extended) of Latin chronicles from the royal abbey of Saint-Denis. Richly illustrated, the *Grandes Chroniques* unlocked the accumulated store of Capetian history and myth in a format which enlarged significantly its potential audience.[56] They were but one among a series of developments in the royalist culture of later Capetian France which encouraged identification of the 'chosen' French people and its 'holy' kingdom with the glorious line of 'Most Christian' rulers.[57] Little wonder, then, that the German treatise-writer Alexander von Roes, in a work composed in the 1280s, described the French monarchs, in the most back-handed of compliments, as more like bishops or abbots than kings.[58]

At around the same time as these currents were flowing together, with an obvious high point in the second half of the thirteenth century, themes become visible in learned legal thought and political philosophy, supportive of the existence of a plurality of political communities under independent kings. Canon and civil lawyers elaborated the idea that certain kingdoms recognised no temporal superior – in political practice at least, and perhaps even in law.[59] Other legists invoked Roman maxims to elucidate the subject's overriding duty to the *communis patria* – the 'common fatherland', or community of the realm – and its prince, with self-sacrifice *pro patria* defined as the noblest of acts.[60] Jurists also expounded the formal principles of consent and representation, smoothing the way for the imposition of general burdens upon entire populations under the king.[61] During the same period, the political writings of Aristotle, with their reasoned case for pluralism, were absorbed into the Latin tradition.[62] The Paris Dominican Jean Quidort (fl. *c.* 1300) was among those who drew from Christian Aristotelianism, reinforced characteristically by liberal doses of law,

---

[55] Beaune, *The Birth*, esp. Chs. 1, 3; Brown, 'Persona'; Binski, *Westminster Abbey*.
[56] A. Vernet, 'Chroniques (Grandes) de France', in *LMA* 2, cols. 2034–5; Moeglin, 'Konstruktion der Nation', pp. 362–5, 374–5.
[57] Strayer, 'France: the Holy Land'.
[58] Alexander von Roes, *Noticia seculi*, cap. 11, ed. Grundmann and Heimpel, p. 158.
[59] Ullmann, 'The development'.
[60] Kantorowicz, *Two Bodies*, pp. 232–72; Post, *Studies*, Ch. 10.
[61] Post, *Studies*, Ch. 3.   [62] Dunbabin, 'Aristotle'.

history and myth, arguments for the existence of distinct, sovereign realms, most specifically the French.[63]

It could justly be objected that these theoreticians were much of the time doing little more than articulate in abstract (and sometimes more extreme) terms convictions which had long been widely held among western Europeans.[64] But it remains significant that such principles found expression when and where they did. For it is striking how very few of the authors of such speculations were German, and how few of their works were composed on German soil. Indeed, at the end of the thirteenth century (and for some decades thereafter), German-speaking Europe remained entirely without universities. Instead, many of the early theorists of the 'state' were to be found working in spheres close to, or under the protection of, the French monarchy, while others took the French king as the object of their theorising.[65] We thus gain an early inkling that, in an age which saw distinct, stable and increasingly self-conscious political communities come into view in Europe, the Germans and their monarchs are conspicuous absentees from the party.

The preceding paragraphs have sought deliberately to unfold in synthetic form a maximalist vision of royal power and nation-making. While it was assembled from arguments well established among historians working in the field, no attempt has been made to raise objections or qualifications, or to indicate possible alternative perspectives to the bold vista of incipient European modernity which such approaches commonly assert or imply. As a result, it has been possible to heap up a whole series of criteria against which, taking the champions of the proto-modern 'nation state' at their word, the development, character and resources of monarchical rule in Germany can now be measured, before proceeding, in the chapters which follow, to evaluate its role in shaping notions of common 'German' identity. The picture which results will amount to a re-examination of the 'state'-centred paradigm for early European nation-making itself.

What, then, of the Germans? The self-same familiar paradigm of rulership and nation-making has often been applied to their medieval past too, but with results wholly unlike those encountered so far.[66] 'Lacking are both national sentiment and the political capacity to forge a

---

[63] Wilks, *The Problem*, esp. pp. 91–2.
[64] A point developed in Reynolds, *Kingdoms and Communities*, pp. 319–29.
[65] See, e.g., Krynen, *L'Empire du roi*.
[66] For the refusal of Germany to conform to the medieval European 'modernisation paradigm', see Reuter, 'The medieval German *Sonderweg*?', esp. pp. 179–80.

centralised state', declared Sylvain Gouguenheim of thirteenth-century Germany, making a by now familiar, though unvoiced, causal connection.[67] The argument is an old-established one, with origins reaching back almost as far as the scholarly quest for the medieval German nation itself. But, unlike that latter pursuit, the lachrymose view of early German 'state'-making has never gone out of fashion or, a handful of dissenters notwithstanding, ceased to command wide agreement.[68] It too was an analysis formed in Germany, during the key middle decades of the nineteenth century. Even while at their most stridently boastful, professorial invocations of the greatness and national pride of their people's medieval forebears were apt quickly to disclose undercurrents of despondency and regret. 'German constitutional history had something hopeless about it from the start.'[69] The medieval German *Nationalstaat* was the great light that failed. 'Too often has our *Volk* experienced the sad consequences of its inner fragmentation', reflected Giesebrecht ruefully, 'not to wish back with the most fervent longing that time of a single, great, powerful Germany.'[70] Most bitterly, failure had come at just the time when Germany's neighbours were embarking, in the manner already observed, on their paths to early national cohesion. 'In France', observed Georg von Below, 'the twelfth century sees the beginning of a restoration of the monarchy, in Germany a period of strengthening of the local powers.'[71] Squabbling princes and emperors had denied the German *Volk* 'the fulfilment of its national longing in a unified *Staatswesen*', compelling the Germans to forfeit their 'place in the sun' to 'those nations whose state-formation had proceeded more rapidly and smoothly'.[72] In truth, the medieval German nation had been all the time but a glorious spectre, all shimmer and dazzle, but, without the solid flesh and bone of institutionalised power, liable at once to dissolve into air. That, it seems, is exactly what it did, at just the time when 'nations' elsewhere were being securely encased within the well-crafted structures of the state. The 'failure' of the Germans in that venture was as abject as their neighbours' 'success' was 'remarkable'.[73]

---

[67] Gouguenheim, 'Les Structures politiques,' p. 47.

[68] For such dissenters, see above, Ch. 1, p. 47.

[69] Heimpel, *Deutsches Mittelalter*, p. 18. The words are from Heimpel's 1933 lecture, 'Deutschlands Mittelalter – Deutschlands Schicksal'. For its context, see Althoff, 'Das Mittelalterbild', pp. 734–6.

[70] Quoted in Schneider (ed.), *Universalstaat*, p. xxxv.

[71] Von Below, *Der deutsche Staat*, p. 365.

[72] Mitteis, *Der Staat*, p. 418.

[73] German 'failure': Schulze, *States*, p. 24; Strayer, *On the Medieval Origins*, p. 35; Hastings, *The Construction*, pp. 7–8; 'remarkable' French 'success': Llobera, 'State', p. 361.

'And so', lamented Johannes Haller, 'we observe everywhere a breaking up and a crumbling away. The course of development [in Germany] moves not towards cohesiveness in great power complexes, but towards separation, division, splintering.'[74]

It was the calamities of the central and later Middle Ages that guaranteed that Germany's long-term historical trajectory would be, in European comparison, so dishearteningly distinctive – 'a history of decline', as Norbert Elias put it.[75] As nation states elsewhere grew apace, the German body politic succumbed to an agonisingly slow process of decomposition. Yet darker shades crowded in after 1945, when a crisis of 'state' and 'nation' rooted in the Middle Ages was invoked by some to explain the allure of dictatorship and ethnic fundamentalism to twentieth-century Germans.[76] So where did things go so fatally wrong? And to whom, or what, was the blame to be apportioned (for it was beyond dispute that such catastrophic misreadings of the historical map required that the guilty be named)? For Heinrich von Sybel, who first set in train the whole melancholy quest, the poison was present almost from the outset. 'In Germany the national unity was shattered by our old emperors' lust for conquest and their defeats.'[77] The trail led all the way back to the tenth century. For von Below, too, it was the Ottonians who first sacrificed 'the objective of *nationalstaatlich* development' to universal goals and ideals.[78] For von Sybel's antagonist, Ficker, the wrong turn was only taken late in the twelfth century, when Barbarossa first entangled his dynasty in its ill-fated Sicilian adventure.[79] In the view of Heinrich Mitteis, meanwhile, not until Frederick II's time did events finally determine 'that the binding together of the German people in a cohesive national *Einheitsstaat* … would be postponed for seven centuries'.[80] How could a path seemingly embarked on from such a position of unmatched strength have thus proved to lead only into the wilderness? Eckhart Müller-Mertens, writing in the DDR from a Marxist perspective, thought he had an answer: German national cohesion under the ruler had simply been attained *too early*, at the Millennium, before the crucial epoch of 'feudal' transformations in power relationships, in the course of which other European states (and nations) were formed. 'It

---

[74] Haller, *Die Epochen*, p. 91.
[75] Elias, *The Germans*, p. 344.
[76] Examples: Elias, *The Germans*, pp. 318–19; Hastings, *The Construction*, pp. 108–9; Winkler, *Germany*, vol. I, p. 4. Barraclough, *The Origins*, sought on a larger canvas to explain modern German history in terms of medieval political developments.
[77] Quoted in Schneider (ed.), *Universalstaat*, p. xvi.
[78] Von Below, *Der deutsche Staat*, p. 362.
[79] Schneider (ed.), *Universalstaat*, p. xvi.
[80] Mitteis, *Der Staat*, p. 400.

would have been better', he ventured, 'if the monarchy had entered this process impotent, and free from all imperial ties and traditions.'[81] Yet for him, too, it was ultimately the siren allure of the south that distracted the emperors' gaze from the task of building at home an 'estates-based monarchy founded principally upon nationality'.[82]

Wherever may have lain the ultimate fault, whether with shadow-chasing emperors, greedy princes, treacherous popes or the hidden hand of history itself, it was at all events clear that by the later thirteenth century, the chance of cohesion under a strong monarchy had passed. Germany had 'missed the opportunity for national development' in that crucial formative era.[83] It is true that some – particularly anglophone and francophone – medievalists have claimed to discern among the Germans a common identity based on shared culture (particularly language), in place of the regnal cohesion of their western neighbours. The validity of this judgement will have to await inspection in a later chapter;[84] but first, the development of rulership itself must be examined. If much of the historiography of early German 'state'-making – whether of recent or older authorship, from German or non-German pens – displays every symptom of teleology run mad, the central charge nevertheless cannot be evaded:[85] that, in a seemingly crucial epoch for the formation of European 'regnal' identities, German society was touched and shaped by monarchical government substantially less than were its main western neighbours.

It is a charge that gathers force from judgements on the nature of German political life recorded in other European kingdoms at the time. The English chronicler Thomas Wykes (who was close to Richard of Cornwall during his rule in Germany) was left open-mouthed by the picture of anarchy which the riotous growth of princely tolls along the Rhine – perhaps thirty-five by the end of the thirteenth century – seemed to reveal: only the 'raging madness of the Teutons', he insisted, could explain such 'extortions', perpetrated from 'impregnable fortresses along the Rhine's course'.[86] The Spanish canonist Vincentius

---

[81] Müller-Mertens, 'Vom Regnum Teutonicum', p. 335. For a comparable judgement from an earlier German medievalist with a decidedly different ideological standpoint, see Heimpel, *Deutsches Mittelalter*, p. 18: 'Die deutsche Verfassung war von vornherein mit den besonderen Schwierigkeiten eines unfertigen Staates belastet.'

[82] Müller-Mertens, 'Vom Regnum Teutonicum', p. 337.

[83] Barraclough, *The Origins*, p. 299; and cf. Huizinga, 'Patriotism', p. 112.

[84] Ch. 11, pp. 484–504.

[85] The anachronistic assumptions of such works are eloquently denounced in Althoff, *Die Macht*, pp. 14–15.

[86] *Chronicon vulgo dictum Chronicon Thomae Wykes*, ed. Luard, p. 222. For the tolls themselves, see Postan, 'The trade', pp. 134–5.

found incredible the pretension of the Germans to universal rule, at a time when in their own lands 'every hut usurps lordship for itself, and every city contends with the Germans for the same'.[87] The impression of division and chaos was likewise invoked by the French lawyer Pierre Dubois, who, writing early in the fourteenth century, affected to perceive in the discords of the Germans an obstacle to the recovery of the Holy Land itself.[88] An effective central authority on the western model was nowhere to be seen. For well-informed Germans, too, their monarchy seemed set on a different trajectory from those of their happier neighbours. Alexander von Roes, whose eyes had been opened by a spell at the French-dominated Curia of the early 1280s, reflected that in the period of roughly fifty years between Frederick II's imperial coronation (1220) and the 1274 Council of Lyon, the 'Roman Empire' had so much declined as to pass almost out of remembrance, reaching by the latter date a point whence 'it cannot decrease any further without being completely destroyed'.[89] That was all in stark contrast to the soaring prestige of the French – to whose monarchy, in a most revealing concession, he ascribed an hereditary sovereignty, without temporal superior, resting upon a grant from Charlemagne himself.[90]

State of dissolution: monarchy and government in Germany

If we take a panoramic view, the political character of the German lands in the thirteenth century appears to reflect the outcome of long-term courses and patterns not unlike those already detected in other European kingdoms. In Germany, too, it seems, the descendants of a plurality of older peoples, each with its own political framework, and shared myths and memories, had over time been drawn together in allegiance to a common ruler: the 'Roman' king or emperor.[91] Yet, as quickly becomes clear, matters are not that simple, and for evidence to support the gloomiest visions of Germany's medieval course, we need do no more than turn over the pages of an historical atlas. As the reader moves from map to map – Europe in c. AD 900, at the time of the First Crusade, in the age of Plantagenet and Valois, on the

---

[87] Quoted in Post, *Studies*, p. 489.
[88] *De Recuperatione*, ed. Langlois, Ch. 13, p. 12.
[89] Alexander von Roes, *Noticia seculi*, cap. 8, ed. Grundmann and Heimpel, p. 154.
[90] Alexander von Roes, *Memoriale*, cap. 24, ed. Grundmann and Heimpel, pp. 125–6. For Alexander's view of French sovereignty, see Scales, 'France and the Empire'.
[91] For a comparison with England, tracing similarities as well as contrasts, see Reuter, 'The making of England', pp. 56–60.

eve of the Reformation – the coloured masses transmute in orderly, well-established succession.[92] The monumental central expanse of the imperial lands first looms large, only to begin shedding its isolated dominance, as the blocks denoting neighbouring and more distant realms and lordships become by stages both fewer and bigger; then, on the closing medieval pages, Europe's hitherto monochrome centre implodes in a riot of coloured shards, tiny and innumerable over much of the west and south, a few bigger fragments to the east and south-east. Yet, so far as the German lands are concerned, this succession of frozen historical snapshots is as misleading as it is familiar.

Some contrasts, of course, are accurate enough. 'Germany', as an assembly of lands under royal rule, did indeed start out big while its neighbours started small. The northern territories over which the Saxon kings and emperors ruled in the tenth century reached already from the North Sea coasts to the Pannonian plains, from the Romance-speaking south-west to the Slavic north-east of Latin Europe. Danish, Polish and Hungarian kings acknowledged the emperor as their overlord. In the second half of the twelfth century, the Empire's German lands were still around twice the size of the realm controlled by the king of France.[93] Although the Empire did not remain unchanged in its territorial extent over the course of the Middle Ages, neither did it grow by stages as did some other European realms; on certain fronts, it contracted.

Most unhelpful, on the other hand, is the impression which the atlases habitually convey, of a Germany once politically unified, which disintegrated into a myriad of separate political elements in the later Middle Ages. In fact, the sharing of rule between the monarch and a plethora of established regional powers was fundamental to the constitutional order of Germany from the first emergence of a separate sphere of rule there out of the ruins of Charlemagne's empire.[94] As Timothy Reuter has pointed out, 'the east Frankish-Ottonian *Reich* was from the start multi-regnal'.[95] The peoples who stood under the monarch in the north (and who, for Wipo, writing in the eleventh century, also raised him to the throne) – Franks, Saxons, Swabians, Bavarians – guarded

---

[92] E.g. Engel (ed.), *Großer historischer Weltatlas*, pp. 18–19, 34–5, 66–7, 78–9; Baldamus, Schwabe and Ambrosius (eds.), *Putzgers Historischer Schul-Atlas*, pp. 66–7, 70–1, 74–5, 78–9; Muir and Philip (eds.), *Philip's Historical Atlas*, pp. 15, 24–5, 29, 36–7, 41.

[93] Reuter, 'The medieval German *Sonderweg*?', p. 199.

[94] See Leyser, 'The German aristocracy'.

[95] Reuter, 'The medieval German *Sonderweg*?', p. 196, as well as Arnold, *Medieval Germany*, part I. For the character and identity of these early medieval realms, see Werner, 'Völker und Regna'.

long the memory of political independence.[96] In the twelfth century, Gerhoh von Reichersberg found it natural to write in the plural, of 'Lotharingians, Bavarians, Saxons and the rest of the German nations [*Teutonicae nationes*]'.[97] Although the imperial monarchy did guarantee, through the Church and the great duchies, a measure of common political life under the ruler, the great secular and spiritual magnates in the far-flung, ancient realms did not regard themselves as his subordinates, still less his subjects, but as rulers in their own right, their power justified in its own terms. True, they came together with the king from time to time in great and solemn assemblies; but not in order to hear his will or bear the strictures of his law.[98] Instead, the monarch's role there was above all to validate, arbitrate within and hold in equilibrium the delicate economy of status and honour within which the German princes moved and acted. It has been truthfully said that the issuing of privileges was the most characteristic act of government engaged in by the Empire's rulers in their high medieval heyday.[99] This was no symptom of incipient decline, or failure of monarchical will, but rather the fundamental unit of political exchange among the elite of the high medieval Reich. It was how things had traditionally been, under 'strong' as well as 'weak' kings.

Established spheres of dynastic predominance were jealously defended, and avidly extended when opportunity arose, while the vast extent of the German lands, set beside the monarchy's relatively modest resources for their domination, ensured that checking the consolidation of princely power would inevitably have been a losing battle. It was not, in any case, a battle which there had traditionally been much call for the king to fight. In face of such facts of life, attempts by the monarch to arrogate to himself unaccustomed powers, or to accumulate lands to the potential harm of Germany's greatest kindreds, had always been liable to end disastrously – as Henry IV had discovered already in the eleventh century.[100] The steps taken by rulers elsewhere in Europe to enlarge the territories under the monarchy's direct control and limit or suppress regional autonomies had no real counterparts in Germany:

---

[96] For Wipo, see Thomas, 'Identitätsproblem', p. 139. Wipo also mentioned the Lotharingians, incorporated into the eastern realm in the tenth century, who might be grouped together with the (eastern) Franks or Franconians. See also the comments of Arnold, *Medieval Germany*, p. 185.

[97] Quoted in Schnell, 'Deutsche Literatur', p. 250 n. 16. For Germany's multi-regnal character in the late Middle Ages, see below, Ch. 11, pp. 504–5.

[98] For this and what follows, see Reuter, 'The medieval German *Sonderweg*?', esp. pp. 193–7. For the political culture of high medieval Germany, see Althoff, *Die Macht*.

[99] Reuter, 'The medieval German *Sonderweg*?', pp. 195–6.

[100] See, e.g., Fuhrmann, *Germany*, pp. 51–69, 84–7.

there was no 'Harrying of the North', nothing to parallel the extension of French royal power under the mantle of the 'Albigensian crusade'.[101] After the eleventh century, the Empire's rulers took little part in the eastward advance of the limits of German settlement. In an age of conquest kingdoms, Germany remained substantially unconquered by its monarchs.

This is not to imply that little changed over the course of the Middle Ages. On the contrary, the foundations of power in Germany, particularly at regional and local levels, were transformed; but the process was deep-rooted and gradual, with no sudden, cataclysmic break in the thirteenth century or any other. The train of developments which saw the 'ethnic' duchies of the early Middle Ages gradually give way to distinct territories under princely government is traceable back to the eleventh century at latest; it had still not wholly run its course in the sixteenth.[102] That series of far-reaching changes, grounded in demographic, economic and cultural advance, from which royal government had drawn power elsewhere in Europe – through the foundation of towns, the control of fiscal resources, and the establishment of new centres of rule, administrative devices and legal principles – was in Germany most evident at the level of the great lordships, not the monarchy. The natural home of medieval German 'administrative' rulership was the principalities.[103] Yet while it would certainly be possible to identify landmark imperial enactments establishing some of the foundations of princely sovereignty, such as Frederick II's celebrated privileges of 1220 and 1232, the raising of boundaries across the landscapes of German-speaking Europe was a process too gradual, too much an extension of ancient, natural and organic tendencies, to permit sharp periodisation, let alone visualisation in tidy blocks of shifting colours.[104]

Most maps likewise fail to capture the distinctive character and spatial rhythms of royal rule in Germany. Since Carolingian times, control had been based on a number of heartlands, in which both royal estates and major monarchical cult sites were concentrated, where the itinerant ruler was most frequently to be seen. These heartlands, which never even came close to encompassing all of Germany, underwent over the course of the Middle Ages transformations in location, extent and

---

[101] Clanchy, *England*, pp. 45–7; Strayer, *The Albigensian Crusade*, esp. p. 142.
[102] See generally Arnold, *Princes*, and, for the later period, Schubert, *Fürstliche Herrschaft*.
[103] Arnold, *Princes*, part III; Näf, 'Frühformen', p. 238.
[104] For Frederick II's statutes in favour of the princes, see Keller, *Zwischen regionaler Begrenzung*, pp. 474–500.

fundamental character.[105] Two key characteristics, however, endured, from the tenth century through to the fifteenth: the concentration of royal power in a limited number of favoured zones with, as a consequence, sharp variations in the intensity with which rulership was experienced between different regions; and the recurrent location of those heartlands of rule towards the margins, very seldom at the geographical centre, of German-speaking Europe.

The more detailed picture, however, is one of recurrent change, with – at any rate from the later Salian period – loss and retreat more visible themes than expansion or consolidation. Already by the end of the eleventh century, the traditional power base of Saxon kingship in the north-east was starting to become closed, its resources lost, to the monarch.[106] After the twelfth century, Bavaria, an ancient zone of transit and periodic stay for the Empire's rulers, fell under the growing territorial domination of the Wittelsbach dukes.[107] The regions where imperial resources (*Reichsgut* in German parlance) were more densely clustered kept their importance longer, but they too were slowly overshadowed, the ruler's material basis depleted. Swabia and Alsace, fundamental to the exercise of kingship throughout the thirteenth century, gradually lost the dominance that they had attained under the Staufer.[108] Even the Rhineland, since Frankish times the indispensable core of royal rule in the east, began to slip from the king's grasp.[109] With the mighty ecclesiastical principalities of Mainz, Cologne and Trier dominating the river's middle and lower courses, the lands along its banks became during Frederick II's later years a centre of organised opposition to the Staufer, their rich resources sustaining anti-kings whom the papacy and its German allies raised up against Frederick's dynasty. The lower Rhine, where the Church of Cologne disputed control with important secular territories such as Brabant, Jülich and Berg, fell earliest out of the king's accustomed orbit, though it did remain throughout the late Middle Ages, in Peter Moraw's phrase, 'open' to him if he made the requisite effort – as Albert I demonstrated in 1302, through successful military operations against the archbishop of Cologne.[110]

---

[105] For overviews, see Mayer, 'Das deutsche Königtum', and more recently, Moraw, 'Die Reichsregierung reist'.

[106] Mayer, 'Das deutsche Königtum', pp. 33–4; Moraw, 'Die Reichsregierung reist', p. 31.

[107] For Frederick I in Bavaria, see Opll, *Das Itinerar*, esp. pp. 144–6.

[108] Mayer, 'Das deutsche Königtum', p. 34.

[109] Ibid., p. 41; Eberhard, 'Herrschaft', p. 107.

[110] Thomas, *Deutsche Geschichte*, p. 117. For Albert's itinerary, see above, Map 2. For the lower Rhine (excluding its furthermost reaches) as *königsoffene Landschaft*, see Moraw, *Von offener Verfassung*, p. 175.

The middle Rhine and lower Main kept their importance longer, but declined somewhat as royal centres after the middle of the fourteenth century, partly in consequence of the loss or surrender by the monarchy of major imperial properties in these regions.[111]

The zones of power on which the Empire's rulers increasingly relied during the late Middle Ages were of a different character from the earlier heartlands. In place of the dwindling clusters of *Reichsgut* on which later thirteenth-century kings were forced to depend, rulership in the fourteenth and fifteenth centuries rested increasingly upon the far-flung dynastic patrimonies assembled by the three families which came over time to monopolise the throne: Habsburg, Luxemburg and Wittelsbach.[112] Of these dynasties, the first two had risen from relatively modest comital beginnings in the western borderlands of German-speaking Europe during the troubled decades after Frederick II's death. In both cases, elevation to the imperial throne had been quickly followed by a dramatic dynastic windfall in regions remote from the ancient family seat. Rudolf I's destruction of Bohemia's 'golden king' Otakar II at the Marchfeld in 1278, and the subsequent break-up of Otakar's vast central European patrimony, had paved the way for settling the Austrian duchies on Rudolf's Habsburg descendants.[113] Luxemburg fortunes rose even faster: the count of Luxemburg who was crowned in Aachen at Epiphany 1309 as Henry VII was able in the following year to marry his son John to the Přemyslid heiress to the immensely rich kingdom of Bohemia.[114]

All three families went on, sustained in varying degrees by spells on the imperial throne, to assemble great dynastic landholdings, spanning and transcending German-speaking Europe, linking the rich western lands with more sparsely settled, but rapidly developing, eastern regions. All of them held or acquired properties west of the Rhine. Looking east, Wittelsbach and Luxemburg gained by turns the margraviate of Brandenburg, and all three families sought lands in the central and eastern Alps; Bohemia had at the start of the fourteenth century lain fleetingly in Habsburg hands, while both the Habsburgs and (more seriously) the Luxemburgs pursued ambitions in Poland.[115]

---

[111] Eberhard, 'Herrschaft und Raum', p. 107.
[112] For context, see Herde, 'From Adolf of Nassau', and Hlaváček, 'The Luxemburgs'. The distribution of the main patrimonial territories is shown on Map 1.
[113] See Krieger, *Die Habsburger*, pp. 38–55.
[114] Hoensch, *Die Luxemburger*, pp. 37–9.
[115] Ibid., pp. 62–84, 155–76, 202–4. For the Habsburg candidature in Bohemia, and resulting opportunities in Poland: Krieger, *Die Habsburger*, pp. 99–109; Grundmann, *Wahlkönigtum*, p. 139.

While a Wittelsbach bid for the Hungarian crown had proved vain, the Luxemburg venture had more success, with the election of Charles IV's second son Sigismund by the Hungarian estates in 1387.[116] Beginning with the early Habsburgs, late medieval rulers commonly sought also to cast composite land bridges across central Europe, built up both from patrimonial lands and from parcels of imperial estates; but these naturally collapsed on the king's death as the crown, and its properties, passed to another family.[117] More durable were those essentially dynastic empires of which the one put together by the Luxemburgs in the east stands out in scale and importance. Charles IV built tirelessly upon the foundations which his father John had laid until, at his death in 1378, the family's lands ranged northwards across east-central Europe from the Austrian marches, through Moravia, Bohemia, Silesia, Upper and Lower Lusatia, to Brandenburg, almost reaching the shores of the Baltic.[118] It is the landed acquisitions made by these new imperial dynasties, above all by the Luxemburger, that most explain the eastward shift in the centre of gravity of rulership visible in the later medieval Reich.

Within their territories, the three great families built up centres of government, residential rule, and dynastic memory and glorification of a kind unavailable to previous occupants of the imperial throne: Munich for the Bavarian Wittelsbachs (and, in certain respects, Heidelberg for that family's Palatinate line); Vienna for the Habsburgs; and, most spectacularly, the glittering Luxemburg metropolis of Prague.[119] It was within these cities that administration, justice and finance were increasingly concentrated; written records heaped up; public spectacle orchestrated to the dynasty's glory; scholars, builders, artists and assorted experts assembled in its service; and institutions of higher learning established to the glory and material benefit of the prince. In ways such as these, rulership over the Empire was able to draw some indirect advantage from those processes of consolidation, centralisation, economic growth and cultural change which in Germany had otherwise mainly benefited the great territories. In one sense, these dynasties were behaving no differently from their predecessors on the

---

[116] For Otto of Wittelsbach's candidature: Spindler (ed.), *Handbuch*, pp. 110–18; for Sigismund: Hoensch, *Die Luxemburger*, pp. 204–5.

[117] For the ambitious plans pursued – in vain – by Albert I, see Thomas, *Deutsche Geschichte*, p. 109.

[118] Engel (ed.), *Großer historischer Weltatlas*, pp. 66–7.

[119] See: Orth, 'München', esp. p. 64; Krieger, *Die Habsburger*, pp. 142–5; Moraw, 'Zur Mittelpunktsfunktion', p. 450.

imperial throne: putting their own interests first, and drawing on their familial resources as a basis for government. Yet the context of their activities had been transformed, in ways which made it more necessary, as well as feasible, to rule the Reich from consolidated spheres of dynastic power (what German historians commonly call *Hausmacht*) in place of, and at the cost of, the properties and incomes attached to the imperial office.[120]

The great change which had taken place was the radical disruption, with the end of Hohenstaufen rule, of the heredity which had characterised succession to the Empire, in fact if not in principle, for much of the long period between the tenth and thirteenth centuries. The statistics speak for themselves. Of the seventeen kings who reigned between 919 and 1254, fifteen came from just three dynasties; son succeeded father on the throne eight times.[121] The thirteen kings who (ignoring absentee and anti-kingships) ruled during the shorter period from the mid-thirteenth century to 1493 were drawn, by contrast, from six – it might be more accurate to say eight – different lineages, with son following father only once.[122] During this period, the geographical focus of royal rule fluctuated sharply and frequently across the breadth of the Empire's northern lands, particularly during the succession of Wittelsbach and Luxemburg tenures of the throne in the fourteenth and early fifteenth centuries. The period of little more than 150 years between 1245 and 1414 contains no fewer than five anti-kingships, three split elections, and two depositions of reigning monarchs. Especially damaging was the long and divisive contest for the throne between Ludwig IV of Wittelsbach and the Habsburg Frederick the Fair, which after 1314 drove a wedge through the Empire's old heartlands in southern and western Germany for the better part of a decade.[123] The kings who came to the throne after 1245 were, in their origins and power, a decidedly mixed bunch, but into the fourteenth century what marked them out was their generally modest familial resources, and the consequent uphill struggles which they had to wage – not always with happy results – to give their rule some substance.

---

[120] For the growing role of *Hausmacht* in the government of the Reich, see Moraw, *Von offener Verfassung*, pp. 229–59; for *Reichsgut*, see Krieger, *König, Reich und Reichsreform*, pp. 31–2.

[121] See Moraw, 'Gedanken zur politischen Kontinuität', p. 47.

[122] The total of eight results from the division of the Wittelsbachs and Habsburgs into two separate lineages in the late Middle Ages.

[123] Thomas, *Ludwig der Bayer*, pp. 43–109.

Rulers of the Empire

Frederick II of Hohenstaufen	1211–50
Konrad IV of Hohenstaufen	1237–54
Henry Raspe, Landgrave of Thuringia	1246–7
William, Count of Holland	1247–56
Richard, Earl of Cornwall	1257–72
Alfonso (X), King of Castile	1257–75
Rudolf I, Count of Habsburg	1273–91
Adolf, Count of Nassau	1292–8
Albert I of Habsburg, Duke of Austria	1298–1308
Henry VII, Count of Luxemburg	1308–13
Ludwig IV of Wittelsbach ('the Bavarian')	1314–47
Frederick ('the Fair') of Habsburg	1314–30
Charles IV of Luxemburg, King of Bohemia	1346–78
Günther, Count of Schwarzburg	1349
Wenceslas of Luxemburg, King of Bohemia	1376–1400
Rupert of the Palatinate (Wittelsbach)	1400–10
Sigismund of Luxemburg, King of Hungary, Bohemia	1410/11–37
Jobst of Luxemburg, Margrave of Moravia	1410–11

What most explains the new climate after 1245 is the emergence during the thirteenth century, within the estate of German princes, of a select group of prince-electors with an increasingly firmly defined and recognised right to nominate the Empire's future ruler.[124] The seven spiritual and temporal magnates who were henceforth to claim this power exclusively are first glimpsed clearly in the double election of 1257.[125] The establishment of the electors at the head of the constitutional order in Germany fostered divisions within the political community. By excluding great secular princes, such as the dukes of Austria and Brabant, as well as the metropolitans of Salzburg, Magdeburg and Bremen, it turned such magnates inward upon their own regional interests and tended further to isolate and insulate their territories from imperial affairs. It also shook the monarchy. Jealous of the power and status which their office brought, the electors resisted actively both the establishment of dynastic continuity on the throne and the elevation

---

[124] See below, Ch. 6, pp. 272–8, as well as Mitteis, *Die deutsche Königswahl*. For the debate on the origins of the electoral college, see: Krieger, *König, Reich und Reichsreform*, pp. 66–71; Ertl, 'Alte Thesen'.

[125] Though only with the Golden Bull of 1356 was the composition of the electoral college formally and definitively settled. See Lindner, 'Die Goldene Bulle', with bibliography.

of a ruler who might prove strong enough to secure it. The German nobles installed as king in the half-century from 1247 to 1298 share in common the fact that, despite the disparities among them in family resources and standing, none was at the time of his elevation an imperial prince. Even a ruler with the solid landed substance of Rudolf I might be described (although with conscious overstatement) by a chronicler as having been 'raised up in Swabia like a speck of dust'.[126]

Kings who augmented their power too markedly, or whose territorial goals were deemed a threat to the electors, were liable, like the capable Rudolf, to find their succession hopes dashed, or even to face ejection from the throne, as did Rudolf's impecunious successor Adolf of Nassau. The ruler's subjugation to the interests of the electors, though never by any means complete, was at its starkest in the decades down to the end of the thirteenth century. The Rhineland archbishops, who with the pope had done most to undermine Frederick II's position in Germany, were also most ruthless in engineering and exploiting the weakness of his successors. It was an era in which, as Heinrich Mitteis put it, 'each candidate had virtually to submit his programme of rule [to the electors] for approval'.[127] Among the numerous privileges to which candidates for the throne in those years put their names, granting individual princes special favours in the event of their elevation, a pre-election document issued by Count Adolf of Nassau for Archbishop Siegfried of Cologne might be singled out to illuminate the respective standing of prelate and pretender.[128] Along with much else, the count had to undertake not to enter the city of Cologne or receive the fealty of its burghers, or to show favour to Siegfried's enemies, some of them named; any breach, Adolf acknowledged, entitled the archbishop to evict him from office – as Siegfried's successor would duly help to do, some six years later.[129] The fact that two of the count-kings installed after 1245 were able, while on the throne, to lay foundations for the future greatness of their dynasties – and, as it turned out, thereby contribute in the longer term to the stabilisation of the imperial office itself – was in spite of the intentions and actions of the princes who chose them.

One theme to emerge strongly from a survey of medieval imperial rulership is therefore the troubled, fluctuating and always partial nature of its relationship with the German lands of the Reich. That relationship, subject from the beginning to sharp periodic changes, became in

---

[126] *Historia Annorum 1264–1279*, ed. Wattenbach, p. 652.
[127] Mitteis, *Der Staat*, p. 416.
[128] *MGC* 3, no. 474, pp. 460–3 (27 April 1292).
[129] Thomas, *Deutsche Geschichte*, Ch. 3.

significant ways more disturbed and incomplete in the decades with which this book is concerned. But in one important respect the involvement of rulers in this period with the Empire's northern lands must be deemed closer than that of their high medieval forebears: they were less often to be found south of the Alps. The contrast is a stark one. From 962 to 1190, all but one of the Empire's rulers had entered Italy and been crowned emperor in Rome by the pope – and the sole exception, Konrad III, was preparing to set off south at the time of his death.[130] Yet of the ten kings who can credibly be said to have ruled between the death of Konrad IV in 1254 and Sigismund's election in 1410, only four entered Italy, of whom three secured a Rome coronation (one of them, Ludwig IV, under highly controversial circumstances). Henry VII was the last emperor to leave his bones in the south (1313). Between 962 and 1190, the Empire's rulers mounted 27 expeditions into Italy, absorbing altogether some 50 years, or roughly a quarter of the total length of their reigns.[131] In the 30 years after 1220, Frederick II was north of the Alps for just 20 months.[132] Between 1254 and 1410, on the other hand, kings spent in total less than 9 years in the south, not much more than 5 per cent of their aggregated time on the throne. But even if such contrasts might appear to endow the reigns of these later monarchs with, in one limited sense, a more visibly 'German' character than their forebears, it must also be a matter for grave doubt whether any of them can be described fully as rulers, let alone governors, of 'Germany'. And since both rulership and government are commonly ascribed by historians such a central part in early nation-formation, it is necessary now to look more specifically at the resources of rule available to late medieval kings, at their scope, and at some of the ways in which the hand of monarchy was (and was not) felt in German society.

Never before, it seems, had royal government in Germany been as ill-matched to its tasks, its institutions as patently incapable of filling its ostensible sphere of rule, as in the thirteenth and fourteenth centuries. True, the problem was – and is – to a large extent one of perceptions and expectations. The German lands were by the end of the Hohenstaufen age more densely peopled and more socially and culturally complex than in times past. More, and different, voices were now raised, and those voices were demanding of the ruler things that had not always been expected in earlier ages. People had more sharply defined and more ambitious conceptions of good and bad government, and were

---

[130] Fuhrmann, ' "Quis constituit Teutonicos?" ', p. 348.
[131] Ibid., p. 348.   [132] Moraw, *Von offener Verfassung*, p. 203.

increasingly ready to give vent to them in forms that have survived for the historian to study. But there had been material decline also: in the resources available to support royal rule; in the standing of the rulers themselves in the view of their contemporaries; and in their capacity to offer, even periodically, a countervailing force to the ascendant territorial power of the princes.

The king's travels through his realm remained an essential foundation of his rule down to the end of the Middle Ages. Particularly for much of the first century after Frederick II's death, rulers were almost continuously in the saddle, lacking as most of them did a centre of power suitable for the long-term support of the monarch and his court. Their situation is not in itself as anomalous or damaging as may appear: itineracy remained in the later Middle Ages an important foundation of rule in other European realms too, in spite of the growth of residential and administrative centres.[133] Into the fourteenth century, the main problems in Germany were rather a continuing lack of alternatives to peripatetic kingship, and – set beside the sheer extent of the Reich – the modest, shrunken and fluctuating character of the itinerary itself. The gradual withering-away of the old imperial estates had made rulership from the saddle more necessary, as well as more troublesome, than ever – at least until the new ruling dynasties of the late Middle Ages had consolidated their family power bases. Much rested upon the ruler's own stamina: as late as 1411, Job Vener had objected to the election of the aged Jobst of Moravia on the grounds that a king of the Romans needed to be a robust and active man.[134] Journeying brought the king the resources of rule. In the unstable climate of post-Hohenstaufen Germany, the most valuable of these was an intangible one: legitimacy. Only by appearing in person to the princes, great lords and – ever more importantly – growing towns of his realm could a monarch hope to gain their acceptance, or to draw them away from any rival claimant to the throne. By the thirteenth century the custom was already long established that the newly created king should tour his German lands, in order to be seen and to garner recognition. By the time of the Golden Bull of 1356, this obligatory circuit had definite landmarks: election in Frankfurt am Main and coronation in Aachen, followed by a journey to Nuremberg for the ruler's first solemn court.[135]

Covering the miles necessary to secure the throne was never easy in the circumstances of the thirteenth and fourteenth centuries, and the ruler

[133] Peyer, 'Das Reisekönigtum', esp. pp. 5–20.
[134] Quoted in Schubert, 'Probleme', p. 141.
[135] *Die Goldene Bulle*, ed. Fritz, p. 87.

could expect to find his progress impeded or his way blocked altogether. Ludwig IV was shut out for several years on end from the heartlands of the Reich in the south-west, which were loyal to the rival pretender to the throne, Frederick of Habsburg. When political divisions were coupled with the king's own lack of experience and resources, his access to his German lands might be small indeed. Richard of Cornwall, an outsider, did not penetrate beyond the Rhineland. If sticking to this rich and populous region made some sense as a short-term survival strategy, it was also an obvious handicap for a king as patently in need of general recognition as was Richard.[136] Observers were not blind to the gap between title and substance, with one chronicler noting dismissively that the king 'came nowhere in the German lands except to the Rhine, and was in fact impotent in the *Reich*'.[137] Some Germans were capable of following closely the movements of their ruler, and sharp-eyed, even harsh, in their verdicts. Even such a well-established and comparatively mobile king as Richard's successor, Rudolf I, became the object of pointed remarks about the allegedly modest horizons of his rule.[138] For one hostile versifier, Rudolf – 'who acts as if he were king' – was really no more than an 'emperor around the Rhine'.[139] A not dissimilar judgement, though without the edge of malice, was returned by an Austrian annalist, in whose view 'the whole of the Frankish and Swabian people' (*gens Francorum et Suevorum*) – but not, by implication, the whole *German* people – 'was governed in peace by King Rudolf'.[140] If the growth of towns had created a new constituency for the monarchy, and an indispensable source of material support for the hard-pressed king, it also nurtured a demanding political public, quick to expect the ruler's presence on the doorstep, and to remark his absence. The chronicler Heinrich von Diessenhoven noted of the visit paid by the exceptionally well-travelled Charles IV to Constance in 1353 that 'he was solemnly received by the clergy and people because he had never before come there, although it was the eighth year since his election'.[141]

If the travelling king seemed destined, under the circumstances prevailing after 1245, always to disappoint, his absence from some parts of Germany was much more protracted, and had deeper, more structural

---

[136] The benefits of his concentration on the Rhineland are emphasised in Moraw, *Von offener Verfassung*, p. 210.

[137] *Sächsische Weltchronik: Sächsische Fortsetzung*, ed. Weiland, p. 284.

[138] For the scope of Rudolf's kingship in Germany, see Riedmann, 'Die leere Mitte', as well as the loose maps appended to Martin, *Städtepolitik*.

[139] 'Schulmeister von Esslingen', in *Politische Lyrik*, ed. Müller, vol. I, p. 87. The poet's verses are examined in Müller, *Untersuchungen*, pp. 142–4.

[140] *Continuatio Claustroneuburgensis VI.*, ed. Wattenbach, p. 744.

[141] *Heinricus Dapifer de Diessenhoven*, ed. Huber, p. 88.

causes and more implacable consequences. The vast, increasingly sovereign, princely territories, such as Austria, Bavaria, and Bohemia, were effectively out of bounds for any king not of the home dynasty; his presence was neither desired nor expected. But these regions apart, the area most conspicuously outside his orbit – most 'remote' from him (*königsfern*), as Peter Moraw terms it – was a broad and growing northern zone, encompassing around a third of the German lands of the Reich.[142] Extending from Brabant, and the Rhine below Cologne, through Westphalia, 'Old' Saxony, Brandenburg, Mecklenburg and Pomerania, to the lands of the Teutonic Order, it corresponded roughly to the regions from which the Hansa drew its members. By the mid-thirteenth century, the days when the lands between Weser, Elbe and Saale had supplied a principal foundation for kingship were long past. After 1245, with the sole exception of William of Holland, no king visited the parts of the realm north of Thuringia for a century.[143] Nor, apart from Albert I's excursion to Nijmegen (1302), did they venture any further down the Rhine than Cologne or Neuß.[144] Goslar in the Harz, site of Henry III's magnificent palace, and in earlier times so important to the imperial progress, had its last visit from a ruler (William of Holland) in 1253.[145] When Charles IV came to Lübeck in 1375, he was the first monarch to enter the rich and bustling imperial city since Barbarossa (the next would be the Bismarckian Kaiser William I).[146] Making an impression of even modest depth or duration upon the political landscape of a region almost always entailed delicate negotiations, which required the king's presence: nothing of any scope was possible by remote control. This explains the absence of the north from the otherwise near-comprehensive series of sworn territorial peaces – *Landfrieden* – which Rudolf I had negotiated in Germany, until the king came personally to Thuringia at the end of the 1280s, when at least some northern regions gained peace-keeping institutions.[147] By contrast, the *Landfriede* established among the Baltic towns at Rostock in 1283 had been made without the king's involvement.[148] In those parts of Germany where he was seldom or never seen, the ruler was

[142] Moraw's scheme for classifying the German regions in terms of their relationship to the ruler, set out in many of his writings, is summarised in *Von offener Verfassung*, p. 175. For the place of the north, see Moraw, 'Nord und Süd'.

[143] Steinbach, *Die Reichsgewalt*, p. 9.

[144] See the maps in Moraw, *Von offener Verfassung*, pp. 215, 223, 225, 227, 231.

[145] Schneidmüller, 'Reichsnähe-Königsferne', p. 19. On Goslar's importance for the Salians, see Bernhardt, *Itinerant Kingship*, esp. pp. 156–60.

[146] See Hoffmann, 'Der Besuch', esp. p. 73.

[147] Redlich, *Rudolf von Habsburg*, p. 449. For a full account of Rudolf's peace-keeping measures, see Gerlich, *Studien zur Landfriedenspolitik*.

[148] Steinbach, *Reichsgewalt*, pp. 98–106.

liable to find himself marginal to the play of power and diplomacy. The Baltic towns waged war on the king of Norway and made alliance with Denmark, all, it seems, without even consulting Rudolf I; nor did he have any hand in the peace settlement of 1285, the work of King Magnus of Sweden.[149] Against a background of protracted absence, an isolated visit was unlikely to make much difference: Charles IV's journey to Lübeck did not in the end prove sufficient to allow him, as he had evidently hoped, to influence the succession to the Danish throne following Waldemar IV's death.[150] Where the ruler had ceased to come, the constitutional position of the Reich was soon eroded. The significant efforts which Rudolf I made to recover authority over imperial towns on the lower Rhine and in Westphalia proved vain without his regular personal proximity or that of his successors.[151] Any contraction of the royal *iter* thus tended, by slackening the monarch's grip on outlying imperial resources, to pave the way for further retreats in the future.

The monarchy's engagement with the German lands was further undermined by sharp fluctuations in the geographical focus of the ruler's journeying between, and in some cases within, individual reigns. The problem lay partly in the sheer number of potentially conflicting demands and priorities – imperial government north of the Alps, plans and ventures in the south, the pursuit of dynastic advantage, the everyday imperatives of mere survival – which any long-lived or ambitious ruler had to balance. A more fundamental difficulty lay in the chronic lack of continuity between reigns which was a consequence of elective kingship, with the result that any advance in the scope of government which a ruler might attain was unlikely to be preserved, still less consolidated, by his successors. Each of these weaknesses is illustrated by the rule of Charles IV north of the Alps.

Charles demonstrates like no one else how an itinerant kingship almost unparalleled in scope could be founded on the resources of dynastic *Hausmacht*.[152] Although by no means all the German lands saw the Luxemburger, his travels did allow him to penetrate regions of the Reich where his predecessors had seldom been seen. At the heart of his rule lay a long axis running east–west through the heart of German-speaking Europe, from the Luxemburg crown lands in Silesia and Bohemia, via Nuremberg, to Frankfurt am Main.[153] All told, Charles spent around

---

[149] Ibid., p. 78.   [150] See Hoffmann, 'Der Besuch'.
[151] Martin, *Städtepolitik*, pp. 60–2, 104.
[152] Eberhard, 'Ost und West', p. 15. Charles made 1,227 known stays in 438 different locations. Among the medieval Empire's rulers, only Barbarossa attained a comparable level of mobility. The extent of Charles's itinerary is shown on Map 3.
[153] Eberhard, 'Herrschaft', esp. p. 106; Moraw, 'Vom Raumgefüge', p. 77.

half his time on the throne moving between towns and castles on this route; and if first place was easily claimed by Prague (where he was to be found for nearly a third of his reign), the German towns on his way also saw a good deal of him. First among them was Nuremberg, where Charles spent in total nearly three years.[154] This central-German corridor provided an unusually promising basis from which to gain access to the regions both to south and north.[155] Yet the appearance of consistency is deceptive, and the geographical focus of Charles's government in fact shifted repeatedly during the course of his long reign.[156] In particular, it was not until the last few years of his life that he was to be found with any regularity in the lands east of the Rhine and north of the Breslau (Wrocław)–Frankfurt axis, through a shift which reflected his acquisition for his family in 1373 of Mark Brandenburg, with the palace at Tangermünde on the middle Elbe.[157]

Nor did Charles's attainments long outlive him. His son Wenceslas lacked his father's energy, and found his reign dogged by domestic political problems. His itinerary until the time of his deposition from the Reich looks like a pale, severely diminished, version of Charles's own, with Nuremberg and Frankfurt the main destinations on his rare, brief forays outside the Bohemian kingdom.[158] But a more radical, and for late medieval Germany more characteristic, breach with Charles's achievements came under Rupert of the Palatinate, raised up by the electors against Wenceslas in 1400. Rupert too based his rule upon dynastic possessions, but his were of much more limited extent than those of the Luxemburger, lying mainly around the middle Rhine, the region in which he thus spent most of his time. The king, observed Dietrich von Niem tartly, appeared to have embraced the student's maxim, that there is no life outside Heidelberg.[159] During Rupert's reign the northern, eastern and – apart from stays at Nuremberg and nearby Amberg – central parts of Germany vanished from the map of kingship.[160] The few supporting points for the travelling monarch to retain some importance throughout the entire period, irrespective of changes of dynasty – towns such as Frankfurt, Mainz and, above all, Nuremberg – were

---

[154] Moraw, 'Zur Mittelpunktsfunktion', pp. 455–6.
[155] A point emphasised in ibid., p. 451.
[156] Emphasised by Seibt, 'Karl IV.', pp. 95–6.
[157] Eberhard, 'Herrschaft', p. 106; Eberhard, 'Ost und West', pp. 20–1. For earlier short forays into central Germany (Thuringia in 1349), see *Die Regesten des Kaiserreiches unter Kaiser Karl IV.*, ed. Huber, pp. 68–9.
[158] Hlaváček, *Urkunden- und Kanzleiwesen*, pp. 440–2.
[159] Cited in Heimpel, *Dietrich*, p. 63.
[160] See *Regesten der Pfalzgrafen am Rhein*, ed. Oberndorff.

insufficient either in number or in geographical span to sustain stable, far-reaching rule.[161]

But the king's itinerary was only one (if the most important) of the means by which he made his presence felt in Germany. The need to travel had always to be offset against the benefits of staying put, at least for a while, and all the more significant late medieval reigns included periods when the ruler based himself in a single location.[162] Rudolf I spent roughly three and a half years in and around Vienna, to Whitsun 1281, and nearly a year in Erfurt at the end of the 1280s. Both towns lay outside (Erfurt to the north, Vienna to the east) of the accustomed routes of the king's travels. Protracted residence allowed for closer relationships to be built up in these comparatively remote parts. Only while at Erfurt was Rudolf able to gain for a while effective lordship over the imperial towns of the north, particularly Lübeck, which was now ready to offer a substantial tax grant in return for the prospect of the king's protection.[163] With time, as the new imperial dynasties deepened their relationships with their patrimonial lands, residential rule took on a more protracted character, raising urgent questions about the ruler's relationship with the German lands. The new pattern first became evident in the time of Ludwig IV. The chronicler Heinrich Taube, writing in Eichstätt, close to the Wittelsbach territories, noted of Ludwig that 'for the greater part of his reign, especially from the time when he departed Italy [1330], he stayed in his own land, something which few of his predecessors had done'.[164] But the habit of ruling Germany for extended periods from dynastic estates was greatly extended under Ludwig's immediate successors. It was a practice which, in the circumstances prevailing in fourteenth-century Germany, could bring as many difficulties as benefits.

Most obviously, it threatened to reintroduce in a new form an old, familiar complication in imperial rulership: the monarch's protracted absence from the German lands of the Empire. Well over half of the known visits paid by Charles IV during his reign were to places east of the Elbe – which meant, in the great majority of cases, locations within his patrimonial lands.[165] The chronicler Heinrich von Diessenhofen

---

[161] Moraw, 'Nord und Süd', p. 53.

[162] The relationship between itineracy and residential rule in medieval Germany is considered in Moraw, 'Die Reichsregierung reist', pp. 29–30.

[163] Thomas, *Deutsche Geschichte*, pp. 46–7; Redlich, *Rudolf von Habsburg*, Ch. 6; Martin, *Städtepolitik*, pp. 56–7.

[164] *Die Chronik Heinrichs Taube*, ed. Bresslau, p. 58.

[165] Eberhard, 'Herrschaft', pp. 107–8. It might be noted, however, that 1351 and 1352 were the only years which Charles spent wholly within the Bohemian crown lands.

noted under the year 1352 that the king was in Bohemia, where 'since the time of the death of his adversary [Günther of Schwarzburg] he stayed more than in the kingdom of Germany' (*regnum Alemannie*).[166] The disparity became more acute under his sons. Wenceslas spent the period from 1389 to 1397 entirely in Bohemia, while his half-brother Sigismund, preoccupied with affairs in his Hungarian kingdom, did not enter the German lands of the Reich at all between his election in 1410 and the summer of 1414.[167] While the Luxemburg territories – the Bohemia–Moravia–Silesia bloc – may have seemed to contemporaries somewhat less sharply distinct from 'Germany' than were the regions south of the Alps, such lengthy absences from the heartlands of the Reich were nevertheless a source of anxiety and disfavour.[168] Charles IV is to be found writing from Prague, assuring his German subjects of his imminent 'arrival in the German lands', just as Frederick II had once deemed it advisable to do.[169] The potentially grave constitutional consequences of staying away are implied by a Nuremberg correspondent of the town of Strasbourg, who wrote in July 1396 recounting how a group of Wenceslas's followers had murdered members of a rival faction at the Bohemian castle of Karlstein, after accusing them of urging the king 'day and night' not to enter Germany, intending thereby, they suggested, 'to bring him from the Roman Empire'.[170] The charge is revealing of contemporary expectations and assumptions. It also proved to be prophetic: Wenceslas's prolonged inactivity in Germany was to contribute to the case for his deposition by the princes four years later.[171]

A major explanation for the impossibility by this time of effectively substituting for the *iter* residential rule from the dynastic territories lies in the fewness and fragility of the institutional ties connecting the ruler's court with the German lands. A further, exacerbating factor was the marginal position, relative to the German regions, of the *Hausmacht* territories themselves. When we recall the importance within processes of nation-making which historians have ascribed to the growth, in

[166] *Heinricus Dapifer de Diessenhoven*, ed. Huber, p. 84.
[167] For Wenceslas, see Hlaváček, *Urkunden- und Kanzleiwesen*, pp. 414–22; for Sigismund, see *Die Urkunden Kaiser Sigmunds*, ed. Altmann, p. 58.
[168] Moraw, 'Wesenszüge', p. 160. Despite not being separated by a barrier to compare with the Alps, Bohemia, Moravia and Silesia were all regarded in this period as quite distinct from Germany. See below, Ch. 9, pp. 396–7, Ch. 10, pp. 454–5.
[169] *Strassburg UB* 5, no. 976, p. 752 (6 July 1371), in the name of Archbishop John of Prague. For further (vernacular) examples from Charles's reign, see ibid., nos. 389, 796, 819, 852, pp. 336, 624, 636, 664. For comparable Latin versions for Frederick II, see *Acta Imperii*, ed. Winkelmann, vol. I, nos. 394, 420, pp. 344, 362.
[170] *Strassburg UB* 6, no. 1064, p. 618.
[171] See the public judgement delivered by Archbishop Johann II of Mainz (20 August 1400, Oberlahnstein): *RTA* 3, no. 204, p. 256.

other medieval realms, of links and dialogues between centre and regions, the implications of their relative absence in Germany become plain. Significantly, none of the urban court centres which grew up within the dynastic territories was able to act as a political and cultural magnet and residential focus for the German nobility, as, for example, Paris did for the French, although it is true that a handful of German princes and nobles close to Charles IV acquired houses in Prague.[172] There is no sign of attempts being made, as they occasionally were elsewhere in western Europe, systematically to draw together at court nobles from different regions of Germany, or to nurture among them a unifying culture and sense of solidarity, focused on service to the ruler (an idea which would in any case, under German conditions, certainly have been doomed to failure).[173] Rulers of the Empire were admittedly sometimes able to exploit dynastic marriages as a means of binding remote regions and their leading families to the crown. It was by marrying his daughter to the Welf duke of Braunschweig (1252) that the hitherto insecure William of Holland gained post facto election by the duke of Saxony and margraves of Brandenburg, which the north German towns had in turn made a condition for their own recognition of the king.[174] The prolific Rudolf I handed out daughters in an especially systematic manner among the leading princely houses of the Reich – to the king of Bohemia, the dukes of Bavaria and Saxony, the count palatine of the Rhine, and the margrave of Brandenburg (as well as Angevin Naples).[175] But the ties thus established were at best skeletal and of uncertain durability, as the failure of the princes to back Rudolf's own dynastic plans in the Empire made clear. Later rulers, moreover, had other priorities: Charles IV, through his own marriages and those of his offspring, showed more concern to augment the Luxemburg patrimony than to establish a presence in the Empire's German territories.[176]

Unlike other European kingdoms, where members of the high nobility competed for access and influence at court, the great men in Germany preferred on the whole to attend on the ruler as little as possible, and to concentrate their energies at home, upon consolidating their regional spheres of dominance; generally speaking, not the strong and ambitious but the weak and threatened sought in Germany the proximity of

[172] Moraw, 'Zur Mittelpunktsfunktion', esp. pp. 463–7.
[173] Moraw, 'Nord und Süd', p. 55. For an instance of the integrative use of the court, see Paravicini, 'The court'.
[174] Moraw, Von offener Verfassung, p. 208.
[175] See the table in Redlich, Rudolf von Habsburg, p. 768.
[176] See the table in Hoensch, Die Luxemburger, pp. 350–1.

the monarch.[177] The princes tended to express opposition to the king not by attempting to overawe his assemblies, as happened elsewhere in troubled times, but by staying away.[178] None of the dynastic capitals was during this period made the site of a formal *Hoftag*, bringing the ruler together with the German princes and nobles.[179] Instead, assemblies were commonly held in the surviving imperial heartlands, in Franconia, around the middle Rhine and lower Main, and in Swabia, regions regarded as neutral ground on which king and magnates could come together.[180] Not that holding assemblies in these core zones ensured the ruler a full, 'representative', turn-out of the great men from across the German lands, however (even had that been the hope or expectation, which probably it was not). Even an assembly as important as the one held at Nuremberg at Christmas 1355 (which saw among other matters the promulgation of the greater part of the Golden Bull) was patchily attended, with few northern princes present.[181] Assemblies convened by a weak ruler were apt merely to show up his weakness: the solemn court which Richard of Cornwall summoned to Worms for April 1269 succeeded in drawing only modest numbers of nobles and clergy, mainly from the lower Rhine.[182]

Although representatives of the towns were summoned to attend *Hoftage* with growing regularity from the thirteenth century, there is no sign that their views were sought, still less that they had a voice of their own in proceedings.[183] All this, it should be recalled, was at a time when in other parts of Europe – notably, in England – assemblies capable of speaking for, and binding in common action, entire regnal communities were emerging as features of the constitutional landscape.[184] Viewed in comparison, the formative power of the *Hoftag* was small indeed. Only at more intimate levels are there occasional signs that by the late fourteenth century new and significant bonds of association and

---

[177] Emphasised, e.g., by Moraw, 'Nord und Süd', p. 60. See also Schubert, 'Probleme', pp. 142–3.

[178] Annas, *Hoftag*, vol. I, p. 147.

[179] For Vienna, see Riedmann, 'Die leere Mitte', p. 52; for Munich, see Orth, 'München', pp. 64–5.

[180] For assemblies in this region under Charles IV, see Moraw, 'Grundzüge', p. 24; for Ludwig IV's preference for Nuremberg and Frankfurt/Sachsenhausen, Orth, 'München', p. 65.

[181] For the 'Golden Bull' *Hoftag*, see: Annas, *Hoftag*, vol. II, pp. 43–55; Moraw, 'Nord und Süd', p. 60.

[182] Weiler, 'Image and reality', p. 1120.

[183] Annas, *Hoftag*, vol. I, pp. 92–4.

[184] Maddicott, *English Parliament*, esp. Ch. 6. As Reuter observed, assemblies were in the Middle Ages 'almost the only occasion when the polity could represent itself to itself': Reuter, 'Assembly politics', p. 207.

common practice were taking shape. These are most evident among the electors, who were bound to meet together annually under the terms of the Golden Bull.[185] While no formal programme of meetings was ever established, the four Rhinelanders in particular did develop habits of increasingly close consultation, first under Wenceslas, whom they eventually joined together to depose, then under Rupert.[186] In this way it is possible to discern by the early fifteenth century the faint outlines of a new type of imperial assembly, which was to take on firmer shape in the decades that followed: one which did not convene at the ruler's will alone, and which might even meet to oppose his designs.[187]

Some regular institutions of government there were, however, attached to the court and maintaining threads of contact and direction, however few and weak, with the German lands of the Reich. The oldest-established and most substantial among them was the chancery. The ties which these institutions were capable of sustaining between court and regions are most clearly visible during the long, busy and well-documented reign of Charles IV. Prosopographical studies have revealed that, over the course of his time on the throne, only around a third of Charles's chancery personnel was drawn from his hereditary lands (above all, from Silesia). Of the rest, it is true, as many as 44 per cent came from the two German regions which, for Moraw, were especially 'close' to the monarch: Franconia and the middle Rhine. But the remaining 20 per cent originated in other parts of Germany.[188] Chancellors included the West Prussian Nikolaus von Riesenburg.[189] A link with western Germany was supplied by the circle of notaries around Archbishop Balduin of Trier (d. 1354), upon which Balduin's great nephew Charles was in his turn able to draw.[190]

Regional social networks, particularly among wealthy burgher families, were clearly an important recruitment base for Charles's officials, an indication of the range of connections which the Caroline court was capable of establishing, at least in the more frequently visited localities.[191] These came to extend beyond the traditional recruitment zones, reaching up particularly into the lands north of the Breslau–Nuremberg axis.[192] Dietrich von Portitz, a burgher's son from Stendal in the

---

[185] *Die Goldene Bulle*, ed. Fritz, cap. 12, p. 68.
[186] Annas, *Hoftag*, vol. I, pp. 142–6, 356–7.
[187] Ibid., pp. 383–4; Moraw, 'Reichstag', in *LMA* 7, cols. 640–3 (here col. 642).
[188] Moraw, 'Grundzüge', pp. 38–9.
[189] Ibid., p. 38.   [190] Ibid., p. 36.
[191] The relationship between chancery personnel and social networks is discussed in Moraw, 'Wesenszüge', pp. 154–7.
[192] See: ibid., p. 157; Lindner, 'Kaiser Karl IV.'.

Brandenburg *Altmark*, became one of Charles's most trusted officials (as well as archbishop of Magdeburg), while the minor Upper Saxon nobleman Thimo von Colditz is another figure from a central German region not hitherto closely linked with the Reich whose fortunes prospered in Luxemburg service.[193] It would be possible to identify yet further brilliant careers attesting to similar social and geographic patterns. Yet the breadth of the recruitment base for Charles's government should certainly not be overstated, and other statistics underline a more restricted picture. Thus, of his 182 counsellors and *secretarii*, a full 54 per cent were from the patrimonial territories.[194] Charles's reign, moreover, was exceptional, and the personnel of other kings shows a still more limited basis. All surviving vernacular documents from the 'curial court' (*Hofgericht*) under Rudolf I appear, for example, to be in the dialect of the king's native Swabia, whence must have come the clerks who wrote them.[195] Nor should it be forgotten how very modest were the numbers of office-holders under the Empire's rulers, in absolute terms or when compared with neighbouring realms. Harry Bresslau was able to identify just eight notaries, along with two chancellors and three protonotaries, for the whole of Rudolf I's eighteen-year reign: in the following century, the kings of England would maintain a hierarchically graded chancery staff of around a hundred *at any one time*.[196]

In their functioning, the institutions of imperial government tended on the whole less to supply a means of transcending the ruler's itinerary than to mirror it and illuminate its limitations. The activity of the chancery illustrates the point starkly. Of the surviving documents issued in the name of Rudolf I, only 5 per cent went to recipients living off the routes of the king's travels.[197] A century later little had changed. Under Charles IV, the whole northern third of Germany (excluding the Rhineland), together with a handful of other regions classified by Moraw as 'remote', accounted for just 15 per cent of the chancery's output, while only 3 per cent of Charles's known writings (and none of an intrusive or mandatory kind) were destined for the vast, tightly closed *territorium* of the Habsburgs.[198] Of the documents issued in the period,

---

[193] Moraw, 'Zur Mittelpunktsfunktion', pp. 469–71 (for Dietrich), p. 475 (for Thimo); Lindner, 'Kaiser Karl IV.', pp. 127–8.

[194] Moraw, 'Nord und Süd', p. 58.

[195] Wohlgemuth, *Das Urkundenwesen*, p. 34. The little that is known about Rudolf's chancery confirms the picture of recruitment from the Habsburg lands, though a Netherlander is also known to have served: Herzberg-Fränkel, 'Geschichte', p. 288.

[196] Bresslau, *Handbuch der Urkundenlehre*, vol. I, p. 570; Carpenter, 'The English royal chancery', p. 35.

[197] Martin, *Städtepolitik*, p. 185.

[198] Moraw, 'Vom Raumgefüge', pp. 70, 73.

solemn privileges form, as in times past, a notable proportion while writings of a routine, standardised character, such as are found in the more developed kinds of administration, are little in evidence.[199] The little which can be discerned of chancery practice suggests a minimum of regular procedure. There is no evidence for the registration of outgoing documents prior to the fourteenth century; and even when this is found, before the reign of Rupert of the Palatinate what survives is fragmentary and limited in extent and in many ways primitive in execution.[200] Even when registers were kept, there was no assurance, particularly given the troubled circumstances in which the throne repeatedly changed hands, that an incoming monarch would be able to gain access to the records of his predecessor.[201] Contemporary portrayals of the Empire's rulers in action conjure up a face-to-face world of spectacle and spoken command (though a Lübeck chronicler does have Charles IV, on his visit to the town, reassuring the council that their city's distinguished status within the Reich is enshrined in 'the old registers of the emperors').[202] As for the total numbers of known documents, these are far from negligible, and they rise markedly over the course of the period, from around 2,500 for Rudolf I to well over 9,000 for Charles IV; but the tally looks less impressive when set beside the achievements of the most prolific medieval bureaucracies – such as the papal chancery, issuing on average 3,646 letters each year under John XXII (1316–24), or that of the English kings, which in 1324 sealed nearly 3,500 standardised writs in a single (admittedly exceptional) *month*.[203] The imperial monarchy's participation in the document revolution of the later Middle Ages was on the most favourable view muted and partial.

It will be patently clear that the Empire's ostensible subjects in Germany did not during the later Middle Ages share, in any but the most notional sense, anything like Reynolds's 'single law and government'.[204] Nor is there much sign of their incipient development. Instead, the broad trend between the thirteenth and fifteenth centuries appears a

---

[199] Moraw, 'Grundzüge', p. 22; and, for the earlier period, Reuter, 'Mandate'.

[200] Hints at earlier record-keeping are collected in Seeliger, 'Die Registerführung', pp. 224–30. However, there is no firm evidence before the reign of Henry VII. For some of the deficiencies particularly of the earlier registers, see ibid., esp. pp. 336–7.

[201] Rupert of the Palatinate thus tried in vain to gain access to the registers of the deposed Wenceslas. Not until 1422 was Sigismund able to obtain Rupert's own imperial registers, which had been retained by his chancellor, Raban von Helmstatt: Moraw, 'Kanzlei und Kanzleipersonal', pp. 443, 451–2.

[202] *Detmar-Chronik*, ed. Koppmann, i.553.

[203] For the imperial totals, see: Moraw, *Von offener Verfassung*, p. 172; Lawo, 'Sprachen der Macht', p. 535; for the papal chancery, Southern, *Western Society*, p. 109; for English writs, Carpenter, 'The English royal chancery', pp. 34–5.

[204] For the weakness of ideas of a single 'German' law, see below, Ch. 11, pp. 505–6.

contrary one: towards the monarchy's increasingly pronounced disengagement from the lives of German-speakers, including the leaders of regional society. By the early fifteenth century, the signs are already apparent that ties between the ruler and the German core of the Reich were dissolving, and giving way to the pattern of regional systems under the princes that would strengthen as the century went on.[205] One major reason for this contrasting course is easily discerned. In other European realms, historians have detected in this period a rising spiral of mutually reinforcing developments. As the scale both of royal resources and commitments grew, the demands of government upon the community of the realm were extended; contacts between rulers and people became more numerous, more intensive and at certain times also more strained; and out of these processes of institutional growth, massive military effort and periodic constitutional crisis, gradually emerged more coherent and politically self-conscious communities under the king. Nothing like this seems to have occurred in Germany. Instead, the spiral ran in the opposite direction, from shrinking resources and institutional atrophy to an overall retreat in the aspirations of government, and the avoidance of conflict and risk. Meanwhile, the new sources of strength which the Empire's late medieval rulers were heaping up, in the form of dynastic *Hausmacht*, tended by their nature at least as much to divide the monarch from his German lands as to bring them together.

Significantly, during centuries which witnessed overall (though with many reverses and sudden dips) a great swelling of royal treasuries in western Europe, the king's poverty was a recurrent theme among German commentators.[206] A Dominican chronicler set down under the year 1276 an arresting anecdote relating to Rudolf I's military preparations against the mighty Otakar of Bohemia.[207] While at Mainz, one of Rudolf's nobles, Walther von Klingen, asked the king who was the keeper of his treasury. Rudolf replied that he had no treasure, except for 5 shillings of bad money, but went on, responding to Walther's further anxious questioning, to declare his confidence that God would provide for him, as he had always done. Even allowing for predictable mendicant enthusiasm for a king who allegedly 'went forth

---

[205] Thus, already in the second half of the fourteenth century the monarchy's relationship with the towns of the middle Rhine was breaking down, as they passed into the hegemonic system of the Rhenish counts palatine: Annas, *Hoftag*, vol. I, pp. 320–1.

[206] Royal incomes in European realms over the late Middle Ages as a whole are estimated in Guenée, *States*, p. 109. There are further figures for France in Le Roy Ladurie, *The Royal French State*, p. 74.

[207] *Chronicon Colmariense*, ed. Jaffé, p. 246. For the *topos* of Rudolf's poverty, see Kleinschmidt, *Herrscherdarstellung*, pp. 229–30.

joyfully and always lived in extreme poverty', the story gives pause for thought, since historians know little more than did Walther about how one of the Empire's more successful late medieval rulers managed his fiscal affairs.[208] Similar in its implications, if altogether less flattering, was a popular rhyme which circulated in Germany over a century later, warning hearers to watch out for the 'wandering trickster' (*goeckelman*), Rupert of the Palatinate, coming with his 'empty purse'.[209] If in some ways the monarchy did attain greater financial sophistication between the thirteenth and fifteenth centuries, especially in its growing recourse to urban credit, the fact remained that governing the Reich had become a burden even for the broadest of shoulders.[210] A hostile chronicler claimed that Sigismund could seldom find the money to pay the innkeeper in the morning.[211]

Not without reason did the image of the Roman eagle plucked of its feathers become a staple of late medieval polemical writings.[212] There is reason to believe that royal income from imperial estates and dues may have plummeted from over 100,000 gulden per annum in the early fourteenth century to somewhere around 17,500 under King Rupert, and maybe 13,000 under Sigismund.[213] That is naturally far from the whole story; the amassing of dynastic *Hausmacht* had emerged in the meantime as a solution to exactly this problem – though, by encouraging rulers to treat imperial properties as dispensable assets, to pledge or alienate as political need dictated, it also contributed to it. Nevertheless, both the decline itself and the means chosen to address it reveal much about the monarchy's scope for action. Giving was invariably easier than taking, sanctioning easier than compelling, and 'state'-building more feasible within the ruler's dynastic patrimony than in the lands of the Reich. Estates, rights and incomes, once granted away, could seldom be recouped. Administrative ties between the German lands and the court were too few and too feeble to function effectively in the king's absence. The regional advocacies established by Rudolf I to recover, safeguard and exploit the remaining *Reichsgut* were mainly confined to areas – the south-west, the middle Rhine and the Wetterau – lying on or close to

---

[208] The meagre evidence is examined in Redlich, *Rudolf von Habsburg*, pp. 479–80, 502–3.

[209] Quoted in Schubert, 'Probleme', p. 178.

[210] For the development of credit, see Stromer, *Oberdeutsche Hochfinanz*.

[211] *Klingenberger Chronik*, cited in Schubert, 'Probleme', p. 181 with n. 333.

[212] Ibid., p. 137; and see below, Ch. 7, pp. 342–3.

[213] Krieger, *König, Reich und Reichsreform*, p. 34. These sums provide a startling contrast with the electors, who in the late fifteenth century were ascribed estimated annual revenues ranging between 40,000 and 80,000 gulden: see Isenmann, 'The Holy Roman Empire', p. 251.

the regular routes of the king's travels.[214] Apt as they were in any case to become enmeshed in the territorial politics of local aristocratic kindreds, the advocacies proved able to do little more than delay for a time the crumbling of the fisc.[215] Much of their point was anyway sacrificed in the massive alienations of *Reichsgut* embarked on by rulers during the fourteenth century. Foremost among them was Charles IV, to whose reign are ascribed nearly a third of all imperial pledges contracted during the Middle Ages.[216] The network of *ministeriales* in their scattered castles, upon which the Salians and Staufer had relied for rudimentary local administration, was quite unsuited to the more complex world of the later Middle Ages, and found no effective successor.[217]

Charles IV even abandoned, for short-term political gain, the responsibility long borne by his predecessors, of protecting Germany's Jews. The pogroms and expulsions of the late Middle Ages ensured that Charles's successors on the throne would derive little benefit from this traditionally significant source of income.[218] In the early fifteenth century, taxes on the Jews were yielding on average only around 800 gulden per annum.[219] Yet more dangerous consequences flowed from the gradual breakdown of relations between the monarchy and the imperial towns. The *Reichsstädte* had enjoyed a first great age of economic growth in the time of the Empire's crisis in the thirteenth century, and the principle of their regular annual taxation (*bede*), first established under the later Staufer, was applied with much vigour and considerable success by subsequent kings.[220] Yet it is revealing that Rudolf I's experiments in the 1280s with new forms of tax were rebuffed by the towns, at precisely the time when rulers elsewhere were starting to extend their power to take their subjects' wealth.[221] The attempts made by Rudolf's successors to add to the burden only antagonised a valuable potential ally, until relations with the towns deteriorated into open war in the troubled final years of Charles IV's reign.[222] Under the circumstances, royal demands for extraordinary subventions in time of emergency

---

[214] See Erkens, 'Zwischen staufischer Tradition', pp. 38–9.
[215] Hofacker, *Reichslandvogteien*, pp. 111, 119, 130, 148–9; Krieger, *König, Reich und Reichsreform*, pp. 42–3.
[216] Thomas, *Deutsche Geschichte*, esp. p. 304; Krieger, *König, Reich und Reichsreform*, p. 32; Isenmann, 'The Holy Roman Empire', p. 254.
[217] See, e.g., Redlich, *Rudolf von Habsburg*, p. 468.
[218] Schubert, 'Probleme', pp. 169–72; Eckert, 'Die Juden'.
[219] Isenmann, 'The Holy Roman Empire', p. 256.
[220] Martin, *Städtepolitik*, pp. 152–3; Redlich, *Rudolf von Habsburg*, p. 487.
[221] Martin, *Städtepolitik*, p. 159; Redlich, *Rudolf von Habsburg*, p. 489; and see generally Watts, *The Making*, pp. 224–33.
[222] Seibt, *Karl IV.*, pp. 332–5.

were at best an uncertain expedient: of the massive sum of 150,000 gulden which King Rupert sought to obtain in this way in 1404, only a tiny fraction was forthcoming.[223] Not before the emergencies of the 1420s did the monarchy even attempt (unsuccessfully) to institute general taxation of the Empire's German subjects.[224]

The military capabilities of the Reich were similarly modest and, in common with the crown's other material resources, showed little development between the thirteenth and fifteenth centuries. This, it should be recalled, was in a period which elsewhere in Europe brought a great expansion not only in the size of royal armies but in their social complexity, developments which have been ascribed much significance in the consolidation of regnal communities.[225] The Empire's rulers lacked both the power and the material means to summon up such extensive forces, and Germany's military classes instead mostly exercised their fabled warlike talents serving other masters with deeper purses, at home and abroad.[226] War mattered much in late medieval German society but had rather little to do with 'state'- (or 'nation'-)making under the king. It is true that the direct vassals of the Reich grew in number during the late Middle Ages.[227] But a more realistic light is shed on the monarchy's military potential when we note that not until the 1430s were attempts made, under pressure of the Hussite menace, to record in detail the service in arms due to the Empire.[228] This admittedly reflects in part the comparative fewness of major outside threats to the German lands before that time; but also absent were the dynamics of governmental growth and constitutional self-assertion which elsewhere in Europe helped to impel kingdoms into conflict.

Nor is there much sign in Germany of those royal 'courts that can give final decisions that bind all the people in a given area', which for Joseph Strayer were a key accompaniment of the incipient 'modern state'.[229] With time, kings gradually retreated even from direct control of the *Landfriede*, probably (despite its limitations) the most effective source of public order at the ruler's disposal, and largely abandoned to

[223] Isenmann, 'The Holy Roman Empire', p. 257.
[224] See Rowan, 'Imperial taxes'.
[225] For the growing size and complexity of European armies, see: Contamine, *War*, Ch. 4; Watts, *The Making*, pp. 219–33; and for their nation-forming potential, Allmand, *Hundred Years War*, pp. 147–8.
[226] For the important role of mercenary service in the south, see Selzer, *Deutsche Söldner*.
[227] Krieger, *König, Reich und Reichsreform*, pp. 76–8. For more detail, see Krieger, *Die Lehnshoheit*.
[228] For this, see Thomas, *Deutsche Geschichte*, p. 417.
[229] Strayer, *On the Medieval Origins*, p. 8.

the regional powers the laborious business of setting up peace-keeping arrangements.[230] The means available to the king to uphold justice were small, particularly when faced with resistance from local men of power. Even the imperial bann was an uncertain instrument. When the English knight John de Harlestone passed through Alsace in 1384, bound for Rome, he found that an imperial safe conduct afforded no protection against seizure and lengthy imprisonment by a local nobleman, Bruno von Rappoltstein. Neither the king of England's supplications nor those of the pope himself were able to speed Harlestone's release. And nor could the injunctions of King Wenceslas do much to coerce Bruno, despite more than one imposition of the imperial bann, to act promptly to free his captive.[231] The history of the 'curial court' (Hofgericht), established in 1235 by Frederick II, illuminates starkly how restricted was the monarchy's scope to provide effective redress to those under its protection. This court, before the fifteenth century the sole appellate tribunal for the Reich, was at best a slow and uncertain source of justice, mostly bound to the ruler's itinerary, open to manipulation by the powerful, impotent against the princes and devoid of local executive institutions.[232] The number of plaintiffs securing redress through the Hofgericht, although showing some growth over the course of the period, seems to have remained almost comically small.[233] It is an indication of the constraints under which royal justice laboured, and of the limited options available for change, that both Rupert and Sigismund lent their support to an institution as murky in its ways and doubtful in its effects as the Westphalian 'free courts', or Veme.[234]

At a time when, the argument goes, ruler and people were elsewhere in Europe being drawn together in organic 'imagined communities' (or, as some prefer, embryonic 'nation states'), the opportunities for any such process to occur in Germany therefore seem modest indeed.

---

[230] Krieger, König, Reich und Reichsreform, pp. 27, 96–7. A more positive assessment of the late medieval monarchy's continuing role at least as a formal guarantor of peace was offered by Angermeier, Königtum, esp. p. 565.

[231] For this incident, see Carter, 'Bruno von Rappoltstein', pp. 62–77. Harlestone appears finally to have secured his freedom at some time in 1389.

[232] See generally Krieger, König, Reich und Reichsreform, pp. 23–4. By the fifteenth century there had developed, by processes that remain obscure, a parallel tribunal, the 'chamber court' (Kammergericht), directly under the monarch. This court is first explicitly mentioned in 1415, but was to grow in importance during the following decades, superseding the Hofgericht altogether from 1452. See J.F. Battenberg, 'Kammergericht', in LMA 5, col. 890.

[233] Thomas, Deutsche Geschichte, pp. 251–3. As late as Charles IV's reign, the Hofgericht may have been hearing as few as 8–10 cases per year.

[234] See generally K. Kroeschell, 'Feme', in LMA 4, cols. 346–9; and for more detail, Lindner, Die Veme.

The capacity of the Empire's rulers to touch, for good or ill, the lives of their German subjects was small and diminishing. Neither common purpose nor organised opposition brought the king face-to-face with a broad spectrum of German political society. Monarchy in Germany lacked dynastic continuity and spatial fixity, as well as material power and the penumbra of success. Whether it headed anything that could be called a German 'state' thus already appears a matter of fruitless semantics; it certainly did not control an effective or a visibly growing 'state' – or, as we might suspect, even a compellingly prestigious one.[235] Little wonder, then, that no pilgrim ever thought of journeying to the court of a Rudolf or a Ludwig to seek the miraculous touch of the Lord's Anointed. Yet the fact remained that Germany *had* a monarchy, which did, at least in principle, lay claim to unique sources of authority and prestige. Did these offer any scope for fashioning relationships with ruler and Reich, in spite of the limitations of royal government? Did there exist any alternative channels, less dependent on the power of the monarchy, through which – imaginatively at least – king and people might be brought together? Might it even be that the very weakness of rulership supplied its own stimuli to popular interest and identification? These are among the matters to which attention must now be turned.

---

[235] Hugelmann, *Stämme*, was at particular pains to demonstrate the applicability of the idea of a (German nation) 'state' to the Reich of the high Middle Ages. He has found few supporters – though see K.-F. Werner, 'Deutschland, A: Begriffe', in *LMA* 3, cols. 781–9 (here col. 782), where 'Germany' is defined as 'der überwiegend von "Deutschen" bewohnten Staat, der seit dem 10. Jahrhundert aus dem ostfränkischen Reich hervorgegangen ist'. For discussion of the problems of viewing the Reich as a state, see: Bowlus, 'The early *Kaiserreich*'; Jenks, 'A capital', esp. pp. 136–7; Keller, *Zwischen regionaler Begrenzung*, pp. 13–53.

3   Realm of imagination: communicating power after the Hohenstaufen

Communicating Landscapes

'I would that Your Grace had heard the king speak', effused a Brandenburg delegate, writing home from the 1507 Constance Reichstag, where Maximilian I had delivered himself of a fiery harangue against the French.[1] The Habsburg monarch, friend, patron and dedicatee of patriotic German humanists, was reputedly capable of moving audiences to tears with his heroically lengthy tirades against those who sought the harm of the Reich.[2] The nation in pre-modern times was at its most substantial when it was a quintessentially *political* community, shaped within structures of power, which in its own form it reflected. About that, most historians appear to agree – although, as we saw, their criteria for identifying such a community have left late medieval Germany singularly ill-placed to join that company of the blessed. But, more fundamentally, the nation is (and was) a product of communications – as Maximilian himself, never slow to beat the patriotic drum, understood better than most. Taken on its own, the point is almost banal. Any historical nation – any, at least, of larger extent than a mere 'political nation' of churchmen and *leudes* huddled around a dark-age warlord – must have embraced people who would mostly never have met, and whose ties to one another were thus of an 'imagined' kind.[3] Even face-to-face encounters – at a great Reichstag, for example – would have been experienced by those present above all imaginatively: their meanings and messages were not axiomatic, but had to be constructed and *communicated*.

What is not obvious, however, is how, beyond the most intimate, face-to-face level, nations themselves have historically *been* communicated,

---

[1] Hollegger, '"Erwachen vnd aufsten"', p. 234.

[2] Ibid., p. 234. On his links with patriotic humanism, see Silver, 'Germanic patriotism'.

[3] For the importance of this quality in defining the nation, see Anderson, *Imagined Communities*, p. 15.

and what preconditions were necessary for the process to begin. If the nation was made in history, certain societies must have acquired resources for its imagining which other, earlier ones lacked. Master propagandist though he may have been, Maximilian's trumpeting of the 'German nation' rested on more than just oratorical talent: in the period to 1500 alone, no fewer than twenty-three printers were in the king's employ.[4] For Eric Hobsbawm, nations exist not only as functions and fictions of 'the state', 'but also in the context of a particular stage of technological and economic development'.[5] For Ernest Gellner, it was precisely the absence of 'lateral communication' between different, isolated communities under the monarch that rendered nations literally unthinkable in pre-modern times.[6] Others would reject as caricature his picture of a profoundly segmented pre-industrial world. But the conviction that some sort of epochal change in the communicative resources of European societies attended the nation's birth is common to many studies, with widely diverse nation-making chronologies. Specific developments repeatedly mentioned include the rise of written vernaculars, the spread of print culture, and the Protestant Reformation, as well as the new communicative possibilities eventually afforded by industrialisation itself.[7] Studies of medieval nation-making, which have often focused disproportionately on the nation as *idea*, have correspondingly thought too little about how (or whether) notions of shared belonging were actually transmitted and received within the communities which they invoked. Yet the emphasis which medievalists have customarily given to the formative role of royal government and its own communicative resources indicates that they, too, recognise the importance of explaining the social dissemination of shared identities. In sum, historians have judged the main result of these various 'breakthroughs' – whether technological, cultural, economic, religious or governmental – as being, by breaking down accustomed barriers and smoothing out old-established differences, to summon into being societies with new levels of cultural interaction and homogeneity – to fashion, we might say, communicating landscapes, corresponding to the nation.

In what degree did post-Hohenstaufen Germany constitute such a landscape? The initial signs hardly look encouraging. What appears to distinguish the German-speaking lands from their European

[4] Hollegger, '"Erwachen vnd aufsten"', p. 224.
[5] Hobsbawm, *Nations*, p. 10.   [6] Gellner, *Nations*, p. 10.
[7] See, e.g., Hastings, *The Construction*, pp. 2–3 (written vernaculars); Anderson, *Imagined Communities*, p. 40 ('print-capitalism'); Gorski, 'The mosaic moment', esp. p. 1451 (printing, popular literacy, the Reformation).

neighbours, apart from their remarkable geographical extent, is their enormous diversity, and the fewness and feebleness of the visible threads binding them together. The sharply contrasting landscapes which in the period were home to German-speakers are reflected in the perceptions of their inhabitants. For the Rhinelander Alexander von Roes, Caesar had founded 'fortresses and cities' in Germany, just as had in an earlier time the younger Priam, émigré nephew of the eponymous king of Troy, who, crossing from Italy (where he had built Verona) into Germany, established Bern, Bonn, and the 'very large city' of Troy Minor: Xanten, north-west of Alexander's native Cologne.[8] His view of urban foundations as the building blocks of history itself makes sense when we note that on the Rhine's lowest courses in the late Middle Ages nearly a third of the population may have dwelt in towns.[9] A century later, the Strasbourg chronicler Jakob Twinger would make of Trier, whose rich, late antique ruins could hardly have failed to stir German imaginations, a lost, pre-Roman 'capital city' (*houbetstat*) for the 'German lands'.[10] Meanwhile, out at the opposite, easternmost limit of German speech, the prospect of the land offered by Nikolaus von Jeroschin, a fourteenth-century chronicler of the Teutonic Order, forms the sharpest of contrasts with these comfortable, well-rooted, mythologised urban visions. The brethren who came east had forsaken 'the sweet land of their birth', 'fertile, tranquil, peaceful', for 'a land of horror, a great desolate wilderness devoid of human cultivation'.[11]

From the Meuse to the Memel was far indeed, imaginatively no less than for the footsore traveller. It was from 'the good towns of Prussia and other far-off lands' that the duke of Brabant in 1350 acknowledged receipt of communications.[12] And while hardship and homesickness were the bitter lot of every holy warrior, the contrasts that would have met the pilgrim going east were real enough. The comparative regional population densities which historians have proposed for German-speaking Europe in the period tell their own stark tale. In the economically advanced, urbanised west, the territory of Brabant, south of the

---

[8] Alexander von Roes, *Memoriale*, cap. 16, ed. Grundmann and Heimpel, p. 109.
[9] Moraw, *Von offener Verfassung*, p. 49. It is thought that over 40 per cent of the inhabitants of the late medieval duchy of Guelders may have inhabited (mainly small) towns: Nijsten, *In the Shadow*, p. 6.
[10] *Chronik des Jacob Twinger*, ed. Hegel, p. 702. For Trier's Roman remains in the Middle Ages, see Clemens, *Tempore Romanorum constructa*, pp. 63–75.
[11] *Di Kronike von Pruzinlant*, ed. Strehlke, p. 342. Nikolaus is here following the Latin chronicle of Peter von Dusburg.
[12] *HUB* 3, no. 677, p. 476.

Rhine delta and west of Alexander's Xanten, may have supported a late medieval population of around forty-five people to every square kilometre.[13] An average figure for all the German regions would certainly be much lower – maybe something over twenty.[14] Moving eastwards, the landscape empties of people, with perhaps eleven inhabitants to each square kilometre in heavily Germanised Silesia in 1350, or just two in the Polish bishopric of Poznań, where German settlement and land clearance were much less.[15]

Other points of view disclose similar contrasts. Of the handful of large German towns with likely population totals in the late Middle Ages in excess of 20,000, most lay in the south and west: none of the greatest cities was located in central Germany, while among the giants the coastal north boasted only Lübeck (to be joined in the fifteenth century by Danzig (Gdańsk)).[16] The most urbanised regions were also, generally speaking, home to more numerous, richer and more ancient religious foundations. In the riparian west and south, social life was old-established, joined at its root to the ancient civilisations of the Mediterranean. On that crucial insight, if not in his Trojan myth-making, Alexander von Roes was quite right – as the Latin names of the towns by the Rhine, Danube and Mosel continued to affirm. Little would happen in the later Middle Ages fundamentally to shake 'old' Germany's cultural predominance, though it is indicative of at least a degree of readjustment to the ancient balance that, of the eight universities of substantially 'German' character founded before 1450, around half – Prague (to 1409), Vienna, Rostock and Leipzig – can be ascribed broadly to the east.[17]

Not even in its geographical extent does German-speaking Europe offer the observer a scene of reassuring fixity. The German lands constituted no natural geographic unity, and their limits were not obvious, but disputable, disputed and shifting; nor did rulership encompass them with any common, authoritatively defining framework. We are confronted with a series of landscapes in flux. If the shaping, fashioning and stabilising hand of royal government was slack in Germany, other social elements were restlessly active and dynamic, ever piling new complexity upon riotous profusion and chaotic variety. Successive

---

[13] Moraw, *Von offener Verfassung*, p. 49.
[14] A study of Saxony discovered 23 persons per km^2 in 1300: ibid., p. 49.
[15] Ibid., p. 50.   [16] Schubert, *Einführung*, p. 97.
[17] Rashdall, *The Universities*, pp. 211–63. The other four are Heidelberg, Cologne, the central-German university of Erfurt and Leuven (Louvain) in Brabant. The total does not include the short-lived university at Würzburg (*c.* 1410–13), discussed in ibid., pp. 253–4.

waves of settlement, intermingling and acculturation, mainly in regions lying to the east of the old German heartlands, had led to the area of Europe inhabited by German-speakers almost doubling in size during the central and later Middle Ages.[18] Demographic growth and land reclamation, clearance and settlement utterly transformed some landscapes, as in the countship of Holland, where the population grew tenfold between 1100 and 1300.[19] At the opposite limit of German speech, the inhabitants of Upper Silesia are thought to have multiplied between five- and sixfold in the century between 1220 and 1320 alone, through a mixture of German settlement and native growth.[20] The spread of towns, which across much of Germany occurred comparatively late, was working its own transformations: by 1400 there were around 4,000 settlements enjoying urban privileges, although many of these admittedly remained minuscule.[21] Between 1180 and 1350, the number of towns in Westphalia increased from 6 to 138.[22] The process had by no means run its course at the time of Frederick II's downfall. In the period 1253–1320, 130 new towns, initially populated mainly by German immigrants, were founded in the Bohemian lands alone.[23] And it was not only in the rapidly developing territories of the east that urbanisation continued into the post-Staufer epoch. On the wealthy lower Rhine, for example, Count Adolf of Berg in 1288 bestowed urban rights upon the obscure riverside settlement of Düsseldorf.[24] But if changes such as these added to the density and complexity of German society in the late Middle Ages, they did little to erode the many and profound contrasts and disunities which still marked the landscapes of German-speaking Europe.

Perhaps the most fundamental, and fundamentally divisive, of these was inscribed upon the land itself. Between the vast lowland belt, which spans northern continental Europe from the North Sea to the Urals, and the Alps, a succession of uplands rising to a thousand metres and more punctuates and divides the human landscape over much of central and southern German-speaking Europe: the Vosges, Black Forest, Hunsrück, Eifel, Taunus and Spessart; the Swabian and Franconian highlands; the Harz, Thuringian, Bavarian and Bohemian forest ranges; the Erzgebirge and Sudeten chains. Other environmental factors, such

---

[18] Thomas, *Deutsche Geschichte*, p. 27; and see below, Ch. 9.
[19] Moraw, *Von offener Verfassung*, p. 49.
[20] Higounet, *Die deutsche Ostsiedlung*, p. 325.
[21] Schubert, *Einführung*, p. 97.
[22] Pounds, *An Economic History*, p. 248.
[23] Higounet, *Die deutsche Ostsiedlung*, p. 172.
[24] Lau, *Düsseldorf*, pp. 9–10.

as climate, soil type and quality, and access to rivers and seas, also varied significantly between different regions of German speech. Taken together, these natural preconditions had all helped ensure that the forms of human life, settlement, economy and culture which by the late Middle Ages had developed among the Germans were marked more visibly by contrasts than by things shared.[25]

The vast extent of the German lands, together with their many natural obstacles and their tendency to fragmentation, ought to have constituted a significant brake upon the movement of people and ideas. A Dominican friar writing in Colmar in Alsace around the year 1300 judged that crossing Germany north–south from the sea to the Alps, or from Fribourg in the west to Vienna ('which is situated near Hungary') in the east, entailed a journey of 4 weeks.[26] His assessment seems realistic. We know that in the mid-fifteenth century it still took travellers on average 34 days to cover the distance between Lübeck and the imperial court in Austria. In the same period, even a journey down the Danube from Regensburg to Vienna took 5–7 days, the return trip against the current 9.[27] Even in the communications-rich west, distance imposed constraints. A messenger going overland from Lübeck to Bruges in 1290 faced a 12-day journey.[28] The time involved in moving through the German lands might be contrasted with the picture in England, where in the fourteenth century a royal envoy was able to traverse the greater part of the realm, from Sandwich on the Kent coast to York, in just 7 days.[29] Of course, the speed of movement of both people and information might vary sharply, depending on the chosen means of transport as well as the time of year. But only rarely in this period were consistent efforts made to master the obstacles of distance. In this respect as in others, the lands of the Teutonic Order occupy an exceptional position. There, a fast and efficient postal system developed during the late Middle Ages, employing post horses and letter boys, and keeping clock time: a letter dispatched to the Order's Grand Master from Königsberg (Kaliningrad) on Good Friday 1420 was logged at Elbing (Elbląg), some hundred kilometres distant, less than 24 hours later.[30] But only towards the close of the fifteenth century would the first foundations be laid for postal communications in the German heartlands in the west.

[25] Some of these contrasts are indicated in Scott, 'Economic landscapes', pp. 1–31.
[26] *Descriptio Theutoniae*, ed. Jaffé, p. 238.
[27] Moraw, *Von offener Verfassung*, p. 47.
[28] Nicholas, *The Northern Lands*, p. 312.
[29] *Oeuvres de Froissart*, ed. Lettenhove, vol. XVIII, p. 155. I owe this reference to Professor Michael Prestwich.
[30] Burleigh, *Prussian Society*, p. 48.

The rhythms of human life, and the cultural landscapes which they fashioned, showed few common elements, and little to sustain an incipient 'German' community. The 'German language' itself, in spoken form, remained into the sixteenth century such a babel of local dialects that Luther was able to observe that people living just 30 miles apart barely understood each other.[31] Obstacles to written communication between the various regional forms of the German tongue also remained substantial, despite the great rise of pragmatic vernacular literacy which had begun in Germany during the thirteenth century.[32] Political and constitutional developments had left their own rich and complex deposit upon the German lands, reinforcing separateness and inhibiting interconnection: in the late Middle Ages, laws and customs, weights and measures might vary not only between different lordships and territories, but also within them – often, indeed, between neighbouring towns and villages.[33] The numerous tolls, by water and land, that greeted the traveller through Germany, and which so agitated Thomas Wykes, were but one irksomely tangible manifestation of the triumph of political multiplicity and the historical absence of authoritarian central regulation.

The fragmented political map, with its restlessly competitive regional and local powers, could make the going hard for the long-suffering traveller in other ways besides. Rivalry spilled over easily into violence, with highway robbery, murder and abduction all finding a comfortable place under the broad, legitimising mantle of feud.[34] Certain regions, and stretches of major public roads, became notorious as the accustomed haunts of predatory, well-armed and often dishearteningly well-connected aristocratic thugs.[35] The castle of Schwanau, destroyed by the burghers of Strasbourg, was according to Matthias von Neuenburg infamous 'throughout Germany' (*in omni Alamannia*) for the great evils done there.[36] Contemporaries persuaded themselves that such horrors were worst in times when the monarchy was enfeebled. Jakob Twinger set down a lurid (and obviously exaggerated) vision of 'war, turmoil and strife in all the lands' during the troubled reign of Adolf of Nassau, such that 'no one dared to go about, and the highways became overgrown

---

[31] Wiesinger, 'Sprachausformung', p. 336. For the development of vernacular communications, see below, Ch. 11, pp. 487–95.

[32] For Germany in European context, see Britnell, 'Pragmatic literacy'.

[33] Schubert, *Fürstliche Herrschaft*, esp. pp. 4, 14–15.

[34] The relationship between political rivalries, 'state-building', feud and violence is well delineated, for a slightly later period, in Zmora, *State and Nobility*.

[35] For such men and their activities, see Rösener, 'Zur Problematik', pp. 469–88.

[36] *Gesta Bertholdi Episcopi Argentinensis*, ed. Hofmeister, pp. 519–20 (1333).

with grass'.[37] The perils of travel find more specific illustration in a letter which the representatives of the Hansa sent from Bruges to the city of Strasbourg in May 1395, begging intercession in favour of 'a poor shipman from the east [ostlant], called Long Claus', a pilgrim, who had been imprisoned by 'the Junker Ludwig von Lichtenberg' and his goods seized as he made his way down the Rhine.[38] Strasbourg, they argued, had a duty to aid the hapless wayfarer, who had recently come from Prussia and 'gets his livelihood from the sea', since he was seized 'on your river and highway'.

But the misadventures of Long Claus point also towards another picture, quite different from the one familiar from the chronicles of ubiquitous, debilitating strife and lawlessness. For these things had not kept the Hanseatic mariner at home; far from it, the letter from Bruges discloses in passing just how widely travelled he was. If the prevailing tone of contemporaries was downbeat, their occasional, incidental remarks hint that the deterrents to movement were maybe less formidable than might be supposed. 'When you get to Basel, do your feet a favour and descend [the Rhine] by ship to Cologne', one schoolboy laconically advises another in an imaginary dialogue about the best pilgrim routes to Rome and back, recorded by the Franciscan Albert von Stade.[39] Albert, whose convent lay beside the Elbe estuary not far from Hamburg, compiled his world chronicle in the time of Frederick II's downfall – a period as disturbed and violent as any in Germany's later medieval history.[40] Yet his fund of practical wisdom for the traveller through Germany and beyond – the expense and poor hostelries when passing through the Pustertal (Val Pusteria), an alternative way south if the Rhine is in flood at Duisburg – already makes such journeying seem a matter of prosaic, if not always comfortable, routine.[41]

Whatever the perils of travel in Germany, and the obstacles strewn in the traveller's way, journeying was by Albert's time becoming in important respects easier.[42] Germany had shared in the European bridge-building boom of the central Middle Ages, while inns and hostelries had proliferated in the German lands as they did elsewhere. In the thirteenth century, German writers give evidence of a burgeoning interest in improving the quality of the public highways, and measures were increasingly being taken, particularly by those who stood to profit

---

[37] *Chronik des Jacob Twinger*, ed. Hegel, p. 454.
[38] *Strassburg UB* 6, no. 937, pp. 556–7.
[39] *Annales Stadenses*, ed. Lappenberg, p. 340.
[40] See H. Patze, 'Albert von Stade', in *LMA* 1, col. 290.
[41] *Annales Stadenses*, ed. Lappenberg, pp. 336, 339.
[42] For what follows, see Spufford, *Power and Profit*, pp. 176, 181, 187–8.

from a growth in traffic. The thirteenth century brought the opening up of the St Gotthard route over the Alps, while a century later the bishop of Chur is to be found arranging for the road at the head of the Septimer pass to be paved. And it was not only by land that efforts were now made to speed the movement of people and goods. In 1398, for example, public celebrations attended the opening of the great canal cut between Lübeck and the Elbe.[43] Little wonder, then, that some characteristically medieval forms of wayfaring now attained powerful new impetus.

The late Middle Ages witnessed in central Europe an unprecedented boom in pilgrimage – a devotional exercise predicated on the ability and willingness of penitent Christians to travel. Some German shrines have left clear testimony to the enormous numbers of pilgrims which they drew in, and to the distances which they came. Noteworthy in this respect is the 'holy blood' cult which flourished at the obscure settlement of Wilsnack in north-western Brandenburg, following the destruction of the church there by fire in 1383.[44] An ornate stone marker, set up some years later by the wayside in Lübeck, points the way thither, and visitors who came included the Englishwoman Margery Kempe (whose devotional journal discloses both the means available for travel in the German lands and some of its perils).[45] If many other cults subsisted from more local traffic, even kings might experience on occasion the press to be met with at the greatest German shrines. Charles IV's entry into Aachen for coronation in 1349 was held up for several days by the crowds – of 'flagellant pilgrims', according to one chronicler – in the city to view the relics of Christ and the Virgin,[46] while Rupert of the Palatinate, crowned in Cologne at Epiphany 1401, cannot have been surprised to find the resting place of the mortal remains of the Magi likewise thronged with visitors.[47]

Not only the number but the social variety of travellers on Germany's highways was growing. The student population of central Europe rose decade-on-decade during the late Middle Ages, and if most preferred to attend institutions in their native regions, this nevertheless remained before the late fifteenth century impossible in much of

[43] Ibid., p. 202.
[44] Bynum, *Wonderful Blood*, Ch. 2.
[45] Goodman, *Margery Kempe*, pp. 158–61; the Lübeck marker is illustrated in Boockmann, *Die Stadt*, p. 255.
[46] *Die Chronik des Mathias von Neuenburg*, ed. Hofmeister, p. 280. For Aachen as the object of Charles's own devotions, see Schmid, 'Vom Rheinland', pp. 457–8.
[47] See Müller, 'Köln und das Reich', p. 612 with n. 66.

Germany.[48] In particular, those universities which were established in major towns lying, like Cologne or Leipzig, on international trade routes, drew recruits from far and wide. In the fifteenth century, the origins of Vienna's students extended far beyond the Austrian lands, embracing Franconia and Swabia and reaching even to the Rhine.[49] And if the most widely travelled academic pilgrims tended to come from wealthy, well-connected families, others had humbler origins. Characteristically, their backgrounds were urban.[50] The heroic journeys attested in the conduct of relatively routine affairs certainly give pause for thought. Sigismund of Luxemburg is found on one occasion enfeoffing six assessors (*scabini*) of the Westphalian *Veme* at Golubac (Taubenburg) in Serbia.[51] But it was in commercial life that the geographical horizons of German-speakers were enlarged most significantly in the two centuries between Frederick II's reign and Sigismund's.

One of the more remarkable aspects of the transformation of German trade and commerce in the central and later Middle Ages was the range of landscapes which it embraced: from Moraw's 'remote' north to the densely peopled riparian west and the growing urban networks of the south and centre. Criss-crossing these regions and spreading out beyond them was a proliferating web of routes, by land and water, bearing local, regional and long-distance traffic.[52] While some of these ways were long established, others, particularly those running eastwards from the German heartlands, reflected developments of more recent origin. But if German commercial expansion, above all in the Hanseatic zone, was closely bound up with the tides of eastward migration, it also carried German-speakers into lands far beyond the limits of concentrated German settlement.[53] The thirteenth century had seen the merchants of the Hansa establish residential bases, or 'counters', in strategic locations across the maritime north, from London and Bruges

---

[48] For the evidence of growing numbers, see Schwinges, 'Admission', esp. p. 188; for the recruitment base of German universities, see Schwinges, 'On recruitment', esp. pp. 36–41.

[49] Schwinges, 'On recruitment', pp. 38–9; and for Vienna, Hesse, 'Der Blick', pp. 105, 109.

[50] The energetic wanderings of the elite are charted in detail in Irrgang, *Peregrinatio Academica*; for recruitment from towns, see Schwinges, 'On recruitment', p. 40.

[51] Lindner, *Die Veme*, p. 436.

[52] For the development of interlinked networks of towns, see Scott and Scribner, 'Urban networks', pp. 113–43; for a map of late medieval trade routes through Germany, see Scott, *Society and Economy*, p. 117.

[53] The links between the Hansa and German settlements in the east are examined in Dollinger, *Hansa*, esp. Ch. 2.

to Novgorod.[54] Their sphere came eventually to extend southward to the Atlantic, with German traders settled on the Portuguese coast.[55] It was under the mantle of the Hansa that Germans penetrated Scandinavia, participating in the thirteenth-century in the foundation of Stockholm, where Germans would eventually comprise up to 40 per cent of the population and occupy half the council seats.[56] In Norway, German merchants and craftsmen made up a quarter or more of the population of late medieval Bergen (the site of a fourth Hanseatic counter).[57] Natives of Cologne were to be encountered throughout the towns of eastern England, with one scion of a burgher family from that city attaining in the later thirteenth century the status of a London alderman.[58] By the fourteenth century, the Hansa was drawing its members from mainly German-speaking towns within a broad arc reaching for 1,500 kilometres over northern continental Europe, from the North Sea coasts to the Gulf of Finland. As a framework uniting communities of Germans around common institutions and outlooks – however tenuous, limited and contested – it had no late medieval rival, and was certainly unmatched by the imperial monarchy.[59]

While the southern towns lacked a comparable overarching organisation, their burghers too were surveying wide horizons. By the 1370s, merchants of Ulm and Augsburg were bringing raw Syrian cotton north from the markets of Milan in volumes large enough to sustain a burgeoning native fustian manufacture.[60] Nuremberg's trade ranged in the late Middle Ages from Sweden to Naples, from Bruges to the Black Sea; and by the fourteenth century, her merchants, along with other southerners, could have recourse to a permanent base at Venice.[61] There was a German quarter in late medieval Zagreb (Agram), and traces of another in still-pagan Vilnius, while in 1382 a German fur trader from Moldova is mentioned in the town books of L'viv in the Ukraine.[62] Nor was it only merchants who were cast up far and wide along the ramified

---

[54] Ibid., esp. Ch. 2.

[55] Ibid., p. 98.

[56] Ibid., p. 36; Nicholas, *The Northern Lands*, p. 190.

[57] Dollinger, *Hansa*, p. 102; Nicholas, *The Northern Lands*, p. 314.

[58] Huffman, *Family*, pp. 162–3. For the alderman Arnold fitz Thedmar, son of a Bremen merchant and grandson of Cologners, see ibid., pp. 189–90. Arnold also wrote a London chronicle and served as custodian of the city's archives.

[59] For the Hansa's identity-forming capacity, see below, Ch. 9, pp. 437–43.

[60] Spufford, *Power and Profit*, p. 254.

[61] For Nuremberg's trade, see Stromer, 'Nuremberg', pp. 210–21; for the German *Fondaco* in Venice, Roeck, 'Venice', esp. p. 48.

[62] For Vilnius, see Rowell, *Lithuania Ascending*, p. 72; for Zagreb, Krahwinkler, 'Der Raum', p. 52; for the Moldovan merchant, Zimmermann, 'Die deutsche Südostsiedlung', p. 60.

commercial routeways of the late Middle Ages. Quite apart from the many mercenaries who found in Italy a congenial second home, by the early fifteenth century German craftsmen are attested in north-eastern towns such as Treviso and Padua, as well as in Venice.[63] In the thirteenth century, miners from the Harz had participated in opening up the copper mines at Falun in central Sweden, while other German miners are to be found working south of Belgrade, as far as Montenegro.[64] There is record of a 'Saxon church' close by the fateful battlefield of Kosovo Polje (1389).[65]

Not, of course, that such signs of growing geographical mobility among German-speakers, taken on their own, necessarily favoured the emergence of any kind of shared 'German' self-consciousness. Far from it: the prevailing impression is of centrifugal movements, scattering Germans across the known globe rather than drawing them towards any common focus. Members of Lübeck's well-travelled merchant elite would generally have known Stockholm, Bruges or London far better than Frankfurt, Strasbourg or Nuremberg. When Charles IV made his rare visit to the Baltic metropolis in 1375, only one of the city's three burgomasters was there to greet him: the others were away, in Denmark and in the maritime west.[66] Yet not all commerce was propelling Germans outwards, into foreign parts. The growth of regional and local markets and the consolidation of regional urban networks encouraged movement, and the gathering and interaction of groups of people, in numerous spheres of varying extent within the German-speaking lands themselves.[67] Meanwhile, a handful of major commercial centres within Germany developed as meeting points for different regional exchange systems. One link between northern and southern commerce was represented by Cologne, a Hansa member, but also a city whose merchants maintained relations with the towns of southern Germany, and beyond.[68] An especially important place was occupied by the fairs of Frankfurt am Main, biennial after 1330, which over time drew in traders from the Hanseatic north and the west, as well as from their established upper German catchment area.[69] About the role

[63] Roeck, 'Venice', p. 46. For German mercenaries in Italy, see Selzer, *Deutsche Söldner*, esp. (for regional recruitment patterns) pp. 217–21.

[64] For Falun, see Dollinger, *Hansa*, p. 36; for miners in Serbia, Zimmermann, 'Südostsiedlung', p. 59.

[65] Zimmermann, 'Südostsiedlung', p. 59.

[66] Moraw, 'Wesenszüge', p. 150 n. 4.

[67] For their development, see Scott and Scribner, 'Urban networks'.

[68] Cologne's relations with north and south in the period are illuminated in Möller, 'Köln'. For the city's Hansa membership, see Dollinger, *Hansa*, esp. pp. 124–5.

[69] Schubert, *Einführung*, pp. 155–6; Moraw, *Von offener Verfassung*, p. 127.

of such markets in the exchange of information and rumour and the formation of political mentalities, we can mostly only speculate. But that the flourishing of trade in Germany and the increasing mobility of its populations helped to foster political discourse is beyond question. Merchants, after all, depended upon knowledge – including knowledge of political affairs – for their livelihoods, and their way of life, urban milieu, wide contacts and literate skills equipped them like few other groups to gather, interpret and disseminate it.[70]

Occasionally we can observe the communicative process at first hand. Already in August 1348, men from Strasbourg were busy spreading tales of well-poisoning against the Jews in Cologne, nearly 400 kilometres downstream from their native city; and Cologne continued to be fed with rumour in the murderous months of pogroms that followed.[71] And where people routinely went, so too might bacilli: a Strasbourg chronicler noted that, whereas the first plague epidemic had come 'down from *Oberlande*', the second, in 1358, 'came up [the river] from *Niderlant*'.[72] Indeed, close study of the Black Death, at its height in Germany in 1349–50, has borne grim testimony to the effectiveness of the communications infrastructures in existence by that time: few if any regions appear to have been spared, and the chroniclers who recounted the plague's passage 'throughout all of Germany [*per totam Alamaniam*]', or observed the great dying 'in all the German lands [*in allen Dudeschen landen*]', probably exaggerated hardly at all.[73]

Some regions naturally sustained more intensive communications, and were thus more favourable to the spread of ideas, rumours and information, than others. That the Rhine and its cities have in this context been mentioned several times already in these pages is no coincidence. What is known of the movement of the Black Death through Germany underlines the importance of great waterways; while the bland self-assurance with which the Limburg notary Tilemann Elhen reported in 1392 the blighting of the vintage 'on the Rhine, the Lahn the Mosel, and everywhere in Germany [*in Duschem lande*]' indicates just how interconnected – in the minds of their inhabitants, as in hard

---

[70] For merchant literacy in Germany, see Isenmann, *Die deutsche Stadt*, pp. 358–63.
[71] Graus, *Pest*, p. 205.
[72] *Fritsche (Friedrich) Closener's Chronik*, ed. Hegel, p. 121. For these terms, see below, Ch. 10, pp. 467–8.
[73] *Die Chronik Heinrichs Taube*, ed. Bresslau, p. 76; *Detmar-Chronik*, ed. Koppmann, i.521. See also, e.g., *Cronica S. Petri Erfordensis Moderna* (Cont. I), ed. Holder-Egger, p. 381, for the plague's spread 'fere in tota Alemania'. The movement of the plague through Germany is reconstructed in detail in Benedictow, *The Black Death*, Chs. 14, 19, 20. For the German evidence and recent historiography, see also Mentgen, 'Die Pest-Pandemie', pp. 300–2.

reality – were the riverine landscapes of the west.[74] But more striking, and certainly more surprising, are the rapidity and comprehensiveness with which certain beliefs, reports, mental dispositions and – under their inspiration – modes of group behaviour proved able at this time to travel through the German lands. We would be wise to take with a pinch of salt the claim of Tilemann Elhen that a new vernacular song was popular 'throughout all of Germany', or his note of changing dress fashions 'in Germany'.[75] But other common impulses and actions of the time are not so easily dismissed, since there the expansive claims of the chroniclers can be corroborated.

The Flagellants are one such instance. These wandering communities of mostly laymen had made their way through the towns and villages in the late 1340s, ahead of the advancing plague, conducting gory and alarming cycles of public penitential devotions. To the appalled eyes of Heinrich von Herford, the Flagellants were 'a headless people' (*gens sine capite*), which in 1349 'suddenly arose from everywhere in Germany' (*ex omnibus ... Theutonie partibus*).[76] The chronicler of St Peter's, Erfurt agreed: the penitents sprang up 'in virtually all of Germany' (*tota Alemania*).[77] Surviving references to the movement are numerous and substantial enough to prove the truth of these startling claims. Originating, it seems, in the far south of Germany, the Flagellants were before long to be encountered in strength from Flanders and Brabant to Silesia, and from the upper Rhine to the middle Elbe, where bands several hundred strong entered Magdeburg.[78] The Erfurt chronicler's claim, that they were active 'in all the cities, towns and villages of Thuringia', has behind it the authority of local knowledge: his own town had (unusually) shut its gates on the penitents.[79] Other parts of western Europe did not remain untouched – with Flagellant songs being translated out of their original German into French in the town of Liège; but, on the whole, the movement was indeed largely a 'German' – and a remarkably *pan*-German – one.[80] So also was the next, more terrible, frenzy of rumour, enthusiasm and common action, which followed rapidly on the penitents' heels: the assault upon the Jews. More than one chronicler reported how, in the time of the plague, Jewish communities were murdered or expelled 'throughout Germany' (*Theutonia*), or 'in

---

[74] *Limburger Chronik*, ed. Wyss, p. 83. For the rapid movement of the plague down the Rhine (300 km in just 3 months), see Benedictow, *The Black Death*, pp. 187–8.

[75] *Limburger Chronik*, ed. Wyss, pp. 36, 37.

[76] *Liber de rebus memorabilioribus*, ed. Potthast, p. 280.

[77] *Cronica S. Petri Erfordensis Moderna* (Cont. I), ed. Holder-Egger, p. 380.

[78] Graus, *Pest*, p. 44.

[79] *Cronica S. Petri Erfordensis Moderna* (Cont. I), ed. Holder-Egger, p. 380.

[80] For Flagellant songs in Liège, see Graus, *Pest*, p. 38 n. 4.

all the realms [*regna*] and cities of Germany' (*Alamania*).[81] Their claims
are supported by the known, often well-documented, facts. Between
late 1348 and early 1350, pogroms occurred in most major towns across
the length and breadth of German-speaking Europe, from Cologne to
Breslau, from Constance to Münster and Stralsund.[82] There is ample
evidence for close consultation and a lively exchange of news between
towns engaged in anti-Jewish violence.[83] Once more, other parts of
Europe were also involved: indeed, the pogrom wave had entered
Germany from the Romance south-west. But again, the picture painted
by the chroniclers, of a movement both centred on and encompassing
Germany, has much justification.

However many and great the hurdles which fragmentation and division, not to mention topography and sheer geographic extent, had
strewn across the landscapes of late medieval Germany, doctrines,
enthusiasms and even popular movements, once combined with fears
or longings of sufficient urgency, were all capable of clearing them with
considerable speed. Within just nine months of her death in November
1231, the cult of St Elizabeth of Thuringia had become sufficiently
widely known to draw pilgrims to her tomb at Marburg from as far
afield as Cologne, Worms and the diocese of Utrecht.[84] Here was no
atomised, locally segmented world, such as Gellner thought characteristic of pre-modern societies. A central element in modernist arguments
against the pre-modern nation – that the prevailing cultural technologies were insufficient to sustain the widespread dissemination and
reception of unifying ideas and sentiments – is not supported by the late
medieval German evidence. But to suggest that conceptions of common identity could in principle have been quite widely communicated
within such a society is not to show that this is what actually occurred.
For the idea of nation is a fundamentally *political* idea, inseparable from
conceptions of rightful order, authority and entitlement. To raise questions of its presence and communication is thus to be drawn back to the
matter of a German *political* community – and to rulership, government
and the problem of power.

[81] *Die Chronik Heinrichs Taube*, ed. Bresslau, p. 92; *Liber de rebus memorabilioribus*, ed.
Potthast, p. 280.
[82] For the areas affected, see Graus, *Pest*, pp. 159–67. Only Austria, along with a handful of individual towns, largely escaped. On one estimate there were 80,000–90,000
Jews in the German lands on the eve of the Black Death, of whom the great majority
were killed between 1348 and 1350: Mentgen, 'Die Pest-Pandemie', pp. 303–4.
[83] Würzburg in particular compiled a systematic dossier of information gleaned from
other towns, covering anti-Jewish rumours and their actions against their own Jewish
communities: Mentgen, 'Die Pest-Pandemie', pp. 304–6.
[84] Werner, 'Mater Hassiae', p. 456.

Monarchy in mind

The medieval nation, we have been told, was a community which emerged most clearly within forms created by the rule of kings, and by institutions of government: the idea of nation, in short, 'closely resembles the medieval idea of the kingdom'.[85] Its substance, for contemporaries, must therefore have borne some relation to the substance of royal rule itself. But in Germany, as we saw, precisely this latter element appears to be lacking in the decades after Frederick II's downfall. In Germany, the rule of kings was variable, shifting, unstable and, in many places for much of the time, nebulous and insubstantial. Their government was a lesser thing than the government at the command of their western neighbours; and because of this, the problems facing them were different, and also in a way smaller, ones. Without great wars to fight or mighty enemies to face down, they had little reason to harangue the populations under their rule on the theme of their common heritage, divine election or shared duties – even had they possessed (as they did not) the means effectively to do so, or an expectation that those who counted would be listening. If the communicative resources of late medieval German society were perhaps more substantial than might at first be thought, those at the disposal of the monarch still look distinctly puny. Whether in his person or through his official writings, the Empire's ruler was, for most people, most of the time, out of sight. What reason then to doubt that he, and the realm – *regnum* – which his official acts invoked, likewise remained largely out of mind?

At best, we must expect, his wanderings would have made a passing and localised impression on those who watched his entourage go by. Viewing the changing scene as the chroniclers captured it, we can follow the king's movements through a succession of regional landscapes and places of stay, bound to each other by little beyond the intangible thread of the *iter* itself, which dissolved into air as the wagons rolled on. 'And ascending to the River Danube, he was received as king by the burghers of Regensburg', writes one chronicler of the recently elected Charles IV. At Nuremberg, the king was met by 'all the princes and nobles of Franconia and Swabia. After that he crossed over to the Rhine, where the cities received him as king'.[86] A Bavarian annalist captured Rudolf I working his way through a similar succession of discrete, adjacent landscapes, as he drew under his rule the nobles and towns 'on the Rhine,

[85] Reynolds, *Kingdoms and Communities*, p. 252.
[86] *Die Chronik Heinrichs Taube*, ed. Bresslau, p. 89.

and in Franconia, Swabia, and Bavaria'.[87] Against this backdrop, the effect of Heinrich Taube's observation (1342) that Ludwig IV 'made a general peace in Germany [*Alamania*], in Swabia, Bavaria, Franconia, and around the Rhine' is merely to render evident the chasm which yawned between the notional scope of Ludwig's rule and the sphere of its actual effectiveness.[88]

It therefore comes as no surprise to find royal government being experienced, perceived and judged within regional and local frames of reference.[89] It is not simply that the most detailed reports of the ruler's doings were often the work of writers living close to the routes which he regularly travelled: what they knew, or deemed worth recording, might also betray on occasion distinctly modest horizons and parochial outlooks. The accounts of Rudolf I's reign to be found in Latin annals of Austrian provenance concentrate heavily upon his early years, tracing in disproportionate detail his struggle with Otakar II, while disclosing little about the remainder of his rule.[90] Chroniclers from the upper Rhine and Alsace, by contrast, gave their closest attention to the king's later years, when he was campaigning in the south-west. Of the detailed narrative unfolded by the Strasbourg notary Gottfried von Ensmingen – unusual, incidentally, in explicitly taking the king's reign as its organising theme – a full three-quarters is devoted to Rudolf's final six years on the throne, whereas his epic clash with Otakar got only perfunctory coverage.[91]

Late medieval treatise-writers, while they generally managed to attain broader, more considered historical perspectives than the chroniclers, were prone to view the monarchy from positions every bit as regionally entrenched. Dietrich von Niem, a native of Westphalia (or, as he would have it, 'old Saxony'), thus missed no opportunity to heap glory on the Empire's Saxon rulers, especially Otto the Great.[92] The Rhinelander Alexander von Roes, by contrast, reserved his praises for the Frankish Carolingians, and scarcely mentioned the Ottos.[93] The

[87] *Hermanni Altahensis Continuatio*, ed. Jaffé, p. 406.
[88] *Die Chronik Heinrichs Taube*, ed. Bresslau, p. 52.
[89] See the comments of Tersch, *Unruhe*, pp. 268–73.
[90] Among the fullest accounts are *Annales Sancti Rudberti Salisburgenses*, ed. Wattenbach, pp. 801–5; *Historia annorum*, ed. Wattenbach, pp. 652–4; *Continuatio Vindobonensis*, ed. Wattenbach, pp. 707–11; *Chronicon Magni Presbyteri Continuatio*, ed. Wattenbach, pp. 533–4.
[91] Gottfried's work bears the title *Gesta invictissimi domini Rudolfi Romanorum regis*: it is printed in *Ellenhardi chronicon*, ed. Jaffé, pp. 122–34. On its significance, see the comments of Kleinschmidt, *Herrscherdarstellung*, p. 123.
[92] See, e.g., Dietrich von Nieheim, *Viridarium*, ed. Lhotsky and Pivec, pp. 47–8; also Jank, 'Die Darstellung', esp. pp. 96–101.
[93] See below, Ch. 7, pp. 339–42.

imperial monarchy's historical inability to subject the German lands to a rule capable of overcoming the gravitational weight of locality and regional tradition is thus obvious even (indeed, especially) from the remarks of the more reflective commentators. Never, it seems, had it been as ill matched to that task as in the two centuries which followed the end of the Staufer.

Germany knew no work of history comparable to the French *Grandes Chroniques*: no centrally produced, synthetic 'official' history of rulership over the German people. Instead, chronicles and annals recounting the deeds of the Empire's rulers were compiled in rich and untidy profusion in many different places in the German lands of the Reich. Yet the picture is perhaps on reflection rather more surprising than may at first appear. For the fact is that rulership and government, whatever their shortcomings, *were* made the subject of many historical accounts; and, while the more detailed of these did tend to cluster where the king was most often to be seen, that was far from being the whole story. The complexity of the picture can be illustrated by beginning in the Baltic port of Lübeck – which, although an imperial city, saw little of the Empire's medieval rulers. Their absence did not, however, inhibit the establishment during the late Middle Ages of a tradition of historical writing, first in Latin, later in the vernacular, which showed a consistent interest in the imperial monarchy.[94] Chronicle-writing in Lübeck rested upon collaboration between the burgher elite and the town's Franciscan convent, which clearly had access to good sources of information – a matter to which we will return. It was a Franciscan by the name of Detmar who, at the behest of the civic elite, embarked during the 1380s upon an extensive vernacular chronicle, incorporating substantial, well-informed and distinctly opinionated coverage of imperial affairs.[95] If their accounts of German politics concentrated mostly upon the north, Lübeck's historiographers also betray a deep-rooted belief in the monarchy's importance, and concern at signs of its enfeeblement.

Lübeck was at least an imperial city, bound by law, obligation and also interest and sentiment, to the Reich. Other chroniclers wrote in places yet more remote from the Empire's rulers. Albert von Stade, whose 'world chronicle' formed a foundation for Lübeck's historiography, was another denizen of the far north (and another Franciscan), who had much to say about imperial affairs under the later Staufer.[96] Other writers in locations well off the beaten track of kingship surpassed

---

[94] Wriedt, 'Die Annales Lubicenses'; Hoffmann, 'Geschichtsschreibung', pp. 298–301.
[95] T. Sandfuchs, 'Detmar von Lübeck', in *LMA* 2, cols. 68–9.
[96] For the character of his work, see H. Patze, 'Albert von Stade', in *LMA* 1, col. 290.

these northerners in knowledge and detail. Their geographical and social range encompassed – to draw examples only from the fourteenth century – a Styrian knight (Otakar uz der Geul), a Cistercian abbot from Carinthia (Johann von Viktring) and a Westphalian Dominican (Heinrich von Herford), each of whom chronicled with knowledge and engagement the affairs of Germany's rulers.[97] Peter Moraw surveyed five major Latin chronicles of the mid-fourteenth century, each of which took kingship as its framework and 'Germany' as its main sphere of interest.[98] While three of these were the work of authors – Matthias von Neuenburg, Johann von Winterthur and Heinrich von Diessenhofen – writing in the old-established heartlands of the southwest, the remaining two – by the Eichstätt canon Heinrich Taube, as well as Johann von Viktring – originated in regions where the presence of royal government was less.[99] Naturally, as Moraw shows, each of these authors had his own particular information sources, and most had contacts with lawyers and learned counsellors close to the ruler.[100] But that only underlines how diverse were the channels which by this date might connect literate Germans with imperial affairs. The important thing about these channels – such as friendship networks and contacts within the religious orders – is that their functioning did not on the whole depend upon the strength of the monarchy itself.

It is even possible (though without some qualification, certainly misleading) to discern by this time the outlines of a specifically 'German' sphere for historical writing, and a 'German' public for history. It is at any rate the case that, with the important exception of universal chronicles, few histories of non-German provenance found a readership in late medieval Germany.[101] There is no doubt, on the other hand, that most German chronicles and annals attained only local or regional circulation (when their reception is attested at all).[102] Yet there are exceptions to this – and suggestive ones, because the works which did reach a geographically broader public invariably ascribed a central place to

---

[97] H. Weinacht, 'Ottokar von Steiermark (O. aus der Geul)', in *LMA* 7, cols. 238–45; Hillenbrand, 'Johann von Viktring', in *LMA* 4, cols. 789–93; Hillenbrand, 'Heinrich von Herford', in *LMA* 3, cols. 745–9.

[98] Moraw, 'Politische Sprache'.

[99] For Taube, see K. Colberg, 'Taube, Heinrich, von Selbach', in *LMA* 9, cols. 628–31.

[100] Moraw, 'Politische Sprache', pp. 698–700, 717; and for Johann von Viktring's relationship with the Habsburgs, Hillenbrand, 'Der Geschichtsschreiber'.

[101] Sprandel, 'Geschichtsschreiber', p. 293. From a different perspective, a study of written portrayals of Rudolf I noted that the king (who was the subject of reports originating in various parts of Germany) attracted little notice from chroniclers outside the Reich: Kleinschmidt, *Herrscherdarstellung*, p. 133.

[102] The importance of regional spheres for the reception of historical writing is emphasised by Sprandel, 'Geschichtsschreiber', p. 291.

rulers and their acts. Two major vernacular histories which demonstrate the point are the *Saxon World Chronicle* from the thirteenth century and the chronicle begun towards the end of the fourteenth by a Strasbourg priest, Jakob Twinger von Königshofen.[103] The evidence of manuscript dissemination and influence upon other writers shows that recensions of the *Saxon World Chronicle* (a work with an exceptionally complex textual history) reached Austria, Bavaria, Bohemia, Thuringia, Swabia and the Rhine, as well as spreading throughout most of north Germany.[104] Manuscripts of Twinger's history, of which over eighty are known, found homes within a broad arc of lands, from the lower Rhine to the Alpine south-east – though with an understandable concentration in the author's native south-west.[105] The tally remains impressive even when it is noted that some copies reproduced only a portion of Twinger's text. Among Latin works, the world chronicle known as *Flores temporum*, compiled towards the end of the thirteenth century by a Swabian Franciscan, reveals a comparable profile, with over a hundred copies so far discovered, traceable to various locations, mainly in southern Germany, from Austria to the Rhine.[106] As the broad dissemination of these works indicates, the history of the Empire's rulers supplied for Germans of the period an impulse to look beyond local horizons, and an element of common interest which, even if most did not know it, they shared with German-speakers elsewhere.[107] The same point can be made by surveying the content of these histories. When north-German chroniclers paid attention to happenings in the south, it was often to note the actions of the monarch – as did Detmar, in his report on the siege of Ulm by Charles IV (1378).[108] By contrast, it is probable that the almost complete silence of south-German chroniclers about events in the north is largely to be explained by the extreme rarity of the ruler's involvement there.[109]

---

[103] See generally: D. Klein and G. Melville, 'Twinger, Jakob, von Königshofen', in *VL* 9, cols. 1181–93; Herkommer, 'Sächsische Weltchronik', in *VL* 8, cols. 473–500.

[104] The evidence for manuscript dissemination is summarised in Funke, *Cronecken*, pp. 35–8; for the chronicle's influence see Herkommer, 'Sächsische Weltchronik', in *VL* 8, col. 495.

[105] Klein and Melville, 'Twinger, Jakob, von Königshofen', in *VL* 9, col. 1183; and see *Chronik des Jacob Twinger*, ed. Hegel, pp. 199–224, for descriptions of the fifty-one manuscripts known at the time of the edition's preparation.

[106] See esp. Mierau, Sander-Berke and Studt, *Studien zur Überlieferung*, esp. pp. 5, 21–2; also P. Johanek, '"Flores temporum" ("Martinus Minorita")', in *VL* 2, cols. 753–8. Knowledge of *Flores temporum* is also attested from central Germany and Poland.

[107] These figures compare favourably with the sample of widely disseminated medieval historical writings tabulated in Guenée, *Histoire*, pp. 250–2.

[108] *Detmar-Chronik*, ed. Koppmann, i.563.

[109] Sprandel, 'Was wußte man?', esp. pp. 220–2.

But if mention is certainly made of the monarchy by chroniclers from various German regions, how great was their knowledge, understanding or even curiosity? In writings from the far north, the Reich as universal idea was at times more to the fore than were specific accounts of rulership in Germany.[110] Elsewhere, in some quarters (perhaps wilful) confusion reigned. 'But in what manner he was elected, or where or when or by which electors, I have never been able easily to discover', wrote a Bavarian chronicler of Charles IV.[111] The three decades of short, feeble and contested reigns which followed Frederick II's deposition proved particularly bewildering for contemporaries, and still more for those who came later. Chroniclers captured to a fault the instability and uncertainty of the period, with an archiepiscopal biographer from Trier recounting – inaccurately, but revealingly – how the election of 'Richard duke [sic] of Cornwall' was followed by the elevation of 'certain others, all of whom ... ruled for [but] a few days'.[112] The chronology of reigns and their interrelation quickly became disordered, with one early fourteenth-century annalist raising up William of Holland as a rival pretender against Henry Raspe (who was in fact his predecessor).[113] Richard of Cornwall underwent some startling transformations, into a 'king of Cornwall', as well as 'king of England'.[114] The usually well-informed Matthias von Neuenburg, writing in the middle years of the fourteenth century, had 'King Richard of England', Frederick II's successor on the throne, meeting his end, in an obvious conflation with Richard the Lionheart, from an arrow while besieging a French town.[115] Only after Richard's demise, in Matthias' account, did the princes choose William of Holland. For Johann von Viktring, writing a little earlier, it had been (just as incorrectly) William who died from an arrow wound, while besieging Aachen.[116]

But it is the extent of chroniclers' knowledge of imperial affairs, and the penetration of reports to remote corners of the realm, that merit more notice than do the predictable cases of ignorance and error. Understandably, the strange and the eye-catching travelled furthest and were remembered best. The short and precarious reign (first in Neuß, then in Wetzlar) of the imposter Tile Kolup, who in 1284 had

---

[110] A point made by Wriedt, 'Annales Lubicenses', p. 577.
[111] *Chronica de ducibus Bavariae*, ed. Leidinger, p. 170.
[112] *Vita Henrici archiepiscopi altera*, ed. Waitz, p. 457.
[113] *Annales Halesbrunnenses maiores*, ed. Waitz, p. 44 (under the year 1261!).
[114] *Die Magdeburger Schöppenchronik*, ed. Janicke, pp. 152–3 ('den koning van Kornuwie'). Elsewhere (ibid., p. 155) the chronicler identifies Richard correctly.
[115] *Die Chronik des Mathias von Neuenburg*, ed. Hofmeister, pp. 10–11.
[116] *Liber certarum historiarum*, ed. Schneider, i.212.

posed as a returning Frederick II, was immortalised in lengthy and circumstantial accounts written up in places as remote from the scene of the action as Austria, Styria and Alsace.[117] But less bizarre happenings might also reach the notice and interest of a distant chronicler. The annals ascribed to Hermann, abbot of the Benedictine monastery of Niederaltaich in lower Bavaria, report in some detail the founding of the Rhenish town league in the 1250s, revealing a grasp of its principles and organisation.[118] The northerner Albert von Stade made an early attempt at explaining the origins of the electors (including even an outline of Trier's foundation myth).[119]

Not only government and politics, but also the persons of the kings themselves were capable of exciting close, often anecdotal, interest. Heinrich von Herford knew that Charles IV had been baptised 'Wenceslas', though he was wrong in thinking that his subsequent change of name was forced on the king by the electors.[120] The rumour that Henry VII had been poisoned while taking communion (although almost certainly untrue) was very widely recounted by German writers, some of whom embroidered the tale to show the piety of the dead emperor, who had supposedly declined to vomit up the fatal Host.[121] Admittedly, certain rulers attracted more anecdotes than others – or at least more that have survived in written form. Rudolf I, the subject of around fifty known tales, is in this respect exceptional.[122] Yet even the modest reign of William of Holland proved capable of inspiring flights of narrative fancy. Abbot Hermann, writing in far-off Bavaria, preserves the story of how the king, while on campaign in Frisia, came to 'a certain town of that province', where he saw a magnificent tomb.[123] Upon asking whose it was, William was informed that the tomb was

---

[117] *Annales Sancti Rudberti Salisburgenses*, ed. Wattenbach, p. 809; *Ottokars österreichische Reimchronik*, ed. Seemüller, pp. 421–7; *Ellenhardi chronicon*, ed. Jaffé, p. 125. On his significance, see Schwinges, 'Verfassung', pp. 177–202.

[118] *Hermanni Altahensis annales*, ed. Jaffé, p. 397. For Hermann's comments, see Kaufhold, *Deutsches Interregnum*, pp. 171–2.

[119] *Annales Stadenses*, ed. Lappenberg, p. 367.

[120] *Liber de rebus memorabilioribus*, ed. Potthast, p. 275; and see Schneider, 'Karolus'. Charles had adopted his new name as a youth at the Capetian court in Paris: see below, Ch. 7, pp. 325–6.

[121] Some examples (from among many): *Die Chronik Heinrichs Taube*, ed. Bresslau, pp. 11–14; *Die Chronik des Mathias von Neuenburg*, ed. Hofmeister, pp. 93–4; *Detmar-Chronik*, ed. Koppmann, i.420–1; and, generally, Franke, *Kaiser Heinrich VII.*, part II. On the circumstances of Henry's death, see Hoensch, *Die Luxemburger*, p. 48.

[122] Martin, 'Das Bild', p. 204; and for more detail, Treichler, *Mittelalterliche Erzählungen*. This was despite Rudolf's evident lack of interest, in contrast to his rival, Otakar of Bohemia, in currying the favour of itinerant vernacular versifiers: Schubert, *Fahrendes Volk*, p. 213.

[123] *Hermanni Altahensis annales*, ed. Jaffé, p. 397.

empty, but that the ancient town fathers had made it in the belief that it would one day hold a king of the Romans. Before long, of course, it was holding William, who was to die at the hands of the Frisians. Attention extended also to the monarch's physical appearance, even if German chroniclers did not on the whole match their Italian neighbours in the vigour and detail of their pen-portraits.[124] Again, the 'thin and lanky' Rudolf was the beneficiary of an exceptional number of portrayals (including one from distant Lübeck), his reputedly unmistakable nose offering a promising butt for burlesque humour.[125] But other kings were not entirely ignored. Heinrich von Herford set down a vigorous sketch of Ludwig IV, with his 'full and abundant black hair and beard' (though 'slightly balding') and 'strong, brawny and muscular arms and legs', 'striding forth like another Romulus'.[126] Even Germans who never saw their ruler in the flesh – among whom we should probably number Heinrich himself – might thus form a mental image of him.[127] Much seems to justify viewing the thirteenth and fourteenth centuries – a period in which more naturalistic portrayals of the human form became established in the visual arts in Germany – as a time when observers learned to look more closely at their social environment, and to describe what they saw in more concrete, specific terms.[128] This developing sensibility, detectable in the writings of the chroniclers and poets, is not without relevance for the capacity of Germans to locate themselves imaginatively within a (human, temporal) political community.

But how *engaged* were German observers by the Reich and its rulers, and how able and willing to ascribe meaning to their contemporary history? Did the imperial monarchy's crises and its weakness move them to passion, or merely to resignation and disaffection? Colourful opinions are certainly not wanting in the vernacular political lyrics which survive in considerable numbers from the thirteenth and early fourteenth centuries, whose main audiences were to be found at the princely and noble

---

[124] For Matteo Villani's description of Charles IV – unequalled in detail or seeming veracity by German portrayals – see Thomas, *Deutsche Geschichte*, p. 218.

[125] For Rudolf, 'mager und lank', see the poet 'Boppe' in *Politische Lyrik*, ed. Müller, vol. I, p. 90. For chronicle accounts of Rudolf's appearance, see: *Chronicon Colmariense*, ed. Jaffé, p. 240; *Annales Lubicenses*, ed. Lappenberg, p. 415 ('fuit enim robustus usque in senectutem eius et sapiens, magnum habens nasum'); *Chronica de gestis principum*, ed. Leidinger, p. 27; *Die Chronik Johanns von Winterthur*, ed. Baethgen, p. 26; *Die Chronik des Mathias von Neuenburg*, ed. Hofmeister, p. 26.

[126] *Liber de rebus memorabilioribus*, ed. Potthast, p. 271.

[127] See the remarks of Thomas, *Ludwig der Bayer*, p. 385.

[128] See the comments of Martin, 'Das Bild', p. 204. Suckale, 'Zur Ikonografie', pp. 327, 330, rightly cautions against overstating such naturalism in images of rulers, or overlooking their stylised and stereotypical elements. Nevertheless, the broad trend remains undeniable.

courts and among elite groups in the towns. Indeed, the later Middle
Ages saw political singers and 'speakers' assume an increasingly independent role in political discourse and opinion-formation, and with it a
new outspokenness.[129] Their judgements on individual kings were by no
means always flattering. Rudolf I, for one hostile poet, made peace with
the success of 'a scarecrow in a barley field'.[130] In verses composed for an
assembly at Passau in 1348, Lupold Hornburg hurled a general impre-
cation at the rulers of his time – 'soft' men, 'cowards' – who did nothing
to 'avenge' the disorders which were plaguing the land.[131] No less opinionated were the political treatise-writers, who, like the poets and singers, embraced contention, and the public airing of trenchant views, as
integral to their genre – as we will see more fully elsewhere.[132] Charles
IV had 'wrecked the imperial chariot' with his alienations, according to
Dietrich von Niem, who also had nothing but scorn for 'the foolishness
and idleness' of Charles's son and successor.[133] But equally forthright
judgements were also uttered in more strictly historiographical writings.
Ludolf, abbot of the house of Augustinian canons at Sagan (Zagań) in
Silesia, shared Dietrich's contempt for Charles's heir. 'What good can
I write of this Wenceslas? Nothing.' Like another Nero, he was 'less a
king than a butcher'.[134] Writers who felt themselves directly touched by
a ruler's acts could be especially scathing: the fiscally voracious Charles
IV, who had appropriated the debts owed by Augsburg's Jews, was for a
chronicler in the town a 'persecutor of Christendom'.[135]

Not only individual rulers and reigns, but whole periods in the monarchy's history might come under the chroniclers' harsh gaze. In the
fourteenth century, Johann von Viktring summed up the period following Frederick II's downfall as a time of 'kings and quasi-non-kings' in
Germany.[136] Johann might, like other writers, have found the political
history of those years impenetrably confusing; but despite – or because
of – that fact, he held a clear view of its significance. A chronicler who
could not always easily check facts remained free to judge, interpret
and ascribe meanings. The impotence and corruption of rulership in

---

[129] Schubert, *Fahrendes Volk*, pp. 206, 211.
[130] 'Schulmeister von Esslingen', in *Politische Lyrik*, ed. Müller, vol. I, p. 89.
[131] Ibid., pp. 196, 198. For Lupold's verse, see F. Schanze, 'Hornburg, Lupold', in *VL* 4, cols. 143–6.
[132] Ch. 5, pp. 243–59.
[133] *Dietrich von Nieheim: Viridarium*, ed. Lhotsky and Pivec, pp. 3, 17. For Dietrich's view of Charles, see Frey, *Pater Bohemiae*, pp. 34–5.
[134] *Catalogus abbatum Saganensium*, ed. Stenzel, pp. 213–15. For Ludolf's attitude to Wenceslas, see Machilek, *Ludolf*, pp. 139–43.
[135] *Chronik von 1368 bis 1406*, ed. Frensdorff, p. 42. For the chronicler's judgement, see Frey, *Pater Bohemiae*, pp. 33–4.
[136] *Liber certarum historiarum*, ed. Schneider, i.197.

Germany during the 'Interregnum' quickly became proverbial in writings of diverse origin. The massive gifts to the princes with which Richard of Cornwall had reputedly purchased the throne attracted particularly widespread comment.[137] Arnold of Trier's biographer took his chance to stress the archbishop's virtue, in turning down a cash sum 'which some said might have been enough to bribe the entire Roman Curia'.[138] The interesting thing about the reports of these goings-on is the indignant tone to be met with, even in histories written far away from the regions where Richard was at work. 'Foolish England, willingly fleeced of so much money', fulminated a Hamburg annalist; 'foolish German princes, who sold their noble right for cash!'[139]

Informed Germans contemplated with anger and alarm the state of the realm; but contemplate it many clearly did. The monarchy remained a talking point during its periodic humiliations and recurrent crises. There is little sign that interest in the ruler and his doings slackened markedly at low points in the fortunes of the Reich; there is more reason to think that controversy and danger stimulated debate. Had they enjoyed the benefit of knowing that the 'Age of the Princes' was dawning in Germany, and that the future of government would henceforth lie for several centuries primarily with the dynastic territories, not the monarchical realm, no doubt writers and singers would have found more appropriate themes on which to expend their words.[140] Without such assurance, they continued to fret at the parlous state of kingship. The anxieties of politically aware Germans around the middle of the thirteenth century are most forcefully captured by surviving political lyrics, which frequently took as their theme the state of the realm and the shortcomings of its leaders. The Staufer had been blamed; but where, one poet demanded to know, was the princes' better king?[141] Their 'rental elections' (*mietekiesen*) had hobbled the Empire like the proverbial mallet bound to a mouse's tail.[142] What was once the Reich (*riche*), punned the poet, was now known as 'poverty', diminished in men, lands and wealth. Chroniclers were hardly less despondent in

---

[137] Examples: *Annales Sancti Rudberti Salisburgenses*, ed. Wattenbach, p. 794; *Annales breves Wormatienses*, ed. Pertz, p. 76; *Ellenhardi chronicon*, ed. Jaffé, p. 122; *Cronica S. Petri Erfordensis Moderna*, ed. Holder-Egger, p. 249.

[138] *Gesta Arnoldi*, ed. Waitz, p. 413.

[139] *Annales Hamburgenses*, ed. Lappenberg, p. 383.

[140] 'The Age of the Princes' was the title chosen by Barraclough, *The Origins*, for the section dealing with the late Middle Ages.

[141] For this and what follows, see 'Höllefeuer' in *Politische Lyrik*, ed. Müller, vol. I, p. 58. Among other examples to be found in Müller's collection, see, e.g., 'Kelin', in ibid., p. 59: the 'high lords' should 'fear God's anger' on account of the absence of peace.

[142] 'Höllefeuer', in ibid., p. 58.

their view of the events of the time. But, with their longer perspective and greater space for reflection, they also provide, by charting the shifting attainments of rulership in Germany, insights of their own: into the expectations projected onto the imperial monarchy and the sphere of action within which the ruler was expected to fulfil them.

Most striking for the reader are the absolute contrasts drawn between periods of weakness and times when royal government was judged to have been more effective. The chronicle of the Bavarian monastery of Fürstenfeld, compiled towards the middle years of the fourteenth century, painted the 'Interregnum' as a calamity of biblical proportions: the land filled with bandits and emptied of cultivators and livestock, the countryside choked with nettles. It was in this wilderness that God then set down a 'saviour', Rudolf I, thereby putting an end to the chastisement of His people – which, the chronicler reflected, had resembled that endured by the Israelites.[143] Other writers agreed that Rudolf's accession marked a revival of kingship. This, they insisted, was not only on account of his unanimous election, and the wide recognition which he secured: Rudolf himself was an able, energetic ruler. 'The king was a good peace-maker', reflected one, 'because he broke all the robber-houses which had damaged the land. In that way, he soon won the German lands [*Daeutscheu lant*], quickly subjugating them by force.'[144] The state of the monarchy had consequences: general order under a capable, vigorous king; anarchy in times of weakness or division. The prize was great, but it was quickly and easily lost. Rudolf had, for Gottfried von Ensmingen, established in Germany (*Alemania*) 'such peace' as 'had never been experienced or seen in that land'. Yet no sooner was the king dead than 'the general peace was broken and dissolved throughout the whole kingdom of Germany [*regnum Alemanie*], as if peace had never existed in that land'.[145] Gottfried was admittedly an unabashed partisan of the Habsburg ruler. But his underlying assumption, that the accessions and deaths of kings might have rapid, dramatic and general consequences for the state of the land, is commonplace among the chroniclers. Following the disputed election of 1314, the Königsaal chronicler claimed, 'conflicts emerged everywhere, violent acts were committed far and wide, and in almost all parts of Germany [*omnibus fere partibus Alemanniae*] there arose infinite dangers'.[146]

---

[143] *Chronica de gestis principum*, ed. Leidinger, p. 28.
[144] *Sächsische Weltchronik: erste Bairische Fortsetzung*, ed. Weiland, p. 328.
[145] *Ellenhardi chronicon*, ed. Jaffé, p. 134.
[146] *Die Königsaaler Geschichts-Quellen*, ed. Loserth, p. 369.

It is not, of course, plausible to suppose that the good times of stable kingship were as generally good nor the bad times of inept or divided rule as unremittingly bad as the chroniclers wished to believe. Lacking the analytical and evidential resources of the modern political scientist, they consistently overrated the capacity of their rulers both to cause and cure the ills of their society. Yet all the signs are that their claims were no mere rhetorical conceits: they were believed by writers and readers alike. The great store which their authors set by the king and his deeds helps explain why these continued to attract such substantial and anxious attention after 1245. But hardly less eye-catching is the scope which German writers ascribe to the acts of monarchy. Their panoramic statements offer little clue to the journeying, campaigning, negotiations, the wearisome, repetitive expenditure of time and energy, which offered the only means for a king such as Rudolf gradually to draw a thin, fragile net of peace-keeping arrangements over his realm. Nor do they acknowledge how distinctly incomplete were the final attainments even of a king of Rudolf's vigour and comparative longevity. On the contrary, observers seem often to have imagined royal government as exercised not over a series of discrete landscapes and localities, but over a single, unitary political community. It will by now be apparent that this community, whether or not equated specifically with a 'kingdom', was commonly identified as *German*. How widely this identification was made, and what it may have signified, is examined in the next chapter.

Rulership and royal government retained the attention of thoughtful Germans during their decades of abasement, crisis and comparative ineffectiveness after the end of the Staufer. They continued to matter in the eyes of many of those who left a record of their attitudes, since they were imagined as acting, in principle, and much of the time in fact also, as fundamental sources of peace, justice and social order. When they appeared to have failed in these tasks, their failures were denounced, not ignored, and remedies demanded. What is more, rulership was at least in some contexts identified with a sphere of action describable in regnal or even ethnic terms: a 'German' sphere – whatever that may have meant. Nor on the whole were the monarchy and its rule conceived merely in a schematic, idealised fashion: on the contrary, specific knowledge about rulers and their deeds was capable of reaching audiences that were geographically and socially diverse. Many Germans, moreover, clearly possessed both the capacity and the motivation to interpret, judge and contextualise the information which came to their notice. All this was in spite of the distinctly limited means available to the ruler himself to make his will known, and to give it effect, within the widely scattered German lands. Despite their divisions and diversities, these lands had by the late Middle Ages come to be criss-crossed and interlinked by many and varied channels of communication, capable of bearing report, rumour and ideas. These did not, on the whole, depend for their functioning upon the effectiveness or intentions of the Empire's ruler. Questions remain, however. How were knowledge, attitudes and assumptions of a specifically *political* kind – those which bore upon the monarchy – transmitted and received? What kinds of media were capable of conveying them? Which social and regional groups were most exposed to them? And what further stimuli, if any, might have induced Germans of the period to pay attention, and react, to such ideas or knowledge as they encountered? It is to these matters that we must now turn.

Communicating power

The inconspicuousness of monarchy in late medieval Germany can be overstated. Modern scholars may have looked with half-closed eyes, their gaze turned down upon their texts, or have let themselves be dazzled by the early 'nation states' apparently taking shape among the Germans' western neighbours; but observers at the time could have detected plenty of signs of the presence of kings and emperors in the German lands. If the peculiar history of monarchical government in Germany goes far to explain its material limitations in the thirteenth and fourteenth centuries, it also underlies an aspect of that institution less often acknowledged: how widely its traces were sown across the landscapes of late medieval Germany. One reason for this is simple: 'the Germans' themselves, as a named political community, may have been among the younger nations of medieval Europe; but the monarchy with which they identified their common fate was, in the thinking of the time, uniquely ancient. The kings who followed Frederick II on the throne were numbered, in the reckoning of literate Germans, in direct succession from the Roman Caesars. From this it followed that the successive dynasties occupying the throne of the medieval Reich were likewise all part of one single, unbroken succession of rulers. The seemingly fractured and discontinuous character of the medieval imperial monarchy is in the end largely a matter of the onlooker's own perspectives and priorities. The modern observer, overwhelmed by the repeated fissures and shifts in the succession to the Reich, is apt to overlook an underlying unity in rulership in Germany without parallel in Europe.

The visible remnants of past imperial rule on German soil left no doubt that here were the works of an illustrious institution. Post-Staufer kings may at times have found themselves deficient in visible majesty; but the vestiges of imperial grandeur were in some places massively planted in the landscape itself. Any person of a little education, contemplating in the thirteenth or fourteenth century the monumental Roman ruins which were visible (in some instances inescapable) in the towns of western Germany, would have been conscious of gazing on the past works of a monarchy which still claimed to rule the land.[147] It was the same with the edifices left behind by medieval ruling houses. Dietrich von Niem knew of Charlemagne's reputed birth at Ingelheim, 'on the river Rhine' close to Mainz, where still stood in Dietrich's time, recently renovated, 'the palace in which he was born'.[148] The fluctuating geographical focus of monarchy in Germany had historically served to pattern the land, across larger and more disparate areas than a more centralised power could easily have attained, with indelible reminders of its claim to rule. The great palace at Goslar may by the mid-thirteenth century have almost ceased receiving the Empire's ruler; but that did not end its importance as a symbol of the Reich for the town's burghers, who jealously guarded their privilege of receiving justice there.[149] Nor did the growing geographical 'remoteness' (to use Moraw's coinage) from the monarchy of Henry III's foundation prevent a fine, multi-towered Goslar from figuring prominently on the Ebstorf world map, datable to the thirteenth or early fourteenth century.[150] Germany was an extensive (if distinctly irregular) palimpsest of many centuries' worth of superimposed reminders of rulership, from Roman fortification to high medieval palace, to late medieval *Reichsstadt* – some of them in places which rulers had long ago ceased visiting. Unlike the king's *iter*, this stratified map of power showed few signs of contraction, and continued rather to put on new layers of complexity.

The absence from Germany of an established royal centre – of anything quite like the 'capitals' which had grown up elsewhere in late medieval Europe – is a deficiency often pointed out. The observation rests upon the same doctrinaire assumptions about the 'proper' course

---

[147] For the widespread presence of Roman artefacts in the landscapes of western Germany in the Middle Ages, see Clemens, *Tempore Romanorum constructa*, esp. part II.

[148] *Dietrich von Nieheim: Viridarium*, ed. Lhotsky and Pivec, pp. 1–2.

[149] Schneidmüller, 'Reichsnähe – Königsferne', p. 12.

[150] Illustrated in *Die Ebstorfer Weltkarte*, ed. Kugler, vol. I, p. 117. For the various proposed datings, see ibid., vol. II, p. 69. Kugler favours a date around 1300 or slightly thereafter. Others have located the map's origins in the early to mid-thirteenth century.

of medieval constitutional development as underlie other judgements about the 'failure' of German 'state-making'. But it omits to acknowledge how differently shaped landscapes of power might have served broadly comparable ends: as one study of Germany's historic 'capitals' has put it, 'the land in the centre [of Europe] was and is the land of numerous central places'.[151] Throughout the Middle Ages, kingship in Germany rested simultaneously upon a plurality of favoured locations, associated with the solemn representation of power, particularly in the context of great public occasions such as coronations, assemblies and the high feasts of the Church. The long-established pattern was perpetuated in the decades after 1245, with the spectacle of monarchy concentrated increasingly in the growing towns. It is true that the German lands remained without an established central place for administration, justice, fiscal control and archive-keeping, in the French or English mould, though Prague did for a time under the Luxemburger start in a limited way to fill these roles.[152] But if we consider instead the other main function of a late medieval 'capital' – the public staging and enactment of monarchy itself – it is less certain that imperial majesty was, in comparison with neighbouring realms, significantly under-represented to the populations under its rule. The sites of memory, tradition and ceremonial associated with the rulers were several, and underwent some elaboration during the late Middle Ages. It was the town's role in the making of kings and as a stage for political spectacle that led Heinrich von Herford to describe Aachen as 'the seat of the kingdom of the Germans' (*sedes regni Theutonicorum*).[153] The same judgement underlay Heinrich von Diessenhofen's description of Frankfurt and Aachen as two 'principal cities' (*principales*) of the realm.[154] The Golden Bull added Nuremberg officially to the list of places where the new king was expected to appear in state.[155] It was with reference to Charles IV's great court at Nuremberg in 1361 that the Eichstätt canon Heinrich Taube carefully enumerated the imperial regalia and relics 'which I saw there'.[156] The plurality of centres of monarchy in Germany may well have increased, rather than diminished, the opportunities for those under the Empire's rule to witness personally the spectacle of rulership.

[151] Schultz, 'Vorwort', in Schultz (ed.), *Hauptstädte der Deutschen*, p. 7.
[152] Moraw, 'Zur Mittelpunktfunktion', pp. 471–4.
[153] *Liber de rebus memorabilioribus*, ed. Potthast, p. 245.
[154] *Heinricus Dapifer de Diessenhoven*, ed. Huber, p. 72.
[155] *Die Goldene Bulle*, ed. Fritz, p. 87; and see above, Ch. 2, p. 80.
[156] *Die Chronik Heinrichs Taube*, ed. Bresslau, p. 118.

The tally of significant sites of power in Germany can be extended. It says much for the imperial monarchy's enduring prestige that the dynasties which came during the late Middle Ages to monopolise the throne were so keen to borrow something of its aura for their own territorial residences. Ludwig IV installed the imperial regalia in what was probably a purpose-built chapel in Wittelsbach Munich, whence the burghers were to prove reluctant to disgorge them to the new king, Charles IV, in the years following Ludwig's death.[157] Charles himself applied energy and ambition without parallel to the task of suffusing with imperial lustre the ancient, already myth-laden Přemyslid metropolis of Prague.[158] The vast New Town which he laid out there, through its scale and magnificence, and its many churches, invoked Rome as well as Jerusalem.[159] The festival of the Holy Lance and Nail, which Pope Innocent VI established at Charles's request in 1354, infused with new salvific power the annual showing of the imperial relics which the king had already initiated in the New Town: in later years they were to be displayed there from the gallery of a purpose-built church.[160] Nor, as we shall see, were these establishments by any means the full extent of Charles's measures in Prague to fuse the symbols of Bohemian and imperial majesty.[161] Dynastic residences like Munich and Prague admittedly had a different status from established sites of imperial memory in the old German heartlands. Any imperial echoes which they were able to raise were destined to die away with the dynasty's tenure of the throne. No family was able during this period to secure a hold on the Empire long or memorable enough to bring about a lasting change of perceptions in Germany: it has already been seen how little attraction their residences exercised for the German princes. Charles IV's achievements were in this respect the most substantial, and given a luckier and more vigorous successor might indeed have brought about the shift of power and perceptions in the Reich that he evidently envisaged. The direction in which, under the emperor's hand, developments were moving is illuminated by an ironic remark by Heinrich von Diessenhofen, who, observing the scene from the far south-west, wrote of the *metropolis regni Bohemie*, 'where is

---

[157] Markschies, 'Ludwig IV., der Bayer', p. 473; Bauer, 'München', p. 120.
[158] See generally Crossley and Opačić, 'Prague'. While some (e.g. Rader, 'Aufgeräumte Herkunft', p. 429) have emphasised the Bohemian focus of Charles's patronage in Prague, imperial motifs were also everywhere prominent – even, e.g., at the Emmaus monastery, despite its Slav patrons and liturgy.
[159] Crossley, 'The politics', p. 126.
[160] Ibid., p. 131.
[161] See below, pp. 232–3, 329–30.

now the seat of the Empire, which once passed to Rome, afterwards to Constantinople, and now to Prague'.[162]

Diessenhofen's remark is certainly a straw in new winds that were blowing over the German lands in the later fourteenth century. But the change should not be mistaken. The densest concentration of legitimising sites still lay in the ancient, urbanised west. These not only maintained their established importance, but underwent in this period further elaboration. Cologne, whose archbishops claimed the right to crown the new king, retained a place in the symbolic landscape of rule in Germany that the city's relative marginality to the royal itinerary seems to belie. It was to Cologne, with its dazzling shrine to the Magi, laden with images and associations of monarchy, that the new king customarily proceeded from his Aachen coronation.[163] Rupert of the Palatinate, as we saw, was actually crowned there on the feast of the Magi in 1401. Two further kings – Charles IV and, before him, the Habsburg Frederick the Fair – were crowned by the archbishop of Cologne in his town of Bonn.[164] And while too much should not be made of Bonn as a site of monarchy, its exploitation does underline further the status of the Rhine's course below Mainz as a king-making landscape. It helps explain why Tile Kolup first appeared in Cologne to seek recognition as the returning Frederick II, before quickly making for nearby Neuß, another of the archbishop's towns by the Rhine. It also highlights in extreme form how in the later Middle Ages the periodically unstable, contested character of kingship in Germany itself encouraged the multiplication of centres linked with monarchy: at a time when the loyalties of Frankfurt or Aachen might well lie with a rival pretender, there was a pressing need for alternative legitimising sites.

The consolidation of the Rhine valley as a monarchical landscape in the period is underlined by the emerging importance of Rhens, just above Koblenz on the river's left bank. An established meeting place for the electors, Rhens not only witnessed two royal elections, those of Charles IV and Rupert; from the time of Sigismund's coronation (1414), new kings making for Aachen are known to have begun calling there for enthronement, with the electors and other princes present, on an open-air riverside throne.[165] Indeed, the whole of the urbanised, populous route which the new ruler travelled between election and

[162] *Heinricus Dapifer de Diessenhoven*, ed. Huber, p. 116.
[163] See Militzer, 'Der Erzbischof von Köln', esp. p. 107.
[164] Volk, 'Von Grenzen', pp. 268, 270.
[165] Ibid., pp. 291–2.

coronation constituted an extended zone of solemn royal display. By tradition, these journeys were stately and magnificent affairs, staged so as to present the king in appropriate style to spectators along the way. There are indications that the element of organised spectacle increased over the course of the later Middle Ages.[166] With all this in mind, Moraw's classification of this part of western Germany as increasingly peripheral (if still 'open') to rulership may understate its importance, at least for the representation of monarchy, its public culture and profile. True, late medieval kings were mostly not to be found regularly in the region below Mainz. But, for a ruler to impress his majesty on those who witnessed him, what mattered was not only how frequently he came to a region, but the manner in which he came, and why. Kingship in Germany was constituted in time as well as space, its 'presence' concentrated in a succession of defining public occasions. Some (like the great Christmas *Hoftage* of 1355 and 1356) followed the rhythms of the liturgical calendar. But the most important ones were crowded into the opening months of a new king's reign. Disproportionately, they were packed into the bustling corridor of routes running between Frankfurt, Mainz, Aachen and Cologne.

Surviving accounts of elections and coronations present an impressive picture of the scale of imperial ceremonial. An Erfurt chronicler believed that 'the prince-electors of the realm and many other princes and nobles from all of Germany' (*Alemania*) had assembled for the election of Henry VII.[167] Assemblies too, while never drawing a full attendance of the princes and towns, could certainly bring together impressive numbers.[168] Contemporary reports make clear that such events attracted lively interest and close observation.[169] Tilemann Elhen's sense of occasion is captured in the dazzling picture which he painted of Charles IV's great court at Nuremberg in 1361, on the occasion of his son's baptism.[170] Chroniclers reveal on occasion a precise grasp of the constitutional forms for king-making. Matthias von Neuenburg remarks that whereas Ludwig IV was crowned 'in the right place [Aachen], but not by the right person', his rival Frederick's coronation had been

---

[166] Ibid., pp. 296–7.

[167] *Cronica S. Petri Erfordensis Moderna*, ed. Holder-Egger, p. 336.

[168] For a list of those known to have been present at Rudolf I's Würzburg assembly of 1287, see *Die Regesten des Kaiserreiches unter Rudolf*, ed. Redlich, no. 2263a, pp. 492–3; for the Nuremberg assembly of February–March 1401, Annas, *Hoftag*, vol. II, pp. 183–91. Annas also analyses attendance at numerous other major assemblies, beginning with the reign of Charles IV.

[169] See, e.g., *Chronik von 1368 bis 1406*, ed. Frensdorff, p. 74, for those attending the assembly held by Wenceslas at Heidelberg in 1384.

[170] *Limburger Chronik*, ed. Wyss, pp. 48–9.

conducted 'by the right person [the archbishop of Cologne], but not in the right place'.[171] Often, those Germans who have left a record appear both to have known and cared about the public rituals surrounding the Empire's ruler. Not only was Charles IV elected and crowned in incorrect locations but, objected Heinrich von Herford, his Bonn coronation was conducted 'as if in secret, without due pomp'.[172]

The towns, growing rapidly in size and number during the thirteenth century, provided a stage on which the king could be witnessed directly by many people, including those of relatively humble standing. The towns supplied an audience for the spectacle of late medieval monarchy which kings and emperors in the glory days of the *Kaiserzeit* had largely lacked. A Bavarian chronicler alleged that, when Frederick the Fair handed over the imperial regalia to Ludwig IV at Nuremberg in 1324, 'many thousands of people' assembled to view them.[173] No wonder that writers of the time emphasised so much the importance to the monarch of urban locations.[174] The rituals for receiving a ruler into a town were by the late Middle Ages well established and, particularly when he visited for the first time, elaborate.[175] The public spectacle that attended Sigismund's entry into the imperial town of Bern in 1414 could stand for many.[176] Already in the suburbs, he was met by a company of 500 liveried boys of the town, garlanded with the arms of the Reich. At the town's gates, the clergy received him with banners and relics. The decorated streets, through which he processed to the pealing of church bells, were reportedly thronged by the entire population, Bern's councilmen at their head. There is little doubt that occasions like this would have been long remembered by those present. Town chroniclers set down for posterity vivid and circumstantial records of the king's visits, like those detailing the reception of Charles IV in Lübeck (1375) and Magdeburg (1377).[177] Their interest extended beyond civic pride: public enactments of rulership in other, neighbouring towns might also command attention. Magdeburg's *Schöppenchronik* records how in 1374 at nearby Tangermünde 'the emperor sat in his majesty in the marketplace and

---

[171] *Die Chronik des Mathias von Neuenburg*, ed. Hofmeister, pp. 98–9.
[172] *Liber de rebus memorabilioribus*, ed. Potthast, p. 275.
[173] *Chronica de gestis principum*, ed. Leidinger, pp. 98–9.
[174] Examples: *Königsaaler Geschichts-Quellen*, ed. Loserth, pp. 335–6 (before entering Italy, Henry VII 'first arranged to visit all the cities of the Empire in Germany'); *Die Chronik Heinrichs Taube*, ed. Bresslau, p. 95 ('all the cities of the Empire in Germany', with three exceptions, gave their allegiance to Charles IV).
[175] See Drabek, *Reisen*, esp. p. 6.
[176] For what follows, see ibid., p. 15.
[177] *Detmar-Chronik*, ed. Koppmann, i.551–3; *Magdeburger Schöppenchronik*, ed. Janicke, pp. 272–4. On these accounts, see Schenk, *Zeremoniell*, pp. 192–3.

enfeoffed the margrave of Meißen's brother … with the banner-fief and regalia of the [arch]bishopric of Mainz'.[178] If political crisis and institutional weakness after 1245 limited the ruler's capacity directly to make his presence felt in the German lands, changes taking place during the same period in society, economy and communications nevertheless had the effect of exposing him to the gaze of new and growing, alert and articulate audiences.

All the signs are that by the fourteenth century the Empire's rulers and those who advised them were coming to understand clearly the wide communicative power of ritual acts and to give increasingly careful thought to the public staging of imperial majesty. Especially on great political and constitutional occasions, the potential offered by urban spaces was now exploited to the full. When Ludwig IV appeared together with Edward III of England at Koblenz in September 1340, it is likely that the site of their meeting, the square before St Kastor's church, was chosen specifically for its capacity to accommodate a large crowd.[179] The choice proved a wise one: according to the English chronicler Henry of Knighton, the heralds estimated a good 17,000 people to have assembled to watch.[180] While it is impossible to corroborate this very high figure, detailed reports of the spectacle set down by chroniclers in various parts of western Europe suggest that the organisers' communicative ends were brilliantly achieved.[181] Maximum visibility had evidently been sought for the key participants, with the emperor himself reportedly seated on a 12-foot-high throne, with the English king and the electors somewhat below him. Ludwig's sumptuous, quasi-priestly garments attracted as much contemporary notice as did the matters enacted, and more than one commentator remarked that the orb which the emperor bore symbolised his title to world rule.

None understood better than Charles IV and his circle how to harness for their image-making ends the ritual street theatre of the late medieval Reich. The wide geographic reach of Caroline self-representation is illustrated by a detailed eye-witness description of the emperor's protracted funeral solemnities in Prague in December 1378. This account, which may have circulated as a newsletter, was incorporated into a chronicle compiled in distant Augsburg.[182] The social estates of

---

[178] *Magdeburger Schöppenchronik*, ed. Janicke, p. 266.
[179] For this and what follows, see Schwedler, *Herrschertreffen*, pp. 50–6, as well as Thomas, *Ludwig der Bayer*, pp. 315–17.
[180] *Knighton's Chronicle*, ed. Martin, pp. 8–9.
[181] Analysed in Schwedler, *Herrschertreffen*, pp. 50–6; and for the orb, see *Knighton's Chronicle*, ed. Martin, pp. 8–9.
[182] *Chronik von 1368 bis 1406*, ed. Frensdorff, pp. 59–63.

Prague which took part in the public mourning are enumerated (7,000 masters and students from the university alone, claims the writer); the armorials of the Luxemburg crown lands which were borne through the streets with the bier are carefully described, as also are the imperial insignia (including shield and banner, the eagle shown head-downward), and the regalia which were placed by the emperor's corpse; even the candles allegedly burned during the extended obsequies are numbered.[183] Noteworthy is the juxtaposition of the symbols of the Reich and of Luxemburg dynasticism, so characteristic of Charles's personal imagery of power. But it is also significant that such detailed information was accessible so far from Prague, and that it was deemed worthy of record.

The absence of any single, established mausoleum and place of memory-keeping for the rulers of the Reich has already been observed. That did not, however, deter writers in Germany from setting down such knowledge as they had relating to the death and burial of kings – though the level of detail found in the Augsburg report is unparalleled. The chronicler of St Peter's, Erfurt, gave a reflective account of Henry VII's reburial in 1309 of his predecessors Adolf of Nassau and Albert I in Speyer cathedral, implying that his act endowed these kings – both of whose reigns had been controversial, and their deaths violent – with new legitimacy.[184] Speyer, where Rudolf I was also laid to rest, had been a site of imperial display since the eleventh century, the burial place of Salian emperors, as well as Philip of Swabia (d. 1208).[185] A German observer in the post-Staufer period was moved to describe Speyer (with some exaggeration) as the place where 'since ancient times kings of the Romans were accustomed to be interred'.[186] The attention which the chroniclers gave to burials there, particularly Rudolf's, suggests that the shift which occurred in the fourteenth century, to interring kings within their dynastic patrimonies, probably did indeed undermine their post-mortem remembrance in Germany.[187] At any rate, the relatively scanty notices which (the Augsburg report notwithstanding) their passing often received seems to reflect lack of information more than any

---

[183] For full discussions of the evidence for Charles's funeral, see: Šmahel, 'Spectaculum et pompa funebris' (pp. 36–7 for order and route of procession); Meyer, *Königs- und Kaiserbegräbnisse*, esp. pp. 100–18; but also, for a critique of Meyer's approach, Meier, 'Königs- und Kaiserbegräbnisse'.

[184] *Cronica S. Petri Erfordensis Moderna*, ed. Holder-Egger, pp. 340–1. See also *Sächsische Weltchronik: Thüringische Fortsetzung*, ed. Weiland, p. 313.

[185] See Ehlers, *Metropolis Germaniae*.

[186] *Ellenhardi chronicon*, ed. Jaffé, p. 134.

[187] See, e.g., the account of Rudolf's burial in *Annales Sindelfingenses*, ed. Pertz, p. 306.

lack of interest.[188] By contrast, even Rudolf I's tomb effigy in Speyer was made the subject of a lively anecdote, set down by a writer in a region remote indeed from the king's burial place.[189]

It was not only in its seeming wrinkles-and-all veracity that Rudolf's portrayal broke new ground.[190] Only one of his predecessors on the throne, Rudolf of Swabia (d. 1080), had been the subject of a funerary image at all. While it is true that tomb sculptures were also far from universal among his late medieval successors, that fact is mainly explained by the turbulent character of the times, and the troubled, impoverished and controversial reigns which they witnessed.[191] The imperial monarchy, its symbolism traditionally directed at the transcendent and the eternal, was still in the thirteenth century well behind its western neighbours in the matter of representing the ruler visually; but in this respect at least, the late Middle Ages saw Germany catch up.[192] Charles IV alone was made the subject of over seventy known depictions.[193] If many of these were made for the eyes of the few, others were on public display; some were monumental. And Charles (though, as ever, exceptional in the number and ambition of his portrayals) took his place in a rich late medieval tradition of depicting living and recently dead monarchs, as well as earlier rulers of the Empire, from Caesar to Charlemagne, Otto the Great, and (St) Henry II – not to mention those biblical 'kings of the Old Law' who were sometimes seen as foreshadowing them.[194] Their making was accompanied by a proliferation in Germany of visual allusions to the Reich and its authority more generally. If the monarch's

[188] Though, e.g., Heinrich von Diessenhofen noted the burial of Henry VII in Pisa and Ludwig IV in Munich: *Heinricus Dapifer de Diessenhoven*, ed. Huber, pp. 61, 95.

[189] *Ottokars österreichische Reimchronik*, ed. Seemüller, pp. 508–9, vv. 39125–194; and see also Meyer, *Königs- und Kaiserbegräbnisse*, pp. 30–1.

[190] See Suckale, 'Die Ikonographie', pp. 327–30, for the possibility that the chronicler (Otakar uz der Geul), in claiming that Rudolf's effigy was made from life, was merely repeating an anecdote told to visitors to Speyer cathedral. Suckale emphasises how little is known about the original form of the tomb image and how weak are the grounds for believing that the image *actually* depicted Rudolf's features.

[191] In addition to Rudolf, near-contemporary funerary images survive for Henry VII, Günther of Schwarzburg and Rupert of the Palatinate, and a later one for Ludwig IV. Curiously, there is no certain evidence that Charles IV was the subject of such a depiction, though it would be remarkable had he not been. For the little that is known, see: Meyer, *Königs- und Kaiserbegräbnisse*, esp. pp. 254–8; Rader, 'Aufgeräumte Herkunft', pp. 422–4.

[192] For what follows, see generally Scales, 'The illuminated *Reich*'. For Germany's traditional imperviousness to image-making: Schenkluhn, 'Monumentale Repräsentationen', p. 374; Dunk, *Denkmal*, pp. 12–13.

[193] Rosario, *Art*, p. 13; also Herzogenberg, 'Die Bildnisse'.

[194] For late medieval monuments to early medieval emperors, see Köster, 'Zwischen Grabmal'; for the assimilation of the Old Testament to medieval rulers, Schenkluhn, 'Monumentale Repräsentationen', p. 370.

personal visibility in the German lands was modest, and the penetrative range of his official writings scarcely greater, other reminders of his rulership were – through processes in which the monarchy itself was often only tangentially involved – becoming increasingly pervasive.

Image-making, the transmutation of stone into flesh, was at the heart of the Gothic style, and its ideological potential for rulers has often been charted in studies of the visual culture of the consolidating western monarchies, above all the French.[195] Its conquest of Germany began rather late, in the time of the Empire's crisis, around the middle of the thirteenth century: equestrian statues of crowned rulers in Bamberg (*c.* 1235–7) and Magdeburg (*c.* 1240–5) were dramatic harbingers of the new mode, while the towns supplied for the image-maker both a site and a rapidly growing audience for display.[196] Particularly in the established centres of imperial spectacle, the monarch's image in stone, or images of his illustrious predecessors, increasingly stood public proxy in his absence. In Aachen, the council's meeting hall on the Fish Market acquired in the second half of the thirteenth century a seven-niched frieze, apparently showing a king – perhaps Richard of Cornwall or Rudolf I – flanked by electors.[197] Aachen's great Rathaus, which incorporated a fragment of Charlemagne's palace, received during the 1370s a façade including thirty figures of the Empire's rulers, of which one is known to have represented Wenceslas; old views show a statue of Charlemagne above the main portal.[198] Some years earlier, Frankfurt's Galgentor, one of the city's main gates, had likewise acquired a sculpture of Charlemagne, along with others of the imperial eagle and St Bartholomew (in whose church the princes met for the election).[199] In Nuremberg, the former Jewish quarter was refashioned following the 1349 pogrom into a site glorifying the monarchy.[200] The chapel of the Virgin erected there (from whose balcony in 1361 the imperial regalia were to be displayed) invoked Charlemagne's Aachen chapel; its decorative scheme incorporated imperial armorials, including those of the electors, and statues of Henry II and his consort Kunigunde.[201] Across

[195] See, e.g., Sherman, *The Portraits*.
[196] For the entry of French Gothic into Germany, see: Sauerländer, 'Two glances', pp. 192–4; Williamson, *Gothic Sculpture*, esp. pp. 174–7.
[197] Grimme, 'Das gotische Rathaus', p. 512; Saurma-Jeltsch, 'Das mittelalterliche Reich', p. 412.
[198] Grimme, 'Das gotische Rathaus', p. 512.
[199] Saurma-Jeltsch, 'Karl der Große', pp. 430–5; Jacobs, 'Das Bild', pp. 78–84. For St Bartholmew's church, see *Die Goldene Bulle*, ed. Fritz, p. 53.
[200] See generally Bräutigam, 'Nürnberg'.
[201] Dunk, *Denkmal*, pp. 38–40; Crossley, 'The politics', p. 124. For the display of the imperial regalia there, see Leistikow, 'Die Aufbewahrungsorte', p. 199. For visual representations of Charlemagne, see below, Ch. 7, pp. 327–30.

the new market square, the theme was taken up on a great ornamental fountain erected late in the fourteenth century, with figures representing the electors, as well as the Nine Worthies (two of them emperors).[202] In imperial towns and in German cities 'close' to the king, representations of particular monarchs, of the electors and of the ruler's insignia, became increasingly familiar sights adorning municipal buildings and civic churches in the decades after 1245.[203]

The new imperial dynasties similarly deployed in their residential cities the full panoply of Gothic public art in order to link their own familial and (in Bohemia) regnal pasts with the symbolism of the Reich. Charles IV's activities in this regard have already been observed. It is important, however, to emphasise just how pervasive were imperial, as well as Bohemian, imagery and memory, particularly in Prague. It was visible in the great sacred and secular building programmes, in the public spaces and processional ways, in a veritable riot of monumental sculpture and carved and painted armorials, and in other forms of representation besides.[204] At the Old Town end of his new stone bridge over the Moldau (Vltava) – a station of key symbolic and dramatic importance on the route linking his metropolis with the ancient castle, mausoleum and cathedral complex beyond the river – was erected what must be interpreted as an immense, neo-Roman triumphal arch, though in the florid Caroline Gothic style. On the town-side façade were set up not only enthroned figures of Charles and Wenceslas (as well as St Vitus, the cathedral's patron), but also a rich array of heraldry, with the imperial eagle prominently displayed together with the armorials of the Luxemburg crown lands.[205] Surviving records mostly do not allow us to discern in detail the nature and extent of Charles's own role in these projects, some of which, including the Bridge Tower, were only completed after his death.[206] But there can be little doubt that he had a major directing part. His personal interest in crafting a monarchical image is well attested; and the role which he ascribed to visual media in attaining his ends is evoked by an observation by the Bohemian chronicler Beneš Krabice, that 'because princes, nobles and great men were streaming to him from all parts of the world', Charles, 'wanting to show the magnificence and glory of his kingdom of Bohemia', had two towers of his castle at Prague – one in the east, the

[202] Dunk, *Denkmal*, pp. 45–6. For the Nine Worthies, see Wyss, 'Die neun Helden'.
[203] For examples, see: Dunk, *Denkmal*, pp. 48–50; Maué, 'Nuremberg's cityscape', esp. p. 36; Kunze, 'Die Königsbilder', esp. pp. 633, 638, 639.
[204] Crossley, 'The politics'; Bachmann, 'Karolinische Reichsarchitektur'.
[205] See Rosario, *Art*, Ch. 7.
[206] For the dating of the Bridge Tower, see ibid., pp. 78–9.

other in the west – covered with lead and gold, in order that they might 'shine forth and reflect the sun … over a very great distance'.[207] It was not only Bohemia's glory that such splendours seemed to magnify, and among those to be found gazing at them would have been many natives of the German lands of the Reich. (We need only think of the thousands of German-speaking students who passed through the university before their exclusion in 1409.) The potential power of concentrated urban image-making was not lost on the emperor's son-in-law, Duke Rudolf IV of Austria (1358–65). Rudolf faithfully followed the Caroline template in developing his own residential city, Vienna, where the collegiate Church of St Stephen soon became thronged with invocations of the imperial monarchy and Habsburg dynasticism alike.[208]

But it was not only where the acts or rituals of power brought him, or where his familial resources were concentrated, that the authority of the Empire's ruler was symbolically present. In Braunschweig, neither an imperial town nor one which in the late Middle Ages saw the king in person, a public fountain set up in 1408 incorporated portrayals of the Empire itself and the electors, as well as, again, the Nine Worthies. (It was to be followed some years later by a sculpted cycle of Saxon kings, as well as Welf dukes, on the town hall façade.)[209] The motive seems in this case to have been a mixture of civic pride and dynastic loyalty – with both sentiments drawing on the reflected glory of the ducal family's imperial heritage. Elsewhere, visual invocation of the Reich in places well off the king's established routes has other explanations. A series of building projects sponsored by Charles IV in east-central Germany doubtless aimed at establishing his visibility in regions where Luxemburg territorial ambitions intruded into rival princely spheres. At Luckau in Lusatia, for example, the Church of St Nicholas became a beneficiary of Caroline largesse, acquiring new fabric and a valuable relic, as well as carved busts depicting Charles and his consort, Elizabeth of Pomerania.[210] At Mühlhausen in Thuringia, where larger-than-life figures of Charles and Elizabeth still incline their heads from above the south portal of the Marienkirche, Luxemburg ambitions may have chimed with the self-protective instincts of a remote and endangered imperial town. According to a later tradition, the incoming

---

[207] *Kronika Beneše z Weitmile*, ed. Emler, p. 541 (for 1370).

[208] Dunk, *Denkmal*, pp. 30–3; Feuchtmüller, 'Die "Imitatio"', pp. 383–4.

[209] Schneidmüller, 'Reichsnähe – Königsferne', pp. 48–9; Dunk, *Denkmal*, p. 50.

[210] Lindner, 'Kaiser Karl IV.', pp. 134–5. More often, however, Luxemburg territorial claims in the German-speaking regions adjacent to Bohemia attained visual expression through statues of St Wenceslas, often paired with carvings of the double-tailed Bohemian lion: Němec, 'Herrscher', pp. 394–5.

town council would assemble each year in the church's shadow to do homage to their petrified lord.[211] The hazards besetting a distant *Reichsstädt* are also attested by the image of Sigismund, resplendent with crown and sceptre, which in the fifteenth century the burghers of Donauwörth set up on their fortifications: a gesture of gratitude for his part in helping the Danubian town escape the lordship of the dukes of Bavaria.[212] The ruler might thus on occasion be invoked visually in precisely those places where he was *not* commonly to be seen, as a mark of vicarious proximity and reassurance. A similar intent seems to have underlain one rather singular genre of monumental imagery: the giant statues of Charlemagne's paladin Roland, usually replete with massive sword, to be encountered in many towns in northern and north-central Germany.[213] The origin of these figures is obscure and possibly remote, and their earliest significance uncertain. But in the late Middle Ages, when some of the originally wooden statues were renewed in stone, it is likely that they had come to stand for imperial law, of which Charlemagne was regarded in Germany as the pre-eminent embodiment (and Roland, as his strong right arm, an enforcer). But more specifically, some at least seem to have invoked *in absentia* the Reich, as source of urban liberties and their guardian against princely and other predators.[214]

Social, economic and cultural changes afoot in Germany in the thirteenth and fourteenth centuries did more to scatter abroad visual invocations of the imperial monarchy than ever did that beleaguered institution itself. The rapid proliferation in Germany of black-on-gold imperial eagles resulted not so much from actions taken by the Empire's rulers as from broad processes of cultural change, which saw the elaboration of a comprehensive visual language of heraldry, embracing the bearers of social and military power throughout Europe. The imperial armorial (strictly, the arms of the ruler himself rather than the Reich) first attained settled form around 1200. During the following decades, it multiplied in media of diverse sorts, and was applied to a growing array of objects, utilitarian as well as stately.[215] A document from Strasbourg records how, on a visit to the city, Charles IV had borrowed a tent decorated with heraldic roses, which one 'Konrad the painter'

---

[211] Dunk, *Denkmal*, p. 52.
[212] Rader, 'Zwischen Friedberg und Eco', p. 269.
[213] For what follows, see: Trusen, 'Rolandsäulen'; Dunk, *Denkmal*, pp. 54–6.
[214] For the changing significance of the Bremen Roland, see Dunk, *Denkmal*, p. 56.
[215] For its development, and for some of the contexts in which it appeared, see: Schubert, *König und Reich*, pp. 358–66; Pferschy-Maleczek, 'Der Nimbus'; Bleisteiner, 'Der Doppeladler'.

was charged to repaint with 'the emperor's armorial'.[216] The black eagle can hardly have been an unfamiliar sight to travellers on Germany's highways. A Frankfurt 'burgomaster's book' from the first half of the fifteenth century shows on its flyleaf an envoy of the town, the imperial armorial on his surcoat, making his way bearing a letter.[217] The growth of written communication speeded its circulation as a seal device, for which it was adopted by imperial towns, as well as by the monarchy itself.[218] Meanwhile, a burgeoning money economy ensured the visibility of monarchical (alongside many other) devices on coins.[219] Charles IV was at pains to emphasise that the new coinage being minted by his uncle, Balduin of Trier, bore *des Rychs zeychen*.[220] That coin images attracted notice is shown by the report (dated 1363) set down by Johann von Guben, town scribe of Zittau in Lusatia, describing the appearance of Charles IV's new (Bohemian) 'heller'.[221] The symbolic power of coins invoking monarchical authority is illuminated by their use in the shadowy rituals of the Westphalian *Veme*, which in the fourteenth and fifteenth centuries claimed to exercise summary blood justice in the Empire's name.[222] Thus, even in Westphalia, another of Moraw's 'remote' regions, where the monarch was scarcely seen at all in the late Middle Ages, his authority – and its potential to legitimise local judicial self-help – was not forgotten. Tangible, portable manifestations of rulership had a part in keeping its memory fresh.

Not only, then, did the Empire's German populations inhabit a common political community under a monarch; they were perhaps less likely to overlook the fact than studies concentrating only on power

---

[216] *Chronik des Jacob Twinger*, ed. Hegel, Beilagen, no. 11, p. 1042. An illustration of a magnificent vermilion tent, adorned with the emblems of King Wenceslas, with the black-on-gold eagle prominent among them, features in a manuscript of Konrad Kyeser's military treatise *Bellifortis* made in 1405: Boehm and Fajt (eds.), *Prague*, p. 234. The tent in which the dead Henry VII is shown lying in the picture chronicle of his expedition to Rome is topped by a large pommel decorated with an eagle: Margue, Pauly and Schmid (eds.), *Der Weg zur Kaiserkrone*, pp. 106–7.

[217] Fricke, *Veme*, no. 128a, p. 153.

[218] Examples in: ibid., nos 156b, 157a, p. 183; Bleisteiner, 'Der Doppeladler', p. 42.

[219] For the diversity of coin types, and the importance of regional mints, in late medieval Germany, see Kluge, 'Das Münzwesen', esp. pp. 380–2.

[220] *MGC* 10, no. 457, p. 351 (28 September 1352).

[221] *Jahrbücher*, ed. Haupt, pp. 16–17. A Metz chronicler similarly described in detail the coins which he claimed Charles IV had struck in the city, probably on the occasion of the 1356 Golden Bull *Hoftag*, with the emperor's portrait on one face and the imperial eagle on the other: Fried, 'Schnöder Mammon', p. 471.

[222] One recondite process, for vindicating a judgement-finder of the court, involved the wronged man appearing with 'an old royal tournois [*eynen alden kunigtornosz*]' in his hand: see Lindner, *Die Veme*, esp. p. 257. A further coin-ritual is recounted in Fricke, *Veme*, p. 81.

and institutions of government might suggest. Given that the medieval idea of nation was located particularly within large political communities under monarchical headship, that observation has a bearing on this book's central concerns. Visible reminders of the authority of the Reich in Germany, of its history and prestige, were not only remarkably many and varied; they also multiplied dramatically, just as their potential audience grew, during the later Middle Ages. There seems no compelling reason to think that either their number or visibility was less than in the more institutionalised realms of western Europe.

Indeed, the involvement of monarchy and Reich in contests of power and authority in Germany helped ensure that their symbols enjoyed on occasion particular notice, were applied with deliberate purpose and were subjected to self-conscious and keenly opinionated scrutiny. A hostile singer recounts how, after rebuffing their lord the bishop of Würzburg, and placing themselves directly under the Reich (1397), the bishop's Franconian towns had 'affixed to every gate the crowned eagle'.[223] In Würzburg itself, a magnificent gilded *Reichsadler* had been hoisted into place, high up on the Rathaus, to the piping of the town's musicians.[224] But the poet was able to add with satisfaction that, with the downfall of the rebels' imperial patron, Wenceslas, the eagle departed its 'shameful' perch among the burghers. Elsewhere, displays of the imperial armorial which observers deemed illegitimate might invite yet more precipitately direct action. When Charles IV came to Passau in 1348, the *signa imperialia aquilarum* which were set up on his lodgings were soon smeared with filth by partisans of his Wittelsbach rivals.[225]

The *Reichsadler* above the town gate therefore had the potential to function as a powerful signifier, capable of evoking for passers-by webs of identification every bit as rich as those summoned up for Roland Barthes by the incidental glimpse of a black soldier saluting the French tricolour.[226] How often it did so is, however, impossible to tell. Without doubt, for most of the time visual representations of ruler and Reich were of a character which one political scientist has termed 'banal': like the national flag, flapping half-noticed on a modern public building, their identity-forming role, if such they had, was largely subliminal.[227] Let us therefore turn to instances where the communication

[223] *Volkslieder*, ed. Liliencron, no. 40, p. 176, vv. 872–3.
[224] Ibid., pp. 176–7, vv. 880–900. For context, see Arnold, 'Im Ringen', pp. 104–7.
[225] *Die Chronik des Mathias von Neuenburg*, ed. Hofmeister, p. 260.
[226] Barthes, 'Myth today', pp. 101–2.
[227] Billig, *Banal Nationalism*, esp. pp. 8, 10.

of information and ideas about the monarchy is more firmly attested, since it has left multiple traces in the written record.

How did chroniclers, and other observers of the state of the Reich and acts of its rulers, come by their information? Can we detect news, comment or gossip circulating on the subject of the monarchy, in forms that could have shaped the awareness and perceptions of individuals or of entire social groups? A number of channels reveal themselves, some reflecting the changing character of German society, and the new forms of communication which it had facilitated. The appeal which writers often made to the authority of oral report certainly went beyond mere literary convention, because occasionally informants are named. In turbulent times, soldiers were a predictably promising source. Johann von Winterthur's account of the battle of Göllheim (1298), at which King Adolf lost his life, was based, he explains, on information supplied by men who were present 'from my homeland' (*patria*) – the German south-west.[228] His knowledge of Henry VII's siege of Brescia (1311) came from a *miles de Alamania*: once again, a knight from Johann's native Swabia.[229] Pilgrims, students and wandering preachers would all have had tales to tell, while strolling players and itinerant versifiers certainly helped to keep the monarchy and its affairs fresh in some minds. The chronicle of the Colmar Dominicans records a prophecy predicting the election and triumphs of Rudolf I, ascribed to an itinerant known as 'Seczere'.[230] Political songs from the period have survived in considerable numbers in written form, though these certainly represent only a small fragment of what was once composed and performed.[231] Quite apart from well-crafted lyrics with some literary pretensions, there is ample evidence (though much of it indirect) for the wide circulation of anonymous ditties on contemporary political themes.[232] Often highly topical, scurrilous and blatantly partisan, these mostly obscure rhymes have been called a 'bridge between high politics and the common man'.[233] Parish priests might render Latin verses

---

[228] *Die Chronik Johanns von Winterthur*, ed. Baethgen, p. 43.

[229] Ibid., p. 60.

[230] *Chronicon Colmariense*, ed. Jaffé, p. 253. He is identifiable as Dietmar Setzer: Schubert, *Fahrendes Volk*, p. 210.

[231] See: Müller, 'Sangspruchdichtung', p. 188.

[232] See the example relating to Rupert of the Palatinate discussed by Schubert, 'Probleme', p. 178. A 'grinning song' (*carmen Smunzil*) at the expense of Ludwig IV, fortuitously recorded by Balduin of Trier's counsellor Rudolf Losse, doubtless stands for many which once circulated: Schubert, 'Ludwig der Bayer', pp. 180–1.

[233] Schubert, *Fahrendes Volk*, p. 210. For evidence of such popular, topical verses reworked in a Latin chronicle, see Schubert, 'Ludwig der Bayer', pp. 170–5. For more on their social functioning, see Schubert, '"bauerngeschrey"'.

on the political ills of the time into the vernacular of the laity.[234] Nor did chroniclers themselves always lead stay-at-home lives. Many in this period belonged to the mendicant orders, while others had travelled in the service of their secular or spiritual lords, or their towns.[235] The far-flung wanderings of Otakar uz der Geul may even have included a stint as an itinerant singer.[236]

The better-connected had their personal correspondents and inform-ants. 'We thank you for the news from [or 'about'] Germany' (*super novis Almanie*), wrote Bishop Johann of Verden to his chaplain Ditmar from the Curia at Avignon in 1338.[237] Some of the chroniclers who had most to report about the affairs of the Reich had their own well-placed friends and contacts: for Johann von Viktring, these included jurists linked with the imperial court and distinguished fellow Cistercians.[238] In the towns, especially in those parts which the ruler often visited, personal networks linked wealthy burgher families with the court and with important individuals, such as prelates and educated counsellors, close to the monarch. Groups of this kind, embracing urban patricians, nobles and (regular and secular) clergy, are detectable in the towns of the upper Rhine and Alsace under the early Habsburgs.[239] Under Rudolf I, Heinrich von Isny – Franciscan friar, royal adviser, and incumbent successively of the sees of Basel and Mainz – acted as a particular con-duit, though not the only one, between such groups, the court and the ruling family.[240] Comparable networks have been traced in the towns of Franconia and the Wetterau in the second half of the fourteenth century, linked to the Luxemburg court.[241] There can be little doubt that the numerous personal relationships which such networks encom-passed had a part in ensuring the circulation of news and rumour about imperial politics, particularly within leading burgher circles in towns 'close' to the king.

---

[234] Otto Baldemann, pastor of the rural parish of Ostheim near Aschaffenburg, thus in 1341 translated (and amplified) Lupold von Bebenburg's *Ritmaticum querulosum* on the state of the Reich: Schubert, 'Ludwig der Bayer', p. 181.

[235] For the wide experience and horizons characteristic of late medieval town chroni-clers, see Du Boulay, 'The German town chroniclers', esp. p. 448.

[236] Weinacht, 'Ottokar von Steiermark (O. aus der Geul)', in *LMA* 7, cols. 238–9.

[237] *Nova Alamanniae*, vol. I, no. 532, p. 352. Johann then continues, 'The news from the Curia is...'

[238] See Moraw, 'Politische Sprache', pp. 717–18.

[239] For Zurich, Basel and Strasbourg, see Peters, *Literatur*, esp. Ch. 2.

[240] Martin, 'Das Bild', p. 208. For Heinrich, see Eubel, 'Die Minoriten'; and for the political public in the south-west in Rudolf's time, see Ritscher, *Literatur*, esp. pp. 28–41.

[241] Moraw, 'Wesenszüge', pp. 154–5, 157.

Indeed, the towns, especially those subject directly to the monarch, merit particular attention as centres for the reception and dissemination of information and ideas about ruler and Reich.[242] A study of the documents issued by Charles IV's chancery has disclosed a year-on-year average of 27 per cent which were destined for an urban milieu.[243] But the imperial and 'free' towns developed during the period an especially close relationship with the high politics of the realm.[244] Their representatives were summoned to assemblies and occasions of high imperial ceremonial. Envoys from the towns were present at many of the key constitutional moments in the monarchy's late medieval history, and duly reported back to their fellow citizens what they had seen. Sigismund's spectacular entry into Aachen in 1414 is captured in an eyewitness account by Eigil von Sassen, burgomaster of the relatively modest imperial town of Friedberg.[245] A letter dated 20 August 1400, sent to a Frankfurt burgher, Jacob Weibe, by a delegate of the city recounts the deposition of Wenceslas, summarising the nine articles justifying his removal from the throne.[246] In July 1411, Archbishop Johann of Mainz and his fellow electors wrote individually to the estates of the Empire to inform them of Sigismund's election. The letter, which included a ringing exposition of the electoral rights of the German princes, survives in copies addressed to six different towns – a small remnant of the number which must have been dispatched.[247] Numerous comparable documents exist. They underline how closely the imperial chancery kept the great urban centres, nodal points in the transmission of news, informed about developments around the ruler.

It was not that the towns were lacking means of their own to discover such things, however. News of the imprisonment of Wenceslas in 1394 reached Augsburg via an envoy from the town of Nördlingen bearing a

[242] Schneider, 'Die Reichsstädte', esp. p. 416; Schubert, '"bauerngeschrey"', esp. p. 890.
[243] Moraw, 'Vom Raumgefüge', p. 77. The study averaged the output in every fifth year, starting in 1350. Under Rudolf I, the imperial towns alone were the addressees of 28 per cent of documents issued by the chancery: Thomas, *Deutsche Geschichte*, p. 48.
[244] For the distinction between imperial and 'free' towns, see Isenmann, *Die deutsche Stadt*, pp. 110–13.
[245] *RTA* 7, no. 167, p. 244.
[246] *RTA* 3, no. 212, p. 271. The reception of such news is confirmed, e.g., by the noting of some of the main charges against Wenceslas (apart from his 'innumerable evils, all of which it would be tedious to write'), by a Mainz chronicler: *Chronicon Moguntinum*, ed. Hegel, p. 239.
[247] *RTA* 7, no. 68, p. 116 (Frankfurt, 21 July 1411). Copies survive addressed to Nuremberg, Strasbourg, Hagenau, Frankfurt, Trier and Rothenburg ob der Tauber, as well as to the Grand Master of the Teutonic Order. For the letter's contents, see also below, Ch. 6, p. 264.

letter.[248] The mercantile and commercial elites had their own sources: the volume of notes and memoirs compiled by the well-connected Nuremberg industrialist Ulman Stromer (d. 1407) discloses a detailed knowledge of imperial affairs extending well beyond his own city.[249] Rulers themselves took advantage of the regular commercial communications which the towns maintained: news of the political crisis afflicting Wenceslas reached the pretender Rupert of the Palatinate by means of (partially encrypted) merchants' letters.[250] We can be confident that reports and speculation were exchanged between burghers from different towns: on the road, at the inn and in the marketplace. Especially along those routes which the itinerant court regularly travelled, they had good reason for keeping a wary eye open. 'And we also let you know that our lord the king came to Nuremberg on the Wednesday after Whitsun, and should be coming to Frankfurt or Oppenheim', wrote a Strasbourg envoy to his town in 1382.[251] Second-guessing the monarch's next move was no idle game: it paid to be prepared. Magdeburg's *Schöppenchronik* records how in 1365 Charles IV had built many ships, and was rumoured to be planning to come into Saxony. 'Some said that he wanted to conquer this land, and specifically this town.'[252] Others proposed a less ominous explanation for the emperor's acts. Nevertheless, notes the chronicler, the burghers took the precaution of strengthening their fortifications and organising their defence.

For the towns of the imperial and dynastic heartlands, kings and emperors were far from being mere ciphers: their acts and plans promised direct and tangible consequences, not all of them welcome; they needed careful scrutiny and reflection. The same Augsburg chronicler who condemned Charles IV's seizure of Jewish debts noted of the taxes which Charles levied on the imperial towns in 1373 that 'no emperor or king had ever before attained this'.[253] Nor was it unknown for the Empire's ruler to take steps directly to influence opinion in Germany in his favour on urgent questions (though none of the post-Staufer kings resorted to issuing general manifestos in the manner of Frederick II).[254] Letters of 1324 from the archbishop of Salzburg to John XXII report how 'in several major cities', Ludwig IV had been present 'in royal pomp'

---

[248] *Chronik von 1368 bis 1406*, ed. Frensdorff, p. 98.
[249] *Ulman Stromer's Puechel,* ed. Hegel; and L. Kurras, 'Stromer, Ulman', in *VL* 9, cols. 457–60.
[250] Moraw, 'Wesenszüge', p. 162.
[251] *Strassburg UB* 6, ed. Fritz, no. 79, p. 52.
[252] *Magdeburger Schöppenchronik*, ed. Janicke, p. 251.
[253] *Chronik von 1368 bis 1406*, ed. Frensdorff, p. 32.
[254] For Frederick's manifestos, see: Segl, 'Die Feindbilder'; Mierau, 'Exkommunikation'.

at great assemblies of the clergy and people, where lengthy polemics were delivered against the pope in Latin, with simultaneous translation into German.[255] Matthias von Neuenburg recounts how in 1338 at Frankfurt, Ludwig had 'affixed to the doors of his court' a 'decree under his great seal, made with the advice of certain Franciscans', the encyclical *Fidem catholicam*.[256] Matthias then summarises the document's challenge to the pope's legal process against Ludwig. No less sustained was the campaign which Rudolf I waged during his early years on the throne, to establish his public credentials as a strong and legitimate king.[257] He was especially concerned to undermine support in the German south-east for the powerful and intractable Otakar of Bohemia. Rudolf's efforts were blessed with remarkable success. False rumours were spread to the effect that Otakar had been excommunicated by the pope. Their circulation and acceptance in Germany are disclosed by their repetition in chronicles from regions as distant as Thuringia and Alsace.[258] A particular obstacle was presented by the Austrian towns, staunchly loyal to the king of Bohemia, from whom they had received great privileges. In these tasks as in others, Rudolf enjoyed the powerful aid of the friars.[259] Franciscans and Dominicans had supported his military campaign in 1276, declaring the Austrians released from their oaths of loyalty to Otakar.[260] The mendicants preached in his favour, and against his Bohemian opponent; they were the main originators of those many, mostly sympathetic, popular tales which circulated about the Habsburg king; and throughout Germany they had a central part in cementing Rudolf's relations with the burgeoning towns, such an important pillar of his rule.[261]

The friars are a prime illustration of how political communications in Germany intensified in the late Middle Ages, even with little direct help from the imperial monarchy. The whole ethos of the mendicant orders centred on the transmission of ideas, doctrines and relevant knowledge, especially to laypeople in the growing towns. The multiplication of mendicant houses marched in step with European urbanisation.

---

[255] *MGC* 5, no. 973, p. 811.

[256] *Die Chronik des Mathias von Neuenburg*, ed. Hofmeister, pp. 157–8. The decree was promulgated at the house of the Teutonic Order in nearby Sachsenhausen. Ludwig's opponents also posted in Frankfurt the papal letters excommunicating him: Kaufhold, *Gladius Spiritualis*, p. 229.

[257] See: Weiler, 'Image', esp. pp. 1130–9; Martin, 'Das Bild', p. 212.

[258] Graus, 'Přemysl Otakar II.', p. 75.

[259] Martin, *Städtepolitik*, pp. 72–3; Graus, 'Přemysl Otakar II.', pp. 73–4.

[260] Redlich, *Rudolf von Habsburg*, p. 276.

[261] Kleinschmidt, *Herrscherdarstellung*, p. 177; Martin, 'Das Bild', p. 204; Martin, *Städtepolitik*, pp. 72–3.

In Germany, their numbers increased dramatically during traumatic times for the Reich in the thirteenth century. In 1250 there were already 38 Dominican and over 100 Franciscan convents on German soil.[262] Nor was there any slackening of the pace (as there was elsewhere in Europe) in the decades that followed, and by the century's close Germany boasted 94 Dominican and around 200 Franciscan houses.[263] In this respect at least, the German lands kept pace with their western neighbours.[264] The mendicant orders were, for the time, unusually well informed about contemporary affairs. They lived close to the people, and they kept an ear to the ground: those chroniclers who gleaned their knowledge from passing soldiers or strolling players are nearly always mendicants. But if they spoke with, and listened to, the lowly, they also from early on moved in the counsels of the great, a further explanation for their close eye for current affairs. In Lübeck, the Franciscan convent had close ties with the ruling burgher elite: the brethren were recruited from among the families of the city's councilmen and served the council as envoys as well as chroniclers.[265] The friars also maintained contacts with royal and princely houses of the maritime north. Lübeck's position as a centre of European commerce, and as a periodic meeting place for the Franciscans' own provincial chapters, further helps to explain the strength, and the wide geographical horizons, of the chronicle tradition there.[266]

The concerns of the friars go far to explain a current in late medieval historiography which in its turn had a substantial part in maintaining and extending awareness of the monarchy in Germany: the tradition of 'universal' chronicles, constructed around parallel or interwoven lists of popes and rulers of the Empire.[267] The writing of world history within a Christian framework, a genre rooted in late antiquity and the early Middle Ages, had enjoyed a revival in western Europe during the eleventh and twelfth centuries.[268] It entered a new phase, however, in the middle decades of the thirteenth, with the assembly of two great compendia of historical materials, by the French Dominican Vincent of Beauvais (d. 1264), and by Martin of Troppau (Opava), a member of the Prague Dominican convent who spent many years in Rome as a

---

[262] Freed, *The Friars*, p. 21.
[263] Ibid., p. 21. At the accession of Rudolf I in 1273 there are estimated to have been around 3,750 Franciscans and 1,800 Dominicans in Germany (ibid., p. 120).
[264] The German figures are broadly comparable with those for France, where by 1275 there were 87 Dominican and 195 Franciscan houses: Lawrence, *The Friars*, p. 103.
[265] For this and what follows, see Wriedt, 'Die Annales Lubicenses', pp. 569–72.
[266] Ibid., p. 569.
[267] See generally Krüger, *Die Universalchroniken*.
[268] For an overview, see Grundmann, *Geschichtsschreibung*.

papal chaplain and penitentiary.[269] Both these handbooks were read in Germany, particularly Martin's, which inspired numerous continuations, elaborations and adaptions, and which has been described as the most influential historical text of the Middle Ages.[270] A broadly comparable work of German provenance was the late thirteenth-century Franciscan compilation known as *Flores temporum*.[271] We have already observed the very large numbers of manuscripts of these and of similar pope-and-emperor chronicles which have survived. They reveal the wide-ranging influence which these handbooks exercised, far beyond the walls of the mendicants' convents. It was precisely their spare, skeletal character, which since the Renaissance drew down on them the scorn of educated readers, that made them so readily adaptable to a variety of historiographical ends.[272] Their compilers' aims, however, were strongly didactic: to provide historical guidebooks for the study of law and, above all, collections of improving *exempla* to support the friars' preaching mission.[273] They owed their existence in part at least to the mendicant objective of teaching and edifying the laity. Important implications therefore arise for the communication of knowledge about the monarchy. It is notable that the descent of imperial rulership – from Augustus Caesar to Adolf of Nassau, in *Flores temporum* – supplied in these works, alongside the Petrine succession, the hard, interlocking vertebrae of history itself. The simple style and structure of these chronicles opened up their contents to readers of only modest literacy, while vernacular translations soon extended their readership further.[274] Meanwhile, mendicant preaching must have played some part – though how great a part is hard to determine – in spreading awareness of the Reich and its rulers among unlettered audiences, particularly in the towns.[275] The friars' compendia took care to make space for the eye-

---

[269] Ibid., pp. 21–2. For Martin, see: A.D. von den Brincken, 'Martin von Troppau', in *VL* 6, cols. 158–66; Brincken, 'Martin', esp. pp. 158–60; Mierau, 'Das Reich', pp. 559–63. And see below, Ch. 6, p. 284.

[270] Brincken, 'Martin', pp. 155–6. For Vincent's chronicle, important in the Netherlands and the north, see Joachimsen, *Geschichtsauffassung*, p. 3.

[271] See above, p. 117, n. 106.

[272] For their structure and adaptability, see Johanek, 'Weltchronistik', esp. pp. 309–10; and for the humanist reaction, Joachimsen, *Geschichtsauffassung*, p. 3. Highly negative judgements have been long-lasting: thus, e.g., Grundmann, *Geschichtsschreibung*, p. 23.

[273] Joachimsen, *Geschichtsauffassung*, p. 6; Grundmann, *Geschichtsschreibung*, pp. 22–3, 69 (though for a more sceptical view of their didactic role, see Mierau, 'Das Reich', pp. 568–9).

[274] Johanek, 'Weltchronistik', p. 327; Mierau, Sander-Berke and Studt, *Flores Temporum*, p. 3.

[275] Johanek, 'Weltchronistik', p. 328.

catching and the entertaining: for stories which would win the attention of a broad, non-learned public.[276] When the Empire's rulers were treated in this demotic, anecdotal way, conditions were created for sowing widely in the German lands some popular recollection, however nebulous, of their lives and deeds.

The imperial monarchy was therefore kept in the minds and before the eyes of the German-speaking populations of the Reich in a range of ways which had little directly to do with its power or effectiveness. In important respects, however, it was precisely the shortcomings of imperial government – its lack of dependable local institutions, and the patent incapacity of certain reigns in particular – that in the post-Staufer period drew some Germans into its workings, set the Reich before them as a problem to contemplate, and compelled them to take steps of their own. While its government was frequently unable to offer reliable legal remedies to those who stood under its rule, the monarchy retained in the late Middle Ages sufficient authority and influence in Germany to trouble gravely any who allowed themselves to fall outside its notional protection. The imperial bann was a particular threat to towns since, once imposed, it exposed their burghers and commerce to the untrammelled depredations of the surrounding nobility and other towns. And precisely the limitations of the Empire's institutions ensured that escaping from such a plight would involve a community in expense and inconvenience enough to concentrate the minds of all concerned upon the Reich and its workings.

Judicial proceedings before the *Hofgericht* under Charles IV and his sons are recorded in detail in the chronicle compiled under the direction of Magdeburg's city council – with good reason. In 1358 a property dispute with Duke Rudolf II of Saxony brought representatives of the town to Mainz, seeking a hearing before Charles and his court.[277] This first entailed a three-day wait, until the emperor arrived from Aachen. Even then, it was only through the mediation of Mainz's councilmen that the Magdeburg delegation was granted admittance. All was in vain, however, since Duke Rudolf's personal intervention before the emperor turned him against the townsmen's cause. The following year thus saw the town's delegates on the road again, helplessly shadowing the court around Bohemia, seeking a hearing.[278] Even Magdeburg's travails seem small beside the fruitless six-week stay in Prague which delegates from Strasbourg claimed to have endured, as part of their vain attempt to

---

[276] Wriedt, 'Die Annales Lubicenses', p. 571; Johanek, ' "Flores temporum" ("Martinus Minorita")', in *VL* 2, col. 757.
[277] *Magdeburger Schöppenchronik*, ed. Janicke, pp. 224–9.
[278] Ibid., p. 229.

escape from the outlawry imposed on the town (wrongfully, in the burghers' view) under Wenceslas.[279] No wonder that a continuator of Magdeburg's chronicle was so anxious to set down, under the year 1394, the correct legal forms (explained to the town's envoys by a scribe of the *Hofgericht*) for appointing procurators to represent a community before the court.[280] This was done, the chronicler notes, in order that 'those who come after us can follow it, and take all the more care'. Care was needful, he went on, because if the burghers themselves were to go before the court, they would have to follow the ruler's entourage for the process's duration, which was unknowable, and could entail great cost. Yet expense also faced those who failed to appear: securing release from the bann, he believed, had eventually cost Strasbourg 40,000 gulden.[281] The chronicler's warnings proved to be prophetic: a later continuation of the same work has Magdeburg's syndic, Master Engelbert Wusterwitz of Brandenburg, in 1418 accompanying the *Hofgericht* 'to Regensburg in Bavaria, into Hungary, [and] into Bohemia'.[282]

If the feeble and unpredictable processes of imperial government made for frayed nerves and heightened awareness in the towns, its outright collapse might provoke more radical acts. In the towns of western Germany, where in the early 1250s Staufer loyalists were still resisting the rule of William of Holland, the Worms annalist paints a picture of abject social breakdown, with 'father divided against son and son against father'.[283] It was in these desperate conditions that, after Konrad IV's death (1254), representatives of the towns of the middle and upper Rhine and the Wetterau joined together to make their own provisions for peace and order in what they viewed as the Empire's vacancy.[284] The grand alliance which resulted, the Rhenish league, was by 1255 claiming the adherence of western German towns from Lake Constance to Westphalia and the North Sea.[285] Its representatives sought co-operation with King William, whom the league came fairly quickly to recognise. But it was in the wake of William's untimely demise that the towns' approach to the problems of rulership and Reich attained their greatest ambition and independence. At an assembly at

---

[279] *Strassburg UB* 6, no. 687, pp. 364–5 (1 October 1392).

[280] *Magdeburger Schöppenchronik*, ed. Janicke, p. 293.

[281] For fines imposed on imperial towns, see Isenmann, 'The Holy Roman Empire', pp. 257–8.

[282] *Magdeburger Schöppenchronik*, ed. Janicke, p. 346.

[283] *Annales Wormatienses*, ed. Pertz, p. 54. For the political situation in western Germany after Frederick II's death, see Demandt, 'Der Endkampf', esp. pp. 157–61.

[284] For the Rhenish league, see esp. Kaufhold, *Deutsches Interregnum*, Ch. 4, as well as: Voltmer, 'Der Rheinische Bund'; Redlich, *Rudolf von Habsburg*, pp. 37–77.

[285] For its scope, see Kaufhold, *Deutsches Interregnum*, p. 169.

Mainz in March 1256, the league laid claim to the status of an imperial regent, responsible while the throne remained empty for the well-being of the Reich and the integrity of its properties – which the towns vowed to protect 'with all our powers, as if they were our own'.[286] True, their entreaty to the princes to unite in choosing William's successor, and their declared intent of shutting their gates on any king raised up in a divided election, failed to prevent just such division from emerging in the months that followed. That did not, however, inhibit the drawing-up of a similar declaration early in 1273, following Richard of Cornwall's death, by a new alliance of western towns, led by Mainz.[287] In the conditions of turbulence which prevailed in western Germany during the 'Interregnum', urban regimes, moved mainly by concern for their own towns' immediate interests, sought – although with little success – briefly to take imperial government into their own hands, and oversee the imperilled *Reichsgut* for themselves. Not the growing strength of the Reich during this 'state-building' century, but its visible collapse, had thus drawn some Germans for a time into more active engagement with its affairs.

It would be dangerously easy, by the selective deployment of evidence, to draw a picture of the relations between rulers and ruled in late medieval Germany just as one-sided as the traditional picture of failed 'state-making' and triumphant princely 'particularism'. If, as this study contends, the imagined bonds between the imperial monarchy and the Empire's German populations were more numerous and significant than often thought, that is but one dimension of a more complex picture. Not everyone gave even passing thought to the Reich: in the countryside, but also in the many small towns under princely or noble control, daily life in Germany took its course without a care for the unseen monarch or his titles. Johann von Guben, town scribe of Zittau, from his vantage point in east-central Germany had much to report, little of it favourable, about Charles IV, 'harsh lord' over a Luxemburg patrimony which included Johann's Lusatia.[288] But his gaze was directed southwards, over the mountains towards Prague, not westwards into the German heartlands of the Reich, which he was seldom moved to mention. Even those chroniclers who were concerned with imperial affairs mostly allotted them relatively modest space among numerous other reports.[289] Moreover, to chart steadily rising levels of imaginative engagement with

---

[286] Voltmer, 'Der Rheinische Bund', pp. 133–4. For their promise to safeguard imperial properties, see Kaufhold, *Deutsches Interregnum*, p. 188.
[287] Redlich, *Rudolf von Habsburg*, pp. 157–8.
[288] *Jahrbücher*, ed. Haupt, p. 23.
[289] A point emphasised by Kleinschmidt, *Herrscherdarstellung*, p. 106.

the monarchy between the thirteenth and fifteenth centuries would be to distort what was a far more ambivalent picture. In some important respects, the German populations of the Reich were closer to their rulers towards the start of the period addressed by this book than at its end. The mendicants, who did so much to propagate the monarch's image, were at the height of their powers in the thirteenth and early fourteenth centuries: it cannot be coincidence that later rulers lack a penumbra of homespun tales and legends such as surround the memory of the friars' friend, Rudolf I. Mortgaging, alienations and political disaffection together ensured that close relations between the monarchy and the imperial towns, likewise characteristic of the thirteenth and early fourteenth centuries, gradually gave way to distance, and in some cases open conflict. The growing dependence of imperial rulership on dynastic *Hausmacht* during the fourteenth century certainly helped, in a complex process of development, to raise cultural barriers, as well as building bridges, between the ruler's dynastic territories and the Empire's remaining German lands. Furthermore, while communications within and between the regions of Germany unquestionably grew in number and intensity between the thirteenth and fifteenth centuries, there is without doubt much to support Peter Moraw's contention, that the real advance came later, in the decades after 1450.[290] Nevertheless, compelling reasons remain for thinking that the imagined relationships between rulers and people in Germany, in their intensity and stimuli, differed less sharply from the patterns found elsewhere in Europe than is often supposed. But did they also find expression in a comparable language of political nation, invoking a distinct 'German' regnal community? Or did traditional doctrines of imperial hegemony, or new ones glorifying dynasty and dynastic patrimony, preclude such developments in Germany? The three following chapters will seek to provide answers.

---

[290] An argument developed in Moraw, *Von offener Verfassung*, esp. pp. 389–94. Moraw's key concept is of the *Verdichtung* of German society in this period.

4   Shades of a kingdom: in search of a German political community

At the Cologne Gate

Early in November in the year 1414 Sigismund of Luxemburg, king of Hungary, king-elect of the Romans, arrived before the town of Aachen, after a three-day journey from Bonn.[1] About the circumstances of his coming and about what followed much is known, for this was no commonplace visit. The king was magnificently accompanied, the duke of Guelders alone sending 4,000 horsemen for his escort; and by the time he entered the town his following had swollen, by the heralds' estimate, to 28,000 horses all told.[2] It is known that, in keeping with a late medieval custom, Sigismund first maintained a three-day camp outside Aachen, with the archbishops of Cologne and Trier among those attending.[3] Events then moved to a climax at the town's Cologne Gate, where the king-elect was greeted by the dean and canons of the minster chapter, bearing a processional cross (probably the 'Lothar' cross, with its sumptuous antique cameo of the emperor Augustus) and the great gilded bust-reliquary of Charlemagne.[4] The king, notes an anonymous reporter, dismounted, kissed the cross and reverently inclined his head to his illustrious Frankish forebear.[5] The procession then moved off, Charlemagne leading the way, the duke of Saxony bearing the sword before the king, through Aachen's bustling streets, to the Carolingian

---

[1] For the journey, see Volk, 'Von Grenzen', p. 274.

[2] For the duke of Guelders, ibid., p. 274; for the heralds' estimate, *RTA* 7, no. 167, p. 244.

[3] Volk, 'Von Grenzen', p. 274. For the late medieval custom of pretenders and kings-elect being expected to hold a legitimising military camp (*Königslager*), to illustrate their support among the great men of the realm, see Weirich, 'Königslager'.

[4] See generally: *RTA* 7, no. 168, p. 245; Schenk, *Zeremoniell*, p. 330. For the 'Lothar' cross, see Grimme, *Domschatz*, pp. 24–8; for Charlemagne's bust-reliquary: Legner (ed.), *Die Parler*, vol. I, p. 137 (essay by Hans Peter Hilger); Kavka, 'Karl IV. (1349–1378) und Aachen'; Grimme, *Domschatz*, pp. 88–90.

[5] *RTA* 7, no. 168, p. 245. For the significance of these actions, see Schenk, *Zeremoniell*, pp. 330–1.

chapel (with its splendid new Gothic choir, begun under Charles the Great's fourteenth-century namesake).[6] Inside, under the ancient octagonal cupola, Sigismund prostrated himself, arms splayed to form a cross, beneath Barbarossa's immense candelabra, fashioned to summon down to earth a radiant, heavenly Jerusalem.[7]

All of this was but a prelude to his anointing and coronation three days later (with the crown taken from Charlemagne's reliquary, first used in 1349 to crown his father), and his installation, in customary fashion, on the Frankish emperor's marble throne.[8] But it was without doubt a spectacular prelude, affording memorable sights to the crowds who thronged the way to witness the new king's entry into 'the golden seat of the realm', as an account of the coronation of Sigismund's great grandfather, Henry VII, had called Aachen, a century before.[9] The progress through the town gate of Sigismund's immense, richly apparelled entourage would on its own have offered a spectacle of elaborately choreographed magnificence.[10] (A protracted one, too, no doubt: when Frederick III and his son came to Aachen in 1486, their procession needed an hour and a half to enter the town.)[11] Onlookers would have been in no doubt that they were witnessing events of deep significance. But what, precisely, *did* they signify? What manner of monarch had the crowds assembled there to gaze upon? Into what tradition of rule was Sigismund being ushered when the great Frankish emperor (from whom the Luxemburger themselves traced blood descent) came out to receive his salutations at the Cologne Gate?[12]

Answering these questions in a few words would hardly have been easier at the time than it is for historians today. Answer them, however, some medieval writers thought they could. Eike von Repgow's *Sachsenspiegel* (1220–35) declared that 'when [the king] is consecrated by the bishops appointed for the purpose, and ascends the seat at Aachen', he gained 'royal power and royal name' (*koningleke gewalt unde koningleken namen*): 'imperial power' (*des rikes gewalt*), by contrast, was

---

[6] For the new choir, see: Legner (ed.), *Die Parler*, vol. I, pp. 121–4 (essay by Leo Hugot); Nussbaum, *Architecture*, pp. 121–3.

[7] See Müller, 'Die Königskrönungen', p. 54; and for the Barbarossa candelabra, Grimme, *Domschatz*, pp. 62–4.

[8] For the crown, see: Petersohn, 'Über monarchische Insignien', p. 84; Minkenberg, 'Der Aachener Domschatz', pp. 59, 63–4; for Charlemagne's throne, Schütte, 'Der Aachener Thron'.

[9] *Gesta Balduini Trevirensis*, cited in Volk, 'Von Grenzen', p. 289.

[10] For the care taken in assembling such processions, see Schenk, *Zeremoniell*, pp. 297–8.

[11] Ibid., p. 298 n. 286.

[12] For Charlemagne's portrayal as Charles IV's ancestor, see: Seibt, *Karl IV.*, p. 386; and below, Ch. 7, pp. 325–30.

conferred only by the pope.[13] Half a century later, the south-German *Schwabenspiegel* repeated the distinction (while also emphasising the electors' part in the king's installation).[14] But over what, and whom, was this 'royal power' to be exercised? To what kind of kingdom did Charlemagne's *aurea sedes regni* hold the key? A German one, perhaps – paralleling the Burgundian and Lombard crowns which the Empire's ruler might receive at Arles and Milan?[15] Certainly, there were those who believed it to be. The diploma of 1166 conferring sainthood upon Charlemagne had named Aachen as 'the head and seat of the kingdom of Germany'.[16] Johannes von Buch, in his gloss on the *Sachsenspiegel* (*c.* 1325), explained that the ruler's first coronation made him 'king over all the German lands'.[17] For Heinrich von Herford, writing in the time of Charles IV, the Frankish emperor himself had decreed that a king was to be crowned in Aachen 'for Germany' (*pro Theutonia*), just as coronation at Monza would make him king of the Lombards, and in Rome 'emperor of the world'.[18]

Such a satisfyingly clear resolution was not, alas, supported by the facts of the chronicler's own day. From the time of his first elevation, the ruler's official titles announced a kingship over the *Romans*, not the Germans, while his public acts assumed from the start the power to rule throughout the Empire's territories.[19] His regalia, including the famous octagonal crown (which tradition identified as Charlemagne's own), were used without distinction both for 'royal' coronations and for the creation of emperors in Rome.[20] It therefore made perfect sense

---

[13] *Sachsenspiegel Landrecht* III, cap. 52 § 1, ed. Eckhardt, p. 237.

[14] *Schwabenspiegel Kurzform*, ed. Eckhardt, *Landrecht*, cap. 118, p. 182, adding that the king is raised to the throne in Aachen 'mit der willen die in erwelt habent'.

[15] For the Lombard crown, see Elze, 'Die "Eiserne Krone"'; for coronation at Arles, see Hilsch, 'Die Krönungen Karls IV.', p. 111.

[16] Cited in Koch, *Sacrum Imperium*, p. 216: 'caput et sedes regni Theutonie'. The claim was repeated in the fourteenth century by Heinrich von Herford that Charlemagne established at Aachen a *sedes regni Theutonicorum*: *Liber de rebus memorabilioribus*, ed. Potthast, p. 78.

[17] *Glossen zum Sachsenspiegel-Landrecht*, ed. Kaufmann, p. 1299 (to *Landrecht* III, cap. 57 § 2): 'So is he koningh ouer alle Dudesche ryke'. In one manuscript tradition the king is said to receive at Aachen 'three golden crowns' for the German realms, though the Aachen coronation is also in some manuscripts designated the 'meanest' (*snodeste*) of the three which he undergoes. For this, see Kannowski, *Die Umgestaltung*, pp. 259–67.

[18] *Liber de rebus memorabilioribus*, ed. Potthast, p. 245. According to Jakob Twinger, Charlemagne had intended Aachen minster as 'the principal church in the German lands' (*die houbetkirche zuo dütschen landen*): *Chronik des Jacob Twingers*, ed. Hegel, p. 406.

[19] The Romanised language of imperial rulership is more fully discussed below, Ch. 5, pp. 224–30; and see Koch, *Sacrum Imperium*, esp. pp. 185–7.

[20] Petersohn, 'Über monarchische Insignien', p. 54.

when another chronicler wrote of 'the advocacy of the Roman Empire' being conferred on the new king at Aachen.[21] The distinctiveness of the Empire's constituent *regna* was further eroded by the shift traceable in German constitutional thinking during the fourteenth century, towards affirming election, not coronation, as the constitutive act in making a ruler.[22] The grounding of imperial government in the will of the princes found clear expression in the 'Declaration of Rhens' of 16 July 1338 and in Lupold von Bebenburg's treatise on the Empire's constitution from the same period.[23] The Golden Bull, in which the elective principle gained its definitive and exhaustive formulation, was to make only the briefest passing reference to the *prima coronacio* which the duly elected monarch customarily underwent, in Aachen.[24]

Yet writings of diverse kinds nevertheless clung firmly to the notion that north of the Alps there existed, in some sense, a 'kingdom', which lay within, but was not identical with, the Empire – even if, in the late Middle Ages, the distinction between the two became somewhat less easily discernible than in earlier times. And a special link between the rule of this kingdom and the German people and their lands seemed, in the eyes of many, as hard to deny as it was precisely to define.

The kingdom in the east

The habit, which long persisted in some quarters, of referring to the Empire's German territories as 'the kingdom of the eastern Franks', encapsulates a fundamental truth. It was under the mantle of Frankish domination, and thereafter the stresses which attended its collapse, that elements of a common political life and (among the greatest magnates) consciousness had first been fashioned in the regions north of the Alps and east of the Rhine.[25] Their government and high politics were Frankish long before anyone thought to call them 'German'. There remains much to be said for beginning, in traditional style, with

---

[21] *Rymkronyk van Jan van Heelu*, ed. Willems, p. 47, vv. 1176–7 ('die voghedye vanden Roemschen rike').

[22] See generally Schubert, 'Königswahl', esp. pp. 270–2.

[23] For the Declaration of Rhens, see *Quellensammlung*, ed. Zeumer, no. 126 (b), p. 156: 'quod electi a principibus electoribus imperii concorditer vel a maiori parte … sibi titulum regium assumserunt ac bona et iura imperii administrarunt, et quod de iure et consuetudine hoc licite facere potuerunt et poterunt…' Lupold von Bebenburg, *Tractatus de Iuribus Regni et Imperii*, in *Politische Schriften Lupolds von Bebenburg*, ed. Miethke and Flüeler. For the relationship between Lupold's thought and the Declaration, see Most, 'Der Reichsgedanke', esp. pp. 477–8.

[24] *Die Goldene Bulle*, ed. Fritz, p. 87.

[25] For constitutional developments, see generally: Schulze, *Grundstrukturen*, pp. 38–42; Werner, 'Deutschland, A: Begriffe', in *LMA* 3, cols. 781–9.

the treaty of Verdun (843), and the division of the vast Carolingian patrimony among the sons of Ludwig the Pious, since from that point onward can be seen opening up the first fissures along lines which later events were to ensure would retain their significance in the centuries that followed. The easternmost of the three new realms, allotted to Ludwig's second surviving son and namesake (who in later times would be called 'the German'), had for its western frontier the Rhine, Aare and Altenbach.[26] The unifying potential of the imperial title waned with the death of Ludwig's elder brother Lothar, who had held the emperorship, in 855. In a further spur to fragmentation, Lothar's own central core of lands was itself split up following his death, creating west of the Rhine in the north the principality that would later be known (from his son, Lothar II) as Lotharingia. The Carolingians who followed Ludwig 'the German' (d. 876) in the east did nothing to reverse the currents that were driving the lands of the old patrimony apart – though they did for a time uphold there the traditional Frankish basis of monarchy.

Internecine strife and external menaces from Northmen and Magyars, as well as the disintegration of the Frankish *imperium* itself, had helped ensure that by the reign of Ludwig 'the Child', the last Carolingian to hold power beyond the Rhine, the eastern peoples nominally under his rule – Franks, Saxons, Bavarians and Alemannians – were consolidating under the headship of an emergent elite of political and military strong-men of their own, the dukes.[27] It is indicative of the separate course on which the eastern duchies appeared set, and of their leaders' incipient ability to act together, that on Ludwig's death in 911 they raised up one of their own number as king.[28] As duke of Franconia, Konrad I may at least have invoked some legitimising ties to the Frankish realm of old; but, unlike his contemporary in western Frankia, Charles 'the Simple', he was not of the royal blood. The emerging integrity of the eastern lands and the break with the past were reinforced when Konrad's death was followed, in 919, by the election as king of the Liudolfing Henry, duke of Saxony.[29] Both these trends were then much advanced by Henry's

---

[26] Fleckenstein, *Early Medieval Germany*, p. 104. Reference to Ludwig as 'the German', although late, is authentically medieval: see *Chronik des Jacob Twinger*, ed. Hegel, p. 890 ('Karleman des dütschen küniges Ludewiges sun').

[27] For the development of the duchies, see: Reuter, *Germany*, Chs. 3, 5; Arnold, *Medieval Germany*, pp. 17–51. Here and in what follows, I propose to avoid rendering the German *Stammesherzog(tümer)* with (the linguistically accurate but in its assumptions and implications potentially misleading) 'tribal duke / duchies' and also to eschew the strange and unfortunate anglicisation as 'stem duke / duchies' sometimes employed in English-language writings.

[28] Ehlers, *Die Entstehung*, p. 16.

[29] Reuter, *Germany*, pp. 137–47.

ordinance of 929 designating his second son Otto, with the assent of the magnates, as his successor in the whole eastern realm.[30] There was henceforth to be no return to the Carolingian custom of dividing up the patrimony between sons: the power balance had shifted decisively, and now *regnum* – the realm – stood beside its *rex*, and the imperatives of blood came under the check of the political community.

The kingdom beyond the Rhine began quickly to gather trappings of constitutional legitimacy and tradition. Henry I acquired from King Rudolf II of Burgundy the Holy Lance and Nail, incorporating them into the regalia, an event still deemed noteworthy by a chronicler in Magdeburg in the late fourteenth century (who, however, ascribed the lance to Constantine).[31] In common with other, subsequent insignia (but in contrast to those of the Carolingians), they were not seen as the property of the ruler or his dynasty, but descended with the realm.[32] The addition of Lotharingia to the kingdom under Henry I gave access to Aachen, with its resources of prestige and legitimacy.[33] Lotharingia also enlarged by roughly a third the territories under the eastern king: the frontiers of the realm thus attained were to change little in the centuries that followed.[34] Within just a few generations the eastern *regnum* had also begun to accumulate its own historical memory. Widukind von Korvey, writing shortly after the middle of the tenth century, was already treating the realm as an established, indivisible whole, while for Thietmar von Merseburg, early in the eleventh, Otto II (961–83) was the third of 'the custodians of our realm [*regni nostri procuratores*]' – the first being Otto's grandfather, Henry I.[35] A new start had been made. A study of historical writings has shown that by the second half of the tenth century the memory of a common Frankish past, though certainly not lost, was already growing pale both east and west of the Rhine beside notions of solidarity based on more recently established ties, and of separation from the 'foreign' realm beyond the frontier.[36]

---

[30] See Fleckenstein, *Early Medieval Germany*, p. 114.
[31] *Magdeburger Schöppenchronik*, ed. Janicke, p. 315. For the Holy Lance, see Schramm, *Herrschaftszeichen und Staatssymbolik*, vol. II, pp. 492–537; for the later Middle Ages, Petersohn, 'Über monarchische Insignien', pp. 88–9. The Lohengrin poet, by contrast, identified it as the lance of Longinus: *Lohengrin*, ed. Cramer, p. 382, vv. 3877–80. Dietrich von Niem was torn between the two identifications: Heimpel, *Dietrich*, p. 226 with n. 3.
[32] Hlawitschka, 'Vom Ausklingen', p. 67.
[33] Reuter, *Germany*, pp. 140–1.
[34] Ehlers, *Die Entstehung*, p. 19; and see below, Ch. 10, pp. 461–7.
[35] Hlawitschka, 'Vom Ausklingen', pp. 71–2.
[36] Bernd Schneidmüller, 'Widukind von Corvey', esp. p. 99. On the fading of Frankish identity in the east, see generally Lugge, *'Gallia'*, esp. pp. 108–16. The view advanced

A kingdom had put down roots, in a series of developments antedating both Otto I's territorial gains in Italy and the subjection of Burgundy to the monarchy under Henry III (1028–56). Before the *imperium* came the *regnum*. But whose *regnum*, and how conceived?

Not, for a long time at least, that of the Germans.[37] The treaty made in 921 between Henry I and Charles 'the Simple', in a boat on the Rhine near Bonn, had styled Henry 'king of the eastern Franks' (*rex Francorum orientalium*), paralleling Charles's kingship over the 'western Franks'.[38] For the post-Carolingian king, Frankishness remained for some time the only identity of rule available – a truth acknowledged by Otto I, when he donned Frankish dress for his coronation at Aachen in 936, and even by that most Romanised of Saxons, Otto III, through his burial in Charlemagne's metropolis (1002).[39] As late as the middle years of the twelfth century, Otto von Freising is to be found insisting upon the kingdom's fundamentally Frankish character. It was to 'the eastern kingdom of the Franks' (*orientale Francorum regnum*) that Bernard of Clairvaux had come in 1146 to preach the crusade – though it says much for the concept's obscurity by this date that Otto had elsewhere felt the need to explain that this eastern Frankia was 'now called the kingdom of the Germans' (*regnum Teutonicorum*).[40] But the propensity of writers already in the tenth century to use on occasion more complex formulations for the lands and peoples under the king – 'Frankia and Saxony', 'the Frankish and Saxon people' – signals a strengthening awareness that the old language of power was no longer adequate.[41] The Liudolfinger were 'Franks' by adoption only, were heirs to their own proud native tradition, and owed their throne to the will of a plurality of eastern peoples and their leaders. By the later tenth century, moreover, the more southerly parts of the kingdom, Bavaria and Swabia, were also being drawn more fully into the political community under the monarch.[42] Already by this time, Ottonian diplomas had started making occasional, tentative reference to a population under

---

by Brühl, *Deutschland – Frankreich*, arguing for a longer-lasting Frankish tradition in both east and west, remains controversial: above, Ch. 1, pp. 41–2.

[37] The complexities of identity and naming in the eastern kingdom in this period are well set out in Werner, 'Les nations', pp. 290–1.

[38] Ehlers, *Die Entstehung*, p. 18.

[39] Keller, 'Die Einsetzung Ottos I.'; Görich, 'Kaiser Otto III.'.

[40] Bernard: *Ottonis et Rahewini Gesta Friderici*, ed. Waitz, pp. 47–8; *regnum Teutonicorum*: *Ottonis Episcopi Frisingensis Chronica*, ed. Hofmeister, p. 277. For the revival of Frankish identity by supporters of the Empire, including Otto, during the twelfth century, see Lugge, '*Gallia*', pp. 202–5.

[41] Müller-Mertens, 'Frankenreich?', p. 50; Beumann, 'Die Bedeutung', p. 336; Lugge, '*Gallia*', pp. 145–7.

[42] Müller-Mertens, 'Frankenreich?', p. 52.

their rule larger than the individual component peoples of their realm: the *Teutonici*.[43] By the beginning of the eleventh century, Bruno von Querfurt was able to call Ottonian Magdeburg 'the new metropolis of the Teutons' (*nova metropolis Theutonum*), and to record how 'the land of the Teutons' (*Theutonum tellus*) had lamented Otto I's death.[44]

Several decades more were to elapse before writers north of the Alps began identifying the kingdom itself as 'German'. Indeed, perhaps the first thing to emphasise about the idea of a bounded, explicitly 'German', political community is that, like many other aspects of medieval German identity, it was constructed from without, and only later adopted and adapted by its intended subjects. What are probably the earliest references to a 'German kingdom' (*regnum Teutonicum*) are found in Italian chronicles from the beginning of the eleventh century.[45] True, the 'great Salzburg annals', which survive in a twelfth-century manuscript, contain a startling entry for the year 920, which has excited attention ever since their discovery in 1921: the Bavarians, submitting to their duke, Arnulf, after Konrad I's death, 'made him to reign in the kingdom of the Germans' (*regnum Teutonicorum*).[46] But the likelihood is that this celebrated – and, if authentic, quite unique – invocation of a German realm (as characteristic of twelfth-century usage as it appears alien to the tenth) was interpolated, probably at the time when the surviving copy was made.[47] Isolated documents from the first half of the eleventh century call the Empire's ruler 'king of the Germans (*rex Teutonicorum*)'; but their origins on the southern and western frontiers of the *regnum*, in Brixen (Bressanone) and Besançon, merely reinforce the impression of a German political community still visible as such to outsiders alone.[48] A solitary German chronicler from around this time does invoke a *regnum Germanum*; but this was not a formulation destined to put down roots.[49]

What changed matters, and gave to writers in the north a 'German' constitutional language, was the dramatic intrusion into the Empire's German territories of the upheaval in political and religious principles that we know as the 'Investiture Contest'. Pope Gregory VII had chosen his words with the conscious aim of stripping away from the

---

[43] See below, Ch. 10, pp. 470–1, noting that these were probably of Italian provenance.

[44] Hlawitschka, 'Vom Ausklingen', pp. 74–6.

[45] Vigener, *Bezeichnungen*, p. 198.

[46] Quoted in Müller-Mertens, *Regnum Teutonicum*, p. 36.

[47] The reasons for doubting the phrase's authenticity are set out in ibid., pp. 36–42; and see also Reuter, *Germany*, pp. 138–9.

[48] Beumann, 'Die Bedeutung', pp. 340–1.

[49] Vigener, *Bezeichnungen*, p. 193.

imperial monarchy the penumbra of sacrality and universalism drawn down around it under the Ottonian and Salian emperors, shrinking Henry IV (1053–1106) to a *rex* like others, ruling his own, finite kingdom – 'of the Germans [*regnum Teutonicorum*]'.[50] The tactic had some hope of success because a distinct territorial kingdom was already deep-rooted north of the Alps while, viewed from the south, its fundamentally 'German' character was also by Gregory's time well established. Indeed, the Gregorian vocabulary was embraced in the north by Henry's princely opponents – or, at least, by their literate champions.[51] If Gregory's own letters did much to spread the idea of a German kingdom, the Concordat of Worms of 1122, which brought the dispute to a close, encased it within clear legal categories. A distinction was drawn between the monarch's powers in 'elections of bishops and abbots of the German kingdom [*Teutonicum regnum*], who pertain to the kingdom', and his more limited entitlements 'in other parts of the Empire' (*aliae partes imperii*). The Concordat thereby rendered visible and significant a distinction which Salian emperorship, with its notion of seamless monarchical rule (*regnum*), had denied: between the ('German') kingdom and the larger agglomeration of lands which had grown up around it, encompassing Italy and Burgundy (the *imperium*).[52] Not for the last time in the Middle Ages, literate Germans cautiously took possession of a corpus of identifying terms and concepts confected by others, beyond their frontiers, for troublesome ends of their own.

The imperial chancery's attempts to resist identifying the Empire's ruler as a mere 'king of the Germans' had considerable success within (though not outside) the German lands, and under the later Salians and the Staufer, the Roman and universal elements in the official language of rulership were elaborated and stabilised.[53] The Germanised titles for the realm – 'German kingdom [*regnum Teutonicum*]' and 'kingdom of the Germans [*regnum Teutonicorum*]' – did, however, gain some limited acceptance, though never regular application, in documents issued in the ruler's name.[54] In the course of the twelfth century, the same terms

---

[50] Müller-Mertens, *Regnum Teutonicum*, pp. 388–9; Fried, *Der Weg*, p. 18.
[51] Müller-Mertens, *Regnum Teutonicum*, pp. 389–90.
[52] Ibid., pp. 375–6; Koch, *Sacrum Imperium*, pp. 111–13, 215–21, 266–76; Appelt, 'Die Kaiseridee', pp. 17–19.
[53] See below, Ch. 5, pp. 210–12.
[54] For this and what follows, see: Vigener, *Bezeichnungen*, pp. 202–11; Schnell, 'Deutsche Literatur', pp. 282–3, but see also the important cautionary notes sounded by Müller-Mertens, 'Imperium und Regnum', esp. p. 566. Of *c.* 1,450 documents issued in the names of Lothar III and the first two Staufer, only ten contain the term *regnum Teutonicum*, and most of these were connected with Italian affairs.

became a familiar part of the vocabulary of chroniclers writing in the Empire's German lands. By the thirteenth, however, they were giving way to another title for a 'German' kingdom: *regnum Alemanniae*.[55] This formulation makes some of its earliest appearances in western German writings, suggesting possible influences from the Germans' Romance-speaking neighbours. The papal Curia, where the form became well established in the thirteenth century, may also have had a part in spreading its use in Germany.[56] But there is also likely to be something in the explanation offered by Alexander von Roes, who ascribed the shift in usage which had taken place, from (as he imagined) *regnum Germanie* – to which later manuscript classes added as alternatives *regnum Theutonie* and *regnum Romanorum* – to *regnum Alamannie*, to the influence of the Hohenstaufen and their Alemannic partisans: it was certainly during the Staufer era that the terminological change took place.[57] Already by the time of Frederick II's demise, therefore, some distinctive elements of a 'German' constitutional vocabulary have become visible: its incompleteness, with the kingdom Germanised more than were its rulers; its comparative lack both of terminological stability and of an anchoring in regular chancery habits; and the influence, attested in its shifting forms, both of external forces and ideas and of the changing geographical basis of royal rule itself.

Nevertheless, the late Staufer era and the years that followed seemed to hold out some prospect of such a language putting down firmer roots, and of a more explicitly German kingdom becoming visible. Frederick II had called his son Henry (VII), raised up to rule under his father north of the Alps, 'king of Germany' (*rex Alemannie*).[58] The idea of Henry as a 'German' king, set over a distinct and separate northern realm (*sîniu Tiuschen rîche*), was strongly articulated by a *Kaiserchronik* continuator, writing in the generation after Henry's death.[59] The same way of thinking is seemingly attested in a Cologne chronicler's description of

---

[55] Vigener, *Bezeichnungen*, pp. 214–17; Schubert, *König und Reich*, pp. 227–8. For the term's late medieval application, see Müller, 'Nationaler Name', pp. 126–31.

[56] Vigener, *Bezeichnungen*, p. 214.

[57] Alexander von Roes, *Memoriale*, cap. 29, ed. Grundmann and Heimpel, p. 134.

[58] See generally: Hugelmann, *Stämme*, pp. 387, 392, 395; Schubert, *König und Reich*, p. 227; and for Henry (VII), Thomas, 'Sprache und Nation', p. 73.

[59] *Kaiserchronik, erste (Bairische) Fortsetzung*, ed. Schröder, esp. pp. 405–6, vv. 613–26, 653–70. The theme of Henry's 'German' kingship was still able to find an echo at the end of the fourteenth century, when Twinger recounted how the emperor had come north to depose 'his son Henry, king *zuo dütschen landen'*: *Chronik des Jacob Twinger*, ed. Hegel, p. 445.

Henry's half-brother and successor, Konrad IV, as 'king-designate of Germany' (rex Theutonie designatus).[60]

The contests for the throne which accompanied the fall of the Staufer brought further invocations of the language of German kingship.[61] A letter of Henry Raspe to the Milanese observed dismissively that Konrad, his rival for the throne, had 'at some time had himself nominated king of Germany' (rex Alamanie).[62] Henry himself had announced in a letter his election 'as king of Germany and prince of the Romans'.[63] It is probable that the unmistakable contraction, during the 'Interregnum', of the sphere of rule commanded by kings, whose hands were kept more than full north of the Alps, encouraged further the perception that theirs was a specifically 'German' monarchy. That, at least, is the impression conveyed by a perusal of the narrative sources of the period, a number of which portray the elevation of pretenders 'as king of Germany' (in regem Alemannie).[64] It therefore appears in tune with the mood of the times when, later in the century, the margrave of Brandenburg promised to act in concord with the king of Bohemia in electing not only an 'emperor of the Romans', but a 'king of Germany' (in eleccione Romanorum imperatoris Alemanie regis).[65]

The impression of a monarchy stripped during these decades of imperial accretions and confined to a purely German base was reflected by chroniclers in the fourteenth century, who saw this as representing

---

[60] Chronica regia Coloniensis, ed. Waitz, Continuatio IV, p. 271 (1237). According to the annals of the Erfurt Dominicans, Frederick set up his son Konrad as ruler in Teutonia: Annales Erphordenses Fratrum Praedicatorum, ed. Holder-Egger, p. 96.

[61] This may reflect in part the adoption in this period of a Germanised vocabulary by the Curia: see Müller-Mertens, 'Imperium und Regnum', p. 576.

[62] Die Urkunden Heinrich Raspes, ed. Hägermann and Kruisheer, no. 7, p. 11 (1246, after 5 August).

[63] Ibid., no. 1, p. 3 (1246, after 22 May). Again, the Milanese are the addressees. The same form of words was repeated in Henry's letter making known his election to Gregory of Montelongo, papal legate in Lombardy (ibid., no. 4, p. 8).

[64] Continuatio Garstensis, ed. Wattenbach, p. 598; Chronicon Imperatorum et Pontificum Bavaricum, ed. Waitz, p. 224 (in regnum Alemannie). Chronica regia Coloniensis, ed. Waitz, Continuatio V, p. 290 (dispatch of a papal legate to Germany following the death of Henry Raspe 'pro novo rege creando in Teuthonia'). See also the much-used compendium of Martin of Troppau: Martini Oppaviensis Chronicon, ed. Weiland, p. 439. All these references are to Henry Raspe and William of Holland, and Martin's usage here may have influenced other writers. A number of chroniclers likewise referred to the elevation of the first post-'Interregnum' king, Rudolf I, as 'king of Germany': see Continuatio Claustroneuburgensis sexta, ed. Wattenbach, p. 744; Annales Halesbrunnenses maiores, ed. Waitz, p. 44; Chronicon Imperatorum et Pontificum Bavaricum, ed. Waitz, p. 225. For further such references, see Hugelmann, Stämme, p. 395.

[65] Regesta Diplomatica, pt. II, ed. Emler, no. 2281 (1291 × 1292?), p. 989. A similar formulation is found in MGC 4.i, no. 5, p. 5 (1298, before 23 June), in which the count palatine mandates the duke of Saxony to elect Albert of Habsburg on his behalf 'in regem Alemanie et futurum imperatorem promovendum'.

the conscious intent of certain post-Staufer kings. 'This one-eyed King Albert', wrote Matthias von Neuenburg, 'powerful in the kingdom of Germany [*in regno Alamannie*], and there acquiring for his offspring all that he could, took no interest in other regions.'[66] But it was Albert's father, Rudolf I, who it was most often said had spurned imperial entanglements for a specifically German sphere of rule. Johann von Winterthur claimed that Rudolf, 'terrified by the example of King Konrad [meaning Frederick II's grandson, Konradin] in Apulia', kept out of Italy, settling instead for governing the *regnum Alamanie* in tranquillity.[67] More than one chronicler has the king tell his followers the fable of the cunning fox (or wolf), which would not enter the mountain, while other beasts went in never to return. Italy was like the mountain: few who ventured in came back without harm to themselves or their fatherland (*patria*).[68]

The fact that such claims were incorrect – Rudolf worked assiduously, if without success, to mount an Italian expedition for coronation at the pope's hands – only reinforces their interest, as it reveals what later observers assumed *must have been* the king's motive for remaining in the north.[69] By and large, German chroniclers seem approving in their judgements on their stay-at-home kings. Beyond the frontier, however, the same perceived behaviour might invite harsher conclusions, as was suggested by the Lübeck annalist, well informed about affairs among the Germans' western neighbours. Writing about Henry VII's accession in 1308, he noted that 'at that time, because kings of Germany [*reges Alemanniae*] after the emperor Frederick made little effort to gain the Empire, it seemed to the French ridiculous that they styled themselves kings of the Romans'.[70] It is no surprise, then, that their western neighbours, disdaining to grant them such risible titles, bluntly heeded instead what seemed the realities of the day. The court of Edward I of England, for example, though careful to honour Rudolf I as *Romanorum rex* in documents intended for his eyes, cheerfully and routinely called him *rei d Alemagne* or *rex Allomanie* behind his back.[71] The papal Curia

[66] *Die Chronik des Mathias von Neuenburg*, ed. Hofmeister, p. 56.

[67] *Die Chronik Johanns von Winterthur*, ed. Baethgen, p. 21. Cf. Johann's ironic observation on Ludwig IV's failure to make good his military alliance with Edward III of England, that Ludwig preferred to be a 'confessor' in Germany (*Alemania*) rather than a martyr in France: ibid., pp. 177–8.

[68] *Alberti Argentinensis Libelluli de Facetiis Rudolfi Regis quae supersunt*, in *Die Chronik des Mathias von Neuenburg*, ed. Hofmeister, p. 548. See also, e.g., *Fritsche (Friedrich) Closener's Chronik*, ed. Hegel, p. 56; *Chronik des Jacob Twinger*, ed. Hegel, pp. 451–2.

[69] For Rudolf's efforts to gain imperial coronation, see Redlich, *Rudolf von Habsburg*, Bk 2, Chs. 2, 6; Bk. 3, Ch. 7.

[70] *Annales Lubicenses*, ed. Lappenberg, p. 421.

[71] *Acta*, ed. Kern, no. 11, p. 6 (1279); no. 43, p. 27 (1283).

continued in time-honoured fashion to set an example to others, mostly avoiding the title 'king of Germany' in solemn diplomatic exchanges with the Empire's ruler, but otherwise employing it freely.[72] Among the Empire's own vassals, those living close to, or beyond, the frontiers of the *regnum*, those who had regular dealings with neighbouring European powers, and those whose own tongue was not German were the ones most likely to refer habitually to their 'German' suzerain.[73] In the decades after 1245, remoteness from the German heartlands of the Reich freed observers, and drafters of formal documents, to disregard constitutional proprieties and speak of their ruler as they found him.

By shrinking the monarch's sphere of rule, Germanising him also diminished him, as the Gregorian papacy had taught the world long before. In an age in which the ruler's hold on his lands was in any case feeble and uncertain, construing his kingship as a merely German one seemed a promising tactic to those who aspired to place themselves outside its bounds. Fritz Kern long ago identified several different lines of argument which were employed in the later thirteenth and early fourteenth centuries by inhabitants of the Reich (as well as by the papacy), all aimed at confining the monarch – particularly when he lacked, as in this period he invariably did, Roman coronation – to the rule of a narrowly drawn 'German' kingdom.[74] When the imperial town of Toul, which lay on the western frontier in Lotharingia, placed itself in 1300 under the protection of Philip IV of France, the treaty of alliance safeguarded only 'the [papally crowned] emperor', not the reigning king, Albert I. For the citizens were, they declared, 'of such free condition that we owe the king of Germany [*roi d Alemaigne*] neither host nor *chevauchée*'.[75] When the Frisian communities of Ostergo and Wangerland petitioned the king of France for market rights, they justified their act by insisting that they had never been subject to any secular lord, 'neither to the king of Germany nor to powers of any nation'.[76] In the decades after the end of the Staufer, the hard facts of

---

[72] For an example of papal usage, see *MGC* 3, no. 237, pp. 225–30 (Nicholas III to Bishop Paul of Tripoli, informing him of the terms for a Habsburg–Angevin alliance, 7 June 1279).

[73] In November 1281, for example, Count Philip of Savoy approached the king of England, seeking assistance against the *rex Alemannie*, who, he claimed, wished to disinherit him: *Acta*, ed. Kern, no. 22, p. 14. For further 'Germanising' references from the frontiers of the realm, see: ibid., no. 63, p. 41 (Count-Palatine Odo of Burgundy); *Acta*, ed. Winkelmann, vol. I, no. 745, p. 589 (Count Henry of Luxemburg).

[74] Kern, 'Die Reichsgewalt', esp. pp. 41–2.

[75] *Acta*, ed. Kern, no. 313, p. 283.

[76] Ibid., no. 1, p. 1 (1271 × 1285).

power were doing much to lend substance and consequences to the notion of a bounded – and, as it seemed, increasingly isolated, and depleted – German kingdom.

There is even evidence (although it is meagre and hard to interpret) which suggests that, in a climate of crisis for the Reich, yet more dramatic changes were envisaged, and that schemes were being entertained for refashioning the Empire's very constitution, and establishing a separate kingdom in the north.[77] That there were at least rumours to this effect, and that they became known in Germany, is at any rate certain. The most substantial reports, however, are found in non-German sources, a sign of the ambitions which western European powers, including the papacy, harboured in this period, to participate in defining the imperial monarchy. In his *Ecclesiastical History*, Ptolemy of Lucca recounted negotiations which he claimed had taken place in 1279 between Rudolf I and Pope Nicholas III, with the aim of breaking up the Empire and establishing an hereditary *regnum Alamannie*, to pass to Rudolf's descendants. In Italy, there were to be new, separate kingdoms for Lombardy and Tuscany, while in Burgundy a further realm was to pass to the son of Charles of Anjou, as a dowry for Rudolf's daughter.[78] The plan, if one existed, was not a wholly new idea. Already in 1273, a former Master of the Dominicans, Humbert of Romans, in a pamphlet on Church reform prepared for the Council of Lyon, had proposed that Germany be sundered from the Empire as a dynastic kingdom, while a separate emperor and rulers for Italy were to be established, under papal control.[79]

It was once thought that splitting the German kingdom off from the Empire was a fully formed papal project, traceable back to Urban IV (1261–4); but the evidence is too meagre and cryptic to allow any such definite conclusion.[80] Nevertheless, it was clearly among the Empire's southern and western neighbours, and particularly in papal circles, that rumours of such a project first took hold.[81] It may be that Alexander von Roes, who was close to the Curia in the 1280s, was seeking to rebuff them when he urged explicitly the importance of maintaining intact all four 'walls' of the Church, by which he meant the Empire's

---

[77] See generally Erkens, *Siegfried*, pp. 266–90, where the older literature is listed.

[78] Quoted in Redlich, *Rudolf von Habsburg*, pp. 420–1; and see also: Busson, *Die Idee*, pp. 17–18; Rodenberg, 'Zur Geschichte', p. 41.

[79] The relevant arguments are set out in Rodenberg, 'Zur Geschichte', pp. 30–1. On Humbert and his pamphlet, see Roberg, *Das zweite Konzil*, pp. 106–12.

[80] Rodenberg, 'Zur Geschichte', esp. p. 2. For some of the problems with this view, see Wilhelm, 'Das Aufkommen', esp. pp. 3, 18.

[81] Erkens, *Siegfried*, pp. 284–5.

four 'principal places': Aachen, Arles, Milan and Rome.[82] Once again, a distinct German realm, whether as objective to be pursued or threat to be resisted, was evidently most readily conceivable from vantage points outside its frontiers. This is not hard to explain. It was particularly at the Curia that during this period solutions were being sought to the grave general problems besetting contemporary Christendom – of which, many agreed, the Empire was among the main ones. Humbert of Romans was not the only churchman to bring forward imperial reform plans for the Council of Lyon (1274).[83] The papacy, after all, had learned at first hand of the dangers which could arise from the imperial monarchy, especially in Italy, and the benefits to be had from bringing it under control. The popes who held office in the decades after 1250 extended as never before their claims to sanction and supervise the Empire's ruler, and to regulate his access to the peninsula.[84] In 1303, Albert I felt compelled to promise Boniface VIII that he would notify the pontiff and 'humbly and faithfully' beg his 'advice' before coming into Italy.[85] And in plain fact, the composition of the Empire did change considerably during this period, principally in response to papal policy: under Nicholas III (1277–80) the Romagna was ceded to the papacy, and negotiations pursued with a view to settling the kingdom of Arles as an imperial fief on the Angevins.[86] If no self-contained German kingdom was deliberately founded, it must nevertheless have seemed at times that such a realm was taking shape by default, as imperial territories were stripped away to benefit the pontiff and the western powers.

Outside Germany, there was in some quarters a greater appetite for contemplating radical steps. If from a German perspective the state of the Reich after 1245 seemed desperate, the view from the Burgundian homeland of Humbert of Romans would have suggested abject collapse.[87] Considered from without, a multi-regnal solution to the Empire's problems doubtless made some sense. Those were, after all, multi-regnal times: as an English historian long ago observed, 'the age of the *regna*, not the *imperium*'.[88] We have seen already just what

[82] Alexander von Roes, *Memoriale*, cap. 25, ed. Grundmann and Heimpel, p. 127. On Alexander's fears for the dismemberment of the Empire, see Heimpel, 'Selbstbewußtsein', pp. 31–2.

[83] For the reform proposals advanced by Bishop Bruno of Olmütz (Olomouc), a supporter of Otakar of Bohemia, see Roberg, *Das zweite Konzil*, pp. 95–101.

[84] Partner, *The Lands*, esp. Ch. 8.

[85] *MGC* 4.i, no. 181, p. 156 (17 July 1303).

[86] Redlich, *Rudolf von Habsburg*, Ch. 6; and see below, Ch. 5, pp. 218–19.

[87] Roberg, *Das zweite Konzil*, p. 112.

[88] Powicke, *The Thirteenth Century*, p. 233.

resources, intellectual and cultural as well as material, were being heaped up on the side of the individual European kingdoms during the thirteenth and early fourteenth centuries.[89] Why not for Germany too? Even if the extent of regnal power there was distinctly modest, what was to prevent Germany at least from being *thought of* as a discrete realm, in an age when the tides of European thought seemed so decisively to favour that form of common life? After all, an appropriate conceptual vocabulary was by this time well established among observers in the western kingdoms. It was quite natural when Pierre Dubois, another pamphleteer with his eye on the reordering of Christendom, urged that the *rex Alemannie* and his kin should in future hold the kingdom in perpetuity.[90] Although Dubois did not argue for the splitting apart of *imperium* and *regnum*, he made clear that he judged the latter community to be both distinct and *German*.[91]

But what of the view from the north? On establishing an independent kingdom, it must first be emphasised that, if the indicators to be found in writings from southern Europe are few and ambiguous, in the Empire's German lands there are scarcely any traces at all. A heavily corrupted passage in the chronicle of the Colmar Dominicans, compiled in circles close to the early Habsburg court, appears to link the king's rule in Germany (*Theutonia*) with the negotiations conducted with Nicholas III over the kingdom of Arles; but if such a connection *was* intended by the chronicler (which from the surviving text is by no means certain), its nature – and the accuracy of his information – can no longer be determined.[92] Events which occurred in 1287 do, however, at least make clear that rumours were by then current in Germany concerning the future relationship between kingdom and Empire. It was in March of that year that a great assembly of the German Church at Würzburg, under the headship of a papal legate, had broken up amid controversy and disorder – with, on one account, the bishop of Toul clambering onto the cathedral font to harangue the assembled prelates.[93] The background to this tumult merits some attention.

Already in January, the archbishop of Cologne, Siegfried von Westerburg, had circulated among the German clergy a document

---

[89] Above, Ch. 2, pp. 58–65.
[90] *De Recuperatione*, ed. Langlois, Ch. 114, p. 103.
[91] Ibid., Ch. 13, p. 12 (*Alemannie regnum ac Imperium*). Dubois' preferred solution was that *regnum* and *imperium* alike be headed by a kinsman of the king of France (ibid., Ch. 116, p. 104).
[92] *Chronicon Colmariense*, ed. Jaffé, p. 205. The passage is examined in Busson, *Die Idee*, p. 35. For the source and its difficulties, see Kleinschmidt, 'Die Colmarer Dominikaner-Geschichtsschreibung'.
[93] The events are narrated in Redlich, *Rudolf von Habsburg*, pp. 703–5.

intended to provide a basis for appeals to the Curia against the activities in Germany of the recently arrived legate, John of Tusculum.[94] John had come north at King Rudolf's request, intending among other matters to prepare the way for the king to travel to Rome for imperial coronation.[95] His fiscal demands, actual and (still more) anticipated, aroused much ill feeling in a German Church which was already, particularly in its westernmost dioceses, groaning under a burden of papal taxation widely perceived as unjust.[96] The ground was therefore fertile for the archbishop's message of resistance. Siegfried, however, did not dwell only on the legate's financial exactions. Although his declared aim was to raise up the Empire, public rumour, widely repeated throughout the kingdom of Germany (*regnum Alemanie*), was that he had come instead to sever that kingdom from the Empire, with which it had always been inseparably united, and massively to diminish the electoral rights of the princes of the kingdom of Germany (*principes regni Alemanie*) by setting up an hereditary king.[97] A salient feature of the document is the insistence with which the archbishop deployed a Germanised language of *regnum*.[98] There are indications that the Cologne protest circulated widely: the surviving text is from Salzburg, while its allegations about an imminent threat to the powers of the electors were echoed by an annalist in Worms.[99] The archbishop's agitation in advance of the Würzburg council, and perhaps also during its sitting, probably helped bring about its rowdy end – though papal fiscal burdens would certainly

---

[94] *MGC* 3, no. 623, pp. 597–9. See also *Die Regesten der Erzbischöfe von Köln*, ed. Knipping, no. 3109, pp. 153–4. A letter from the church of Minden, a suffragan of Cologne, dated 28 February 1287, promises to support Cologne's protest: ibid., no. 3115, p. 155; *MGC* 3, no. 624, pp. 599–600.

[95] Redlich, *Rudolf von Habsburg*, pp. 697–705.

[96] For the background in papal fiscal exactions, see: Kern, *Ausdehnungspolitik*, p. 84; Hauck, *Kirchengeschichte*, esp. p. 458; Redlich, *Rudolf von Habsburg*, pp. 617–18, 700–1. For the bishopric of Toul, see Eubel, 'Die Minoriten', esp. p. 666.

[97] *MGC* 3, no. 623, p. 598: 'Insuper attendentes, quod licet dominus predictus legatus asserat [se] ad hoc ad partes Alemanie a sede apostolica destinatum, ut alteram mundi lucem, videlicet sacri Romani virutem imperii, que iam dudum consopita extitit, excitaret, tamen vox est, verbum et fama publica per regnum Alemanie multipliciter divulgata, quod idem dominus legatus regnum ipsum semper imperio inseparabiliter unitum intendit constituendo regem hereditarium, quantum in eo est, ab imperio separare et sic alteram mundi lucem, videlicet honorem culminis imperialis, si fas est dicere, extinguere et excecare ac iuri principum regni Alemanie ecclesiasticorum et secularium, ad quos spectat eleccio regis eiusdem promovendi postmodum in imperatorem, enormiter derogare.' The protest echoes the words of Innocent III's decretal *Venerabilem* (1202), recognising the electoral rights of the German princes. For this, see below, Ch. 6, pp. 282–3.

[98] Schubert, *König und Reich*, p. 229.

[99] *Annales breves Wormatienses*, ed. Pertz, p. 77.

have weighed more heavily with most of those present than fears for the Empire's constitution.

What do Siegfried's public 'rumours' signify? If nothing else, the archbishop's claims indicate that by the late 1280s some Germans were becoming acquainted with notions similar to those circulating in the south in the preceding decade. Could they have contained any truth? In answering this question, it is important to distinguish between the matter of the hereditary crown and the kingdom's separation from the Empire. It is likely that Rudolf's endeavours to gain coronation at the pope's hands were impelled above all by the aim of securing his son's succession in the Reich.[100] As will become clear elsewhere, the idea of a hereditary monarchy was far from dead in post-Staufer Germany, despite the opposition put up by the electors and their supporters.[101] By the later thirteenth century the principle had become established that only a crowned emperor was entitled to seek his son's elevation to the throne.[102] This goes far to explain the tenacity of Rudolf's negotiations with a succession of popes to arrange a journey south.[103] But there is no solid evidence to support the idea that the king or his ministers ever seriously considered abandoning the Empire for a mere German kingdom. Indeed, as will shortly become clear, the signs are that such a prospect would have been unthinkable. Why Archbishop Siegfried would have perceived in the elevation of Rudolf's son the seeds of a threat to the electors is easily enough explained: any resumption of dynastic continuity on the throne might quickly have come to be interpreted as a custom of heredity in favour of the Habsburgs, binding in future the princes' hands. Why he linked it with the more remote spectre of the Empire's dissolution is less clear. But it is likely that, in Siegfried's view, the very prospect of hereditary succession would have threatened to strip the Reich of its unique character and mission, and reduce it to the status of one royal patrimony among many.[104] Exactly that argument had only a few years before been deployed by Alexander von Roes, himself a native of Cologne and champion of the princes.[105] The Germans were fated to rule no commonplace *regnum*.

Once established among the Germans, the notion of a separate dynastic kingdom was able periodically to return to haunt them. Those

---

[100] Redlich, *Rudolf von Habsburg*, p. 697.
[101] Below, Ch. 6, pp. 289–92.
[102] Schubert, 'Königswahl', pp. 291–2; Erkens, *Siegfried*, p. 267 and n. 38. The principle was of recent origin, emerging in the years following the fall of the Hohenstaufen.
[103] Redlich, *Rudolf von Habsburg*, esp. Ch. 7.
[104] Erkens, *Siegfried*, pp. 288–90.
[105] For Alexander's case, see below, Ch. 6, p. 291.

writers who invoked it invariably perceived it as a danger, and linked it with threats to German possession of the Empire and with schemes to strip away territories from the monarchy. It remained a favoured phantom of the Rhineland archbishops in their struggles with the early Habsburg kings. In December 1299 Albert I had met for negotiations with Philip IV of France at Quatrevaux, a remote woodland spot on the Franco-imperial frontier in Lotharingia.[106] The context for their meeting lay in preparations which were under way for the marriage of Albert's son Rudolf to the French king's sister, Blanche.[107] Just what was discussed and resolved when the two kings met was left undisclosed at the time, and has largely remained a mystery to historians.[108] The Rhineland princes were, it seems, quickly at work filling the void with rumour. A manifesto issued by the archbishops of Mainz, Cologne and Trier declared that they would never assent to the treaties being drawn up with France, since these clearly aimed at dividing up the Empire.[109] As in 1287, Cologne appears to have taken a lead, and again the keenest suspicions probably centred on Albert's aspiration to raise his son to the throne. (One of the Habsburg king's diplomas for the French had rashly implied that his 'heirs' were to succeed him 'in the Roman realm' (*in Romano regno*).)[110]

Once again, however, contemporary report made the leap to imagining more lurid changes. A chronicle fragment from the lower Rhine preserves the rumour, seemingly of French origin, that Albert had surrendered to the king of France the Empire's lands west of the Rhine, with their cities, including Trier, Mainz and Cologne.[111] There can be no question of this fantastic tale reflecting undertakings actually made at Quatrevaux. Its source reinforces the suspicion that it was propagated for political ends by the king's enemies close to the Rhineland electors.[112] Yet it remains in its way revealing, reflecting, it seems, a view

---

[106] See now: Schwedler, *Herrschertreffen*, pp. 93–108; Jones, *Eclipse?*, pp. 300–6. The classic account is Kern, *Ausdehnungspolitik*, pp. 200–13, but see the criticisms of Thomas, *Deutsche Geschichte*, pp. 112–14. A concise, clear narrative of Franco-imperial relations at this time is provided by Grundmann, *Wahlkönigtum*, pp. 130–3.

[107] For these negotiations, see Thomas, *Deutsche Geschichte*, pp. 111–12.

[108] For the resolution of frontier questions there, see below, Ch. 10, p. 464.

[109] *MGC* 4.i, no. 80, pp. 61–2 (5 December 1299): the negotiations constituted a *dilapidacio imperii* (p. 62). See also Kern, *Ausdehnungspolitik*, p. 204.

[110] *MGC* 4.i, no. 76, pp. 59–60 (5 September 1299). Arnold Busson believed that the negotiations of 1299 involved renewed plans to break up the Empire for the sake of establishing a hereditary kingdom: Busson, *Die Idee*, pp. 65–6. There is no firm evidence for such a scheme.

[111] Discussed in Kern, *Ausdehnungspolitik*, p. 212.

[112] Thomas, *Deutsche Geschichte*, p. 112. For the rumour in French writings, where it appears to have begun, see Jones, *Eclipse?*, p. 303.

of the Empire's lands as a historical confection, assembled over time, which might also therefore, given different historical circumstances, in time be dismantled. Heinrich von Herford, in the fourteenth century, imagined Charlemagne as the ruler of an original 'kingdom of the Teutons' (*regnum Theutonicorum*), to which he had added by stages the 'kingdom of the Lombards' and, with his Rome coronation, the 'kingdom of the Romans'.[113] And even the narrower realm, as it existed in the late Middle Ages, was not timeless: the incorporation of Lotharingia under Henry I was recalled and celebrated by German champions of the Empire from Alexander von Roes in the thirteenth century to Dietrich von Niem in the fifteenth.[114] Under Albert I, it seems, some were ready to imagine the tides of change rolling back a depleted *regnum* to its earliest limits, in a late Carolingian East Frankish kingdom terminating at the Rhine.

There is no sign that anyone with a political voice in late medieval Germany, or whose own thoughts are recorded, viewed the idea of the Reich stripped down to a mere German realm other than with hostility and alarm. Some clearly judged it understandable, even laudable, when monarchs appeared to shun commitments beyond the Alps, and to content themselves in practice with a more specifically German sphere; but that did not imply any demand for them to cast aside the penumbra of imperial titles and doctrines which still illuminated and legitimised their rule. According to Heinrich von Herford, Charlemagne legislated that the king of Germany (*rex Theutonie*) should remain in perpetuity king both of the Lombards and the Romans.[115] German observers differed in their level of awareness of the Empire's non-German lands, and in the importance which they ascribed to them. Few were as strident as Dietrich von Niem in denouncing the weakness and vice of those rulers – in his eyes, Charles IV, Wenceslas and Rupert – guilty of their neglect.[116] The long years which Dietrich spent at the Curia had given him a consciousness of the Empire's historic rights in Italy and Burgundy beyond the grasp of most observers north of the Alps. But it remained the common view that the Empire's properties should be maintained intact. If few German contemporaries showed any awareness of Rudolf I's cession of the Romagna to the papacy, Matthias of Neuenburg, reviewing the king's action some decades later, would insist that it was

---

[113] *Liber de rebus memorabilioribus*, ed. Potthast, p. 245.
[114] Alexander von Roes, *Memoriale*, caps. 23, 27 (manuscript classes E–G), *Noticia seculi*, cap. 11, ed. Grundmann and Heimpel, pp. 123, 131, 158–9; Dietrich von Nieheim, *Viridarium*, ed. Lhotsky and Pivec, pp. 10–11.
[115] *Liber de rebus memorabilioribus*, ed. Potthast, p. 245.
[116] Dietrich von Nieheim, *Viridarium*, ed. Lhotsky and Pivec, pp. 3, 17, 18–19.

'to the grave harm of the Empire'.[117] Heinrich von Diessenhofen meant no compliment to Charles IV when he contrasted, under the year 1359, the parallel reigns of pope and emperor, with 'the pope recovering the Holy See's property, the emperor relinquishing imperial property to its occupiers'.[118] The Styrian knight Otakar uz der Geul, whose rhymed chronicle was taking shape around the time of the Quatrevaux meeting, lambasted the French king's encroachments on western imperial holdings (*des rîchs guot*), to which he had 'no right'.[119]

Failure to hold the line against such infractions dishonoured a ruler. Medieval etymology insisted that the true *augustus* was one who 'augmented' his realm. Dietrich von Niem contrasted pointedly Otto I (*augustus*), founder of the Empire's territorial power, with the *augustulus* Charles IV, under whom began its dissolution.[120] The principle was made explicit in the post-Staufer period in the chancery's vernacular forms for imperial titles, which lauded the monarch as an 'augmenter of the Empire' (*merer des reichs*).[121] That there was more to this idea than mere words is shown by its invocation in the judgement of deposition promulgated against Wenceslas in the names of the Rhineland electors (20 August 1400). There, the king was accused of 'grave dismemberment and diminution [*mynneruenge*]' of the Reich, 'against the dignity

[117] *Die Chronik des Mathias von Neuenburg*, ed. Hofmeister, p. 37. It is an indication of sensitivies on the imperial side at the time of the Romagna's surrender that a letter of Nicholas III to Rudolf, calling for the mandating of plenipotentiaries with full powers, insisted that this should be 'absque conditionali adiectione "salvo iure vel demembratione imperii" aut alia simili, cum tales clausule captiose plurimum videantur': *MGC* 3, no. 195, p. 184. In appointing Edward I of England as mediator in his dispute with Savoy, Rudolf had insisted that any settlement was to be *absque demembratione imperii*: *Die Regesten des Kaiserreiches unter Rudolf*, ed. Redlich, no. 942, p. 233 (3 May 1278).

[118] *Heinricus Dapifer de Diessenhoven*, ed. Huber, p. 114: 'papa bona sedis recuperans, imperator bona imperii occupantibus relinquens'.

[119] *Ottokars österreichische Reimchronik*, ed. Seemüller, p. 986, vv. 74800–11. Johann von Winterthur regarded Ludwig IV's abortive alliance with Edward III of England in the late 1330s as a lost opportunity to recover imperial cities which the king of France 'imperio ... illicite et indebite abstraxit': *Die Chronik Johanns von Winterthur*, ed. Baethgen, p. 177.

[120] Dietrich von Nieheim, *Viridarium*, ed. Lhotsky and Pivec, p. 3. For the medieval roots of the *augeo-augustus* linkage, see: Kleinschmidt, *Herrscherdarstellung*, p. 38 n. 157; Koch, *Sacrum Imperium*, p. 217.

[121] The vernacular chancery form was noted in the *Schwabenspiegel*, where it was linked with the king's coronation oath: *Schwabenspiegel*, ed. Eckhardt, *Landrecht*, cap. 121/125, pp. 184–5: 'als man den kunig kieset so sol er dem reich hulde sberen ... das er ... das reich alczeit mere vnd nit ermer. dicz schreibet der kunig an allen seinen brieffen die er sendet das er das reich zu allen zeiten mere vnd reicher vnd nicht ermer mache'. A historical account of the origins of *merer des reichs* is provided in *Chronik des Jacob Twinger*, ed. Hegel, p. 335, telling how the Romans acclaimed Augustus as 'ein merer des riches und des gemeinen nutzes'.

of his title'.[122] Wenceslas, the electors went on, had neglected and alienated towns and estates not only in the German (*Dutschen*), but also the Romance (*Welschen*), lands of the Empire. Especially in northern Italy, where French forces had been allowed to seize the city of Genoa, the Luxemburger's lassitude was for the princes a matter of scandal. Particular notoriety attached to the king's bestowal upon Giangaleazzo Visconti, lord of Milan, of a hereditary duchy in return for massive sums.[123] These and similar infractions were high on the electors' list of charges. The continued integrity of *all* imperial territories mattered; their dispersal justified the sternest sanction.

The constitutional logic of this position was set out in a declaration of imperial rights, directed against papal encroachments, drawn up in 1338. If, as a statute of John XXII had claimed, Italy had no connection with the kingdom of Germany (*regnum Alemanie*), then the candidate raised up by the German princes could not be termed (in customary fashion) 'king of the Romans'. But neither would he be a king of Germany (*rex Alemanie*), as the princes had no constitutional power to elect such a one. And since the pope sought also to deny his authority in the Empire's French lands, he would be 'like a crowned statue, having neither rulership nor realm [*regimen neque regnum*]'.[124] When the territorial dismemberment of the Reich was invoked, suspicions were never far away that the historical relationship between the German people and the Empire itself was under threat. Dark plots were divined repeatedly, invariably of French, papal or Franco-papal authorship. A letter sent in 1380 to the town of Strasbourg by Archbishop Kuno of Trier sought the banishment of preachers favourable to the Avignon pope Clement VII: these men were seeking nothing but the annihilation of the Empire and (as a natural consequence) the perpetual servitude of all the German lands (*alle Dúytsche lant*).[125] From German perspectives, the Romance-speaking territories of the Reich supplied a basis for the imperial authority of its ruler which threatened to crumble with their subtraction. This danger was ever present. The spectre of a separate, dynastic German kingdom admittedly lost during the fourteenth century such small substance as it had possessed in Germany, as

[122] *RTA* 3, ed. Weizsäcker, no. 204, pp. 255–6. The point was developed explicitly by Jacob Twinger, who explained that Wenceslas 'was nüt ein merer des heilgen riches, also sich ein roemesch künig schribet, sunder er was ein minrer und ein versumer und unnütze man des heilgen riches': *Chronik des Jacob Twinger*, ed. Hegel, p. 495.

[123] See Thomas, *Deutsche Geschichte*, pp. 330–9. The sale of the Milanese duchy to the 'tyrannical' Giangaleazzo was specifically condemned, e.g., by Dietrich von Niem: Dietrich von Nieheim, *Viridarium*, ed. Lhotsky and Pivec, p. 16.

[124] *Nova Alamanniae*, vol. I, no. 583, p. 396.

[125] *Strassburg UB* 5, ed. Witte and Wolfram, no. 1368, p. 999 (3 February 1380).

the growth of dynastic *Hausmacht* placed the ruler's dealings with the German lands on a new footing, setting a greater imaginative distance between dynasty and *regnum*. What lived on, however, was a more general fear that the Empire would be subverted through the erosion of its broad landed base. This fear, as will shortly become apparent, was intimately linked with conceptions of a specifically 'German' political community.[126]

One fact above all renders implausible the notion that rulers in the post-Staufer period aspired to a German kingship distinct from the Empire: the pains which their own chanceries took to avoid mentioning such a kingship in their documents. Even Frederick II's sons were almost always styled, in traditional fashion, 'king of the Romans' in their public acts, as were the 'Interregnum' kings: official invocations of their 'German' kingship, if in some ways suggestive, are few, indeed anomalous. Nor did conventions change in the decades that followed. The official language of kingship and emperorship in the Reich employed sonorous Latin formulae, which by the later thirteenth century had been in use in the chancery for around 300 years. *Dei gratia Romanorum rex* [or *imperator*] *semper augustus*: the weighty penumbra of Christian *Romanitas* which surrounded the ruler's acts was not lightly to be conjured away. Indeed, it was jealously upheld when need arose: Henry VII judged it a dishonour to be addressed, disregarding his Roman title, as 'king of Germany' (*rex Alamannie*).[127] Invocations of a 'German' kingship are almost entirely absent from Latin documents in the ruler's name; and the few examples which do occur are usually identifiable as the product of special circumstances.[128] The signs are that the term was consciously avoided.[129] It is found only slightly more often in writings issued by the electors and other princes.[130]

---

[126] Below, Ch. 5, pp. 218–19.
[127] 'Bannitio Florentiae', in *MGH Leges* 2, ed. Pertz, p. 520: 'His etiam non contenti, per civitatem eamdem publice, alta voce preconis, banniri fecerunt, quod unicuique licitum foret impune offendere in personis et rebus gentes illius, qui se gerit pro rege Alamannie, ipsum nolentes suum ac Romanorum regem aliquatenus adpellare, supprimentes ipsius veri nominis dignitatem in ipsius opprobrium et despectum.'
[128] See, e.g., *Acta*, ed. Böhmer, no. 633, p. 441 (17 June 1311), a document in Henry VII's name concerning the homage traditionally done by counts of Burgundy *predecessoribus nostris Alamanie regibus*. The language may reflect Burgundian usage; or its point may have been to underline to a distant and independent-minded vassal that homage was not owed only to crowned emperors. The same considerations apply to Richard of Cornwall's act enfeoffing Countess Margaret of Flanders with the fiefs previously held by the counts *ab imperatoribus seu regibus Alamannie*: *Acta*, ed. Winkelmann, vol. I, no. 571, p. 458 (2 July 1262).
[129] Schubert, *König und Reich*, pp. 230–1.
[130] See the examples cited above, pp. 162, 168.

If taboos against invoking a 'German' monarchy were somewhat less among the chroniclers, its use was still hardly common.[131] It was favoured by the Franciscan Johann von Winterthur, who refers repeatedly to the *rex Alemanie*, whose rule he viewed as the foundation for ascent to Roman emperorship.[132] The same phrase finds occasional use in another chronicle from the mid-fourteenth century, compiled at the Cistercian monastery of Königsaal (*Aula regia*), near Prague – although there, conventional invocation of the monarch's Roman titles remained the norm.[133] Occasional reference is made to a 'German' king by the Carinthian abbot Johann von Viktring, and further isolated instances are to be found scattered in other historical writings.[134] On the whole, however, Latin historiographers knew well their monarchs' official styles, and evidently felt bound by them. Only among the treatise-writers, who took a long view of the Empire and its rulers, reaching beyond the conventions of their day, is somewhat greater flexibility to be discerned. Alexander von Roes, an acute observer of the changing relationship between power and title in German history, wrote of the Frankish monarchs prior to Charlemagne's Rome coronation as 'kings of the Franks or Germans [*reges Francorum vel Germanorum*], which is one and the same'.[135] He was quick, however, to point out that the title was not used by their successors, who in his day were called 'kings or emperors of the Romans'.[136] Lupold von Bebenburg, writing towards the middle of the fourteenth century, had altogether less inhibition about naming the Empire's rulers as *reges Germanie*.[137] Lupold, like Alexander, was well aware both of the Roman titles claimed by monarchs in his own day and of the fact that in former times those titles were not used.[138] Unlike Alexander, however (though in common with Johann von Winterthur), Lupold deemed the 'German' royal title which he invoked to be quite compatible with an imperial mission. Dietrich von Niem contrasted

---

[131] For a survey, see Müller, 'Nationaler Name', pp. 132–9.
[132] *Die Chronik Johanns von Winterthur*, ed. Baethgen, p. 156 (1338): 'Accersitisque principibus electoribus regis Alamanie et per consequens imperatoris Romanorum.' For further examples, see ibid., pp. 8, 21, 53, 68, 156, 201, 211–12, 218.
[133] *Königsaaler Geschichts-Quellen*, ed. Loserth, pp. 38, 136, 174, 368–9.
[134] Thus *Liber certarum historiarum*, ed. Schneider, i.130, 184, 301; and see also, e.g., *Gesta Boemundi archiepiscopi Treverensis*, in *Gesta Treverorum*, ed. Waitz, p. 471.
[135] Alexander von Roes, *Memoriale*, caps. 20, 26, ed. Grundmann and Heimpel, pp. 115, 128.
[136] Ibid., cap. 26, p. 128.
[137] Examples: Lupold von Bebenburg, *Tractatus de Iuribus Regni et Imperii*, caps. 2, 3, 5, in *Politische Schriften Lupolds von Bebenburg*, ed. Miethke and Flüeler, pp. 257, 267, 295.
[138] Ibid., cap. 5, p. 295. Their adoption, he insisted, was not on account of the Empire's Italian lands, but 'propter reverenciam sacrosancte Romane ecclesie'.

Wenceslas' weakness in the face of heresy with the resolve shown by his predecessors, 'Catholic kings and emperors of Germany' (*catholici reges et imperatores Germanie*), such as Frederick II.[139] Conceptual distance from the day-to-day events of rulership, like physical distance from the German lands themselves, freed a handful of writers to discern a 'German' monarchy which most of their contemporaries in the north could or would not acknowledge. But their viewpoint, like the broad historical knowledge on which it rested, was in their day most untypical.

Any expectation that the chancery's growing use of the German language in the later Middle Ages might have been accompanied by the introduction of an explicitly German vocabulary of rule quickly proves vain. On the contrary, the styles for kingship and emperorship employed in vernacular documents were even more unbendingly Roman than in the Latin tradition, and translated forms of 'king of Germany' are wholly absent. Among chroniclers writing in the vernacular, they are met with only exceptionally, and without standard form. The Braunschweig Rhymed Chronicle, composed late in the thirteenth century, invokes occasionally a 'king of the Germans' (*dher Dhudeschen koninc*).[140] Jakob Twinger used the language of German kingship only historically, never of contemporary or recently dead rulers. He thus explains how, following the division of the Carolingian empire, 'the German kings [*die dütschen künige*] were more powerful than the kings of France', and consequently gained the Empire.[141] As Twinger's usage here indicates, there existed in the late Middle Ages no vernacular term for a discrete 'German' political community, comparable to *Frankreich*, *Engelant* or *Schottenlant*. Fashioning such a term meant clumsy adaption of the Latin, as in the Brabanter Jan van Heelu's reference to Rudolf I as *van Almaengen coninc*.[142] Vernacular political lyrics entirely avoided speaking of 'German' kings or emperors, instead lauding the ruler in traditional fashion as 'king of Rome [*künic von Rome*]', 'protector of Rome [*vot von Rome*]' or similar forms.[143]

---

[139] Dietrich von Nieheim, *Viridarium*, ed. Lhotsky and Pivec, p. 19.

[140] *Braunschweigische Reimchronik*, ed. Weiland, pp. 478, vv. 1492–5 (Konrad II), 555, vv. 7745–7 (William of Holland). For a further example, see *Detmar-Chronik*, ed. Koppmann, i.276 (1198): Innocent III favoured Otto of Saxony for the throne 'unde let en kronen koninghe der Dudeschen to Aken'.

[141] *Chronik des Jacob Twingers*, ed. Hegel, p. 705.

[142] *Rymkronyk van Jan van Heelu*, ed. Willems, p. 326, v. 8941.

[143] Examples in *Politische Lyrik*, ed. Müller, vol. I, p. 55 ('Von Wengen': *vot von Rome*), pp. 74–5 (Friedrich von Sonnenburg: *künic von Rome*); cf. *Lohengrin*, ed. Cramer, p. 320, v. 2629: *der roemisch vogt* (for Henry I!). And see Schnell, 'Deutsche Literatur', pp. 287–8.

As we have seen already, the terminology of a 'German' kingdom, by this time almost invariably rendered as *regnum Alemanniae*, did attain a modest, and short-lived, prominence in the post-Staufer period, particularly in the context of rumours about the future constitution of the Reich.[144] But, across the thirteenth and fourteenth centuries as a whole, its invocation in writings issued by the monarch, or by other bearers of power in Germany, is only slightly more frequent than are references to a 'German' king. It occurs in only a small minority of surviving documents.[145] In some instances, the phrase's application seems straightforwardly political, comparable with its use for other European kingdoms. Henry VII, for example, refers in an encyclical to his steps, before departing for Italy, to put in order 'the kingdoms of Germany and Bohemia [*regna Alamagnie Boemieque*]'.[146] Occasionally, it appears to express a more abstract notion of political community. Thus, a document of 1344, originating in Balduin of Luxemburg's circle, objects to papal terms for reconciliation with Ludwig IV which, if accepted, would have constituted 'the destruction of the Germanic people and polity' (*destructio Germanici populi atque regni*).[147] We thus encounter – not for the last time – the uncertain relationship which some late medieval writings indicate, between *regnum* and the apparently broader *imperium*. Other applications, however, suggest instead that a German *regnum* commanded no settled place at all in the Empire's constitutional vocabulary, since it was evidently in some contexts interchangeable with formulae making no reference to a 'kingdom'. There seems no compelling reason why, for example, Rudolf I should in 1288 have sought from Edward I of England the protection specifically of 'the merchants of *the kingdom of* Germany [*mercatores regni Alemannie*]', rather than simply the 'merchants of Germany [*mercatores Alemanie*]', on whose behalf his son Albert I was to petition the doge of Venice.[148] Nor can the pattern of its use be distinguished with any clarity from the far more common (though, it would seem, less constitutionally precise) references in royal

---

[144] Though for a rare documentary reference to a *regnum Germanie*, see *MGC* 3, no. 85, p. 76 (an encyclical of Rudolf I to the Empire's subjects in Italy). See also Hugelmann, *Stämme*, p. 396.

[145] See generally Müller-Mertens, 'Imperium und Regnum', pp. 569–87.

[146] *MGC* 4.ii, no. 801, p. 803 (29 June 1312).

[147] *Nova Alamanniae*, vol. II.i, no. 773, p. 498. *Germanici* is a subsequent addition to the text, evidently by Balduin's counsellor Rudolf Losse.

[148] Rudolf's letter is printed in *Urkundliche Geschichte des Hansischen Stahlhofes zu London*, vol. II (1851), p. 14, quoted in Hugelmann, *Stämme*, p. 394; Albert's is in *MGC* 4.i, no. 214, p. 185 (29 March 1307). For a further regnal example, see *HUB* 2, no. 266, p. 103 (28 October 1315): Duke John II of Brabant grants trading privileges to 'mercatores regni Almanie seu Theutonie'. Elsewhere, Hansa merchants were commonly designated merely as 'German': see below, Ch. 9, pp. 437–8.

documents to the 'regions of Germany' (*partes Alemannie*).[149] On occasion, invocation of a German *regnum* may have had a specific object, such as reminding non-German imperial vassals of their subjection to the king they habitually called 'German', no less than to an emperor.[150] In other instances, the choice of *regnum* probably reflects ecclesiastical usage, as when Archbishop Werner of Mainz informed his suffragans of the temporal penalties which the king of the Romans was bound to apply in support of excommunications imposed 'by the prelates of the *regnum Alamanie*'.[151] The term's adoption by the German clergy may have been fostered by its common use in communications from the papal Curia.[152] Often, however, the reason for its choice is simply obscure.

Mention of a German *regnum* is hardly commonplace among Latin chroniclers, but neither is it especially rare. And, as it is applied in their narratives, the political and constitutional ideas which the phrase adumbrated find clearer and more frequent expression. True, chroniclers too might employ it as, so it seems, a mere alternative to 'Germany': in 1346, the newly elected Charles IV slipped into Bohemia in disguise, fearing the power of his rival, Ludwig IV, 'throughout the *regnum Alamanie*'.[153] But in other instances, its associations with government are more explicit. Rudolf I 'in his days gloriously governed the *regnum*

---

[149] Thus their seeming equivalence in the formulation, evidently aimed at comprehensiveness, *regnum et partes Alemann(ie)*: *MGC* 5, no. 952, p. 792 (treaty of Duke Leopold of Austria with the king of France, 27 July 1324).

[150] Thus *MGC* 3, no. 319, p. 312 (1282), to Count Philip of Savoy, concerning imperial properties in Burgundy, over which the king claimed jurisdiction 'ratione imperii seu regni Alamannie'. See also Schubert, *König und Reich*, p. 230. For possible uses of *rex Alemannie* in this way, see above, n. 127.

[151] *MGC* 3, no. 111, p. 102 (7 July 1276). And see also ibid., no. 28, p. 29 (for the Teutonic Order); *MGC* 4.i, no. 449, p. 392 (provisions to churches). The testimony provided by the Cistercian abbot of Kamp to a papally instigated inquiry of 1290 into the mistreatment of Archbishop Siegfried of Cologne by his townsmen and their allies included the claim that the matters of which he spoke were common knowledge 'per totum regnum Allemannie et etiam alibi in diversis mundi partibus': Düsseldorf, Urk. Kurköln 179, membrane ii. See also Archbishop Siegfried's protest letter, discussed above, as well as the programme which Bishop Bruno of Olmütz prepared for the 1274 Council of Lyon: *MGC* 3, no. 620, pp. 589, 590.

[152] As examples, see: *MGC* 3, nos 78, 79, pp. 67, 68; *Codex Epistolaris Rudolfi I*, ed. Bodmann, pp. 19–23. Gregory X, in a communication with Alfonso X of Castile, referred to the crown which the Empire's ruler received at Aachen as *corona regni Alamanie*: Wilhelm, 'Das Aufkommen', p. 4.

[153] *Heinricus Dapifer de Diessenhoven*, ed. Huber, p. 54. The author of the late fourteenth-century *Cologne World Chronicle* recounted how, within the *regnum Germanie* (a term which he used repeatedly), there had arisen that 'very dangerous and detestable sect of laymen', the Flagellants: *Die Kölner Weltchronik*, ed. Sprandel, p. 89 (and cf. pp. 55, 91, 99).

Alemannie'.[154] Ludwig of Wittelsbach and Frederick of Habsburg, elected in discord in 1314, each 'interfered in the administration of the realm in Germany [*regnum in Alamania*]'.[155] Following Ludwig's establishment on the throne, his former rival Frederick hoped, during his absence in Italy, 'to gain the realm and rule of Germany' (*Alemanniae regnum et regimen*).[156] The sense specifically of a 'German realm' seems also to underlie Gottfried von Ensmingen's claim that the imposter Tile Kolup aspired to bring under his rule *tota regio Alemanie*.[157] Johann von Viktring, in writing 'Of the corrupt state of the realm in Germany (*De statu regni in Alemannia corrupto*)', appears to draw together notions of territory, community and the general good in a way which looks forward to later applications of the concept of 'state'.[158] We have already observed how German chroniclers invoked a *regnum Alemannie* to encompass what they saw as the geographically less ambitious rule exercised by post-Staufer monarchs. Occasionally one of them might look deeper, discerning a distinct 'German' political community around the king, which became visible especially in relation to the ruler's efforts to establish peace, and took concrete form at great assemblies under his headship.[159] This community's existence, and its common acts, were then located within the *regnum*. In 1355, for example, Charles IV 'summoned to him at Nuremberg the electors and burghers in the kingdom of Germany' (*in regno Alamannie*), and commanded that peace be kept throughout the *regnum*.[160] Yet, for all the suggestiveness of such remarks, it is the relative fewness of references to a German realm, and the instability of the term's use, that must above all be kept in mind. The trends, apparently strong at the time of Frederick II's downfall, towards the emergence of a more clearly conceived German kingdom out of the ashes of the Hohenstaufen Reich, found no real consolidation in the century that followed.

---

[154] *Vita Henrici archiepiscopi altera*, ed. Waitz, p. 457.

[155] *Die Chronik Heinrichs Taube*, ed. Bresslau, p. 31.

[156] *Königsaaler Geschichts-Quellen*, ed. Loserth, p. 451.

[157] *Ellenhardi chronicon*, ed. Jaffé, p. 126.

[158] *Liber certarum historiarum*, ed. Schneider, i.211. The phrase appears as a heading to book ii, recension (a). For *status regni* as a basis for 'state', see K.-F. Werner, 'Regnum', in *LMA* 7, cols. 587–96 (here col. 587). Johann also invokes elsewhere a German realm with solid constitutional substance, identifying the south-eastern frontier of the *regnum Theutonicum*: *Liber certarum historiarum*, ed. Schneider, i.149.

[159] For the composition of this community, see below, pp. 186–9.

[160] *Heinricus Dapifer de Diessenhoven*, ed. Huber, p. 101. As further examples, see ibid., pp. 72 (Charles IV met at Speyer with the nobles and urban delegates of the *regnum Alamannie*, 1349), 88 (Charles IV commanded 'nobiles et civitatenses per regnum Alemannie' to swear a three-year peace, 1353).

In part, the problem lay with the concept of *regnum* itself. The term carried in the Middle Ages, depending on context and authorial intent, an unusually wide range of possible meanings.[161] Nor was it applied consistently or predictably. *Regnum*, wrote Isidore of Seville, 'is named from kings', and 'kingdom' is indeed in many cases clearly the proper translation.[162] It has even been suggested, with good reason, that *regnum* brings us closest to a medieval conception of the '(national) state': king, kingdom and people (*rex*, *regnum*, *gens*) had a natural affinity in medieval minds.[163] Yet Isidore himself had also numbered the Roman Empire among the *regna*.[164] And it was in broadly similar spirit that Lupold von Bebenburg would invoke a *regnum Germanie*: to signal not a narrowly drawn German territorial realm but a larger (though still finite) imperial domain, within which the German element predominated.[165]

Writings from the thirteenth and fourteenth centuries (in which *regnum* is far more often found on its own than linked to any designation for 'Germany') reveal a similar complexity. In some instances, it seems clearly to denote a political community within, but distinct from, the *imperium*: one which, it is reasonable to suppose, would for contemporaries often have borne a 'German' penumbra. Among the questions put to the new king at his Aachen coronation was the demand to know whether he would preserve and recover the rights and properties of *regnum et imperium*.[166] Gottfried von Ensmingen tells how the imposter Tile Kolup summoned Rudolf I to appear before him for investiture with the *regnum*, 'as if from a true emperor'.[167] In a diploma of 1282, Archbishop Siegfried of Cologne was careful to exempt *regnum* as well as *imperium* from the principalities to whose settlement on Rudolf's sons

---

[161] For something of its range, see: Niermeyer and Van de Kieft, *Mediae Latinitatis Lexicon Minus*, part II, p. 1177; Koch, *Sacrum Imperium*, p. 12.

[162] *Isidori Hispalensis Episcopi Etymologiarum*, ed. Lindsay, I.9.3.1: 'Regnum a regibus dictum'; and see Werner, 'Regnum', in *LMA* 7, col. 587.

[163] Moeglin, 'Die historiographische Konstruktion', p. 354; Reynolds, *Kingdoms and Communities*, pp. 323–4.

[164] Werner, 'Regnum', in *LMA* 7, col. 587.

[165] For Lupold's conception of the Empire and its relation to German identities, see below, Ch. 6, pp. 267–8.

[166] 'Vis iura regni et imperii, bona eiusdem iniuste dispersa conservare et recuperare et fideliter in usu regni et imperii dispensare?' The question first appears in a coronation ordo of 1309, but it has been convincingly shown that the same question was put to Rudolf I in 1273: see Schubert, 'Königswahl', p. 321 with n. 27.

[167] *Ellenhardi chronicon*, ed. Jaffé, p. 126. See also *Vita Henrici archiepiscopi altera*, ed. Waitz, p. 462, indicating that the pseudo-emperor intended Rudolf to rule under him as king: '[Tile Kolup] misit litteras suas Rodolpho Romanorum regi, ut ipsum tamquam dominum suum recognosceret tali intersigno et quod rex quondam sub ipso militasset.'

he was prepared to assent.[168] The chronicler Heinrich von Diessenhofen depicted Pope Benedict XII commanding Ludwig IV to lay down 'the governance of *regnum* and *imperium*' as a precondition for reconciliation.[169] Matthias von Neuenburg, while seldom speaking explicitly of a 'German' realm, did employ the dual form *regnum et imperium*.[170]

Elsewhere, however, Matthias himself reveals some of the term's troublesome depths and ambiguities. He thus tells how in 1315 Frederick of Habsburg put on display at Basel the imperial insignia, 'which are called "*regnum*"'.[171] Yet in a later passage, Matthias recounts how in 1350 the Wittelsbacher surrendered up to Charles IV the self-same insignia, 'which are called "*imperium*"'.[172] In the writings of Alexander von Roes, the term's 'imperialising' is complete: the *regnum* was the secular counterpart of the Christian priesthood (*sacerdotium*), with a comparable world mission; it was thus an *imperiale regnum*, describable in its full universal scope as 'the unity of the *imperium* or *regnum*'.[173] But, despite all this, territorial kingdoms were also for Alexander *regna*.[174] A similar picture is observable in documents from the royal chancery, where *regnum* again often appears interchangeably with *imperium*, and is found combined in much the same range of standard phrases.[175] The distinction between 'royal' and 'imperial' titles was further elided in the common forms *regnum Romanum* and *regnum Romanorum*, to be found in both documentary and narrative sources.[176] By the early fourteenth century the process of blurring reached a new stage with the tautological *regnum seu imperium*.[177]

Discerning a 'German' kingdom with any clarity and consistency through the opaque Latin terminology is no easy matter. It grows harder with the passage of time, as events and changing habits of usage combined to wear away such distinctions as there had once been. Yet turning to vernacular documents and texts discloses a whole new field

---

[168] *MGC* 3, no. 340, p. 326 (27 July 1282).

[169] *Heinricus Dapifer de Diessenhoven*, ed. Huber, p. 26.

[170] *Die Chronik des Mathias von Neuenburg*, ed. Hofmeister, pp. 10–11, 54, 273.

[171] Ibid., pp. 100–1.   [172] Ibid., p. 444.

[173] Alexander von Roes, *Memoriale*, cap. 10 (*imperiale regnum*), cap. 12 (*regnum – sacerdotium*); *Noticia seculi*, cap. 8 (*unitas imperii sive regni*): ed. Grundmann and Heimpel, pp. 101, 102, 155.

[174] E.g. *Memoriale*, cap. 16, p. 111, for the Thuringian kingdom established by the Franks.

[175] Such as *status, reformatio, consuetudo*. For an example of each, see: *Eine Wiener Briefsammlung*, ed. Redlich, no. 247, pp. 244–5; *MGC* 3, no. 15, p. 19; *Urkundenregesten*, ed. Diestelkamp and Rödel, no. 522, p. 362.

[176] E.g. *MGC* 3, nos. 427, 433, pp. 412, 421; *Ellenhardi chronicon*, ed. Jaffé, p. 127; *Continuatio Vindobonensis*, ed. Wattenbach, p. 704.

[177] Schubert, *König und Reich*, pp. 235–6.

of problems, and opens up perspectives on the constitutional assumptions of thirteenth- and fourteenth-century Germans largely invisible from Latin writings. In the vernacular, even the façade of a unitary German *regnum*, reassuringly familiar in its seeming parallels with other European kingdoms, crumbles entirely. The term had no direct German translation, a handful of rare and anomalous formations apart.[178] The specific form 'kingdom' (*künicrîche*), though in other contexts well established in Middle High German, was seldom used to denote the Empire's German lands in their political aspect.[179] Instead, we find vernacular counterparts – *lant* and, less commonly, *rîche* – which often appear in the plural when combined with a 'German' appellation. Thus, to cite for the moment just a single example, Jakob Twinger claimed that Henry VII was accompanied on his Italian expedition by contingents 'from all the towns in the German lands' (*in dütschen landen*).[180] But consideration is more conveniently given elsewhere to the rather different, more flexible, conceptions of a German community which the vernacular permitted. Let us therefore turn now to another framework within which a German realm might find expression: in the broadest sense institutions, and the forms of political life more generally.[181]

German government, German society

Offices of the Reich with a 'German' title were few and insubstantial. One which at least had tradition on its side was the archchancellorship exercised by the archbishops of Mainz 'throughout Germany' – *per Germaniam*, or, in the plural form customary in the vernacular, *in Dutschen landen*.[182] The Mainz archchancellorship already had quite a long, if fluctuating, history by the thirteenth century, and the forms through which it was invoked were standard and commonplace in archiepiscopal and other documents.[183] In the fourteenth century, Mainz's title was set in stone through its acknowledgement in the Golden Bull

---

[178] See Hugelmann, *Stämme*, p. 397.
[179] *Mittelhochdeutsches Handwörterbuch*, ed. Lexer, i.1775. For a rare example of its use, see *Sächsische Weltchronik: erste Bairische Fortsetzung*, ed. Weiland, p. 328: because of Rudolf of Habsburg's fame *uber elliu Dautschen lant*, the electors bestowed on him *daz chuenichrich*.
[180] *Chronik des Jacob Twinger*, ed. Hegel, p. 462.
[181] For vernacular forms, see below, Ch. 10, pp. 472–3.
[182] For an example of each form, see: *MGC* 3, no. 1, p. 7; *RTA* 1, ed. Weizsäcker, no. 2, p. 10.
[183] Buchner, 'Die Entstehung', p. 4 with n. 2. Mainz's archchancellorship attained a renewed prominence in the late Staufer period.

(as also were the archchancellorship for Italy pertaining to the archbishop of Cologne and Trier's archchancellorship for Gaul and Arles).[184] But Mainz's office, like the others, was largely ceremonial, despite the ambitions occasionally shown by its incumbents to exploit it as a basis for intervention in imperial politics.[185] There is in this period no sign that the Empire's territorial divisions were reflected in the organisation or work of the chancery itself. Above all, the title reflected the honorific primacy to which the archbishops laid claim when the monarch was in Germany: the Golden Bull confirmed his privilege of sitting at the ruler's right hand throughout the lands of his 'Germanic chancellorship' (*cancellariatus Germanicus*), Cologne province excepted.[186]

Suggestive of the more territorially limited view of the Empire which gained ground in the later Middle Ages, with its tendency to confuse the bounds of *imperium* and *regnum*, is a limitation which was applied to the Mainz archchancellorship (an indication, it might be added, that at least some Germans kept the office in mind).[187] The Strasbourg chronicle of Fritsche Closener (completed in 1362) declared that Mainz's title covered *Germania*, 'that is to say, from Hungary to the Rhine'. Trier's archchancellorship, meanwhile, was for Gaul (*Gallia*), 'namely, here on this side of the Lombard mountains in the German lands'.[188] Alexander von Roes, writing several decades before, while acknowledging Trier's authority over Gaul, had glossed Mainz's *archicancellarius Germanie* as 'all of Germany' (*totius Alamanie*): a less obviously restricted application.[189] It seems to have been during the 'Interregnum' that the archchancellorship over the kingdom of Arles, traditionally exercised by the archbishops of Vienne, was transformed into an office in Trier's hands.[190] On one early view, Trier's responsibility was likewise for

---

[184] *Die Goldene Bulle*, ed. Fritz, pp. 54, 57.
[185] Particularly Archbishop Gerhard II in the time of Adolf of Nassau: Bresslau, *Urkundenlehre*, vol. I, pp. 518–19. Mainz's archchancellorship was also, however, invoked as providing a constitutional foundation for the archbishop's right to the first voice in elections: thus, *MGC* 4.i, no. 17, p. 15 (23 September 1298).
[186] *Die Goldene Bulle*, ed. Fritz, p. 57. Mainz's privilege in *Germaniae partes* was noted by the Königsaal chronicler, who also listed the three archchancellorships: *Königsaaler Geschichts-Quellen*, ed. Loserth, p. 273.
[187] See Stengel, 'Regnum', pp. 194–5.
[188] *Fritsche (Friedrich) Closener's Chronik*, ed. Hegel, p. 35; and see also below, Ch. 10, p. 458. The same bounds were given by Twinger, following Closener: *Chronik des Jacob Twinger*, ed. Hegel, pp. 425–6.
[189] Alexander von Roes, *Memoriale*, cap. 24, ed. Grundmann and Heimpel, pp. 124–5.
[190] Bresslau, *Urkundenlehre*, vol. I, pp. 513–17. The matter is uncertain since, as Buchner emphasised, there is no evidence of a Trier archchancellorship under the 'Interregnum' kings, and the archbishop himself only appears to have begun using the title early in the fourteenth century: Buchner, 'Entstehung', pp. 25–7.

Arles.[191] But another version, popularised by the chronicle of Martin of Troppau, names the archchancellor's sphere of action, more ambiguously, as 'Gaul'.[192] The triad of archchancellorships for the Empire's three main territorial blocs – Germany, Italy and Burgundy – had thus become confusingly overlaid with a division of responsibilities *within* the northern *regnum* itself.[193] By the time of the Golden Bull, Trier's title had in fact been enlarged to include both 'Arles' and 'Gaul', and the same expanded form was employed by the archbishops themselves.[194] But Closener's limitation of Mainz's *Germania* to lands beyond the Rhine (which had on its side the authority of classical geography) is revealing, pointing, as it seems, to a free-floating, subjective quality in the archchancellor's office: a capacity for silent readjustment in line with shifting perceptions of the Reich itself. This in turn underlines just how bereft was Mainz's title both of institutional anchoring and of everyday importance in government.

A 'German' administrative sphere of a still less stable kind was conjured fleetingly into being in the numerous vicariates which the Empire's rulers bestowed upon native and foreign princes, to administer the northern properties of the Reich, particularly in times of the monarch's own absence. These were by their nature temporary, without institutional foundations of their own. Their substance and consequences differed widely. Examining the scope ascribed to them reveals much variety, geographical as well as terminological, though seldom real precision. Sometimes a vicar's responsibilities extended beyond 'Germany', to include the kingdom of Arles, or, as in the vicariate bestowed in 1327 on John of Bohemia, *Sclavia*, meaning the more easterly parts of the *regnum*.[195] Or a vicar might be charged more generally to act 'in the German lands [*in Tutschen landen*] and in all the other lands on this side of the Lombard mountains'.[196] The complete dispensability of *regnum* in contexts signifying 'German' government is clear from its absence from the terms of vicariates – although its rough vernacular counterpart,

[191] *Schwabenspiegel*, ed. Eckhardt, *Landrecht*, cap. 128/132, p. 192: 'der bischof von trierl ist chantzeler ze dem chvnichriche ze arle'. The archbishop of Mainz is also listed, as 'chantzeler ze tvetschen landen'.

[192] Bresslau, *Urkundenlehre*, vol. I, p. 514 with n. 5, rejecting Buchner's view (Buchner, 'Entstehung', pp. 6–8) that Martin *invented* Trier's archchancellorship for Gaul.

[193] The significance of the change was underlined by Kern, *Ausdehnungspolitik*, p. 20; and see also the comments of Schnell, 'Deutsche Literatur', pp. 263–5.

[194] *Die Goldene Bulle*, ed. Fritz, p. 50; Buchner, 'Entstehung', pp. 37, 41–4.

[195] *Acta*, ed. Böhmer, no. 622, p. 434 (13 September 1310); *Nova Alamanniae*, vol. I, no. 175, p. 98 (February 1327).

[196] *Acta*, ed. Winkelmann, vol. II, no. 908, p. 585 (24 February 1367).

the plural 'German lands', was regularly employed.[197] In Latin documents, the hesitancy and confusion which tended to surround the use of *Germania* emerges sharply. In 1349, Charles IV appointed the son of the duke of Brabant to govern in the king's absence 'in our kingdom of the Romans [*Romanorum regnum*] throughout *Germania* or *Theutonia*'.[198] While the addition of a second German title might here have been intended to denote the vicar's powers in 'German' lands on both sides of the Rhine, elsewhere it appears merely tautological. The huge vicariate which in 1396 Wenceslas entrusted to his half-brother Sigismund included among its territories all of both *Germania* and *Alemania* (as well as, listed separately, Brabant, Lotharingia and Flanders).[199] In fact, there are signs that we may be ill-advised to put too much stress on the precise wording of such documents, or agonise too long over their terminological nuances. In 1338, Ludwig IV made known the appointment of King Edward III of England as imperial vicar 'throughout all of *Alemannia* and *Germania*'; yet in a document issued at the same time for Edward himself, the king's office is described – with the evident aim of advancing the English king's political objectives – as extending 'throughout Germany [*Alemannia*] and Gaul [*Gallia*], and all their provinces or regions'.[200] Whether 'Gaul' here denotes merely the Empire's German lands in the west or (as is more likely) some larger, less determinate sphere, is impossible to establish conclusively.[201] Merely the fact that it was not felt necessary to accord such seemingly critical matters written clarification is itself suggestive. But even more startling is the use of different terms, denoting, it seems, an office of quite different geographical scope, in two writings concerning the self-same appointment. Not only was there no territorial continuity between vicariates; even within a single grant, the surviving documents attest a strange and disconcerting lack of fixity.

Especially opaque was the 'German' sphere of responsibility periodically ascribed to the Count Palatine of the Rhine. This prince, whose office was held to descend from the Carolingian mayors of the palace, was credited with a range of duties, filling an absent ruler's place, within

---

[197] For the political meaning of 'German lands', see below, Ch. 6, pp. 263–6.
[198] *Acta*, ed. Winkelmann, vol. II, no. 716, p. 445 (January? 1349).
[199] *RTA* 2, no. 247, p. 429 (13 March 1396).
[200] For both texts, see Offler, 'England', pp. 611–13. Matthias von Neuenburg echoed the terms of the public notification of Edward's appointment, as imperial vicar-general 'per Germaniam et Theutoniam': *Die Chronik des Mathias von Neuenburg*, ed. Hofmeister, p. 150.
[201] See Schwedler, *Herrschertreffen*, p. 62; and for Anglo-imperial objectives west of the imperial frontier at this time, Offler, 'England', p. 613.

a fluctuating field of action. According to the *Schwabenspiegel*, compiled in southern Germany in the 1270s, he could be empowered to act as judge in the affairs of princes on the king's departure from Germany (*vert der chvenich von tvetschem lande*).[202] Ludwig IV's quarrel with John XXII raised questions about the right to administer the Empire's lands during vacancies, with Ludwig's supporters insisting that this power belonged to the Count Palatine, 'especially in Germany' (*in partibus Alemanie*).[203] In the Golden Bull, however, his sphere of action as regent during vacancies is confined to the Rhineland, Swabia and lands under Frankish law (with the duke of Saxony holding parallel powers in Saxon-law regions).[204] This, it might be added, is but one illustration of the almost complete invisibility in the Golden Bull – arguably the single most important constitutional document in the entire history of the Reich – of any explicitly German governmental sphere.

But in other aspects of the Empire's constitutional life, and in other legal texts, the German lands are credited with more substance, and with a more binding constitutional character. The vernacular *Sachsenspiegel* informed its readers that feudal service was owed to the Reich only 'within the [lands of the] German tongue, which are subject to the Roman king and Empire'.[205] The obligation on the princes to answer the ruler's summons to court was confined to 'German soil' (*dudescher art*), a limitation subsequently reinforced in the *Schwabenspiegel*, where it was stated that princes and other nobles 'are to attend court in the German lands [*ze tvetschen landen*] and not beyond'.[206] A diploma of Charles IV stipulated that fiefs were to be received 'on German soil' (*auf einem duetschem ertreiche*).[207] Frederick II's contention, that a 'German court' (*curia Alemanie*) was in session wherever the emperor and his princes happened to be, proved vain, and those of his successors who found their way into Italy did not attempt to summon Germans to assemblies there.[208] The

---

[202] *Schwabenspiegel*, ed. Eckhardt, *Landrecht*, cap. 123/127, p. 188.

[203] *MGC* 5, no. 909, p. 732 (22 May 1324); and see also *Nova Alamanniae*, vol. I, no. 583, p. 392 (after 16 July 1338). Heinrich von Herford, who also mentions the Count Palatine's powers, ascribed their origin to Charlemagne, who transferred the Empire *in Theutonicos*: *Liber de rebus memorabilioribus*, ed. Potthast, p. 240.

[204] *Die Goldene Bulle*, ed. Fritz, p. 59.

[205] *Sachsenspiegel Lehnrecht*, cap. 4 § 1, ed. Eckhardt, p. 22. For the equation of 'German tongue' and 'German lands', see below, Ch. 10, p. 481.

[206] *Sachsenspiegel Landrecht* III, cap. 64 § 1, ed. Eckhardt, p. 249. Cf. *Schwabenspiegel*, ed. Eckhardt, *Landrecht*, cap. 139/143, p. 203.

[207] *MGC* 10, no. 4, p. 3 (8 January 1350).

[208] Hugelmann, *Stämme*, p. 447. See also ibid., pp. 438–40, for the struggle (1226) between the bishop and burghers of Cambrai, with Frederick's rebuttal of the latter (who had insisted that their obligation to answer was confined to *curia Alemanie*), with the declaration that 'ibi sit Alemanie curia, ubi persona nostra et principes imperii consistunt'.

inability, already noted, of the Luxemburger to draw the nobles and towns of the Reich to meetings in Bohemia or elsewhere in their dynastic lands lends further substance to the perception that there existed a German political community, with which rulers were bound by custom to meet on 'German soil'.

The vernacular law codes of the thirteenth century, while they emphasise the distinctiveness of ancient legal communities such as the Saxons and Swabians, therefore also present the 'German lands' as together constituting a sphere within which certain legal acts had force.[209] An important question, then, is whether this view found reflection in the public documents of the Empire's rulers. In some significant cases it did. It was from 'the bounds of Germany' (*de finibus Alemannie*) that Frederick II's constitution on heretics (1232) had declared it the emperor's will to eradicate 'the brood of heretical perdition'.[210] And just as the *Schwabenspiegel* had included stipulations about the quality of coins to be minted 'in the German lands' (*in tvtschen landen*), so royal legislation on the subject explicitly adopted these same bounds.[211] 'The German lands' were invoked in a statute issued by Wenceslas in 1382, as the sphere within which controls on the coinage were to have force.[212] The king's actions were nothing new: a decree of Rudolf I from 1282 had likewise regulated mints *in regno Alamanie*.[213] Other acts of rule similarly had effect within a German legal landscape. It was specifically from 'the German lands' (and not from the Reich more generally) that in 1403 King Rupert banished two knights implicated in the death of the duke of Braunschweig-Lüneburg.[214] Similar assumptions seem to underlie a chronicler's report of how, after overcharging Rudolf I's queen for a carriage, the bishop of Speyer 'had to vacate the German lands until after the king's death'.[215]

Germany also provided the frame for an array of specific mandates and concessions issued by rulers. Frederick II had in 1237 forbidden

---

[209] For Germany as a sphere of law, see also below, Ch. 11, pp. 505–6.

[210] *MGC* 2, no. 158, p. 197.

[211] *Schwabenspiegel*, ed. Eckhardt, *Landrecht*, cap. 204, p. 273.

[212] *RTA* 1, no. 201, pp. 354–5. See also ibid., no. 257, p. 474, in which Wenceslas instructs the town of Rothenburg ob der Tauber to allow his counsellor Johann von Leuchtenberg to strike coins in the town 'mit sulchen korne und ufsacz als wir in Dutschen landen zu slahen zu rate worden sein...' (15 January 1385).

[213] *MGC* 3, no. 335, p. 322.

[214] *RTA* 5, no. 333, p. 452. The terms of the banishment reveal further interesting assumptions. The two men were to depart German soil 'und in Dutsche lande nicht wiederkommen in zehen jahren'. But after the first four years had elapsed, Rupert retained the right to permit them to return 'home' (*herheim zu ziehen*).

[215] *Sächsische Weltchronik: erste Bairische Fortsetzung*, ed. Weiland, p. 329.

counts 'throughout Germany' (*per Teotoniam*) to place the townspeople of Constance under the imperial bann.[216] A century later, it was to all the Faithful living 'in Germany' (*in Almania*) that Ludwig IV made known the right of Goslar's burghers to hold fiefs.[217] A grant of May 1346 permitted imperial towns 'in the German lands' to impose on the Venetians and other Italians the same dues as were levied on them.[218] A list of promises which Charles IV made in 1374 to Archbishop Kuno of Trier included an undertaking to protect the clergy 'in the German lands'.[219] A German sphere was also sometimes invested with binding force within political agreements: Charles IV promised, in a treaty with Count Palatine Rudolf, 'at no time to ally with anyone in the German lands', without excluding Rudolf as a possible adversary.[220] Wenceslas, as arbitrator between the bishop of Speyer and the Count Palatine, was to give judgement 'at Mainz or Frankfurt, or wherever he chooses *in Dutschen landen*'.[221] The towns of the Wetterau and Alsace promised in 1387 faithfully to aid the king 'in these German lands and here on this side of the mountains' against anyone seeking to oust him from the throne.[222]

Declarations of a more general kind concerning royal government might also take a German frame of reference. In December 1378 Wenceslas wrote to the town of Strasbourg, announcing his imminent arrival 'in the German lands' where, with the advice of the princes, he would 'ordain what is good and useful for the lands and the Reich'.[223] Specifically, this would doubtless have been taken as a promise to uphold the public peace. Establishing and safeguarding peace and order, in the eyes of Germans of the day the main duty which lay upon their ruler, was itself ascribed a German setting, in official acts and, more commonly, in contemporary imagination. Wenceslas declared in his *Landfriede* of March 1383 that he had allied with the princes and towns against all peace-breakers 'here on this side of the Lombard mountains, in all German lands and in our kingdom of Bohemia'.[224] Henry VII was a 'king of justice' (*rex iustitiae*), 'who placed all regions of Germany [*omnes partes Alemanniae*] under perfect tranquillity and peace'.[225] Rudolf I, for one observer, had made 'a great peace throughout Germany, from the

[216] *Acta*, ed. Winkelmann, vol. II, no. 1236, p. 889.
[217] *Acta*, ed. Böhmer, no. 795, p. 536 (3 November 1340).
[218] Ibid., no. 818, p. 549.   [219] *RTA* 1, no. 3, p. 13.
[220] *Acta*, ed. Winkelmann, vol. II, no. 771, p. 480 (15 July 1353).
[221] *RTA* 1, no. 172, p. 297 (8 September 1380).
[222] Ibid., no. 307, p. 551.   [223] Ibid., no. 125, p. 230.
[224] Ibid., no. 205, p. 372.
[225] *Königsaaler Geschichts-Quellen*, ed. Loserth, p. 335.

mountains of Italy to the waters of the English sea'.[226] Other remarks in similar vein have already been encountered elsewhere.[227]

And if 'Germany' supplied a measure for the establishment of peace, it was also made the backdrop to its collapse. Of the war which accompanied Albert I's clash with the Rhineland electors an Erfurt chronicler wrote, with by now familiar exaggeration, that 'this plague infested the bounds of almost all Germany' (*tocius fere Alamannie fines*).[228] The king, insisted a petition from the city of Cologne to the Curia, could not ignore the 'clamour of the entire population of Germany' (*tocius populi Almanie*), raised against the new tolls which his princely opponents had established on the Rhine.[229] Germany was not only the zone within which the good ruler built harmony, but also the stage upon which a bad one might oversee its destruction. A report which reached Nuremberg at the time of Wenceslas's deposition told of how, at a meeting in Kuttenberg (Kutná Hora) in Bohemia, the herald 'Sassenlant' had excoriated the king to his face for letting himself become 'a negligent and wicked man, and idle in the German lands'.[230] An envoy of the town of Frankfurt similarly recorded among the grounds for Wenceslas's removal that 'he permits robbery, arson [and] murder throughout the length and breadth of Germany' (*als wide als Dutschelant ist*).[231]

But the 'Germany' which late medieval writers summoned up was more than just a flat backcloth onto which the actions or omissions of the Empire's rulers were at times projected. It was also a community of political actors, with and through whom the monarch was bound to rule. It was from 'the German lands' that participants were drawn to assemblies to discuss the affairs of the Reich.[232] The main components of such a German community were the princes, headed by the electors, other members of the nobility and the towns, especially those which were subject directly to the Reich. Heinrich von Diessenhofen repeatedly noted Charles IV's dealings with 'the electors and burghers' or 'the nobles and burghers' of the *regnum Alemannie*.[233] Each of these groups,

---

[226] *Ellenhardi chronicon*, ed. Jaffé, p. 124. The same chronicler subsequently made another, similar claim for Rudolf's peace-keeping: 'Et sic facta est pax in tota terra Swevie, ab Alpibus montium Ytalie usque ad Traiectum [i.e. Utrecht] super fluvium Reni, et quievit omnis Alemania in conspectu eius.'

[227] Above, Ch. 3, pp. 123–4.

[228] *Cronica S. Petri Erfordensis Moderna*, ed. Holder-Egger, p. 322 (for 1301).

[229] *MGC* 4.i, no. 131, p. 106 (May 1301).

[230] *RTA* 3, no. 250, p. 305.

[231] Ibid., no. 212, p. 272 (20 August 1400).

[232] A meeting at Frankfurt am Main arranged for 13 May 1397 was to be attended by 'fursten geistlich ind werentlich graven herren und steden van Duytschen landen': *RTA* 2, no. 251, p. 440.

[233] *Heinricus Dapifer de Diessenhoven*, ed. Huber, pp. 72, 88, 101.

it should be stressed, was routinely identified as German. About the princes and their constitutional role, it will be necessary to say more elsewhere.[234] The assimilation of the towns to the Empire's established bearers of power is characteristic of the times. An article in the statutes of the imperial town of Dortmund (1250) invoked 'all the cities of Germany [*civitates Teutonie*] which are in the Roman Empire'.[235] A continuator of the vernacular, rhymed *Kaiserchronik* lauded Rudolf I's rapid mastery over all the imperial towns in Germany – *übr al des riches stete / die er in Tiutschen landen hete*.[236] Without acceptance by this German political community, or at least a substantial portion of it, a king, in practice, could not rule. With this in mind, a hostile chronicler observed how Ludwig IV 'draws to him with threats and blandishments the ecclesiastical and secular princes and the cities of the Empire in Germany'.[237] In 1401 King Rupert instructed an envoy to reassure Pope Boniface XI that, as regards the state of Germany (*de statu Almanie*), he believed the king to have the obedience of all the imperial towns.[238] At times when the throne was disputed, where these key – German – political actors chose to bestow their allegiance was a matter of grave importance, to be studied keenly. 'All the cities of the Empire in Germany gave their support to King Charles [IV], except for three which assisted [Günther] of Schwarzburg, namely Frankfurt, Friedberg, [and] Gelnhausen', noted a chronicler for the year 1349.[239]

Late medieval writers persisted in viewing the German lands, despite all the evidence for their divisions and diversity, as constituting a single community of experience under the monarch, all alike thriving under a good ruler and suffering together under an evil or unlucky one. But they also treated Germany, more prosaically, as a natural and appropriate frame within which to narrate, explain and evaluate the deeds of their kings, and the political fortunes of the Reich. The imposter Tile Kolup 'led a great part of Germany into error'.[240] Ludwig IV raised forces to expel his rival, Charles of Moravia, 'from the bounds of Germany' (*a finibus Alamanie*).[241] Several years later, with peace established between the Luxemburger and his former Wittelsbach foes, we read instead of how 'Margrave Ludwig [of Brandenburg] allowed

---

[234] Below, Ch. 6, pp. 270–8.
[235] *Hansische Geschichtsquellen* 3, cited in Hugelmann, *Stämme*, p. 394.
[236] *Kaiserchronik*, ed. Schröder, pp. 415–16, vv. 406–11.
[237] *Königsaaler Geschichts-Quellen*, ed. Loserth, p. 483.
[238] *RTA* 4, no. 11, p. 30.
[239] *Die Chronik Heinrichs Taube*, ed. Bresslau, p. 95.
[240] *Annales Sancti Rudberti Salisburgenses*, ed. Wattenbach, p. 809.
[241] *Die Chronik Johanns von Winterthur*, ed. Baethgen, p. 263.

King Charles to travel freely throughout Germany' (*per Theutoniam*).[242] Germany was also a space within which, rhetorically at least, writers could offer comparative judgements through implicit appeal to common memory. The forces which Albert I raised against Bohemia were, for the Lübeck chronicler Detmar, so large that 'no greater army upon great horses had at that time ever been seen in the German lands'.[243] In the *Saxon World Chronicle*, a more remote military engagement, Otto I's triumph at the Lech in 955, was recalled as 'one of the greatest victories ever won on German soil'.[244] Not only events, but also rumours about the monarchy were given a German setting. Johann von Winterthur records under the year 1343 how 'the word went around quite commonly throughout the whole land of Germany' (*per universam terram Germanie*) that the electors were raising up Ludwig IV's brother-in-law, Count William of Holland, as a rival pretender to the throne.[245] An Austrian annalist noted for 1284 how 'very great rumours resounded throughout almost all of Germany, about the coming of a certain emperor Frederick'.[246] The 'German lands' not only attained for late medieval writers a kind of unity, however nominal, when the deeds of their monarchs were recounted; they also, it seems, constituted a space for imagining the politics of the Reich fitting and obvious enough not to require great reflection or justification. The imperial monarchy, its attainments and its crises, had a home in Germany.

Germany came first. Not only was the new king obliged to begin by securing the backing of the leading political actors there; his first duties of government lay in Germany also. It was his care for 'noble *Germania*, our illustrious young bride', that Ludwig IV emphasised in a mandate of February 1327.[247] The Königsaal chronicle tells how numerous envoys came to Henry VII from Italy, inviting the king to 'their most

---

[242] *Liber de rebus memorabilioribus*, ed. Potthast, p. 284.

[243] *Detmar-Chronik*, ed. Koppmann, i.404. For a similar report, see *Limburger Chronik*, ed. Wyss, pp. 81–2: in 1388 the king of France entered Germany with forces which, in size and magnificence, had never been seen *in Duschen landen*.

[244] *Sächsische Weltchronik*, ed. Weiland, p. 162. The account follows that in the universal chronicle of Ekkehard, which, however, does not have the *Saxon World Chronicle*'s Germanising language: *Ekkehardi chronicon universale*, ed. Waitz, p. 189.

[245] *Die Chronik Johanns von Winterthur*, ed. Baethgen, p. 201. See also, e.g., the claim of Heinrich Taube, under the year 1333, that a rumour current in *Alamania* expected Ludwig IV to renounce the realm in favour of Duke Henry of Lower Bavaria: *Die Chronik Heinrichs Taube*, ed. Bresslau, pp. 45–6.

[246] *Continuatio Vindobonensis*, ed. Wattenbach, p. 712.

[247] *Nova Alamanniae*, vol. I, no. 175, p. 98. For Charles IV, in a commission of vice-regal powers in the Empire's northern lands to Balduin of Trier (9 December 1346), 'noble *Germania*' was the 'youthful bride of the Roman realm and Empire': *MGC* 8, no. 144, p. 224.

strong cities'. But before setting out Henry 'first arranged to visit all the cities of the Empire in Germany, and to establish in them a fitting state of affairs'. Only then did he prepare for his journey into Italy.[248] Rulers themselves acknowledged in their official acts the same order of priorities. In a letter of 1338, Ludwig IV informed the Venetians that he would be coming south once he had dealt with 'German business' (*negocia Alemanie*).[249] 'Having resolved all things throughout Germany', declared a letter of Rudolf I, 'we are turning our minds to Tuscany.'[250] Germany was the prime locus of imperial power politics, to be mastered before all else: so much was beyond dispute. With King William of Holland dead, claimed a fourteenth-century chronicler – characteristically, mistaking the facts but not the imperatives of political life in the 'Interregnum' – Konrad of Hohenstaufen was able to set out for Sicily, 'because he no longer faced any obstacle in Germany'.[251] No king was well advised to tarry south of the Alps when the work of government urged him north. King Rupert's own hasty departure from Italy had been necessary, he explained, 'because we … were at that time better able to promote the benefit and advantage of the holy Reich from here in the German lands than we believe, even with God's help, we could have done had we remained in Lombardy'.[252] Not to recognise this basic truth of power could have fatal consequences. 'Because the emperor Frederick [II] was in distant parts, and died so suddenly that he did not defend himself in the German lands against his opponents, the common people said that he had been driven out, and that no one knew where he was.'[253]

More positive considerations also urged the priority of the Empire's German territories. Their human and material resources, insufficient though these may have been, remained indispensable to any large-scale ventures which the Empire's rulers might aspire to undertake. In *Heinrich von Kempten*, a chivalric tale dating from the time of Rudolf I, the poet Konrad von Würzburg had the abbot of Kempten inform the eponymous hero that the emperor – at the time in the south – 'has sent

---

[248] *Königsaaler Geschichts-Quellen*, ed. Loserth, pp. 335–6. See also: *Die Chronik Johanns von Winterthur*, ed. Baethgen, p. 60 (Henry VII pacified *tota Alemania* before entering Italy); *Liber de rebus memorabilioribus*, ed. Potthast, p. 227 (having set things in order in *Thetonia*, Henry crossed into Italy). For a similar turn of phrase in relation to Frederick II's departure for Italy (*ordinatis regni Alemanie negociis …*), see *Die Chronik der Grafen von der Mark*, ed. Zschaeck, p. 36.

[249] *Acta*, ed. Böhmer, no. 780, p. 527.

[250] *MGC* 3, no. 371, p. 353.

[251] *Liber certarum historiarum*, ed. Schneider, i.193 (under the year 1251!).

[252] *RTA* 5, no. 255, p. 337 (16 June 1402).

[253] *Detmar-Chronik*, ed. Koppmann, i.333.

into the German lands for warriors'.[254] Art here reflected life with precision. In 1354 Charles IV, from Mantua, 'wrote to the cities of Germany and to the bishops and others, that they should send him armed men as was the custom'.[255] Hard experience taught just how fundamental was the ruler's dependence on his German realm for expeditions beyond its bounds. In 1405, King Rupert's envoy was charged with informing Pope Innocent VII, to excuse his master's continued failure to come to Rome, that 'the princes and lords spiritual and temporal who belong to the Empire in the German lands are neither ready nor prepared to journey with our lord at their own cost into Lombardy'.[256]

Yet the primacy which the German lands attained when thought was given to the Empire's government rested on more than just the common-sense imperatives of power. It was also, it is clear, an *ideal* primacy – albeit, for many writers, one taken for granted, rather than explicitly named or reflected upon. In important ways, precisely the fact that imperial government was about more than just Germany served to place its German component in a starker relief than would otherwise have been attainable. Rulers are repeatedly to be found bestowing grateful rewards on nobles who had served them faithfully 'both in Italy and in Germany' (*tam in partibus Ytalie quam Alamanie*), or 'here in the German lands' and in Lombardy.[257] To invoke the Empire characteristically meant invoking Germany. Rudolf I, in one annalist's terse valedictory jottings, 'ruled for seventeen years in Germany [*Alemannia*], and did not enter Italy'.[258] When the king or emperor did set off south, the German lands might be named by chroniclers noting his departure, characteristically at the head of an armed force. But far more commonplace were references to Germany in context of his return – 'over the mountains into *Dudeschland*', wrote Detmar in Lübeck, his gaze set on the distant Alps.[259]

The Alps rose up as an elemental barrier, before which constitutional terminology and German political imagination alike made pause, in order to mark a significant transition. The archbishop of Cologne, as Italian archchancellor, thereby became in one documentary formulation 'archchancellor of the Reich for beyond-the-mountains' (*van overberge*).[260] A letter from Strasbourg contemplating withdrawing the

---

[254] Konrad von Würzburg, *Heinrich von Kempten*, p. 30, vv. 439–40.
[255] *Die Chronik des Mathias von Neuenburg* (AU Cont.), ed. Hofmeister, p. 482.
[256] *RTA* 5, ed. Weizsäcker, no. 470, p. 682.
[257] *Acta*, ed. Böhmer, nos. 644, p. 451 (20 March 1312), 783, p. 528 (30 June 1338). See also *Acta*, ed. Winkelmann, vol. II, no. 648, p. 395 (15 June 1344).
[258] *Continuatio Ratisbonensis*, ed. Jaffé, in *MGS* 17, p. 416.
[259] *Detmar-Chronik*, ed. Koppmann, i.463.
[260] *Originalurkunden*, vol. I, no. 25, p. 265 (1275).

town's troops from King Rupert's army aired the view that 'in serving our lord the king beyond the mountains', Strasbourg had already 'done enough', and that it was time for her men to 'ride back home'.[261] 'Home' meant Germany. The idea is strongly suggested in Heinrich von Herford's description of how Ludwig IV, at the end of his Italian expedition, 'returned to Germany [*in Theutoniam*] in strength and with joy, and was received with very great pomp'.[262] It was to 'the German lands' that in 1402, Rupert explained, he had 'come back' from his own dismal Italian adventure.[263] Not only the ruler, but those who went with him on the Empire's affairs were moved to acknowledge Germany as their 'home' in context of journeys beyond its limits. A letter from Mainz explained how that city's contingent with Rupert's army had been given leave to 'ride back into the German lands'; and now that they were 'back home again', Mainz declared, the city was no longer willing to send men into Lombardy – to, as the letter phrases it, 'such a far-off land'.[264]

Plural though the 'German lands' may have been, under their kings, past, present and future, they became nonetheless a significant unity. It was not just that late medieval writers persisted, often against the clear facts, in making them the site of shared political experience. More profoundly, they were also from time to time invoked as a community of political identification and destiny, headed by the ruler of the Reich. The victorious campaign which Rudolf I led, in 1289, into Romance-speaking Burgundy, was for Gottfried von Ensmingen undertaken 'in order to recover the honour and good name of all of Germany'.[265] Ludwig IV declared that, were he to fail to intervene in Italy, to protect her populations against foreign oppression, his neglect would redound to his own shame, that of the electors, the house of Bavaria and the entire German nation.[266] And the 'whole nation of Germany' (*nacio tota Germanie*) was indeed, according to Rudolf Losse, threatened with disgrace through Ludwig's own failure to honour his English alliance.[267] The repute, and with it the common identity, of the German territories was deemed to rest, for good or ill, directly on the triumphs and

---

[261] *RTA* 5, no. 199, p. 261 (14 November 1401).

[262] *Liber de rebus memorabilioribus*, ed. Potthast, p. 246.

[263] *RTA* 5, no. 230, p. 312.

[264] Ibid., no. 206, p. 267 (13 March 1402).

[265] *Ellenhardi chronicon*, ed. Jaffé, p. 128. The report is rendered into the vernacular in *Fritsche (Friedrich) Closener's Chronik*, ed. Hegel, p. 51.

[266] *MGC* 6, no. 266, p. 174.

[267] *Nova Alamanniae*, vol. I, no. 581, p. 389 (September–December 1338). For Lupold Hornburg's argument, in similar vein, to the princes met at Passau in 1348, see below, Ch. 6, pp. 269–70.

humiliations of their kings and emperors. But this was no mere passive relationship, and the Empire's German subjects also had a share in upholding the prestige which accrued to their land within the Reich. The protocol of a meeting of towns at Speyer in 1402 thus averred that those communities 'seek always the honour and benefit of our lord the king, of the Reich, and of Germany'.[268] To fail in that duty was, for writers of the time, to bring disgrace on a polity at once imperial and German.[269]

The German populations under the ruler had, by virtue of their very Germanness, an especially urgent concern for his doings and his fate: that at least is the strong implication of remarks to be encountered in the writings of historiographers and poets. Short, often anonymous, occasional verses thus enjoined 'Germany' to rejoice at a ruler's election to the Empire or his victories in battle, or to weep at his untimely death.[270] A Latin poet perceived in the short-lived Henry VII the 'splendour of realms, radiant light of the Teutons', while for Matthias von Neuenburg Henry was 'the flower of the German race' (*flos germinis Germanorum*).[271] Rhetorical outpourings of emotion might even be extended to other members of the dynasty – at least when that dynasty was the Hohenstaufen. 'All of Germany' (*tota Germania*), as one chronicler imagined, mourned the passing, in 1268, of Frederick II's hapless grandson Konradin.[272] Charles IV's advice to his son and successor was thus reportedly to 'make the Germans your friends'.[273] To do so was no more than tradition required: Charles's own imperial grandfather, Henry VII, was remembered as a 'lover of the German people'.[274] Whatever may have been their accustomed titles, the Empire's rulers were clearly perceived by observers in the north as heading a German political community: in a significant, if not a strictly constitutional, sense they *were* German kings and emperors.

Or were they? Reaching such a view would mean overlooking the polyglot assortment of monarchs and pretenders who contribute so

---

[268] *RTA* 5, no. 347, p. 489: '… unsers herren des koeniges des richs und Dutsches landes ere und frommen…'

[269] See the comments of the Salzburg annalist on the failure of Rudolf I's nobles to be present with him in fitting numbers at the battle of the Marchfeld, cited below, Ch. 8, p. 367.

[270] Examples in Ritscher, *Literatur und Politik*, pp. 16, 18, 21.

[271] Ibid., p. 23; *Die Chronik des Mathias von Neuenburg*, ed. Hofmeister, p. 94.

[272] *Ellenhardi chronicon*, ed. Jaffé, p. 122. And see ibid., p. 133, where the (pro-Habsburg) chronicler reports the death of Rudolf I's son, also Rudolf, in 1290 as being mourned by *Germania*.

[273] *Chronik des Jacob Twinger*, ed. Hegel, p. 493.

[274] In valedictory verses on Henry in Augsburg monastic annals: *Annales SS. Udalrici et Afrae*, ed. Jaffé, p. 435 ('Glorius imperator, Germane gentis amator').

much to the prevailing mood of disjuncture in the history of the post-Staufer Reich. Here, moreover, is surely disjuncture of a kind peculiarly inimical to any idea of 'national' cohesion – an idea which rested, in the Middle Ages, upon the imagined identification of king, kingdom and people.[275] In the Declaration of Arbroath, the case for sovereign independence which representatives of 'the whole community of the realm of Scotland' had in 1320 set before the pope, it was claimed that in the kingdom of the Scots 'one hundred and thirteen kings of their own royal stock have reigned, the line unbroken by a single foreigner'.[276] German partisans of the late medieval Reich could scarcely make a comparable boast. Among the princes raised to the throne were a king of Castile and a brother of the king of England. Members of the French royal dynasty were several times contenders, as were the English kings Edward III and Richard II.[277] For a time, the crown had seemed destined to fall to the Přemyslid Otakar II. Indeed, viewed from one angle, the history of the Reich in the two centuries after 1250 fits a pattern of power which for some scholars characterises the close of the Middle Ages in western Europe: the rise of large, composite dynastic empires, which, it is alleged, came increasingly to overlay, deny and frustrate the nascent 'national' polities formed during the previous centuries.[278]

Few families seem better to embody this spirit of patrimonial empire-building than the restlessly acquisitive house of Luxemburg, under which the imperial title took its place among a dazzling, pan-European array of regnal trophies. Hardly another dynasty appears so loftily to soar above the fray of medieval nation-making. The Luxemburger illuminate in outstanding fashion the international horizons of a European high nobility whose members did not seek their identity in narrow ethnic categories. Associating them with a specifically 'German' sphere of power and culture, moreover, seems singularly inappropriate. Henry VII is thought barely to have understood the language, while his grandson and great-grandsons invested much of their energy in winning allegiance in the lands of their eastern crowns.[279] The Hungarian kingdom held by Sigismund at the time of his election to the Reich was not even within its bounds. The primacy accorded to familial prestige seemed even to seep into the monarch's relationship with the Empire, previously

---

[275] Werner, 'Regnum', in *LMA* 7, col. 587.
[276] The full text is translated in Duncan, *The Nation of Scots*, here p. 35.
[277] For French candidatures, see Zeller, 'Les rois'; for Edward III, Offler, 'England'; for Richard II, Tuck, 'Richard II'.
[278] For this view, see Werner, 'Les Nations', pp. 303–4.
[279] For Henry VII, see Hoensch, *Die Luxemburger*, pp. 25, 31. Henry had spent his formative years at the court of Philip IV of France.

unqualified and absolute. Charles IV, in a break with tradition, incorporated the phrase 'king of Bohemia' into his imperial titles and paired the imperial eagle with the double-tailed Bohemian lion on his seals, thereby conflating imperial and dynastic frames of reference.[280]

German observers were not blind to the new symbolism of power, and seem often to have concurred that the proper categories for understanding the Luxemburg monarchs were first and foremost patrimonial, not national, ones.[281] In this spirit, we find Charles IV referred to as *Karolus Bohemus* or *keiser Karl van Behmen*, while his luckless eldest son was 'king of Bohemia', 'Roman king of Bohemia' or 'King Wenceslas of Bohemia and [almost, it seems, as an afterthought] also Roman king'.[282] In July 1414 a member of the well-informed Veckinchusen merchant family wrote from Cologne to a kinsman in Bruges, reporting on the whereabouts of 'the king of Hungary' – although by that date Sigismund's elevation as king of the *Romans* had enjoyed general recognition for at least three years.[283]

Against such understandable verdicts must, however, be set not only the widespread conviction, to which late medieval writings attest, that the Empire's ruler should rightfully be German, but also the pains which commentators sometimes took to Germanise even the most apparently unpromising candidates. Alexander von Roes was explicit on the matter, demanding that the electors raise to the throne 'a German knight ... just like Charlemagne'.[284] According to the author of the final book of the fourteenth-century *Karlmeinet* compilation, such a principle had been laid down by the Frankish emperor himself. Charles (portrayed as a member of a *French* dynasty!) had stipulated that, after the death of his son Louis, no one who was not 'a German man' should be raised to the throne.[285] Accounts of particular elections indicate a widespread

---

[280] As examples, see the plates in Seibt (ed.), *Kaiser Karl IV.*, pp. 327–8.

[281] It was not only the Luxemburger who might now be treated in this way: for 'koningz Ropert van Beigeren' (Rupert of the Palatinate), see *Cölner Jahrbücher*, ed. Cardauns, p. 95.

[282] For Charles: *Liber de rebus memorabilioribus*, ed. Potthast, p. 274; *Fritsche (Friedrich) Closener's Chronik*, ed. Hegel, p. 101; *Magdeburger Schöppenchronik*, ed. Janicke, p. 330; for Wenceslas: *Cölner Jahrbücher*, ed. Cardauns, p. 85; *Magdeburger Schöppenchronik*, ed. Janicke, p. 296; *Chronik von 1368 bis 1406*, ed. Frensdorff, p. 98. For Wenceslas's own documentary titles, see Hlaváček, *Urkunden- und Kanzleiwesen*, pp. 94–100.

[283] *Hildebrand Veckinchusen: Briefwechsel*, ed. Stieda, no. 98, p. 116; and see also *Cölner Jahrbücher*, ed. Cardauns, p. 51. For the circumstances of Sigismund's elevation and recognition, see Thomas, *Deutsche Geschichte*, pp. 378–9.

[284] Alexander von Roes, *Noticia seculi*, cap. 18, ed. Grundmann and Heimpel, p. 165.

[285] *Karl Meinet*, ed. Keller, A 535, p. 825, vv. 22–7 ('Hey en wer eyn duysch man, / Den vromsten, den man vinden kan'). See also Jostkleigrewe, *Das Bild*, pp. 168–9; and for the Carolingians as a French dynasty, below, Ch. 6, pp. 284–6.

belief that those involved in choosing the monarch endeavoured to see that this was done. And – at least in German imagination – not only the electors: Siegfried von Balnhausen depicted Pope Gregory X sharply demanding of Otakar II, in a rebuff to his imperial pretensions, 'why should we wish to raise up a Slav to the Empire, when we have many princes and counts in Germany?'[286] Outsiders expected to find a German on the throne. A treatise in the name of King Robert of Naples observed (with much distaste) the fact that 'by custom kings of the Romans are generally elected from the German tongue'.[287]

Often, it is in the more unreflective reports of the princes' deliberations that their authors' assumptions are best revealed. Gottfried von Ensmingen portrays the electors, in an attempt to break their deadlock over the choice of Richard of Cornwall's successor, 'recalling to mind all the nobles throughout all the realm of Germany' (*per omnem gyrum Alemanie regionis*); and yet, he explains, 'none of the princes of Germany wanted to assume the rule of the Roman realm'.[288] An occasional remark hints at similar assumptions among the electors themselves: Count Palatine Rupert, in a document promising his vote to Wenceslas, declared that, in his fitness for the Reich, the Luxemburger was 'the best and most beneficial [candidate to be found] in the German lands'.[289]

The colourful array of princes who sought, or actually gained, the throne in the decades after 1250 seems to have done little to shake the conviction that the Empire's rulers were – or at least should be – scions of its German lands. The warning to the princes sounded by the singer 'Meißner', not to let the Reich fall into foreign hands, may have been sounded with a view to the 1257 election.[290] But perhaps not quite all Germans were certain that this was in fact the outcome of that contest. Konrad von Würzburg may have thought he could discern at least the palest shades of a 'German' identity in the English prince Richard of Cornwall. That would, at any rate, be a plausible deduction from his chivalric poem *The Tournament at Nantes*, which pitted a team of princes of Germanic speech, under one 'King Richard of England', against

---

[286] *Sifridi presbyteri de Balnhusin historia*, ed. Holder-Egger, p. 707.
[287] Cited in Jäschke, 'Reichskonzeptionen', p. 432.
[288] *Ellenhardi chronicon*, ed. Jaffé, p. 122. Similar assumptions underlie the lament of the poet Tannhäuser, that no monarch was in his day to be found 'in allen tiutschen richen' to compare with Frederick II: *Politische Lyrik*, ed. Müller, vol. I, p. 47.
[289] *RTA* 1, no. 20, p. 45 (22 February 1375).
[290] 'Meißner', in *Politische Lyrik*, ed. Müller, vol. I, p. 68. The poet urges the German princes ('Diutsche zunge'), 'Gib niht din erbe in vremdiu lant, daz dir din schepfer hat an geerbet.'

Romance-speaking opponents led by the king of France.[291] Even the impossibly cosmopolitan Luxemburger might, it transpired, be made to qualify as Germans. Peter von Zittau, abbot of the Bohemian royal monastery of Königsaal, seems to point the way, with his assertion that the countship of Luxembourg itself lay *in partibus Germaniae*.[292] From such a view, the step was not perhaps a large one to the blunt and startling claims of Jakob Twinger, writing some decades later: 'thus, Charles IV and his son Wenceslas possessed the Reich and were kings of Bohemia; yet they were of German dynasty [*von dütschem geslehte*] – and *had to be* of German dynasty'. They were, he explains, in this respect no different from the Carolingians, who, despite being 'kings of France', were likewise of German stock.[293] Germanness, for the Strasbourg chronicler, was indispensable in those who were to be raised to the throne. Yet its terms were evidently drawn generously enough to accommodate the most unlikely candidates, and thereby to cast a mantle of (ethnic) continuity over that singularly discontinuous institution, the late medieval imperial monarchy.

Peoples – *gentes* – were first and foremost the dark shadows cast upon medieval political mentalities by kingdoms – *regna*: such, it seems, was a prevailing pattern, reproduced throughout Latin Europe.[294] Prevailing, perhaps, but not invariable. 'Reich, state and nation', we are informed, 'never came to coincide in Germany', in the Middle Ages.[295] Let us for now set aside the problem of defining the character and membership of

---

[291] Konrad von Würzburg, *Das Turnier von Nantes*, ed. Schröder, esp. pp. 49–61. The 'Germanic' (*tiusch*) party includes the kings of Denmark and *Schotten*, as well as a number of (German-speaking) imperial princes. The king of Spain (= Alfonso of Castile?), by contrast, is placed among the Germans' opponents, and subordinated to the king of France – a sign, it has been suggested, that the poem was intended to rally support for Richard's kingship, and against his rival. For the work's probable connections with the English candidature and dating (1257/8), see Brunner, 'Das Turnier von Nantes'. (Another view of the poem, however, ascribes to it a later date, linked to the Plantagenet–Habsburg marriage negotiations of 1277–9: Ritscher, *Literatur*, p. 61.)

[292] *Königsaaler Geschichts-Quellen*, ed. Loserth, p. 331.

[293] *Chronik des Jacob Twingers*, ed. Hegel, p. 422. Dietrich von Niem also regarded the Luxemburger as a German dynasty: Heimpel, *Dietrich*, p. 155 n. 1. In Hartmann Schedel's Nuremberg chronicle, from the end of the fifteenth century, Sigismund is identified as 'Bohemian by birth, German in origin' (*natione bohemus, origine theutonicus*): *Liber chronicarum*, p. cclxix. The view was not universal, however. A Mainz chronicler appears to ascribe the crisis of Wenceslas's reign to his Bohemian identity, as well as his proverbial uselessness. The princes met to consider what action to take, 'ex quo ille Bohemus fuit et est inutilis': *Chronicon Moguntinum*, ed. Hegel, p. 229 (1397).

[294] Ehlers, 'Natio. 1. N. (Nation)', in *LMA* 6, col. 1037, as well as Reynolds, *Kingdoms and Communities*, Ch. 8.

[295] Ehlers, 'Natio. 1. N. (Nation)', in *LMA* 6, col. 1037.

the German 'nation': that will concern us in due course.[296] Let us set aside also the unquestionable complicating element of the Reich, the Empire. What, then of the *regnum*, kingdom – or, in a commonplace if not unchallenged extension – the 'state'?[297] That such a kingdom existed north of the Alps should not be lost sight of. It had come into being, like other European realms, within the shifts and chances of late Carolingian dynastic politics, and its existence predated the acquisition of those far-flung 'imperial' appendages with which it was destined subsequently to become bound up. So far, we might say, so straightforward. But almost at once the complexities crowd in. The impulse to name the kingdom as 'German', or to link it with a 'German' people, came relatively late, in the context of its rulers' ventures beyond its frontiers. The impulse came initially from without – and, not for the last time, the papal Curia took a central role. And it came, in part at least, submerged within political currents which seemed to threaten fundamentally the status and powers of the Empire's rulers. Invoking the Germans as political actors was, from early on, bound up with notions both of imperial adventure and of the monarch's abasement and limitation; indefinite prestige and sharply focused taboo, neither favouring the establishment of a stable constitutional language mapping kingdom onto people. The shifting geographic basis of government within the *regnum* was a further inhibition. Consequently, the vocabulary which evolved, of a distinct, 'German', rulership and realm, was simultaneously complex and incomplete, and generally devoid of binding constitutional force. There were, in official contexts, few compelling reasons to deploy it, and some sound ones for avoiding it. To the inherent 'softness' of this German constitutional vocabulary must, moreover, be added by the late Middle Ages the growing opaqueness of the northern *regnum* itself.

The Carolingian successor-kingdom beyond the Rhine never boasted a hard shell of institutions of the kind to whose evolution elsewhere has been ascribed such importance in moulding the nation within the realm.[298] Without it, there was little to inhibit the realm's own contours from slipping and dissolving under the changing shocks and pressures of history. Its territorial outlines, first relativised by the growth in the central Middle Ages of a composite Empire, were subsequently to be blurred and confused with the Empire's erosion in the thirteenth and fourteenth centuries.[299] Faced with such shifts, the semantic instability

[296] Below, Chs. 10, 11, pp. 452–69, 487–506.
[297] For the problems in the way of equating medieval kingdoms with 'states', see: Davies, 'The medieval state'; Foot, 'The historiography'.
[298] See above, Ch. 2, pp. 57–62.
[299] Stengel, 'Regnum', pp. 194–7.

of the term *regnum* itself was exposed, while the emergence in the later Middle Ages of a parallel, but imperfectly matched, political vocabulary in the vernacular added a further layer of conceptual uncertainty. In the same period, the very notion of a German *regnum* was in some quarters tainted by its association both with rumoured plans to partition the Reich and with challenges to the powers of the ascendant prince-electors.

Invocations of a discrete 'German' sphere of government and politics were left, by and large, to force their way out through the cracks in a triumphal Roman façade of Christian monarchy, which allotted them only a limited and somewhat obscure place. With this substantial restriction in mind, the number and variety of references to be found, which place the monarchy in a German sphere of action, or which view it in relation to an explicitly German political community, is remarkable and thought-provoking. If an explicitly constitutional language, invoking a German *regnum* and (more problematically) *rex*, is only occasionally on display, this was not the sole means available to delineate a specifically German sphere of political life. The Empire's German lands were portrayed, by chroniclers and treatise-writers, and to some degree also in chancery documents, as representing axiomatically the prime location of imperial government and monarchy. They supplied the bounds within which a variety of legal enactments and political relationships had effect. They were taken, most often unreflectively, as a frame within which to narrate, to measure and to judge the events of imperial politics. Germany was the natural home of the Empire's rulers, the main site of their creation, the venue for their most urgent tasks and the rightful place of their return. Its peace or disorder were regarded as principal indices of a ruler's glory or shame. The populations of the German lands had an especially close relationship with the monarchy, were bound to it in identification and service, and were held to share its fate in good times and ill. Its polyglot late medieval incumbents were themselves deemed to be Germans when the evidence could be stretched approximately to fit. Beneath its, by the late Middle Ages somewhat discoloured, neo-Roman cladding was to be found a more venerable political structure which, while itself unstable and imperilled, nevertheless lent a measure of shape and support to the larger, more grandiose whole.[300] Late medieval observers did not doubt that this inner structural core was German. In giving voice to their perceptions,

---

[300] On this, see the comments of Werner, 'Deutschland, A: Begriffe', in *LMA* 3, col. 787.

they were, it seems, able to circumvent relatively easily the constraints of the constitutional vocabulary available to them.

One reason why the imperial monarchy was so susceptible to being viewed within a German frame was that it seemed to the outward gaze naturally to fit such a frame. At no time in the Middle Ages was this as true as in the two centuries following the death of Frederick II. The main constitutional acts in creating the Empire's ruler – election, coronation and the round of legitimising journeys that customarily followed – took place on German soil, under the direction of German high dignitaries. Apart from Rome, the principal centres of public spectacle and political memory in the late medieval Reich lay in Germany. The attention which kings and emperors gave to their German territories may have been slight and fitful; but, as a whole, Germany still saw far more of most of them than did other regions of the Reich. That is especially true of the post-Staufer period, when both the number and the duration of expeditions into Italy declined. The decades after 1250 also saw the Romance-speaking territories of imperial Burgundy fall increasingly under the sway of the French crown.[301] The Empire's surviving properties and revenues, modest and dwindling though they were, lay mainly in the German lands, which also supplied most of the monarchy's servants. The armies which kings and emperors led on campaign were mainly German in composition, and were so perceived by contemporaries. In the course of the later Middle Ages it became increasingly common for the imperial chancery to address the Empire's German subjects in their own language.[302] Terminological developments, in both Latin and the vernacular, had their own part in bleeding the German identity which enclosed the *regnum* into the imperial monarchy at large, at a time when conceptual distinctions between the Empire and its northern core were growing harder to sustain.[303]

The imperial monarchy, despite all indications to the contrary, was at its heart a German institution: such, it appears, was the common view among writers in its northern territories in the decades after 1250. The evidence of their own eyes, their experiences and their everyday assumptions assured them that this was so. Yet their viewpoints went beyond pragmatically registering the facts of political life in the Reich. Indeed, as we have seen, their Germanised view of the monarchy was in significant ways starkly at odds with those facts.

[301] For more on this, see below, Ch. 5, pp. 218–19.
[302] The growing use of the vernacular is discussed below, Ch. 11, pp. 492–3.
[303] For the ambiguous use of *Reich* in this period, see below, Ch. 5, pp. 220–1.

German perspectives on rulership and government were moulded by the stubborn persistence of doctrines, convictions and hopes at least as much as by the shifting scene on the ground. They expressed not merely how literate Germans believed things to be, but how they felt things *ought* to be. Understanding their viewpoints will mean looking beyond the nebulous *regnum*, to the grand, if unstable, edifice of the *imperium*.

5   The matter of Rome: universalising political identities

A lesson from Viterbo

The papal resort town of Viterbo is pleasantly situated in a region of upland lakes, some 80 kilometres north-west of Rome, from whose foul air and disease it offered during the Middle Ages a welcome retreat. A fine palace and loggia still bear witness to the papal court's protracted residence there in the second half of the thirteenth century.[1] Several popes were buried and no fewer than five elected in the town. As the focus of papal politics, as a place where decisions were taken with importance for all of Latin Europe, Viterbo became a destination for people of varied origin, outlook and motivation. It is not only the influential few whose presence there has left a mark on the historical record. One of the less conspicuous visitors was a German, the treatise-writer Alexander von Roes, who probably came to the town in the entourage of the Ghibelline cardinal Giacomo Colonna.[2] The only surviving trace of his time there is the mention which he himself makes of it in one of his works; but that is enough to make clear the formative importance for his outlook and writings of his stay in the bustling hill town.

In most respects, Alexander von Roes remains a shadowy figure, and little can be known of him with certainty. Even his name is only tenuously preserved, in a single manuscript of his writings, in which he identifies himself as a canon of the convent of St Maria on the Capitol in Cologne.[3] Alexander was evidently a priest, since he recounts a

---

[1] See Radke, *Viterbo*.
[2] For Alexander and his works see generally: M. Hamm, 'Alexander von Roes', in *VL* 1, cols. 222–6; Grundmann, 'Über die Schriften'; Scales, 'Alexander of Roes'.
[3] Alexander von Roes, *Memoriale*, ed. Grundmann and Heimpel, p. 91 ('Alexander de Roes, canonicus sancte Marie in Capitolio Coloniensi...'). For the manuscript in which it appears, now in the Nationalbibliothek in Vienna, see ibid., pp. 54–5. Significantly, this is not only among the earliest surviving manuscripts of Alexander's writings but also the only one to include all his known works. For St Maria on the Capitol, see: Levison, 'Zur Geschichte', pp. 504–5; Johag, *Klerus*, pp. 53–7; Schäfke, *Kölns romanische Kirchen*, pp. 166–80.

discovery which he made in Viterbo while celebrating mass. Attempts
to locate him within the ecclesiastical community of thirteenth-century
Cologne have had some modest success. He has been plausibly identified with an individual mentioned in the city's records, and it is likely
that he had links with one of Cologne's patrician clans.[4] Yet even the
scantiest outline portrait quickly fades out in speculation. As to the reasons for his presence at the Curia, there are again some likely indicators
in the Cologne sources, but no certain information.[5] Only fleetingly,
through his own words, do we catch a more three-dimensional view of
Alexander's character and experience; and that relates not to his roots
on the Lower Rhine, but to his time in the south.

It was during the recent papal vacancy occasioned by the death of
Nicholas III (22 August 1280), he recalled, that the awareness dawned
that the missal which had been supplied to him from the papal chapel,
from which he was celebrating mass, lacked the customary prayers for
the monarch. Nor, he noted, could this be explained as mere scribal
error, since he had found the same omission in other missals, in use
both within the city of Rome and without.[6] The inclusion of prayers
for the king or emperor in the canon of the mass, alongside supplications for the priest and for other orthodox Christians, had become
increasingly common after the ninth century, but during the later
Middle Ages they began to be removed, at a time when the imperial
power was waning. The missals in use at the Curia had led the way in
excluding the monarch's remembrance.[7] For Alexander, the change had
more than liturgical significance: it pointed towards the grave danger
which, he contended, the entire Christian community would face, were
the clergy to reach the view that they could dispense with the Empire

---

[4] Identification with one Alexander von Leysberg (or Leysburg), born in 1225, was
first proposed in Schraub, *Jordan*, pp. 47–8. The evidence is explored in more detail
in Grundmann and Heimpel, 'Einleitung', pp. 2–4. This Alexander von Leysberg
received a canonry at St Maria on the Capitol from Archbishop Konrad von Hochstaden
(1238–61) and became parish priest of the village of Effern, south-west of Cologne.
Grundmann also made a plausible case for an association between Alexander and the
patrician family de Rosse, which probably had its name from the house zum Ross on
Cologne's Rheingasse and had links with St Maria on the Capitol: ibid., pp. 4–6. For
the close links between this convent and the Cologne patriciate, see Schäfke, *Kölns
romanische Kirchen*, p. 177.
[5] The presentation of Alexander von Leysberg to the Cologne Church of 'Little'
St Martin by the abbess of St Maria on the Capitol brought him into dispute with
Cologne's civic notary and chronicler Gottfried Hagen, who had been presented to
the same living by the commune; both parties pursued the matter at the Curia. See
Grundmann and Heimpel, 'Einleitung', pp. 2–4.
[6] Alexander von Roes, *Memoriale*, cap. 2, ed. Grundmann and Heimpel, pp. 92–3.
[7] Ebner, *Quellen*, esp. pp. 398–9; and see generally Hirsch, 'Der mittelalterliche
Kaisergedanke', esp. p. 16.

and its protection.[8] Here was the ancient, classic 'two swords' doctrine, pressed urgently into action.

Alexander's evident shock at his discovery suggests that he had not at the time been long at the Curia. But by the time he came to set his thoughts down, the papal vacancy was over and the Frenchman Simon of Brie was pope, as Martin IV. His elevation took place in Viterbo, and those who were present recorded the anger aroused in some quarters by the naked triumphalism of the new pontiff's Angevin partisans.[9] It is highly likely that Alexander was present, and that this occasion, too, impressed upon him the gravity of the dangers which seemed to menace his view of the Empire. There were people, he observed, both clerics and laymen, who were asking why the pope transferred the Empire, through Charlemagne, to a people as coarse and unruly as the Germans. Surely the imperial title should have remained with the Romans or, if it had to be transferred, then rather to the French, especially since Charles himself was king of the Franks.[10] For the Cologne canon, such loose talk threatened the Empire's very future – and thereby promised, on the authority of an ancient tradition, to open a way to the coming of Antichrist and the lurid terrors of the Last Days. Martin IV's recent installation was just the sort of occasion on which Alexander would have heard subversive views being bandied about among the pope's French-speaking adherents.

Alexander was still south of the Alps seven years later when he compiled a further prose treatise on the Empire. His *Noticia seculi* of 1288 is dedicated to an unnamed Roman nobleman, likely to be once again Giacomo Colonna.[11] Characteristically historical in perspective and argument, it drew upon written sources apparently unknown to Alexander when he wrote his first imperialist tract, and which probably came to his notice in his new southern milieu.[12] Foremost among them was an eschatological treatise from the early thirteenth century, *De semine scripturarum*, which was to supply the argumentative spine for his new work.[13] Alexander's later writings also show signs of a keener

---

[8] Alexander von Roes, *Memoriale*, cap. 2, ed. Grundmann and Heimpel, p. 93.

[9] Grundmann and Heimpel, 'Einleitung', pp. 7–8. For the background, see Runciman, *The Sicilian Vespers*, pp. 210–12.

[10] Alexander von Roes, *Memoriale*, cap. 14, ed. Grundmann and Heimpel, pp. 104–5.

[11] Alexander von Roes, *Noticia seculi*, cap. 1, ed. Grundmann and Heimpel, p. 149; and see Grundmann and Heimpel, 'Einleitung', p. 9.

[12] Grundmann, 'Über die Schriften', pp. 172–5; Grundmann and Heimpel, 'Einleitung', p. 10.

[13] On this work, see: Kampers, 'Zur "Notitia saeculi"'; Hirsch, 'Zur "Noticia saeculi"'. It is thought that *De semine*, which exists in numerous manuscripts and has never been published in full, was written in the years 1204–5 at Bamberg, probably by a monk of

awareness of world events and their significance: in the *Noticia seculi*, as in his *Pavo* of three years before, he took the chance to note, with ill-concealed satisfaction, the nemesis of Angevin global ambitions in the 'Sicilian Vespers'.[14] The signs are that protracted residence in a cardinal's household in one of the storm-centres of European power and diplomacy had opened Alexander's eyes, broadened his horizons and lent to the assumptions about the political order which he had brought with him from the north a new edge of polemical urgency.

There can be little doubt that his new home would have given him much to ponder. Even his patron, Giacomo Colonna, appears – at least to the modern view – a contradictory as well as a central figure. A Roman aristocrat, fully at home in the urban jungle of factions and intrigues, Giacomo owed his high spiritual offices to familial deal-making under the Orsini pope Nicholas III.[15] In time, he was to earn, with the rest of his kin, the bitter wrath of Boniface VIII. Yet before that, in 1294, he would vote, however reluctantly, for the elevation to pope of the holy fool Pietro di Morrone. He was brother to the saintly Margherita, and protector of the Roman convent which was home to her female followers. Sympathetic tradition made of him a friend of the humble and the poor. The most prominent Ghibelline in the sacred college, Giacomo was also close to the spiritual wing of the Franciscan order – hardly noted in this period for its friendship towards the Empire. It seems likely, indeed, that Alexander's later writing was influenced by his contacts with Franciscan radicals around the cardinal.[16] The Cologne canon would therefore have had ample opportunity while in Viterbo to reflect on the complex relationships between ideas and actions, convictions and external pressures in which the *imperium* was enmeshed.

Alexander von Roes was among the first of a succession of literate Germans who in the decades after 1250 were moved to pick up their pens in the Empire's defence. Extended tracts, largely of German origin, aimed explicitly at defending the Reich, were at this time a relatively new phenomenon, but were to become characteristic of the late Middle Ages.[17] Alexander's motivations, and even his experiences, were

the Michelsberg. For its origins, see also: Grundmann, 'Über die Schriften', p. 161; Hirsch-Reich, 'Alexander von Roes', esp. p. 305.

[14] Alexander von Roes: *Pavo*, vv. 265–72; *Noticia seculi*, cap. 15, ed. Grundmann and Heimpel, pp. 161–2, 191; Heimpel, 'Über den "Pavo"', pp. 198–200. For the context, see Runciman, *Sicilian Vespers*, esp. Ch. 13.

[15] For what follows, see: F. Simoni Balis-Crema, 'Colonna' and 'Colonna, Giacomo', in *LMA* 2, cols. 52–5; Brentano, *Rome*, pp. 177–80, 245.

[16] Grundmann and Heimpel, 'Einleitung', p. 9; Hirsch-Reich, 'Alexander von Roes', esp. p. 313.

[17] See below, pp. 243–58.

not untypical of their writers, although few others present quite such a clear view of the relationship between environment and authorial purpose. The treatise-writers have much to reveal about the importance of the imperial idea after the Staufer, about its social workings and about its relationship with conceptions of German identity. It will therefore be necessary, in a later part of the present chapter, to examine in some detail the lives, interactions and mental worlds of these assorted imperialists. They illustrate particularly clearly a paradox at the heart of late medieval German identities. The period between the thirteenth and the fifteenth centuries stands out, on any objective reckoning, as a distinctly un-imperial age. In the 170 years between 1245 and 1415, there was a western Roman emperor, crowned in Rome and generally recognised, for fewer than 25 years.[18] At no time in this long period, moreover, did an emperor reign who had been installed in the traditional fashion, by a pope in person. And yet it can be cogently argued that in no previous era had the imperial idea been so widely and urgently present in the minds of the Empire's German populations, or so central to their notions of who they were. This paradox must be explored, by examining the social penetration of imperialist thought and sentiment, and the means and impulses for its reception. This too will be our concern in what follows. First, however, the character of the imperial idea itself needs to be gauged, and consideration given to its lineaments and fortunes in Germany after the end of the Staufer.

Imperium

'To trace its career with any minuteness', wrote James Bryce in his essay on *The Holy Roman Empire*, published in 1864, 'would be to write the history of Christendom from the fifth century to the twelfth, of Germany and Italy from the twelfth to the nineteenth.'[19] Bryce's own more modest goal, as he explained in later editions of the work, was 'to speak less of events than of principles, and endeavour to describe the Empire not as a State but as an Institution, an institution created by and embodying a wonderful system of ideas'.[20] For Bryce, whose adult life was lived out in the high summer of British imperialism, the historical importance of the imperial idea was as axiomatic as its grandeur.[21]

---

[18] The figure appears all the more stark when it is noted that, taking the long period between 962 and 1493 as a whole, the number of years with an emperor (283) exceeds the number without (248): Schneidmüller, *Die Kaiser*, p. 47.

[19] Bryce, *The Holy Roman Empire* (1864), p. 5.

[20] Bryce, *The Holy Roman Empire*, rev. edn, p. 2.

[21] Harvie, 'James Bryce'.

But the idea of empire was destined to shed much of its lustre in the decades following Bryce's death in 1922, and its German incarnation to suffer in the middle years of the twentieth century a precipitate fall from grace. The 'Europeanisation' of medieval Germany, which was such a pronounced theme in European historiography after 1945, went hand-in-hand both with the relativisation of the medieval imperial tradition and with its marginalisation. Imperialist thought, a widespread view now insisted, was neither the exclusive property of the Germans nor did it dominate medieval imaginations as was once supposed.[22] The Germans' medieval *Sonderweg* was, in its imperial lineaments at least, largely illusory; the Reich really was, as the Gregorians had long before alleged, just another kingdom.

It is naturally important that rhetoric be kept distinct from hard realities, and beyond doubt that medieval people were themselves able to make the distinction. The medieval western Empire, as a power among others, was at all times a different and lesser thing than the fanfares of its public acts or the cosmic fantasies of some of its literate champions made it out to be. Whatever might have been the teaching of Roman civil law on the subject, there is little sign that anyone seriously believed the kingdoms of Latin Europe to be subject to the emperor's rule, and plenty of evidence that thoughtful people did not.[23] The idea that they were, or should be, under him was at most a knotty legal fiction to occupy jurists, never a substantive threat or (except perhaps, fleetingly, under Henry VII) the basis for a ruler's policies.[24] By Henry's time, in any case, a powerful body of legal opinion, canonist and increasingly also civilian, was insisting that kingdoms (or, more cautiously, certain specific kingdoms) were free of the Empire in law, just as they were in fact.[25] But already in the Empire's heyday, under Barbarossa, the overblown doctrines of the Reich had moved to anger and scorn a man of John of Salisbury's wide experience and learning. 'Who', John had demanded to know, 'set up the Germans as judges over the peoples of the earth?'[26]

---

[22] A view trenchantly expressed in Werner, 'Das hochmittelalterliche Imperium', esp. pp. 20–1, 54.

[23] Werner, 'Das hochmittelalterliche Imperium'; Kienast, *Deutschland*, vol. II, esp. pp. 390–2.

[24] Even the lawyers were perhaps less exercised by the question than was once thought: Pennington, *The Prince*, esp. p. 36.

[25] Canning, *Medieval Political Thought*, pp. 124–5, 165–6, 170–1; Canning, 'Ideas', esp. pp. 3–5, 8–10; Walther, *Imperiales Königtum*, pp. 78–85; Post, *Studies*, esp. p. 492.

[26] See: Fuhrmann, '"Quis constituit Teutonicos?"', pp. 344–5; Reuter, 'John of Salisbury', esp. pp. 344–5.

Yet John's own words point towards another truth, too easily obscured by the concern of post-war medievalists to set aside the Reich-centred nationalism of their immediate forebears: the medieval Roman Empire laid claim – whether or not, in the eyes of contemporaries, realistically or justly – to a unique heritage. No other western prince wrote, even rhetorically, of his 'world monarchy' (*monarchia mundi*) or 'world government' (*regimen mundi*), or explained, as had Frederick II in his 'Golden Bull of Rimini' (1226), how he and his forebears were raised up above the kings of the earth to benefit all mankind.[27] It was an English chronicler who recounted how as 'ruler of all' (*dominus universorum*) Frederick's father, Henry VI, had enfeoffed Richard the Lionheart with his realm.[28] Frederick himself had, as emperor, laid claim to the headship of Christendom's secular princes, whom he aspired to lead in his struggle with the spiritual power.[29] Only the imperial chancery could have thought – however fleetingly and doubtless ill-advisedly – to speak of the crowned heads of the west as 'rulers of the provinces' (*reges provinciarum*) or to call the king of France himself a 'kinglet' (*regulus*).[30] Other kings might also drape themselves, to varying degrees, in Roman imperial finery; yet none but the Empire's bearers could muster a full, consistent vocabulary of rulership infused with Roman styles and titles. A 'Roman Empire' from the eleventh century, a 'Holy Empire' from the mid-twelfth, and a 'Holy Roman Empire' with growing regularity from the mid-thirteenth, its chancery forms tracked a steady course, undiminished in the late Middle Ages, towards an ever-more-fulsome universalism.[31]

Nor was the Empire's special *Romanitas* a matter only of words. No other monarch could realistically aspire to enter in state the city of Rome itself, for coronation by the pope or his delegates. That the codified Roman law viewed the emperor as the sole *princeps* remained

---

[27] Kirfel, *Weltherrschaftsidee*, pp. 160, 164–5; Kienast, *Deutschland*, vol. II, p. 270. For the universalist tradition in thought on the Empire, see: Folz, *The Concept*, pp. 4–5; Kölmel, *Regimen Christianum*, esp. p. 66; for the Golden Bull of Rimini: *Historia Diplomatica Friderici Secundi*, ed. Huillard-Bréholles, vol. II.i, pp. 549–52; Hageneder, 'Weltherrschaft', p. 266.

[28] Roger of Howden, quoted in Kienast, *Deutschland*, vol. II, p. 345.

[29] See: Kirfel, *Weltherrschaftsidee*, esp. p. 199; Wieruszowski, *Vom Imperium*, pp. 36–7.

[30] Kirfel, *Weltherrschaftsidee*, p. 18. These terms are discussed and contextualised in Benson, 'Political *renovatio*', p. 378.

[31] For the development of titles, see: Schwarz, *Herrscher- und Reichstitel*, pp. 59–66, 69–70, 86–96, 104–10, 189–211, 235–43; Koch, *Sacrum Imperium*, esp. pp. 111–13, 215–21, 266–9, 275–6; Weisert, 'Der Reichstitel', esp. pp. 449–60; Müller-Mertens, 'Imperium und Regnum', esp. pp. 572–5; Appelt, 'Die Kaiseridee', pp. 11–18; and for their late medieval vernacular counterparts, Zeumer, *Heiliges römisches Reich*, pp. 15–16.

for its medieval students and interpreters an inescapable, if not in the end invincible, fact.[32] Roman legal doctrines had reputedly moved Barbarossa to ask his Bolognese legists whether he was indeed lord of the whole world, just as they allowed his grandson to pose as a lawgiver in the footsteps of Justinian.[33] The emperors of antiquity furnished the governors of the medieval Reich with an ancestry as exclusive as it was illustrious. Roman imperial history was their history. Otto von Freising was among those to insist that the Roman Senate's right to choose the monarch had passed to the German princes.[34] Their protracted military expeditions south of the Alps seemed to place the emperors of the high Middle Ages squarely in the tradition of their Roman forebears – whose reputation as exemplars of the martial virtues was acknowledged throughout Latin Europe.[35] Rome's cultural heritage too was, as it seemed, theirs for the taking if they had a will. Towards the close of the twelfth century Konrad, bishop-elect of Hildesheim, had written from Sicily to friends in the north: all that they had read in Virgil and Horace was true, as they might discover for themselves without leaving the Empire's bounds.[36]

'And it came to pass in those days', recounts St Luke's Gospel, 'that there went out a decree from Caesar Augustus, that all the world should be taxed.'[37] Medieval Roman emperorship was able to look for its sanction to the New Testament, where the emperor's illustrious ancient predecessor was to be seen establishing the conditions for Christ's coming. The Roman Empire's universal mandate appeared to be validated by Christ's own words.[38] Old Testament prophecy was called on in proof of its world-historical role, and of the necessary intermixing of its ultimate fate with that of all humankind.[39] From Barbarossa's time onward,

---

[32] Kienast, *Deutschland*, vol. II, esp. pp. 311–22; Canning, 'Ideas', esp. pp. 7–8.

[33] For Barbarossa and his legists, see: Fögen, 'Römisches Recht', pp. 73–9; Pennington, *The Prince*, pp. 10–16; for Frederick II as Justinian's successor: Folz, *The Concept*, p. 112; Schaller, 'Kaiseridee', p. 122; for codified Roman law under Frederick: Kienast, *Deutschland*, vol. II, pp. 286–7.

[34] Goez, *Translatio Imperii*, p. 175.

[35] See Keen, *Chivalry*, Ch. 6.

[36] Thomas, 'Das Identitätsproblem', p. 147.

[37] Luke 2:1. For the passage's significance, see Hageneder, 'Weltherrschaft', p. 261. The words of the Gospel were paraphrased by Johann von Winterthur, reporting the decree that went out 'a cesare augusto Ludwico' – Ludwig IV – forbidding observation of the papal interdict on Germany (1338): *Die Chronik Johanns von Winterthur*, ed. Baethgen, p. 158.

[38] The *locus classicus* was Matthew 22:21: 'Then saith he unto them, Render therefore unto Caesar the things which are Caesar's; and unto God the things that are God's.'

[39] For the Old Testament legacy, see: Kampers, *Kaiseridee*, esp. pp. 5–6; Cohn, *Millennium*, esp. Ch. 1.

the *sancta ecclesia* had a titular counterpart in the *sacrum imperium*.[40] The Empire's ruler was held to enjoy a unique relationship with the Christian commonwealth, with its institutional manifestation, the Catholic Church, and with its head. There was, as a letter of 1159 in Barbarossa's name had put it, 'one God, one pope, one emperor'.[41] Just two powers had from ancient times sufficed to govern the world; alongside the spiritual authority of prelates had been placed for its support the emperor's temporal *potestas*: so, at least, still ran a common interpretation of a famous late antique papal decretal.[42] 'Two swords' were, by divine providence, 'enough' for the care of human affairs.[43] And the 'temporal sword' was with the emperor – a principle whose establishment was the first concern of that most hard-headed and widely read of German law codes, the *Sachsenspiegel*.[44]

The 'reform' or 'renewal' (*reformatio, renovatio*), which imperial documents portrayed as the emperor's particular duty, seemed to make of him an agent of positive change extending beyond the narrowly political, and encompassing also the sphere of the Church.[45] Opinions differed as to the proper relationship of the two powers, with each other and with God. Alexander von Roes insisted that not only the Empire's ruler, but the entire German people as its custodians, deserved to be treated by the pope 'like a brother and equal partner'.[46] Disputation did not remain confined to a Latinate milieu: the *Sachsenspiegel*-glossator Johannes von Buch gathered authorities to show that the papal sword was not set over the imperial.[47] But all agreed that affairs were rightly ordered when their relations were governed by harmony. Under the year 1367, the Limburg chronicler Tilemann Elhen was able to note that, with pope and emperor together in Italy, 'the two swords of the world were in agreement'.[48] And while canon law had come over time to insist

[40] For the development of this title, see the works listed above, n. 31.

[41] Kirfel, *Weltherrschaftsidee*, p. 162; Benson, 'Political *renovatio*', pp. 378–9.

[42] For Gelasius I's decretal *Duo sunt* and its transmission to the Middle Ages, see Robinson, 'Church', pp. 288–300.

[43] For the doctrine of 'two swords', see Watt, 'Spiritual and temporal powers', pp. 370–4. Its source, in Luke 22:38, remained well known: see, e.g., its elucidation by Johannes von Buch: *Glossen zum Sachsenspiegel-Landrecht*, ed. Kaufmann, pp. 133–4 (to *Landrecht* I, cap. 1).

[44] *Sachsenspiegel Landrecht* I, cap. 1, ed. Eckhardt, p. 69.

[45] For the conjunction of imperial and Church reform in the fifteenth century, see Engels, 'Der Reichsgedanke', p. 97.

[46] Alexander von Roes, *Noticia seculi*, ed. Grundmann and Heimpel, p. 162.

[47] *Glossen zum Sachsenspiegel-Landrecht*, ed. Kaufmann, pp. 134–5 (to *Landrecht* I, cap. 1); and see Kannowski, *Die Umgestaltung*, pp. 278–81.

[48] *Limburger Chronik*, ed. Wyss, p. 55: 'da waren di zwei swerte von der wernde eintrechtig'.

ever more sharply upon the subjection of emperor to pope, a strong current also emphasised the comprehensiveness of the emperor's – as the pope's – sphere of action, and the gravity of the duties with which he was charged.[49] He was, for the thirteenth-century canonist Hostiensis (an eloquent champion of papal hierocracy), 'God's earthly vicar in temporal affairs'.[50] Despite the alarmed discovery of Alexander von Roes, the emperor was in fact generally to retain the special place in the liturgy that he had enjoyed for many centuries already.[51]

While the Empire's repeated conflicts with the high medieval papacy undoubtedly contributed to its long-term institutional weakness, the imperial *idea* was not only shaken, but also deepened, complicated and enriched by these bruising encounters. Although the crusading movement, with its roots in the doctrines of the Gregorian papacy, had at first left the emperor out in the cold, that had in the end merely spurred the Staufer to assimilate the mission to the Holy Land to the emperor's traditional duty of holy strife.[52] The final decades of Christian rule in the east were consequently to witness the last Hohenstaufen emperor, as if in fulfilment of his prophetic destiny, wearing the crown of universal monarchy in the Holy Sepulchre itself, an act of Christian-Roman *renovatio* of fitting grandeur for a self-styled imitator of Constantine the Great.[53] Supporters responded by lauding Frederick as an inaugurator of the Golden Age, comparable to another King of Jerusalem, Christ himself.[54]

The clashes with the Curia under the later Staufer helped ensure that, in a time of fervent eschatological speculation, the Empire's rulers became ever more closely enmeshed in prophetic schemes which appeared rapidly to be moving towards a consummation. For better or – as with time it increasingly seemed – for worse, the *imperium* took up its place at the heart of the drama of human salvation.[55] A Prague manuscript of the mid-fourteenth century, informed by the prophetic writings of Abbot Joachim of Fiore (d. 1202), depicts an apocalyptic dragon whose seven heads are marked with the names of seven evil

---

[49] For the Empire in canon law, see Muldoon, *Empire*, Ch. 3, as well as Kölmel, *Regimen Christianum*, esp. p. 65.

[50] Watt, *The Theory*, p. 112. For the papal monarchy's role in reinforcing *imperial* universalism, see Baethgen, 'Zur Geschichte', p. 199.

[51] See below, p. 222.   [52] Schaller, 'Kaiseridee', p. 113.

[53] For the significance of Frederick's Jerusalem crown-wearing, see Abulafia, *Frederick II*, pp. 186–7; for prophecy, Schaller, 'Endzeiterwartungen', p. 309; for Frederick as a Christian holy warrior in Constantine's footsteps, Schaller, 'Kaiseridee', p. 118.

[54] Schaller, 'Endzeiterwartungen', p. 309; Schaller, 'Kaiseridee', pp. 126–7.

[55] See generally Reeves, *Prophecy*.

monarchs, of which, no fewer than four – Nero, Constantius II, (St!) Henry II and Frederick II – were ancient or medieval Roman emperors.[56] The high medieval Reich of the Staufer ended with neither a bang nor a whimper, but with a silence which commentators were moved for decades thereafter to fill with speculations of their own.

Whatever the shocks and blows to which the imperial idea was in the thirteenth century exposed, the fact that other royal dynasties, above all the Capetians, were at pains to appropriate some of its core tenets and motifs, and even to attain the imperial throne itself, underlines its continuing relevance – indeed, transcendent prestige – during the first century of the 'modern state'.[57] The candidature of French royal princes was promoted, with variable levels of vigour and conviction, though always in vain, in 1273/4, 1308, 1313 and 1324–8.[58] Learned champions of the monarchy from the period, notably Pierre Dubois and Jean de Jandun, also periodically banged the drum for a French emperor. The belief in deep-laid French plans (often, it was imagined, with papal backing) for a new *translatio* in favour of their own people remained a spectre among German writers throughout the late Middle Ages.[59] Far from extinguishing the imperial idea, therefore, the upheavals of the mid-thirteenth century served, it seems, to scatter it abroad, for European princes to apply in service of their rule at home. In 1259 King Jayme I of Aragon felt it necessary to point out that the election of Alfonso X of Castile as king of the Romans did not entitle him to set himself up as 'emperor of Spain' (*ymperator Hispaniae*).[60] Even the most vociferous champions of constitutional pluralism and nascent regnal sovereignty paid back-handed tribute to the lingering power of those ancient doctrines from which they sought to secure their king's escape: he was '*emperor* in his own kingdom'.[61]

But if 'the Roman eagle' was not yet the 'dead duck' of one scholar's formulation, it remains obvious why Robert Folz should have located the post-Staufer imperial idea 'beyond the realm of reality'.[62] There

[56] Patschovsky, 'Henry "the First"', p. 291.
[57] For the historiography, see above, Ch. 2, pp. 58–60.
[58] See: Roscheck, 'Französische Kandidaturen', esp. pp. 16–31, 55–118, 119–35; Zeller, 'Les rois'; as well as Jones, 'Understanding', esp. pp. 5–7.
[59] For the persistence of such rumours, see below, Ch. 7, p. 349, as well as Roscheck, 'Französische Kandidaturen', pp. 193–208.
[60] Stengel, 'Kaisertitel', p. 271.
[61] For this phrase and its origins, see: Kienast, *Deutschland*, vol. II, pp. 469–75; Stengel, 'Kaisertitel', p. 273; Pennington, *The Prince*, pp. 3, 35–6.
[62] Burns, *Lordship*, p. 97; Folz, *The Concept*, Bk. IV ('The concept of empire beyond the realm of reality'). For the gulf between idea and reality in the Empire at the beginning of the fourteenth century, see also: Moraw, 'Reich (Das späte Mittelalter)', cols. 448–9; Fößel, 'Die deutsche Tradition', esp. pp. 23–5.

were but few who sought seriously to defy the logic of power in Europe after 1250, and those few were, it seems, destined to be brought low. The emperor Henry VII was to expire before Siena, not five years into his reign, with his grandiose designs for imperial *renovatio* in ruins.[63] Just ten years before that, the career of Boniface VIII had ended in humiliation for that most imperial of pontiffs, at the hands of a mob.[64] The universal fantasies of the 'two powers' had never been shown up as more hollow. Even the Empire's staunchest German defenders, despite their general adherence to traditional doctrines, found themselves unable to ignore the realities of their day. Most of the treatise-writers of the late thirteenth and fourteenth centuries made space for arguments, not always fully reconciled with their prevailing universalism, which acknowledged the legitimate independence of certain other realms.[65]

We have seen already that the Roman Empire's custodians were less often to be found in Italy after 1250, and that such visits as they made were less lavishly supported, less warlike in style, and of shorter duration and less glorious outcome than in times past. The Empire's late medieval rulers were a source of recurrent disappointment to learned Italian Ghibellines, with their dreams of a new imperial dawn in the south.[66] For Dante, Rudolf I and his son, 'German Albert', in remaining beyond the Alps, had betrayed their most noble calling.[67] Rudolf, the sly fox of admiring German chroniclers, was a mere neglecter of his duties.[68] Petrarch had met with Charles IV in Mantua early in 1355, as the Luxemburger made his way south for imperial coronation.[69] But all his pleas that Charles take in hand Rome's renovation were not enough to deter the newly crowned emperor from departing the city, faithful to his promise to the pope, at the close of his coronation day. Within three months he was back on German soil.[70] Indeed Charles, who knew

---

[63] For Henry's death, see Bowsky, *Henry VII*, pp. 303–4.
[64] On Boniface's imperialism, see Kölmel, *Regimen Christianum*, p. 491; on his fate, Boase, *Boniface VIII*, Ch. 13.
[65] For Alexander von Roes and France, see Scales, 'France and the Empire', esp. pp. 404–5; for Engelbert von Admont and Lupold von Bebenburg: Ubl, 'Die Rechte', esp. pp. 362, 373–5.
[66] See generally Kölmel, *Regimen Christianum*, pp. 491–2.
[67] See Scott, *Purgatory*, esp. pp. 102–5, 123–4.
[68] For German views, see above, Ch. 4, pp. 162–3. A letter of Dietrich von Niem to Rupert of the Palatinate (1408) criticised the king as a neglecter of the Empire's southern territories in terms similar to Dante: Heimpel, *Dietrich*, pp. 61–2.
[69] Grundmann, *Wahlkönigtum*, p. 225.
[70] Seibt, *Karl IV.*, pp. 238–9. Charles was crowned in Rome on 5 April; on 3 July he was in Augsburg: *Die Regesten des Kaiserreiches unter Kaiser Karl IV.*, ed. Huber, pp. 163, 175. The brevity of his stay in the south struck the chronicler Heinrich von Diessenhofen, who observed, 'Et sic infra novem menses ingressus Italiam Tusciam

from his youth the tortuous ways of northern Italy as did few among the Empire's rulers, had already sought to disabuse the poet laureate of his humanist fantasies in a letter of 1351: emperors had learned from experience that all things were to be tried before iron.[71] For a hard-headed and hard-pressed monarch, Italy's cities were in the fourteenth century less a venue for glorious deeds than a reservoir of much-needed cash – that, and a storehouse of sudden hazards to be sidestepped, just as Charles himself had fled before a revolt in Pisa, on his hurried 'imperial' progress back from Rome.[72]

In his bull *Pastoralis cura* (1313), Pope Clement V ruled that the kingdom of Sicily, whose king, Robert of Anjou, the emperor Henry VII had sought to arraign for treason, lay 'outside the Empire's bounds' (*extra districtum imperii*), and thus beyond the reach of imperial justice.[73] Some decades later another pope, Clement VI, preached in consistory that no temporal realm had limits as extensive as the Empire.[74] Yet the underlying message was again the same: the *imperium*, like any other kingdom, was a finite agglomeration of territories. The observation (though not the conclusion which Clement V drew from it) was uncontroversial enough: writings from the imperial chancery also spoke freely of the ruler's duty to protect 'places under the Roman Empire', and referred to the Empire's 'bounds'.[75] Some Germans at least were moved, in unpromising times for a universal Empire, to rally in defence of the monarchy's powers within this territorial core. For Lupold von Bebenburg, in a treatise written at the height of Ludwig IV's clash with the Curia, the Reich was at heart a great, composite realm, fundamentally Germanic, but with Italian and other appurtenances. Within its limits – set, historically, by the conquests of Charlemagne – its monarch was to rule as free from outside interference as did any other crowned

---

et Romam et in imperatorem coronatus reversus est unde venit...': *Heinricus Dapifer de Diessenhoven*, ed. Huber, p. 99.

[71] Printed in Burdach, *Vom Mittelalter*, vol. VII, no. 2, p. 15, in a manuscript written by Cola di Rienzo.

[72] Grundmann, *Wahlkönigtum*, p. 225. It has been estimated that during the course of his reign Charles IV obtained more than 850,000 florins from Italy on the basis of imperial rights: Thomas, *Deutsche Geschichte*, p. 239.

[73] Walther, *Imperiales Königtum*, pp. 215–19 (for the bull's relationship with the thought of Oldradus); Wood, *Clement VI*, pp. 146–7; Schubert, *König und Reich*, p. 211. For the matters at stake in the action against Robert, see Pennington, 'Henry VII', pp. 81–3.

[74] Wood, *Clement VI*, p. 148.

[75] Examples: *Acta*, ed. Winkelmann, vol. II, no. 91, p. 80; *MGC* 3, no. 649 (47a), p. 638. In a proclamation of 27 February 1379, Wenceslas, together with the four Rhenish electors, declared it the king's duty to combat divisions among Christians in the world 'so weyt das heilige Romische reich begriffen ist': *RTA* 1, no. 129, p. 234.

prince.[76] Just like his western neighbours (whose effective sovereignty Lupold explicitly recognised), he had an inherent right at least to rule as emperor within his own realm – to which, like them, he had lawfully succeeded.[77]

And, even viewed solely in its territorial aspect, the medieval Reich remained impressive. To the original East Frankish *regnum* and its appurtenances had been added lands in northern and central Italy in the tenth century and the kingdom of Arles or Burgundy in the eleventh. With each of these territorial clusters was associated a crown, which the Empire's ruler might hope to obtain, through coronation respectively at Monza or Milan and at Arles (though neither crown was generally regarded as a precondition for his exercise of rule in those regions).[78] The northern *regnum* had itself grown in size and complexity during the central Middle Ages, as its eastern marchlands were settled and stabilised. By the thirteenth century, Bohemia was established as a hereditary kingdom of substantial wealth, power and independence, linked to, yet also distinct from, the neighbouring 'German' realm.[79]

But the Roman Empire's late medieval custodians enjoyed at best mixed success in maintaining the integrity of their far-flung realms, and showed little prospect of adding to them, as a good *augustus* was etymologically bound to do. Some extensions of the Empire's frontiers there were, as in the far north-east, where Livonia, subjected in the thirteenth century to conquest and Christianisation, was an imperial fief.[80] On the eastern marches of the *regnum*, the progressive incorporation of the Silesian duchies into the Bohemian crown, ratified by treaty between the Bohemian and Polish kings in 1335, had brought these previously Polish territories within the frontiers of the Reich.[81] Although not within the Empire territorially, Prussia, subjected militarily by the Teutonic Order in the thirteenth century, was linked in more opaque ways with the Reich, whence had come the Order's main

---

[76] For Lupold, see below, p. 244; for his view of the Empire as a territorial realm among others: Most, 'Der Reichsgedanke', esp. pp. 457–8; Fößel, 'Die deutsche Tradition', pp. 25–7.

[77] Lupold von Bebenburg, *Tractatus de Iuribus Regni et Imperii*, cap. 9, ed. Miethke and Flüeler, p. 320: 'Et hec opinio ex hoc maxime videtur habere veritatem, quod reges alii christianitatis, qui tamen hodie ut plurimum non recognoscunt imperatorem Romanorum nec aliquem alium superiorem in temporalibus...' Cf. ibid., cap. 8, p. 315.

[78] See above, Ch. 4, p. 154. Opponents of the monarch in the Empire's non-German lands were more likely to base resistance upon his not having undergone *imperial* coronation in Rome: Kern, 'Reichsgewalt', pp. 70–8.

[79] Richter, 'Die böhmischen Länder', pp. 300–5.

[80] Moraw, *Von offener Verfassung*, p. 45.

[81] Seibt, 'Die Zeit der Luxemburger', pp. 378–80.

charter for conquest, and whence came also most of its recruits.[82] Yet all these gains were, in different ways, incidental; none resulted from efforts specifically to extend the Empire's bounds. And elsewhere, the signs pointed to impending fragmentation. In the south-west, in the Alpine marchlands of the German and Burgundian kingdoms, the towns and peasant communities of the Swiss Confederation were in the fourteenth century laying the foundations of future independence, in a series of bloody military triumphs over their Habsburg lords.[83] In the urbanised north-west, an old-established westward concentration in commerce and culture gained after the later fourteenth century the lineaments of a more sharply political cohesion and separateness, under the influence of the Valois dukes of Burgundy.[84]

But the western Roman Empire's most conspicuous losses during the post-Staufer period occurred in those regions where the cultural ties to Roman antiquity remained most visible: in southern Gaul and in Italy. Territorially at least, the later Middle Ages were an era of depleted *Romanitas*.[85] Particularly in the kingdom of Arles, the decades after 1250 witnessed the gradual disintegration of imperial lordship.[86] The Romance-speaking south of the Burgundian kingdom had already been considered a potential diplomatic pawn by the Staufer, so the plans laid under Rudolf I, to settle the territory as a fief on the Angevins (who already held from the Empire the countship of Provence), had precedent on their side.[87] The advance of French administration into the Lyonnaise west of the Saône had been proceeding by stages since the twelfth century; by the end of the thirteenth, the town of Lyon had passed beyond the Empire's control.[88] Imperial suzerainty over Avignon was ceded to the pope in 1348.[89] A seal was set upon the reconfiguration of rule in the region when, at the end of his reign, Charles IV granted the imperial vicariate in Arles for life to the French dauphin – who also held, by custom, the countship of Vienne, and was to

---

[82] Though not an imperial fief, Prussia was described in the Golden Bull of Rimini as pertaining to the *monarchia imperii*. For its constitutional status, see: Boockmann, 'Die Eroberung', pp. 94–5; Schulze, *Grundstrukturen*, pp. 81–3.

[83] Peyer, 'Eidgenossenschaft', esp. pp. 198–202.

[84] Berg, *Deutschland*, esp. pp. 29–30, 32–3.

[85] For the surrender of the Romagna to the papacy in 1278, see above, Ch. 4, pp. 166, 171.

[86] See Fournier, *Le Royaume*, esp. pp. 229–55.

[87] Resmini, *Das Arelat*, p. 11. Henry VI was the first Staufer ruler to contemplate splitting up the kingdom of Arles to secure diplomatic objectives; the same policy was considered by Philip of Swabia and Frederick II.

[88] Resmini, *Das Arelat*, esp. pp. 283–4; Fournier, *Le Royaume*, p. 299; Wood, 'Regnum Francie', p. 139.

[89] Schmugge, 'Kurie und Kirche', p. 75.

retain imperial powers in Arles following his elevation to the throne as Charles VI.[90] There had been plans before to draw the region under the French crown; but on this occasion Valois rule, under the long-lived Charles, was able finally to obliterate the tradition of subjection to the Reich.[91] Dietrich von Niem was in no doubt that the Luxemburger was to blame for allowing Arles, 'so noble a member of the said Empire', to pass under French control.[92] While the extent of the Empire's territorial contraction should not be overstated, its relative modesty is explained more by an absence of aggressive neighbours than by successful defence by the Empire's rulers, despite their professed concern for the integrity of the *imperium*.[93] Had the French monarchy really pursued the systematic *Ausdehnungspolitik* identified long ago by Fritz Kern, its gains at the expense of the Reich would have been greater than they were.

Paralleling the Empire's retreat from its south-western lands was the trend, most marked in those same regions, for imperial territories to become merged with the northern ('German') realm. As early as 1281, a document in the name of Duke John of Saxony observed that the bounds of the kingdom of Arles had almost passed out of memory, an indication of its fading constitutional distinctiveness.[94] We have seen already how around the same time the imperial archchancellorship for Arles, previously held by the archbishops of Vienne, became conflated with a new office in Trier's hands, for 'Gaul', encompassing also the western lands of the *regnum*.[95] Northern Burgundy, largely German in language and culture, lay close to the German south-west, a region regularly visited by the Empire's rulers, and was intimately bound up with the territorial interests of German princely dynasties, notably the Habsburgs.[96] Its relationship with the Reich was therefore of a different, closer kind than that of the Romance south of Arles, where imperial rule had ceased to have material consequences long before the region finally dropped out of the Empire's territorial ambit. The town of Basel, for example, although constitutionally part of the Burgundian realm, and a suffragan of the metropolitan see of Besançon, belonged politically

---

[90] Seibt, *Karl IV.*, pp. 350–60; for the establishment, after 1349, of the status of the dauphiné of Vienne as an imperial fief held by the heir to the French throne, see ibid., p. 352.

[91] For earlier plans, see: Thomas, *Deutsche Geschichte*, p. 187; Seibt, *Karl IV.*, pp. 352, 357; Jones, *Eclipse*, p. 306.

[92] Dietrich von Nieheim, *Viridarium*, ed. Lhotsky and Pivec, p. 17.

[93] For clauses against the Empire's 'dismemberment', see above, Ch. 4, p. 172.

[94] *MGC* 3, no. 258, p. 253 (5 September 1281).

[95] Ch. 4, pp. 183–4.

[96] Redlich, *Rudolf von Habsburg*, esp. pp. 544–641; and, more generally, Krieger, *Die Habsburger*, Ch. 7.

to the *königsnah* zone around the Upper Rhine.[97] The distinction was reflected in imperial diplomacy: the kingdom of Arles which it was proposed under Rudolf I to settle on the Angevins was to exclude the free countship of Burgundy in the north.[98] Charles IV was acknowledging a process of fragmentation already long under way when in 1361 he detached from the kingdom of Arles the countship of Savoy, with its strategically important Alpine passes.[99] If one element in the special status claimed by the imperial monarchy had traditionally lain in its hegemony over a plurality of realms (the 'walls' of Christendom's 'house', the 'wheels' of the imperial 'chariot'), there are thus clear signs of that hegemony dissolving in the decades after 1250.[100]

The language of imperial rule itself provided a mantle of comfortable obscurity beneath which such changes could take place. The increasing conflation, after the thirteenth century, of *imperium* and *regnum* has been observed elsewhere.[101] In the vernacular, meanwhile, a designation was to hand which straddled both Latin terms, while carrying a range of meanings broader and less distinct than either: *rîche*. Encompassing a rich assortment of related notions (rulership, power, government, reign, realm, political community), the spheres of rule which it might be drawn on to designate extended from the heavenly *rîche* itself to the smallest local jurisdiction.[102] Applied to the Empire, it tended to highlight the abstract and general. The compiler of the *Book of Kings of the New Law* cited 'ancient writings' to the effect that the *rîche* – hegemonic rule itself – 'first arose in Babylon', before passing in succession to the Persians, Greeks and Romans.[103] The term could

---

[97] For Basel's ambiguous position, see Kern, 'Reichsgewalt', p. 51.

[98] *MGC* 3, no. 258, p. 253; Kern, 'Reichsgewalt', p. 43. Alexander von Roes likewise set the *comitatus Burgundie* conceptually apart from the *regnum Arelatensium*: Alexander von Roes, *Noticia seculi*, cap. 11, ed. Grundmann and Heimpel, p. 159.

[99] Seibt, *Karl IV.*, pp. 350–1; and see Birken, 'Deutschland', p. 289. However, difficulties in interpreting Charles's purpose here are highlighted by Müller-Mertens, 'Imperium und Regnum', pp. 583–4.

[100] Dietrich von Nieheim, *Viridarium*, ed. Lhotsky and Pivec, pp. 10–11; Alexander von Roes, *Memoriale*, cap. 25, ed. Grundmann and Heimpel, p. 127. For Dietrich's adoption of Alexander's metaphor of the Empire's 'walls', see Heimpel, *Dietrich*, p. 154.

[101] Above, Ch. 4, p. 181.

[102] Jesus thus informs Pilate, 'ez ist hie nicht mein reich / in diser werlt': *Die Weltchronik Heinrichs von München*, ed. Shaw, Fournier and Gärtner, p. 96, vv. 1756–7. For *rîche*, see: Grimm, *Deutsches Wörterbuch*, vol. VIII, pp. 573–8; Moraw, 'Reich (Das späte Mittelalter)', pp. 423–4; *Mittelhochdeutsches Handwörterbuch*, ed. Lexer, vol. II, pp. 416–17. For the term's complex constitutional significance in the late Middle Ages, see: Schubert, *König und Reich*, pp. 245–54; Annas, *Hoftag*, vol. I, pp. 78–82.

[103] *Der kunige buoch*, ed. Massmann, p. cxxi, following *Sachsenspiegel Landrecht* III, cap. 44 § 1, ed. Eckhardt, p. 229.

be used to encode artefacts and institutions embodying the Empire's authority – even, for one chronicler, an imperial army – as well as designating the monarch's own person.[104] In late medieval titles, the Reich might, like its Latin counterparts, be both 'holy' (*heilig*) and 'Roman' (*Roemisch*), and was virtually never explicitly linked with the German people or their lands.[105] But in most cases *daz rîche* was employed alone, without further elucidation. Its use in written form increased rapidly after the thirteenth century, in step with the growing importance of the written vernacular. But its popularity may well also reflect the conceptual merging of Empire and ('German') realm in this period, a process which, by its ambiguity, it also encouraged.[106]

Changes in the place of Latin Europe within a wider world ensured that some established elements of imperial doctrine became during the late Middle Ages harder to realise than in earlier times. Richard of Cornwall had distinguished himself as a Holy Land crusader in the decade before his election to the Empire; but the times would not for much longer favour such extravagant ventures. The king-emperor's traditional role as holy warrior was to be thwarted not only by the modesty of his own military resources but by the contraction of the crusading movement itself, and changes in its character, after the fall of the Latin East in 1291. The Empire's ruler could no longer realistically hope to lead great armies to the Levant. Such experience as late medieval emperors gained of crusading was, in its modesty, diffuseness and lack of success, characteristic of the age. In the winter of 1344–5, Margrave Charles of Moravia, the future Charles IV, embarked with his father, King John of Bohemia, on a campaign with the Teutonic Order against the Lithuanians. False rumour and bad weather quickly conspired to thwart the venture, however.[107] Charles's son Sigismund, as king of Hungary, was to play a prominent part in the doomed Nicopolis expedition of 1396, where his abandonment of the field roused the military engineer Konrad Kyeser to mock him as a coward (and, less predictably, a hermaphrodite).[108] There is no doubting particularly Sigismund's personal commitment to the crusading ideal.[109] But no crowned ruler of

---

[104] *Limburger Chronik*, ed. Wyss, p. 47: '... da lag daz riche vur Velmar...' For Ludwig IV as *daz rich*, see Schmid, 'Die Hoftage', p. 446.

[105] Though for the plural use of *rîche* in connection with German designations, see below, Ch. 10, p. 472.

[106] See Schubert, *König und Reich*, esp. p. 236.

[107] For a full account, see Werunsky, *Geschichte Kaiser Karls IV*, vol. I, pp. 373–7; for Charles's own account of the expedition, *Karoli IV Imperatoris Romanorum Vita*, ed. Nagy and Schaer, pp. 154–9.

[108] *Conrad Kyeser aus Eichstätt, Bellifortis*, ed. Quarg, vol. II, p. 4.

[109] See Hoensch, *Kaiser Sigismund*, esp. pp. 79–87.

the Reich in this period took the field against the infidel.[110] The Empire's late medieval custodians could boast no feats of Christian slaughter and triumph to set beside the legendary deeds of Ottonian and Staufer emperors, not to mention those linked with the name of Charlemagne. Yet imperial leadership in holy war lived on as ideal and aspiration. Indeed, the collapse of Latin rule in the East brought for a time an intensified focus on the Empire as a possible element in a western counteroffensive. Following the fall of Acre, Church councils in France and even England expressed the hope that the German princes would quickly choose a new king, to speed the Holy Land's prospect of relief.[111] Schemes for the recovery of Outremer identified the Empire as a problem in need of solution as a prelude to any new expedition.[112] And the duty of war for the Faith remained central to conceptions of imperial rulership. Rudolf I's electors in 1273 announced that the king-elect was 'vigorous in body, and blessed with success in warfare against the wicked'.[113] The king himself observed that the Empire's recent weakness had been 'to the exultation and joy of heathens and other perfidious people'.[114] Adolf of Nassau justified his imperial candidature as enabling him more effectively to realise his aim of aiding the Holy Land, and his successors, Albert I and Henry VII, were also to conjure the prospect of a campaign in the East to underpin their rule in the Reich.[115] The supplication in the Good Friday liturgy, for the Empire's triumph over 'barbarian [here, meaning pagan] peoples', continued to be invoked in imperial documents, as well as the writings of the chroniclers.[116] The duty of holy war which lay upon the Empire's bearer was reaffirmed in both the Aachen and Roman coronation rites.[117] The acts

---

[110] Although Sigismund himself was to crusade later in his reign against his own Bohemian subjects as Hussite heretics.

[111] Denton, *Philip the Fair*, p. 7.

[112] *De Recuperatione*, ed. Langlois, Ch. 13, pp. 12–13; and see the report on conditions in Germany prepared by Bishop Bruno of Olmütz (Olomouc) for the 1274 Council of Lyon: *MGC* 3, no. 620, pp. 589–94 (16 December 1273).

[113] *MGC* 3, no. 14, p. 18. A similar formulation was employed to announce to the Empire's subjects the election of Rudolf's son Albert in 1298: *MGC* 4.i, no. 8, p. 7.

[114] *MGC* 3, no. 22, p. 25 (22 December 1273).

[115] Ibid., no. 474, p. 460; and for Albert and Henry, Weiler, 'The *Negotium Terrae Sanctae*', pp. 29–30.

[116] As examples, see: *Chronicon Magni Presbyteri Continuatio*, ed. Wattenbach, p. 533; *Chronicon Colmariense*, ed. Jaffé, p. 249; *MGC* 3, no. 23, p. 26; *Acta*, ed. Böhmer, no. 401, p. 322. For the origin of these words, see: Hirsch, 'Kaisergedanke', esp. pp. 2–3; *The Gelasian Sacramentary*, ed. Wilson, pp. 75–6. For the Carolingian and Ottonian foundations of the imperial duty of holy war, see Robinson, 'Church', pp. 292–3.

[117] For the Aachen coronation *ordo*, see *MGH Leges* 2, pp. 386–92, where it is ascribed to the coronation of Rudolf I. The printed version has since been identified, however, as the *ordo* used for Henry VII's coronation in 1309: *Die Regesten des Kaiserreiches unter Rudolf*, ed. Redlich, no. 4d, pp. 18–19.

of a successful or admired ruler might still be enfolded in the imagery of the crusade, even when performed far away from Christendom's frontiers or in war against fellow Christians. More than one chronicler told of how a cross, or cross-shaped cloud, had appeared in the sky above Aachen at the time of Rudolf I's coronation. This was but a prelude to the treatment accorded the king's triumph over Otakar II at the Marchfeld in 1278.[118] Accounts of the battle (fought on Holy Cross day) endowed the imperial forces with the full panoply of invocations of Christ's sacrifice: insignia, banners, battle cries. Even the theme of conversion was drawn in, with the pagan Cumans of Rudolf's ally, Ladislas IV of Hungary, portrayed as willingly taking up the Christian symbols and chants.[119] According to the Salzburg annalist, there were many in the imperial army who had taken the Cross (as had their king, at Lausanne in 1275), intending to journey to the Holy Land.[120]

With time, however, the Empire's rulers accommodated themselves to a more complex world, in which war against the heathen could no longer command its earlier prominence. Ludwig IV admittedly still backed the Teutonic Order's mission to the extent of issuing, in November 1337, a visually magnificent diploma, enfeoffing the Order's Grand Master with the (yet unconquered) land of Lithuania.[121] The Wittelsbachs enjoyed close relations with the German Knights, allies in Ludwig's struggle with Avignon: one of the Order's castles on the Lithuanian front bore the name 'Bayernburg', while the fantastic prospect was mooted of naming a planned Lithuanian archbishopric after Bavaria. But the late Staufer tradition which had bound the German Order closely to the imperial dynasty itself could find no continuation amid repeated changes of ruling house in the Reich during the two centuries which followed.[122] Charles IV's relations with the German crusaders were ambivalent at

---

[118] For the cross above Aachen, see Friedrich von Sonnenburg's verse in *Politische Lyrik*, ed. Müller, vol. I, p. 75.

[119] *Continuatio praedicatorum Vindobonensium*, ed. Wattenbach, p. 731. According to the Fürstenfeld chronicler, writing several decades later, the bishop of Basel instructed a certain Franciscan to preach to Rudolf's army before the battle, saying that they were doing God's work and fighting for justice, that those who died would gain the martyr's crown, but that the dead from Otakar's army would be damned, as rebels against justice, to eternal torment: *Chronica de gestis principum*, ed. Leidinger, pp. 33–4.

[120] *Annales Sancti Rudberti Salisburgenses*, ed. Wattenbach, p. 803. For Rudolf himself, see *Die Regesten des Kaiserreiches unter Rudolf*, ed. Redlich, no. 438b, p. 122.

[121] For what follows, see Boockmann, 'Die Eroberung', p. 174. The diploma was adorned with an illuminated initial showing the emperor, with sceptre and orb, investing the kneeling Grand Master (Dietrich von Altenburg) with a vassal's banner: Suckale, *Die Hofkunst*, p. 37.

[122] For the Staufer and the Order, see Boockmann, 'Die Eroberung', esp. p. 92.

best: the emperor's negotiations with the Lithuanian princes, to secure their peaceful conversion, potentially threatened the Order's interests, indeed its *raison d'être*.[123] In 1395, following the dynastic union with Christian Poland, Charles's son Wenceslas went so far as to prohibit the Order from waging holy war against Lithuania.[124] A thought-provoking, if apocryphal, sidelight on changing values, in some quarters at least, is provided by Jakob Twinger, who tells how Charles IV was urged by certain nobles to mount an expedition to recover the Holy Land, since his resources were greater than those of any of his forebears.[125] (Twinger himself believed Charles to have been the richest emperor for many hundreds of years.) The Luxemburger conceded that he had indeed the means to launch a great crusade, but judged that to do so would be merely to waste his warriors' lives. History showed, after all, that while (as Charles, or Twinger, imagined) kings and emperors had often won the Holy Land, as soon as they returned home the heathen rose again and took it back, killing or expelling its Christian occupiers. Reality, it seems, was slowly but inexorably catching up with the *Reichsidee*.

The persistence of imperialism

But if the imperial idea's material foundations were less substantial, and the circumstances for its realisation less propitious, than before, its vocabulary and motifs endured, commanding a measure of acknowledgement even in surprising quarters, and were extended and infused with new meanings in the decades after Frederick II's death. Beyond reality the concept of Empire may have lain; but in a sense it always had, and in an age of constricted and disheartening realities its seeming capacity for defying their gravitational pull, and its strong element of the fantastic, held for some a considerable appeal. If the grandiloquent universalism of Henry VII's coronation encyclical is startling to the modern eye, hardly less so is its generally well-mannered reception by the ('sovereign') crowned heads to whom it was sent.[126] The judgement of the German canonist Johannes Teutonicus, that the independence which kingdoms enjoyed from the Empire was merely *de facto*, and not

---

[123] For Charles's dealings with the Lithuanians, see Seibt, *Karl IV.*, pp. 379–81. It should be noted, however, that Charles also confirmed Frederick II's 'Golden Bull of Rimini', in the Order's favour (ibid., p. 381).

[124] Boockmann, 'Die Eroberung', p. 177.

[125] *Chronik des Jacob Twinger*, ed. Hegel, p. 492.

[126] Edward II of England appears to have accepted the imperial rhetoric without demur, while the French raised no general objection, insisting only on their own realm's exceptional standing: Baethgen, 'Weltherrschaftsidee', pp. 192–3. For the encyclical itself, see Pennington, *The Prince*, pp. 167–8.

grounded in law, had been endorsed by incorporation into the ordinary gloss to Pope Gregory IX's authoritative *Liber Extra* of 1234.[127] It was subsequently to find pungent expression in Boniface VIII's denunciation of the lying pride of the French, for claiming just such independence.[128] Particularly within the powerful but ambiguous realm of ritual, the reception of the Empire's ruler in neighbouring kingdoms continued to demand careful handling. When the aged and gout-ridden Charles IV set out for Paris late in 1377, the emperor's French hosts were at pains to delay his crossing of the frontier, in order that Charles's Christmas Eve reading of the resonant passage from St Luke's Gospel invoking the mandate of Caesar Augustus should not occur on French soil.[129] According to one tradition, when Charles's son Sigismund came to England in 1416, the English king's brother, Humphrey Duke of Gloucester, met him at Dover bearing a sword, and refused to let the king of the Romans disembark until he had given assurance that he did not seek to assert imperial lordship over England.[130]

The city of Rome itself, while it unquestionably saw less of the Empire's rulers than in times past, retained much evocative power. Some German chroniclers took Rome's foundation as a chronological datum.[131] If military glories in the south were few indeed for Caesar's impoverished fourteenth-century heirs, imagination could still paint larger and more stirring scenes. The picture-chronicle of Archbishop

---

[127] Kienast, *Deutschland*, vol. II, pp. 307–11; Pennington, *The Prince*, pp. 32–3. This was despite a growing current of canonist dissent during the thirteenth century, and despite the fact that Innocent III himself had famously noted the king of France's non-recognition of a temporal superior: Canning, *Medieval Political Thought*, pp. 124–5.

[128] *MGC* 4.i, no. 173, p. 139 (Boniface's recognition of Albert I as king of the Romans, 30 April 1303): 'Nec insurgat hic superbia Gallicana, que dicit, quod non recognoscit superiorem. Mentiuntur, quia de iure sunt et esse debent sub rege Romano et imperatore ...' Boniface's words were quoted at length by Heinrich von Herford: *Liber de rebus memorabilioribus*, ed. Potthast, p. 217.

[129] Heimpel, 'Königlicher Weihnachtsdienst', pp. 162–9; Schwedler, *Herrschertreffen*, pp. 298–300.

[130] Allmand, *Henry V*, pp. 104–5. The subsequent mythical elaboration of this story seems to attest its contemporary resonance: see Kingsford, 'A legend of Sigismund's visit to England', pp. 750–1. For Sigismund's image in England (where one chronicler recalled him as *princeps superillustrissimus*), see Scales, 'Rose without thorn', p. 34.

[131] Thus, e.g.: *Martini continuatio Coloniensis*, ed. Waitz, p. 355 ('Anno Domini 1274. Urbis vero condite 2112 ...'); *Sächsische Weltchronik: Sächsische Fortsetzung*, ed. Weiland, p. 285 ('Rudolf von Havensberg quam an daz riche nach gotes gebort 1273 jar unde von Rome stiftunge 2031 jar'); *Liber de rebus memorabilioribus*, ed. Potthast, p. 213 ('Adolfus comes de Nassov ... cepit anno mundi 5253., Urbis 2042'): the discrepancies in dating are striking. Dating *ab Urbe condita* was the established practice among late Roman historiographers, but fell out of use at an early date in much of the post-Roman West: Guenée, *Histoire*, p. 154. In the late Middle Ages its use outside Germany was comparatively rare, though not unknown.

Balduin of Trier shows the forces of Balduin's brother, Henry VII, battling their way across the Milvian Bridge, with its memories of an earlier, epochal imperial triumph, to gain entry to the city.[132] The inconclusive street fighting in which the Luxemburger had in fact found himself embroiled when he reached Rome in 1312 was transformed by the chroniclers into a sanguinary vindication of German *animositas*: men waded up to their knees in blood and the Tiber flowed red.[133] Italy was invoked in imperial documents as the Empire's 'garden', or its 'orchard', and the monarch's prestige was enhanced when he was imagined, however implausibly, masterfully plucking its fruits.[134] When Rome fell to Ladislas of Naples in April 1408, Dietrich von Niem was shocked and appalled that a monarch other than the Empire's ruler should have entered the city.[135]

The soaring aspirations with which, in official rhetoric, the imperial title had traditionally been joined continued to be proclaimed by the Empire's champions. Indeed, in times of crisis, they were enunciated more fully and explicitly than ever. A letter of Rudolf I to the town of Vienna announced the king's intention to pacify and set to rights 'the affairs of the Holy Empire and the entire Christian Commonwealth'.[136] For the poet Friedrich von Sonnenburg, the same king was a 'guardian of all Christendom'.[137] In the Styrian Rhyming Chronicle one of the nobles campaigning with Rudolf I against the Burgundian countpalatine is portrayed expressing the view that every prince 'who has been baptised and is called Christian' must receive 'land, sceptre and crown' from the Empire's ruler.[138] The imperial chancery after 1250 found nothing incongruous about continuing to invoke the words of Pope Gelasius I, with their vision of a Christian world shared between papal and imperial governance.[139] The principle of two universal

---

[132] Margue, Pauly and Schmid (eds.), *Der Weg zur Kaiserkrone*, pp. 70–1.

[133] *Die Chronik Johanns von Winterthur*, ed. Baethgen, pp. 62, 68. For events in Rome, see Bowsky, *Henry VII*, pp. 159–70. The one full-scale battle which took place during Henry's time in Rome, on 26 May 1312, was a defeat for the Luxemburger.

[134] *MGC* 3, nos. 100, 266, pp. 90, 260; for further examples, see Schubert, *König und Reich*, pp. 223–4. Dietrich von Niem wrote of Lombardy 'que solebat vocari Viridarium imperiale': Dietrich von Nieheim, *Viridarium*, ed. Lhotsky and Pivec, p. 16.

[135] Heimpel, *Dietrich*, pp. 42, 61–2.

[136] *Codex Epistolaris*, ed. Bodmann, no. 99, p. 253.

[137] *Politische Lyrik*, ed. Müller, vol. I, p. 75 ('vogete ... aller kristenheit').

[138] *Ottokars österreichische Reimchronik*, ed. Seemüller, p. 433, vv. 33123–9; and see Tersch, *Unruh*, pp. 264–6.

[139] *Acta*, ed. Winkelmann, vol. II, no. 165, p. 125 (Rudolf I to the bishop of Liège, seeking the excommunication of Guy of Flanders, 27 March 1287: 'Quoniam duo sunt, quibus principaliter regitur orbis terre, sacra videlicet pontificis auctoritas et regalis

powers collaborating harmoniously for the general good proved tenacious in Germany, despite the rifts of the Staufer era. The principle of co-operation was prominently enshrined in the *Sachsenspiegel*, which emphasised at the start the duty upon the Empire's ruler to assist the Church in enforcing spiritual sanctions.[140] In 1287 Rudolf I urged upon the visiting papal legate that excommunication should follow imposition of the imperial bann.[141] An Erfurt chronicler believed, although mistakenly, that the short-lived Innocent V (January–June 1276) had actually excommunicated those illegally holding imperial properties.[142] The logic of this relationship is visible behind the words of Magnus von Reichersberg's continuator, for whom Otakar II was a rebel not merely 'against *regnum* and *imperium*' but also against 'Holy Church'.[143]

The Empire's rulers continued to be regarded by German writers as the custodians of a special mandate of unique scope. Their protective duty towards Church and Faithful was a major theme in the pro-imperial treatises which multiplied in the decades after 1250. Konrad von Megenberg underpinned with an array of canonist authorities his insistence that 'to the emperor pertains the office of defending the Church of Christ and delivering all her sons from molestations and oppressions'.[144] But the same idea had also impressed itself on less reflective minds. A chronicler in the early fourteenth century observed how after Frederick II's passing '*the Church* lacked a king of the Romans'.[145] And, as in times past, to act as the champion of Church and Faith meant treading a grand stage. According to Heinrich von Herford, at the time of Charles of Moravia's elevation as anti-king, supporters of his rival, Ludwig the Bavarian, had contested the validity of his election, partly on the grounds that Charles had not been raised up for the right reasons. These included 'the general good of the commonwealth ... the well-being and protection of the whole world, and the spreading of the Gospel and the Christian Faith'.[146] Nevertheless, it was as a 'world monarch' (*mundi monarcha*) that Charles himself subsequently called upon

---

potestas...' For another example of the use of *Duo sunt*, see *MGC* 3, no. 386, pp. 366–7.

[140] *Sachsenspiegel Landrecht* I, cap. 1, ed. Eckhardt, p. 69. The principle was reiterated some decades later in the south-German *Schwabenspiegel* (ed. Eckhardt, *Landrecht*, 'Vorwort', pp. 42–3).

[141] *Die Regesten des Kaiserreiches unter Rudolf*, ed. Redlich, no. 2076, p. 453.

[142] *Cronica S. Petri Erfordensis Moderna*, ed. Holder-Egger, p. 276.

[143] *Chronicon Magni Presbyteri Continuatio*, ed. Wattenbach, p. 533.

[144] Konrad von Megenberg, *De translacione Romani imperii*, cap. 1, ed. Scholz, p. 254.

[145] *Heinrici de Heimburg annales*, ed. Wattenbach, p. 715.

[146] *Liber de rebus memorabilioribus*, ed. Potthast, p. 275.

the Lithuanians to accept baptism.[147] Charles's own Golden Bull gave the matter authoritative formulation: the prince-electors were charged with appointing 'a temporal head for the world ... [and] the Christian people, namely a king of the Romans, to be raised to Caesar'.[148]

The graver the troubles facing the Church, the more urgently some at least looked to the Empire's ruler to fill his world-historical role.[149] The summons was not without danger for those who failed to answer it. According to Jakob Twinger, Wenceslas was deposed in part because he did nothing to end 'the great and lamentable crises, conflicts and schisms in Holy Church, which had persisted for many years ... [and] which it is a Roman king's duty to avert and resolve'.[150] In the time of the Councils, Dietrich von Niem was still belabouring the hapless Luxemburger, and Rupert of the Palatinate, for their failure to carry holy war to the heathen.[151] With imperialist diehards, the 'statesman-like' restraint of a Charles IV cut no ice at all. But when the Empire's governor did come to the Church's aid, his actions could still reap for him unparalleled prominence and stature, such as were garnered by Wenceslas's half-brother Sigismund, convenor and protector-designate of the Council of Constance.[152] While his powers were by no means uncontested, and Sigismund himself hardly consistent in asserting the claims of his imperial title, the king of the Romans was nevertheless able to observe the Council's sessions, 'in imperial dress', from a raised chair in Constance Cathedral. When John XXIII announced his intention to resign the papacy, Sigismund was at the pope's right hand, seated in a special seat.[153] Here, it seems, was at least fleeting support for Twinger's dogged reiteration, at the same late date, that 'an emperor or Roman king is the supreme head of Christendom'.[154]

---

[147] Schneider, 'Karls IV. Auffassung vom Herrscheramt', pp. 147–8; Seibt, *Karl IV.*, pp. 379–81. Further examples of universalising claims in Charles IV's writings are collected in Lindner, 'Es war an der Zeit', pp. 123–30.

[148] *Die Goldene Bulle*, ed. Fritz, p. 54.

[149] For Dietrich von Niem's response to the Great Schism, for example, see Heimpel, *Dietrich*, esp. p. 153.

[150] *Chronik des Jacob Twingers*, ed. Hegel, p. 495. 'All this was done while there was a twenty-year schism in the holy Roman Church', fulminated a Mainz chronicler, listing the Luxemburger's alleged enormities: *Chronicon Moguntinum*, ed. Hegel, p. 239. Wenceslas's inactivity in spite of his insistence that resolving the Schism pertained to him alone: Engels, 'Der Reichsgedanke', p. 81.

[151] See Heimpel, *Dietrich*, pp. 160, 163.

[152] For Sigismund's status at Constance, see Engels, 'Der Reichsgedanke', esp. pp. 93–4.

[153] Ibid., p. 89.

[154] *Chronik des Jacob Twinger*, ed. Hegel, p. 248; and cf. ibid., p. 401.

The language of Christian-Roman universalism retained, for German writers, its hegemonic, legitimising power. It remained during the later Middle Ages the recourse of the most solemn documents in the ruler's name. Ludwig IV's statute *Licet iuris* of August 1338, conceived as a definitive public statement of the monarch's powers, declared the Empire's head to be without temporal superior, 'but to him all nations [*nationes*] are subject', as 'the Lord Jesus Christ himself' had attested, through the familiar words of St Matthew's Gospel.[155] 'The majesty of the Holy Empire', insisted the Golden Bull, had power over 'the laws and governance of diverse nations, distinct in customs, mode of life, and language.'[156] That such grandiloquent doctrines retained some imaginative power is indicated by their repetition outside the formal clauses of imperial diplomas. Through her marriage to Henry VII's son John, noted Peter von Zittau, the Přemyslid heiress Elizabeth became 'daughter-in-law to the lord and prince of the whole world'.[157] Sometimes, late medieval writers introduced new universalising touches of their own. The king's Rome coronation, remarked Johannes von Buch, fourteenth-century glossator to the *Sachsenspiegel* (which had had nothing to say on the matter), made of him 'emperor over all the world'.[158] In a tradition first attested in the fifteenth century, the king-elect, on reaching the doors of Aachen minster, received instruction from the dean and senior canon on the symbolic significance of the chapel's ancient bronze sculptures: he was to protect his Reich as the Roman she-wolf guarded her young, and to rule over an Empire of as many languages as the pine-cone fountain had 'tongues'.[159]

But the pervasiveness, the axiomatic quality, of the vocabulary of Empire which enfolded the monarchy is better illustrated through its more routine expressions. Richard Plantagenet, Earl of Cornwall, gazes serenely out from his great seal, by the Grace of God neither more nor less an Ever-August King of the Romans, in title at least, than were the middling German noblemen who preceded and followed him in that office.[160] From within this language it was no less natural unblinkingly

---

[155] *Quellensammlung*, ed. Zeumer, no. 127, p. 156, citing Matthew 22:21. On the statute and its context, see Stengel, *Avignon und Rhens*, pp. 153–61. For an earlier imperial document insisting on the monarch's elevation 'super gentes et regna', see *Acta*, ed. Winkelmann, vol. II, no. 124, p. 102 (9 July 1280).

[156] *Die Goldene Bulle*, ed. Fricke, cap. 31, p. 90.

[157] *Königsaaler Geschichts-Quellen*, ed. Loserth, p. 264.

[158] *Glossen zum Sachsenspiegel-Landrecht*, ed. Kaufmann, p. 1300 (to *Landrecht* III, cap. 57 § 2); and see Kannowski, *Die Umgestaltung*, pp. 260–7.

[159] Müller, 'Die Königskrönung', p. 54. For the Empire's multi-lingual character, see below, Ch. 11, pp. 491–2.

[160] Illustrated in *Die Siegel*, ed. Posse, p. 37.

to recognise in 'Adolf, Count of Nassau' the Romans' hundredth ruler since Caesar.[161] The 'pope-and-emperor' chronicles so widely copied in late medieval Germany laid out in overview this unique continuity, just as they privileged the Empire's rulers by yoking their descent, and theirs alone, to the succession of pontiffs from Peter.[162] Another new development of the thirteenth century, they projected into a still-unfolding present a visibly unbreakable parallelism of Christian-ecclesiastical and Roman-imperial histories.[163] Evolved, ramified and deeply rooted in medieval and earlier imperial history, the lexicon of *imperium* thus imparted to the monarch's acts, in times of change and disjunction, an aura of timelessness. Although itself not entirely unchanging, the official language of sacred *Romanitas* offered the Empire's late medieval custodians a quality which they sought: the appearance of continuity. Not without cause did the imperial chancery continue to quarry the formularies, just as it reaffirmed the diplomas, of 'the blessed emperors and kings, our predecessors'. We look in vain for a 'German' constitutional language even remotely comparable in stability, richness of conjunctions, official acceptance, habitual usage or legitimising power. No such language existed.[164] As a general rule, the more elevated a document's style and fundamental its content, the more encompassing would also be the language of *Romanitas*. What distinguishes many of the most resonant and extensive public statements on the Empire's status and character – Henry VII's coronation encyclical, for example, or the constitutional utterances of emperor and princes in the year 1338, or the Golden Bull – is, by contrast, the almost complete absence of specific reference to the German people, its habitation or political form.

It was in imperial, Roman, or Christian-Roman, certainly not in any explicitly 'German', traditions that those most in need of legitimacy still sought it.[165] Such a need was felt particularly keenly by those who found themselves raised to the imperial throne. It received fulfilment in remarkable, multi-media amplifications of sacralised *Romanitas* under the three crowned *imperatores* of the fourteenth century, Henry VII, Ludwig the Bavarian and Charles IV – and under the last two particularly. For all three monarchs, the imperatives of settling a new dynasty

---

[161] *Liber de rebus memorabilioribus*, ed. Potthast, p. 213.
[162] For universal chronicles, see above, Ch. 3, pp. 146–8.
[163] For the genre and its importance in Germany, see Mierau, 'Die Einheit', esp. pp. 283–5, 289; for its role in sustaining the doctrine of universal Empire in the late Middle Ages, Mierau, 'Das Reich', esp. pp. 563–70.
[164] See the comments of Eggert, 'Bemerkungen', pp. 305–6.
[165] For appeals to a legitimising Roman past by German princely and noble dynasties, see below, Ch. 7, pp. 308–9.

upon the throne were coupled with an urgent need to generate ideological cover for delicate – in Ludwig's case, bitterly controversial and divisive – relations with the Church and its head. Each of them, moreover, gained first-hand acquaintance with the wellspring of imperial legitimacy and reservoir of image-making artistic talent that was Italy, such as their stay-at-home predecessors had long lacked.

Driven by the imperatives of doctrinal self-assertion, particularly in the face of ecclesiastical programmes and censures, and buoyed up by new ideological and presentational resources, fourteenth-century monarchs promoted an inflationary spiral of imperial image-making. Prototypes for their authority were invoked, with a newfound spirit of ambition, both in antiquity and in the Old Testament. The lion throne of Solomon now made its appearance on the imperial great seal, and under Ludwig IV was augmented, for good measure, by a throne flanked by large and lifelike Roman eagles.[166] The monarch's ceremonial dress evolved in line with the new imagery. Already under Henry VII, the crown (or crowns) had begun to attain an increasingly mitre-like aspect, a development which proceeded further under Ludwig.[167] The Wittelsbacher also commissioned sumptuous new vestments, combining priestly attributes with Byzantine references and, over all, a characteristically prominent scattering of imperial eagles. Such innovations, with their carefully elaborate public staging, aspired to make an impression in Germany, and chronicle reports indicate that they were successful in this.[168] *Romanitas* was central. Ludwig introduced Roman architectural motifs into the north, following his return from Italy, just as his golden bull, probably the work of a Pisan goldsmith, featured on its reverse, with a novel accuracy of observation, the antiquities of the city of Rome itself.[169]

The fusion of sacrality with an imperial vision of antiquity, firmly established as a legitimising visual programme under Ludwig IV, was to be taken up and much extended by his Luxemburg supplanter. Under Charles, dynastic prestige and imperial tradition were brought together under powerful osmotic pressures, in which relics and cults had the main role. The Přemyslids' patron, St Wenceslas, was borne beyond the

[166] For the Solomon throne and eagles, see: Suckale, 'Die Hofkunst im 14. Jahrhundert', p. 326; Saurma-Jeltsch, 'Zeichen', p. 338; and for illustrations: Suckale, *Die Hofkunst*, pp. 31–2, ills. 16a, 17; *Balduin von Luxemburg*, p. 42 (lion throne of Henry VII).

[167] For crowns and vestments, see: Kintzinger, 'Zeichen', pp. 358–63; Suckale, 'Zur Ikonografie', pp. 338–9.

[168] As an example, see above, Ch. 3, p. 132.

[169] The knights' hospital at Ettal in the Bavarian Alps, begun in the 1330s, echoed the Pantheon: Suckale, 'Die Hofkunst im 14. Jahrhundert', p. 326. For Ludwig's golden bull, see Suckale, *Die Hofkunst*, p. 31 with ill. 16b.

Bohemian frontier to infuse the lands of the Empire, through altars and other foundations in centres of imperial memory such as Nuremberg, Aachen, Ingelheim and Rome itself.[170] Meanwhile, the scattered territories of the Reich were symbolically woven together into a composite sacral landscape, through the transplanting of holy objects, and the fostering of associated cults, in regions far remote from their places of origin.[171] In this way, the cult of the obscure, sixth-century Burgundian martyr Sigismund, which Charles had discovered at the monastery of Einsiedeln, was able to spread through the Empire – and, characteristically, gain incorporation into the public devotions of the Luxemburger themselves.[172] Charles's conception of Prague as a second Rome (as well as a new Jerusalem) found expression in his many church foundations, some, like the Carmelite convent of Our Lady of the Snows, harking back to a Roman prototype, while others alluded to the 'New Rome' of the Byzantine east or to the southern lands of the medieval Roman Empire.[173] The numerous ancient and sacred objects which Charles brought together in the city proclaimed the self-same message. As well as accumulating Byzantine and antique gems and cameos, the emperor, for all his sceptical words to Petrarch, was delighted to receive the poet laureate's gifts of Roman coins.[174] Yet more numinously potent were the many relics which he heaped up. Some, like the portion of St Peter's pastoral staff which Charles brought from Trier, or the widely scattered remains of the soldiers of the Theban Legion, linked the Luxemburger with Christian and imperial Rome, while others bestowed proximity with Christ himself.[175]

In his funeral oration, Archbishop Jan Očko called Charles 'another Constantine', and it seems likely that the emperor's patronage aimed deliberately at associating him with early Christian Roman emperors, such as Heraclius and Constantine himself.[176] The avidity with which he sought out relics with connotations of Christian triumph, such as the

[170] Machilek, 'Privatfrömmigkeit', p. 91.
[171] Ibid., pp. 94, 99.
[172] Schneider, 'Karls IV. Auffassung', p. 130; Herzogenberg, 'Bildnisse', p. 333.
[173] Machilek, 'Privatfrömmigkeit', pp. 91–2; Chadraba, 'Der "zweite Konstantin"', p. 508.
[174] Fried, 'Schnöder Mammon', pp. 465–6; Macek, 'Die Hofkultur', p. 238.
[175] Schmid, 'Vom Rheinland nach Böhmen', esp. pp. 448–56 (Theban Legion); Machilek, 'Privatfrömmigkeit', p. 90; Chadraba, 'Kaiser Karls IV. devotio antiqua', p. 56. Charles's practice of collecting relics and spiriting them away to Bohemia attracted the notice of contemporaries: Die Chronik des Mathias von Neuenburg, ed. Hofmeister, pp. 469–70; Heinricus Dapifer de Diessenhoven, ed. Huber, p. 89.
[176] For the funeral oration, see Chadraba, 'Der "zweite Konstantin"', pp. 505, 515 n. 3; for his imitation of Christian Roman emperors, Chadraba, 'Kaiser Karls IV. devotio antiqua', pp. 62–4.

remains of early martyrs and, above all, objects connected with Christ's Passion, may well reflect a desire to imitate a late antique tradition of Christian emperorship.[177] The theme of Christian-Roman imperial victory, renewed and made manifest in the house of Luxemburg, also found visual expression in the emperor's public monuments, such as the cycle of sculpted figures on his Prague 'triumphal arch'.[178] It was represented with startling directness in a magnificent gilded image set up above the doorway of his private chapel in the castle of Karlstein. There, Charles and a splendidly attired female figure, probably Anna von Schweidnitz, his third consort, together raise aloft a great bejewelled cross, in unmistakable *imitatio* of Constantine and his mother, Helena.[179] Viewed in its totality, Karlstein's rich and complex decorative scheme can be understood as a microcosm, set within carefully co-ordinated architectural spaces, of the three ages of Christian history, at the centre of each of which was placed the emperor himself.[180] From Bohemia's forests to Rome and Constantinople – not to mention the prophetic Jerusalem – was far indeed; yet it was the shades of those cities, their holy places and objects, their ancient Christian monarchs, their eschatological promise, that Charles sought to summon to his hilltop fastness.[181]

Such marvels were reserved for the privileged few, like the Brabantine envoy Edmund Dynter, whom Wenceslas in 1413 led 'by the hand' to view the painted Luxemburg genealogy in Karlstein.[182] The innermost sacred spaces of Charles's 'spiritual pleasure palace' were, indeed, for the monarch's eyes only.[183] What, then, of the larger audience for the imperial idea? How far could it reach beyond the small circles of the powerful, their advisers and servants? Despite the institutional weakness of imperial government, the signs of its capacity for social penetration are in fact varied and substantial. The armies which followed the Empire's rulers invoked the Roman heritage and Christian mission of the Reich as they faced the king's enemies. More than one account of the battle of the Marchfeld has King Rudolf's forces raising cries of

---

[177] Chadraba, 'Kaiser Karls IV. devotio antiqua', pp. 54–5.
[178] Chadraba, 'Der "zweite Konstantin"', pp. 513–15.
[179] Ibid., p. 510.
[180] For Karlstein as a progression through 'sacred time', see Crossley, 'The politics', pp. 143, 147.
[181] The mosaic, set up at Charles's behest, which adorns the Golden Portal of his rebuilt cathedral of St Vitus in Prague places Charles within the Last Things, in company with the Christ of the Last Judgement: Herzogenberg, 'Bildnisse', p. 324.
[182] Crossley, 'The politics', p. 143. For the genealogy, see Herzogenberg, 'Bildnisse', p. 331.
[183] His 'geistliches Lustschloß': Seibt, *Karl IV.*, p. 392.

'Rome' and 'Christ' against the Bohemians' shouts of 'Prague'.[184] It is hard to dismiss as merely conventional the talismanic utterances of men facing the urgent prospect of violent death. Mention of the imperial battle cry of 'Rome' in German vernacular romances of the time discloses its broad familiarity among the warrior classes.[185] And the fact that German knights continued to invoke the Empire's name, even when not fighting under the imperial banner, underlines its power of identification: German mercenaries in Milanese pay are reported in 1344 to have called out *'Romaric, Romaric'.*[186] A still more complete example of the Empire's internalisation as a component of martial, aristocratic identity is provided by Count Adolf of Berg, a middling nobleman whose estates lay in the uplands east of the lower Rhine, well off the track of the monarch's travels. A near contemporary account of the battle of Worringen in 1288, which pitched the archbishop of Cologne against a confederation of the regional nobility, has the count's forces joining the fray to shouts of *'Berge Romerike!'*[187]

The wide and in the later Middle Ages growing visibility of the ruler's armorial, the black-on-gold eagle, has been observed already.[188] Its familiarity is confirmed by its frequent invocation in writings of varied kinds. What these also make clear, however, is its common association not merely with the Empire as idea and institution, but specifically with the Roman character of the Reich. Rudolf I was for one contemporary poet 'the eagle of Rome' (though another versifier glossed allegorically the forms of *'des riches schilt'* only to observe sharply that the king was no eagle but a mere woodpecker tapping at a rotten tree).[189] An Austrian annalist likewise pointed out the Roman connotations of the eagle on the king's banner, while Alexander von Roes, who in his allegorical *Pavo* (1285) employed an eagle to represent and speak for the

---

[184] *Continuatio Vindobonensis*, ed. Wattenbach, p. 709; *Continuatio praedicatorum Vindobonensium*, ed. Wattenbach, p. 731; *Chronicon Magni Presbyteri Continuatio*, ed. Wattenbach, pp. 533–4. On the battle generally, see Redlich, *Rudolf von Habsburg*, pp. 320–1.

[185] *Lohengrin*, ed. Cramer, p. 444, v. 5119; Konrad von Würzburg, *Partonopier und Meliur*, ed. Bartsch, p. 220, vv. 15170–1; and see Thomas, 'Nationale Elemente', p. 362.

[186] Selzer, *Deutsche Söldner*, p. 99.

[187] *Rymkronyk van Jan van Heelu*, ed. Willems, p. 233, vv. 6287–90: 'Soe trocken si al ghescaert / Dapperlike ten stride waert, / Crierende blidelike: / "Hya, Berge romerike!"'.

[188] Above, Ch. 3, pp. 138–40.

[189] Konrad von Würzburg in *Politische Lyrik*, ed. Müller, vol. I, p. 89 ('Dem adelarn von Rome werdeclichen ist gelungen'); and for the hostile verdict of 'Schulmeister von Esslingen', see ibid., p. 89 ('Ir nement des riches schiltes war ... in golde ein ufreht adelar hat uf den schilt gestrecket sich'). For Konrad's praise of Rudolf, see also Ritscher, *Literatur*, pp. 51, 59.

Empire, lauded elsewhere the matchless deterrent power of 'the eagles of the Romans and the Germans'.[190] But it was a Roman rather than a German Empire that the language and symbols of military allegiance appeared to contemporaries overwhelmingly to proclaim. Little wonder, then, that the imperial herald to the end of the Middle Ages went by the name of *Romreich*. Only in the sixteenth century did he start to be known as *Deutschland*.[191]

Imperial crisis, imperial public

What perhaps most of all infused the Empire's name and its symbols with a commanding imaginative power, capable of reaching out beyond elite circles, was its association with a politicised Christian eschatology staking universal claims. While the Reich was not the only European monarchy to be made the subject of prophetic hopes and fears, the tradition of envisaging Roman emperors as central actors in an impending world-historical transformation was a uniquely rich and ancient one, and the stimuli to its perpetuation and elaboration during the Middle Ages particularly many and urgent.[192] Once again, the late medieval imperial monarchy was nourished as an ideal, even as its material shortcomings were being savagely exposed, by a peculiarly venerable and illustrious antique heritage. Speculation about the Empire's future historical role rested on an amalgam of Roman Sibylline prophecy and early Christian doctrines plotting the expected course of the drama of human salvation, and it was underlain by still more ancient ideas about a coming messiah and his transformative works.[193]

Byzantine prophecies anticipating a last Roman emperor, the inaugurator of an age of peace, whose passing was to herald the reign of Antichrist and the loosing of the armies of Gog and Magog, had reached western Europe by the eighth century. They attained new urgency with the revival of the western Empire in the time of Charlemagne.[194] In the centuries that followed, eschatological speculation attached itself to these northern Caesars, as well as to the Carolingians' successors in

---

[190] *Annales Sancti Rudberti Salisburgenses*, ed. Wattenbach, p. 803, for Austrian forces bearing 'vexillum Romane aquile'; Alexander von Roes, *Memoriale*, cap. 33, ed. Grundmann and Heimpel, p. 142. For his *Pavo*, see Heimpel, 'Über den "Pavo"'.
[191] Schubert, *Einführung*, p. 33.
[192] For other monarchies as the subject of prophecy, see Kurze, 'Nationale Regungen', esp. pp. 6–7 (for France).
[193] See generally Kampers, *Kaiseridee*; also: Struve, 'Die falschen Friedriche', esp. pp. 326–7; Reeves, *Prophecy*, esp. pp. 295–300.
[194] See Kampers, *Kaiseridee*, esp. pp. 23–4, 33–5.

western Frankia.[195] The Staufer, however, were to be written by their supporters like no dynasty before them into the fabric of salvation history, while their detractors were perceiving in the Swabian emperors the agents of a coming Antichrist long before their final fall from grace. Abbot Joachim's eschatological schemes, meanwhile, had had the effect of making the Last Things appear startlingly imminent.[196] That impression was lent force by their dissemination, through the new mendicant orders, in the time of Frederick II's clash with the Curia, years which also saw the Mongols advancing upon Europe like a long-awaited apocalyptic scourge.[197] Joachim's followers did not hesitate to identify in the emperor Antichrist's precursor, or Antichrist himself. Frederick's partisans, for their part, preferred to view him as he presented himself, as the righteous chastiser of a corrupt Church, and to hurl the name of Antichrist back at the pope.[198] The Staufer were to be the final imperial dynasty, divinely elected to rule until the end of human history.[199] What these contending viewpoints shared was a conviction that the fate of the entire Christian community, and the future course and consummation of human affairs, were bound up with the contemporary struggle of emperor and pope.

When Frederick died with the eschatological drama – scheduled, on Joachimite reckoning, for a climax in the year 1260 – still uncompleted, the field was thrown open to yet more luxuriant prophecy, and even to fantastic attempts at re-enacting a Staufer monarchy.[200] Some speculated that the emperor would arise again, or that he had never died. Others looked for a 'third Frederick', of Hohenstaufen blood, to punish or purify the clergy, with attention falling for a time on the young margrave of Meißen.[201] Already before Frederick's death, a group in the town of Schwäbisch Hall was denouncing the pope as a heretic and looking to the emperor and his son to restore the Church to

---

[195] Ibid., esp. pp. 43–61; Reeves, *Prophecy*, pp. 301–2. The identity-forming role, among both the Germans and the French, of rival, Carolingian-derived, emperor prophecies is emphasised by Kurze, 'Nationale Regungen', pp. 6–8.

[196] Töpfer, *Das kommende Reich*, p. 48; Gloger, *Kaiser*, p. 194; Schaller, 'Endzeiterwartungen', p. 306; and see generally Reeves, *Prophecy*.

[197] For the role of the mendicants, see Reeves, *Influence of Prophecy*, pp. 161–90; for the Mongols as the peoples of Gog and Magog, Schaller, 'Endzeiterwartungen', p. 313.

[198] For the rival views of Frederick, see: Schaller, 'Endzeiterwartungen', pp. 314–16; Töpfer, *Das kommende Reich*, pp. 155–6. In 1239 the emperor had compared his birthplace, Jesi, to Bethlehem.

[199] Schaller, 'Kaiseridee', p. 130.

[200] For the significance of 1260, see: Schaller, 'Endzeiterwartungen', p. 306; Reeves, *Prophecy*, pp. 53–4; Kampers, *Kaiseridee*, p. 72.

[201] For speculation on this theme, see: Töpfer, *Das kommende Reich*, pp. 160, 168–9; Kampers, *Kaiseridee*, p. 98.

apostolic simplicity.[202] Around the same time, the writings of a certain Brother Arnold, a German Dominican, reflect the same agitated mood. Adapting Joachim's teachings, Arnold foresaw a purge of the clergy at the hands of the friars preachers, aided by the emperor.[203] But the disappearance of Frederick, and then of his offspring, brought a strange new twist to the association of the Staufer with the Empire's prophetic future.[204]

In 1269 a young man briefly created a stir in the German southwest by claiming to be Frederick's grandson Konradin, who had lost his head in Naples a few months before.[205] His appearance turned out to be but the prelude to the emergence in Germany of a veritable clamour of would-be Staufer – though the others of whom we know all insisted they were Frederick II himself. The first of them was noted in 1284 in the south-west.[206] There was another 'Frederick' in Utrecht around a year later, and still others in Lübeck in 1287 and Esslingen in 1295.[207] Each of these figures either was quickly apprehended and executed, or slipped back into obscurity as silently as he had emerged. One such 'reign' merits fuller consideration, however: that of the imposter, whose name is recorded as Tile Kolup or Dietrich Holzschuh, who held court in Frederick's guise, first at Neuß and then in the imperial town of Wetzlar, for several months in 1284 and 1285.[208] Although at first driven from Cologne as a madman, he proved able for a time to maintain himself in style and to acquire at least some of the trappings of rulership; and he evidently possessed both grandiose political ambitions and some notion of the material steps needed to give them effect.[209] Envoys came

[202] Kampers, *Kaiseridee*, p. 96; Töpfer, *Das kommende Reich*, pp. 159–60; Struve, 'Utopie', pp. 73–5.

[203] For Arnold, see: Töpfer, *Das kommende Reich*, pp. 156–9; Kampers, *Kaiseridee*, p. 96.

[204] For what follows, see generally: Struve, 'Die falschen Friedriche'; Struve, 'Utopie'; Schwinges, 'Verfassung'; Cohn, *Millennium*, pp. 113–18.

[205] *Flores Temporum: Imperatores*, ed. Holder-Egger, p. 241; *Notae Weingartenses*, ed. Waitz, p. 831.

[206] *Annales Colmarienses maiores*, ed. Jaffé, p. 211.

[207] For the Utrecht 'false Frederick', see *Annales Blandinienses*, ed. Bethmann, p. 33; for those in Lübeck and Eßlingen: *Detmar-Chronik*, ed. Koppmann, i.367; *Annales Colmarienses maiores*, ed. Jaffé, pp. 221–2.

[208] On Tile Kolup, see: Struve, 'Die falschen Friedriche', pp. 319–20; Schwinges, 'Verfassung', pp. 180–1; Redlich, *Rudolf von Habsburg*, pp. 529–41; Martin, *Städtepolitik*, pp. 161–5.

[209] On his style of rule, see: *Martini continuatio Coloniensis*, ed. Waitz, p. 357; *Annales Sancti Rudberti Salisburgenses*, ed. Wattenbach, p. 809. The Styrian Rhyming Chronicle paints a vivid picture of the magnificence of his court: *Ottokars österreichische Reimchronik*, ed. Seemüller, p. 422, vv. 32197–9. The imposter was evidently aware of the constitutional importance of Frankfurt in the making of the ruler and, according to the biographer of Archbishop Henry of Trier, intended to summon the

from Lombardy, and powerful Germans established links with the obscure monarch.[210] Tile Kolup's reception in Wetzlar, which at the time was resisting Rudolf I's taxation, spurred the king to undertake a lengthy journey to confront him in person.[211] Only then was the pseudo-emperor handed over and burned. His strange rise and precipitate fall attracted notice and wonder throughout the length and breadth of Germany.[212]

Physical impersonation of an allegedly still-living Frederick II seems to have ended with the thirteenth century (by which time the emperor would have been over 100 years old). But speculation around the coming of a transformative emperor Frederick rumbled on, if for much of the time obscurely. In 1348, during troubled times in Germany, Johann von Winterthur reported rumours anticipating the advent of such a one, who would marry poor women to rich men and so chastise the clergy that they would hide their tonsures beneath cow dung.[213] Neo-Sibylline prophecies in the time of Charles IV foresaw 'wailing and distress' under the Luxemburger, and further imperial decline, but also the advent of a heaven-sent Frederick to liberate Jerusalem and convert the heathen.[214] 'Manifestos for a future Frederick', as Norman Cohn called them, were to become more extended, and more lurid, in the century preceding the Lutheran Reformation.[215] As the Empire of solid fact receded in the decades after the fall of the Staufer, a spectral Empire of hope, fear and anticipation gathered substance in the minds of some Germans.[216]

German princes to a *generale concilium* there: *Vita Henrici Archiepiscopi Altera*, ed. Waitz, pp. 462–3. The Styrian Rhyming Chronicle (as above, p. 426, vv. 32541–6) depicted the false emperor instructing his followers to go to Frankfurt and wait for him there. See also the comments of Schwinges, 'Verfassung', p. 186.

[210] For embassies from the Lombard cities and the marquis of Este, see *Chronica Fratris Salimbene de Adam Ordinis Minorum*, ed. Holder-Egger, p. 537. For the many visitors who came to Neuss 'ex variis provinciis', and for the style of their reception, see *Cronica S. Petri Erfordensis Moderna*, ed. Holder-Egger, p. 289. Abbess Bertha of Essen had the privileges of her convent confirmed by the imposter: Erkens, *Siegfried*, p. 263.

[211] For Wetzlar's resistance to Rudolf, see Schwind, *Die Landvogtei*, pp. 183–4; for the king's response, Redlich, *Rudolf von Habsburg*, pp. 531–9.

[212] For the chronicle references, see above, Ch. 3, p. 118. 'No corner of the world', claimed Henry of Trier's biographer, remained untouched by the news of the pseudo-emperor's deeds: *Vita Henrici Archiepiscopi Altera*, ed. Waitz, p. 462.

[213] *Die Chronik Johanns von Winterthur*, ed. Baethgen, pp. 280–2. See also Töpfer, *Das kommende Reich*, p. 179; Struve, 'Utopie', pp. 76–8.

[214] Herkommer, 'Kritik', pp. 78–9.

[215] Cohn, *Millennium*, pp. 118–26.

[216] As Friedrich Baethgen observed, 'Es ist, als suchten sich die Völker in ihren Träumen einen Ersatz für das, was die Gegenwart nicht zu bieten vermochte.' Quoted in Struve, 'Utopie', p. 92.

The emperor prophecies merit attention here for what they reveal about the social penetration of the imperial idea in late medieval Germany. The heretics of Schwäbisch Hall were in all likelihood sustained in their convictions by powerful pro-Staufer families in the region, and by the town's direct contacts with the emperor and his son.[217] But subsequent outbreaks of enthusiasm rested upon rumour and speculation alone, and these evidently attained at times considerable intensity and dissemination.[218] Mostly, they would have spread by word of mouth. 'At that time it was said', noted the *Saxon World Chronicle* for 1251, 'that the emperor Frederick was dead; but part of the people insisted that he lived on.' 'The doubt', added the chronicler, 'long persisted.'[219] Peter von Zittau, a native of east-central Germany, recalled a 'popular prophecy' (*vulgare vaticinium*) from his youth, according to which Frederick of Meißen would become a mighty emperor and visit 'marvels' upon the clergy.[220] 'Some people say', remarked Alexander von Roes, following a prophecy long current in Germany (*Germania*), that from the stock of Frederick II would spring forth a 'sinful root', another Frederick, to humble the German clergy and the Roman Church.[221] Even forty years after his death, reflected the compiler of *Flores temporum*, men were still claiming that the emperor was alive, and would shortly return in great power.[222] The rumours were to rumble on for some time longer.[223] A babel of voices, detectable now through the wondering commentaries of the literate few, talked the Staufer *imperium* back to imagined life in the decades after 1250.

Such talk was highly mobile, and many, it seems, had their ears open. Pro-Staufer prophecies quickly made their way north over the Alps from Italian Ghibelline circles, just as the tale of Frederick's reappearance went south.[224] The false emperor executed at Utrecht was claimed to have arisen after three days from the ashes of the imposter burned

---

[217] Kampers, *Kaiseridee*, p. 76.
[218] For rumours about Frederick II, see generally Gloger, *Kaiser*, pp. 198–9.
[219] *Sächsische Weltchronik*, ed. Weiland, p. 258.
[220] *Königsaaler Geschichts-Quellen*, ed. Loserth, pp. 424–5.
[221] Alexander von Roes, *Memoriale*, cap. 30, ed. Grundmann and Heimpel, p. 136. See also Töpfer, *Das kommende Reich*, pp. 186–7.
[222] *Flores Temporum: Imperatores*, ed. Holder-Egger, p. 241. The Viennese chronicler Jansen Enikel, probably writing in the 1270s, also noted the great *strît* which Frederick's death stirred up: some said that he was dead and buried, and others that 'er leb noch in der werlt wît'. *Jansen Enikels Weltchronik*, p. 574, vv. 28945–57.
[223] For fourteenth-century references to such rumours, see: *Chronica de gestis principum*, ed. Leidinger, p. 35; *Die Chronik Johanns von Winterthur*, ed. Baethgen, p. 209.
[224] For Ghibelline prophecies in Germany, see: Reeves, *Prophecy*, pp. 311–12; Kampers, *Kaiseridee*, p. 98.

shortly before at Wetzlar.[225] Most remarkable about Tile Kolup himself was the extent of his knowledge; on this above all rested his imposture.[226] Many nobles came to him, observed an Erfurt chronicler, 'all of whom, by means of necromancy, he greeted by their own names'.[227] How else but by black magic was an obscure man's access to such information to be explained? The pseudo-monarch was able even to acquire the means of making plausible imitations of imperial documents, authenticated with a seal based on Frederick's own.[228] The *imperium*, as ideal, and even as style of rule, was evidently widely accessible, and not only in elite circles. The false rulers themselves were, so far as we can tell, men of humble origin, as were many of their supporters.[229] More than one chronicler insists that the poor were Tile Kolup's most loyal adherents.[230] That is not to suggest that such figures appealed specifically to the destitute. On the contrary, contemporaries were struck by the breadth of their support. In the view of one Austrian annalist, Tile Kolup 'led a great part of Germany into error', and 'many lords', as another chronicler notes, gave him their allegiance.[231] The point is rather that social stratification, like geographical distance, was clearly little obstacle to the spread of their fame and appeal.

The rumours, the enthusiasm, the imposters: all had their main home in the Empire's German lands. Yet the ruler they invoked was to be no 'German' but a universal one, who would extend his rule to the ends of the earth. His God-given power was to 'reach over all kingdoms'.[232]

---

[225] *Annales Blandinienses*, ed. Bethmann, p. 33.

[226] The means by which he legitimised himself are analysed in Schwinges, 'Verfassung', pp. 198–200.

[227] *Cronica S. Petri Erfordensis Moderna*, ed. Holder-Egger, p. 289. The remarkable extent of his knowledge is also emphasised in *Vita Henrici archiepiscopi altera*, ed. Waitz, p. 462.

[228] *Vita Henrici archiepiscopi altera*, ed. Waitz, p. 462. And see Struve, 'Die falschen Friedriche', p. 322 n. 22.

[229] *Vita Henrici archiepiscopi altera*, ed. Waitz, p. 462: 'quidam rusticus'; *Martini continuatio Coloniensis*, ed. Waitz, p. 357: 'quidam nacione rusticanus'. See also Schwinges, 'Verfassung', pp. 180–1. Johann von Winterthur, writing towards the middle of the fourteenth century, identified Tile Kolup as a smith: *Die Chronik Johanns von Winterthur*, ed. Baethgen, p. 22. The 'false Konradin' was allegedly a smith's son: *Notae Weingartenses*, ed. Waitz, p. 831.

[230] According to the Styrian Rhyming Chronicle, the poor resisted handing Tile Kolup over to King Rudolf: *Ottokars österreichische Reimchronik*, ed. Seemüller, pp. 424–5, vv. 32422–38. See also Struve, 'Die falschen Friedriche', p. 324.

[231] *Annales Sancti Rudberti Salisburgenses*, ed. Wattenbach, p. 809; *Cronica S. Petri Erfordensis Moderna*, ed. Holder-Egger, p. 289. See also: *Ellenhardi chronicon*, ed. Jaffé, p. 125 ('excecavit cum eo multos nobiles Alemanie'); *Continuatio Vindobonensis*, ed. Wattenbach, p. 712 (he attracted to him 'fere omnes Renenses').

[232] See Kampers, *Kaiseridee*, p. 102, for the prophecy recorded *c.* 1300 by Heinrich Hessler regarding a future monarch, whose power 'sal werden also vol, / daz sein heil wirt also gestalt, / daz von gote sin gewalt / sal uber alle riche reichen'. The prophecies

Only such a monarch, it was clear, would prove equal to the ills of the time. It is likely that, particularly in the growing towns, escalating social tensions, and the patent incapacity of the Empire's elected rulers to resolve them, fuelled the longing for a great peace-bringing emperor, and stoked speculation and controversy over the time and manner of his coming.[233] Tile Kolup's own career illuminates these rifts: both in Neuß and in Wetzlar, there are signs that he divided the burgher community, or threw into relief divisions already present.[234] Elsewhere, urban life in the decades after 1250 was disrupted by struggles between regimes dominated by patrician clans and the groups which they shut out from government, including craftsmen organised in guilds. Social conflict emerged early in Cologne, where the Dominican scholar Albertus Magnus had during the 1250s twice been called upon to arbitrate in clashes, in which the archbishop was also embroiled, between prominent families and other elements in the city.[235] Not only was the imperial monarchy unable to resolve such disorders; in the course of its protracted conflicts with the papacy the Empire itself became, especially in the towns, a source of widespread division for the German populations under its rule.

The closing years of Frederick II's reign saw excommunications, interdicts and even crusading armies directed at those parts of Germany which remained loyal to the emperor and his kin. No less intensive was the barrage of sermons, letters, pamphlets and prophecies maintained by both sides, which already surely merits the name of propaganda, and which contributed to the febrility of the public mood.[236] People were moved to act. In Oppenheim, a messenger from Archbishop Siegfried of Mainz, at the time papal legate in Germany, was dragged from church by the hair to have his nose cut off by a burgher mob. In Strasbourg, Staufer partisans set upon the Dominicans, hanging one and throwing another into the river Ill.[237] The renewal of strife under Ludwig IV brought a return of anguished speculation and desperate acts. Dreadful

---

which circulated in Germany in the late 1260s, probably of Italian Ghibelline origin, anticipating the coming of a new emperor Frederick, also expected him to bring peace to the whole world and to extend his rule to the ends of the earth: Töpfer, *Das kommende Reich*, pp. 168–71. See also Schreiner, 'Die Staufer', esp. p. 251.

[233] Struve, 'Die falschen Friedriche', esp. pp. 326–30; and, for the importance of towns, Schwinges, 'Verfassung', p. 190.

[234] For Neuß see Erkens, *Siegfried*, p. 263; at Wetzlar it was the *potiores civitatis* who agreed to hand the imposter over to King Rudolf: *Ellenhardi chronicon*, ed. Jaffé, p. 126.

[235] Groten, *Köln*, pp. 180–206.

[236] See: Segl, 'Die Feindbilder'; Mierau, 'Exkommunikation'.

[237] For Oppenheim, see Demandt, 'Der Endkampf', pp. 133–4; for Strasbourg, Freed, *The Friars*, p. 160.

portents were seen.[238] For one imperialist writer, the attacks on Jewish communities which spread through southern Germany in the late 1330s signalled the fate awaiting the clergy.[239] Events appeared to be proving his point. One senior cleric, who at papal behest had urged the people of Berlin and Cölln to withhold fealty from Ludwig's son as margrave of Brandenburg, was murdered and his corpse burned. A papal envoy, who came to Saarburg to promulgate the Curia's legal process against the Bavarian, was still being held captive there by 'agents of the Devil' many months later.[240] In Frankfurt am Main, the struggle of the 'two powers' was given succinct and very public expression when Ludwig's opponents put up papal letters of excommunication on church doors beside the emperor's decrees.[241] Ludwig's own learned champions also went to work, circulating inflammatory writings and kindling helpful rumours in their master's cause.[242]

The papal interdict was a particular source of division. After the emperor's death, Lupold Hornburg was still fulminating against the 'false bann' from which 'the poor' found no release.[243] Ludwig himself had forbidden its observation.[244] In Landshut, Ludwig von Teck had led armed men into the Dominican convent, threatening to burn it down if divine services were not resumed.[245] The contests for the throne which in each case accompanied these clashes added their own note of division. One theme recurs: the populations of the Empire's German lands, and particularly their urban component, were repeatedly called upon to form a view on the events of the time, and to decide where their own loyalties lay. Ludwig IV had in 1338 marshalled his supporters

---

[238] From the Upper Rhine, for example, there were reports of 'sweating' images of Christ: Kaufhold, *Gladius Spiritualis*, pp. 210, 236; and see, for a plague of grasshoppers and other ominous contemporary 'afflictions', Lupold Hornburg, *Die Landpredige*, in *The Poems of Lupold Hornburg*, ed. Bell and Gudde, p. 182, vv. 125–33.

[239] Konrad von Megenberg, *Planctus*, pars I, cap. 27, ed. Scholz, p. 46.

[240] For these incidents, see Schubert, 'Ludwig der Bayer', p. 190.

[241] Kaufhold, *Gladius Spiritualis*, p. 229. On the importance of the church door as a venue for the display of constitutional and polemical writings by both Ludwig IV and his papal opponents, see Schubert, 'Ludwig der Bayer', pp. 178–9. As Heinrich von Diessenhofen remarked, the emperor thus proclaimed his case 'as if by the herald's cry': *Heinricus Dapifer de Diessenhoven*, ed. Huber, pp. 29–30. As Schubert observes, Ludwig's public documents would have been visually impressive on account of their length alone, even to spectators to whom their learned Latin texts were inaccessible: 'anyone who could list so many arguments had to be right'.

[242] Schütz, 'Der Kampf Ludwigs des Bayern', p. 390, for the 'forged' plaint put into circulation by Ludwig's protonotary Ulrich Wild, accusing John XXII of heresy.

[243] Lupold Hornburg, *Die Landpredige*, in *The Poems of Lupold Hornburg*, ed. Bell and Gudde, p. 185, vv. 229–30; and see the comments of Schubert, 'Ludwig der Bayer', p. 184.

[244] Kaufhold, *Gladius Spiritualis*, p. 227.

[245] Ibid., p. 245.

to assail the Curia with petitions on his behalf. When proctors from the town of Aachen came before Benedict XII at Avignon, the pope conceded that he had already received thirty-six identical letters from other imperial towns, professing loyalty to the emperor.[246] Choices of a similar kind were being faced throughout the German lands. Whether an interdict was to be observed, an excommunicate prince shunned or an anti-king backed were decisions with potentially grave consequences for those called on to take them and for those in whose names they acted.[247] In the century following Frederick II's reign no institution did more than the papacy to ensure the Empire's continuing, periodically urgent, relevance to Germans, well beyond the ambit of their monarch's dwindling means of rule.

The Empire in debate

On one measure of the Empire's significance, the signs are clear. Never before had the medieval *imperium* been made the subject of such numerous, extended and reflective writings, elucidating its character and justifying its existence, as it came to be in the two centuries following the end of the Staufer. While the doctrines which the treatise-writers propounded were in essence traditional, well rooted in authoritative textual pasts, their lengthy elucidation of the imperial idea was new.[248] It is true that polemical tracts in the Empire's defence were being written as early as the 'Investiture Contest'.[249] Writings glorifying the *imperium* multiplied under the Staufer; Frederick II's reign had seen the agitational texts come thick and fast. Yet it was only in the crisis decades following his fall that works of a more developed kind, replete with extended historical, legal and philosophical proofs, were piled up in the Empire's support. That thinkers of the stature of Dante, Marsilius and Ockham were now among their authors underlines the continuing intellectual potency of the imperial idea, at least in the regions most affected by the Empire's affairs.[250] But a greater number of these tracts were the work of Germans, who have traditionally held far less starry

---

[246] Ibid., p. 219. For context, see Stengel, *Avignon*, pp. 85–184.
[247] For the role of excommunication in forming public opinion see Mierau, 'Exkommunikation', pp. 69–71.
[248] For the character of these works and their links with earlier imperialist traditions, see: Heer, 'Zur Kontinuität', esp. pp. 336–7; Dempf, *Sacrum Imperium*, part III, cap. 3; for their novelty and its significance, Walther, *Imperiales Königtum*, pp. 220–9.
[249] Suchan, 'Publizistik'; Robinson, *Authority*, Chs. 2, 3; Melve, *Public Sphere*.
[250] See generally: Miethke, 'Politisches Denken', pp. 121–44; Folz, *The Concept*, Chs. 11, 12.

places in the history of political thought.[251] From the 'Interregnum', and the uncertain times which followed, to the period of Ludwig IV's clash with Avignon, and thence to the era of the Schism and that of the Councils, the flow of imperialist writings from German pens mapped with precision the recurrent crises of the Reich and, in later periods, that of its spiritual counterpart, the papacy. To survey the origins, careers and experiences of their authors – figures such as Alexander von Roes, Lupold von Bebenburg, Konrad von Megenberg and Dietrich von Niem – is to discover much about the workings, and enduring penetrative powers, of the imperial idea itself.

Noteworthy first of all is the diffuseness of the picture which they present. The Empire's German defenders were the opposite of the tight-knit and high-ranking coterie around the throne that some views of medieval political culture might lead us to anticipate.[252] Of their social origin it can be said that, while most came from families commanding at least a measure of local standing, none was born into the ruling circles of the great. Beyond that, however, few common elements stand out. Some were the offspring of ministerial families, well connected, as was Lupold von Bebenburg's kin, or impoverished like Konrad von Megenberg's.[253] Others came from the towns, Gobelinus Persona from Paderborn burgher stock, Dietrich von Niem from Brakel, where his father was probably a councillor.[254] Though respectable enough, such men can scarcely be said to have entered the world predestined for high affairs. Geographically too, they were provincials. While Lupold and Konrad hailed from *königsnah* Franconia, others had their roots in regions peripheral to royal government. The Cologne of Alexander von Roes, though an important station on the new king's ceremonial travels, saw the monarch only spasmodically. Westphalia, which produced a succession of imperialist treatise writers, among them Jordan

---

[251] For generally negative judgements, see: Ullmann, *Political Thought*, p. 186; Morrall, *Political Thought*, p. 95; Barraclough, *The Origins*, p. 299. Their main common characteristic was an 'anxious conservatism': Dempf, *Sacrum Imperium*, p. 494.

[252] Thus, e.g., Althof, *Spielregeln*, esp. p. 256. Althof's evidence is drawn overwhelmingly from the earlier Middle Ages.

[253] For Lupold, see: K. Colberg, 'Lupold von Bebenburg', in *VL* 5, cols. 1071–8 (esp. cols. 1071–3); P. Johanek, 'Lupold (Leopold, Liupold) v. Bebenburg', in *NDB* 15, pp. 524–5 (here p. 524); Krüger, 'Lupold', esp. pp. 49–52; Miethke and Flüeler, 'Einleitung', pp. 1–61; for Konrad: G. Steer, 'Konrad von Megenberg', in *VL* 5, cols. 221–36 (here col. 221); Krüger, 'Einleitung', pp. xii–xvii; Krüger, 'Das Rittertum', esp. p. 302. See also the bibliographies for the substantial older literature on both writers.

[254] For Gobelinus, see K. Colberg, 'Person, Gobelinus', in *VL* 7, cols. 411–16; for Dietrich: Heimpel, *Dietrich*, pp. 13–14; Colberg and Leuschner, 'Einleitung', pp. vii–viii.

von Osnabrück, Dietrich von Niem and Gobelinus Persona, saw him hardly at all.[255] While the Empire's government made its way through Germany with short and leaden steps, the imperial idea was carried far and wide, on other currents.

Most of the treatise-writers occupied responsible offices in the Church, and a handful won significant honours and titles; but these were generally the fruits of long and busy years spent in administration and law, rather than marks of privileged birth. The bishopric of Bamberg which eventually fell to Lupold von Bebenburg set a seal on more than two decades devoted to the affairs of the church of Würzburg, as well as reflecting his contacts with Balduin of Luxemburg's circle.[256] A comparable period spent toiling in the papal bureaucracy preceded Dietrich von Niem's unhappy tenure of the bishopric of Verden.[257] Here, then, were men who could plausibly claim, as Dietrich repeatedly did, that their understanding of the problems of the day rested upon *experience*.[258] On occasion, that experience must have been deeply troubling. In unstable times, even churchmen of relatively humble rank and origin sometimes found themselves disconcertingly close to the centre of events. Dietrich von Niem had been present at the torture of five cardinals, carried out at the behest of the violent Urban VI (1378–89).[259] Among the troubles impinging on their lives were the Empire's crises and its periodic rifts with the Curia. Not until the 1350s was Lupold von Bebenburg finally released from the multiple excommunications which he had incurred in the time of Ludwig IV.[260] Engelbert von Admont had been forced abruptly to terminate his studies in Prague when the mood in King Otakar's capital turned ugly following Rudolf I's elevation to the Reich.[261] The salutary shocks to which Alexander von Roes was exposed in papal Viterbo were not wholly untypical of the experience of other thoughtful Germans of his time, of comparable status and outlook.

On the whole, these traditionalist champions of the Reich led active and varied – on occasion, indeed (as a biographer of Dietrich observes), 'almost adventurous' – lives.[262] But even when they fell

---

[255] For Jordan, see: Grundmann and Heimpel, 'Einleitung', pp. 16–18; Koch, 'Jordanus'; for Westphalia's importance in imperialist thought, Grundmann, 'Westfalen'.

[256] Johanek, 'Lupold (Leopold, Liupold) von Bebenburg', in *NDB* 15, p. 524.

[257] Heimpel, *Dietrich*, Ch. 2.

[258] Colberg and Leuschner, 'Einleitung', p. viii.

[259] Heimpel, *Dietrich*, p. 20.

[260] Miethke and Flüeler, 'Einleitung', pp. 53–4.

[261] H. Zinsmeyer, 'Engelbert (Poetsch) von Admont', in *LMA* 3, cols. 1919–20 (here col. 1919); Fowler, *Intellectual Interests*, p. 20.

[262] J. Leuschner, 'Dietrich von Nieheim', in *VL* 2, cols. 140–4 (here col. 141).

short of high drama, their days were not lived out in ivory towers. Konrad von Megenberg's appointment in 1342 as rector of the school at St Stephen's in Vienna brought with it a general responsibility for schooling in the city.[263] Dietrich's charitable works included founding a hospital at Hameln as well as endowments for the German hospice in Rome, where he was the first rector.[264] Other imperialist writers busied themselves with local monastic reform.[265] Canonries and other offices in collegiate churches would have reinforced their familiarity with ecclesiastical government and with its sociable and communal duties and bonds. Especially striking is the recurring place which long-distance travel occupied in their lives. Konrad von Megenberg went repeatedly to papal Avignon, as a young man at the behest of the university of Paris, later on behalf of the town of Regensburg and of the emperor himself.[266] Trips back to Germany, of varied destination and purpose, punctuated Dietrich von Niem's long career in the south.[267] It was in all likelihood a legal dispute which had set Alexander von Roes on the long road from Cologne to Viterbo.[268] University studies above all brought such men, in impressionable youth and early adulthood, to foreign lands and cities. Engelbert von Admont's time in Prague was followed by several years in Padua.[269] Lupold's student years were spent in Bologna (whence he departed a *doctor decretorum*); Dietrich's in Avignon.[270] The lack, before the later fourteenth century, of universities on German soil compelled youthful careerists to seek their education in distant parts. The remarkable ascent of Rudolf Losse, as diplomat and theoretician in Balduin of Luxemburg's service, was founded upon study at Montpellier: far indeed from his Thuringian homeland, though handily close to Avignon.[271] Often, it is clear, these university years left a lasting impression. Konrad von Megenberg, who as student and teacher spent nearly a decade in Paris, lauded the city as a scholar's paradise.[272] It may have been similar formative experiences that induced Alexander von Roes – about whose education, however, nothing certain is known – to incorporate the Paris *studium* into his tripartite

[263] Steer, 'Konrad von Megenberg', in *VL* 5, cols. 221–2.
[264] Heimpel, *Dietrich*, pp. 14–15; Colberg and Leuschner, 'Einleitung', pp. vii–viii.
[265] K. Colberg, 'Person, Gobelinus', in *VL* 7, col. 411.
[266] Steer, 'Konrad von Megenberg', in *VL* 5, col. 221.
[267] Heimpel, *Dietrich*, pp. 20, 40, 44–5.
[268] Grundmann and Heimpel, 'Einleitung', pp. 3–4.
[269] Zinsmeyer, 'Engelbert (Poetsch) von Admont', in *LMA* 3, col. 1919.
[270] Colberg, 'Lupold von Bebenburg', in *VL* 5, col. 1072; Heimpel, *Dietrich*, pp. 22–3.
[271] Burgard, 'Rudolf Losse', p. 49.
[272] Steer, 'Konrad von Megenberg', in *VL* 5, col. 221; and see Konrad von Megenberg, *Ökonomik*, lib. 3.i, cap. 3, ed. Krüger, vol. III, p. 22.

scheme for the government of Christendom.[273] Engelbert von Admont would later remark upon some of the marvels of Venice which he had taken the opportunity to view while studying in Padua.[274] Lupold was to return later in life to his north Italian *alma mater* to consult his old tutor, Johannes Andreae, in a matter of law.[275]

If these German treatise-writers were men of thought and learning, few among them could be described as cloistered intellectuals. Mostly they were clerks not only of broad experience but of wide and varied reading and writing. Tracts on the Empire usually form only a portion – and not always a large portion – of their known works. Engelbert von Admont listed in a letter thirty-three writings of which he claimed authorship, divided between works of theology, and natural and moral philosophy.[276] Konrad von Megenberg's extensive *oeuvre* encompassed theological, hagiographic, pedagogical and encyclopaedic texts, alongside his repeated treatment of imperial matters.[277] A concern for the education of the young, which led him to cast his eyes outwards, beyond narrow learned circles, may in part reflect his own difficult early years.[278] Was this omnivorous quality replicated in their writings on the Empire? And did the *imperium* as a theme characteristically draw to it commentators of broad learning and experience? What can certainly be said is that their approaches to the imperial idea varied considerably in character and focus. Engelbert's writings, abstract, idealised and grounded in Aristotelian philosophy, were quite different from Lupold's, with their roots in law and history, or from the even more markedly historical treatises of Alexander von Roes.[279] Some works display considerable rigour and organisation; others, like the many, repetitive tracts dashed off by Dietrich von Niem, were little more than shapeless compilations.[280] Imperialist thought, we might say, shared in this period some of the 'openness' which Peter Moraw has perceived in the imperial constitution itself: various routes into it could

---

[273] Alexander von Roes, *Memoriale*, cap. 25, ed. Grundmann and Heimpel, pp. 126–7; and see Grundmann, 'Sacerdotium'.

[274] Fowler, *Intellectual Interests*, p. 23.

[275] Colberg, 'Lupold von Bebenburg', in *VL* 5, col. 1072.

[276] Zinsmeyer, 'Engelbert (Poetsch) von Admont', in *LMA* 3, col. 1919. For his writings, see Ubl, *Engelbert*.

[277] Listed in Steer, 'Konrad von Megenberg', in *VL* 5, cols. 222–34.

[278] For his pedagogical interests, see ibid., cols. 231–4. Concern for the upbringing and development of poor boys of knightly family is a recurrent theme in his writings on military matters: Krüger, 'Das Rittertum', esp. pp. 312–14.

[279] For the character of Engelbert's political writings, see S. Krüger, 'Engelbert (Pötsch?) von Admont', in *NDB* 4, pp. 509–10 (here p. 510), and generally Ubl, *Engelbert*.

[280] See the comments of Colberg and Leuschner, 'Einleitung', pp. viii, liv.

be followed, and not all of them were open only to individuals of highly technical and specialised intellectual formation.

Of course, the number of writers who engaged systematically with the imperial idea was not in absolute terms very great; and it would be wrong to overstate the significance of the handful of assorted texts which they left behind. It is easy to understand the dismissiveness with which historians of political ideas have mostly treated their defences – tired and hackneyed defences, as they must often seem – of an apparently obsolete institution. Was anyone at the time listening to them? Were they even listening to one another? The initial signs are not promising. Indeed, the general obscurity of their works seems to belie their frequent modern description as 'publicist' tracts. If it was ever their authors' aim to secure wide attention for their writings, or to agitate broadly on the Empire's behalf, we can only be struck by their lack of visible success.

It would be hard to imagine works less well suited to a general propaganda end. First of all, they were written without exception in learned Latin: even Konrad von Megenberg, who sought through use of the vernacular to extend the public for some of his other works, attempted nothing of the sort in his imperialist tracts.[281] All these treatises were in varying degrees constructed in conformity with the contemporary rules of learned exposition: they made few concessions to readers lacking their writers' academic backgrounds and mental habits. Most of them survive only in small numbers of copies; for some there is just a single manuscript.[282] In this respect they resemble other works of similar character and intent, from the same and earlier periods.[283] The polymathic Konrad von Megenberg, who had no difficulty attracting a readership for other works (most notably his heterogeneous *Book of Nature*), could stimulate no comparable demand for his thoughts on the Empire.[284]

---

[281] For his vernacular works, see Steer, 'Konrad von Megenberg', in *VL* 5, cols. 231–4.

[282] For the single surviving manuscript of Dietrich von Niem's *Viridarium Imperatorum et Regum Romanorum*, see Lhotsky and Pivec, 'Einleitung', p. vii. For the three works edited in *Dietrich von Nieheim: Historie de Gestis Romanorum Principum*, ed. Colberg and Leuschner, there survive in total fourteen manuscripts: Colberg and Leuschner, 'Einleitung', ibid., p. ix.

[283] For late medieval political treatises generally, Jürgen Miethke suggests that about thirty surviving manuscripts is a typical number: Miethke, 'Das Publikum', p. 7. For imperialist tracts, the numbers were often much smaller. Of William of Ockham's eleven known polemical writings, for example, six survive in only a single manuscript: Offler, 'The "influence"', p. 348. For the fewness of manuscripts for controversialist works from the 'Investiture Contest', see Suchan, 'Publizistik', p. 30.

[284] For a full account of manuscripts, see Drossbach, 'Neue Forschungen', esp. pp. 3, 7, 12. The four copies of *De translatione Romani imperii*, two texts of the *Yconomica*, or the single exemplar of his *Planctus ecclesiae in Germaniam* can be contrasted with over eighty known manuscripts of the *Buch der Natur*.

And it is not only from a modern perspective that their writers' milieu seems fragmented and remote. Konrad, writing in Regensburg in the early 1350s, found himself unable to get his hands on tracts written in the preceding decades by Ludwig IV's learned partisans at his Munich court, hardly more than 100 kilometres distant. It is not even certain that Konrad knew at first hand the writings of his polemical *bête noire*, Ockham.[285] Similarly, the absence of reference by Konrad and his contemporaries to the works of Alexander von Roes, which ought to have been highly relevant to their concerns, suggests that these remained unknown among south-German imperialists half a century after their writing.[286]

But this is only half the picture. The other half is glimpsed when we recall why it is that we know of Konrad's failure to locate the works of the Munich imperialists: because, as he states himself, he was *looking* for them. However we are to account for the obscurity of most of these writings, lack of contemporary interest does not supply a full explanation.[287] Alexander's works were clearly valued by those who happened upon them, such as Dietrich von Niem, who wrote with respect of the 'presentient German' responsible for the *Memoriale* (whom he mistook for a fellow-Westphalian, Jordan von Osnabrück).[288] Indeed, the fate in Dietrich's time of this particular work illustrates how the public for an imperialist text might under certain circumstances expand spectacularly. The *Memoriale*, in stark contrast to most of its counterparts, survives in a full seventy manuscripts, and there must once have been considerably more.[289] Most of the surviving texts, it is true, are relatively late, but the circumstances under which they proliferated are revealing nonetheless. Copying was at its height in the time of the Church

---

[285] Konrad von Megenberg, *Ökonomik*, lib. 2.iii, cap. 1, ed. Krüger, vol. II, p. 87; Miethke, 'Das Publikum', pp. 9–10.

[286] What is known of the provenance of the handful of early manuscripts of Alexander's writings offers no indication that they circulated in the Wittelsbach sphere. The earliest known copy is of Austrian origin, but most of the others were made in the western and north-western regions of the Reich: Grundmann and Heimpel, 'Einleitung', pp. 40–2, 81; and for a further early manuscript, not listed by Grundmann and Heimpel, of Cologne origin: Powitz and Buck (eds.), *Die Handschriften*, pp. 266–8. I am grateful to Professor Jürgen Miethke for drawing this manuscript to my attention.

[287] The *Defensor pacis* at least became the subject of rumour and oral report which carried some knowledge of its contents to those without direct access to Marsilius's text. A Strasbourg priest even felt able to offer in his vernacular chronicle a summary of its argument: *Fritsche (Friedrich) Closener's Chronik*, ed. Hegel, p. 70.

[288] *Alemannus presagus*: Dietrich von Niem, *Nemus unionis*, tractatus vi, cap. 33, p. 483.

[289] Grundmann and Heimpel, 'Einleitung', pp. 40–80, where sixty-three manuscripts are listed; Miethke, 'Politisches Denken', p. 134 n. 53, lists a further six; see Miethke, 'Das Publikum', p. 8 n. 31, for one more. The manuscript tradition makes clear that there were once other copies besides.

councils at Constance and Basel: in one formulation, 'the great book fairs of the Middle Ages'.[290] Different readers were drawn to it for different reasons. One basis of its appeal was historical: roughly half of the surviving manuscripts of the *Memoriale* describe it as a 'chronicle'.[291] Appreciation of its value as a window on the past was by the time of the Councils not wholly new. Already in the 1360s it had been drawn on by the compiler of a vernacular town chronicle in Magdeburg: an early instance of an imperialist tract exerting influence beyond the rigorously Latinate milieu of its origin.[292] Other manuscripts were bound together with constitutional works, such as the Golden Bull, suggesting a legally minded readership. One copy, which found its way into the archive of the margraves of Brandenburg, seems to have been read as a guide to Germany's constitutional and ethnic geography, to underpin the jurisdiction of an imperial law court.[293] What all this suggests, surely, is the work's comparative 'openness' – both in the sense that its exposition was, in fact, quite accessible to the lettered non-specialist, and that it was amenable to readings supporting a considerable range of interests and perspectives.

Alexander's treatise is unusual not only for its broad dissemination but also for the lightness of its formal structure and its strong emphasis on historical proofs, qualities which go far to explain its wide appeal. The seepage of an imperialist treatise into a German vernacular milieu is not unparalleled in this period. Jakob Twinger appears to have known Lupold von Bebenburg's tract on the imperial constitution; and again, it was the work's historical matter which caught his eye.[294] On the whole, however, these post-Staufer defences of the Empire were not in any general sense 'public' – still less 'propaganda' – works. That is not, however, to say that they did not seek, and often find, a public of a more specific kind. Characteristically, it was made up of men not unlike the treatise-writers themselves: clerics in the main, thoughtful and educated, but not secluded from the affairs of their time. The significance of this audience ought neither to be exaggerated – numerically, it can

---

[290] Schubert, 'Zur Konzeption', p. 338. And see generally Lehmann, 'Konstanz und Basel'.

[291] See Grundmann and Heimpel, 'Einleitung', pp. 42–80.

[292] Grundmann, 'Über die Schriften', p. 198.

[293] Schubert, 'Zur Konzeption', esp. pp. 338–41.

[294] *Chronik des Jacob Twinger*, ed. Hegel, p. 624, lamenting the habit of some Rhenish nobles of calling themselves 'Rhinelanders', rather than taking pride in their (German) Frankish identity and Trojan descent. For Lupold on the same theme: Lupold von Bebenburg, *Tractatus*, cap. 3, ed. Miethke and Flüeler, pp. 264–5. Twinger also made use of the history of the Schism by his contemporary Dietrich von Niem: Heimpel, *Dietrich*, p. 171.

never have been large – nor dismissed. The social philosopher Jürgen Habermas famously identified as characteristic of modern societies the existence of 'spaces' within which 'public' sociability and discourse might take place. The Middle Ages, by contrast, knew only the hierarchical representation of a ruler's power to the limited 'public' assembled at his court, not the dynamic exchange and contest of opinions.[295] But the few glimpses which we gain of the treatise-writers in their natural habitat suggest that modern social theorists may here have been (not uncharacteristically) guilty of setting barriers too high and too absolute between post-Enlightenment Europe and the centuries that went before. Fourteenth-century Germany may have been lacking in coffee houses, but it was not without social spaces permitting, and even fostering, political discourse and contention, at least within specific, limited spheres.[296]

It is the contentiousness of German imperialist texts that often stands out. Alexander von Roes made clear that he was writing to rebuff opinions which had come to his notice, doubtless in papal Viterbo, and with which he vehemently disagreed. Alexander's adversaries remain spectral, but that is not always the case. Konrad von Megenberg's antipathy to Ockham was as frank as it was implacable. In a tract dedicated to Charles IV, Konrad recounted how in a dream vision he had personally rescued the Roman king, along with popes and cardinals, from the clutches of an apocalyptic monster representing the English friar.[297] The imperial idea had by the late Middle Ages become irretrievably enmeshed in controversy: to take a view on it was to take a stand. The proper relationship of the imperial monarchy with the Church and its head invited particular contention, as Konrad's agitation makes plain. While all could agree that dealings between the 'two powers' ought to be collaborative and, ideally, harmonious, establishing the terms for that collaboration meant touching upon what were historically some of the most painful points of division in medieval political thought. It would be a caricature to suggest that the problem of relations between emperors and popes formed the central matter of late medieval imperialist writings. It does not, in fact, bulk as large as might be supposed,

---

[295] Habermas, *Public Sphere*, esp. pp. 5–9. For medievalists' critiques of Habermas, see: Thum, 'Öffentlich-Machen'; Thum, 'Öffentlichkeit'; Haverkamp, ' "…an die große Glocke hängen" ', esp. pp. 83–4; Althof, *Spielregeln*, pp. 229–57; Hruza, 'Propaganda'; Melve, *Public Sphere*, vol. I, pp. 6–17.

[296] For the constituting of a 'public sphere' through *modern* forms of sociability, see Eley, 'Nations', esp. p. 291.

[297] On Konrad's *Tractatus contra Occam*, see Miethke, 'Konrads von Megenberg Kampf', esp. pp. 73–5.

and some Germans, such as Alexander von Roes, had little directly to say about it. For others, however, it did represent an important principle. Lupold von Bebenburg, faithful to the doctrine of the electors at Rhens (1338), thus offered a view of the *regnum et imperium Romanorum* which, in placing them on a par with other sovereign realms, was designed in part to rebuff papal claims to scrutinise the princes' choice for the throne.[298]

Sometimes we can not only observe the clash of opposing texts but also discern the interactions of their authors. If Konrad von Megenberg found certain imperialist works elusive, others came more readily to hand. His treatise *On the Translation of the Roman Empire* (1354) followed closely Lupold von Bebenburg's tract on the Empire, with which, however, Konrad fundamentally took issue over the relationship between the 'two powers' and the pope's role in making the Empire's ruler.[299] Relations between the two polemicists – so similar in a number of ways – were, it seems, amicable despite their disagreements: Konrad dedicated his voluminous treatise on the household (*Yconomica*, 1348–52) to the bishop of Bamberg, whose patronage he may have been seeking.[300] Not the temperature of the dispute but the closeness of the intellectual exchange is interesting here. It is no isolated instance. Ockham's *Octo quaestiones*, composed early in the 1340s while the Englishman was under Ludwig IV's protection, took firm though courteous exception to Lupold's judgement on the ruler's power before papal coronation.[301] Lupold himself had come close to soliciting such criticism: at the close of his *Treatise on the Rights of Kingdom and Empire*, he had called on his patron, Balduin, to submit it for amendment by wiser heads. 'It looks very much as if he was taken at his word.'[302] There is good reason to think that Lupold and Ockham had engaged in verbal disputations, which subsequently found reflection in the writings of both men.[303]

[298] Ubl, 'Die Rechte', esp. pp. 367–8; Miethke and Flüeler, 'Einleitung', pp. 61–97.
[299] Scholz, *Streitschriften*, pt. I, pp. 95–127.
[300] Konrad von Megenberg, *Ökonomik*, 'Widmung', ed. Krüger, vol. I, p. 15. For the work's dating, see Krüger, 'Einleitung', ibid., pp. xxviii–xxix. The dedication to Lupold, bishop from 1353, must be a later authorial addition. For Konrad's quest for patronage, see Miethke, 'Konrads von Megenberg Kampf', esp. p. 83.
[301] See: Miethke, 'Wirkungen', pp. 207–9; Offler, 'Ockham's *Octo Quaestiones*'. The list of 'questions' probably originated in Balduin of Trier's circle. The existence of a second, independent, attempt at answering them, of German authorship, is further evidence for the liveliness of contemporary debates on the imperial constitution (ibid., pp. 325–8).
[302] Offler, 'Ockham's *Octo Quaestiones*', p. 331; Lupold von Bebenburg, *Tractatus*, cap. 19, ed. Miethke and Flüeler, p. 408.
[303] Wittneben, 'Lupold', esp. pp. 585–6. Lupold made subsequent additions to his *Tractatus* which, as Wittneben shows, engage with Ockham's views as expressed in his *Octo Quaestiones*, but without ever directly citing this work. Wittneben proposes

Since the English friar was at the time in Munich, and Lupold in the circle of the metropolitan of Trier and Mainz, this prospect would imply that contacts among the Empire's heterogeneous champions were sometimes livelier than might otherwise be suspected.[304] On occasion, they may have grown lively indeed: Ockham himself is reputed to have dispatched a fellow friar to seek out Konrad von Megenberg and warn him to desist from personal attacks.[305]

Within and between these small groups of educated imperialists, written texts were clearly but one element in a culture of debate in which the spoken word also had much importance.[306] The colophon to one manuscript of Lupold's treatise reveals that in 1341 its author presented his work orally to an audience at the episcopal *curia* at Eichstätt.[307] Verbal exposition of the imperial idea was extended to a rather different public when the poet Lupold Hornburg declaimed his lengthy vernacular 'complaint' for the Empire to the German princes assembled at Passau.[308] Gauging the part played by the spoken word in the making, revision and dissemination of imperialist writings must inevitably remain a speculative venture; but there is no reason to doubt that it was substantial.[309] Beside the general fewness of surviving copies of imperialist tracts needs to be set an awareness that, for the influence of imperialist thought in this period, manuscripts were by no means the whole story.

A larger view is needed: one which relates the Empire's champions and their writings in more complex ways to the various groups, networks and patterns of experience within which imperialist ideas were nurtured, exchanged and, through controversy, animated. In Germany, these relationships had a distinctive structure, reflecting the political character of the Empire's German lands. This found reflection in the form and social scope of the literate discourse which in the late Middle

---

that both Lupold's amendments and Ockham's treatise arose out of a bout of verbal sparring.

[304] Wittneben proposes Munich as the possible site of Lupold's encounter with Ockham: ibid., p. 585.

[305] Miethke, 'Konrads von Megenberg Kampf', p. 87.

[306] For different ways of experiencing written texts themselves, see Briggs, *Giles*, p. 6.

[307] Miethke, 'Wirkungen', p. 209. In 1328 a cleric in the service of John XXII alleged that Ludwig IV had permitted Marsilius's *Defensor pacis* to be read out and elucidated in his presence: Miethke, 'Das Publikum', pp. 1–2.

[308] *Politische Lyrik*, ed. Müller, vol. I, pp. 189–201. Lupold's work was based ultimately upon Latin verses by Lupold von Bebenburg, his *Ritmaticum querulosum*: ibid., pp. 174–8.

[309] Lupold von Bebenburg's *Tractatus de Iuribus Regni et Imperii* probably reflects protracted discussion of its theses between Lupold and Balduin of Trier: Colberg, 'Lupold von Bebenburg', in *VL* 5, col. 1075.

Ages was conducted around the *imperium*. Among the main characteristics of the frameworks within which the Empire was debated were
plurality, 'openness' and a marked absence of authoritarian direction.[310]
The monarchy itself was not powerful enough to exercise the kind of
hegemonic control over ideas which Habermas thought characteristic
of the Middle Ages. Only under Ludwig IV, at a time of bitter controversy and division in the Church at large, did the ruler's own court
become an important centre for anti-papal and (in some instances, for
that reason) imperialist writers.[311] Ludwig's Munich provided a home
for a colourful assortment of learned polemicists, outsiders as well as
Germans, unusual by German standards in their diversity and distinction.[312] The emperor's quarrel with Avignon allowed various axes to be
ground, not only the familiar German ones. The range of competing
perspectives and policies which jostled for a hearing at Ludwig's court
serves to underline how limited was the scope for doctrinal direction
from the centre. It is revealing that under Charles IV, an emperor distinguished by the energy and the resources which he devoted to crafting and manipulating images of his rule, no major imperialist treatise
(unless we include in that category the Golden Bull) was composed in
court circles. That Konrad von Megenberg, who dedicated two tracts
to Charles, was able, in his naive and one-sided papalism, so to misjudge the temper and needs of the Luxemburg court is itself eloquent
testimony to the absence of central orchestration.[313] Writings on the
Empire did not, in any direct way, serve the ends of royal power, but
arose from other, more varied impulses.

Regarding Germany as a whole, the picture is diffuse and polycentric. The imperial idea was made the object of sustained reflection in

---

[310] The discourse of literate groups in late medieval Germany, and its structures and
forms, lend themselves well to analysis applying the 'dialogical approach' formulated by Leidulf Melve in his important study of debate and communication in the
'Investiture Contest' – though, as Melve acknowledges, the number of 'public arenas' within which such discourse might take place had grown by the late Middle
Ages: see esp. Melve, *Public Sphere*, vol. I, 'Introduction'; vol. II, p. 657.

[311] See, in addition to the essays by Miethke ('Wirkungen') and Schütz, cited above, De
Boer, 'Ludwig the Bavarian'.

[312] The heterogeneous, fractured character of Ludwig's court is emphasised by Pfaff,
'Die Münchner Minoriten', esp. p. 54. For a fourteenth-century German view of
Ludwig's circle and its works, see *Chronica de ducibus Bavariae*, ed. Leidinger, pp.
164–5. Matthias von Neuenburg was aware that Ludwig's decree *Fidem catholicam* had been drawn up 'with the counsel of certain Friars Minor': *Die Chronik des
Mathias von Neuenburg*, ed. Hofmeister, pp. 157–8.

[313] *Tractatus contra Occam*, *De translatione Romani imperii*. For these writings and their
likely reception at Charles's court, see Miethke, 'Konrads von Megenberg Kampf',
esp. pp. 95–7. There is no indication that Charles ever acknowledged receipt of these
works or showed Konrad any favour on account of them.

a number of different locations, and through various forms of association, at different times and under different circumstances. Courts other than the ruler's might sponsor imperialist writings, as did that of Balduin of Trier. Alexander von Roes, although writing in the south, set out a view of the Empire which appears closely to reflect the perspectives of the contemporary archbishop of Cologne.[314] Less formal, more intimate networks are also occasionally to be glimpsed, such as the one centred on the Würzburg notary and historiographer Michael de Leone, with which Lupold von Bebenburg was linked.[315] To speak, as some medievalists have done, of groups such as these as constituting 'closed', 'partial' or 'internal' publics captures well their intimacy, plurality and exclusivity, and thus the inevitably small social impact of their thought.[316] But to suggest that medieval political culture was by its nature inimical to the discursive, argumentative qualities of modern public communication would, for Germany in the post-Staufer era, be wide of the mark.[317] On the contrary, within these groups the indications which we possess point to dynamism and interaction, and to a climate of lively personal and textual exchanges. Group-specific sociability and the interconnected movement of people and manuscripts supply the keynotes. The world chronicler Dietrich Engelhus can be captured on student journeys to Prague (1373) and Erfurt (1392), in each case, characteristically, in the company of a group of fellow scholars from his native Einbeck.[318] What occupied their conversation during those long hours on the road we cannot say. What we do know is that Dietrich subsequently managed to consult the *Garden of Emperors and Kings of the Romans* of his fellow Westphalian Dietrich von Niem in a form different from that preserved in the only surviving manuscript.[319] Webs of personal and textual interconnection were denser and more complex than the fragmentary witness of known works suggests; and imperialist writings, too, evidently had a place in those webs.

---

[314] See Erkens, *Siegfried*, pp. 287–8.
[315] See: G. Kornrumpf, 'Michael de Leone', in *VL* 6, cols. 491–503; Peters, *Literatur*, pp. 138–68.
[316] Faulstich, *Medien*, Ch. 1 ('partial public'); Miethke, 'Das Publikum', pp. 11–12 ('closed public'); Suchan, 'Publizistik', p. 30 ('internal public'). For the polycentric, fluid and situational qualities of medieval political publics, see Thum, 'Öffentlichkeit', esp. pp. 67–70.
[317] The view of Gerd Althof, who, concentrating on the earlier Middle Ages, has emphasised the primacy of ritual over discursive forms of public communication: Althof, *Spielregeln*, pp. 229–31. For the contested character of the *modern* 'public sphere', see Eley, 'Nations', p. 306.
[318] Irrgang, *Peregrinatio Academica*, p. 72. In 1394 Dietrich is still to be found intervening on behalf of an Einbeck graduate in Prague.
[319] Lhotsky and Pivec, 'Einleitung', p. viii.

Thoughtful Germans were able to take the chances which an age of growing intellectual mobility was making available. Dietrich von Niem's scrapbook writings are the surviving deposit of innumerable encounters, with books and documents, tales and legends, significant places and people, in the course of a much-travelled life.[320] Manuscripts changed hands, and personal collections grew, as a result of travel, student friendships and times spent at the great focal points of debate and controversy in Europe.[321] In the history of the imperial idea in the post-Staufer period, and especially its more developed and controversial forms, the role of the Church is unmistakable. Serious debate about the *imperium* remained largely a debate between clerks. The Church provided such men, for all their sometimes obscure origins, with a career ladder and an entry into the universities. It furnished them with key conceptual tools, notably, a command of canon law.[322] Just as the Church, and its head, had done most to charge the imperial idea with controversy, so it was the Church which endowed at least a handful of the Empire's German-speaking inhabitants with the means to take part in the argument for themselves. It also supplied the main venues for its conduct. The courts at which ideas about the Empire were nurtured and challenged were mostly under the headship of high ecclesiastics. One above all drew in German partisans of the Reich, and confronted them with challenges urgent enough to impel them to formulate their thoughts on parchment: the papal Curia. It was at Avignon that Konrad von Megenberg composed the first, and most stridently partisan, of his imperialist tracts.[323] Within the household of the schismatic Roman popes Dietrich von Niem found both material and intellectual sustenance for his polemicist works. The unexpected stimuli which the papal court at Viterbo had in store for Alexander von Roes have already been observed. Each of these writers was impelled, through experience of one of the two universal 'powers' of the Middle Ages, to think and to write more urgently about the other.

---

[320] See Colberg and Leuschner, 'Einleitung', p. xv. As Haskins long ago observed, 'the history of ecclesiastical travel has much to tell us': Haskins, 'The spread', p. 21.

[321] It was while at Montpellier and Avignon that Rudolf Losse had begun to assemble his wide-ranging manuscript collection: Burgard, 'Rudolf Losse', p. 51. Archbishop Nicholas of Gniezno is known to have brought back manuscripts from the Council of Constance, including the writings of Gottfried von Viterbo, while Heinrich Toke later recounted how he took the opportunity of attendance at Basel in 1432 to explore local libraries. For these and other examples, see Lehmann, 'Konstanz und Basel', pp. 256–7, 263, 271.

[322] For the importance of canon law for fourteenth-century imperialist treatise-writers, see Ubl, 'Die Rechte', esp. p. 386.

[323] See Steer, 'Konrad von Megenberg', in *VL* 5, cols. 224–5.

Rome, as idea, still mattered – and mattered more than might be expected: the imperial theme proved remarkably resilient in post-Staufer Germany. This was despite the Empire's territorial shrinkage and conceptual blurrings, despite the absence of imperial triumphs beyond the Alps or beyond the seas, and despite even, for most of the period, the lack of a crowned and generally recognised emperor. Thoughtful Germans showed a marked realism in their judgement of the Empire's limitations and the bounds of the possible, and gave a new, more explicit recognition to the legitimacy and unshakability of their neighbours' claims to a separate political existence. Yet in the face of all, the idea of *imperium* did not contract. Instead, its presentation grew more magnificent, its titles more resonant and encompassing, while its social reach and its capacity to nourish hopes and expectations, at least in moments of particular tension, also expanded. The Empire itself, moreover, now became the subject of systematic scrutiny and justification, in a manner unseen in the days of its power. Explaining these phenomena means paying attention both to the character of the imperial idea and to developments in German politics and society. Not least, it requires that account be taken of the unique, doctrinally interwoven and (at least until Charles IV's time) still periodically troubled relationship between the imperial monarchy and the Church.

It was its antiquity, and its unmatched legitimacy and prestige, indeed, in the eyes of some, its indispensability to the unfolding scheme of human history, that allowed the imperial idea to maintain its potency despite (and in certain respects, even under the stimulus of) the monarchy's weakness and periodic crises. The circumstances under which the Hohenstaufen departed the stage had energised and polarised opinion, and sown the expectation of strange days ahead. In a period which saw rising social tensions in the German towns, and an increasingly lively circulation of news, rumour and specialised knowledge, the imperial idea was able to become detached from the ruler and his court and, at least fleetingly, linked to the persons of a succession of wild adventurers and opportunists. The 'false Fredericks' are just one, outlandish, manifestation of a more general phenomenon: the way in which the relative absence in Germany of central, authoritarian direction or co-ordination allowed the Empire as idea to proliferate in a variety of forms, for a range of publics.

Among these were small, literate and Latinate groups, sustained at various times by centres of patronage and discourse, propounding a range of viewpoints on the Empire, reflecting the interests and concerns of their patrons. In addition, there were also more isolated figures, such as Konrad von Megenberg, whose imperialist writings appear not to have been produced within such a local support-system, but rather in the hope of joining one. Others, as Alexander von Roes demonstrates, could be moved to write in order not so much to articulate or propagate a patron's views as to shape them, on the basis of pressing concerns of their own. Among such figures, as a recent study of an earlier medieval controversy remarked, 'a manuscript culture in no way constitute[d] an insurmountable hindrance for public-sphere formation'.[324] Discourse was able to occur within, but to a degree also between and beyond, such circles, reflecting a culture of debate in which both the written and the spoken word had a part. Such discourse, and the urgent, occasionally acrimonious, contests of opinion to which it gave rise, drew sustenance from the fundamentally controversial qualities of the imperial idea itself.

It was not only comparatively learned Germans whom the Empire's dealings with the Church and its head periodically moved to take sides. The administrative and disciplinary institutions of the Church commanded a social reach and penetration far beyond that of the imperial monarchy.[325] So too did its propaganda: the influence exerted by the language of Curial polemic, even upon Germans who resisted its arguments, underlines its penetrative scope.[326] While *Königsnähe* may have been constrained, *Papstnähe*, at least as mediated through the long arm of the Church's agents, was much more ubiquitous. But, in times of division, the pope's commanding proximity inevitably also drew the king-emperor closer to his German subjects. The imperial monarchy itself was stimulated, partly in response to the controversies of the early fourteenth century, to attend more closely to its own communicative and opinion-forming resources – visual and ritual, as well as verbal and textual. Particularly under Ludwig the Bavarian, many people felt directly the consequences of their monarch's rift with the Church, and found themselves impelled to act, and doubtless often also to reflect, upon the significance of their actions. A handful of lettered Germans, meanwhile, attained an identity-forming *Papstnähe* of a more intimate kind, through the opportunities afforded by the highly mobile worlds of clerical learning and careerism. That some were moved to reflection by their experiences far from home, we know from their writings. If, viewed from within Germany, the crises besetting the Reich appeared troubling enough, Avignon, or Paris or Rome (or, indeed, the hilltop

[324] Melve, *Public Sphere*, vol. I, p. 8.
[325] The role of the Church's communications structures in the context of the struggle with the Empire is emphasised by Mierau, 'Exkommunikation', pp. 54–5.
[326] Sommerlechner, *Stupor Mundi?*, pp. 147–50.

vantage-point of Viterbo) offered larger, starker, more salutary – and, it would seem, more self-consciously *German* – perspectives.

Not invariably, it is true. Engelbert von Admont found it entirely possible to reflect at length upon the *imperium* with barely ever a word about its relationships, past, present or future, with the German people. Others, however, had a great deal to say on these matters, as will shortly become plain. That they did so, and that other late medieval Germans likewise spoke so readily of their people in relation to the affairs of the Reich and its rulers, appears hard to explain when we consider the character and development of the late medieval imperial idea as encountered above. For, as we saw, the public styles and titles of the Christian-Roman *imperium* contracted not at all between the thirteenth and the fifteenth centuries. They hardly changed, and such change as did occur was towards a yet more resonant universalism. Not until the days of Maximilian of Habsburg would chancery clerks start to recognise with any consistency the existence of a 'German' king, while the 'Holy Roman Empire of the German nation' (whatever that title may originally have meant) is scarcely younger.[327] How and why late medieval people were able to perceive as German their avowedly universal Empire is the concern of the next chapter.

---

[327] Weisert, 'Der Reichstitel', p. 449; and for the early usage and interpretation of the Empire 'of the German nation': Zeumer, *Heiliges römisches Reich*, esp. pp. 17–22; Nonn, 'Heiliges Römisches Reich', esp. pp. 141–2.

6   Roman Empire, German nation: the German imperial tradition

A German world order

'The medieval empire', one distinguished commentator has written, 'was not in any sense the German nation in its medieval guise.'[1] An English-language overview of Germany's political development in the Middle Ages reaches a similar conclusion, cautioning that 'the western Empire had very little to do with any notion of German statehood or nationhood'.[2] 'Such concepts', readers are assured, 'are too modern for a reasonable match in the sources.' The Empire, it appears, occupied among the Germans not only the constitutional ground on which elsewhere in Europe nascent 'sovereign states' would arise but also the emotional space which in other realms was to be colonised by the nation. In Europe at large, it has often been argued, the later Middle Ages 'witnessed the death of old "universal" values ... and the rise of "national" ones in their place'.[3] These latter, however, were reserved for more fortunate lands. The Germans, lulled by dreams of imperial glory, had sleepwalked past the turnings which led to state and nation alike.[4] In place of those desiderata, they found themselves 'burdened' with the Reich.[5]

But was their imperial 'burden' really such a barrier to nationhood? It requires only the briefest reflection on more recent epochs in the German past to make clear that, medievalist nation-making paradigms notwithstanding, there is no fundamental incompatibility between, on the one hand, imperialist dreams and fantasies and, on the other, a strongly developed sense of common identity. Indeed, far from being

---

[1] Matthew, 'Reflections', p. 367.
[2] Arnold, *Medieval Germany*, p. 119.
[3] Allmand, *Hundred Years War*, p. 141.
[4] For this theme in Germanophone historiography, see above, Ch. 2, pp. 66–8.
[5] Waley and Denley, *Later Medieval Europe*, p. 67. The view is also powerfully presented, as a perspective for understanding the *longue durée* of German history, in Winkler, *Germany*, vol. I, p. 4.

antithetical, each of these sentiments was destined in the twentieth century powerfully to nourish and reaffirm the other. A people which believes itself called to an imperial mission is likely to possess a heightened, not an impoverished, sense of its own existence *as* a people. Particularly during the Nazi era, it became the fashion in Germany to perceive in the 'first Reich' of the Middle Ages the same combination of universal ambition and German self-consciousness that was impelling contemporary German foreign policy. Hitler himself affected to find in the medieval Reich a direct sanction for his own Germanocentric imperialism. 'One thing at any rate is clear', he announced in 1942. 'If we want to stake any kind of claim in the world, we will have to make appeal to the history of German emperorship.'[6] Nazi public culture made much of the memory of the medieval Empire, exploiting its surviving artefacts and monuments and interpreting the rituals of contemporary politics so as to construct visible continuities.[7] In 1938, following the *Anschluß*, the imperial regalia were brought from Vienna to Nuremberg, their home between the fifteenth and eighteenth centuries and a city rich in associations both with the medieval and the contemporary Reich.[8] When Hitler travelled to Italy to meet with Mussolini, the event was interpreted in the German press as re-enacting the *Romzüge* of the emperors of old.[9] An article which appeared in 1942 in the *Frankfurter Zeitung*, headed 'The Reich as Mission', identified the medieval Empire as the template for a new European order. 'With the constitution of the Reich idea the German people have become bearers of a supra-State responsibility. In this sense the traditions of the Holy Roman Empire of the Germanic race are today revived and renewed. A new Reich has grown out of these relationships.'[10]

Some of the most eminent German medievalists of the time were on hand to underpin official goals with interpretations presenting the first Reich as a heroic venture in Germanic dominion and a charter for contemporary national ambition. 'Internal consolidation, expansion of the Reich, and regaining that position at the heart of Europe which history,

---

[6] Wolf, *Litteris*, p. 249.

[7] For one of the more exotic manifestations of Nazi medievalism, see Helzel, *Ein König*, esp. Chs. 9, 10.

[8] Fillitz, 'Die Reichskleinodien', p. 147; and for the conjunction of civic self-promotion and imperialistic Nazi image-making which formed the event's background, see Brockmann, *Nuremberg*, pp. 186–90. The symbolic continuity of German imperialism received due emphasis at the time, with one newspaper commenting that 'the Holy Empire of the German nation has arisen in a new form, and the insignia of the former Reich once again have life and meaning' (ibid., p. 189).

[9] Klemperer, *The Language*, p. 108.

[10] As translated in *The Times*, 21 July 1942.

[its] achievements and qualities grant the German people are the great tasks of the German future', wrote Hans Erich Feine in 1935.[11] 'Only now that the German Reich has once again taken up its great historical task as a European ordering power', reflected Karl Jordan in 1942, 'has the deepest meaning of the imperial politics of the Middle Ages revealed itself.'[12] Walther Kienast anticipated 'the morning of a new Reich, a new order', which would put an end to the 'titanic struggle' of sovereign states with its origins in the Middle Ages.[13] But, for all its universalism, it was to be a *German* order, fashioned by qualities which Germans alone possessed. For Hermann Heimpel, whose work was to inaugurate the systematic study of the late medieval treatise-writers, the national make-up of the Germans suited them uniquely to universal rule. Of course, the attainments of the emperors of old had transcended nation, corresponding rather to 'the needs of humanity itself at that time'.[14] Yet they remained solely German attainments. It was the Saxon Henry I's 'Germanic will to world order', Heimpel insisted, that rendered his reign 'an eternally valid example'. 'Heroes' like Henry were 'the first German Führer, of the blood that is still our blood'.[15] It was exactly their combining of a universal vision with belief in the Germans' special destiny and capacity to fulfil it that, for Heimpel, rendered post-Staufer imperialist writers like Dietrich von Niem and Alexander von Roes historically so significant.

The matter of Germany

Little is to be gained, surely, from setting the imperialist bluster of Hitler's Reich beside the venerable and prestigious political vocabulary of the late medieval *imperium*. The universal doctrines of the latter, with their invocations of a Christian and Roman heritage, had on their side a time-hallowed solemnity and inherent legitimacy which seem to forbid comparison with the opportunistic boasting of a murderous and short-lived dictatorship. Added to this, the language of medieval emperorship was framed, in many of its most stately and deliberate formulations, so as specifically to exclude invocation of the Germans and their lands. Banners, battle cries and the longings to which imperial eschatology gave voice – all were infused, no less than the *arengae* of the monarch's own most solemn *diplomata*, with a *Romanitas* so implacable

[11] Feine, *Tausend Jahre deutscher Reichssehnsucht*, p. 64.
[12] Cited in Schönwälder, *Historiker*, p. 224.
[13] Wolf, *Litteris*, p. 244.   [14] Ibid., p. 254.
[15] Heimpel, 'König Heinrich der Erste', in Heimpel, *Deutsches Mittelalter*, pp. 48, 49.

as to leave few spaces into which the elements of ethnic particularism might intrude. And yet the modern parallel is not in all respects fatuous, since the public rhetoric of the post-Staufer Reich, like that of far more recent imperialisms, did in fact, in specific but highly revealing ways, bind up claims to universal dominion with notions of common German ethnicity. And it included, at least among the Empire's more outspoken champions, appeals to virtues and aptitudes imagined as being specifically German. Such claims seem startlingly to anticipate – and in certain instances may even have inspired – those encountered several hundred years later.

Ideas of this kind were most fully and frankly articulated by the treatise-writers – the appeal of whose works to German medievalists of the mid-twentieth century, as well as their comparative neglect subsequently, is not hard to understand. For Alexander von Roes, it was to 'the Germans' (*Germani*) that 'the government of the world has been translated and the direction of the Church committed'.[16] As the custodian of the Empire, the German people became, in Alexander's account, a central element in the divine plan for human salvation, the instrument of 'that government which God placed as a marvel upon earth'.[17] In a Latin verse polemic, *The Church's Lament over Germany* (1337–8), Konrad von Megenberg had a personified *Ecclesia* praise 'Germany' (*Germania*) as her sole rightful protector, who in times past had 'illustriously saved me, with great endeavour and, indeed, with blood'.[18] But examination of other writings from the period makes clear that these German polemicists were by no means eccentric in the assumptions on which they rested their claims. The *Lohengrin* poet has Henry I warn his followers, before joining battle with the pagan Hungarians, that should the German lands (*diutschiu lant*) fall tributary to the infidel, 'so will the [Christian] Faith be trampled'.[19] 'The Germans' (*Theutonici*), noted the chronicler Heinrich von Herford, had, through the transfer of the Empire into their hands, 'attained world dominion' (*dominium mundi*).[20] 'They have the governance of the Roman Church.' An array of canonist authorities was heaped up to affirm that their ruler was set 'over all kings' and that 'all nations are under him'.[21] A specifically German role

---

[16] Alexander von Roes, *Memoriale*, cap. 10, ed. Grundmann and Heimpel, p. 100: 'Germani, ad quos mundi regimen est translatum et ecclesie regimen est commissum.'

[17] Ibid., cap. 10, p. 101: 'Germani, ad quos et in quos imperiale regnum est translatum … quod dominus posuit in prodigium super terram.'

[18] Konrad von Megenberg, *Planctus*, ed. Scholz, pars I, cap. 8, p. 29.

[19] *Lohengrin*, ed. Cramer, p. 315, vv. 2524–30.

[20] *Liber de rebus memorabilioribus*, ed. Potthast, p. 39.

[21] Ibid., p. 39, invoking also the Germans' 'regimen Romane ecclesie'.

on the world stage was even the subject of occasional (though, admittedly, hardly frequent) allusion in public documents from the Reich. It was, as the Rhineland princes explained in announcing Sigismund's election, their 'stern hardness of firm and constant loyalty' which had won 'the princes of the German lands' (*Dutscher lande fursten*) the right to elect a Roman king and future emperor 'and a temporal head for the whole world'.[22] Invocations of the German people were linked in late medieval writings not merely with the imperial idea, but with some of its more ambitious and grandiloquent expressions.

Especially noteworthy is the frequency with which the Germans and their lands found mention in texts of various sorts bearing upon the conflicts of the 'universal' powers, Empire and papacy. In some ways, this is easily explained. The German lands were the imperial monarchy's main power base, and it was natural that, under both Frederick II and Ludwig the Bavarian, the popes should have concentrated on breaking their opponents' support there – with highly disruptive consequences for German society. A letter from Strasbourg insisted to John XXII that its burghers would be unable to travel safely in Germany (*in partibus Alamanie*) if the papal legal process against the emperor was promulgated in the town.[23] The grave divisions which resulted from the interdict in Ludwig's time have already been observed.[24] A letter in the emperor's name, urging that the cardinals summon a general council to resolve the matter, alleged that 'almost all the churches, and especially in Germany, are greatly oppressed by the sentences of excommunication'.[25] Ludwig's dispute with the Curia, as Balduin of Luxemburg informed Benedict XII, had been a source of 'no small scandals and dangers to souls, both in *Alamania* and in other parts of the world'.[26] Konrad von Megenberg, writing at Avignon in the late 1330s, described the helpless vacillation of a German higher clergy torn between allegiance to their spiritual lord and to a schismatic emperor. Perhaps, he reflected, the Germans (*Germani*) might secede from the Catholic Church altogether, as had the Greeks when the Empire was taken from them.[27]

---

[22] *RTA* 7, no. 68, p. 116 (Frankfurt, 21 July 1411). For this document see above, Ch. 3, p. 143 n. 247. For another documentary reference to the universal role of the Germans, see *Nova Alamanniae*, vol. I, no. 583, p. 391, an official compilation of imperial rights (after 16 July 1338), here concerning the electoral rights exercised by the princes 'a tempore, quo Theutonicis regnum Romane ecclesie concessum est'.

[23] *MGC* 5, no. 889, p. 704 (1 April 1324).

[24] Above, Ch. 5, pp. 242–3.

[25] *Nova Alamanniae*, vol. I, no. 338, pp. 181–2 (29 June 1334).

[26] Ibid., no. 547, p. 366 (16 July 1338). Stengel believed that the letter was never sent.

[27] Konrad von Megenberg, *Planctus*, ed. Scholz, pars I, cap. 36, p. 51.

In part, therefore, the stress which German writers laid upon the harm done to Germany in the course of the struggles between pope and emperor merely reflected the contest's actual focus and consequences. That is not, however, the whole story. As we have seen elsewhere, the repeated identification of 'Germany' as the sphere within which events of fundamental importance to the imperial monarchy – events whose impact, however, varied substantially between different regions and localities – had their effect cannot be taken as axiomatic: it requires explanation. And at least in some of the more programmatic writings which resulted from the clash of the 'two powers', the Germans and their lands were ascribed clear and fundamental importance. A number of revealing assumptions and connections underlie Ludwig the Bavarian's third appeal against the pope's legal proceedings, drawn up in May 1324.[28] John XXII is condemned as an egotistical schemer and fomenter of dissensions, convicted by his own words of thirsting after Christian blood. 'He is, however, reported particularly to have said that discord among the princes, nobles and people of Germany [Alemannia] is the safety and deliverance of the Roman pontiffs and Church.'[29] When war and bloodshed spread in Germany, as a result of divided royal elections, the pope had appointed no envoy to avert these evils, though he could easily have chosen one from among the many collectors of revenues he kept there. In declaring the imperial throne vacant, John had infringed the 'rights and liberties' of 'all Germany', as well as those of the electors, princes and other subjects and vassals of the Empire.[30] What the pope – that 'malicious subverter of canons and violator of rights' – sought was nothing but 'the complete destruction of the holy Empire and its liberty and dignity, and the extermination and annulment of the Empire's prince-electors, all the Empire's subjects, and all Germany' (totius Alamanie).[31] 'Germany' was the Empire's foundation and principal member, ideally no less than materially. Its honour and standing, its identity – indeed, its very survival as a political concept – depended directly upon the Empire's well-being. Yet the pope, far from showing that solicitude towards Germany which as her ruler's spiritual counterpart he owed, had cynically worked for

---

[28] MGC 5, no. 909, pp. 723–44 (22 May 1322). The appeal, drawn up in the Teutonic Order's convent at Sachsenhausen, near Frankfurt, survives in two versions (for the second, see ibid., no. 910, pp. 745–54, of the same date). All the passages cited here are common to both versions. See also Thomas, Ludwig der Bayer, p. 164; and, for the importance of Ludwig's reign for the multiplication of references to the Germans in imperial documents, Thomas, 'Sprache und Nation', p. 81.
[29] MGC 5, no. 909, p. 724.
[30] Ibid., p. 727.   [31] Ibid., p. 726.

her destruction. Indeed, John had announced publicly his intention of bending every effort to crushing 'the brazen serpent, the Empire of the Germans' (*imperium Alemannorum*).[32]

If the ideal of papal–imperial relations continued in the late Middle Ages to be envisaged by German commentators as the harmonious collaboration of two great, universal monarchies, it is remarkable how ready some were to explain its breakdown in terms of ethnic antagonisms and grievances. A famous early example is seen in the denunciation of papal oppression of the Empire's German lands which the poet Walther von der Vogelweide composed, dated to 1213.[33] His bitter portrayal of the pope – Innocent III was meant – gleefully stirring up divisions in the Reich (bringing 'two Germans under one crown') and cynically duping *die tiutschen* out of their silver in some ways anticipates Ludwig's appeal against John XXII. Not only the pope's German victims, moreover, but also his Romance-speaking partisans and co-conspirators (*Walhen*) were imagined by Walther in broadly ethnic terms.[34] Not merely two 'powers', but two *peoples* were in conflict. This way of thinking was to be reinforced among German writers in the later thirteenth and fourteenth centuries, as the papacy fell increasingly under the domination of the Germans' powerful and assertive western neighbours, the French. It was not only at times when the spiritual and secular powers were in open collision that observers now came to regard their dealings as patterned by inter-ethnic rivalries. Alexander von Roes, who had observed with disquiet the elevation to the papal throne of the Frenchman Simon of Brie, would deliver, in his *Noticia seculi* of 1288, a withering valedictory judgement on the late pope. 'Of Gallic birth', Martin IV had thrown into confusion the whole Church and faith, 'wanting to govern the entire world in the French manner' (*modo Gallicorum*).[35] And with an immoderate love of his own people had gone, according to a view which gained currency in Germany, a loathing of their eastern neighbours. The pope 'greatly hated the Germans', observed the Lübeck annalist simply.[36] In Latin annals of Austrian provenance we learn that this 'enemy of the Teutons' often expressed the wish that he were a stork and the Germans frogs to devour, or himself a pike and

---

[32] Ibid., p. 732. The allegation was repeated verbatim by the chronicler Heinrich von Herford – an indication of the document's circulation and reception in Germany: *Liber de rebus memorabilioribus*, ed. Potthast, p. 240.

[33] See Walther von der Vogelweide, *Die Lieder*, ed. Maurer, no. 73, p. 222.

[34] Thus ibid., p. 72, for the juxtaposition: 'ir *tiutschez* silber vert in mînem *welschen* schrîn. / ir pfaffen ezzet hüener und trinket wîn, / unde lât die *tiutschen* ... vasten'.

[35] Alexander von Roes, *Noticia seculi*, cap. 16, ed. Grundmann and Heimpel, pp. 162–3.

[36] *Annales Lubicenses*, ed. Lappenberg, p. 415: 'Iste Teutonicis multum invidebat.'

the Germans fishes to gulp down.[37] Papal dealings with the Empire's German lands and their rulers became overlaid, in contemporary political rhetoric, with a dense vocabulary of interrelated ethnic stereotypes, pitting the Germans collectively against a hostile, Romance-speaking Curia. When the legate John of Tusculum (whose controversial stay in Germany has been noted already) saw how by his behaviour he had aroused 'the fury of the Alemannic people' he was soon wishing himself, according to one chronicler, back in his father's house in Rome, eating Lombard cabbage.[38] In Konrad von Megenberg's *Lament*, composed at the height of Ludwig the Bavarian's rift with Avignon, both the pope's attack on the Germans, as custodians of the Empire, and the defence of them mounted by a personified 'Church', were couched in terms of their alleged ethnic qualities, measured against other European peoples.[39] As we will see elsewhere, ethnic stereotypes were to be drawn on extensively in this period, both by Germans and their neighbours, to articulate fundamental constitutional arguments.[40] For now, however, it will suffice to note how axiomatically the Curia – imagined as quintessentially Romance-speaking, and for much of the time specifically French – was pitted against an *imperium* conceived of as fundamentally German.

For some of the Empire's sternest critics, precisely the strength of its bond with the Germans lay at the heart of the problem. A short tract composed in support of King Robert of Naples deployed Aristotelian and Thomist doctrines to urge the outright abolition of a universal monarchy which was irredeemably Teutonic.[41] Others, as we have seen, held out the hope that the tie between Empire and people might be broken after all.[42] German writers were no less convinced of their people's organic bond with the *imperium*, and some were at pains to argue for its preservation. In *Lohengrin*, a vernacular grail romance, probably dating from Ludwig IV's time but set in that of Henry I (919–36), the Saracens ominously announce their aim of installing their caliph as

---

[37] *Continuatio Vindobonensis*, ed. Wattenbach, pp. 712–13.
[38] *Ellenhardi chronicon*, ed. Jaffé, p. 130. The legate, according to the Colmar annalist, 'furorem Theutonicorum non immerito metuebat': *Annales Colmarienses maiores*, ed. Jaffé, p. 213.
[39] Konrad von Megenberg, *Planctus*, ed. Scholz, pars I, cap. 8, pp. 28–9.
[40] Below, Ch. 8, pp. 363–82.
[41] Jäschke, 'Reichskonzeptionen', esp. p. 432. Joachim of Fiore had regarded the Roman Empire in German hands as interchangeable with the rule of Islam as an enemy of the Church in the fifth age of the New Testament: Patschovsky, 'Henry "the first"', p. 312.
[42] Above, Ch. 5, p. 214, for French imperial candidatures.

'emperor in Rome in the German's stead'.[43] The imperial monarchy, for all its universalism, was rooted in German soil. In Latin verses, Lupold von Bebenburg had a personified Empire declare that 'I inhabit the Germans' fatherland for my seat.'[44] An antiphon on the Holy Lance and Nails, composed following Innocent VI's institution of their feast in 1354, urged the German people to rejoice at the honour which Christ had done them in bestowing specifically on them the instruments of his Passion, which were kept with the imperial regalia.[45] For the Strasbourg chronicler Fritsche Closener, Konrad I (911–18) had been 'the first German Kaiser', ruling for seven years 'in the German lands'. Applied to Konrad's modest northern reign, such language seems reasonable enough; but more revealing is Closener's insistence that the mighty Otto I was 'the first *powerful* German Kaiser'.[46] Jakob Twinger, Closener's Strasbourg heir, lent some substance to Otto's 'German' emperorship, recounting how the Saxon had journeyed south to restore Lombardy and Italy to 'the rule of the Germans and the Reich'.[47] Nor, in the fourteenth century, was this way of thinking consigned only to past history. Ludwig IV, in a letter to John of Bohemia, explained the motivation behind his projected journey to Rome: his Italian subjects had implored his aid, appealing to his coronation oath *pro conservando statu imperii*, lamenting their plight, and 'putting the blame on us, on the prince-electors, on other princes and subjects of the Empire, *and on the Germans generally*' (*Theutonicis universis*).[48] The German character of imperial lordship in Italy, invoked by Ludwig, might on occasion be given highly concrete expression. A letter of 1282 in the name of Rudolf I's chancellor and imperial vicar suspended judicial proceedings in Tuscany pending the arrival there 'of his German-speaking vicar-general ... with a company of five hundred German knights of the same tongue'.[49] German identity was here woven into the everyday application of imperial rule itself, self-evident proof of its authenticity.

[43] *Lohengrin*, ed. Cramer, p. 415, vv. 4520–1; and see Thomas, 'Das Identitätsproblem', p. 151.

[44] Lupold von Bebenburg, *Ritmaticum Querulosum et Lamentosum Dictamen de Modernis Cursibus et Defectibus Regni ac Imperii Romanorum*, in *Politische Lyrik*, ed. Müller, p. 175.

[45] See Heimpel, *Dietrich*, p. 226 n. 3: 'Gaude pia plebs iustorum / Gensque omnis Germanorum / Tantis de muneribus. Nam iocalia salutis / Tibi dedit rex virtutis / Suis de vulneribus / Claves, lanceam et crucem, / Hec sacra magnolia, / Ergo Christum vite ducem / Excole per omnia.'

[46] *Fritsche (Friedrich) Closener's Chronik*, ed. Hegel, pp. 34, 35.

[47] *Chronik des Jacob Twinger*, ed. Hegel, p. 419.

[48] *Nova Alamanniae*, vol. I, no. 173, p. 94 (24 February 1327).

[49] *MGC* 3, no. 608, p. 570. The idea that the Empire's authority south of the Alps found embodiment in the German identity of its representative lived on in the fifteenth

If Germanness could be called on to authenticate imperial government, the Empire in its turn endowed German identity with meaning and, in the eyes of literate Germans, their people with an honourable and prestigious place among an imagined plurality of Catholic peoples. The universal found a focus in the German. That a general council of the Church was being held (under imperial protection) on German soil was to the 'great glory of Germany' (*magna Alamanie gloria*), King Sigismund was informed in an address delivered in 1414 on behalf of the University of Cologne.[50] It was, he professed, his 'fervid zeal for the German fatherland' (*patria Germaniae*) that had moved Lupold von Bebenburg to compile his treatise on the Empire's constitution.[51] The need to stand up to those who would impugn or undermine the honour which the Germans gained through the Empire therefore became, in times of crisis and danger, a recurrent theme. In a letter of 1409, King Rupert informed an unknown town that the treaty recently made between Wenceslas of Luxemburg and the Pisan cardinals, which had sown 'new confusion, disunity and war in the Roman Empire', was to the 'great dishonour' of 'all the German lands' (*aller Dutscher lannde*).[52] The letter's addressees were urged to have regard to their 'dignity, honour and status', as well as Rupert's own, and not to recognise the cardinals' action. 'Should the German tongue lose its right [to the Empire], its *honour* will be undermined', the poet 'Meißner' had insisted, in verses probably composed during the troubled years preceding Rudolf I's elevation.[53] As Ludwig the Bavarian's manifesto against the pope contended, once the Empire was subverted, 'Germany' herself – here envisaged, it seems, as a community of political actors under the monarch – faced the prospect of *exterminium*. The Germans, represented by their political elite, might bring down on themselves exactly that fate – collective loss of status, and thus identity – through their own failure to live up to the high charge laid upon them. That was Lupold Hornburg's

century. When Enea Silvio Piccolomini came to Milan in 1449 to negotiate the city's submission to Frederick III, one of the proposed terms was that 'the emperor should appoint a German to administer justice in Milan itself', whereas in other, lesser, towns he might install 'anyone he pleased': Pius II, *Commentaries*, ed. Meserve and Simonetta, pp. 90–1. For more on the visible Germanness of Germans when in the south on imperial campaigns, see Ch. 8, pp. 368–9.

[50] Universitätsbibliothek Erlangen, MS 533, f. 20r. I am grateful to Professor Robert Swanson for drawing my attention to this manuscript.

[51] Lupold von Bebenburg, *Tractatus*, cap. 19, ed. Miethke and Flüeler, p. 408. Lupold went on to speak of his devotion particularly to his native Franconia: *Francia Germanica*. For this passage, see below, Ch. 10, p. 480.

[52] *RTA* 7, no. 371, p. 702 (Heidelberg, 13 October 1409).

[53] *Politische Lyrik*, ed. Müller, vol. I, p. 68. Problems of dating are discussed in Müller, *Untersuchungen*, pp. 121–2.

grim message to the princes in 1348: through the softness and cowardice of its great men, Germany stood 'in small regard'.[54] Alexander
von Roes had a similarly stark message for 'the Germans', exalted as
they were through the Roman Empire: let them by their actions show
themselves duly grateful.[55] But who were the 'Germans', upon whose
deeds the collective standing, indeed the very existence, of their people
as a whole was portrayed as depending? On this, treatise-writer and
poet were at one: the warrior nobility, pre-eminently the princes, and
above all those who were charged with choosing the Empire's ruler.
The German aristocracy – and not the 'Roman' kings and emperors –
were the element which, more than any other, in late medieval imagination bound the Empire and its fate to the Germans and theirs.

Imperial princes, German princes

A chronicler records how the imposter Tile Kolup, as the crowning
masterstroke of his grand deception, laid plans for a 'general council' to assemble at Frankfurt where, having summoned 'the princes
of Germany' (*principes Alimanie*), he was to be formally 'restored' to
his rule.[56] The pseudo-emperor's constitutional grasp, at least as the
archbishop of Trier's biographer reports it, is not to be faulted: for his
solemn affirmation as ruler he had identified not only the right place,
but the indispensable political actors too. To the German nobility, and
above all the princes, was ascribed responsibility – in partnership with
the monarch or even, in time of crisis, in his stead – for fundamental constitutional matters in the Reich.[57] A letter of Ludwig IV to the
cardinals, urging them to convene a general Church council, declared
that 'we also wish and intend solemnly to assemble [for such a meeting]
all the secular and ecclesiastical princes of Germany'.[58] A decade later,
draft proposals for repairing the emperor's rift with Avignon envisaged
'that Ludwig will procure that the princes and barons of Germany
swear and give letters to the effect that if [he] does not honour all things
they will not assist him, but will be against him'. Another article raised

---

[54] *Politische Lyrik*, ed. Müller, vol. I, p. 198; and see the comments of Herkommer,
'Kritik', pp. 75–7.
[55] Alexander von Roes, *Memoriale*, cap. 10, ed. Grundmann and Heimpel, pp. 100–1:
'Utinam exaltati per Romanum imperium ... intelligerent et non essent ingrati!'
[56] *Vita Henrici Archiepiscopi Altera*, ed. Waitz, p. 463.
[57] For the development of the high nobility as an independent constitutional factor in
the Reich in the late Middle Ages, see Annas, *Hoftag*, vol. I, esp. pp. 137–57.
[58] *Nova Alamanniae*, vol. I, no. 338, p. 182 (Überlingen, 29 June 1334: '... principes
Alem(anie) seculares et ecclesiasticos universos volumus et intendimus ... solemniter
aggregare'.

the prospect 'that the princes and barons of Germany will supplicate for Ludwig's absolution'.[59] Alongside many general references to the Empire's 'princes' (*principes imperii, principes Romani imperii*, and so on), it was invariably the *German* political elite – and not, by contrast, those of Italy or Burgundy, never explicitly mentioned in such contexts – which in imperial and other documents was made the bearer of the Empire's affairs. The same ethnic (or ethno-constitutional) frame of reference is encountered in the reports of the chroniclers on imperial politics.[60] The *Saxon World Chronicle* records an abortive assembly at Bern in 1238 to which Frederick II 'had summoned the German princes and nobles'.[61] In a Bavarian continuation of the same chronicle, 'all the German princes of the Holy Roman Empire' urged Ludwig IV to stand firm for the territorial integrity of the Reich, in face of John XXII's excommunication.[62] It was 'the princes of the German lands' who, in Tilemann Elhen's account, met at Frankfurt in 1397 and established a *Landfriede*.[63]

Among the many references in the sources to the political and constitutional roles of the German princes and nobility, one thing stands out: the absence of a formulaic, 'official', vocabulary for their naming, comparable to the highly standardised, and Romanised, chancery language to which the monarchs themselves were subject. Instead, the reader encounters, in disordered profusion, invocations of *principes Alamanie, principes Theutonie, principes Germanie, proceres Alemannie, principes et comites de Germania, comites et nobiles de Alemannia, nobiles et barones regni Alamannie, Daeutsche landesherren, fursten von Dutschen landen* – to name but some of the richly varied forms through which the ruler's aristocratic companions were identified. It does not seem fanciful to suggest that precisely the absence of an authoritative terminology for referring to the Empire's political elite opened the way for its routine designation as 'German'. The contrast with their ruler's binding

[59] Ibid., vol. I, no. 773, pp. 496, 497 (August 1344).
[60] These terms, particularly in chancery documents, often referred primarily not to an ethno-cultural but a constitutional community: the princes of the northern *regnum*, among whom were some, particularly along the western frontier, who were not German-speakers. For this usage, see Begert, *Böhmen*, pp. 50–3, following Julius Ficker, *Vom Reichsfürstenstand*, 2 vols. in 4 parts (Innsbruck, 1861–1923). However, as will become clear in what follows, these princes were nevertheless routinely linked with the Empire's translation to the German people *and* regarded as the particular embodiment of that people's defining qualities.
[61] *Sächsische Weltchronik*, ed. Weiland, p. 252: '... de Dudischen vorsten unde de herren...'
[62] *Sächsische Weltchronik: Dritte Bairische Fortsetzung*, ed. Weiland, p. 345: '... allen Dutschen fursten des heiligen Romischen riches...'
[63] *Limburger Chronik*, ed. Wyss, p. 93.

imperial *Romanitas* is evident, for example, in an account of Rudolf I's election, by the *principes imperii*, set down by a monastic annalist in Lower Bavaria: the Habsburger was 'elected king of the Romans by the princes of Germany'.[64] The widespread currency of this distinction is underlined by its repetition in contexts still further removed from the dry formulae of chancery clerks. In Konrad von Würzburg's vernacular romance *Partonopier und Meliur*, the unhorsing of the (Roman) emperor at a tournament provokes the indignation of his attendant *German* nobles (*der Tiutschen ungehabe*).[65]

For the electors themselves, it might be supposed that different, more elevated, principles would have applied. That the Empire's princes were recognised as rightfully choosing its ruler was no constitutional novelty in the late Middle Ages.[66] But until around the middle of the thirteenth century, the principle was maintained that the northern magnates as a whole had a voice.[67] And indeed, although a narrowing and stratification process can be seen at work from the end of the twelfth century at latest, substantial groups of magnates of changeable composition nevertheless long continued to have a hand in choosing the new monarch. Sixteen temporal princes took part in the double election of 1198.[68] Konrad IV of Hohenstaufen was formally elected in 1237 by the archbishops of Mainz, Trier and Salzburg; the bishops of Bamberg, Regensburg, Freising and Passau; the king of Bohemia; the Rhenish Count Palatine; the landgrave of Thuringia and the duke of Carinthia.[69] But after mid-century, in a process whose detailed stages and dynamics still remain opaque, the exclusive right of a small circle of princes became established, no longer merely to promulgate formally the election, but to choose a ruler on behalf of all.[70] By the 1270s, observers were able to

---

[64] *Hermanni Altahensis Continuatio*, ed. Jaffé, p. 410.

[65] Konrad von Würzburg, *Partonopier und Meliur*, ed. Bartsch, p. 219, vv. 15153–4.

[66] For the importance of the idea of princely election under the Staufer, see Koch, *Sacrum Imperium*, pp. 191–2.

[67] Italian and Burgundian princes, however, did not take part. The last recorded instance of Italian participation was at the election of Otto III in Verona in 983: Begert, *Böhmen*, p. 61 with n. 211.

[68] Wolf, *Die Entstehung*, pp. 15–16. However, Wolf's underlying thesis here, that this group, and thus the emergent body of electors, was defined by consciousness of shared Ottonian descent, has met with a broadly sceptical reception: Ertl, 'Alte Thesen', esp. p. 627.

[69] *MGC* 2, no. 329, p. 440 (February 1237); Wolf, *Die Entstehung*, p. 35.

[70] The distinction between participation in choosing the monarch (*Wahl*) and public declaration of the choice (*Kur*) is more succinctly made in German than English. In the thirteenth century, a group of princes who had already gained the right of *Kur* gradually secured also the exclusive power of *Wahl*. How and why this came about has long been regarded as one of the foremost riddles of German constitutional history, and in recent times has become the subject of lively controversy and attracted diverse

identify a group of seven, who before the century's end were already being referred to as a distinct *collegium* and distinguished as 'electors' (*kurfursten*).[71] In the years that followed, their special constitutional standing within the princely estate became increasingly clearly defined. The Golden Bull, which set out in detail the electors' privileges, compared them to the seven golden candlesticks of the Book of Revelation.[72] They were – in a metaphor whose origins, applied to the princes, lay in the Staufer era – the 'main columns', by which the 'holy edifice' of the Empire was upheld.[73] In choosing a king and future emperor, 'for the well-being of the Christian people', they acted under the guidance of the Holy Spirit.[74] Amid the apocalyptic universalism in which the Golden Bull enfolded the electors, not a word was said about their German identity.

But in fact a broader view of the sources reveals that the vocabulary employed to designate the electors, while it certainly changed over time, reflecting their evolving constitutional distinctiveness, was hardly more regular than that used for the princes generally. And, away from the solemn clauses of the Golden Bull, it was no less ready to invoke for them an explicitly German identity. If the electors were often designated simply as 'princes of the Empire', or *principes electores imperii*, they were also 'the princes of Germany'. Albert I wrote in September 1298 of his recent election *ab illustribus Allemannie principibus*.[75] The German political elite had a special responsibility for ensuring that the imperial office was filled. 'You, German princes, be warned: see that an emperor is consecrated', admonished the 'Meißner', in verses composed in the troubled times following the end of the Staufer.[76] It was specifically to his archchancellorship for Germany that appeal was made to justify the archbishop of Mainz's claim to the first voice in elections.[77] As the terminology for the electors' designation grew more specific, in the later thirteenth and early fourteenth centuries, ethnic points of reference were worked into the expanding formulations. Gregory X had, according to the *Braunschweig Rhyming Chronicle*, in 1273 sent his mandate

---

and ingenious attempts at a resolution. For surveys of the debate, judicious critiques and proposals, see: Krieger, *König, Reich und Reichsreform*, pp. 66–71; Erkens, *Kurfürsten*, esp. pp. 5–13; Ertl, 'Alte Thesen', as well as Wolf, 'Seit wann?', esp. pp. 410–33. Also still fundamental: Mitteis, *Die deutsche Königswahl*, esp. Ch. 6.

[71] Ertl, 'Alte Thesen', p. 635.
[72] *Die Goldene Bulle*, ed. Fritz, p. 45; and cf. Revelation 1:12–13.
[73] *Die Goldene Bulle*, ed. Fritz, p. 56. For the origins of the 'columns' metaphor, see Koch, *Sacrum Imperium*, pp. 193–4. Again, the image is traceable back to Revelation.
[74] *Die Goldene Bulle*, ed. Fritz, p. 53.
[75] *MGC* 4.i, no. 17, p. 15 (23 September 1298).
[76] *Politische Lyrik*, ed. Müller, vol. I, p. 68.
[77] *MGC* 4.i, no. 17, p. 15.

to choose a new king to 'the princes who had charge of election to the Empire in the German lands'.[78] A supplication drafted by imperial towns for dispatch to Avignon on behalf of Ludwig IV spoke of the ruler's elevation 'by the princes of Germany, electors of the Empire' (*principes Alamanie electores imperii*).[79] The Rhenish Count Palatine was able to number himself among 'the most excellent princes of Germany [*Germanie principes*] who by law and ancient custom have the right and power to elect the Roman king, afterwards to be raised to emperor'.[80] In the seven electors, the historic responsibility for the Empire's well-being which rested on all the German princes – indeed, on the entire German nobility – was now concentrated. Alexander von Roes, in exhortatory mood in the longest of his works, was able to move in seamless progression from his opening, 'Would that the Germans...!' (*Utinam Germani*), to a more pointed, 'Would that the princes, especially those to whom pertains the right and power of electing the king afterwards to be raised to emperor...'[81]

Yet the electors' recurrent identification with 'Germany' is, on the face of it, rather odd. In reality, their German identity was no more axiomatic than that of the monarchs whom they raised up. On the contrary, it was perceived as a problem from the first emergence of a more stable and limited group of princes with the prime voice in choosing a ruler. A celebrated passage in the *Sachsenspiegel* had insisted that the king of Bohemia, despite his office of imperial cupbearer, had no part in elections because he was not German.[82] Not the least startling thing

---

[78] *Braunschweigische Reimchronik*, ed. Weiland, p. 567, vv. 8731–2. The pope 'bot dhen vursten, dhe dha phlagen des riches kore an Dudeschen lande'; cf. the formula, evidently derived from a letter of Otakar II, in which the electors are the 'principes ... Alemannie, quibus est potestas cesares eligendi': *Regesta Diplomatica nec non Epistolaria Bohemiae*, ed. Emler, no. 2619, p. 1145.

[79] *Nova Alamanniae*, vol. I, no. 520, p. 340 (around 17 May 1338).

[80] *MGC* 4.i, no. 5, pp. 4–5 (1298, before 23 June).

[81] Alexander von Roes, *Memoriale*, cap. 10, ed. Grundmann and Heimpel, pp. 100–1.

[82] *Sachsenspiegel Landrecht* III, cap. 57 § 2, p. 243: 'De scenke des rikes, de koning van Behmen, de ne hevet nenen kore, umme dat he nicht dudisch n'is.' A number of historians have sought, on various grounds, to argue that this passage is a later interpolation: thus, e.g., Wolf, 'Seit wann?', pp. 404–5. However, an array of evidence, including indications of the early influence of Eike's words, now makes this appear highly unlikely: the passage was almost certainly part of the original text. Thus: Ertl, 'Alte Thesen', esp. p. 626; Erkens, *Kurfürsten*, esp. pp. 20–1. Alexander Begert has objected to prevailing readings of the passage on different grounds, arguing that Eike judged the Bohemian ineligible not on the basis of ethnicity but on the narrower constitutional principle that – with the 1220 elevation of Henry (VII) fresh in mind – as a king in his own right he could not take part in choosing another (and particularly not a narrowly 'German') king: Begert, *Böhmen*, pp. 80–1. However, such ingenious complexity seems superfluous here: Eike appears explicitly to target the Bohemian's

about this claim is its patent contradiction of the facts of the day. The Bohemian king had been one of Philip of Swabia's electors in 1198 and had also given his voice in the election of Frederick II. He was thenceforth to be recurrently involved in choosing the monarch.[83] The view of the *Sachsenspiegel*, that there were six electors only, and that the Bohemian was not of their number, found in the later thirteenth century an echo, in somewhat different form, in the canon law of the Church.[84] In the annals of Albert von Stade, compiled around mid-century, we encounter again the claim that the Bohemian did not elect, 'since he is no Teuton'.[85] It was expressed in a more extreme form at the time of King Otakar's rebellion against Rudolf I in the 1270s, when it seemed for a while that the duke of Lower Bavaria might supplant the Bohemian among the core of electors.[86] The *Schwabenspiegel*, compiled in the mid-1270s, duly substituted the Bavarian for the Bohemian, while insisting, with an ethnocentrism more strident than Eike's, that the temporal prince-electors must be 'German men, all four'.[87] Probably as late as Ludwig IV's reign, the *Lohengrin* poet, doubtless swayed by the rulings of such weighty and widely known authorities, is still to be found ascribing an electoral voice to Bavaria while ignoring Bohemia's title (which by then had long since been publicly confirmed beyond all doubt).[88]

---

ethnicity, and that is certainly how the passage was read a generation later, by the compiler of the *Schwabenspiegel*.

[83] Richter, 'Die böhmischen Länder', p. 303; Zeumer, 'Kur', pp. 210–11.

[84] The canonist Hostiensis, in his gloss to Innocent III's *Venerabilem* (1262 × 1271), noted that in the view of some the Bohemian only participated if the other six electors could not reach agreement: Zeumer, 'Kur', pp. 212–13. For the relevant passage, see Buchner, 'Die Entstehung', p. 63 n. 1. The view that the king of Bohemia's role was to establish concord if the others were divided proved durable. It was reiterated in the fourteenth century by writers as various as the *Sachsenspiegel* glossator Johannes von Buch (below, n. 90) and the chronicler Heinrich von Herford: *Liber de rebus memorabilioribus*, ed. Potthast, pp. 94–5. In the vernacular tradition, it proved still longer-lasting: Schnell, 'Vorstellungen', pp. 133–41.

[85] *Annales Stadenses auctore Alberto*, ed. Lappenberg, p. 367: 'Rex Boemiae, qui picerna est, non eligit, quia Teutonicus non est.' This passage too has been targeted by Armin Wolf and others as a later interpolation. Again, however, the balance of evidence argues against such a view: Erkens, *Kurfürsten*, pp. 23–4.

[86] For the Bavarian claim, see Zeumer, 'Kur', esp. pp. 224–9.

[87] *Schwabenspiegel*, ed. Eckhardt, *Landrecht*, cap. 128/132, pp. 192–3: '... vnd die svlen tuetsche man sein alle vier von vater vnd von muoter oder von eintwederem'. Only a minority of manuscripts allow for descent from a German as one or other parent, however, with others insisting that both parents must be German in order to establish a voting right (though, in spite of this, some later manuscripts still include Bohemia among the electors): Begert, *Böhmen*, pp. 76–7. Over 300 manuscripts of the *Schwabenspiegel* (*Landrecht*) survive or are attested: P. Johanek, 'Schwabenspiegel', in *VL* 8, cols. 896–907 (here col. 896).

[88] *Lohengrin*, ed. Cramer, p. 287, vv. 1961–80. The *Lohengrin* poet's contemporaries did not follow him in his view: for verses by the singer Frauenlob, probably from the early

With time, the Bohemian king's vote did gain general recognition – which is to say, the Bohemian himself was gradually drawn beneath the Germanising mantle of the electoral college. The Germanness of the electors was cut from the same pliable fabric as that of the monarchs they chose. Letters of Ludwig IV appointing John of Bohemia as imperial vicar did not shrink from naming the king, in a reference to his electoral office, as 'one of the limbs of Germany' (*unum ex Alem(anie) menbris*).[89] The passing of the Bohemian crown from the ancient Přemyslids to the Luxemburger had doubtless eased the shift in perceptions. Johannes von Buch, in his widely read gloss to the *Sachsenspiegel*, dealt bluntly with the claims of his source on the matter: the king of Bohemia did indeed have a vote, because he *was* German.[90] An important part in changing outlooks had been played by the ubiquitous chronicle of Martin of Troppau, which in a much-cited verse numbered the Bohemian among the electors.[91] Most significantly, however, the electors' 'German' identity is revealed by the Bohemian case as a protean, shifting thing: less an attribute which individual princes brought with them to their electoral role than one projected onto them in consequence of their participation in the most fundamental constitutional affairs of the Reich.

It was not only the Bohemian vote which seemed hard to reconcile with the electors' common German identity. Albert von Stade

---

fourteenth century, which list the Bohemian among the seven, see *Politische Lyrik*, ed. Müller, vol. II, p. 138. For the poem's dating, see Thomas, 'Der Lohengrin', esp. p. 174; for definitive imperial recognition of the Bohemian vote, in documents from the period 1285–90: Begert, *Böhmen*, p. 77; Zeumer, 'Kur', pp. 244–5.

[89] *Nova Alamanniae*, vol. I, no. 175, p. 98 (Trent, February 1327). In the same context, of electoral powers, Pope Urban IV had already written to Otakar II as one of the 'principes regni Theutoniae, ad quos Romanorum regis in imperatorem promovendi spectat electio': *Regesta Diplomatica nec non Epistolaria Bohemiae*, ed. Emler, no. 370, p. 142 (3 June 1262).

[90] *Glossen zum Sachsenspiegel-Landrecht*, ed. Kaufmann, p. 1300, to *Landrecht* III 57 § 2: 'Wente he hir secht, dat de koningh van Bemen dar vmme nenen kore en hebbe, dar vmme dat he nicht Dudesch en ys, so hefft he nun den kore, nach / deme dat he Dudesch is.' However, Johannes did go on (ibid., p. 1301 with n. 48), citing the canon-law tradition originating with Hostiensis, to limit the Bohemian's role to the resolution of elections where the other six participants were equally split. On this, see Kannowski, *Die Umgestaltung*, pp. 258–9. For the dissemination of his gloss, see I. Buchholz-Johanek, 'Johannes von Buch', in *VL* 4, cols. 551–9. The gloss survives in 136 manuscripts, and was translated at an early date from its original Low German into Middle and Upper German.

[91] *Martini Oppaviensis Chronicon: Imperatores*, ed. Weiland, p. 466: 'Maguntinensis, Treverensis, Coloniensis, / Quilibet imperii fit cancellarius horum, / Et palatinus dapifer, dux portitor ensis, / Marchio prepositus camere, pincerna Boemus: / Hii statuunt dominum cunctis per secula summum.'

appealed to Trier's special antiquity to justify her prince's electoral voice, although the city was 'not of *Alemannia*'.[92] Albert's argument, invoking a legendary Assyrian foundation, is a reminder of the rich resources of myth and memory concentrated in the Empire's western lands.[93] But it also highlights a problem not confined to Trier. Geographical notions of Roman origin, which made the Rhine a frontier between 'Germany' and 'Gaul', left a full three of the seven electors with their main seats on the Gallic side of the line.[94] Their location raised obvious questions about the identity of the princes themselves, which Alexander von Roes, as a native of Cologne, deemed it prudent to tackle head-on. 'And note', he cautioned, 'that the populations of the cities and dioceses of Trier, Cologne and Mainz are Germans [*Germani*], and their archbishops are held to elect the king.'[95] The emphasis is unmistakable, and easily explained. More interesting is the assumption on which Alexander rests his case: the peoples under the three Rhineland archbishops could not be other than German, *because* their princes had electoral votes.[96] For Alexander, 'German' identity was no changeless datum, but the layered deposit of historical processes. Not the Empire's rulers but the electors provided him with a measure and an explanatory model for its accretion in time. Originally, under Charles the Great, there were just four of them, all princes of the Frankish Rhineland, at a time when the eastern principalities had scarcely begun to accept Christianity.[97] Only subsequently, after their conversion, and the intermixing of the Frankish and Saxon elites, after the Saxons had proven their loyalty and worth to the Empire, did 'the Germans' (*Germani*) decide to add to the electors' number. The Saxon princes – the duke of Saxony and margrave of Brandenburg – were thus henceforth to take part, along with

---

[92] *Annales Stadenses auctore Alberto*, ed. Lappenberg, p. 367.
[93] For the Trier origin myth, see below, Ch. 7, p. 319.
[94] See below, Ch. 10, pp. 455–61.
[95] Alexander von Roes, *Memoriale*, cap. 11, ed. Grundmann and Heimpel, pp. 101–2.
[96] Essentially the same argument was advanced independently shortly afterwards by the Tuscan chronicler Tolomeo da Lucca: the region to the left of the Rhine was known as *Teutonia* and accounted to the *regnum Alamanniae* 'because it elects the emperor'. See Begert, *Böhmen*, p. 47.
[97] Alexander von Roes, *Memoriale*, cap. 12, ed. Grundmann and Heimpel, pp. 102–3. Later MS classes also number the king of Bohemia among the princes subsequently added to the electoral college. However, his name is not mentioned in the earliest form of the work, composed in 1281, at a time when the status of the Bohemian vote was uncertain: Grundmann and Heimpel, 'Einleitung', pp. 25–6.

the *principes Germanie* (to whom they had now been assimilated), in choosing the ruler.[98]

'The Germans' emerge from such writings as a political community which took shape within history, as a series of separate warrior aristocracies, and their leaders were progressively conjoined beneath the unifying mantle of the Empire. It was this common trust and burden, whose main bearers were the princes, which rendered their shared Germanness visible and significant. It was his constitutional status within the Reich that, for all Albert von Stade's equivocation on the matter, set a seal on the archbishop of Trier's 'German' identity, enabling Balduin of Luxemburg to write of 'the princes of Germany, electors of the Holy Roman Empire, of whom we are one'.[99] Alexander's account of the origins of the electors, while unusually full and sophisticated, was but one – Rhenish, Frankish – variant of a more pervasive master-myth. A different chronology, but the same historical model, was invoked in a letter of Ludwig IV to Count Berthold von Henneberg, empowering him to raise the Saxon nobility for Ludwig's Italian campaign. The princes, magnates and nobles of Saxony, the letter explained, had been the Empire's founders, who through their warlike deeds and glorious triumphs had established and magnificently exalted it.[100] Not Charlemagne but the Ottonians (whose rule was much lauded by Ludwig's German partisans) are on this view the originators of a German political community.[101] The Saxons were 'incorporated before all others into the Empire of the Teutonic people'. This, and the burdens which they had to shoulder, explained why the Saxons alone had two prince-electors, for their own glory and the Empire's defence.

Translatio imperii

But how was it that *German* princes were to be found raising up a *Roman* king-emperor at all, and even, as it seemed, giving proof of their Germanness by that very act? Not the least remarkable element in late medieval Roman emperorship, surely, was the notion that Caesar's nomination should rest with men whose homes lay not beside the Tiber,

---

[98] Alexander von Roes, *Memoriale*, cap. 27, ed. Grundmann and Heimpel, pp. 130–1.

[99] *Nova Alamanniae*, vol. I, no. 547, p. 366 (1338, soon after 16 July): '... principes Germanie sacri Romani imperii electores, de quorum numero unus sum et fui ...'

[100] *MGC* 6, no. 326, p. 239 (6 August 1327). E.E. Stengel identified Berthold von Henneberg, regent of the Mark Brandenburg from 1323, as the person responsible for awakening Ludwig IV's interest in the Saxon *Kaiserzeit*: Thomas, 'Der Lohengrin', p. 173.

[101] For the championing of the Ottonians by fourteenth-century imperialists such as Lupold von Bebenburg, see below, Ch. 7, pp. 340–2.

but by the Rhine, Elbe, Oder or Moldau. The hold which the German people had gained over the Roman Empire, which was deemed to have its most tangible constitutional expression in the electoral rights of their princes, became between the thirteenth and fifteenth centuries the subject of a body of historical myth of uncommon political urgency and social penetration. If it was also to a startling degree complex, tangled and contradictory, those qualities are better viewed as attesting to its wide importance than as betraying the alleged weaknesses upon which modern scholarship has so often chosen to concentrate.

Some of the salient qualities of the legends recounting the Empire's transfer to the Germans stand out to the most cursory inspection. Not least is its epochal significance, in the judgement of some late medieval Germans. The Dominican Heinrich von Herford routinely invoked the *translatio imperii in Theutonicos* (which he believed had occurred under Charlemagne), alongside the foundation of the world and the city of Rome, and the birth of Christ, for basic chronological orientation.[102] In one account, the passing of rule from the 'Franconians' to the 'Saxons', with Henry I's accession, was distinguished by the appearance of a comet.[103] Equally noteworthy is the habitual ethnocentrism of the accounts which German writers gave of the constitutional order which the Empire's translation had established. Lupold von Bebenburg insisted that it was to 'the Germanic Franks' (*Franci Germanici*) that, 'not without the merits of virtues', the *imperium* had passed.[104] In the post-Staufer era the case for the Empire's possession specifically by the Germans – on the basis, it was argued, of uniquely favourable character traits – was made more explicitly, at greater length and with greater urgency than ever before.[105]

Lupold's choice of language underlines another recurrent element in late medieval legends linking the Germans with the Reich: the formative influence of regional perspectives and traditions, and thus the diversity, even incompatibility, of the visions of nation-making which they unfolded. For the Franconian Lupold, the Empire's translation was proof of 'the special nobility of the *Franks* of Germany'.[106] Against his viewpoint might be set that of the Westphalian Dietrich von Niem, for whom it was only with the accession of the Ottonian dynasty, and the Empire's 'mutation' *away from* the Franks, that it came at last to 'the

---

[102] Thus, e.g., *Liber de rebus memorabilioribus*, ed. Potthast, p. 54 (reign of Lothar).
[103] *Martini Minoritae Flores*, ed. Eccard, p. 1612.
[104] Lupold von Bebenburg, *Tractatus*, cap. 3, ed. Miethke and Flüeler, p. 264.
[105] For purported German characteristics, see below, Ch. 8, pp. 363–73.
[106] Ibid., p. 263.

Germans or Saxons'.[107] One result of such a diversity of regional and social standpoints was to introduce controversy and open contention into accounts of the Empire's passage to the Germans. Further matter for argument arose, moreover, from the diversity of sources upon which writers were able to draw, and their different ways of understanding them. Jakob Twinger, in his much-copied vernacular chronicle, thus summarised the version of the story as set out by his Strasbourg predecessor Fritsche Closener – that the Empire was first held by the French, then divided, and not reassembled in German hands until the tenth century – only to declare that this 'should not be believed', since the Reich had in fact been with the Germans since Charles the Great's day.[108]

The right understanding of *translatio imperii* was no trivial matter. The Franciscan Johann von Winterthur, reporting schemes for a settlement with Avignon, has the princes tell Ludwig IV that the pope's proposed terms would mean them giving up rights of election 'which have belonged to us since Charles's time' and their transfer to foreigners.[109] The Empire's bestowal upon the Germans, it was widely contended, was rooted in cosmic historical processes reflecting God's will for his people. But there was no guarantee that history had reached a standstill, or that the Germans' sway over the Empire would be any more immutable than had those of earlier 'imperial' peoples – the obvious cautionary example being that of the Byzantine Greeks.[110] In troubled times, the signs were that it would not. 'If you grant the [imperial] eagle to this rude people [i.e. the Germans]', the pope urges a personified Church in Konrad von Megenberg's polemical *Lament*, from the 1330s, 'you can if you wish also take it from them again.'[111] A contemporary sense of the tentativeness of things is captured in the qualification added by more than one chronicler that the Germans, having gained the Empire, still hold it 'up till now'.[112] Throughout the two

---

[107] Dietrich von Nieheim, *Viridarium*, ed. Lhotsky and Pivec, p. 34: '... mutacio imperii de Francis in Germanos sive in Saxones...'

[108] Closener, following Martin of Troppau and Frutolf-Ekkehard, explained that, with Charlemagne's Rome coronation, 'sus kam daz romesche rich an die Frantzosen über' (from the Greeks): *Fritsche (Friedrich) Closener's Chronik*, ed. Hegel, p. 34. Cf. *Chronik des Jacob Twinger*, ed. Hegel, pp. 421–2.

[109] *Die Chronik Johanns von Winterthur*, ed. Baethgen, pp. 245–6.

[110] Thus Lupold Hornburg, *Dyse rede ist von des Ryches clage*, vv. 504–7, in *Politische Lyrik*, ed. Müller, p. 199, in which a personified Reich says of the Germans: 'Lant sie niht vntat balde, / Ir vntruwe vnd ir groz vnart, / So forht ich, daz ich muze eine vart / Farn, als ich tet von kriechen.'

[111] Konrad von Megenberg, *Planctus*, ed. Scholz, pars I, cap. 14, p. 34.

[112] *Martini Minorita Flores Temporum*, ed. Eccard, p. 1613; *Fritsche (Friedrich) Closener's Chronik*, ed. Hegel, p. 35.

centuries which followed Frederick II's death, German commentators, from kings to polemicists and vernacular chroniclers, repeatedly insisted that plans were afoot to strip their people of the imperial title and transfer it to another.[113]

Several factors ensured a comparatively large public for the idea of the Empire's translation. One was its identification as an epochal moment in the universal chronicles in which the German lands were so prolific, and which from the thirteenth century were linked particularly with the didactic aims of the mendicant orders.[114] With the reception of the pope-and-emperor chronicle genre in Germany in the late thirteenth century, universal history took an ethnocentric turn, in writings which now accorded greater prominence to the place of the Germans in a Christian-Roman past.[115] The myth of the Empire's transfer in this way reached out beyond the learned few, to larger, more varied audiences. Its circulation was speeded by the crises which repeatedly beset the imperial monarchy and the doubts and anxieties which these stirred up. The process was encouraged, moreover, by the way in which the *translatio* legend had first entered the political consciousness of German-speakers, and the sustenance which it thereafter received from the Empire's great doctrinal counterpart and protagonist, the Catholic Church.

The notion that rulership had passed, over time, between a succession of (conventionally, for medieval writers, four) hegemonic peoples was in origin an ancient one. It is to be found in the Old Testament, but entered the medieval Latinate tradition above all through late antique Christian historiography.[116] It gained, in consequence, a central place in eschatological schemes depicting the course and end of human affairs, resting upon the prophetic vision of the Book of Daniel.[117] The idea that hegemonic power in the world had mapped within history, through a succession of epochal changes, a broadly east–west trajectory became during the central Middle Ages a component in larger, more amorphous narratives reflecting cultural change and growth in Latin Europe.

---

[113] See above, Ch. 5, p. 214 and below, Ch. 8, pp. 376–7.

[114] Goez, *Translatio Imperii*, pp. 106–7; for mendicant historiography, see Guenée, *Histoire*, pp. 55–8.

[115] Thus Mierau, 'Die Einheit', esp. pp. 289, 299, examining the adaption of the chronicle of Martin of Troppau (for which, see below), by the south-German Franciscan author of *Flores temporum*.

[116] Goez, *Translatio Imperii*, pp. 19–20; and see also H. Thomas, 'Translatio Imperii', in *LMA* 8, cols. 943–6.

[117] For Nebuchadnezzar's vision, see Daniel 2:31–3; for its interpretation, Goez, *Translatio Imperii*, p. 7.

By the thirteenth and fourteenth centuries it was an established point of reference for German writers of history.[118] Especially noteworthy about the *translatio* myth is its natural propensity to locate power and change in notions of ethnicity. Already in the ninth century it was being claimed that with the Carolingians the Roman Empire had come to the Franks.[119] But it was not until the second half of the eleventh that the idea began to take shape that the *imperium* had passed into the hands of the 'German' people.[120] Once again, the Investiture Contest, and the controversies which it fuelled, offered powerful stimulus to what was destined to become a central element in German political identity. And it was above all the papacy which in the constitutional crises of the two following centuries was to infuse substance and authority, though also doubt and controversy, into the idea of the Empire's historic transfer to the Germans.

The most important single judgement on the subject came in 1202, in Innocent III's decretal *Venerabilem*, which explained how the Apostolic See, which translated the Roman Empire, through Charles, from the Greeks to the Germans, had also granted the princes 'the right and power of electing the king, afterwards to be raised to emperor'.[121] The pope's pronouncement soon became widely known, and was much cited.[122] The gloss to *Venerabilem* made explicit that the 'princes' who had benefited from the Empire's transfer were the electors.[123] In 1303, Boniface VIII offered his own sonorous, hierocratic, summation of a developing tradition, insisting that:

the vicar of Jesus Christ and successor of Peter transferred imperial power from the Greeks to the Germans, so that those same Germans [*ipsi Germani*], namely the seven princes (four laymen and three clerics) might elect a king of the Romans, to be promoted to emperor and monarch over all earthly kings and princes.[124]

---

[118] See thus, as examples, *Der kunige buoch*, ed. Massmann, p. cxxi, following *Sachsenspiegel Landrecht* III, cap. 44 § 1, ed. Eckhardt, p. 229; *Sächsische Weltchronik*, ed. Weiland, p. 78, identifying the four empires as those of the Chaldeans, Persians, Greeks and Romans, noting the modest beginnings and subsequent greatness of the Roman Empire, and anticipating its coming *cranchait*.

[119] Müller-Mertens, 'Römisches Reich', p. 10.

[120] The earliest known instance of this view is from Adam von Bremen, writing in the 1070s. See the comments of Thomas, 'Das Identitätsproblem', p. 140, as well as Müller-Mertens, 'Römisches Reich', pp. 17–18.

[121] Printed in *Corpus Iuris Canonici*, ed. Friedberg, vol. II, cols. 79–82. And see: Kempf, *Papsttum*, pp. 48–55; Folz, *Le Souvenir*, pp. 272–5; Goez, *Translatio Imperii*, Ch. 7.

[122] Schubert, *König und Reich*, p. 22.

[123] Buchner, 'Die Entstehung', pp. 62–3.

[124] *MGC* 4.i, no. 173, p. 139 (30 April 1303).

Such rulings naturally did much to shape the course of subsequent debate on the Empire's translation.[125] As binding canonical judgements, they lent the Germans' claim to the political heritage of ancient Rome a firm constitutional status. In so doing, they powerfully legitimised an idea both inherently surprising and, outside Germany, not universally accepted.[126] They underlined the principle that the Reich was a dignity to be earned, thereby concentrating attention upon the putative collective qualities and qualifications both of the German people and its late medieval rivals. And they reinforced the focus, which already lay at the heart of German constitutional doctrines, on the princes as the Empire's main repositories and custodians.

But these papal *loci classici* also carried more troubling implications, encased as they were within doctrines emphasising the unlimited power of Christ's vicar to provide as he saw fit for the well-being of his people. What the pope had given, the pope might take away. And the papal account of the Empire's passage to the Germans was destined to become, for all its importance, just one narrative among several. This was inevitably so, not least because the Innocentian version raised as many questions as it answered. When had the general transfer of the Empire to the German princes, of which *Venerabilem* spoke, taken on concrete constitutional shape in the form of the electoral college? Did this occur already under Charles, or only at some later time? Indeed, not everyone was ready to be assured that imperial rule had itself come to the Germans 'in the person of the magnificent Charles', about whose own ethnic identity there were fundamental doubts.[127] In the eyes of some, moreover, the *translatio imperii* of the canonists, with its stress upon the pope's historic centrality to that event and on the firm papal control under which the German princes were accordingly to act in nominating a ruler, seemed dangerously to serve the ends of papal hierocracy. The papal version provided, in any case, at best a basic framework of key themes and events. Much narrative and explanatory work remained to be done.

Matters were complicated by the wide circulation and great influence in Germany of another, more detailed (though still far from complete), account of the Empire's transfer and of what had followed. Like

---

[125] See thus the canonical authorities heaped up by Heinrich von Herford to explain the origins of the *dominium mundi* of the *Theutonici*: *Liber de rebus memorabilioribus*, ed. Potthast, p. 39.

[126] Thus, in 1256, Italian supporters of Alfonso X denied the validity of election by the German princes, insisting on the right of the whole Roman people to participate in elections if they chose. For this and comparable examples, see Wilks, *Sovereignty*, pp. 188–9.

[127] For these, see below, Ch. 7, pp. 333–6.

the papal-canonical tradition, it too was of non-German origin.[128] The Dominican Martin of Troppau is known to have lived for over twenty years in Rome, where he held office as a chaplain and penitentiary at the Curia.[129] It was there, between 1268 and 1277, that he compiled and reworked his chronicle of popes and emperors, destined to become the most widely used historiographical handbook of the late Middle Ages. Martin's main purpose was to provide a chronological reference work for scholars, particularly jurists and theologians: at once a compendium of post-biblical history to supplement Peter Comestor's *Historia scholastica* and a handy companion-volume to Gratian's *Decretum*.[130] The Roman Empire's passage to the Germans in itself concerned him little, and found no mention in the brief, conventional account of the four historical 'world empires' (*regna maiora*) – Babylon, Carthage, Macedon, Rome – with which he prefaced the third, final recension of his chronicle.[131] Elsewhere, however, Martin, did deal both with the transfer of imperial power (from the Greeks) to northern Europe and with the establishment of the electoral college – which he treated as two quite distinct, almost unconnected events. Under Charles the Great, as *rex Francorum*, the Empire came to the Franks, whom Martin equated with the French (*Francigene*).[132] In the later Carolingian period, it was divided, with separate rulers in Italy, and only reassembled under Otto I, 'the first emperor of the Teutons' (*imperator Theutonicorum*). 'The Empire having been taken away from the Italians', he went on, 'only Teutons have ruled down to the present time.'[133] Down to Otto III, the imperial title descended by hereditary succession, but with his death 'it was instituted' – by whom, Martin does not say – 'that the emperor be elected by the office holders of the Empire': the three Rhenish archbishops, and the four temporal electors, occupants of the main honorific court offices.[134]

---

[128] It has been proposed that Martin may have hailed from the German-speaking element in Bohemia, and that this might explain his adoption of an imperial frame of reference: Moraw, 'Das Mittelalter', p. 109. This cannot be established, however, and the most visible influence upon Martin's outlook is Roman, not northern.

[129] See above, Ch. 3, pp. 146–7.

[130] For his objectives, see Brincken, 'Martin von Troppau', in *VL* 6, cols. 162, 165.

[131] *Martini Oppaviensis Chronicon*, ed. Weiland, p. 398; and see the comments of Mierau, 'Die Einheit', esp. pp. 300–1.

[132] *Martini Oppaviensis Chronicon*, ed. Weiland, p. 461. Elsewhere, Martin sought, inspired by *Venerabilem*, to trace the Empire's passage, under Pippin, to the Germans: ibid., p. 426.

[133] Ibid., p. 465.

[134] Ibid., p. 466. For Martin's account of the origins of the electors, see generally Buchner, 'Die Entstehung', pp. 68–9. The role of the electors' ceremonial functions (*Erzämter*) in the emergence of the electoral college has been controversial and remains much discussed: Ertl, 'Alte Thesen', esp. pp. 624–5, for the historiography.

For Martin, both Charles and Otto I were solicitous champions of Roman (and not merely papal) interests, and it was at the will of the Roman clergy and people, as well as the pope's, that they gained their imperial titles. His viewpoint was a southern, more specifically Roman, one and the precise character of the shifting constitutional arrangements in the north, to which Martin alludes, is not made clear. It was left to Germans to supply what was lacking. In doing so, they had to grapple with a narrative of the Empire's transfer which was hard to reconcile with the papal-canonist picture. Little wonder, then, that there arose such a luxuriant variety of competing explanations. Different commentators, moreover, felt themselves bound in varying degrees by Martin and the papalists, now following them closely, now extending or twisting their accounts to suit their needs. Some felt free to contradict or simply ignore these pervasive authorities.

The two main questions on which German writers sought clarity concerned the role of Charles the Great in the Empire's transfer to the Germans and the relationship of that event to the powers of the prince-electors. Nowhere were these matters more tersely dealt with than in the *Schwabenspiegel*: 'the Germans elect the king; King Charles gained this for them'.[135] As early as the 1230s the south-German poet Stricker had portrayed Charles bestowing on the German aristocracy as a whole the right to choose the Empire's ruler.[136] But it was only with the *Book of Kings of the New Law*, probably composed in the 1270s, that the Frankish emperor was made the inaugurator specifically of the college of electors.[137] A document from Ludwig IV's reign enumerating the Empire's rights insisted that the electors could trace their powers back to the time when the governance of Christendom (*regnum Romane ecclesie*) was first granted to the Germans – though without specifying when that time was.[138] The (probably contemporary) *Lohengrin* poet, who rated highly the powers of the electors, whom he deemed capable of bestowing the title of emperor itself, was explicit in making Charles their originator.[139]

For others, accounting for the German constitutional landscape of the time meant tracing more protracted and complex processes of *translatio*. For Heinrich von Herford, it was first the kingdom of the Franks that was transferred to the 'Germans', under Pippin, followed by the

---

[135] *Schwabenspiegel*, ed. Eckhardt, *Landrecht*, cap. 120/124, p. 182.
[136] Folz, *Le Souvenir*, pp. 368–9.
[137] *Der kunige buoch*, ed. Massmann, p. clxxix.
[138] *Nova Alamanniae*, vol. I, no. 583, p. 391 (after 16 July 1338).
[139] *Lohengrin*, ed. Cramer, p. 287, v. 1977: 'Mit den siben vürsten Karl daz rîche kunde stiften.'

Empire under his son Charles.[140] Konrad von Megenberg, for whom the papacy was the author of the Empire's translation, proposed a graduated, three-stage passage to the Germans (represented, again, by the early Carolingians) under three popes, Stephen II, Hadrian I and Leo III: it would not, on account of 'the people's inexperience' (*inexperiencia gentis*), have been proper for it to come to them in a single act.[141] Alexander von Roes, as we have seen already, felt able to grant only the four Rhineland electors an origin under the Frankish emperor; the others were added later, as historical change and their own proven merits came to justify their accession. Nevertheless, for Alexander it was in Charles' person that the Empire had come to the Germans.

Others reached a different view, and followed Martin of Troppau in discerning only in the tenth century the origins of the Germans' hold on the Reich. Precisely *when* in the tenth century itself drew divergent judgements. For the composer of the *Braunschweig Rhyming Chronicle*, the Carolingians were a French dynasty; only with the accession of the first Saxon king, Henry I (919–36), did imperial rule pass to the Germans.[142] The *Saxon World Chronicle* identified his predecessor Konrad I's reign as the turning point.[143] In Strasbourg, Fritsche Closener found his hands tied by close adherence to Martin's account, with its insistence that neither Henry nor Konrad had exercised fully imperial power, since neither had ruled in Italy, nor been crowned by the pope.[144] Only under Otto I did the age of German emperorship dawn. Yet Closener, while acknowledging these constraints, fought against them: *daz rich*, which had already come to the Germans 'in part' under the Carolingian Ludwig the Child, passed to them 'fully' under Konrad and Henry – even as he conceded that neither ruler was accounted a true emperor.[145]

Not all of those who argued for the Empire's transfer to the Germans in the person of Charles also believed that the Frankish emperor had given the princes their constitutional powers. Martin of Troppau's

---

[140] *Liber de rebus memorabilioribus*, ed. Potthast, p. 19.

[141] Konrad von Megenberg, *De translacione Romani imperii*, cap. 4, ed. Scholz, pp. 258–9.

[142] *Braunschweigische Reimchronik*, ed. Weiland, p. 470, vv. 903–10. Around a century later, the Mecklenburg chronicler Ernst von Kirchberg likewise told how Charlemagne had brought the Empire to 'France'. *Mecklenburgische Reimchronik*, ed. Cordshagen and Schmidt, p. 12, vv. 167–8: 'sus brachte Karl daz keysirrich / von Krichin hyn geyn Frangrich.'

[143] *Sächsische Weltchronik*, ed. Weiland, p. 157.

[144] *Martini Oppaviensis Chronicon: Imperatores*, ed. Weiland, p. 464.

[145] *Fritsche (Friedrich) Closener's Chronik*, ed. Hegel, pp. 34–5: '...Cuonrat und Heinrich, die zalt man nüt für rehte keiser, wande sü von dem bobest nüt gekronet wordent'.

account of the late tenth-century origins of the electoral college proved highly influential, and a number of writers who dismissed or ignored his ascription of a French identity to the Carolingians found his picture of developments under the later Ottonians more compelling. No one insisted more vehemently than Lupold von Bebenburg upon Charlemagne's Germanness, or argued more firmly that the Empire's passage to the (Carolingian) Franks marked also its translation to the Germans.[146] But for Lupold, who cited Martin's authority specifically on the point, the electors were only instituted upon the death, without heirs, of Otto III.[147] A late origin for the electoral college was likewise proposed by other vigorous proponents of a *translatio* to the Germans under Charles, such as Konrad von Megenberg (who followed Martin more slavishly in this than had his exemplar, Lupold), Heinrich von Herford and Jakob Twinger.[148] Predictable confusion reigned as to precisely when and by whose acts the new institution came into being. Lupold implied that Otto himself was responsible, and this view was developed more explicitly by Twinger. The emperor, he explained, took timely action to forestall the conflicts which would otherwise have followed his death, since all the nobles of the Reich would have wanted a say in the choice of ruler – 'just as' (and here the townsman's voice is heard) 'the populace of a free city might itself elect a leader, and sometimes wars and quarrels arise therefrom'.[149] For Heinrich von Herford, meanwhile, the electors were only instituted after Otto's death, at the urging of Archbishop Heribert of Cologne.[150] Dietrich von Niem made Henry II (1002–24) their originator.[151]

The guiding authorities available on the matter of the Empire's translation did not, therefore, make things easy for literate Germans in the post-Staufer epoch, who found themselves forced to think hard, sometimes to argue, to accommodate themselves to complexity, and to make uncomfortable choices between contradictory narratives. That a number still judged the effort worthwhile speaks for the subject's contemporary importance. How and why the *imperium* had come to the Germans were questions which they felt mattered. This is attested by the disagreements into which the subject plunged German commentators at all

---

[146] See below, Ch. 7, pp. 335–6.
[147] Lupold von Bebenburg, *Tractatus*, cap. 2, ed. Miethke and Flüeler, pp. 258–9.
[148] Twinger was explicit about the distinction: 'It has thus been shown why and how the Empire came from the Greeks to the Germans. But the Empire's election came over two hundred years later to the seven electors.' *Chronik des Jacob Twingers*, ed. Hegel, p. 404.
[149] *Chronik des Jacob Twinger*, ed. Hegel, pp. 424–5.
[150] *Liber de rebus memorabilioribus*, ed. Potthast, p. 94.
[151] Thus his treatise *On the Schism*: Heimpel, *Dietrich*, p. 66.

points – reflecting in part their own varied perspectives and motivations in writing. Few others, for example, would have endorsed without quibble Konrad von Megenberg's claim that the whole process reflected the unalloyed authority and directive power of the papacy.[152] The contours of the translation legend remained indeterminate enough to allow its manipulation to reflect different writers' conscious convictions, just as it tended to shape itself to their regional and social perspectives.

Prominent in most versions of the translation legend is the role of the German aristocracy, particularly the princes, as the main bearers of an imperial mandate understood as divinely sanctioned violence. The Empire, noted the *Saxon World Chronicle*, after coming first to the Carolingians, had passed to 'the German nobles'. The chronicler took care to emphasise both their military attainments and their identity as Germans. Henry I's great victory over the Hungarians led to Henry being 'hailed as emperor and *augustus* and the land's father by the princes and by all the German lords'.[153] The reference to their ethnicity was the chronicler's own: his exemplar, the eleventh-century universal chronicle of Ekkehard, told only of Henry's elevation by 'the army'.[154] The Empire's commission to the Germans, in late medieval imagination, was essentially a military commission, to a band of warrior-protectors and servants, from among whose ranks was to be chosen a leader with the self-same warlike duties and qualities. The *Sachsenspiegel* glossator Johannes von Buch recounted how under Charles the Great the monarch's election, which had previously lain with 'the senators in Rome', was transferred to 'the army' (*de herlude*).[155] The change was motivated by military practicality, allowing *dat volk* – the 'people' in arms, the warrior stratum – to provide for the ruler's replacement, should he die on campaign 'in foreign lands'. In this way the Empire came to the Germans (*de Dudeschen*). In loyal service under arms – to the Roman Church, just as it was claimed they had once served Roman Caesars – lay the justification for *translatio imperii in Germanos*.[156] The idea is recurrent in German writings. The German Franks, reflected Lupold von Bebenburg, might be 'not inappropriately commended for their invariable constancy and fealty' to the Empire's rulers down the centuries.[157] Lupold devoted an entire treatise to delineating the 'zeal' of the

---

[152] For Konrad's pro-papal view and its background, see Scholz, *Streitschriften*, pt 1, pp. 103–4.
[153] *Sächsische Weltchronik*, ed. Weiland, p. 160.
[154] *Ekkehardi chronicon universale*, ed. Waitz, p. 183.
[155] *Glossen zum Sachsenspiegel-Landrecht*, ed. Kaufmann, p. 1251 (to *Landrecht* III 52 § 1).
[156] See below, Ch. 7, pp. 339–41.
[157] Lupold von Bebenburg, *Tractatus*, Capitulatio, ed. Miethke and Flüeler, p. 236.

German princes, throughout history, for Christendom's defence.[158] The Germans, Alexander von Roes declared simply, were Christendom's *militia*.[159] Thus did the Empire pertain to them – or they, through their military endeavours, to it.

Election and identity

The German princes therefore stood at the centre of conceptions of the Reich as a political community, and constitutional change in the thirteenth century served to reinforce that centrality. The prince-electors were incorporated with remarkable speed into the fabric of German political culture. The earliest depictions of them in public art are to be found already in the second half of the thirteenth century, and these became numerous in the German lands, particularly in the imperial towns, in the decades which followed.[160] It would be wrong, however, to suppose that the fall of the Staufer and the rise of the electors spelt the end of the dynastic idea in the public life of the Reich. Quite apart from the ambitions, real and suspected, of princely families themselves to gain a lasting grip on the crown, we can discern in German writings a more pervasive interest in the dynastic element in imperial affairs, and a keen alertness to familial bonds.[161] Heinrich von Diessenhofen noted in passing that Gerlach von Nassau, provided to the see of Mainz in 1346, was the grandson of King Adolf, who had died half a century before.[162] Blood continued to seem historically significant. More than one chronicler observed that the contestants to the throne who met in battle at Mühldorf in 1322 were both grandsons of Rudolf I.[163] Hugo von Reutlingen imagined that only with the death of Konrad IV (1254) was a principle of dynastic succession broken which had pertained since the time of Charlemagne. Albert of Habsburg had become King Adolf's enemy because the electors had not chosen him as successor to his father, Rudolf I, 'as had been the custom up till then'.[164] Significant as was the historical breach represented by the end of the Staufer, moreover, there are signs of the emergence in the fourteenth century of a new

---

[158] Lupold von Bebenburg, *Libellus de Zelo*, ed. Miethke and Flüeler.
[159] Alexander von Roes, *Noticia seculi*, cap. 14, ed. Grundmann and Heimpel, p. 160.
[160] Hoffmann, *Die bildlichen Darstellungen*, Ch. 3; Saurma-Jeltsch, 'Das mittelalterliche Reich', pp. 411–18.
[161] For the controversies around the idea of a hereditary crown, see above, Ch. 4, pp. 165–71.
[162] *Heinricus Dapifer de Diessenhoven*, ed. Huber, p. 49.
[163] *Chronica de gestis principum*, ed. Leidinger, p. 41; *Die Chronik des Mathias von Neuenburg*, ed. Hofmeister, p. 121.
[164] *Excerpta ex Expositione Hugonis de Rutlingen*, ed. Huber, pp. 130–1.

imperial-dynastic datum, represented by the reign of the first Habsburg king.[165] Not only were both Ludwig IV and Frederick the Fair King Rudolf's descendants: Heinrich von Diessenhofen tells of the magnificent reception accorded to Charles IV when he came to Strasbourg, 'in the manner of the ancient kings and emperors from whose blood he was descended'.[166] As well as being the grandson of an emperor and the son of a (Bohemian) king, through his mother and his maternal grandmother, Charles too could trace his line back to the first Habsburg on the throne.[167] To be able to boast royal and imperial ancestors remained a powerful argument for the crown, and one which received regular reiteration as succession stabilised within the Habsburg–Luxemburg–Wittelsbach triad during the fourteenth century.[168]

As to why the imperial crown did not descend within a single family, as did other European crowns, German writers offered two explanations. One was historical, and rested on the authority of Martin of Troppau. Under the Ottos in the tenth century, emperorship was conveyed *in erbendes wise*; but with Otto III's death without heirs, another solution had had to be found, hence the institution of the college of electors.[169] The other view, by no means incompatible with this, concentrated on idoneity: given the Empire's nature, it was not appropriate that it should pass from father to son. The establishment of an elective monarchy after Otto III took place, explained Dietrich von Niem, for 'the welfare of the Church of God and the Christian people'.[170] Heinrich von Herford concurred that principle, not mere pragmatism, had determined the founding of the college of electors.[171] For Alexander von Roes, it was Charlemagne himself who had determined that the *regnum ecclesie*, as the 'sanctuary of God', was not to be possessed *iure hereditario* – though he was happy to accord his heirs a portion of the realm to hold in this way, thus instituting the kingdom of France.[172]

Elective monarchy, on this view, was superior to mere dynastic kingship. Why it seemed to be so has a number of explanations. The rule

---

[165] For the contemporary historical significance of the end of the Staufer, see below, Ch. 7, pp. 344–6.

[166] *Heinricus Dapifer de Diessenhoven*, ed. Huber, p. 62.

[167] For the same connection (and Charles's wider royal affiliations), see *Die Chronik des Mathias von Neuenburg*, ed. Hofmeister, p. 237.

[168] Thus see *MGC* 4.i, no. 8, p. 7 (28 July 1298), in which the electors justify their choice of Albert of Habsburg as being *de regali prosapia procreatus*.

[169] Thus: *Fritsche (Friedrich) Closener's Chronik*, ed. Hegel, p. 35; *Chronik des Jacob Twingers*, ed. Hegel, pp. 424–5; and see *Martini Oppaviensis Chronicon: Imperatores*, ed. Weiland, p. 466. Martin offered no explanation for the change.

[170] Dietrich von Nieheim, *Viridarium*, ed. Lhotsky and Pivec, p. 18.

[171] *Liber de rebus memorabilioribus*, ed. Potthast, p. 94.

[172] Alexander von Roes, *Memoriale*, cap. 24, ed. Grundmann and Heimpel, pp. 124–5.

of ancient Rome, republic and principate, was thought to have had an electoral basis comparable to the late medieval Reich: Augustus was 'elected' *keiser*.[173] For chroniclers and pamphleteers of mainly clerical background, the fact that canon law was on the side of election represented a powerful affirmation: Heinrich von Herford was among those to appeal to the authority of *Venerabilem* on the matter.[174] To legal ruling was added imperialist political theology, with the insistence that the temporal head of Christendom, like any prelate, must have his suitability tested in an *electio canonica* (in the revealing formulation of Alexander von Roes).[175] The more historically versed could appeal to past instances to show how the infiltration of the hereditary principle inevitably brought corruption. The historical *cause célèbre*, cited by Alexander von Roes, was that of the Merovingians. Yet Charles's own descendants, Alexander went on to insist, had failed in their duty to the Church once they began to think that they ruled by dynastic right.[176] The Staufer too had shown the worst consequences of imperial power being monopolised by a mere familial (and thus, importantly, regional) faction.[177]

Principled defences of a blood descent for the imperial crown are seldom to be met with in German sources. There was naturally no shortage of literate champions of individual dynasties; and there were those, too, such as the Habsburg partisan Johann von Viktring, whose accounts of imperial affairs had little, and certainly little positive, to say about the electors.[178] Dynasties remained important in understanding the changing (and enduring) patterns of politics and rulership in the Reich. What was generally resisted, however, was making dynasty conceptually coterminous with the imperial monarchy itself. The basis of this aversion is revealed by some of the contemporary and historical criticisms which German writers made of imperial dynasticism. These indicate the nature of the fears which the prospect of hereditary rule excited in some quarters, and they also help to explain why imperial

---

[173] *Sächsische Weltchronik*, ed. Weiland, p. 82; and for the 'election' of Augustus, *Der kunige buoch*, ed. Massmann, p. cxxiv.

[174] *Liber de rebus memorabilioribus*, ed. Potthast, p. 94.

[175] Alexander von Roes, *Memoriale*, caps. 24, 27, ed. Grundmann and Heimpel, pp. 124, 129. The principle of canonical idoneity was also emphasised by Konrad von Megenberg: Scholz, *Streitschriften*, pt 1, pp. 105–7.

[176] Alexander von Roes, *Memoriale*, ed. Grundmann and Heimpel, pp. 116, 129.

[177] Ibid., cap. 29, pp. 133–4; and see below, Ch. 7, p. 348.

[178] Moraw, 'Politische Sprache', esp. p. 716. A rare German argument for the *inherent* superiority of hereditary over elective rule (specifically, as a guarantor of peace) is found in the vernacular *Chess Book* of the monk Konrad von Ammenhausen (1337), see Werminghoff, 'Zur Lehre', esp. 155.

political culture after the Staufer gave such weight to the princes – and their German identity.

Within a composite – indeed, multi-ethnic – political sphere, such as the northern territories of the Reich, dynastic ambition quickly came to look like partiality, a partiality potentially highly subversive of good order. Dietrich von Niem objected to the uniting under Charles IV of the Bohemian and Brandenburg votes in Luxemburg hands, as under-mining the elective principle for mere familial ends.[179] Some perceived a clear polarity of interests at work. According to Jakob Twinger, Charles 'was very covetous of property, land and men, and whatever property came his way he bestowed upon the kingdom of Bohemia and not on the Reich'.[180] Past examples reveal contemporary mentalities still more fully. The *Saxon World Chronicle* recounts how the emperor Henry VI had asked the princes to agree that the Empire should descend by hered-ity, as other kingdoms do. The princes assented, but the Saxons judged it shameful and instituted a great legal process, forcing the emperor to back down.[181] No provision for the Empire's rule which perman-ently denied a voice to some or any of the historical-ethnic communi-ties under the monarch (as heredity inevitably did) could be permitted to stand. Ultimately, dynastic succession might lead to the loss of the Empire altogether, as had occurred at the end of the Carolingian period, when the title passed for a time to Italian rulers. The German princes, constitutionally embodied in the electors, were by contrast a composite community, representing – in imagination, though very imperfectly in reality – the historically composite character of the Empire's northern (but only its northern) lands.[182] If the idea of their 'German' identity was a somewhat opaque construct, it was a constitutionally useful one, expressive of an ideal unity transcending the formidable force fields of region and family, and thus constituting a viable imagined basis for a political community – viable, precisely on account of its opaqueness.

The Empire had a good deal to do with German nationhood in late medieval estimations: altogether too much, in fact, for some critical observers. The Germans enjoyed a special distinction as a people, in the recognition which canon law accorded them as collective bearers of the *imperium*, and beneficiaries of its translation. The elective character of the crown focused attention not only, or not even always mainly, upon the monarch but also on the political community which raised him up.

---

[179] Dietrich von Nieheim, *Viridarium*, ed. Lhotsky and Pivec, p. 19.
[180] *Chronik des Jacob Twingers*, ed. Hegel, p. 491.
[181] *Sächsische Weltchronik*, ed. Weiland, p. 235.
[182] An idea most cogently expressed by Alexander von Roes, above, pp. 277–8.

That community was imagined – even in the face of evidence to the contrary – as an ethnic unity. The German military aristocracy, with whom the Empire had come to rest, was not subjected to a Romanising political vocabulary to the same degree as were the rulers they created, but remained explicitly grounded in the soil of the north. That is not to suggest that the character and composition of the German elite, or the origin and extent of its titles and specific powers, were clear or agreed. On the contrary, these matters were the subject of diverse and contending judgements, reflecting the confusions and contradictions of the sources and the varying perspectives of different commentators. The fact that key elements in the doctrine of the Empire's passage to the Germans were the coinage of outsiders complicated further its adoption by German writers. But, as modern studies of national discourse have argued, contention, rather than bland consensus, is the hallmark of a developed ethno-political identity.[183]

The crises and conflicts in which the imperial monarchy was embroiled in the thirteenth and fourteenth centuries resulted in greater emphasis being placed upon its German elements. The consolidation of the college of electors focused attention upon those northern princes with whom the choice of ruler primarily lay and on the German political milieu within which they subsisted. The doctrine of *translatio imperii*, whose underlying assumptions were ethnic (reflecting the ancient notion of a succession of hegemonic peoples), became the subject of urgent and extensive discussion, in a political climate which seemed to invite speculation about the Empire's custodianship and about its future more broadly. Just as some sought the root of the recurrent quarrels between emperors and popes in the German identity of the Empire's bearers, others were led to argue for the conservation of the status quo, through a positive view of the entitlements of those same German custodians. The relations of the universal powers of Christendom were read through an increasingly ethnocentric lens, as the papacy too came to appear, in German estimations, a channel for national interests, particularly those of the French.

What, though, of the *German* nation? Its character (explicitly for a handful of literate champions, more vaguely for larger groups) as an imagined basis for the post-Staufer Reich, two centuries before that

---

[183] Thus Breuilly, 'Changes', p. 83: 'If national values mattered politically I would expect *contention* over them. In the modern period, as soon as the language of nationality becomes politically important it is contested. Consensus suggests unimportance.' While the discourse of nation in late medieval Germany was much less intensive than those modern instances on which Breuilly concentrates, it was certainly not consensual.

principle received its celebrated formulation as a constitutional title, is clear. Yet expressed, as it was, for example, in *Venerabilem*, merely as the bearer of the Roman Empire's east–west translation, the idea of a community of German political actors appears a pale and amorphous thing: little more than a name, a constitutional fiction – albeit one evidently capable of exciting strong views in some quarters. To establish whether it was anything more will mean examining some of its elements in greater detail. This is the concern of the chapters which follow.

7 Trojans, giants and other Germans: peoplehoods forgotten, remembered and relocated

Wild men

A tapestry woven at some time around 1400 shows wild men in a battle scene. Immense, blond- and red-haired, they are assailing a castle defended by black-skinned Moors.[1] The tapestry was probably made to seal the union through marriage of two rich Strasbourg kindreds. At first sight, the image is unremarkable enough: wild folk had a well-established place in the chivalric imagination of late medieval aristocrats and their imitators in the towns.[2] Yet the theme of holy war suggests a weightier message than polite, upper-class amusements; and the depiction of the outsized holy warriors is also eye-catching. Are they, perhaps, specifically *German* wild men? German writers of the time never tired, after all, of calling for their people to take the front rank in war against the infidel, and they cited in justification not only the Germans' zeal for the Faith but their boundless physical vigour.[3] Even a French agitator for the crusade felt compelled to concede, in this spirit, the Germans' potential value in holy war, as *robusti*.[4]

At the century's close, a new generation of patriotic Germans was to discover in the wild man an embodiment of the pure and noble spirit of an ancient, sylvan Germany. He would become in their hands the standard-bearer for a self-consciously Germanic counter-Renaissance, pitting the wholesome primitivism of the northern forests against the urban ways of a soft and over-civilised south.[5] By that time, literate Germans had the *Germania* of Tacitus to cheer their spirits and affirm their moral judgements. Yet the humanists were not the first Germans to imagine a people of outsized archaic supermen as their

---

[1] Husband, *The Wild Man*, pp. 24–5 (illustration), 77–81 (commentary).
[2] See generally Bernheimer, *Wild Men*, Ch. 5.
[3] For their physical stature, see, e.g., Konrad von Megenberg, *Ökonomik*, lib. 2.iv, cap. 3, ed. Krüger, vol. II, pp. 200–1; and for their energy in war, below, Ch. 8, pp. 363–72.
[4] Kämpf, *Pierre Dubois*, p. 84.
[5] See: Silver, 'Forest primeval', esp. p. 27; and, for German soldiers as wild men, Hale, *Artists*, pp. 53, 67.

earliest forebears. As early as the twelfth century, the vestiges of such an idea seem to lurk behind the words of a chronicler from Alsace, who proposed an etymological link between Teutonic speech and the Celtic deity Theutates.[6] The pagan gods of northern Europe, like their counterparts in the ancient Mediterranean, might be conceived of as giants. Just such an equation appears to underlie the claim of Thomas of Cantimpré, in his *Liber de natura rerum* (*c.* 1225/6–41), that Germany (*Theutonia*) had its name from a giant called Theutanus.[7] For Thomas, Theutanus had some imaginative substance and popular repute. It was reported that his grave and physical remains could still be viewed, in a village beside the Danube some two miles from Vienna. The giant's skull, it was said, was more than two sword lengths across. Appealing to the authority of Lucan, Thomas insisted that there were once many giants in Germany. Around 1270, his report of Theutanus was repeated in the Middle Netherlandish vernacular by Jakob van Maerlant, and some years after that, in summary form, by a Dominican from Colmar in Alsace.[8] The ancient giant's remains, observed the Alsatian friar, were actually displayed to travellers.

Around the same time, Alexander von Roes was planting an aboriginal founder-giant more solidly in the first German soil. A band of Trojan refugees under King Priam's nephew had settled in the lands west of the Rhine and driven out the native Gauls.[9] Quite different, however, were their dealings with the indigenous Teutonic women whom they encountered. These they had married, since they were 'big, and fit for the begetting of very powerful offspring', being descended 'from the giant Theutona, from whom the Teutons [*Theutonici*] are named'. From the union of Trojans and giant Teutons sprang the earliest Germans. It was a tale to inspire the patriotic fancy of a later generation of Germans, into whose hands Alexander's account eventually passed. For Johannes Rothe in the fifteenth century, it was obviously the coupling of Priam's warriors with the giant-women that begot 'the mighty Siegfried, Hagen and Kriemhild, of whom men still sing'.[10] Immense and unbounded, the progeny of Theutona were the first root of a famous race of German heroes. Christendom, as the Strasbourg tapestry appears to insist, could wish for no stouter defence.

[6] *Chronicon Ebersheimense*, quoted in Kästner, ' "Theuton" ', p. 81.
[7] Ibid.
[8] For Jakob van Maerlant, see ibid., p. 82 with n. 58; for the Colmar Dominican, *Descriptio Theutoniae*, ed. Jaffé, p. 238 (where the giant is named as *Theuto*).
[9] Alexander von Roes, *Memoriale*, cap. 16, ed. Grundmann and Heimpel, pp. 108–9.
[10] Quoted in Kästner, ' "Theuton" ', p. 93. For Rothe, see S. Tebruck, 'Rothe, Johannes', in *NDB* 22, pp. 118–19.

Amnesia

Highly coloured they may have been; but the threads for a German collective myth were neither many nor durable. Alexander's 'Germans', with their Trojan blood, were really just Frankish Rhinelanders writ large; and such an obviously regional perspective was hardly suited to sustaining a unifying myth for the many distinct communities of tradition and memory in the German lands. Its dissemination was therefore slow and limited; and yet, as a vision of the earliest 'German' past, Alexander's tale had no real rival before the humanists took the matter up in the late fifteenth century. Moreover, as will become clear elsewhere, staking a claim to shared roots in a race of primeval giants – creatures with a deeply troubled reputation in medieval tradition – was a potentially risky venture.[11] Of an all-embracing German origin legend there were few traces in the late Middle Ages; and those that there were posed as many questions as they answered.

A great oblivion seemed to cover the German past at the close of the Middle Ages. Supplying durable histories to dispel it was a prime objective of the humanists, who never tired of pointing out the evils that had come from their forebears' forgetfulness of their glorious common heritage.[12] That forgetfulness seemed to explain Germany's contemporary weakness, since the great deeds of old had no recollection, and could no longer inspire emulation, while only the calumnies heaped on the Germans by neighbours and rivals were heard.[13] In fact, the humanists' own writings partially refute such a bleak vision, drawing as they do upon the works of late medieval writers such as Lupold von Bebenburg and Alexander von Roes.[14] Yet if many of their favoured themes – the stirring deeds of emperors past, and the peculiarly German virtues which had nourished them – were old-established ones, the humanists

[11] Below, Ch. 8, esp. pp. 359–60.
[12] Heinrich Bebel thus informed Maximilian I in 1501 that Germany 'does not lack for a past of glorious deeds. We miss only the historians who should have recorded those deeds': Strauss (ed. and trans.), *Manifestations*, p. 69; and see also: Silver, 'Germanic patriotism', esp. pp. 38–41; Strauss, 'German history', pp. 667–8. The theme is already encountered among pre-humanist German historiographers in the fifteenth century: see Sieber-Lehmann, *Nationalismus*, pp. 195–6. For some German humanists, moreover, this absence of early German histories was the result of their deliberate suppression by the Germans' Italian rivals. 'Let them give back to us the entire *History* of Tacitus which they have hidden away', thundered the Saxon chronicler Albert Krantz. 'Let them return Pliny's 20 books on Germany!' Strauss, *Sixteenth-Century Germany*, pp. 8–9.
[13] See Konrad Celtis's 1492 'Ingolstadt address', in *Selections from Conrad Celtis*, ed. and trans. Forster, pp. 36–65.
[14] See: Borchardt, *German Antiquity*, Ch. 5; Münkler and Grünberger, 'Enea Silvio', pp. 180–3 (for Lupold).

did bring a new urgency and rigour to their exposition. They also drew upon an unprecedented abundance of both ancient and rediscovered medieval sources and, following their Italian exemplars, supplied a vision of history itself as a noble, distinct and necessary undertaking.[15] The humanists largely created 'national' history as a genre.[16] It is therefore understandable that the attainments of earlier writers in the field should have seemed to them so inadequate.

The oblivion to a common German past with which Renaissance historians charged their medieval forebears has been a prominent theme for more recent scholars, too. In the second half of the twentieth century many medievalists came, like the humanists, to regard a shared past as the fundamental source and touchstone of nationhood.[17] They too were impressed by the weakness of this element in medieval Germany.[18] Unlike the humanists, however, modern scholars have taken the view that there simply was no common, 'German' past to be attained in the Middle Ages. The explanation for this lay in the character of German society itself, and in the historical development of its institutions. History in the German lands was irredeemably polarised. On the one hand was an *imperium* which far transcended them, and was in principle limitless: a monarchy which drew its unparalleled prestige from no German but a Roman past.[19] On the other stood the very many imagined histories of different towns, regions and dynastic territories – the last consolidating their existence, and their narratives of separate, legitimising pasts, even as the powers of the post-Staufer *imperium Romanum* waned.[20] Behind a contemporary world of political multiplicity, moreover, still loomed the shades of a more remote, formative ethnic multiplicity: of Franks, Saxons, Bavarians and Swabians, whose common and distinct pasts continued to be invoked and interpreted.[21] Under such circumstances,

---

[15] For German humanists' sources, see: Borchardt, *German Antiquity*, Chs. 4, 5; Stadtwald, *Roman Popes*, pp. 75–6.

[16] Mertens, 'Mittelalterbilder', pp. 35–6; Helmrath, 'Probleme', pp. 341–2: 'das "deutsche Mittelalter" ist eine patriotische Entdeckung der Humanisten!'

[17] As Rees Davies observed, 'A people without a history was a contradiction in terms': Davies, 'Language', p. 20. Sense of common past is placed first among the 'elements of medieval national consciousness' identified by Ehlers, 'Natio. 1. N. (Nation)', in *LMA* 6, col. 1036; and see also: Ehlers, 'Die deutsche Nation', p. 23, and 'Elemente', p. 570; Guenée, *States*, pp. 58–9; and, for a broader perspective, Smith, *Ethnic Origins*, p. 2.

[18] 'Deutschland ... bekam im Mittelalter keine Darstellung seiner Volksgeschichte, als fehlte ihm der Blick auf eine gemeinsame Vergangenheit.' Grundmann, *Geschichtsschreibung*, p. 17.

[19] Ibid., p. 17. The absorption of German into Roman history is also argued by Moeglin, 'Die historische Konstruktion', pp. 371–2.

[20] Ehlers, 'Die deutsche Nation', p. 26.

[21] Ibid., p. 29. For region and identity, see below, Ch. 11, pp. 504–24.

there was – *could* be – no discrete 'German' history: only something more, or less, something more ancient, or more tangible.

Absent from the literature of medieval Germany, therefore, was any inclusive myth of shared origins to compare with those which had been set down in favour of other European peoples, first during the early Middle Ages and then with renewed vigour in the twelfth and thirteenth centuries.[22] Absent was a mythical founder-figure in the style of Brutus of Albion, Hengist and Horsa, Francio or old father Čech, or an archaic nation-maker to compare with Clovis in France, the Bohemian seeress Libussa, Piast the wheelwright or Arthur of the Britons.[23] Charlemagne's historical place for German writers, while significant, was variable and disputed – particularly when compared with his established home in the 'fair France' of chivalric epic. The *translatio imperii in Germanos*, with which some accounts linked Charles's name, had the two-dimensionality of a constitutional act – historically important, without doubt, and sharply contested, as we have seen; but on its own scarcely the stuff of richly mythic history. In this respect, it hardly bears comparison with the myths of divine election, exalting Chosen People and blessed homeland, to be found elsewhere in Europe.[24]

Above all, the Germans of the late Middle Ages seem to lack that most potent of mythic wellsprings of identity, a common *sacred* past.[25] There is little sign that the Germans were identified as a special people of God, or made the beneficiaries of that potent Old Testament narrative of common election which was projected onto some other medieval European peoples.[26] The sacred protagonists of early Christian history – figures such as St George or St Andrew, or the Virgin Mary or Christ himself – were rarely claimed as their partisans and patrons, as they conspicuously were by others.[27] Germans looked back upon no dark-age royal saint as community-builder, on the pattern of St Wenceslas,

---

[22] On medieval origin legends, see generally: Reynolds, 'Medieval *origines gentium*'; Kersken, *Geschichtsschreibung*, pp. 778–816; Plassmann, *Origo gentis* (pp. 24–7 for earlier work). On the functioning of these legends, see also the comments of Remensnyder, *Remembering*, pp. 6–7.

[23] Graus, *Lebendige Vergangenheit*, p. 24; Beaune, *The Birth*, Ch. 2; Gillingham, 'Geoffrey', pp. 105–6.

[24] On this theme, and some of its problems, see Garrison, 'Divine election'.

[25] On this, see generally Smith, *Chosen Peoples*; and for a specific instance, Roshwald, *The Endurance*, esp. pp. 14–22.

[26] For the celebrated instance of France, see Strayer, 'France: The Holy Land'; for the model's early application to England, Wormald, '*Engla lond*'; and for its late medieval form, Ruddick, 'National sentiment', pp. 8–9, 13–16.

[27] For the Virgin, see Schreiner, '*Maria patrona*'.

St Margaret or St Olaf.[28] (The cult of the emperor Henry II and his consort, Kunigunde, canonised in the twelfth century, was never of much more than local importance.) Nor did the Germans boast a glorious ruler-saint of more recent times to invoke unity, as did the memory of Louis IX in late medieval France.[29] How could they hope to do so, when the history of the monarchy itself appeared so fragmented? In a land under the rule of elected kings and emperors, even the narrative core of dynastic history was lacking.[30] If the central Middle Ages had periodically brought the tentative linking of dynastic and imperial histories, such threads were all eventually broken, and the ascendant power of the prince-electors after 1245 offered little prospect that they might be remade. Lacking too, in consequence, were the stable sites of memory and prestige which elsewhere provided a home for the fabrication of illustrious, all-embracing, official pasts.

The construction and obliteration of memory have in recent times become central themes in the study of the Middle Ages.[31] Medievalists now stress how fundamentally the past (or rather, very many, overlapping and competing, pasts) mattered to medieval people in fashioning their imagined worlds and accounting for and justifying power relationships on all levels.[32] Medieval people lived in and through these constructed pasts, in which all significant bonds were in some sense grounded. Relationships not figured in past time can have had little significance or durability. In the decades after World War II, moreover, an influential group of Germanophone scholars came to ascribe fundamental importance to collective memory and its construction in the emergence of new peoples in Europe in the late Roman period and the centuries that followed. To strip the Germanic *gentes* of their dangerous mythic allure, Reinhard Wenskus and his disciples developed a model of ethnic formation stressing the creation of fictive common pasts and their projection onto the heterogeneous military followings of kings and warlords.[33] By these means, it was argued – and not on any basis of primal blood affinities – were formed the new peoples of Dark-Age Europe. This 'ethnogenesis' model has been highly influential, particularly in

---

[28] Graus, *Lebendige Vergangenheit*, pp. 180–1.
[29] For the political use of Louis's memory, see Hallam, 'Philip the Fair'.
[30] Emphasised by Ehlers, 'Natio. 1. N. (Nation)', in *LMA* 6, col. 1037; and see also Graus, *Nationenbildung*, p. 141.
[31] Examples include: Geary, *Phantoms*; Remensnyder, *Remembering*.
[32] Thus, e.g., Remensnyder, *Remembering*, p. 3.
[33] 'As soon as a community has developed its own historical-ethnic traditions ... its ethnic existence begins. Tradition-building is the precondition for historical existence': Wenskus, *Stammesbildung*, p. 54. On the significance of the new model, see Schneidmüller, 'Ordnung der Anfänge', pp. 291–2.

Germany, and as a template for the historically grounded nation it has proved transferable to later medieval times.

The medieval nation, and its historical basis, viewed in this way took on a particular character. It was small, cohesive and exclusive, and located primarily at the royal court and at religious institutions with close ties to the court. It was in these places that the nation was given historical form, in extended Latin chronicles purporting to trace common origins and recounting epochal events and shared achievements. The social and geographical extension of the nation was thence conceivable as spreading ripples from the monarchical centre, sometimes accelerated, in the late Middle Ages, by texts of a more widely accessible character (the vernacular *Grandes Chroniques* being a salient example) which thus fulfilled an essentially propagandist function.[34] Fundamentally, however, the nationalised past was the business of a powerful few.[35] Aristocratic courtiers and prelates close to the ruling dynasty characteristically made up the 'kernel of tradition' which kept the nation's memory. This is a functionalist view, in which constructions of the collective past serve clear political ends – and can be judged by modern scholars in terms of their apparent success in promoting those ends. It is not only in Germany that medievalists have in recent times found such an approach compelling.[36] Judged in this way, coherence and power of vision are virtues in medieval historical writing; diffuseness and contention are not. The medieval writers who fashioned these parchment peoples were themselves characteristically learned, often socially powerful figures, well qualified to educate their ruling elites in their high destinies and in the illustrious, obligatory and unifying pasts in which they were rooted. Monarchs themselves are even credited on occasion with propagating historical visions of common identity among leading groups, in the cause of integration under their rule.[37]

Late medieval Germany conspicuously failed to conform to this success template. There was no stable monarchical centre, and therefore no centralised, official version of the past. With the end of the Staufer came an end to historical writing in the ruler's entourage.[38] Charles IV, alone among the Empire's fourteenth-century rulers in patronising

---

[34] The centre-periphery approach to medieval (French) identity-formation is criticised by Remensnyder, *Remembering*, pp. 106–7. For medieval historiography as 'propaganda', see: Guenée, *Histoire*, pp. 332–46; Given-Wilson, *Chronicles*, esp. pp. 202–7.

[35] Ehlers, 'Nationsbildung in Frankreich', pp. 585–6.

[36] For a prominent anglophone instance of its application, see Geary, *The Myth of Nations*, esp. Ch. 3.

[37] For an English example (Alfred the Great), see Foot, 'The making of Angelcyn'.

[38] Indeed, this was lacking already for the last Staufer: Frederick II left behind no court historiography. See Sommerlechner, *Stupor Mundi?*, p. 11.

chroniclers, cultivated (with feeble enough results) Bohemian and dynastic, not imperial, and still less 'German', history.[39] The late Middle Ages have been judged as bringing a sharp fall in both the quality of historical writings in Germany and the characteristic social status of their authors.[40] And the decline of both seems in turn to mirror the enfeeblement of the Reich – just as the powerful historiographies being unfolded close to the centre in other European kingdoms appear to reflect, and perhaps partially to explain, their late medieval ascent.

Precisely here, however, lies the problem. Not only does the template not fit Germany: it actually draws attention to those elements in the German scene – multiple foci and voices, the absence of distinguished court historiographers – which seem to signal political weakness and fragmentation; and it thus invites circular thinking. The humanists, as we saw, had been there first, undergirding narratives of national decline with one of historiographical impoverishment, betokening in its turn an enervating collective amnesia – for what people which cherished its past could have fallen into such a state? Modern scholars have at times been guilty of building similar chains of unwarranted assumption, and thus reading the historiography of medieval nationhood with the nationalist's eye for success and failure. To show that powerful, centralised realms became the subject of nationally framed histories is not, after all, to show that *only* such realms could sustain historically grounded nationhoods. Indeed, on closer inspection, there was in fact no European template. The *Grandes Chroniques*, and the more ancient Saint-Denis tradition on which they rested, were exceptions, and no western European norm.[41] Other realms and peoples had other resources of memory, and discovered different pasts in different places. In late medieval England, where sentiment of nationhood is fairly widely attested, histories of realm and people tended to highlight conflicts, breaches and divisions (not least, that of 1066) and lacked an 'official', dynastic voice.[42]

Accounts of a common history could take more than one form and might draw on diverse sources of nourishment. Who is to say that the anxieties, fractures, contests and disappointments which mark the political climate in the Empire's German lands after the end of the Staufer cannot have provided stimuli of their own to reflect upon shared pasts,

---

[39] Macek, 'Die Hofkultur Karls IV.', p. 240.
[40] Grundmann, *Geschichtsschreibung*, pp. 69–70.
[41] Comparing Germany with the more favourable course of medieval French nation-making has been a major focus of post-war Franco-German approaches: thus Moeglin, 'Die historiographische Konstruktion', esp. pp. 374–5; Ehlers, 'Nationsbildung in Frankreich'.
[42] Given-Wilson, *Chronicles*, Ch. 8.

on the bonds and divisions made through history – and on the roots of common destinies not vindicated but frustrated? Whether, and how, they may have done so is the subject of this chapter. If such pasts did not display the lineaments of nation-making familiar from modern studies in the field, then perhaps they had others – which the prominence of specific national paradigms, most notably that of the French, has led scholars to underrate or overlook. For, whatever the humanists may have thought, it is remarkable just how prolific was medieval Germany in historical writings: a survey covering the period 1347–1517 has found history being written, at one time or another, in some 110 locations.[43] Also striking, in a land of diminished monarchy, is the continued (or even growing) importance of monarchs, particularly within the proliferating genre of schematic pope-and-emperor chronicles, in supplying a narrative spine for imagined pasts. No less remarkable, moreover, in a realm marked, as we are told, by acute political discontinuity, are the powerful claims which such chronicles stake to a past not only illustrious but ancient and fundamentally unbroken.[44] Whether it was in any sense a *German* past remains to be seen. Given the character of the German lands themselves, however, the approach usually favoured by medievalists, concentrating upon extended and authoritative written narratives and on their elite authors and sponsors, will clearly not suffice. Instead it will be necessary, drawing inspiration from studies of collective memory in the more recent European past, to take a broader and more flexible view of the media and sites which might embed historically grounded identities.[45] It will be important to give due weight, in the construction of such identities, to the perspectives and imaginative capabilities of diverse potential audiences.

Origines gentium

Germanic prehistory, that subject which, from the late fifteenth to the mid-twentieth century, was periodically to absorb those who went in quest of the origins of the Germans, possessed little substance for late medieval writers. A mere handful of works, as we have seen already, depict the German lands as the habitation, in ancient times, of an aboriginal population of 'Teutons', with whom the warrior bands which

---

[43] Sprandel, 'Geschichtsschreiber', p. 290.

[44] Writing in the vernacular in the fourteenth century, Fritsche Closener thus promised readers a 'chronicle of all the popes and all the Roman emperors there have been since Christ's birth': *Fritsche (Friedrich) Closener's Chronik*, ed. Hegel, p. 15.

[45] As examples, see: Green, *Fatherlands*, Ch. 3; Sayer, *The Coasts of Bohemia*, Ch. 4; Zimmer, *A Contested Nation*, Ch. 2.

came north over the Alps were to intermarry. Only in this highly limited form do we encounter an idea roughly comparable to the modern
notion of the 'Germanic': an identity, anterior to and more limited than
the fully 'German', but nevertheless supposedly forming a common historical foundation upon which such Germanness would eventually be
built. Even on the rare occasions when chroniclers, usually following
late antique exemplars, invoke the names of particular peoples from
the ancient north, they show little capacity, or will, to go beyond such
names – and little discernible sense of political multiplicity existing in
remote times combined with an underlying and significant cultural
unity. Unusual in this respect is the compiler of a universal chronicle
from thirteenth-century Bavaria, who observes how the ancient political units of the German lands and their names (of which he offers
a long list, following Isidore) have changed since ancient times.[46] But
there is also continuity, in the name of the Teutons (*Teutonici*) themselves, which derives from two pagan idols, namely Theuto, idol of
the Turingi, and Thon, worshipped by the Saxons.[47] The insensitivity
with which even an erudite commentator might read the ethnic map
of ancient Germany is disclosed by Dietrich von Niem's rendering of
the triumph of Clovis over the Alemanni, as attested in his late antique
source, as a shock 'French' victory over the 'Germans' (*Germani*).[48]
Typically, however, the distant pasts invoked by German writers were
more selectively peopled – with the proud, singular and thoroughly
mythologised forebears of the Saxons, the Franks and their ilk.

Tales recounting the deeds of warrior-heroes, set in an archaic past,
were probably widely told. Dietrich von Niem refers to the 'songs which
are still sung today among the peasants and artisans', and himself singles
out Dietrich von Bern as a mighty German to stand beside Barbarossa
or Frederick II.[49] By the late Middle Ages such tales had also attained
written form.[50] For most people, however, the epic past was less directly
historical, and far less explicitly 'German', than appeared to a learned
curialist like Dietrich or a chronicler of the wide interests of Johannes
Rothe. The more its heroes were drawn back into the sober light of history, moreover, the less German they were apt to seem: the historical
'Dideric van Bern' whom the *Saxon World Chronicle* captures subjugating

[46] *Chronicon Imperatorum et Pontificum Bavaricum*, ed. Waitz, pp. 221–3.
[47] Ibid., p. 221.   [48] Heimpel, *Dietrich*, pp. 222–3.
[49] Ibid., p. 219. Twinger likewise refers to the heroic tales which *die geburen* 'sing and
tell': *Chronik des Jacob Twinger*, ed. Hegel, pp. 376–7.
[50] For their later medieval development, including the transition to written form, see
Müller, 'Wandel von Geschichtserfahrung'.

Italy was *der Gothen koning*.[51] While a less bookish, partially oral, memory culture clearly also existed, this is mostly impossible to recapture, and even to contemporaries its epic heroes did not always seem amenable to reconciliation with, or integration into, more extended accounts of the past.[52] For Jakob Twinger (writing in the vernacular, but in a learned, clerical tradition), the dragon-slaying feats of 'Lord Dietrich', and of Hildebrand, found no confirmation in Latin sources and were therefore 'lies'. They could have no place within his multi-layered histories of Church and Reich, Germans, Franks and Rhinelanders, while the hero of Bern himself was undoubtedly 'in Hell'.[53]

Germany's epic champions of old had not acted in the cause of nation-building or for the defence of an imagined common homeland, as did their counterparts elsewhere. There was no German Arthur, and no medieval attempt to fabricate one. And yet the materials for such a venture lay close at hand, as the humanists were to show when their researches in long-forgotten manuscripts led them to the figure of the legion-slaying Arminius.[54] There was much that a patriotic reader might have gleaned about the ancient *Germani*, even from those antique texts long familiar to medieval scholarship; and as the fifteenth century was to disclose, further rich pickings were easily to be won if only the will was there. The will, however, was not there: the Lucan-inspired tag *furor Teutonicus* spoke eloquently to late medieval Germans; the tragic fate of the ancient *Teutones* apparently did not.[55] Yet, to suppose that what late medieval Germans needed was detailed patriotic history, and that in failing to hunt it down they betrayed an impoverished political identity, is surely to fall into the error of the Renaissance bibliophile or Wilhelmine schoolmaster. For common identity in the late Middle Ages did not depend upon close and accurate histories, but on powerful myths – which Germans were able to locate within imagined pasts even more illustrious, and certainly more authoritative, than those to be found in the forests of *Germania*.

---

[51] *Sächsische Weltchronik*, ed. Weiland, p. 133. For late medieval attempts to reconcile epic and historical narratives, and the difficulties which these occasioned, see Kornrumpf, 'Heldenepik', esp. p. 97.

[52] A rare early attempt at achieving such a reconciliation is represented by the world chronicle of Heinrich von München: see ibid., p. 109, and *Weltchronik Heinrichs von München*, ed. Shaw, Fournier and Gärtner, pp. 397–406.

[53] *Chronik des Jacob Twingers*, ed. Hegel, p. 380. The 'lying' nature of the epic tradition was an established view among chroniclers, expressed already in Frutolf-Ekkehard and the *Kaiserchronik*: see Kornrumpf, 'Heldenepik', esp. pp. 99, 108.

[54] Borchardt, *German Antiquity*, Ch. 3, with references.

[55] See the comments of Thomas, 'Warum', p. 176; and, for *furor Teutonicus*, below, Ch. 8.

Germans in search of a common past turned their eyes southwards. In spite of this, the widespread view which sees Roman history as filling for Germans the place occupied among their neighbours by accounts of a 'national' past is in important respects mistaken. In fact, German writings on Roman antiquity were characteristically limited and selective in focus, and often vague, derivative and perfunctory. They betray little curiosity about the history, topography or antiquities of Rome itself, of the kind that was already stirring among some Italians, and they made little attempt to appreciate its ancient institutions, way of life, thought or literature.[56] Twinger for one showed himself frostily unsusceptible to the myth of Rome: the ancient city's days of greatness were long gone, and 'as I have seen it I estimate that the people of Strasbourg or Mainz or Cologne are as powerful as those of Rome'.[57] Imaginative engagement with the world of the ancient Mediterranean in general was less in Germany than in some other parts of the north; in the thirteenth century, the history of the Romans was being written with greater learning, concentration and urgency of purpose in northwestern France than in the lands to the east.[58] By the late Middle Ages, German writers could turn to much-copied earlier chronicles treating Roman history, such as the Frutolf-Ekkehard compilation from the end of the eleventh century, or the vernacular *Kaiserchronik* from the middle of the twelfth, as well as more recent compendia.[59] On the whole, they settled for reproducing, varying or elaborating on what they found in these canonical texts, rarely attempting to go much further.

If German chroniclers sometimes took as their datum the founding of Rome, the long histories which they unfolded were scarcely even-handed. Their accounts of the city's mythical origins and early kings were mostly perfunctory.[60] The *Flores temporum* compiler edited ruthlessly the material on Rome which he found in his source, Martin of Troppau.[61] The remote and alien Roman past only commanded the

---

[56] Enikel, following the *Kaiserchronik*, made confused mention of the Pantheon (*Rotundâ*), 'which is [still] to be seen today': *Jansen Enikels Weltchronik*, ed. Strauch, p. 389, vv. 20373–82; but specific references to the city's monuments are generally rare in German writings of the period.

[57] *Chronik des Jacob Twinger*, ed. Hegel, p. 321.

[58] Thus the accounts of Roman antiquity in the French vernacular examined in Spiegel, *Romancing*. For the richness of the antique sources upon which, e.g., the early thirteenth-century *Faits des Romains* rested, see ibid., p. 120.

[59] *Ekkehardi chronicon universale*, ed. Waitz, esp. pp. 48–138. The importance of Frutolf-Ekkehard for late medieval historiography is emphasised by Brincken, 'Geschichtsschreibung', pp. 309–10. *Kaiserchronik*, ed. Schröder.

[60] Thus *Sächsische Weltchronik*, ed. Weiland, pp. 79–82, for Rome's foundation and kings, largely following Frutolf-Ekkehard.

[61] Mierau, 'Die Einheit', pp. 292–3.

engagement of German writers when it seemed to speak to their own perspectives and understanding. In this spirit, Romulus was repeatedly identified as the originator of knighthood.[62] The Republic was cited by one chronicler as an illustration of the superiority of elective over hereditary rule, while the *proemium* to the Golden Bull invoked its downfall to warn of the evils which come from division.[63] The Viennese patrician Jansen Enikel interpreted its institutions in the categories of the medieval town.[64] Predictably, the emperors were accorded more detailed coverage, as they had been in earlier chronicles. Not only were late medieval writers able to interweave their reigns with the formative events of Christian history; the emperors were generally regarded as the direct forebears of men who still ruled in the German lands: as the first links in a chain of rulers which ran unbroken, as it seemed to Jakob Twinger, 'from the first emperor, Julius, down to the Roman king Rupert of Bavaria'.[65] The Empire's earliest history remained inscribed within the vocabulary of late medieval emperorship and in the German language of its bearers. More than one chronicler explained how the term *caesar* or *keyser* had at first been personal to Julius, before being adopted by the Empire's subsequent rulers (on one account, in conscious imitation of their valiant forebear).[66]

Whenever the Roman past did not obviously illuminate a familiar present, its treatment in German accounts tended to be mechanical, lacking in urgency and narrative shape. In the thirteenth-century *Book of Kings of the New Law*, Roman emperorship is reduced to a series of disembodied, moralising anecdotes drawn from the lives of individual rulers, united by no discernible sense of the unfolding of an interconnected history. The treatment accorded to different emperors in the chronicles admittedly reveals at least a broad sense of their relative historical importance: Constantine, for understandable reasons, commanded disproportionate space.[67] But of any conception of ancient Roman history as having a shape and meaning of its own, there is little trace: the story, after all, continued. The city's sack by Alaric's Goths in AD 410 possessed for German writers none of the epochal significance

[62] Thus, e.g., *Chronik des Jacob Twinger*, ed. Hegel, p. 319.
[63] *Sächsische Weltchronik*, ed. Weiland, p. 82; *Die Goldene Bulle*, ed. Fritz, p. 45.
[64] Discussed in Tersch, 'Frühgeschichte', pp. 60–2. Despite this, the overall tone of Enikel's chronicle is courtly rather than bourgeois: Wenzel, *Höfische Geschichte*, p. 96.
[65] *Chronik des Jacob Twinger*, ed. Hegel, p. 231.
[66] Ibid., p. 332; and, for shorter accounts: *Sächsische Weltchronik*, ed. Weiland, p. 86; *Martini Minoritae Flores Temporum*, ed. Eccard, p. 1563. For Latin usage, see *Die Goldene Bulle*, ed. Fritz, pp. 53, 54.
[67] Thus, e.g., *Martini Minoritae Flores Temporum*, ed. Eccard, pp. 1580–3.

with which it would later be invested, and received scant and cursory notice, or none at all.[68] Nor was much historical importance ascribed to the eventual extinction (or rather, from the chroniclers' perspectives, interruption) of Roman emperorship in the west, and the accession of Odoacer, 'from the land that is now called Austria'.[69]

It was not that the Roman past was unimportant to late medieval Germans: far from it; but its importance lay in its imagined role in shaping the subsequent development of political relations and loyalties north of the Alps. This role appeared extensive, and was readily invoked: *Romanitas* bestowed *legitimacy*. It was more than antiquarian motives that led German towns to trace their origins, often with at least broad accuracy, to the time of Roman rule by Danube and Rhine, or promoted Trier to the status of a second Rome.[70] The first known instance of a German noble family claiming Roman ancestry comes in the twelfth century.[71] By the early fourteenth, even the counts of the Mark, a dynasty of only regional significance in *königsfern* Westphalia, were being traced back to Rome.[72] Monarchs also stood to benefit. Around the same time a legend took shape locating the origins of the Habsburg dynasty with two brothers, exiles from Rome.[73] The Roman Colonna family, with which the Habsburgs came to be linked in myth, derived its own descent from the Julian imperial house.[74] This was not the only instance of fabricated Roman history being called upon to set a seal on Habsburg aspirations. During the winter of 1358–9 an unknown supporter of Duke Rudolf IV of Austria brought together a great compilation of constitutional documents, among them forged

---

[68] See thus the brief note in *Sächsische Weltchronik*, ed. Weiland, p. 132. The event's significance was downplayed by *Martini Minoritae Flores Temporum*, ed. Eccard, p. 1587, following Orosius. For its establishment as historically significant, see Ferguson, *The Renaissance*, Ch. 1.

[69] *Sächsische Weltchronik*, ed. Weiland, p. 133, following Frutolf-Ekkehard.

[70] For characteristic lists of Roman foundations, see: *Der kunige buoch*, ed. Massmann, p. cxxiv; *Jansen Enikels Weltchronik*, ed. Strauch, pp. 405–6, vv. 21152–70; *Chronik des Jacob Twinger*, ed. Hegel, p. 330. Evident here is the influence of the *Kaiserchronik* (ed. Schröder, p. 87, vv. 379–94). For high medieval antiquarianism on the subject, see Clemens, *Tempore Romanorum constructa*, part III, Ch. 3; and for Trier as *Roma secunda*, Hammer, 'The concept', pp. 57–60.

[71] Thomas, 'Julius Caesar', pp. 257–8.

[72] *Die Chronik der Grafen von der Mark*, ed. Zschaeck, p. 13, tracing them to the Orsini; and see Patze, 'Mäzene', p. 366.

[73] The legend was recounted by Matthias von Neuenburg: *Die Chronik des Mathias von Neuenburg*, ed. Hofmeister, pp. 8–9; and see: Lhotsky, 'Apis Colonna', esp. p. 27; Busch, 'Mathias'.

[74] Lhotsky believed that already by c. 1300 the Habsburgs had come to regard themselves as a German branch of the Colonna: 'Apis Colonna', p. 32; and see also Busch, 'Mathias', p. 113.

diplomas of Caesar and Nero, conferring on Austria a generous degree of freedom from imperial rule, and many other distinctions besides: the so-called *Privilegium Maius*.[75] The forgery's aim was unquestionably less to detach the Habsburg lands from the Reich than to bolster the relative standing of their Habsburg rulers – who, in the wake of the Golden Bull, were conspicuous in lacking an electoral vote – within it.[76] The *Privilegium Maius* offers excellent illustration of what ancient Rome had to offer late medieval Germans – and why they wanted it, and how they might get it. Probably no educated German of the time could have debunked its forgeries: that took the forensic skills of a Petrarch (although it was suspicions raised at Charles IV's court that had set him onto the trail);[77] the counterfeiting of an ancient Roman past, on the other hand, is characteristic of the time and place. The larger the gap that appeared between perception and aspiration, the more likely it was that mythologised visions of Rome would be called upon to fill it. Charles IV himself, whose claim to the Reich at first stood in doubt (and whose family's title to Bohemia was troublingly recent), was identified with a whole array of illustrious ancient emperors – quite apart from a fantastic genealogy, which projected his ancestry even into the stratosphere of the antique gods.[78]

The figure of Julius Caesar interested late medieval Germans greatly, although in characteristically selective and myth-making ways.[79] Not only did they believe that Caesar had been widely present in Germany, and that the marks of his presence were still to be made out in the landscape; the first Kaiser was understood by some as the source and origin of the 'German' people itself. A lasting foundation for this idea was established by the *Annolied*, a vernacular account of the life of St Anno of Cologne, from the close of the eleventh century, a time in which origin myths of various kinds were starting to proliferate across the length and breadth of Europe.[80] The *Annolied* poet first recounted the separate origin legends of the four principal peoples in the German lands (Franks, Swabians, Bavarians and Saxons), before telling of their valiant resistance to Caesar and then, after Caesar had subjugated them, of how they joined together to aid him militarily in winning supreme rule

[75] Lhotsky, *Privilegium Maius*.
[76] Niederstätter, *Die Herrschaft Österreich*, p. 149.
[77] For translation and discussion of Petrarch's letter to Charles IV (misdated to 1355), see Burke, *Sense of the Past*, pp. 50–4.
[78] For Charles's fanciful genealogy, see: Seibt, *Karl IV.*, p. 387; Crossley, 'The politics', p. 143.
[79] See generally Thomas, 'Julius Caesar'; Graus, *Lebendige Vergangenheit*, pp. 221–2.
[80] *Das Anno-Lied*, ed. Opitz; and see E. Nellmann, 'Annolied', in *VL* 1, cols. 366–71.

from the Senate.[81] Julius rewarded his northern followers with treasure and privileges. 'Henceforth, German men were loved and esteemed in Rome.'[82]

What ensured the story's survival and proliferation was its incorporation, in an expanded form, into the widely read *Kaiserchronik*.[83] Down this route, versions of the legend were able to gain entry into some of the universal emperor-chronicles made in Germany during the late Middle Ages – thereby overshadowing their accounts of the Roman Empire, from its inception onward, with the memory and promise of German arms.[84] Can we therefore identify in Caesar's alliance with the peoples of ancient Germany an *origo gentis Teutonicorum*, to compare with the nation-making myths of Germany's medieval neighbours?[85] In important respects, the answer must be no. Caesar himself is a rather different figure from the founding patriarchs to whom other peoples looked back: no home-grown hero, but an alien conqueror. The German people which he helps to forge also appears anomalous, a unity defined not through common blood but military alliance, and overlaying a series of other, already well-established political-cultural identities.

But while these elements of distinction certainly highlight the difficulty of generalising about the sources of medieval nation-making, their significance in supposedly inhibiting that process among the Germans can be exaggerated. The arrival of mighty warriors from elsewhere – typically, the Mediterranean south – was a formative moment in many origin legends, not a German anomaly. The difference in the German case is rather that the warrior interloper, Caesar, does not annihilate or expel the native populations, but eventually embraces them as friends and near-equals. And nor should the composite character of these newly minted 'Germans' necessarily be taken as a sign of their imagined weakness or divisions. Caesar's northern followers may have been of diverse origin, but they are presented as displaying comparable (and highly prestigious) values and qualities in his service, and

---

[81] A comparable account of Caesar's activities in the north was set down in Latin at Trier around the same time: *Gesta Treverorum*, ed. Waitz, pp. 136–43.

[82] *Das Anno-Lied*, ed. Opitz, xxviii, p. 32.

[83] *Kaiserchronik*, ed. Schröder, pp. 83–92, vv. 217–596; and see E. Nellmann, 'Kaiserchronik', in *VL* 4, cols. 949–64. The chronicle survives in nearly forty complete or fragmentary manuscripts, the largest number for a German-language text of the twelfth century: ibid., col. 949. See also: Thomas, 'Julius Caesar', pp. 256–7; Moeglin, 'Die historische Konstruktion', p. 368.

[84] See Thomas, 'Das Identitätsproblem', p. 145; and, for instances of the legend's late medieval reception: *Der kunige buoch*, ed. Massmann, pp. cxxi–xiii; *Jansen Enikels Weltchronik*, ed. Philipp Strauch, pp. 401–7, vv. 20968–21270; *Chronik des Jacob Twingers*, ed. Hegel, pp. 329–32.

[85] The phrase is that of Thomas, 'Julius Caesar', p. 253.

thereby winning a common reward. The explicitly political character of their unity, in service to a common leader, seems indeed to reflect a remarkably realistic view of the processes by which new peoples were *actually* made during the Middle Ages, in Germany and elsewhere. Also revealing, however, is how the tale of Caesar's venture in the north and his triumphal return to Rome gained in its late medieval retellings an increasingly German hue.

The *Annolied* account was itself significant in this respect, as one of the earliest instances, and the first in the vernacular, of the word 'German' (*diutsch*) being used in a clearly political sense. Yet the poet's main concern was still with the proud *separate* pedigrees of Caesar's northern followers, who were 'German' only in occasional, limited and adjectival ways.[86] Starting with the twelfth-century *Kaiserchronik*, however, and increasingly so in subsequent accounts, 'the Germans' become a more substantial and familiar element, and the tale's emphasis shifts from diverse roots to common achievements. Jansen Enikel depicts Caesar meeting by the Rhine with 'the German princes' (*di tiutschen fürsten*), under whom a great army assembled for the march south, just as imperial armies were to do in later times.[87] For Jakob Twinger, it was 'the whole German army' (*dütsche volg*) under arms that accompanied him to Rome.[88]

For the majority of these late medieval writers, it was 'the Germans' collectively, and not the pre-existing peoples individually, who benefited from their association with Julius. Alexander von Roes – who did not tell the story of the march on Rome, but did present Caesar as settling his native Rhineland with Romans – was unusual in confining the identity-forming results of the encounter to a more limited, western and Frankish, *prima Germania*.[89] More extensive was the scale of Caesar's impact as recounted by Enikel. Not only did he impose 'good peace' on 'all the German lands' (*al der Diutschen lant*), as an emperor ought, and later rulers would fail to do; he drove out the monstrous 'flat-feet' and Cyclopses (*die einougen liut*). The Germans themselves he marked out collectively with unique honours: only they, apart from Julius himself,

---

[86] Ibid., p. 259.
[87] *Jansen Enikels Weltchronik*, ed. Strauch, p. 406, vv. 21186–8; and see also his judgement on the fall of Rome to Caesar's forces (ibid., p. 406, v. 21200): 'den Diutschen was wol gelungen'.
[88] *Chronik des Jacob Twinger*, ed. Hegel, p. 332.
[89] Alexander von Roes, *Memoriale*, cap. 11, ed. Grundmann and Heimpel, p. 102. A broader, though still Rhineland-centred, view of the Roman settlement is presented by Twinger, for whom 'many thousands of people from Rome and from Italy settled in the German lands, and most of all by the Rhine, and became intermingled with the Germans': *Chronik des Jacob Twinger*, ed. Hegel, pp. 702–3.

were to be addressed with the respectful plural *Ihr*, and the tongue to be cut out of anyone omitting so to honour them.[90]

The most conspicuous honour, to which the tale inescapably looks forward, is the eventual transfer of the Empire itself into German hands. It is notable, in a legend which originated in the time of the Investiture Contest, that the precocious link which it forges between a nascent 'German' people and imperial rule contains no religious element and is sanctioned by no Christian or proto-Christian authority. Nor does it make of the Germans mere servants of Roman masters: the relationship is rather one of hard-won parity. Indeed, in one portrayal of the transalpine alliance, not only are the Empire's translation and the electoral powers of a German warrior aristocracy projected into a Roman past; in conceding them, Caesar bows to superior force. On this account, found in a version of the *Saxon World Chronicle*, 'the nobles of the German lands' (*die herren von Duczschen landen*), having helped Julius to victory over Pompey's more numerous forces, ask him to grant them a wish.[91] This turns out to be for nothing less than the Reich itself, which Caesar reluctantly concedes, when his counsellors assure him that 'otherwise you are dead'. In return, the Germans choose him as their ruler. 'Thus did the Empire's election first come into the power of the German nobles.'

Far from their dealings with the first *keyser* merely Romanising the peoples of the ancient north, it Germanised them – and, in late medieval imagination, illuminated and reaffirmed those elements which set them apart from the world of the south. Caesar himself gave the distinction constitutional force, according to Enikel, by exempting the Germans from written Roman law: every 'man of German birth' was to be subject only to the judgement of his fellow Germans.[92] Among the rewards heaped on Julius' followers, this was 'the crown of honour'. Their relationship with Rome, for late medieval writers, did not subsume but guaranteed, and gave form to, their independence. German identity found expression, just as it did in accounts of *medieval* emperorship, in the comings and goings of armies across the Alps: northerners heading south, and Romans coming north. Only some of these interactions were collaborative: others were antagonistic; and it is through their resistance as well as through co-operation that the Germans are presented as winning their status as the peers and heirs of Rome. Opposition

---

[90] *Der kunige buoch*, ed. Massmann, p. cxxii.
[91] *Sächsische Weltchronik*, ed. Weiland, p. 86. The story appears in only two manuscripts known to the *MGH* edition.
[92] *Jansen Enikels Weltchronik*, ed. Strauch, p. 407, vv. 21259–65.

and conflict are recurrent themes, and do not end with the triumphs of Caesar. The much-repeated tale of Julius' wars and alliances had itself begun with insurrection in the north (literally) setting alarm bells ringing in Rome.[93] For Jakob Twinger, it was only through 'cunning', and not greater valour, that Caesar had, after a long siege, captured the ancient German capital (*houbetstat*) of Trier.[94] Another story, of a Bavarian duke who rebelled against the emperor Severus, ascribes his victory over Roman arms to his superior force of 'German knights'.[95]

If the destruction of the legions at the Teutoburg Forest in AD 15, as detailed history, was submerged until the time of the humanists, its memory survived more obscurely in the late Middle Ages.[96] It underlies Twinger's recounting of how Tiberius had sent an army into the German lands, which were resisting his demands for tribute. The ensuing battle, which he locates near Augsburg, was the deadliest which the Romans had ever fought, costing them more than 30,000 men, while the victorious 'Germans' (*Dütschen*) came away almost unscathed.[97] If the events themselves were blurred and their recollection minimal, their significance was no less clear: German military might had in ancient times opposed and proved a match for the power of Rome. The Empire's northern peoples (pre-eminently the Franks), moreover, were in late medieval memory responsible, through their military endeavours, for the final destruction of Roman power in the west.[98] It was 'with the aid of the Germans' (*der Dudischen*) that Theoderic had built his new regime upon the ruins in Italy.[99] The historical roots of the medieval Reich, it was clear, were not only in freedoms gained through Rome, but in freedom wrested *from* Rome, out of which a new political order was able eventually to emerge.

But it was the Roman colonisers themselves who had sown a widely visible legacy across the landscapes of late medieval Germany, enabling its transmission and elaboration even beyond the audience for

[93] The story of the bells set up in Rome to ring when a province rebelled originated with the *Kaiserchronik* (ed. Schröder, p. 83, vv. 245–6); later works which recount versions of it include: *Der kunige buoch*, ed. Massmann, pp. cxxi–ii; *Jansen Enikels Weltchronik*, ed. Strauch, p. 401, vv. 20968–82.

[94] *Chronik des Jacob Twinger*, ed. Hegel, pp. 330, 702.

[95] *Der kunige buoch*, ed. Massmann, pp. cxxxvi–vii.

[96] On this, see generally Thomas, 'Nationale Elemente', p. 348 n. 14.

[97] *Chronik des Jacob Twinger*, ed. Hegel, p. 335.

[98] Thus Lupold von Bebenburg, *Tractatus*, ed. Miethke and Flüeler, cap. 1, p. 245, on the Franks' destruction of Roman rule in Gaul, following Gottfried von Viterbo, *Pantheon*, and Frutolf-Ekkehard; and see also *Chronik des Jacob Twinger*, ed. Hegel, p. 625.

[99] *Sächsische Weltchronik*, ed. Weiland, pp. 133–4, following Frutolf-Ekkehard, though the reference to 'German' aid is the chronicler's own insertion.

written histories. Julius, with his legitimising power as the first *keyser*, was memorialised above all. As one of the chivalrous Nine Worthies, he was to be met with in effigy in public places in a growing number of German cities.[100] A fifteenth-century source, which identifies the visible fortifications of towns in western Germany as Caesar's work, clearly reflects local tradition.[101] Particular locations provided nodal points for the elaboration of memory. Jakob Twinger recounted how, following his subjugation of the Rhineland towns 'and all the German lands', Caesar gave thanks to Mercury at the temple, which he adorned and renewed, at Eberheimmünster, near Strasbourg. The recollection of its location was preserved by the 'magnificent monastery' afterwards built there.[102] The recording of local memory and the ascription of continuity with an ancient imperial past attained in some places more monumental form. At the Valkhof at Nijmegen, a written inscription from the fifteenth century claimed Julius as the castle's founder (and Charlemagne and Barbarossa as its renovators).[103] Once again, imperial memory is localised: here, through insertion into this proud heritage (as *Caesar Willelmus*, no less) of the thirteenth-century count of Holland who for a time headed the Empire.

Caesar had, through acts of power, remade the German landscape, within which he remained visible and memorable – not at a central, monarchical seat, but more widely and diffusely. Imagination lent him mobility: if Julius could be made the author of constitutional documents he had never issued, he might also easily have his power, and his visible legacy, extended to the remotest places. Jansen Enikel, in characteristically fantastic fashion, projected Caesar's rule in the north as far even as Poland.[104] It was not only Enikel who ascribed to Julius a northern itinerary of almost limitless scope. For Ernst von Kirchberg, he had

---

[100] See above, Ch. 3, p. 136.
[101] *Dispatches*, ed. Kendall and Ilardi, vol. II, p. 118 (2 March 1461). Among the 'numerous glorious memorials' to Caesar which a Milanese envoy claimed to have viewed in the region, he made specific mention of the gatehouse of 'a town in lower Germany, which is called Julius Caesar'. The town in question was probably Jülich, whose literary association with Caesar is traceable back to Widukind von Korvei. For the medieval evidence and recollection of Jülich's Roman origins, see Clemens, *Tempore Romanorum constructa*, pp. 343–4, as well as Graus, *Lebendige Vergangenheit*, esp. p. 222.
[102] *Chronik des Jacob Twinger*, ed. Hegel, p. 702. The tradition originated with the *Chronicon Ebersheimense*, from the mid-twelfth century: Clemens, *Tempore Romanorum constructa*, pp. 351–2.
[103] Nijsten, *In the Shadow*, p. 324. A manuscript tradition of Gottfried von Viterbo's *Pantheon* had already identified Nijmegen as a foundation of Caesar: Clemens, *Tempore Romanorum constructa*, p. 352.
[104] *Jansen Enikels Weltchronik*, ed. Strauch, p. 404, vv. 21083–4.

reached Mecklenburg, founding Wollin and Demmin.[105] According to Peter von Dusburg, he made war on the Prussians, thereby setting an example for Peter's own brethren in the Teutonic Order.[106] Even at settlements far remote from the Romans' historical orbit, his presence had allegedly left a mark. At Magdeburg, according to the fourteenth-century *Schöppenchronik*, Caesar established a temple to Diana, whose virgin attendants (*megede*) supplied the name for the new town, which he had hastily fortified with walls (*leimwenden*) before marching south for Rome.[107] The *Saxon World Chronicle* similarly tells how Caesar had happened by moonlight upon the site of Lüneburg, thus dedicating it to 'the god of the moon', and naming it accordingly. The golden moon which, the chronicler claims, he set up there on a stone pillar – 'which all the people of those lands worshipped, even the Danes and Wends' – is duly shown, above the town's battlemented walls, on the (on one view, roughly contemporary) world map from nearby Ebstorf.[108] Not only had the Germans gone to Rome for Caesar's sake; he too, for theirs, had extensively and memorably come to them.

The Germans, as late medieval writers conceived of them, were a composite, political people, whose origins were in a mythologised construction of political history. Their relationship with early imperial Rome constituted an *origo gentis*, a story whose characteristic twin refrains were what the Romans did for the Germans and their lands, and what the Germans did *to* the Romans. In Caesar, they did indeed have a formative military hero in many ways comparable to those to whom their western neighbours looked back. Largely absent, however, are the myths of common blood, migration and settlement which have seemed such a significant and revealing foundation for ideas of nationhood elsewhere in medieval Europe.[109] Even when the vestiges of such ideas appear in German writings, they are heavily influenced and constrained by the shades of the older, more limited, common pasts which they had once been fashioned to recount. None of this seems very surprising, given

---

[105] *Mecklenburgische Reimchronik*, ed. Cordshagen and Schmidt, p. 8, vv. 67–70; p. 22, vv. 31–4.

[106] *Cronica terre Prussie*, ed. Töppen, p. 39.

[107] *Magdeburger Schöppenchronik*, ed. Janicke, pp. 7–8. The account of the town's foundation by Caesar rested upon twelfth-century Latin annals: see Funke, *Croneken*, p. 68.

[108] *Sächsische Weltchronik*, ed. Weiland, p. 86; *Die Ebstorfer Weltkarte*, ed. Kugler, vol. I, p. 129; ibid., vol. II, p. 279. (Kugler, however, argues for a later dating.) The story originates in a recension of the chronicle produced in either Braunschweig or Lüneburg: Funke, *Cronecken*, p. 114.

[109] Emphasised by Graus, *Lebendige Vergangenheit*, p. 378; and see also Münkler and Grünberger, 'Origo et Vetustas', esp. pp. 235–6.

that the Roman foundation myth of 'the Germans' itself drew attention to their original ethnic multiplicity. Yet, even among histories as fractured and irreconcilable as these, multiplicity emerges on closer inspection as just one element in a more complex web of ideas.

First, in myth, came the several peoples of the German lands. The Saxons, already ascribed a common origin in the ninth century, were in the tenth traced by Widukind von Korvei to the disbanded armies of Alexander the Great.[110] Roughly a century later, the Bavarians acquired an Armenian ancestry at the hands of the *Annolied*-poet, who also granted a less explicit common origin to the Swabians.[111] Oldest and most influential of all was the myth which traced the ancestry of the Franks back to those prodigious fathers of nations, the Trojans. The people of Trier were ascribed a uniquely remote beginning, with Trebata, son of the Assyrian king Ninus, who had come with his followers half a millennium before the Romans, at a time when, according to Jakob Twinger, 'there was no one dwelling on this side of the sea in the German lands'.[112] Among the ancient warrior-peoples who settled, and thus helped to make, the German landscape of medieval tradition might also be added, in more historical time, the Romans themselves. Just like other European peoples in their mythic pasts, like the Empire in its *translatio*, or like culture, learning and political institutions more broadly, the ancestors claimed by the historic communities of the German lands had once taken a westward and northward course. Thus far, Germany was typical. More distinctive is the coexistence there of multiple separate regional origin myths – and none, as it seems, encompassing the German populations as a whole.

Myths of migration and settlement appeared to explain and justify the formation of medieval polities in a number of ways, which help to account for their appeal. They legitimised the emergence of new powers on the political stage. The Saxons seem in this way to have acquired an origin story (indeed, more than one) around the time of the emergence of the Liudolfinger as successors to the Carolingians in eastern Frankia. They imbued with meaning and tradition those communities of power – institutionalised, territorially distinct, grounded in a common law and

---

[110] Widukind proposed an alternative origin for the Saxons in the Danes and Northmen. The earliest, ninth-century, account of the Saxons' origin is by Rudolf von Fulda. See Grau, *Der Gedanke*, p. 13.

[111] *Das Anno-Lied*, ed. Opitz, pp. 23–4; and see Grau, *Der Gedanke*, pp. 17–18, 21–2. The poet's explanation of the Swabians' origin follows Isidore's elucidation of the name of the *Suebi*, 'a monte Suevo': *Etymologiarum sive Originum libri XX*, ed. Lindsay, I.9.2.98.

[112] *Chronik des Jacob Twinger*, ed. Hegel, p. 700.

jealous of their autonomy – which were attaining increased substance in some parts of Europe in the central and later Middle Ages.[113] In France, the Trojan myth offered a historical foundation for constitutional claims to independence.[114] The interpretation of origin legends might provide a means of addressing the rival claims of different polities to sovereign power within the same territory.[115] In an age of conquest kingdoms and colonial ambitions, moreover, origin myths constituted a charter for domination and expropriation.[116] They spoke of civilisation, and of the empowering deeds of mighty ancestors. They raised potent Old Testament echoes, with their stories of harsh journeys made to lands of plenty, whose control had to be won in military struggle against primitive and monstrous inhabitants. It is no coincidence that those most restless of high medieval conquerors, the Normans, were recurrently made the subject of such tales.[117] Origin myths offered a powerful foundation for dynastic realms, affirming the titles of ruling houses by tracing their bloodlines to the migrant heroes of old.[118] In the genealogies projecting his dynasty back to the Trojans, Charles IV was following in the footsteps of the Přemyslid rulers of Bohemia, who had derived their own descent from the first mythical rulers in the Czech lands.[119] Migration and settlement legends thus also supplied a foundation for claims to status within larger, imagined hierarchies of peoples, whose ancient interactions and interconnections were capable of interpretation to disclose relative antiquity and worth.[120]

The character of the Empire's German territories did not appear to favour an all-encompassing settlement legend. Germany was no discrete and sovereign polity, with clear channels of common political life within which such a legend might solidify, as settlement myths did elsewhere. Instead, it was the several imagined pasts of the more ancient peoples of the Reich that dominated. Only relatively rarely, very generally and not as a distinct community of power, were 'the Germans' as a whole ascribed a single root: in the remote division of the world among the sons of Noah, and the confusion of tongues which followed. The

---

[113] Reynolds, 'Medieval *origines gentium*', p. 380.
[114] Beaune, *The Birth*, Ch. 8; Baldwin, *The Government*, pp. 372–3; Berges, *Die Fürstenspiegel*, pp. 76–7.
[115] Waswo, 'Our ancestors', p. 289.
[116] Ibid., pp. 282–7.
[117] Loud, 'The *gens Normannorum*', esp. pp. 113–15.
[118] Baldwin, *The Government*, p. 372.
[119] Charles IV and the Trojans: Crossley, 'The politics', p. 143; Graus, *Lebendige Vergangenheit*, Ch. 3.2.
[120] Beaune, *The Birth*, p. 228; Baldwin, *The Government*, p. 373: the Trojan myth served 'to situate the French kings and their people in the mythological cosmology of the genesis of nations'.

author of a fragmentary Bavarian popes-and-emperors chronicle from the thirteenth century traced in detail the migration and subdivision of the peoples of Shem, Ham and Japheth, which he conceived as communities of language. 'All the peoples [*gentes*] of *Germania*, *Alemannia*, and of Gaul' were accordingly of Japhethite descent – a quality which linked them with the English, Scots, Scandinavians and Romans, but set them apart from the Hamitic Slavs and Semitic Byzantines.[121] When medieval people speculated about their own beginnings, they commonly reflected also on the descent of others. The late eleventh-century *Gesta Treverorum*, whose history of the population of Trier remained influential in the late Middle Ages, located the origins of city and people within broader reflections upon the races (*gentes*) sprung from Noah's sons.[122] Biblical genealogies had the further advantage of disclosing not only bonds and divisions between peoples but also their hierarchical ordering, from which might be derived claims to rule. It was a commonplace that from Shem, Ham and Japheth came not only peoples but social estates, respectively freemen, slaves and nobles.[123] With this in mind, the compiler of the Bavarian popes-and-emperors chronicle was able to insist that all the western Empire's historic rulers, whatever their *gens*, are called Romans because all were from Japheth.[124]

The Noachid descent myth allowed only a general ordering of peoples, however. It mostly did not answer those questions which periodically concerned medieval people, about the relationship of their communities and rulers with neighbours, rivals, subjects and overlords. Historical myths of this more secular and political character are what the Germans as a people seem to lack.[125] Yet traces of this sort of myth are not in fact wholly absent, although it is true that attempts to establish a common 'German' origin are few in number and invariably partial and problematic. Such attempts multiply in the period after the fall of the Staufer. Locating them means scrutinising some of the varied forms in which the well-established legends concerning the origins of the component peoples of the German lands were recounted.

Some of the characteristics of such tales are illustrated by the version incorporated into the *Book of Kings of the New Law*.[126] Taking up

---

[121] *Chronicon Imperatorum et Pontificum Bavaricum*, ed. Waitz, p. 221.

[122] *Gesta Treverorum*, ed. Waitz, pp. 130–1.

[123] Borst, *Der Turmbau*, vol. II.ii, pp. 655–6. The interpretation originated with Honorius Augustodunensis.

[124] *Chronicon Imperatorum et Pontificum Bavaricum*, ed. Waitz, p. 221.

[125] The absence of such a myth for the Germans is emphasised by Graus, *Lebendige Vergangenheit*, p. 378.

[126] *Der kunige buoch*, ed. Massmann, p. cxxiii.

the Saxon myth, the chronicler tells how, following Alexander's death, his army fled in 300 ships, of which only 54 survived to reach northern shores. Eighteen shiploads settled Prussia and another 12 came somehow to Bohemia. The remaining 24 landed on German soil (*ze tiutschem lande*), which they seized, killing the native populations apart from the peasants, whom they kept alive to work on the land. Interestingly, the chronicler claims that it was only long after other regions that 'the German lands' (*tiutschiu lant*) were thereby brought under cultivation. The form of this account – extending a well-established ethnic origin myth outwards to fill a larger and less distinct ('German') frame – is characteristic. More unusual is the bleakness of its vision of ethnic slaughter and replacement, modelled upon the Saxons' reputed massacre and displacement of the ancient Thuringians.[127] The landscape is barren and empty, late to enter the civilised fold.

The larger corpus of settlement myths which concentrated on the westernmost territories of German-speaking Europe had more ancient and complex visions of human habitation and interaction with which to work. Collective identities were conceived as the deposit of layered processes of settlement by several warrior peoples from the ancient south, over the course of a long period. As recounted by Jakob Twinger, the first colonists arrived in the Rhineland around twelve hundred years before the Romans, after Trebata, son of the Assyrian king Ninus, fled his homeland with an armed following, having killed his stepmother, Semiramis. The realm which he then established, centred on Trier, was the first German polity, and included the cities of Cologne, Mainz, Worms, Strasbourg and Basel, all founded by Trebata's companions.[128] The unifying element was language, since Trebata had commanded that his disparate followers should all use German (*dütsche sproche*).[129] As also in the story of Caesar's alliance with the northern peoples, therefore, Germanness, here conceived linguistically, is made to serve as an overarching identity expressive of the political-military unity of a series of supposedly ethnically distinct warrior bands.

The Trier legend, if not wholly confined to a local audience, remained firmly rooted in place and local tradition.[130] Much more generally current

---

[127] *Sächsische Weltchronik*, ed. Weiland, p. 78.

[128] *Chronik des Jacob Twinger*, ed. Hegel, p. 700. For the origins of the Trebata legend in the Latin historiography of high medieval Trier, see Thomas, *Studien*, pp. 190–2.

[129] *Chronik des Jacob Twinger*, ed. Hegel, p. 700. This claim is traceable back to the *Chronicon Ebersheimense*: Schnell, 'Deutsche Literatur', p. 306.

[130] A version of it was referred to by the Bohemian Peter von Zittau, who perhaps knew of it via Archbishop Balduin's circle. According to Peter, Trebeta (*sic*) was 'of the blood of Aeneas': *Königsaaler Geschichts-Quellen*, ed. Loserth, p. 273. It was also known, e.g., to the north-German Albert von Stade (above, Ch. 6, p. 277).

was the story of the fall of Troy. The poet Konrad von Würzburg, who wrote verses in praise of Rudolf I, thus also composed a massive, unfinished, account of the *Trojanerkrieg*, following a French model.[131] The story of that ancient struggle belonged to all cultured Europeans, and in Germany the 'romance of Troy' was a well-established (albeit derivative) literary genre;[132] but Troy's putative political legacy there had a more limited applicability. Some of the Empire's late medieval rulers were able to claim it for their families: in addition to the Luxemburger, the early Habsburgs may also have been credited with a Trojan origin.[133] But the argument made in Konrad IV's election decree of 1237, that the same imperial rule whose disposal had passed to the German princes (*principes Germanie*) was traceable back to Troy, was not to be widely repeated in subsequent generations.[134] In contrast to other parts of Europe, where the Trojan myth provided a legitimising core for the theme of political solidarity under a monarch, its role in poly-ethnic Germany was constrained by an inescapable link with just one historic people: the Franks.

Those late medieval writers whose conceptions of political community made appeal to the legacy of Troy came characteristically from the Frankish regions of Germany. The limitations of their materials are unmistakable. Even the questions of when and under what circumstances the Trojan refugees, or their descendants, had settled north of the Alps drew divergent answers. Alexander von Roes followed a tradition traceable back ultimately to the seventh-century Fredegar in locating their arrival in the immediate aftermath of the city's fall. Warrior bands under Aeneas and the younger Priam, the Trojan king's nephew, had fled their homeland, with Aeneas' forces settling Italy, while Priam's made their way north over the Alps.[135] For Lupold von Bebenburg, following the influential account of Frutolf-Ekkehard, it was only in late Roman times that the Trojan *Franci* had set out northward, from their settlement in Pannonia, to enter *Germania*, coming

---

[131] H. Brunner, 'Konrad von Würzburg', in *VL* 5, cols. 272–304 (here cols. 298–9).

[132] Another major Trojan history was composed by Jakob van Maerlant, in the same broad period as Konrad's (second half of the thirteenth century), and following the same French source: I.E. Biesheuvel, 'Jacob van Maerlant', in *VL* 11, cols. 737–51 (here col. 749). On the legend's treatment in German vernacular literature generally, see: Bumke, *Geschichte*, pp. 249–55; Bumke, *Höfische Kultur*, pp. 120–35. Universal chronicles also paid attention, in varying degrees, to the Trojan wars: thus *Jansen Enikels Weltchronik*, ed. Strauch, pp. 255–321.

[133] Such a link may have been made in the lost history of the Habsburgs by Heinrich von Klingenberg, Rudolf I's protonotary: Lhotsky, 'Apis Colonna', p. 50.

[134] *MGC* 2, no. 329, p. 440.

[135] Alexander von Roes, *Memoriale*, cap. 16, ed. Grundmann and Heimpel, pp. 108–9.

first into Thuringia and then moving west across the Rhine.[136] Jakob Twinger made clear that of three migrant peoples which had shaped the Rhineland, the Franks – that is to say, 'the people which came from Troy' – were the latest, coming after the Romans, and long after the ancient men of Trier.[137]

Whenever they may first have come north, it was clear that the zone of their settlement was far from corresponding to 'Germany'. Those 'first Franks' (*primi Franci*), Alexander explained, had dwelt 'towards Gaul, in Mainz, Cologne, and Trier dioceses'.[138] It was, indeed, into *Gallia*, left of the Rhine, that they had come, a region at that time ethnically mixed, out of which Priam's followers had expelled westwards the native Gallic population. Yet those incomers themselves might properly be termed 'long-haired Gauls' (*Gallici comati*), no less than Germans (*Germani*) or Franks.[139] Some of them would eventually journey further west still, to settle in the region between the Seine and Loire and to intermarry with Gallic women.[140] According to the *Saxon World Chronicle*, it was under Valentinian that the Franks, having rebelled against the Roman Empire, made their way into Germany (*voren in Dudischeme lande*), winning all the land around the Rhine and all France (*Vrancrike*).[141] A similar map of settlement was plotted by Lupold, whose Franks reached Rheims, Soissons and Orleans, eventually subjugating 'all of Gaul and Germany, from Aquitaine to Bavaria'.[142]

Trojan blood, for late medieval writers, forged affinities which in extent were both more and less than German. Its enduring remembrance in Germany, moreover, was limited and localised, reflecting authorial viewpoints which were themselves rooted in locality. In contrast to other parts of western Europe, the German lands claimed in late medieval report only a tiny handful of settlements as putative 'new Troys', clustered in the narrow Frankish heartlands by the Rhine.[143]

---

[136] Lupold von Bebenburg, *Tractatus*, cap. 1, ed. Miethke and Flüeler, pp. 244–5, following Frutolf-Ekkehard and Gottfried von Viterbo, *Pantheon*. The Franks' departure from Pannonia, on this account, was occasioned by their refusal of tribute to the Romans and the resulting war.

[137] *Chronik des Jacob Twinger*, ed. Hegel, p. 703.

[138] Alexander von Roes, *Noticia seculi*, cap. 11, ed. Grundmann and Heimpel, p. 158. For *primi Franci*, see Lugge, '*Gallia*', pp. 205–6.

[139] Alexander von Roes, *Memoriale*, cap. 18, ed. Grundmann and Heimpel, p. 113.

[140] Ibid., p. 114. Manuscript classes E–G have the migrants settling around the Seine only.

[141] *Sächsische Weltchronik*, ed. Weiland, p. 128.

[142] Lupold von Bebenburg, *Tractatus*, cap. 9, ed. Miethke and Flüeler, p. 245.

[143] Alexander von Roes, *Memoriale*, cap. 16, ed. Grundmann and Heimpel, p. 109 (*Troia minor*: Xanten); Jakob Twinger identified a castle of 'Nuwe Troeye' at Kirchheim, west of Strasbourg, whose foundation he ascribed to Dagobert: *Chronik des Jacob*

Not refugees from Troy but Roman emperors had, in contemporary imagination, sown the German lands widely with towns. It was Caesar, and no incoming Brutus or Francio, who it was believed had given the Germans laws, chased away monsters and planted, as a founding father, the seeds of a common existence *as* Germans.

Yet, many and substantial though the barriers were to extending the Frankish Trojan myth to a larger 'German' origin, such an extension was repeatedly attempted.[144] Terminology encouraged this. The incoming Trojans were *Germani*, as Alexander von Roes explained, an appellation which he invested with the added weight of historic meaning: they were so called in recognition of a shared origin (*germen*), and thus parity, with those descendants of Aeneas, the Romans.[145] Only those Trojans who intermarried with native Teutons, insisted Lupold von Bebenburg, were called Franks [*Franci*]; those who joined with the Gauls he distinguished by the derivative *Francigene*.[146] According to the *Saxon World Chronicle*, 'those who settled the German lands [*to Dudischeme lande*] were called Franks [*Vranken*], those in France, French [*Franzoisere*]'.[147] 'Frank-land [*Franken*] and France are two different things', cautioned Jakob Twinger.[148] Alexander was particularly anxious to police the terminological frontier between German Franks and Gallic *Francigene*, which, as we will see, formed part of the explanatory underpinnings of his scheme for a functional division of Christendom. It was 'the German Franks on the Rhine', insisted Twinger, who gained the Empire under Charlemagne. An obligation lay upon their descendants proudly to cherish their heritage. Twinger therefore followed Lupold in taking to task those Rhenish nobles who happily settled for being called mere Rhinelanders, forgetful of their Frankish and Trojan origins.[149]

Twinger, ed. Hegel, p. 554. In Italy, by contrast, at least a hundred towns traced their origins to the migrations of Aeneas and Antenor: Beaune, *The Birth*, p. 242.

[144] See Moeglin, 'Die historische Konstruktion', pp. 366–7.

[145] Alexander von Roes, *Memoriale*, cap. 16, and *Noticia seculi*, cap. 11: ed. Grundmann and Heimpel, pp. 111, 157.

[146] Lupold von Bebenburg, *Tractatus*, cap. 1, ed. Miethke and Flüeler, p. 245, following Gottfried von Viterbo, *Pantheon*. For the *Franci–Francigene* distinction in German writings, see Lugge, *'Gallia'*, pp. 207–8.

[147] *Sächsische Weltchronik*, ed. Weiland, p. 128; and see also *Chronik des Jacob Twinger*, ed. Hegel, p. 623: '[Die Franken] die sich in welschen landen nyder liessent und kint mit den Walhen die lantlüten mahtent, die kint wurden genant Francigene das sint Franzosen, also sü ouch noch heissent die in Frangrich sint. Aber die Franken die sich in dütschen landen nydersattent und kint mit den Dütschen mahtent, die kint und ire nochkumen heissent Franken von der Troeyer ursprunge.'

[148] *Chronik des Jacob Twinger*, ed. Hegel, p. 424.

[149] Ibid., p. 624; Lupold von Bebenburg, *Tractatus*, cap. 3, ed. Miethke and Flüeler, pp. 264–5.

The idea that the eastern ('German') Franks were collective beneficiaries of the Empire's translation encouraged their conceptualisation as a group whose settlement extended well beyond the Rhineland. The concept of a greater Frankia, equated with a 'German' political community under the imperial monarchy, had already found expression in an older but still influential tradition, articulated in the twelfth century by Otto von Freising and Gottfried von Viterbo.[150] Late medieval writers from the west of Germany wondered at the historic reach of Frankish identity even as they registered its limits. For Twinger, the Trojan migrants (who at their arrival had spoken a Romance tongue) intermingled so extensively with the native *Dütschen* that 'now all Germans are really called Franks – apart from Swabians, Bavarians, Saxons, Thuringians, and Frisians, who are not called Franks'.[151]

The widespread, identity-forming, presence of Frankish blood within the German lands was explained in part by the ancient peregrinations of the warrior itinerants themselves. A group of Franks had settled Franconia, 'of which Würzburg is the capital', under their own duke, Francio *(Franke)*.[152] They had entered Thuringia where, according to Alexander von Roes (here following Gregory of Tours), they established a realm under long-haired kings.[153] For Alexander, the movement east of the Rhine of offshoot bands from the swelling Trojan core foreshadowed the making of a German political community – so that in course of time, the whole of *Theutonia* came to be known, 'from the more important' element in its population (i.e. the Trojan *Germani*) as *Germania*.[154] The same process was later extended further when Charlemagne, in subjugating the heathen Saxons, settled in their lands ten thousand Franks.[155] The eastward march of Frankish-Trojan Germanness possessed for Alexander a quasi-constitutional significance, preparing the way for the absorption of the eastern princes into the college of electors.[156]

However problematic was the Frankish origin legend as a mould for the mythic prehistory of the Germans (and no medieval origin myth was without problems), it possessed considerable allure, at least for

---

[150] Lugge, *'Gallia'*, pp. 203–4; Folz, *Le Souvenir*, p. 255.
[151] *Chronik des Jacob Twinger*, ed. Hegel, pp. 623–4.
[152] Ibid., p. 624. Alexander von Roes was another writer to recount the settlement of 'eastern Franks' *(Franci orientales)* in Franconia: Alexander von Roes, *Memoriale*, cap. 18, ed. Grundmann and Heimpel, p. 113.
[153] Alexander von Roes, *Memoriale*, cap. 16, ed. Grundmann and Heimpel, p. 111.
[154] Ibid., cap. 16, p. 111.
[155] Ibid., cap. 27, p. 130. Alexander was here following and adapting Einhard, *Vita Karoli*.
[156] See above, Ch. 6, pp. 277–8.

writers in the Frankish lands and for those making a polemical case for the German people. It discloses in its late medieval applications just how strongly German identity was in this period refracted through the lens of region, and also how region might provide a standpoint from which to conceive of the Germans. Most conspicuously of all the settlement legends which German writers recounted and adapted, the Frankish myth came to serve political ends comparable to those for which such legends were applied elsewhere in Europe. It located the Germans – those of them, at least, who could plausibly be linked with migrant Trojans – in relation to other European peoples, notably the Italians and the French, in a manner which allowed questions of hierarchy and title to be discussed. The Germans, insisted Twinger, were 'just as noble as the Romans', since both peoples had the same Trojan ancestry.[157] Specifically, the Trojan myth allowed a case to be made, on the basis of national character and aptitude, for continued German possession, in troubled times, of the Roman Empire. Both the universalising (and Germanising) potential of Frankish myth and its inherent difficulties are illuminated by its most illustrious medieval embodiment: the emperor Charlemagne.

The great Charles

The Europeanisation of Germany's medieval memory after World War II brought no change as radical as the remaking of Charles the Great. To the German medievalist elite who had rallied to defend his honour in 1935 – in part, against the naive strain of Nazi Teutonophilia which made of him an un-German interloper and 'slaughterer of the Saxons' – the Frankish emperor appeared as a quintessentially Germanic bulwark for the West.[158] As late as 1956 Charles still managed to win a place in the new edition of the compendium *Die großen Deutschen* (co-edited by the medievalist and one-time doyen of Strasbourg's Reichsuniversität, Hermann Heimpel).[159] With time, however, the figure of Charles became increasingly de-nationalised, identified (though this was in itself nothing new) with the advance and protection of 'European' culture, and

---

[157] *Chronik des Jacob Twinger*, ed. Hegel, p. 624.

[158] Hampe *et al.* (eds.), *Karl der Große oder Charlemagne?* For the defamation of Charles by Nazi ideologues, see See, *Deutsche Germanen-Ideologie*, pp. 94–5.

[159] Löwe, 'Karl der Große'. The author himself (p. 19) admittedly based his case for Charles's inclusion on his historical 'greatness', despite the fact that he was 'kein "Deutscher"'. As late as the 1970s, however, the octogenarian Walther Kienast was still to be found chiding Rahewin for getting Charles's identity 'wrong' by making him a western Frank: Kienast, *Deutschland*, vol. II, p. 529.

located more firmly within early medieval contexts. With these trends came another, as German medievalists began ruefully to note how little significance Charles's memory appeared actually to have had for medieval Germans, particularly when compared with its vigorous and varied celebration among their western neighbours. Non-Germans, meanwhile, have on occasion seemed happy enough to concur in depicting a reign, and legacy, with little significance east of the Meuse.[160]

Charlemagne's legacy in Germany could not directly be projected, via claims to dynastic continuity, onto the political community under its monarchs. This was in contrast to the situation beyond the western frontier, where the Capetian kings came in the late twelfth and early thirteenth centuries to claim that (as prophecy had foretold) the French monarchy had 'returned' through marriage to the blood of Charles.[161] By the early fourteenth century, this conviction was tenacious enough in France to survive a change of dynasty.[162] In Germany, however, where succession to the Carolingians had been claimed for the Staufer, the link appeared broken with their demise.[163] The saviour-emperor by the name of Charles, a descendant of Charlemagne, whose rumoured imminent coming Alexander von Roes reported, was to be of French royal blood.[164] Late medieval Germany, in contrast to Naples, Hungary or France itself, was mostly not a land ruled by Charleses. Rudolf I's choice of the name for a son (born in 1276) probably reflected contemporary Angevin influence as much as any desire to invoke a Carolingian connection.[165] The sole monarch to bear the name, Charles IV, as he records in his autobiography, received it from his Capetian namesake

---

[160] Thus, e.g., Gabriele and Stuckey (eds.), *The Legend of Charlemagne*.

[161] Kienast, *Deutschland*, vol. II, pp. 506–11.

[162] Beaune, *The Birth*, pp. 182–3; Baldwin, *The Government*, pp. 392–3.

[163] For the descent of the Hohenstaufen from Charlemagne (and Clovis), see Sommerlechner, *Stupor Mundi?*, p. 105 (Burchard von Ursberg). Not everyone thought the association of Carolingian blood with the monarchy ended with the Staufer, however. Sifrid von Balnhusin observed that with the death of King Henry Raspe in 1247 expired 'those noble princes of Thuringia, who traced their origin to the dynasty of Charlemagne': *Sifridi presbyteri de Balnhusin historia universalis*, ed. Holder-Egger, p. 704.

[164] Alexander von Roes, *Memoriale*, cap. 30, ed. Grundmann and Heimpel, pp. 136–7. For the Angevin Charlemagne prophecies current in Italy in Alexander's time, see Folz, *Le Souvenir*, pp. 298–9; for their application by Alexander, Mohr, 'Alexander', pp. 280–1.

[165] See the comments of Resmini, *Das Arelat*, pp. 117–18, arguing against the older view of Redlich, *Rudolf von Habsburg*, p. 748, that a Carolingian reference was indeed intended. This is in marked contrast to Rudolf's near-contemporary on the French throne, Louis IX, whose identification with Charlemagne included wearing one of the Frankish emperor's coins on his seal chain like an amulet: Kienast, *Deutschland*, vol. II, p. 513.

during his youth at the French royal court, superimposed upon his baptismal name of Wenceslas.[166] Again, the influence of the western neighbour, rather than the Carolingian title itself, was decisive, though Charles did seek subsequently to exploit the connection.[167]

The vernacular literary tradition which preserved in Germany the Frankish emperor's name and deeds was mainly derived, directly or indirectly, from French models. It was more limited, thematically and in richness of material, than the French.[168] The great Carolingian had entered German writings with a ready-made French pedigree, which Germans, it seems, were mostly unable, and perhaps unconcerned, to contest. From the south-German Charlemagne epics of the early thirteenth century, Wolfram's *Willehalm* and Stricker's *Karl*, to the more diffuse *Karlmeinet* compilation, probably assembled in the Aachen region in the fourteenth century, the emperor was seen to move in a French milieu.[169] The geographical diffusion of tales of Charles, moreover, was partial and uneven, and in the late Middle Ages concentrated in the west and north: in Frankish and Saxon Germany, where the emperor's memory had particular resonance, and where the French and Netherlandish texts which underpinned German accounts of him lay close at hand.

Recent approaches to Charlemagne's place in German political culture have tended, therefore, to cast doubt on the extent of his visibility and importance, on his political centrality, and on his identification with an explicitly German political community. There are indeed good grounds for caution on all these matters. Yet excessive, or selective, scepticism brings its own distortions. No bygone monarch exercised in medieval memory an influence as socially pervasive as do the invented traditions of modern nationalism.[170] If Charles's commemoration in Germany was limited, partial and contestable, that of other mythologised rulers – Arthur in England (but also Wales!), for example – was hardly less so.[171] The pervasiveness of Charlemagne's French tradition

---

[166] *Karoli IV Imperatoris Romanorum Vita*, ed. Nagy and Schaer, pp. 22–3: the French king 'imposed' (*imposuit*) on him his new name; and see also the comments of Schneider, 'Karolus', esp. pp. 365–6, 372, 374, 380.

[167] The ordinal number *quartus*, of which Charles's title made regular use, itself drew implicit attention to his Carolingian predecessors: Eggert, 'Bemerkungen', pp. 306–7.

[168] Bastert, '"der Cristenheyt als nücz"', esp. pp. 127–8. For the French Charlemagne tradition, see Morrissey, *L'empereur*.

[169] For this and what follows: Lohse, 'Das Nachleben', esp. pp. 342–4; Bastert, '"der Cristenheyt als nücz"', esp. pp. 137–43.

[170] For their role in modernity, see Hobsbawm, 'Mass-producing traditions'.

[171] For the problematic character of Arthur, see Gillingham, 'The context and purposes', esp. pp. 116–18.

can also be overstated: systematically remembering kings past was in most places and contexts an act of the few, not the many. On each count – presence, political relevance, identity – the balance sheet is more mixed than either the bookish German patriots of times past or their more assiduously *communitaire* successors have allowed.

In several ways, the presence of Charles in Germany grew in the late Middle Ages.[172] The proliferation of his image, in stone, paint, goldsmiths' work and other media, is striking: some salient examples have been encountered already.[173] If portrayals of the emperor clustered most densely at sites linked to his name (notably Frankfurt and, above all, Aachen), more ubiquitous forms for his representation – as a Worthy beside Caesar, or vicariously, through his paladin Roland – brought him to places more varied and remote. Charlemagne's cult had a particular importance, as it infiltrated many (though far from all) regions of Germany from the twelfth century onward.[174] A number of centres, besides Aachen, became particular sites of veneration, among them Zurich, as well as major churches in the north which were linked (accurately or not) with the Saxon mission. Although never a major popular votary, St Charles attained some local prominence in this way, in the form of liturgical commemoration, chapels, altars, images, relics and collections of objects associated with his person.[175] The textual tradition likewise continued to grow. Of the vernacular epics of the thirteenth century, numerous manuscripts are known, and the influence of these works reached beyond their own genre to infiltrate more rigorously chronological histories.[176] The twelfth-century *Kaiserchronik*, in which Charles was given more space than any other emperor, had a particular influence upon late medieval historiography. Einhard's *Vita* was also much copied and read.[177]

In some of its most visible and prestigious elements, the German Charlemagne tradition was without western rival: in possession of the emperor's mortal remains and in occupation and continued constitutional use of the most numinous site of his monarchy, Aachen.[178] Charles himself remained central to the rituals and the visual style of kingship.

---

[172] Still fundamental for the German tradition is Folz, *Le Souvenir*.
[173] Ch. 3, pp. 135–6.
[174] For what follows, see Zender, 'Die Verehrung'.
[175] See the gazetteer in ibid., pp. 106–12.
[176] For numbers of manuscripts (well over seventy for *Willehalm*, for example), see Lohse, 'Das Nachleben', pp. 342, 343.
[177] For its dissemination, see Schneidmüller, 'Sehnsucht', pp. 293–4.
[178] Some of the peculiarities of the German tradition are identified by Graus, *Lebendige Vergangenheit*, pp. 192–4; for the importance of Aachen as a legitimising site, see Schneidmüller, 'Sehnsucht', esp. pp. 292–9.

The new monarch was installed upon 'the throne of King Charles the Great', as an Erfurt chronicler noted at Rudolf I's elevation.[179] The octagonal imperial crown was (mistakenly) believed in the late Middle Ages to have been worn by Charles, and the ceremonial sword was also ascribed to him.[180] Aachen preserved his memory like nowhere else. Alexander von Roes urged 'anyone wishing to know of the manifest virtues of this holy man, and of how through rule in this world he merited the company of the angels' actually to go there and read of his deeds.[181] But Germans of Alexander's day could also observe how Aachen had, in a sense, long ago come to them. The central Middle Ages had seen the widespread reproduction of the form and architectural features of Charlemagne's chapel, elements of which were observable in the eleventh-century fabric of Alexander's own convent church, St Maria on the Capitol in Cologne.[182] The appeal of Aachen minster as a model endured, as we will see, in the late Middle Ages.

The remembrance of Charles continued to flourish and develop in the late Middle Ages in Aachen itself, where visible commemoration of the sainted emperor and its physical setting were substantially the work of the thirteenth and fourteenth centuries.[183] Frederick II, on the occasion of his coronation there in 1215, had closed up the sumptuous reliquary casket, with its gilded figures of Charles and his successors in the Reich.[184] Richard of Cornwall in the 1260s endowed Aachen with a new set of regalia, including crown and sceptre.[185] Under Charles IV, further reliquaries were created for his Carolingian namesake's remains, including the magnificent gilded bust, adorned with enamelled imperial eagles and fleurs-de-lys, to house a fragment of his skull.[186] Also under Charles, work began on the chapel's Gothic choir, with its architectural parallels, hardly accidental, to the Capetians' sacred treasury of kingship, the Sainte-Chapelle. Around the same time, the dilapidated

---

[179] *Cronica S. Petri Erfordensis Moderna*, ed. Holder-Egger, p. 263.
[180] Schramm, *Herrschaftszeichen*, vol. III, p. 881. For Richard of Cornwall's coronation with *diu kunic Karles krône*, see *Ottokars österreichische Reimchronik*, ed. Seemüller, p. 163, v. 12332; for contemporary identification of the sword with Charles, Dietrich von Nieheim, *Viridarium*, ed. Lhotsky and Pivec, pp. 17–18.
[181] Alexander von Roes, *Memoriale*, cap. 22, ed. Grundmann and Heimpel, p. 123.
[182] See generally Verbeek, 'Die architektonische Nachfolge'.
[183] See Grimme, 'Karl der Große'.
[184] For the Charlemagne shrine, see Nilgen, 'Herrscherbild', pp. 361–2, as well as Saurma-Jeltsch, 'Karl der Große', pp. 423–4, with references.
[185] Groten, 'Richard von Cornwall', pp. 437–8.
[186] For Aachen's Charlemagne reliquaries of this period, see generally Kavka, 'Karl IV. (1349–1378) und Aachen', pp. 480–1. It is rarely possible, however, to find clear evidence for Charles IV's role as patron.

Carolingian palace was rebuilt as a civic hall, its new portal guarded by a monumental figure of Charlemagne himself.

Charles IV's appropriation of the legacy of his holy forebear was unprecedented in extent: not even Barbarossa had invoked him in such varied, visible and magnificent ways.[187] The Frank's ideological power for the monarchy therefore not only remained substantial, but attained new importance in the context of the weak and contested reigns of the post-Staufer era. Charles of Luxemburg had attained the throne in 1346 as the candidate of a papally backed faction while the excommunicate Ludwig IV still lived and reigned. Aachen had been closed to Charles: his first coronation was in Bonn. However, in pursuit of the legitimacy which installation at Charlemagne's seat promised, he not only underwent a repeat coronation, at Aachen in 1349 (by which time his challengers for the throne were dead, and his own acceptance more widespread): his coronation, on 25 July, was just two days before the feast of the Frankish monarch's translation.[188] Charles clearly felt he owed his great predecessor much: following the birth of his son Wenceslas in 1361, he sent to Aachen a thanks offering of 17 gold marks.[189] Charles visited Aachen repeatedly in his later years (as Richard of Cornwall had done, in the 1260s): a sign that the town's legitimising draw remained sufficient, periodically at least, to override the late medieval 'remoteness' from the monarchy of this western corner of the Reich.[190]

Aachen, however, was just the start. Within months of his second coronation, Charles had established in Nuremberg (on the site of the Jewish quarter, razed in a pogrom perpetrated with his own knowledge and assent) a chapel to the Virgin which invoked, in Gothic guise, Charlemagne's minster church.[191] The Aachen chapter had in 1349 granted Charles three of the Frankish monarch's teeth, which he took with him into Bohemia.[192] (One would eventually be embedded in a painted image of the emperor-saint in the Holy Cross chapel, the religious summation of Charles's castle at Karlstein.) In 1351 he founded in the Prague New Town a community of Augustinian canons dedicated to the Virgin and St Charlemagne: the form of the church again echoed Aachen.[193] Such a visibly political invocation of the saint's

---

[187] See generally Machilek, 'Karl IV. und Karl der Große'.
[188] František Kavka, 'Karl IV. (1349–1378) und Aachen', p. 478.
[189] Fajt, 'Karl IV.', p. 491.
[190] For *Königsferne* in late medieval Germany, see above, Ch. 2, p. 82; for Charles and the Aachen Charlemagne cult, Machilek, 'Karl IV. und Karl der Große', pp. 129–34.
[191] Crossley, 'The politics', p. 124.
[192] Machilek, 'Privatfrömmigkeit', p. 92; Fajt, 'Karl IV.', p. 491.
[193] Kavka, 'Karl IV. (1349–1378) und Aachen', p. 478.

memory, binding the Reich to the ruler's patrimonial lands, was something new, though wholly characteristic of Charles IV. It was extended
in 1354, when the king established another Augustinian convent, at
the site of Charles the Great's palace at Ingelheim, by the Rhine. The
dedication, to SS Charlemagne and Wenceslas, embodied a recurrent
merging of east and west, dynasty and imperial rule, as did the stipulation of the foundation diploma that the four canons were to be Czech-
speakers and subject to the provost of Charles's Prague foundation.[194]
So, too, moreover, did Charles's bringing of the imperial regalia, with
their links to Charlemagne, to Prague, and their annual display there.
Seldom before had the Frankish saint-emperor been so prominently, or
politically, on show.

It seems generally to have done his Luxemburg imitator little good.
A desire for good relations with Charles IV may on occasion have had
a part in advancing his namesake's cult. Thus, at Frankfurt am Main
in 1356 a *passionale* was compiled for St Bartholomew's church (confirmed in the same year in the Golden Bull as the rightful place for
all future royal elections), exhaustively detailing Charlemagne's merits and miracles.[195] The Frankish emperor's depiction on Gulden coins
minted in Frankfurt is a further symptom of the flourishing of his
memoria in the town at this time, under monarchical stimulus.[196] But
Germans, so far as we can tell, mostly did not take up the implied invi-
tation to compare Charles with his illustrious forebear – at least, not
favourably. Dietrich von Niem knew of the Ingelheim foundation, and
appreciated its significance; but that did not deter him from roundly
condemning Charles as a bad emperor, who had destroyed rather than
exalted his venerable *imperium*.[197] German writers were not blind to the
aptness of Charlemagne as a model and measure for later rulers; but
the comparison had to seem justified. Circumstances might make it
so. The long, largely uncontested rule of Rudolf I, following the confusion of the 'Interregnum', seems to have been greeted by some, perhaps encouraged by the king's own partisans, as an epochal moment

---

[194] Ibid., p. 478. There are indications from Charles's reign of Charlemagne being
directly associated with St Wenceslas – and of both these holy namesakes and prototypes thus being linked with Charles. In Frankfurt am Main, the Galgentor figure
of Charlemagne, datable to the 1360s, was invested with visual attributes of the
Bohemian saint: Jacobs, 'Das Bild', pp. 81–4.

[195] Kötzsche, 'Darstellungen', p. 162. It was only under Charles IV that Charlemagne's
feast became firmly established at Frankfurt. For the role of political considerations
in the making of images of Charlemagne at Frankfurt in this period, see Jacobs, 'Das
Bild', esp. pp. 73–84.

[196] Saurma-Jeltsch, 'Karl der Große', p. 435.

[197] Dietrich von Nieheim, *Viridarium*, ed. Lhotsky and Pivec, pp. 1–2.

of renovation redolent of Charlemagne's reign. The singer 'Meister Boppe' drew comparison between the two monarchs.[198] According to another poet, Friedrich von Sonnenburg, the pope had sent letters throughout Christendom announcing that no king had been so dear to a pontiff 'since King Charles's day'.[199] The chronicle of the Colmar Dominicans records a prophecy ascribed to an itinerant seer, 'Seczere', that although Rudolf would not attain full emperorship, there would be no one like him in glory, power, honour and riches 'since the time of Charlemagne'.[200] A contemporary continuator of the *Saxon World Chronicle* likewise judged the time auspicious: Rudolf had received at Aachen 'the holy Roman crown, which no king has attained, as is [wrongly!] said, since King Charles the Great'.[201]

Charlemagne was remembered as the source of titles, powers and institutions which remained important, sometimes urgently so. A number of princely dynasties in the northern lands of the Reich traced their ancestry to him.[202] Charles remained politically relevant, a recommended pattern for late medieval rulers of the Reich. For Konrad von Megenberg, he still encapsulated the basic template of political virtues against which any candidate for the imperial throne had to be measured.[203] Johann von Viktring, whose chronicle may have been conceived as a work of instruction for contemporary Habsburg princes, explained how Charlemagne had established peace and order in the land, as an ideal emperor should.[204] It was in gratitude for the aid which they had rendered him in (appropriately, and significantly) forcing an entry into Aachen for his coronation that in November 1248 William of Holland confirmed to the Frisians the rights and freedoms granted them by Charles, 'our predecessor, of blessed memory'.[205]

---

[198] *Politische Lyrik*, ed. Müller, vol. I, p. 91.

[199] Ibid., p. 75.

[200] *Chronicon Colmariense*, ed. Jaffé, p. 253.

[201] *Sächsische Weltchronik: Sächsische Fortsetzung*, ed. Weiland, p. 285.

[202] For the dukes of Brabant, see Ridder, 'Gefühl', pp. 197–9; for the Luxemburger, Seibt, *Karl IV.*, p. 386. Siegfried von Balnhausen traced the landgraves of Thuringia back to the Carolingians: *Sifridi presbyteri de Balnhusin historia universalis*, ed. Holder-Egger, p. 704.

[203] Konrad von Megenberg, *De translacione Romani imperii*, cap. 12, ed. Scholz, p. 289: 'Porro illa requiruntur esse bona in Romanorum principe electo, que Magnum Karolum dignum fecerunt imperio Romano, videlicet ut non sit tyrannus et pauperum oppressor, set pocius eorundem iudex equus et pius defensor.'

[204] See Hillenbrand, 'Der Geschichtsschreiber', esp. p. 449. Johann also held up to the Habsburgs their forebear Rudolf I as an imitator of Charles, comparing his defeat of Otakar II with Charlemagne's subjugation of Tassilo: *Liber certarum historiarum*, ed. Schneider, i.231.

[205] *Die Urkunden Heinrich Raspes und Wilhelms von Holland*, ed. Hägermann and Kruisheer, no. 48, pp. 82–4 (3 November 1248).

Away from his more derivative and strictly literary representations, Charlemagne was often remembered in post-Staufer Germany as a political figure, who had shaped in lasting ways the constitutional and institutional landscapes of his eastern lands. Late medieval depictions of Charles not uncommonly show him bearing the sword of justice;[206] and it was as a custodian of the judicial order in his lands that he was particularly imagined. This might take fanciful and anecdotal form, as in Enikel's story, one of several which he told of the emperor, of Charles coming to the aid of a snake, which summoned him to remove a toad from its eggs.[207] But the emperor was also made the source of concrete measures and institutions. In the *Saxon World Chronicle*, he is seen instituting the imperial bann, while by the fourteenth century he had also become the originator of the Westphalian *Veme*.[208] The laws and privileges of the Saxons and Swabians, as well as the Frisians, were traced back to him.[209] Viewed in this light, the transfer of the Empire to the Germans, for which he was celebrated by some, was but one among a series of characteristic acts by the Frankish emperor, raising up through powerful and lasting legal provisions those communities and groups which had earned a special distinction.[210]

Heavily mythologised though his relations with the German lands clearly were, Charlemagne remained in late medieval report a tangibly historical figure. He stood for an Empire which had itself been made and shaped within history – not least, through its translation to a new bearer-people. Charlemagne's Reich appeared material and finite, its shades, for German observers, still recognisable in their own day, in ways that the ancient Roman Empire was not. He may not have been as active as Caesar in founding towns; but for the Saxon Dominican Heinrich von Herford he had spanned the newly Christian east with bishoprics, while fertile local tradition continued to add to his purported

---

[206] See the numerous examples identified in Kötzsche, 'Darstellungen'; and for more, Fricke, *Veme*, nos. 6, 8–11, pp. 18, 20–3.

[207] *Jansen Enikels Weltchronik*, ed. Strauch, pp. 515–18, vv. 26383–532; Charles thus showed himself to be the 'best rihtaere' (v. 26384); and see Geith, *Carolus Magnus*, pp. 222–3, 235.

[208] *Sächsische Weltchronik*, ed. Weiland, p. 152; *Liber de rebus memorabilioribus*, ed. Potthast, p. 30; and see Lindner, *Die Veme*, pp. 466–8.

[209] Thus *Schwabenspiegel*, ed. Eckhardt, *Landrecht*, cap. 30, pp. 80–1, for the Swabians' privilege that time should not run against their right, as it does not against the king's, granted by Charles in gratitude for the aid which the Swabian duke Gerolt rendered him against the Romans. See also *Deutschenspiegel und Augsburger Sachsenspiegel*, cap. 32, § 3, ed. Eckhardt and Hübner, pp. 110–12. For Charlemagne and written law, see generally Lück, 'Der Sachsenspiegel', esp. p. 266.

[210] That is how it is presented in the *Schwabenspiegel* (ed. Eckhardt, *Landrecht*, cap. 120 / 124, p. 182).

monastic foundations.[211] Charles's Empire was also, for all its trans-
alpine appendages, more visibly northern than that of the Caesars. It
is hardly coincidence that Charlemagne was ascribed a central place
in the arguments of German publicist writers, such as Alexander
von Roes, Lupold von Bebenburg and Konrad von Megenberg. The
Empire's learned non-German protagonists, such as Ockham, tended
by contrast to ignore him, preferring to found their claims for imperial
power upon the more glorious, and abstract, name of Rome. Lupold,
among the treatise-writers the one most disposed to view the Empire as
a bounded, territorial polity, made much of Charles and said nothing of
substance about his Roman forebears.[212] In a handful of works – typically, products of the Saxon lands such as the late thirteenth-century
Braunschweig Rhyming Chronicle – the Empire's history, or the chroniclers' engagement with it, began not with Rome but with the Frankish
emperor and his deeds in the north.[213] But if Charles had done much to
shape the political map of Germany, what was to be concluded about the
identity of the man himself – ruler, according to the same Braunschweig
chronicler, of 'the kingdom of the French'?[214]

This was a view commanding wide assent in Germany, as it did outside. In addition to the French-derived traditions of epic and romance
(for Wolfram, Charles was 'the noblest *Francoys* ever born'), it was also
affirmed in more deliberately historical writings.[215] Whatever claims
William of Holland may have made, to grant charters as the Frankish
emperor's successor, the Frisians themselves repeatedly turned to the
French kings for confirmation of their freedoms, insisting that it was
to them, and not the *rex Allimanie*, that Charles's power had passed.[216]
Charlemagne's Frenchness found acceptance particularly in vernacular
works, like the *Braunschweig Rhyming Chronicle*.[217] Likewise for Fritsche

---

[211] *Liber de rebus memorabilioribus*, ed. Potthast, p. 44; Zender, 'Die Verehrung', pp.
102–3, 106–12.

[212] For Charlemagne's centrality to Lupold's conception of the Empire, see Most, 'Der
Reichsgedanke', esp. pp. 454–9; for the contrast between his view of the Empire's
historic character and Ockham's, Wittneben, 'Ludwig', pp. 578–80.

[213] See Runge, 'Die fränkisch-karolingische Tradition', p. 1.

[214] *Braunschweigische Reimchronik*, ed. Weiland, p. 461, vv. 185–7: '... Karl, vil werdich-
liche / untphenc daz konincriche / der Franzoysere und dhe krone'.

[215] For Wolfram, see Schnell, 'Lateinische und volkssprachliche Vorstellungen', p. 131.

[216] *Acta*, ed. Kern, no. 1, p. 1 (1271 × 1275): The Frisian communities of Ostergo and
Wangerland petition King Philip III for a new market, declaring their independence, which they owe to the French king's ancestor, Charlemagne ('ex quo nostrum
gentem, ymmo totam Frisiam, attavus Regis Francie, Karolus Magnus beatissime
memorie liberavit'); and for a later example (*c.* 1337), see *HUB* 3, no. 647, p. 441.

[217] *Braunschweigische Reimchronik*, ed. Weiland, p. 470, vv. 903–10, telling how 'dhe
Franzoysere' had held the Empire since Charlemagne's coronation. See also
Mecklenburgische Reimchronik, ed. Cordshagen and Schmidt, p. 12, vv. 159–60 ('Her

Closener, writing in fourteenth-century Strasbourg, Charles was *künig zuo Frangrich*.[218] Some Latin writers also hesitated to Germanise the Frankish emperor. Dietrich von Niem observed that he had been born and raised, died and been buried within Germany (*Germania*); yet he remained, as a Frank, less fully German in Dietrich's eyes than were subsequent emperors of Saxon and Swabian origin.[219] Many, of course, saw no reason to discuss the emperor's ethnicity at all.

Why should they have done so? What mattered, surely, was less what Charles *was* than what he *did*. Even *translatio imperii* implied no compulsion to judge the emperor's own identity. According to the fourteenth-century *Upper-Rhenish Chronicle*, the emperor was the son of Pippin *kuning zuo Francrich* and victor of Roncesvalles *and* the Empire's translator *ze túschem lande* and founder of the college of electors.[220] Like Caesar, Charles was a conqueror, whose wars were a defining moment for the German warrior bands which, in following him, proved their title to the Empire: his own 'nation' was no more obviously relevant to that identity-forming process than was Caesar's. It was in any case hardly common for medieval writers to agonise over such matters. And, for Charles, the sources spoke with discordant voices, while the known facts of his life and reign seemed likewise to preclude a simple view. Characteristically, German writers had to grapple with judgements on his identity, often of non-German origin, which came laden with the weight of authority. It was not only the poets' sources that made of Charlemagne a *Francoys*; the ubiquitous handbook of Martin of Troppau also ruled that the Carolingians were a French dynasty (*Francigene*).[221] Yet other voices, no less weighty, bore a different

ward funden vnd irkant / in Frangrich vnd was Karl genant'). The general absence of a German Charlemagne from vernacular literature is emphasised by Schnell, 'Lateinische und volkssprachliche Vorstellungen', esp. pp. 131–2; and see similarly, Geith, *Carolus Magnus*, p. 204. For analysis and explanation, stressing the importance of sources and authorities, see Jostkleigrewe, *Das Bild*, pp. 162–70. An early exception is represented by the *Kaiserchronik*, in which Charles appears as 'der êrste kaiser ... ze Rôme / von Diutisken landen': *Kaiserchronik*, ed. Schröder, pp. 349–50, vv. 14818–19. The chronicler's identification of Charles is ambivalent, however, since he also describes him as the son of Pippin of Karlingen (ibid., p. 340, v. 14309).

218 *Fritsche (Friedrich) Closener's Chronik*, ed. Hegel, p. 33.
219 Dietrich von Nieheim, *Viridarium*, ed. Lhotsky and Pivec, p. 1: 'Et licet dictus Carolus Magnus esset rex Francorum, fuit tamen natus in Germania...'; and see the comments of Heimpel, *Dietrich*, pp. 221–2. Dietrich, however, took a more decided view in his *Nemus unionis* (1408), referring to Charles as *natione et lingua Theutonicus*: see below, Ch. 11, p. 496 n. 81.
220 *Die Oberrheinische Chronik*, ed. Maschek, pp. 51–2; and see the comments of Jostkleigrewe, *Das Bild*, pp. 168–9.
221 *Martini Oppaviensis Chronicon*, ed. Weiland, p. 463. Martin is not entirely consistent, however, as elsewhere, following *Venerabilem*, he writes of the Empire's translation *in Germanos* in Charles's person: ibid., *Pontifices*, p. 426.

message. Had not Innocent III described the Empire as coming to the Germans in Charles's own person? The native Staufer legacy lent further support to a Germanist reading: for Gottfried von Viterbo, the emperor was a *Theutonicus* in the paternal line.[222]

Much required explanation. To some, such as Alexander von Roes, the accession of the Carolingians marked a significant moment, when power among the Franks shifted eastwards, from its previous centres within Gaul.[223] Yet their realm remained multi-ethnic. 'Nor is there any doubt that Charles was German [*Theutonicus*]', Alexander felt obliged to insist, 'even though he ruled over Gauls'. In the *Book of Kings of the New Law*, what mattered was the eastward emphasis of his rule. Charles persuaded the princes to recognise his son Louis as his successor by reassuring them of his own continued presence as guardian, since 'I intend to be more in the German lands [*ze tiutschem lande*] than in France [*Vrankriche*]'.[224] Yet in his person no less than his rule, he seemed to straddle two worlds. His 'daily dress' when in the east was a plain and modest garment, lined with fur in winter; only when he went to *Vrancriche* did he wear 'immoral clothing, after the custom of the land'.[225] Interpreting the significance of Charlemagne's legacy was a further problem. Both Alexander and Lupold von Bebenburg took exception to what they deemed the usurpation of Frankish titles by the French and their kings. Yet Lupold and Alexander nevertheless each felt compelled to concede to the western neighbour a share of Charles's constitutional legacy – in Alexander's account, a portion of the historic *regnum Francorum* to hold by hereditary title, free of all temporal superiors.

In the two centuries between the Staufer and the age of the Councils, the number of writers to claim Charlemagne explicitly as a German was rather small. Alexander von Roes did so most cogently and fully. Lupold appealed to Gottfried von Viterbo in proof of his claim that Charles was a *Franco Germanicus*, and noted his birth at Ingelheim, his

[222] Grau, *Der Gedanke*, p. 34; Thomas, 'Julius Caesar', p. 257.

[223] Alexander von Roes, *Memoriale*, cap. 21, ed. Grundmann and Heimpel, pp. 117–18, explaining how, before his elevation as king, Pippin as *maior domus* had his main seat in Cologne (in contrast to the Merovingians, who 'frequenter habitabant in Gallia togata': ibid., cap. 20, p. 116); and see *Chronik des Jacob Twinger*, ed. Hegel, p. 883, insisting that Charlemagne and his ancestors had the seat of their rule in the German lands, from which they subjected *welsch Frangrich* to the Germans, 'et non e converso'. The Carolingians 'were of German dynasty and had their seat most of all in Aachen, Worms, Metz, and by the Rhine' (ibid., p. 705).

[224] *Der kunige buoch*, ed. Massmann, p. clxxxix; and for Charlemagne's treatment in this work, see Geith, *Carolus Magnus*, pp. 210–20.

[225] *Der kunige buoch*, ed. Massmann, p. clxxxiii.

naming of the months and winds in his native tongue, and his granting to the Germans of laws in their vernacular.[226] Lupold was followed in this by his contemporary and contestant, Konrad von Megenberg. The Dominican Heinrich von Herford supplies a rare chronicler's voice. Charles was 'the first emperor of the Teutons' (*primus imperator Theutonicorum*), who thus 'raised up with many privileges and dignities his homeland, Germany [*Theutoniam patriam suam*], and Aachen in particular'.[227] In the vernacular, it is not until the start of the fifteenth century that a chronicler (Jakob Twinger) is found to identify the Frank unequivocally as German. Advocates of this view were to become more numerous, particularly within the Latin tradition, during the fifteenth century. Claiming Charles for the Germans was to be a recurrent theme among the humanists – who were affirmed in this conviction, as in others, by the late medieval publicists on whose works they drew.[228]

Before the humanists, the few voices arguing explicitly for a German Charlemagne are hardly representative of German writers more broadly. There must be several reasons for their rarity, not least the pervasive power of genres and authorities originating beyond Germany and urging a different conclusion. Hardly less remarkable, however, is that the argument was pursued at all, despite – or partly on account of – the fact that the materials for its support appeared so contestable. To lay such vehement claim to the ethnic ascription of a long-dead monarch was, in European comparison, unusual. Why the point, for its advocates, seemed important, and why it came to matter when it did, will be returned to in the next chapter. But equally significantly, whatever their judgements on his own identity, German writers frequently ascribed to Charles a fundamental place in the historical development of (*specifically*) the northern lands of the Reich and of post-Roman western emperorship. For all these reasons, it is instructive to consider the emperor and his age in light of the current of history – German history – which on some views they inaugurated.

---

[226] Lupold von Bebenburg, *Tractatus*, cap. 3, ed. Miethke and Flüeler, pp. 260–1. Alexander von Roes similarly claimed in proof of Charles's Germanness his naming in his *lingua materna* of the months and days of the week: Alexander von Roes, *Noticia seculi*, cap. 18, ed. Grundmann and Heimpel, p. 165. For Gottfried and for the high medieval tradition of linking German monarchs with Charlemagne, see Kienast, *Deutschland*, vol. II, pp. 516–19.

[227] *Liber de rebus memorabilioribus*, ed. Potthast, pp. 45, 78.

[228] For fifteenth-century and humanist views, see: Schnell, 'Lateinische und volkssprachliche Vorstellungen', p. 130; Mertens, 'Mittelalterbilder', pp. 35–6; Münkler and Grünberger, 'Enea Silvio', pp. 176–8.

The course of German history

The imperial monarchy appeared to late medieval eyes as an institution with a venerable and continuous history. Yet it was a history with distinct phases, of which a new and significant one was entered with the passage of imperial power to the Franks and Germans.[229] The names of the monarchs themselves – Henry, Ludwig, Frederick and indeed Charles – invoke connections with an imperial past which reached back to the ninth century, but no further. Beginning with the Carolingian era, or at latest with the tenth-century Ottonians, the treatment of the Empire's history by German writers changes. Thenceforward, down to the authors' own day, it assumes a more defined shape, with a more detailed and fully historical periodisation. It is recounted, by some at least, with a new polemical edge and ascribed more explicit meanings. It is given a stronger ethnic colouring – as *German* history, we can in certain cases start to say.

Such works admittedly form only a minority among the writings from German pens which addressed themselves to, broadly speaking, imperial history. Even universal chronicles, that genre so characteristic of the German lands, often contributed less to forming views of the Empire's post-antique history in the west than might be thought. Many of the manuscripts of these much-copied compendia are fragmentary, or concentrate only on particular periods (often, reflecting their religious, didactic ends, the earlier ones) within the long history of God's people under two 'Laws'.[230] Much of the appeal of the universal chronicle format in the late Middle Ages, moreover, lay in its adaptability to supply a basic framework within which local or regional histories could be recounted. Even when the Empire's more recent past was made a focus, it was not always recounted in a manner well suited to disclosing larger meanings. Jansen Enikel's account of the period between Charlemagne and Frederick II comprised little more than a heap of anecdotes about Charles and Frederick themselves, without visible shape or unifying significance.[231] In the printed edition of Fritsche Closener's chronicle 'of all the popes and all the Roman emperors that there have been since the birth of Christ', the reign of Henry IV (1056–1105) claims just four lines (recording the crusaders' capture of Jerusalem), with no word

[229] A view signalled explicitly by Heinrich von Herford, who dated reigns *imperii Theutonicorum*, as well as from the creation of the world, the foundation of Rome and the birth of Christ: above, Ch. 6, p. 279.

[230] Bumke, *Geschichte*, pp. 345–50.

[231] *Jansen Enikels Weltchronik*, ed. Strauch, pp. 498–574, vv. 25539–28958; and see the comments of Wenzel, *Höfische Geschichte*, p. 99.

about Henry's struggle with the reformed papacy. His fatal son, Henry V (1106–25), receives three lines.[232] It is possible to see the force of the remark, made by Closener's Strasbourg successor Jakob Twinger, that while people prefer to read about recent rather than remote things, it is about noteworthy events in the more recent past that the least has been written.[233]

Nevertheless, both the raw materials for reflecting on the Empire's more recent history and the stimuli to doing so increased markedly in the decades after the mid-thirteenth century. Pope-and-emperor chronicles, with their visible insistence on the enduring primacy, within a providential historical scheme, of the western *imperium*, became ubiquitous, particularly in Germany, during the Empire's post-Staufer crisis. While they did not themselves always provide clear judgements on the shape or meaning of imperial history, they offered readers considerable stimuli to fashioning their own. The numbering of late medieval reigns in imperial chancery documents attests to a generally impressive, although not flawless, institutional memory of the Empire's rulers back to the Franks.[234] We have already seen how widely scattered in the German lands were lasting reminders of the rule there of Frankish, Saxon, Swabian and other imperial monarchs.[235] To travel was to encounter the Reich; and it was its post-Roman history that often spoke most clearly and eloquently. Dietrich von Niem was able to transcribe Henry II's tomb inscription in Bamberg cathedral.[236] And to local survival must be added the force of localism and the defence of local privilege. These factors help to explain why, for example, the memory of Charlemagne continued to be cultivated, and visibly elaborated, in places far remote from the travels of late medieval kings.[237] Charles's diplomas, meanwhile, generally proved more amenable to fabrication

---

[232] *Fritsche (Friedrich) Closener's Chronik*, ed. Hegel, p. 36. The massive 'Heinrich von München' compilation offers just 20 verses on Henry IV, concentrating on his reputed personal vices ('er was ein hürer / und ein rechter spiler'): *Weltchronik Heinrichs von München*, ed. Shaw, Fournier and Gärtner, p. 542, vv. 1–20. For the humanists, by contrast, Henry IV and his fate commanded much attention: Strauss, *Sixteenth-Century Germany*, pp. 7–8.

[233] *Chronik des Jacob Twingers*, ed. Hegel, p. 230.

[234] Eggert, 'Bemerkungen', p. 309. A comparably precise sense of succession is evident in Sifrid von Balnhusin's designation of the anti-king Henry Raspe as 'Henry VII': *Sifridi presbyteri de Balnhusin historia universalis*, ed. Holder-Egger, p. 704.

[235] For the location of memory in the medieval landscape, see Geary, *Phantoms*, p. 124.

[236] Heimpel, *Dietrich*, p. 226. Dietrich also, e.g., visited Hildegard of Bingen's monastery, where he was able to see both her remains and her books; he cites her prophecies concerning the future of Empire and Church: ibid., p. 247.

[237] See generally Kötzsche, 'Darstellungen'. On the relationship between the memory of kings and the monarch's protracted physical absence, see the comments of Remensnyder, *Remembering*, pp. 10–12.

to suit local ends than were those of Caesar, the Austrian *Privilegium Maius* notwithstanding.

Recurrent crises infused the history of the *imperium* with contemporary relevance, and because these tended (at least implicitly) to touch upon possession of the Empire, as well as on its powers, the centuries since the accession of the Franks spoke particularly eloquently to current concerns. It is no coincidence that some Germans in the time of Ludwig the Bavarian, when debate centred on the power of the emperor and the German princes to act free from papal constraint, turned so avidly to the Ottonian period, when monarchs were seen to have done just that.[238] Nor was it only German views that were influential. In interpreting the Empire's past, as in other things, the Church and its papal head provided an ongoing framework and counterpoint. Canon law itself supplied a golden seam of historical *causes célèbres* from the Empire's post-antique history in the west, concentrated upon defining moments of interaction and conflict with Rome. This was a past, moreover, which in troubled times popes continued publicly to interpret. The turbulent history of the Reich since Frankish times proved indestructible and for some, it seems, inescapable.

The creation of a number of extended and structured accounts of the Empire's Carolingian and post-Carolingian past (as well as the reproduction of older ones) is a noteworthy feature of the post-Staufer era. This was despite, or in several cases clearly because of, the visible diminution of the Empire's power and prestige when compared with previous centuries. Much of the material which late medieval writers assembled was itself extracted, often largely verbatim, from earlier sources; but the combination and directing purpose were their own. Here was history with a point and, in certain instances, a directly political end. Beginning with the Carolingians, the Empire's rulers are seen to take on a number of activities which, while mostly implicit in the idea of Christian emperorship itself, were not ascribed in comparable detail to earlier monarchs. Kings and emperors are shown extending the frontiers of the Reich, and recovering its lands where these were lost. They fight the heathen, take the vanguard in crusading, and defend and enrich the Church. They march south to aid the pope against his local adversaries (just as their ancient forebears had once crossed the Alps to assist Caesar against his). They bring the peoples of northern Europe, at the sword's point, within the Christian fold.[239] And they do these

---

[238] Thomas, 'Der Lohengrin', pp. 174–5.
[239] Lupold von Bebenburg, *Libellus de Zelo*, cap. 2, ed. Miethke and Flüeler, p. 423. The German princes of old showed their zeal 'in extending the Catholic faith, not only within their realm, but also in neighbouring regions'.

things as *Germans*: representatives of a people which, as embodied in its military aristocracy, it was thought could boast unmatched achievements in the service of the Faith.

A new era dawned, for some, with the accession of the Carolingians, whose seizure of power was presented as finding justification in their protection of the Church. Lupold von Bebenburg's catalogue of 'great acts of defence by ancient German princes towards the church of Rome, against tyrants' began with the campaigns of Pippin against the Lombard king Aistulf and Charles Martel against (*sic*) the Goths.[240] By his aid to Leo III, Charlemagne was continuing an established dynastic tradition. Frankish (or German) north and Roman south were again linked, as they were in the Trojan legend, through the idea, first asserted in the *Kaiserchronik* and much repeated thereafter, that the pope was Charles's brother.[241] Armed protection for the see of Rome thenceforth continued, under Otto I, against Berengar, Otto III against the consul Crescentius, and Lothar III (1125–37) against Roger of Sicily.[242] Journeying south to liberate the Church had become by the late Middle Ages an identifying attribute of the Empire's Carolingian and post-Carolingian rulers, familiar even beyond the Latinate milieu of the treatise-writers. In *Lohengrin*, a much-mythologised Henry I is portrayed defeating a Saracen army outside Rome.[243] The emperor's historic responsibility for the Church, moreover, was not confined to service at the papacy's bidding. Dietrich von Niem, writing in the time of the Schism, explained how Otto I (to his fellow Saxon Dietrich, the greatest of all emperors) had healed an earlier rift in the Church by deposing Pope John XII.[244]

To some late medieval commentators, hardly less than to the patriotic professors of a much later age, the period between the tenth and twelfth centuries was a veritable *Kaiserzeit*, filled with splendid figures and glorious deeds (if also with the gathering shades of troubles ahead). By the fourteenth century, Otto I had joined Charles as *magnus* for German writers, although Otto never attained the complex and many-

---

[240] Lupold von Bebenburg, *Tractatus*, cap. 4, ed. Miethke and Flüeler, pp. 281–2.

[241] Thus, e.g., *Sächsische Weltchronik*, ed. Weiland, p. 149; and see Folz, *Le Souvenir*, p. 162.

[242] Lupold von Bebenburg, *Libellus de Zelo*, cap. 4, ed. Miethke and Flüeler, pp. 436–43.

[243] *Lohengrin*, ed. Cramer, pp. 429–85.

[244] Dietrich von Nieheim, *Viridarium*, ed. Lhotsky and Pivec, p. 14; and see Heimpel, *Dietrich*, pp. 218–19. Konrad von Megenberg, responding to Ockham's use of this apparent instance of unlimited imperial power, had emphasised that Otto only acted against the pope as executor of the decision of a Church council: Konrad von Megenberg, *Tractatus contra Wilhelmum Occam*, cap. 9, ed. Scholz, p. 378.

sided remembrance accorded to the Frank.[245] Otto III was the 'wonder of the world'.[246] Comparatively little significance – certainly, little positive significance – was accorded the Salians, while the achievements of twelfth- and (more rarely) thirteenth-century emperors, though highly judged in certain accounts, appeared overshadowed by mounting crises.[247] Most glorious of all, for some at least, were the Ottonians. Modern scholarship has judged the style of rule of these east-Frankish monarchs as quite different from that of their Carolingian forebears.[248] Late medieval writers, however, were impressed by the parallels and seeming continuities, at least in their attainments. These extended to the sphere of law – or so it was supposed. According to Johannes von Buch, only some parts of the *Sachsenspiegel* were traceable back to Charlemagne: other clauses had originated with the Ottonians (and with Frederick Barbarossa).[249] The Ottonians themselves – Henry I and Otto III, the sainted Henry II and 'red' Otto II ('bloody death' and 'pale death to the heathen', as Fritsche Closener calls him) – also appeared fundamentally alike in late medieval judgement.[250] What united them, and linked them to the Frankish past, was triumph – historically formative triumph – in Christian warfare.

Their achievements were both superlative and comparable. Just as Charlemagne had converted the Saxons 'by the material rather than the spiritual sword', so Henry I 'made the Northmen and Danes subject to him by arms and, calling them back from their primal error, taught them to bear the yoke of Christ'.[251] Charlemagne's Christianisation of 'the entire population of Germany' (*totus populus Germaniae* – though specifically the Saxons are meant) had constituted 'an immense divine

---

[245] Jank, 'Die Darstellung', pp. 86, 94–5.

[246] *Fritsche (Friedrich) Closener's Chronik*, ed. Hegel, p. 35.

[247] For a glowing assessment of Lothar III (1125–37), who imitated in his virtues 'his forebears Constantine, Charles the Great and Otto the Great, whose descendant he was', see *Sächsische Weltchronik*, ed. Weiland, p. 205. The crusading achievements of the Staufer were emphasised by Dietrich von Niem, who was also the earliest German writer to present an unambiguously positive view of Frederick II: Dietrich von Nieheim, *Viridarium*, ed. Lhotsky and Pivec, pp. 72–3; Heimpel, *Dietrich*, pp. 227–8; Pivec and Heimpel, *Neue Forschungen*, pp. 28–56. Previously, German writers' judgements on Frederick, though seldom unequivocally negative, tended to be ambivalent and self-contradictory: Sommerlechner, *Stupor Mundi?*, esp. pp. 480–4.

[248] See esp. Reuter, 'The Ottonians'.

[249] *Glossen zum Sachsenspiegel-Landrecht*, ed. Kaufmann, p. 125; and see Lück, 'Der Sachsenspiegel', pp. 270–1.

[250] *Fritsche (Friedrich) Closener's Chronik*, ed. Hegel, p. 35; and see also *Sächsische Weltchronik*, ed. Weiland, p. 165.

[251] For Charles, see Alexander von Roes, *Memoriale*, cap. 27, ed. Grundmann and Heimpel, p. 130; for Henry I, Lupold von Bebenburg, *Libellus de Zelo*, cap. 2, ed. Miethke and Flüeler, p. 428, following *Annalista Saxo*.

blessing'. Yet the Christian frontier continued to advance under successive emperors – none of whom, according to the *Lohengrin* poet, extended it as much as did Henry II. Just as Otto I had established the church of Magdeburg, Henry II founded Bamberg.[252] As Charlemagne had waged war against the Saxons, and Henry I and Otto I against the Danes and Obodrites, so Henry II overcame 'Bohemia, Poland, and those Slav regions that were pagan'.[253] The tenth-century emperors, in late medieval report, assembled afresh, on new foundations, the landed dominium dissipated under Charlemagne's descendants. As to who had done most, opinions might differ. Evident, however, was that these monarchs had brought together the territorial *imperium* which, although depleted, still endured. Also clear, to some at least, was that they did all this as *German* monarchs. Otto I, claims the *Saxon World Chronicle*, 'exalted the Empire [*dat rike*] more than any other German *keiser*. He freed the land from the Hungarians; he won for the Empire Bohemia, Poland and Lombardy, Burgundy and Lotharingia.'[254] The resulting polity, extensive, composite and finite, invited the structural metaphor. The imperial 'chariot', for Dietrich von Niem, was assembled at this time, with its four great wheels (threatened with loss in his own day): Germany (*Alamania*), along with Lotharingia, and Luxembourg, Arles and Italy.[255] Its construction was the work of 'very powerful Roman princes of German origin'.[256]

The Empire was also capable of metaphorical depiction through the figure of the eagle. Here, the images which came to German writers in the post-Staufer era were often sorry ones. For Konrad von Megenberg, writing for Charles IV, it was malicious foreigners who were seeking with coarse fingers to pluck the Roman eagle.[257] Just such an act had been dramatised by Alexander von Roes in his *Pavo* (1285), which culminates with the papal Peacock strutting in the humiliated Eagle's feathers – an inescapable allusion, whatever its wider meanings, to

---

[252] *Lohengrin*, ed. Cramer, p. 567, v. 7557; cf. *Sächsische Weltchronik*, ed. Weiland, p. 164.

[253] *Martini Minoritae Flores Temporum*, ed. Eccard, p. 1616; and see *Lohengrin*, ed. Cramer, p. 567, vv. 7551–6.

[254] *Sächsische Weltchronik*, ed. Weiland, p. 164.

[255] Dietrich von Nieheim, *Viridarium*, ed. Lhotsky and Pivec, p. 3. For Dietrich's interpretation of the *currus imperii*, see Funder, *Reichsidee*, pp. 245–63, underlining the importance of the number four. See also the similar structural metaphor employed by Alexander von Roes, in which the Empire's four 'principal places', Aachen, Arles, Milan and Rome, represent the four 'walls' of the house which is the Church: Alexander von Roes, *Memoriale*, cap. 25, ed. Grundmann and Heimpel, p. 127.

[256] Ibid., p. 49.

[257] Konrad von Megenberg, *De translacione Romani imperii*, ed. Scholz, p. 249.

the fate of Frederick II.[258] The glorious achievements of old had not lasted. The Empire's history since Carolingian times, for some observers, possessed a shape and progression which derived in part from its crises and relative decline in the most recent past. This view found support in the eschatological expectations which lay particularly upon the Roman Empire and which encouraged attempts to identify the moment at which the inevitable process of decline set in. In the *Saxon World Chronicle*, from around the mid-thirteenth century, a description of the feet of Nebuchadnezzar's dream-figure, of iron mixed with clay, is followed by the reflection that 'this betokens the infirmity of the Roman Empire, which it will suffer before its end, as every rational man can now see'.[259] The Empire's historic abasement, moreover, meant above all that of Germany. In Konrad von Megenberg's *Lament*, it is a personified *Alemania* which complains to the pope that 'I now live miserably among the beggars, [whereas] once I numbered among your friends.'[260] Discerning the meaning of the Empire's decline, apportioning blame and proposing remedies constituted the purpose particularly of some of the publicist tracts. In their view of the German past, and in the polemical concerns which led them to attain it, they anticipated the German humanists – as well as, more remotely, foreshadowing the view of the medieval Reich, its ascendancy and putative betrayal, unfolded centuries later in the age of German nationalism.

The shaking of the Empire's ascendancy in Christendom was ascribed various periodisations, reflecting the diverse regional and social positions and explanatory schemes of different commentators. To Germans in the post-Staufer era, the Empire's troubled relations with the papacy were a prominent theme. The recurrent nature of these conflicts, as well as the gravity of their consequences, had begun by the late Middle Ages to disclose historical patterns and, to some, lessons. Ludwig IV's quarrel with Avignon brought a particular sense of *déjà vu*. Ludwig, observed Konrad von Megenberg, in the earliest and most impassioned of his polemical works, was enduring the same fate as had 'Henry, Konrad, [and] Frederick' before him.[261] In a more mature tract from the 1350s, Konrad insisted to Charles IV that *experiencia*, the teacher in all things, disclosed how uniquely deadly was the poison spread by 'discord between the supreme pontiff and the Roman emperor'. In

---

[258] Alexander von Roes, *Pavo*, ed. Grundmann and Heimpel, p. 190, vv. 248–50. Alexander's detailed knowledge of, and reference to, the actual circumstances of Frederick's deposition are underlined by Heimpel, 'Über den "Pavo"', p. 186.
[259] *Sächsische Weltchronik*, ed. Weiland, p. 78.
[260] Konrad von Megenberg, *Planctus*, ed. Scholz, pars I, cap. 60, p. 64.
[261] Ibid., pars I, cap. 35, p. 50.

addition to the lamentable cases of the late Staufer and Henry VII, there was the recent memory of 'how all Germany [*tota Germania*] was fragmented and divided through schism in the time of Ludwig IV, your predecessor'.[262] Occasional attempts were made to look further back. An unusually far-reaching judgement was passed by the *Saxon World Chronicle*, which ventured as far as the eleventh century and the accession of 'Hildebrant': Pope Gregory VII. 'Then broke out for the first time dissension between the see of Rome and the Roman Empire, such as endures to the present day.'[263] The source of later ills did not lie only with the papacy, however. Of Henry V's elevation against his father, the chronicler observed, 'from this election the Empire never subsequently recovered; it was clearly against God'.[264] The search for fatal turning points in the history of the Reich did not begin only in the nineteenth century, or even with the humanists: already in the crisis-torn thirteenth century occasional voices were beginning to ask when and how the axial moment had come.

Particular attention was directed at the reign of Frederick II and at the decades which followed. For Dietrich von Niem, it was during the contest for the throne between Frederick and Otto IV (1198–1215) that the Empire's material basis, alike in Italy, in Germany and in its western lands, was 'almost irrecoverably lost and alienated'.[265] For Alexander von Roes, the decline of the Empire to almost nothing (as well as the rise of the Roman papacy to universal dominion) had occurred within the half-century between Frederick II's imperial coronation and the 1274 Council of Lyon.[266] The Staufer legacy marked the Empire's German lands particularly deeply, and the dynasty's downfall came over time to be invested to a peculiar degree with significance. The rumoured survivals and recurrent impersonations which we have already encountered were but one aspect of this.[267] The fate of Konradin at the hands of Charles of Anjou and (as it was alleged) Pope Clement IV became the stuff of recurrent, late medieval fable.[268] In their recollection, these events gained a marked flavour of ethnic antagonism. An annalist

---

[262] Konrad von Megenberg, *De translacione Romani imperii*, ed. Scholz, p. 251.
[263] *Sächsische Weltchronik*, ed. Weiland, p. 175.
[264] Ibid., p. 185. For medieval constructions of the eleventh century as a watershed, see more generally Geary, *Phantoms*, p. 22.
[265] Dietrich von Nieheim, *Viridarium*, ed. Lhotsky and Pivec, pp. 32–3.
[266] Alexander von Roes, *Noticia seculi*, cap. 8, ed. Grundmann and Heimpel, p. 154.
[267] Ch. 5, pp. 236–41.
[268] For example, see *Die Chronik des Mathias von Neuenburg*, ed. Hofmeister, pp. 11–12. Charles of Anjou writes to the pope, identified as 'Martinus', asking what he should do with his captive. The latter writes back: 'Vita Conradini mors Karoli, mors Conradini vita Karoli', whereupon Charles has Konradin executed.

in Worms recounted how 'this Konradin, beautiful as Absalom, was cruelly decapitated, along with several German counts and nobles, by Charles with the advice of the pope, through hatred of the German name [*ob invidiam Theutonici nominis*] and on account of his grandfather, Frederick'.[269] The long remembrance of the wrongs done to the last Staufer,[270] and the enduring obligation to right them evidently still felt by some to lie on the imperial monarchy, are illuminated by a story preserved by Matthias von Neuenburg. This tells of how Ludwig IV, in the course of his expedition to Rome in the late 1320s, came upon the castle in which Konradin was (mistakenly) believed to have been beheaded, and had it razed to the ground.[271]

Specific factors combined to lend the period, when viewed from some distance, the character of a watershed. A significant number of chroniclers, among them Matthias von Neuenburg, the monk of Fürstenfeld and the Styrian rhyming chronicler, Otakar, commenced their narratives with Frederick II's downfall and what followed, or with the election of Rudolf I in 1273. Others stopped there – such as Jansen Enikel and the 'Heinrich von München' compilator, who ended their world chronicles with the deaths of Duke Frederick of Austria in 1246 and Frederick of Hohenstaufen in 1250.[272] On the whole, these were no mere annalistic compilations, such as might break off suddenly for various reasons, but extensive, structured histories, created with a coherent purpose. Martin of Troppau allowed the emperor series of his highly influential chronicle to fade out inconsequentially, after making

---

[269] *Annales breves Wormatienses*, ed. Pertz, p. 76. A similarly ethnically coloured account was given by Dietrich von Niem: Konradin was put to death along with 'several German magnates and nobles'; Manfred too was *nacione Germanus*; and the Angevin dynasty had a recurrent record of perpetrating acts of cruelty 'contra aliquos nobiles Germanie': Dietrich von Nieheim, *Viridarium*, ed. Lhotsky and Pivec, p. 14. By the time of the humanists, the story of Konradin's betrayal was ripe for transformation even into a scurrilous woodcut, which was to circulate with Luther's writings, showing the pope himself swinging an immense two-handed sword at the neck of the kneeling and prayerful youth· illustrated in Stadtwald, *Roman Popes*, p. 201.

[270] Dietrich von Niem, in the early fifteenth century, was still able to reproduce songs which he claimed were in popular circulation concerning Konradin: Heimpel, *Dietrich*, pp. 227–8.

[271] *Die Chronik des Mathias von Neuenburg*, ed. Hofmeister, p. 370. Intended here may be the Torre Astura, a fortified residence held at the time by the Frangipani family and lying some 50 km south of Rome. It was here that Konradin was handed over to Charles of Anjou.

[272] See Liebertz-Grün, 'Erzählte Zeitgeschichte'. The manuscript tradition of 'Henrich von München' is complex: only one redaction announces Frederick II as its end point, and only one surviving manuscript actually sees this programme through: *Weltchronik Heinrichs von München*, ed. Shaw, Fournier and Gärtner, pp. xv, 3. Another historiographical watershed, though less strongly politically coloured, was formed by the years 1348–9: Sprandel, 'Geschichtsschreiber', pp. 289–90.

the stark observation that, with Frederick's deposition and death, the Empire had fallen 'vacant'.[273] Dietrich von Niem, writing early in the fifteenth century, closed his detailed histories with the Staufer, reserving little beyond angry invective for the kings who came after.[274] Other perspectives were possible, of course. Johann von Winterthur's chronicle begins with Frederick II's early years, passes over his downfall and what came after, and concentrates on the divided election of 1314 as epochal calamity. But it is nevertheless noteworthy how many literate Germans arrived, apparently independently, at broadly the same dividing point in the Empire's history: the ending of the high medieval *Kaiserzeit*, with which the patriotic historians of a later age would also lay down their pens.

The decisions made by chroniclers therefore played a part in constructing for their readers, and for subsequent writers, a history of the Reich which changed course after the eleventh century, and particularly in the thirteenth. The chroniclers' perspectives reflected in their turn, at least in part, an interpretation disseminated by the imperial monarchy and its supporters. Rudolf I, after coming to the throne, had faced fundamental problems in locating himself in relation both to his immediate predecessors and to a Hohenstaufen legacy both authoritative and tainted. Although Rudolf could claim a more substantial reign than those who went directly before him, the problems of continuity were nevertheless real, with one chronicler observing specifically that the king was 'not of Staufer birth'.[275] The significance of the breach which appeared to exist is indicated by the attempt made by the pro-Habsburg Matthias von Neuenburg, writing in the fourteenth century, to close it, with his claim that Rudolf was Frederick II's godson. The language of Rudolf's government was conceived so as to position his reign in relation to the immediate past and to reinterpret that past in light of his reign. Rudolf's chancery adopted elements of

---

[273] *Martini Oppaviensis Chronicon*, ed. Weiland, p. 472; and see the comments of Sommerlechner, *Stupor Mundi?*, pp. 38–9. On the significance of Frederick's reign, Martin followed Vincent of Beauvais.

[274] Dietrich praised Frederick II as, through his crusade and royal installation in Jerusalem, advancing the *honor imperii*. This was contrasted with the subsequent poor state of the *imperium*, which 'valde in eius statu, gloria et honor ac potencia diminutum est': Dietrich von Nieheim, *Viridarium*, ed. Lhotsky and Pivec, p. 3; and see Funder, *Reichsidee*, p. 215.

[275] 'Der was von Stoufen niht geborn' – though, the chronicler immediately adds, Rudolf was 'an manhait ûzerkorn': *Kaiserchronik: zweite (Schwäbische) Fortsetzung*, ed. Schröder, p. 413, vv. 176–81, 190–99. That Rudolf was indeed related to Germany's leading princely dynasties – and that the electors, if not others, were aware of this – is emphasised, against older scholarship, by Busch, 'Mathias', p. 221.

the late Hohenstaufen documentary style, while his *Landfrieden* drew heavily upon the model of Frederick II's Mainz peace of 1235.[276] In particular, Rudolf's government took pains in its official utterances to brand the kings who had come to the throne following Frederick's deposition as illegitimate, when it did not ignore them altogether.[277] Their acts and grants were null and void, as the throne had been 'vacant' since Frederick.[278]

The message was evidently quite widely received, and proved able to reinforce already established perceptions of the times as marked by weakness and misrule. We have already seen how bewildering contemporaries found the succession of post-Hohenstaufen kings.[279] Some went further. 'Down to King Rudolf the kingdom of the Romans had lain in confusion, without emperor and without king, for twenty-two years, as if given up to oblivion.'[280] Rudolf's reign inaugurated the reform, at least temporarily, of a realm 'which had long been vacillating'.[281] More than one commentator quoted the Book of Judges to the effect that 'in those days there was no king in Israel'.[282] Looking back on the period from the vantage point of the fourteenth century, Closener commentated that *daz rich* was at that time 'so infirm, that it had never before been so much derided'.[283] Schiller's 'kaiserlose, schreckliche Zeit' was first constructed in literate German memory in the period following its ending.

Where (beyond the natural progress of human wickedness) ought to lie the blame for the Empire's late medieval state was mostly addressed cautiously or, more often, not at all. The events surrounding Frederick II's life and downfall in particular appeared for a long time too confused,

---

[276] For chancery borrowings, see Ladner, 'Formularbehelfe', esp. pp. 191, 193; for Rudolf's *Landfrieden*, and their heavy dependence on the 1235 Mainz peace: Gerlich, *Landfriedenspolitik*, Angermeier, *Königtum*, pp. 53–78; Redlich, *Rudolf von Habsburg*, pp. 429–50.

[277] See generally *Die Regesten des Kaiserreiches unter Rudolf*, ed. Redlich, p. 9. As an example, see the ruling of the *curia* at Nuremberg in November 1274, allowing Rudolf to recover by force imperial properties 'que Fridericus quondam imperator, antequam lata esset in ipsum deposicionis sentencia, possedit et tenuit pacifice et quiete'.

[278] *Urkundenregesten*, ed. Diestelkamp and Rödel, no. 9, p. 7 (16 January 1274): Rudolf remits to the burghers of Bern all rights and privileges 'quas vacante imperio de reditibus, censibus vel obvencionibus imperii recipistis...'

[279] Ch. 3, p. 118.

[280] *Cronica S. Petri Erfordensis Moderna*, ed. Holder-Egger, p. 263.

[281] *Catalogi archiepiscoporum Coloniensium: Continuatio postrema*, ed. Cardauns, p. 357.

[282] *Iohannis abbatis Victoriensis Liber certarum historiarum*, ed. Schneider, p. 211 ('De statu regni in Alemannia corrupto'); *Cronica S. Petri Erfordensis Moderna*, ed. Holder-Egger, p. 263.

[283] *Fritsche (Friedrich) Closener's Chronik*, ed. Hegel, p. 150.

and too enmeshed in doctrinal standpoints both vehement and irreconcilable, to permit clear or far-reaching assessments.[284] The proper apportioning of blame among the protagonists in Ludwig the Bavarian's intractable struggle with the Avignon popes was likewise often unclear to those Germans who lived through it. With time, however, short- and longer-term patterns of events began to clarify sufficiently to allow some commentators to identify the villains on the world-historical stage.

Some located the historic source of present ills within the northern territories of the Reich. For the Rhinelander Alexander von Roes, it was the period of Hohenstaufen domination that had brought the fatal turning. Those emperors neglected the counsel of the princes, preferring instead to rule through 'Swabians, Bavarians, and Upper-Germans' (*ulteriores Alamanni*). 'In this way, under Swabian domination [*sub Suevorum imperio*], imperial power and authority ceased to grow, and began sharply to decline.'[285] Others attached varying degrees of opprobrium to those who followed the Staufer on the throne.[286] None equalled in virulence Dietrich von Niem's denunciations of the Empire's diminution at the hands of the Luxemburg *reguli* Charles IV and Wenceslas.[287] Some pointed accusing fingers at the German princes, with whom lay the choice of ruler – 'stupid' men, for the Hamburg annalist, in greedily taking Richard of Cornwall's foreign gold. The venality and short-sightedness of the German princes was a theme among vernacular versifiers in the immediate post-Staufer era.[288] Alexander von Roes, who could look back on the Interregnum from the 1280s, began his longest treatise by wishing upon the Germans, embodied in the electors, that 'wisdom' and sense of historic responsibility which he clearly felt they lacked. It was usurpations by the princes which, for Dietrich von Niem, had 'within [the last] two hundred years' reduced the monarch to a mere 'cipher or bean-king' among his subjects.[289]

---

[284] As examples, see Sommerlechner, *Stupor Mundi?*, pp. 107–11.

[285] Alexander von Roes, *Memoriale*, cap. 29, ed. Grundmann and Heimpel, pp. 134–5.

[286] Thus, e.g., Mathias von Neuenburg qualified his generally positive picture of Rudolf I's reign by noting that Rudolf's concessions of imperial territory in Italy to the papacy were 'to the Empire's grave harm': *Die Chronik des Mathias von Neuenburg*, ed. Hofmeister, p. 37.

[287] Heimpel, *Dietrich*, p. 66. It was *propter negligenciam imperatorum* that the *imperium* was diminished: Dietrich von Nieheim, *Cronica*, in *Dietrich von Nieheim: Historie de Gestis*, ed. Colberg and Leuschner, p. 251.

[288] Thus, e.g., on the *girikeit* of the German elite, Meißner in *Politische Lyrik*, ed. Müller, vol. I, p. 68.

[289] Dietrich von Nieheim, *Cronica*, in *Dietrich von Nieheim: Historie de Gestis*, ed. Colberg and Leuschner, pp. 251–2.

Longer historical perspectives tended to disclose the root of the evil as lying beyond the Germans' frontiers, among their ancient counterparts and competitors. The idea that the French were laying hold of the Carolingian inheritance (of which, it was widely acknowledged, they were indeed entitled to some share) in unwarranted and subversive ways is one we have encountered already. French machinations towards the Reich went back a long way. 'After the German princes gained the [imperial] election, the kings of France (and other kings) greatly hated it', explained the *Saxon World Chronicle*. As a result, 'they liked to undermine the Empire'.[290] It was a jealousy with clear historical roots, in the contested legacy of Carolingian *translatio imperii*, and one which might find material outlet. According to an entry dated 1379 in the Magdeburg *Schöppenchronik*, 'the king of France wanted to return the Roman Empire to the French crown, as it was in former times'.[291] The idea of a historic French plot against the German hold on the Reich was widely disseminated in political society.[292] Three addresses issued by King Rupert in 1409, to the princes, nobles and towns, explained how the French had long been working, with money and great cunning, to bring the Empire into their own hands, as well as annexing imperial properties in various regions.[293] The underlying vision did not have to reach back all the way to the Carolingians. Rupert, as Rhenish count palatine, had had a memorandum drawn up in 1397, warning King Wenceslas not to attend a projected meeting with King Charles VI at Rheims. For it was to be feared that the French 'seek in one way or another to supplant you; and this is nothing new, for since the time of your great-grandfather, the emperor Henry [VII], they have always sought to draw the Empire to themselves.'[294] The danger was especially great because the French had not always acted alone. At the start of the Schism, Rupert went on fantastically to allege, the cardinals had thought of making Charles V of France pope, 'and then, as pope, he would have been able to make his son emperor and transfer the Empire from Germany [*Alemannia*] to France'.

That the papacy had historically been guilty of anti-German bias, and that it had periodically been co-opted to serve specific interests, notably those of the French nation, are views we have encountered already. Belief in the papacy's ideal universality, like that of the Empire

---

[290] *Sächsische Weltchronik*, ed. Weiland, p. 150.
[291] *Magdeburger Schöppenchronik*, ed. Janicke, p. 279. The king is therefore portrayed as turning to the Avignon pope, Clement VII.
[292] For rumours, see also Roscheck, 'Französische Kandidaturen', pp. 193–208; for actual candidatures, above, Ch. 5, p. 214.
[293] *RTA* 6, no. 280, p. 468.   [294] *RTA* 3, no. 23, p. 55.

itself, remained strong, providing a foundation for the enduring conviction that the spiritual and temporal heads of the world should work together as partners. However, the long period of French domination of the Curia in the late thirteenth and fourteenth centuries had encouraged some Germans to detect a persistent ethnic partisanship and underlying hostile intent.[295] Individual pontiffs were accused of deliberately fomenting strife in Germany, as Ludwig IV charged John XXII with doing. To argue, however, that the popes had acted *consistently* to undermine the Empire was a step further, and one which, despite a recurrent pattern of conflict, few German commentators yet wished to take. The idea doubtless had some currency outside learned circles, especially in times of tension. When the Lübeck chronicler Detmar alleges that the pope schemed for Henry VII's deposition 'because he worked for the Empire's advancement', he is implying a form of papal ill-will deeper rooted and more implacable than any mere product of particular tensions.[296] Konrad von Megenberg reassured Charles IV that the Church had no intention of damaging the Empire, whatever *tota Germania* might say.[297] The *Saxon World Chronicle*, as we saw, traced the Empire's woes back to 'Hildebrant'. But it was Dietrich von Niem, who knew the Curia from the inside, who came closest to making of the papacy a long-term agent of imperial decline. The popes, he argued, had undermined the Empire's rulers through the oaths with which they bound them on accession.[298] Undue alienations of imperial property to the Church had also, down the centuries, from the days of Henry V to those of Frederick II, Konradin and Ludwig the Bavarian, been a recurrent source of conflicts, as rulers strove to get back what was rightfully theirs.[299] Full histories of alleged Roman tyranny and false dealings with the Germans and their monarchs would only come with the age of humanism.[300] Yet the modes of historical argument which the humanists were to deploy, and the fund of resentments upon

---

[295] See above, Ch. 6, pp. 266–7.

[296] *Detmar-Chronik*, ed. Koppmann, i.420. The context is an account of Henry's Italian expedition.

[297] Konrad von Megenberg, *De translacione Romani imperii*, cap. 14, ed. Scholz, p. 301. Konrad was here defending the principle of papal approbation against the contention of Lupold von Bebenburg, that the delays which this entailed could prove dangerous: Charles IV himself, Konrad points out, had been quickly approved.

[298] These, as Dietrich argued, conflicted with the monarch's coronation oath, to conserve the properties entrusted to him: Funder, *Reichsidee*, pp. 219–20; Heimpel, *Dietrich*, p. 165.

[299] Dietrich von Nieheim, *Viridarium*, ed. Lhotsky and Pivec, p. 49.

[300] For these, see generally Stadtwald, *Roman Popes*.

which they drew, had already begun to take shape by the start of the fifteenth century.

The argument, widely encountered in modern scholarship, that any sense of a 'national' past among late medieval Germans must have been, in comparison to their western-European neighbours, weak and impoverished, draws attention to some important distinctions between Germany and other parts of Europe. In Germany, other common identities, grounded in the construction of other, often older, shared histories, had particular importance.[301] The common past which united the German territories of the Empire was, necessarily, an imperial past, which, in space and time, seemed to extend far beyond anything that might be called 'German' history. The elements of a discrete and continuous national tradition, such as we find elsewhere – continuity of dynasty, national saints, a well-defined historical homeland – are all, by contrast, less in evidence in Germany.[302] Some of these differences – and thus, limitations upon any sense of a unifying 'German' past – are without question real enough. Literate Germans were not able to construct a common mythic origin which convincingly transcended the separate origin legends of the more ancient component peoples of the German lands – though it is revealing that some nevertheless tried to do so. The history of the western *imperium* was, axiomatically, a Roman, not (or not simply) a German, history.

The problem, however, is also one of perception. Modern scholars, like the German humanists long before, have found what they set out to find, and have constructed models well adapted to helping them find it. Like the humanists, their arguments possess a circular quality, resting upon a belief in the power of national myths and histories to forge common political bonds. Where such bonds appear weak – as they do in late medieval Germany – so, too, it is assumed, must necessarily have been any empowering sense of a common past. A survey of the development of accounts of German history in the post-Staufer period underlines the shortcomings of such circular reasoning. All the signs are that conceptions of 'the Germans' as a community of political actors with a shared history were in fact gaining in strength in the time of the Empire's crisis and weakness, and partly *on account of* that weakness. By the fourteenth and fifteenth centuries, the visions of German history being unfolded by the most self-consciously political writers were replete with larger-than-life national heroes, false turnings and collective stabs-in-the-

---

[301] See below, Ch. 11, pp. 516–17.

[302] The absence in Germany of a historical relationship with a clearly defined territory is emphasised by Graus, *Lebendige Vergangenheit*, pp. 141–2. For more on this, see below, Ch. 10, pp. 452–69.

back – to the extent that they sometimes seem startlingly to foreshadow the nationalist narratives of a much later age.

On closer examination, some of the purported elements of German difference emerge as rather less distinctive (or less debilitatingly so) than is often claimed. Caesar and Charlemagne, as formative figures for a German identity, have more in common with the mythic founders and nation-makers encountered elsewhere in medieval Europe than some have allowed. Diffuseness, multiplicity of voices, even regionalism and localism, did not in every case inhibit the development of notions of a larger common past – and were capable of furnishing resources and stimuli of their own for perceiving such a past. Different forms of political life might nurture comparable modes of thought. If the Germans were not, in quite the sense that the French were, a chosen people under a holy race of kings, their literate champions were able to discern other sources of divine favour: most prominently, the grant of the Roman Empire itself. Explaining and justifying that uniquely illustrious form of common election meant, for late medieval writers, the close construction of a German national character – and of the supposed qualities of the Germans' neighbours and rivals.

8 Rome's barbarians: accounting for the Germans

Thinking with monsters

By the end of the Middle Ages, western Europeans felt sure that they knew the Germans. Medieval churchmen and scholars, who through their writings had taken the main part in constructing the Germans as a people, thereby taught themselves, and taught others, by what signs they might recognise them. Germans stood out. The Venetian painter Veronese was to be summoned before the Inquisition to answer for allegedly populating a painting of the Last Supper with 'buffoons, drunkards, Germans, dwarfs, and similar vulgarities'.[1] By Veronese's time the habit among some of the Germans' southern and western neighbours, of representing them as gross and grotesque, and even as less than fully human, was already several centuries old. The image seems to have begun taking shape among western Europeans in the tenth and eleventh centuries, around the time when westerners first named the Germans as a distinct people, and it probably reflects the same factors which had rendered Germans visible to them as such.

The image had a number of recurrent elements. Germans were wild and furious. Addicted as they were to warfare, their mode of fighting was brutal, chaotic and predatory. Their domestic politics reflected the same turbulent and disorderly spirit: according to Pierre Dubois, every succession to the throne brought 'innumerable occasions for strife in Germany'.[2] They were a people of immoderate appetites, for food and particularly drink. 'The Germans can endure any hardship', went one late medieval aphorism: 'would that they could endure thirst.'[3] With gluttony and drunkenness went physical coarseness and disregard for

---

[1] Burke, *The Italian Renaissance*, p. 130.
[2] *De Recuperatione*, cap. 12, ed. Langlois, p. 12.
[3] Walther, 'Scherz', p. 274, no. 73; and for gluttony, see ibid., no. 77, and for ironic reference to 'German abstinence', p. 281, no. 134. For these images in Italian writings on the Germans, see Amelung, *Das Bild*, pp. 31–2.

personal appearance.[4] Pierre Roger, the future Pope Clement VI (and tutor to the youthful Charles IV), was said to have interpreted Ludwig IV's epithet 'the Bavarian' as meaning 'unable to wipe his beard clean'.[5] The same absence of moderation, refinement and due order character-ised their language, likened by westerners to the roaring of lions or a terrible thunder, but also to the barking of dogs, howling of wolves and croaking of frogs.[6] The Germans partook of the unbounded, elemental violence of nature itself, just as their native climate, in urbane west-ern caricature, was notoriously harsh. It was in this spirit that Petrarch imagined the clouds from the German north shedding an 'iron rain' of criminal soldiery upon his native Italy.[7] Germany lacked the amenities for fully civilised living, as the primitive social manners of its inhab-itants purportedly made plain. The German who aspired to move in the fashionable world of Francophone chivalry was a comical figure in French report, just as Italian humanists mocked the neglect of fine let-ters which they claimed to find in the north.[8] Not every element in the picture was black: there was much acknowledgement of the bravery, as well as the ferocity, of Germans under arms, while the wonder excited by their physical stature and strength has been observed already.[9] None of this, however, subtracted from the overall judgement that the Germans were a backward people – a *gente ritrosa*, as Petrarch put it.[10]

Such were the perspectives of some cultivated westerners. How did Germans themselves respond to these generally unflattering portray-als? What account did they give of themselves – and how did they locate themselves in relation to their purportedly more advanced neigh-bours? To answer these questions, it is first necessary to understand why the Germans had come to be depicted as they were. A part of the explanation lies in the fragmentation of the Frankish patrimony in the ninth and tenth centuries and in the geographical separation of the Empire's – east-Frankish and German – bearers from its ideological

---

[4] For French views of the Germans, see: Zimmermann, 'Die Beurteilung'; Remppis, *Die Vorstellungen*; and for further specific examples: Walther, 'Scherz', nos. 73, 74, 77, 134, pp. 274, 281; Black, 'An accidental tourist', pp. 182–5.

[5] *Die Chronik des Mathias von Neuenburg*, ed. Hofmeister, pp. 188–9.

[6] Thompson, *Feudal Germany*, vol. I, p. 372; Dümmler, 'Über den furor Teutonicus', p. 119; Chaytor, *From Script*, p. 24; Meyvaert, ' "Rainaldus" ', p. 754; Zimmermann, 'Die Beurteilung', pp. 281–2. Language was a fundamental measure of humanity (and its lack, an indicator of monstrosity): Friedman, *The Monstrous Races*, p. 29.

[7] *Vita Solitaria*, quoted in Amelung, *Das Bild*, p. 42.

[8] For French mockery of German chivalry, see Thomas, 'Nationale Elemente', p. 367; for Petrarch on the state of German letters, Amelung, *Das Bild*, pp. 39–40.

[9] Ch. 7, p. 295 (*robusti*); and see the examples in: Thompson, *Feudal Germany*, vol. I, pp. 369–70; Zimmermann, 'Die Beurteilung', pp. 235–6.

[10] Amelung, *Das Bild*, pp. 40–1.

heart and material resource-base in Italy. These circumstances had made of the Germans' west-Frankish neighbours long-standing rivals, with an imperial claim of their own, and they made of the populations of Italy recurrent victims for the bands of armed men heading over the Alps in the emperor's service. Imperial military expeditions came south most frequently and in greatest force between the tenth and the thirteenth centuries, during which time the caricature of the brutal and uncouth German became entrenched.[11] When the abbot of Siegburg came to Rome in 1181, seeking the canonisation of Archbishop Anno of Cologne, a cardinal reportedly wondered aloud at the idea that a land so fertile in armed men might also produce saints.[12] From the eleventh century, there was a further element, in the recurrent conflicts of principle and interest between the Empire's rulers and the reformed papacy, which polarised opinion across Latin Europe and which were fought out in the south by military means.[13] It was in the time of Barbarossa's clash with Alexander III that John of Salisbury hurled his famous rhetorical barbs at the universal pretensions of the Germans – 'this brutish and unruly people'.[14] Even when the power of the imperial monarchy receded, after the mid-thirteenth century, a strong German military presence in Italy remained, in the form of the mercenary companies, employed by the consolidating regional powers of the peninsula, but widely unpopular. Germans, as it seemed, were men of blood, whose violent deeds served causes of questionable legitimacy.

What else were they? In an increasingly complex Latin Europe after the Millennium, a reputation for indomitable martial prowess no longer seemed a sufficient title to rule. Indeed, except when combined with other desirable social and cultural attainments, it was starting to sound like a reproach. The remark, in a Dublin parliamentary statute of 1297, that the Irish are a people who 'rush instantly to war', was not intended as a compliment.[15] The expanded geographical horizons of some Europeans, greater mobility and a quickening pace of communications both within Europe and beyond, nourished perceptions of difference – including difference between peoples.[16] The strengthening of spiritual and secular authorities, with their sharpened concepts of

---

[11] For imperial armies in the south in this period, see Schneidmüller, *Die Kaiser*, Chs. 5–7; for the identity-forming role of imperial expeditions, Thomas, 'Das Identitätsproblem', pp. 138–9.

[12] Schmugge, 'Über "nationale" Vorurteile', p. 458.

[13] For representations of the Germans by the Gregorian party, see Thompson, *Feudal Germany*, vol. I, p. 374.

[14] For John's words, see above, Ch. 5, p. 209 n. 26.

[15] Quoted in Lydon, 'Nation and race', p. 104.

[16] Larner, *Marco Polo*, Ch. 1; Jackson, 'Christians'.

distinction and more advanced instruments for their enforcement, in the same period lent to certain boundaries a new compulsive force.[17] The language of collective stereotype now attains heightened visibility and urgency in the sources, at a time when members of different political and cultural communities were coming together in more regular proximity and rivalry – on crusade or pilgrimage, for example, at the schools, in the growing towns or at multi-national princely courts.[18]

The high medieval vocabulary of inter-ethnic caricature, boasting and denigration also constituted an eloquent and flexible *political* vocabulary, suitable for underpinning arguments and staking claims. So pervasive did clichés of national character become that by the thirteenth century much of the European political order was capable of description in terms of the purported – complementary, contrasting or competing – collective attributes of its component peoples under their various rulers.[19] Indeed, before the century's end Alexander von Roes was able to confect an entire model for universal Christian government, founded on the premise that different peoples have different capabilities and defects.[20] In a time of bitter anti-Roman invective, and then of French-speaking popes, even the see of St Peter became conceivable as an aggregate of the supposed national virtues and (particularly) shortcomings of its occupants. The trade in ethnic stereotypes was further quickened by a shifting balance of power in western Europe. Military triumphs against imperial forces at Bouvines (1214) and Tagliacozzo (1268) helped affirm the clear ascent of the French to become the foremost continental power. The wars of the later Middle Ages, meanwhile, saw the competition of European realms translated into rival, tendentious accounts of collective character, deployed with the object of legitimising territorial claims and blackening the names and undermining the titles of others.[21] Enemies were now made monstrous and

---

[17] Moore, *The Formation*; Richards, *Sex*; Boswell, *Christianity*, esp. Ch. 10.

[18] For the role of increased mobility in the formation of stereotypes, see Schmugge, 'Über "nationale" Vorurteile'; for a theoretical approach to stereotyping, Gilman, *Difference*.

[19] See, e.g., Frederick II's encyclical letter of 1241 to the rulers of Latin Christendom regarding the Mongol threat, invoking Germany, 'fervent in arms'; France, 'the mother and nurse of chivalry'; Spain, 'warlike and bold'; 'active' Wales; 'bloodstained' Ireland; and so on: *Matthaei Parisiensis, Chronica Majora*, ed. Luard, pp. 112–19 (here p. 118).

[20] For an explicit enunciation of this principle, see Alexander von Roes, *Noticia seculi*, cap. 16, ed. Grundmann and Heimpel, p. 162: 'Whoever wanted to govern the Italians in the same way as the Germans and the French are to be governed, and vice versa ... would without doubt be perverting the right order of governance.'

[21] Allmand, *Hundred Years War*, Ch. 6; Menache, 'Symbols'.

ascribed monstrous intentions.[22] Fundamentally dynastic contests were rewritten as inter-ethnic struggles for survival.

The rhetorical construction of French pre-eminence within Latin Europe is especially noteworthy, as it reveals how culture and learning were being linked to military power to define an ideal people. It highlights the importance of the high medieval revolution in scholarship, with its new institutional settings, as a stimulus to the more intensive application of collective stereotypes.[23] Modes of perception and standards of judgement were changing: reason was becoming an attribute of power in its own right – and an indispensable one.[24] The idea became established in the thirteenth century that higher learning itself – the *studium* – had been 'translated' by Charlemagne, just as the Empire passed to the Germans, to Paris and the French.[25] In 1229 Pope Gregory IX had declared that the chivalric and military qualities in which the French excelled were only beneficial because they were wedded to learning.[26] The contemporary prestige of French knighthood rested as much upon its fashionable style and cultural trappings – language, and a courtly literature much imitated in Germany – as on French feats of arms, impressive though these seemed. And in an age of crusader kings, it was plain, to their own literate champions at least, that French military successes were won for the benefit of Church and Christendom. According to the Saint-Denis chronicler Guillaume de Nangis, the two outer leaves of the fleur-de-lys stood for Learning and Knighthood, which protected the central leaf, representing Faith.[27]

The new learning provided fresh stimulus to the rhetorical contest of national character, by directing the attention of literate Europeans to the Graeco-Roman tradition of ethnographic writing and to the ancient scientific ideas with which it was linked.[28] It was these that enabled Pierre Dubois to argue that the disposition of the heavenly bodies ensured that men conceived and born in the Paris region were 'better constituted, appointed and endowed than those of any other district'.[29]

---

[22] For enemies as monsters, see Scales, 'Central and late medieval Europe', pp. 287–96.

[23] For an example, see Bartlett, *Gerald*, p. 3.

[24] Murray, *Reason*, esp. Ch. 5.

[25] During the late Middle Ages the idea entered German vernacular historiography. Thus, the late fourteenth-century *Österreichische Chronik von den 95. Herrschaften* (ed. Seemüller, p. 26) tells how 'der chünig [Charles] pracht die grozz schuol von Röm gen Paris'.

[26] For this theme, see Grundmann, 'Sacerdotium', p. 17.

[27] Ibid., pp. 14–15.

[28] Friedman, *The Monstrous Races*, esp. Ch. 1; Bartlett, *Gerald*, Part III.

[29] *De Recuperatione*, cap. 139, ed. Langlois, pp. 128–9.

French domination of Christendom was written in the stars.[30] Italians were by the late Middle Ages beginning to voice claims of their own to cultural pre-eminence, founded upon a uniquely rich inheritance from antiquity.[31] And against those fortunate peoples, favoured as the French were by nature or the Italians by history, enjoying advanced cultures, and presenting a vision of perfected humanity, was now opposed the barbarian, devoid of such blessings and barely human at all.[32] The Welsh, declared one English chronicler, were 'men of an animal type'.[33] The classical revival of the twelfth century had helped to transpose the barbarian – previously, characteristically a pagan – from beyond the Christian frontier, deep into Latin Europe itself.

The barbarian was not urbane (or urban) and he was not reasonable. He was moved, as Albertus Magnus explained, 'by unreasoning fury, lust, and self-delusion'. The barbarian was he 'whom neither law, nor civility, nor discipline disposes to reason'.[34] Such a one could not be left to rule himself, still less be permitted to rule over others. Constructions of the barbarian thus became, from the twelfth century onward, a favoured strategy among apologists for those militant European regimes which were engaged in bringing neighbouring peoples into subjection.[35] The Other was named and described in order to justify its expropriation and colonisation.[36] Yet the charge of barbarism could not be levelled arbitrarily. Like other elements in the classical ethnographic canon, including those constituting the idea of 'civilisation', it was no empty tag, but a literary artefact bearing the authority of antiquity. As such, it could be applied with conviction only to groups which might plausibly be said to display the appropriate common qualities and modes of life. Literate medieval people constructed their own

---

[30] For the medieval application of astral and other ancient scientific theories of national character, see Strickland, *Saracens*, Ch. 1.

[31] For the growth of Italian awareness of the antique heritage, see Weiss, *The Renaissance*, esp. Chs. 2–4.

[32] See generally, Jones, 'The image of the barbarian'; and for the proliferation of barbarian stereotypes in writings in Europe in the high Middle Ages, Meyvaert, '"Rainaldus"'.

[33] *Gesta Stephani*, cited in Gillingham, 'The context and purposes', p. 106.

[34] Both citations in Jones, 'The image of the barbarian', p. 398. For unreason as the essence of barbarism, see Murray, *Reason*, p. 256.

[35] For the role of stereotyping in this process, see Bartlett, *Making of Europe*, Ch. 4; for the reputed incapacity of peoples in colonial regions for self-government: Bartlett, *Gerald*, pp. 162–3; Gillingham, 'English imperialism', p. 392. This is a perspective which historians of twelfth-century Britain have found particularly compelling.

[36] Said, *Orientalism*, esp. pp. 1–28. For 'the Other', see McDonald, 'The construction of difference', pp. 231–2.

common identities, and those of their adversaries and victims; but they did not do so wholly on terms of their own choosing.

The image of the Germans confected by their southern and western neighbours was a barbarian image. For a people like the Germans, who collectively laid claim to the legacy of ancient Rome and to the grandest titles of monarchy, such an image was to say the least problematic; yet the ability of Germans to counter it with more positive self-representations was constrained, as ancient authority bound their hands. 'The customs of the northern peoples are wolfish', cautioned Albertus Magnus, himself a German, following antique science.[37] Still more troublingly, for some Germans, the evidence of their own eyes and ears appeared to prove ancient authority right. Even to the seasoned observer, the old caricatures seemed to fit. 'There are many peoples in Germany' (Germaniae nationes), explained the Franciscan Bartholomaeus Anglicus, who taught at Magdeburg in the 1230s, 'with huge bodies, strong in their powers, bold in spirit and fierce, unconquered, [and] absorbed in plunder, predations and hunting.'[38] Those Germans who travelled beyond the western and southern frontiers of their lands might be made uncomfortably aware of the damaging implications of their people's reputation for primitiveness. There were those, lamented Alexander von Roes, who invoked the Germans' disorderly dress, as well as their behaviour, to call into question their title to the Empire itself.[39]

The 'German' national character which, by drawing on the testimony of antiquity, their cultivated neighbours delineated, proved in many respects irresistible even within the German lands. The Germans – their common identity constructed, in this respect as in others, from without – became their own Other.[40] If monsters were, as Peter Burke has remarked of early modern Europe, 'good to think with', late medieval Germans summoned them on occasion for assistance in thinking about themselves.[41] Monstrous beings – giants, dwarfs, hags, wild

---

[37] Friedman, The Monstrous Races, p. 53.

[38] Schönbach, 'Bartholomaeus Anglicus', p. 69; his choice of word for the Germans' physical size – immania – follows Isidore, and has connotations of the monstrous and barbarous: cf. Etymologiarum sive Originum libri XX, ed. Lindsay, I.9.2.97. For Bartholomaeus himself, see C. Hünemörder and M. Mückshoff, 'B. Anglicus', in LMA 1, col. 1492.

[39] Alexander von Roes, Memoriale, cap. 14, ed. Grundmann and Heimpel, p. 104: '... cum se ipsos neque in ornatu vestium neque in morum compositione regere sciant...' Coarse clothing, or lack of clothing, it might be noted, was a recurrent attribute of 'monstrous' peoples: Friedman, Monstrous Races, p. 31.

[40] For the idea of medieval people having an inner Other (though expressed here in terms of demonic possession, not barbarism), see Classen, 'Introduction', p. xvi.

[41] Burke, 'Frontiers', p. 37.

men – crowd the literary and visual imagination of medieval Germans in bewildering profusion.[42] Their presence was at times inescapably political. We have encountered (perhaps self-consciously German) wild men already, and we have seen how giants, and mighty giant women, were sometimes imagined as founding ancestors of the Germans themselves.[43] The Trojans who came to Britain had, just like the ancient Israelites, famously expelled or destroyed the indigenous ogres whom they encountered in their new homeland; Priam's settlers by the Rhine married theirs, and thereby perpetuated something of their outsized capacities in future generations.[44] Whereas other lands had long since dealt with their monstrous infestations, disorderly and hybrid beings were able, in fourteenth-century Germany, to infiltrate the political symbolism of the monarchy itself. Elaborately helmeted wild men bearing the arms of the Reich and Bohemia clamber at the foliated margins of King Wenceslas's psalter. They even insinuate themselves into his *de luxe* copy of that most solemn of his father's public acts, the Golden Bull, where one provides hairy companionship for the king, as he peeks from behind his monogram.[45]

This chapter is the first of two which concentrate upon the relationship between German identity and the Other. It seeks to show how Germans reconciled their people's claim to the political inheritance of Rome with constructions of their own collective character which seemed to make of them thoroughgoing anti-Romans and (by history and temperament) to debar them from that inheritance. It will also be necessary to explain why accounts of the purported common qualities of the Germans became more numerous and extended in German writings during periods of crisis for the imperial monarchy, from the thirteenth century onward.

That late medieval German identity was relational is a premise underlying the present book throughout; but it finds particular application and support in the current chapter and the next. It was through encountering the Other that Germans learned to know themselves – *as* Germans.[46] And a developing sense of common selfhood in its turn

---

[42] Examples in Bernheimer, *Wild Men*, esp. Ch. 2.
[43] Ch. 7, pp. 295–6.
[44] For Trojan colonisation and the destruction of monsters in Britain, see Cohen, *Of Giants*, pp. 32–7.
[45] Boehm and Fajt (eds.), *Prague*, p. 225 (and cf. p. 223: Wenceslas Bible); Legner (ed.), *Die Parler*, vol. III, p. 104.
[46] For the Other and medieval identity-formation, see Classen, 'Introduction', p. xi: 'Without the foreign there would be no familiar, and vice versa, as the confrontation of the self with the non-self constitutes identity by way of negotiation and interaction'; also Scior, *Das Eigene*, esp. 'Einleitung'.

supplied a foundation for judging and classifying outsiders. These points are easily demonstrated. Without exception, the late medieval writers who offered the fullest and the most impassioned accounts of German identity wrote in close proximity to the non-German Other. Either, like the Strasbourg chroniclers, for example, they lived and worked in an ethno-cultural frontier zone or they had been exposed to identity-forming encounters and insights beyond the frontier.[47] As we have observed already, the most opinionated tended also to be the best travelled.[48]

Each of the frontiers of the German lands, and of the plethora of ethnic and political groups dwelling beyond them, made some contribution to conceptions of Germanness. However, the content and perceived meaning of the 'cultural differences' that were thus communicated varied between different frontier regions. To the west and south lived peoples with whom some believed the Germans themselves to be related through blood as well as history. These were peoples which could make cogent claims of their own on the Roman imperial legacy, and whose advanced cultures challenged the Germans' sense of identity, inviting a response (as the current chapter will show). The peoples dwelling to the north and east, by contrast, had historically related to the Germans and their rulers primarily as the subjects of conquest or dominion (actual or claimed), or had no close relationship with them at all. Literate Germans conceived of these peoples via a quite different set of categories from those which they associated with their neighbours in the west and south (as the next chapter will show). Bonds, whether of kinship or historic rivalry, seemed less great.

However, the process of 'continuing dichotomisation between members and outsiders' crucial to identity-formation did not take place only in encounters with human groups and individuals, but also with texts and textual traditions.[49] Germans, we might say, came to understand themselves as such not only because Italians, Frenchmen, Czechs or Poles told them they were German, and explained to them what it meant, but because Aristotle, Caesar and Isidore, and numerous other venerable authorities, told them. Those same authorities also helped them ascribe identities to their neighbours. In the present chapter, therefore, the emphasis is upon engagement with a textual tradition, in

---

[47] The role of bruising contacts with non-Germans in sharpening Alexander von Roes's sense of political identity is underlined by the fear which he expresses that his patriotic account will provoke *derisio Gallicorum*: Alexander von Roes, *Noticia seculi*, cap. 18, ed. Grundmann and Heimpel, p. 165.

[48] Above, Ch. 5, pp. 254–9.

[49] The phrase is that of Barth, 'Introduction', p. 14.

light of which contemporary developments were understood. The next chapter will be concerned with a more diverse range of encounters.

In concentrating upon the textual construction of identity and alterity, treated here as inseparable processes, I pay considerable attention to a category of evidence which modern studies in the field have mostly ignored or consciously rejected: literary *topoi* of selfhood and difference. German scholars in particular have, since the late twentieth century, been at pains to argue against any attempt at drawing significant conclusions from ethnic stereotypes and caricatures.[50] Here, alongside a general distaste for what can appear as mere clichéd outbursts of ethnocentric boasting and denigration, more specific considerations are discernible. Trawling the medieval sources for supposed expressions of racial self-assertion was a prominent element in the *Volksgeschichte* of the 1930s, geared to the objectives of Nazi ethnography and reflecting its social-Darwinist world view. This goes far to explain why German medievalists after 1945, and more markedly since the 1960s, tended to concentrate instead upon internal factors in their accounts of early nation-making.[51]

Yet, as social anthropologists in particular have emphasised, collective identities do not self-generate: a people entirely isolated from other peoples would possess no consciousness of its own common being.[52] There are also, however, a number of other reasons to take seriously *topoi* of identity and alterity, relating to their role within textual traditions. As found in medieval writings, stereotypical accounts of the qualities of different peoples should not be read merely as crude expressions of unthinking prejudice (though they were no doubt capable of becoming that too and, particularly in verbal exchanges, must often have done so). Instead, they represented to literate people accounts of the nature of human society resting upon the authority of ancient

---

[50] Thus Ehlers, 'Nation und Geschichte', p. 208; Ehlers, 'Die deutsche Nation', pp. 24–5. For a sophisticated restatement of the case, see Jostkleigrewe, *Das Bild*, pp. 391–8 (acknowledging, however, that his picture of mutual cross-border respect and fair judgement fits the French better than the German evidence). An important German exception is Schmugge, 'Über "nationale" Vorurteile'. Some late twentieth-century French medievalists, whose approach to nation-making closely resembled that of their German counterparts, likewise dismissed the relevance of stereotyping. Colette Beaune thus omitted French attitudes to neighbours from her study of late medieval French nationhood as 'not integral to the subject in hand': Beaune, *The Birth*, p. 6.

[51] See above, Ch. 1, pp. 28–30. As Norbert Elias has observed in the context of contemporary debates, 'the hypersensitivity towards anything that recalls National Socialist doctrine results in the problem of a "national character" being largely shrouded in silence': Elias, *The Germans*, p. 2.

[52] Thus Eriksen, *Ethnicity*, p. 34.

ethnography: their deployment was a sign not of a writer's ignorance, but of his learning. As such, they functioned as elements in coherent world views. They were not adopted at random: particular peoples were recurrently (though not invariably) endowed with broadly the same sets of attributes – usually those which ancient authority seemed to prescribe.[53] Ethnic stereotypes, moreover, were no aberration, but were inseparable from other elements in medieval constructions of identity, such as accounts of common pasts. For the Empire's German champions, therefore, Germans had always fought boldly in defence of the Church and the Roman Empire, as countless historical instances showed: it was in their character to do so. These qualities helped to render such *topoi* peculiarly suitable for underpinning titles and claims and rebuffing the claims of others. The painted monsters of medieval ethnic stereotype were good not only to think about but to argue with.

It is not enough, however, only to examine the textual construction of medieval peoples. A common weakness in medievalists' approaches to the subject lies in their tendency to concentrate solely upon demonstrating through textual analysis the currency of the nation as idea in the Middle Ages, without considering that idea's application and reception, or exploring the social effects of medieval ethnic thought.[54] The present study aims to transcend these limitations. The current chapter thus examines constructions of the Germans and their neighbours as dynamic elements in political controversy, while the next considers the role of German ethnicity within multi-ethnic societies as a basis for social action. In so doing, it will be necessary to attempt, so far as the available evidence permits, to gauge the temperature of late medieval invocations of ideas of German peoplehood: to ask not only what they meant to people, but how much.[55]

Men destined for war

In many ways, the Germans' well-established reputation as born warriors is only to be expected.[56] Indeed, it is hard to imagine how they could have laid convincing claim to the Roman Empire without it. Excellence in arms was what the imperial title pre-eminently demanded of its

---

[53] The Germans, who were ascribed rather different characteristics by respectively their western and southern and their eastern neighbours (although there was consistency between different writers within each group), provide an example of their capacity for variation. For the eastern accounts, see below, Ch. 9, pp. 410–12.

[54] Tracing their influence through to action is generally very difficult from the evidence surviving from pre-modern Europe: Ranum, 'Introduction', p. 12.

[55] For the nation as sentiment, see Smith, *National Identity*, Ch. 4.

[56] On this, see generally Scales, '*Germen militiae*'.

bearers. That had been the greatest claim of the Romans themselves, who in medieval memory were above all matchless soldiers. The duties of Christian Roman monarchy, as these came to be elucidated in political theology and canon law, were by general agreement of a strongly military character. The Empire's ruler bore the secular sword.[57] Prayers for the monarch besought his triumph over the pagans, while the imperial coronation liturgies referred to his duty to extend by successful war the limits of the Christian community.[58] And precisely that was what the greatest emperors – the greatest *German* emperors – of times past were remembered for having done. 'Once no one could protect me, I know it, nor did they wish to; but *Germania* illustriously saved me, with great effort and, indeed, with blood', Konrad von Megenberg's personified Church tells an unsympathetic Pope.[59] We have already surveyed the tale of high medieval military triumphs, won as it was claimed for the sake of the Christian commonwealth. It was therefore only natural that the electors emphasised the martial prowess of their chosen candidate, while sympathetic chroniclers affirmed his outstanding *manhait*.[60]

The monarch's own manly vigour was that of his people. The doctrine of the Empire's translation ensured that questions about the suitability of its bearers would necessarily be answered in ethnic terms. Although *Venerabilem* was silent as to why specifically the Germans had been granted this honour, the bull's interpreters were more forthcoming. All were to acknowledge, as the German canonist Johannes Teutonicus urged, 'that the Teutons by their virtues have won the Empire'.[61] The nature of those virtues was never in doubt. Sacred violence, in late medieval memory, had forged the German people. It was in recognition of service done to the monarch in arms that, for Alexander von Roes, the Saxons and Brandenburgers, with their princes, were drawn within an expanding German political community.[62]

At the same time as Germanising them, memories of the armed service rendered to emperors past gave occasion for commemorating, and

[57] For 'two-swords' doctrine, see above, Ch. 5, pp. 212–13; for its application in the imperial chancery, *Acta*, ed. Winkelmann, vol. II, nos. 85, 193, pp. 76–7, 140–1.
[58] See Ch. 5, p. 222.
[59] Konrad von Megenberg, *Planctus*, ed. Scholz, pars I, cap. 8, p. 29.
[60] For the electors, see Ch. 5, p. 222. The petition to Pope Clement V seeking recognition of Henry VII cited his proven ability to pacify even the Germans (*Theutunici*): *MGC* 4.i, no. 294, p. 256 (26 July 1309). For Rudolf I's *manhait, Kaiserchronik: zweite (Schwäbische) Fortsetzung*, ed. Schröder, p. 413, vv. 194–200. Other chroniclers likewise emphasised the new king's military capabilities: thus, for the Königsaal chronicler, the electors chose in Rudolf a 'virum utique bellicosum et strenuum': *Königsaaler Geschichts-Quellen*, ed. Loserth, p. 47.
[61] Post, *Studies*, p. 488. For *Venerabilem*, see above, Ch. 6, pp. 282–3.
[62] See above, Ch. 6, pp. 277–8.

distinguishing with privileges, the special warlike achievements of individual component peoples. The much-repeated legend of the ancient Germans' military aid to Caesar had exactly this dual effect. The ubiquitous etymology of 'Franks' as 'free' (from tribute) on account of that people's armed support for Valentinian – reproduced even in a fourteenth-century Magdeburg town chronicle – offered a template for subsequent award-winning feats of arms, serving other emperors.[63] Vernacular law codes, the *Schwabenspiegel* and near-contemporary *Deutschenspiegel*, record the singular benefits which the Swabians enjoyed in recognition of the valiant aid which their duke, Gerolt, rendered Charlemagne before Rome: time does not run against them in legal matters; and they are to have the front rank in the Empire's military campaigns.[64] This second, specifically martial, honour seems to have been widely remembered.[65] Chroniclers record how, after the duke of Austria refused a request from Johann Windloch, bishop of Constance, that the Swabians should fight in the van under the bishop's banner on the duke's 1354 expedition against Zurich, the bishop led his troops away. 'For the Swabian people [*gens Swevorum*] earned by their vigour and merit, from the time of Charlemagne and other rulers, the right to be in the van.'[66] War in the Empire's name made the Germans one, but it did so by celebrating the proud, distinct histories of the pre-German *gentes*. These too were of a belligerent kind.

It was not without reason that the arms-bearing stratum in German society, the nobility, was singled out as the beneficiaries of the Empire's translation. In their martial virtues they stood for the German people as a whole. Germans, like aristocrats, were born to arms: they were a 'warrior race' (*germen milicie*), punned Konrad von Megenberg.[67] It was not only imperialist polemicists who thought in this way. For the military engineer Konrad Kyeser, a natural aptitude for war was what set Germans apart from other peoples:

[63] *Magdeburger Schöppenchronik*, ed. Janicke, p. 10.
[64] *Schwabenspiegel*, ed. Eckhardt, *Landrecht*, cap. 30/34, p. 80; *Deutschenspiegel und Augsburger Sachsenspiegel*, ed. Eckhardt and Hübner, cap. 32 § 4, p. 112. The events before Rome are also recounted in *Der kunige buoch*, ed. Massmann, p. clxxiv. The story goes back to the *Kaiserchronik*: *Kaiserchronik*, ed. Schröder, pp. 345–6, vv. 14597–14628; and see Mertens, 'Spätmittelalterliches Landesbewußtsein', pp. 140–1. As Klaus Graf observes, for the Swabian nobility, the legend fulfilled the role of an origin myth: Graf, 'Souabe', p. 300.
[65] The Lohengrin-poet thus depicted the Swabians as enjoying the *vorstrit* in Henry I's army against the Hungarians: *Lohengrin*, ed. Cramer, p. 395, vv. 4128–30.
[66] *Die Chronik des Mathias von Neuenburg (AU Cont.)*, ed. Hofmeister, p. 478; and cf. *Heinricus Dapifer de Diessenhoven*, ed. Huber, p. 93.
[67] Konrad von Megenberg, *Planctus*, ed. Scholz, pars I, cap. 31, p. 48.

Just as India is famous for gems ... Arabia for gold, Hungary for cowardice ...
Italy for trickery ... England for riches, France for nobility and all affability,
Germany glories in a stern, robust, and powerful knighthood (*milicia*).[68]

'The Germans are better knights than all other nations under heaven',
insisted Konrad von Megenberg.[69] We have seen already how important
it was, from German perspectives, to uphold the Germans' collective
'honour', as vindicated through violence.[70] The Strasbourg chronicler
Gottfried von Ensmingen records how 'the good name of the knighthood of the German realm' was tarnished by the flight of a German
nobleman, Count Egino of Freiburg, before an army under the French-
speaking count of Montbéliard.[71] Alexander von Roes, who thought he
could discern a rational order of peoples in the world, reflecting God's
purpose, explained the Germans' place in that order. 'Just as there is
a time of peace and a time of war', he reflected, 'so also there are men
destined for peace and men destined for war.'[72] First among these latter
were his fellow countrymen. In his allegorical *Pavo*, the birds of prey
are *Teutonici* and *Alamanni*.[73]

Teutonic warriors are no less to the fore in accounts of contemporary
affairs in the post-Staufer period than they were in late medieval imperial memory. Again, however, it is a specific type of military actions that
causes reference to be made to their martial qualities: actions in the cause
of the Reich and led by its ruler. It was with an *imperatoria Germanorum
militia* that Henry VII laid siege to Florence.[74] Letters in the monarch's
own name invoked his subjects' military potential. Rudolf I, complain-
ing at French encroachments on the church of Viviers, threatened King
Philip III with the *potentia* that *Germania* brings forth.[75] The same
theme was still being sounded in the fifteenth century.[76] The chroniclers
placed similar boasts in the monarch's mouth. More than one account
of Rudolf I's siege of Besançon in 1289 has the king frightening off a

[68] *Conrad Kyeser aus Eichstätt, Bellifortis*, ed. Quarg, vol. II, p. 3. The reference to
Hungarian 'cowardice' relates specifically to the behaviour of King Sigismund and
his forces at the battle of Nicopolis (1396), where they were said to have fled the field.
For similar allegations, see the verses of Peter von Rez in *Politische Lyrik*, ed. Müller,
vol. II, pp. 59–63.
[69] Konrad von Megenberg, *Ökonomik*, lib. 2.iv, cap. 12, ed. Krüger, vol. II, pp. 200–1.
[70] Above, Ch. 6, pp. 269–70. For honour in medieval German political culture, see
Scales, '*Germen militiae*', pp. 54–9.
[71] *Ellenhardi chronicon*, ed. Jaffé, p. 128.
[72] Alexander von Roes, *Memoriale*, cap. 33, ed. Grundmann and Heimpel, pp. 141–2.
[73] Alexander von Roes, *Pavo*, ed. Grundmann and Heimpel, p. 173.
[74] *Königsaaler Geschichts-Quellen*, ed. Loserth, p. 348.
[75] *Acta*, ed. Kern, no. 53, p. 34.
[76] For examples from the chancery of Frederick III, see Sieber-Lehmann,
Spätmittelalterlicher Nationalismus, p. 191.

projected French intervention with the mere mention of his German forces.[77] The Colmar chronicler imagined Rudolf, when he confronted Otakar of Bohemia in 1276, urging on his knights to 'show the glory of Teutonic arms to the barbarian peoples'.[78] It was in service of the Empire that, in late medieval report, 'German' military might was pre-eminently on display. Faithfully rendering such service in time of need was the highest duty placed upon the princes, while withholding it imperilled the prestige of the entire German people. That, at least, was the judgement of one Austrian annalist, for whom the glory of 'our illustrious Germany' (*nostra clara Germania*) was placed in doubt, in spite of Rudolf I's great victory at the Marchfeld, on account of the fewness of the German princes who had accompanied him there.[79]

Accounts of imperial affairs in the period refer repeatedly to Germans as warriors. References multiply in the decades after 1250, in spite of the general weakness of the imperial monarchy, and the consequent fewness of resounding triumphs to celebrate. It was with 'an army of Teutons' (*Theutonicorum exercitu*) that, according to one chronicler, Rudolf overcame Otakar at the Marchfeld in 1278.[80] The force which Henry VII's son John led into Bohemia in 1310 was selected from 'the flourishing knighthood which *Germania* germinates'.[81] The ethnocentric note is pervasive in such contexts. Indeed, facts were sometimes bent and complexities ignored in order to draw a clear ethnic dividing line. Gottfried von Ensmingen radically simplified and misrepresented Rudolf I's political objectives in the south-west in the 1280s, in order to portray a stark confrontation between 'Germans', led by the king, and opposing 'Gauls'.[82] It was 'in order to recover the honour and the good name of all of Germany' (following the count of Freiburg's shameful flight) that Rudolf campaigned triumphantly in the region in 1289.[83] No complex territorial goals, but vindicating the

---

[77] *Liber certarum historiarum*, ed. Schneider, i.260, 301; *Die Chronik des Mathias von Neuenburg*, ed. Hofmeister, pp. 39–40.

[78] *Chronicon Colmariense*, ed. Jaffé, p. 249.

[79] *Annales Sancti Rudberti Salisburgenses*, ed. Wattenbach, p. 803.

[80] *Gesta Adolfi regis*, printed in Jäschke, 'Zu den Gesta Adolfi Regis' (here p. 239). In fact, Rudolf's army also contained a substantial force of Hungarians.

[81] *Königsaaler Geschichts-Quellen*, ed. Loserth, p. 305 ('ex omne florida militia germinantis Germaniae').

[82] *Ellenhardi chronicon*, ed. Jaffé, pp. 130–2. According to Matthias von Neuenburg, Bishop Peter of Basel's conflict of 1287 with the count of Montbéliard was *cum Gallicis vicinis*: *Die Chronik des Mathias von Neuenburg*, ed. Hofmeister, pp. 40–2.

[83] *Ellenhardi chronicon*, ed. Jaffé, p. 128. And see above, Ch. 4, p. 194 for the reflections of a Salzburg annalist on the implications for the standing of *nostra clara Germania* of the German princes' failure to aid Rudolf I against Otakar II of Bohemia.

honour of German arms, was for this chronicler the purpose of the king's military action.

The Germanness of imperial armies and the militancy of the Germans themselves each attained special visibility on the monarch's journeys into Italy. The chroniclers' portrayals of these events in particular constitute a remarkable triumph of sanguinary wish-fulfilment over sharply diminished (if often still distinctly bloody) reality. Johann von Viktring thus recounted how Ludwig IV had 'entered Italy, to the wonder of many, attended by a noble and outstanding retinue of knights of German stock'.[84] It was 'after mustering an invincible army from Germany' that, in another near contemporary account, Henry VII crossed the Alps in October 1310. What was in the chronicler's mind's eye can be recaptured in a fourteenth-century picture-book narrative of Henry's expedition, where we see the king of the Romans toiling up a stylised Alpine ridge amid a dense, mail-shirted throng bristling with lances and bright with banners.[85] The emperor's summons to Germany for armed men when he headed south was a theme familiar enough to have become a literary trope: there was much more to it than just logistics.[86]

The parading of German military hardware was what was expected and required, even by some Italians: it lent legitimacy to the king's presence among them.[87] For the monarch and his entourage, appearing in the south in high martial style was therefore a matter of principle. During preparations for an aborted Italian expedition under Rudolf I, the bishop of Basel wrote to the king from Rome, urging him to assemble 'a band of warriors such as mighty *Germania* can nurture'.[88] He took pains to impress on Rudolf the need for a truly magnificent show of force, 'thereby gaining infinite glory for Germany and renown that will endure for many generations'. Where mere display did not suffice, those same forces could naturally also be applied coercively; but even outright violence tended to appear as heavily choreographed and ritualised, at least to the eyes of commentators in the north. Henry VII, as

---

[84] *Liber certarum historiarum*, ed. Schneider, ii.92. This is in contrast to the modest retinue which Ludwig actually brought from Germany. See Pauler, *Die deutschen Könige*, pp. 144–64; Offler, 'Empire and papacy', pp. 36–7.

[85] Margue, Pauly and Schmid (eds.), *Der Weg zur Kaiserkrone*. The picture-chronicle, datable to c. 1340, reflects the patronage of Archbishop Balduin, whose depiction is almost as prominent as that of his brother, Henry. For the army crossing the Alps, see p. 47.

[86] For its incorporation into vernacular chivalric literature, see Ch. 4, p. 192.

[87] For an example of this, see above, Ch. 6, p. 268.

[88] O. Redlich, 'Ein oberrheinisches Formelbuch aus der Zeit der ersten Habsburger', *ZGORh* NF, 11 (1896), cited in Thomas, 'Nationale Elemente', p. 365.

the Königsaal chronicler tells it, did more than just successfully besiege Brescia.[89] He showed his 'fury' and brought before the city 'the invincible eagles of Germany'. A 'great fear and trembling' came upon the citizens, who therefore made their way to his camp 'in the manner of mourners', with bare feet and cords about their necks, there to throw themselves on their faces and profess themselves his *servi*.[90] The drama being enacted had well-established, traditional roles, each conceived of in ethnic terms. Caesar triumphant expresses himself with dark and violent humour, just as Otto von Freising had written of Barbarossa, making rhetorical play of the same juxtaposition of northern steel and southern moneybags.[91] His Italian subjects are seen in the subjection to which nature fits them, since they are, as Alexander von Roes put it – mapping ethnography onto the ideal types of social rank – the 'common people' (*populus*) to Germany's *militia*.[92] Congenitally unable to match the Germans militarily, they cannot act otherwise. 'For that people [the Germans] was accustomed always to be victorious, and was therefore very ready to assail and put to flight the soft and feminine spirit of the Gauls' (here, Italians).[93] Even their lands – the Empire's 'garden', its 'orchard' – were feminine and thus subject: soft, and ripe for exploitation.[94]

The king and his followers, for their part, were required to display the specific hallmarks of the Germans at war. There seems to have been much agreement as to what these were. Their courage, at least in their own estimation, was different in degree from that normally expected of soldiers, attaining to elements of the heroic: Germans were exemplars of *strenuitas, animositas, audacia*.[95] In vernacular descriptions, their capabilities readily acquired epic overtones: a successful or

---

[89] For what follows, see *Königsaaler Geschichts-Quellen*, ed. Loserth, pp. 342–3 (and on the king's *furor*, cf. *Liber de rebus memorabilioribus*, ed. Potthast, p. 229); for Henry before Brescia, Bowsky, *Henry VII*, pp. 115–27.

[90] Balduin of Luxemburg's picture-chronicle of the expedition actually portrays the Brescians abasing themselves before Henry in this way: Margue, Pauly and Schmid (eds.), *Der Weg zur Kaiserkrone*, p. 63.

[91] For Otto's quip, that Barbarossa's army paid the Romans for the imperial crown not in Arabian gold but Teutonic iron, see *Ottonis et Rahewini Gesta*, ed. Waitz, p. 113; for purported remarks by Henry VII in comparable spirit: *Die Chronik des Mathias von Neuenburg*, ed. Hofmeister, p. 83; *Die Chronik Johanns von Winterthur*, ed. Baethgen, p. 62.

[92] Alexander von Roes, *Noticia seculi*, cap. 14, ed. Grundmann and Heimpel, p. 160.

[93] *Königsaaler Geschichts-Quellen*, ed. Loserth, p. 348. For the south's 'fear' of the north, see Konrad von Megenberg, *Planctus*, ed. Scholz, pars I, cap. 8, p. 28.

[94] For this imagery, see above, Ch. 5, pp. 225–6.

[95] As examples, see: *Königsaaler Geschichts-Quellen*, ed. Loserth, p. 348 (*animositas, audacia*); *Conrad Kyeser aus Eichstätt, Bellifortis*, ed. Quarg, vol. 2, p. 2 ('Theutunia vero gloriatur strenui robusti et forti milicia').

admired ruler – a Rudolf I or a Henry VII – was for the poets a *helt* ('hero') or *degen* ('mighty warrior').[96] The Germans' aptitude for fighting was no mere reflection of skill and training, but the manifestation of an innate love of violence: 'joy in war' (*belli letitia*), as one chronicler put it.[97] Their powers on the battlefield were literally superhuman. Indeed, 'it was often seen how ten Germans would attack, wound and slaughter a thousand or more in pitched battle'.[98] And underlying all, as the energy source for these fearsome feats, was the element which, for friend and foe alike, set Germans apart: their inborn *furor*.

The trope of 'Teutonic fury' (*furor Teutonicus*) encapsulated the people's military vigour.[99] In 1336, according to Johann von Winterthur, the king of Hungary abandoned his campaigning and went home because he dreaded the advent of the Germans (especially, adds the southerner Johann, the Swabians), and fled 'as if before a whirlwind or a raging tempest' (*tempestatem furiosam*).[100] The *topos* had infused portrayals of imperial campaigns in Italy since Staufer times, and it continued to define the spirit of late medieval accounts. In 1310, imperial forces had rampaged through Milan, 'raging in the Teutonic fashion' (*more quasi Theutonico furentes*).[101] 'Teutonic fury' thus claimed a central part in those rhetorical constructions of difference, pitting Germans against Romance-speaking peoples, which constitute some of the most developed statements of 'German' identity from the period. The trope's currency grew, rather than diminishing, in the post-Staufer era, and by the fifteenth century had become the recourse of chancery clerks as well as chroniclers and pamphleteers.[102] It was not applicable only on the battlefield. More than one writer tells of the 'fury' with which Germans resisted the – insidious, treacherous and thus in the

---

[96] For examples, see 'Der Unversagte', in *Politische Lyrik*, ed. Müller, vol. I, p. 86 (Rudolf as 'ein helt an tugenden unverzaget'); Lupold Hornburg, 'Dyse rede ist von des Ryches clage', ibid., p. 198 (Henry VII as 'der gotes degen'). For the use of these words in German heroic literature, see *Der Nibelunge Nôt*, ed. Bartsch, vol. II.ii, pp. 51–3 (*degen*), 146–7 (*helt*).

[97] *Ellenhardi chronicon*, ed. Jaffé, p. 131.

[98] *Königsaaler Geschichts-Quellen*, ed. Loserth, p. 348. Rudolf I is reported as boasting, following his victory at Besançon, that with just four hand-picked German knights and forty foot soldiers he could overcome any multitude: *Die Chronik des Mathias von Neuenburg*, ed. Hofmeister, p. 42. The theme of Germans fighting against overwhelming odds is, again, old-established: see Thompson, *Feudal Germany*, vol. I, p. 370.

[99] See generally: Dümmler, 'Über den furor Teutonicus'; Kirn, *Aus der Frühzeit*, pp. 45–6, 51–9.

[100] *Die Chronik Johanns von Winterthur*, ed. Baethgen, p. 130.

[101] *Liber de rebus memorabilioribus*, ed. Potthast, p. 228.

[102] Sieber-Lehmann, *Spätmittelalterlicher Nationalismus*, esp. p. 191.

chroniclers' portrayal quintessentially Italian – machinations of the papal legate John of Tusculum in the north.[103]

Furor Teutonicus was thus, for literate Germans, mostly (though not, as we shall see, invariably) a thoroughly admirable thing. Yet this seems a surprising response to a Latin tag, of Roman origin (it is first encountered in Lucan's *Pharsalia*), which had been coined to characterise an alien – non-Roman – style of war.[104] Applied to the Germans (rather than the ancient *Teutones*), its earliest recorded use is in the era of the Investiture Contest, its meaning pejorative. And as applied to Germans by their neighbours, a term of collective blame (and inferiority) is what it remained: Petrarch distilled what he saw as the difference between Italian and German character into a disdainful antithesis, *vertù contra furore*.[105] Despite all this, for German writers, their people's innate fury became in the late Middle Ages a central argument in their claims to a special political status. It is in light of those claims, and of the opposition which they incurred, that we must understand the proliferation, in the decades after 1250, of accounts of German national character more generally.

It was therefore in war that the innate difference between the Germans and the Romance peoples was most clearly revealed. Left to themselves, the latter – in German account, most often French armies – typically melted away in the face of danger. Tilemann Elhen tells how the French-speaking count of Saint Pol had entered Luxembourg with a strong army.[106] But when Count Dithart von Katzenelnbogen, appointed guardian of the region by King Wenceslas, opposed him, the French (*di Walen*), slipped away under cover of darkness, leaving their pipers playing and torches burning to hoodwink their adversary. The juxtaposition of courage and cunning implicit here is recurrent in

---

[103] Above, Ch. 6, p. 267. For *furor* in the context of German resistance to the Church's fiscal demands, see Kirn, *Aus der Frühzeit*, p. 46; for the legate's activity and the controversy which it aroused, above, Ch. 4, pp. 167–9. German 'fury' at Roman exactions would have recalled, for literate contemporaries, the legendary refusal of the Franks (as *feroces*) to recommence tribute payments to the Romans at the end of their ten-year respite: thus Lupold von Bebenburg, *Tractatus*, cap. 1, ed. Miethke and Flüeler, p. 243.

[104] For Roman representations of the ancient Germanic peoples, see Sherwin-White, *Racial Prejudice*, esp. Ch. 2.

[105] Amelung, *Das Bild*, p. 41. In Ambrogio Lorenzetti's fresco cycle of 1338–9 in the Palazzo Pubblico in Siena, illustrating the nature and effects of good and evil government, the allegorical figure of *furor* appears in company with tyranny, division and war: see Skinner, 'Ambrogio Lorenzetti', p. 33.

[106] *Limburger Chronik*, ed. Wyss, p. 87. And see also ibid., pp. 53–4, for 'di große gelseschaft uß Welschem lande' which entered Alsace (1365), only to take flight 'wider zu Welschlant' upon the appearance of a German army.

German writings.[107] Yet even Romance-speaking armies might acquit themselves adequately if only they were under German leadership. Peter von Zittau tells of how a force of 22,000 Pisans, marching to the aid of Henry VII, had been unable to make headway until Henry dispatched to them 'barely eighty German knights', who infused the army with 'boldness of spirit' and thereby secured its passage.[108] The real calamity arose, in German eyes, when their neighbours failed to appreciate the value of such robust military tutelage and, adding pride and treachery to a native want of spirit, snatched the Germans' rightful place for themselves. Matthias von Neuenburg recounts how at Crécy (1346) the defeated French had first seized the van, only to flee the field, abandoning their German allies (who naturally stood firm) to be slaughtered.[109] The victorious Edward III – who as a warrior-king himself was qualified to speak on such matters – is portrayed honouring the fallen Germans and reflecting how much better they had deserved than the treacherous dealings of the French.

Value-laden narratives of this sort, not uncommon in the chronicles, were suitable for projection by imperialist treatise-writers onto a global backdrop, to allow the drawing of global conclusions. For Dietrich von Niem, the defeat of the western crusading force at Nicopolis in 1396 was due to the French usurping the place in the van that traditionally belonged to the Germans 'in all wars against the Saracens'.[110] Alexander von Roes had already made the same point allegorically:

Birds sing and rejoice when they see flowers [the French lily!], but at the sight of the eagle they fall silent and flee. Therefore, all barbarian peoples [*omnes barbare nationes*] despise the insignia of other kings, but they naturally fear and abhor the eagles of the Romans and the Germans.[111]

Crusader-kings notwithstanding, inborn aptitude and the lessons of history alike made war for the Faith a German, not a French, affair.

---

[107] The Poles were occasionally subjected to comparable depiction by German writers in the eastern lands: they were *Lechi* or *Lechite*, since they triumphed in war more through trickery than prowess. Thus, *Chronica principum Poloniae*, ed. Stenzel, pp. 39, 42.

[108] *Königsaaler Geschichts-Quellen*, ed. Loserth, p. 348.

[109] *Die Chronik des Mathias von Neuenburg*, ed. Hofmeister, pp. 205–7. This is not the only instance from the chronicles of a Romance people allegedly fleeing the field while their German allies stand and fight to the death: that, according to Twinger, was what had happened when German and Italian forces faced the Saracens in Italy under Otto II: *Chronik des Jacob Twingers*, ed. Hegel, p. 422. Matthias von Neuenburg's account of Crécy was also repeated by Twinger: ibid., pp. 474–5.

[110] Quoted in Heimpel, *Dietrich*, p. 156.

[111] Alexander von Roes, *Memoriale*, cap. 33, ed. Grundmann and Heimpel, p. 142.

Not only holy war, however. The fundamentally military character of the imperial office ensured that the same arguments – and symbols – applied here also. Konrad von Megenberg's allegorical Church thus warns the pope not to 'charge the shield [of the Empire] with those lilies, which are soft and womanish'.[112] To Alexander von Roes, writing in 1288, in the aftermath of the downfall of Charles of Anjou, the same argument had recent history on its side:

Although there are many reasons for the past tribulations of the French ... this however is the most important, that ... the French are assuming for themselves habits which the natural order of things denies to them and their profession forbids. For they ought to be peaceful and harmonious, and concerned with the well-being of body and soul; but they strive like Teutons [*more Teutonico*] and like warriors, to become cruel and bellicose men and plunderers.[113]

Precisely what social role Alexander had in mind for the French we will see shortly; but the main point here was that it could never be an imperial one.

Alexander's arguments invoked webs of old-established Gallophobe stereotype. Some of these were common to other Romance-speaking peoples, notably the Italians – who, like the French, were *Walhen* or *Walschen* in the vernacular and, on occasion, *Gallici* in Latin.[114] Each of these peoples, in recurrent German report, joined cunning and deceit to cowardice, lasciviousness and effeminacy.[115] The French added further vices: vanity, garrulity, frivolity, lethargy and, particularly in reaching out their hands for the Empire, pride.[116] None of these calumnies was exclusive to the treatise-writers: they recur in northern writings of diverse sorts.[117] Taken together, they added up to a familiar caricature, which some Germans believed they could discern in the personalities of their own time. Jakob Twinger wrote of Jean de Luxembourg-Ligny

---

[112] Konrad von Megenberg, *Planctus*, ed. Scholz, pars I, cap. 31, p. 60.
[113] Alexander von Roes, *Noticia seculi*, cap. 15, ed. Grundmann and Heimpel, p. 161. The same events receive allegorical treatment in his *Pavo*, vv. 263–72 (ibid., p. 191).
[114] For *Walhen, Walschen*, see *Mittelhochdeutsches Handwörterbuch*, ed. Lexer, iii.649; for vernacular reference to Italians, *Acta*, ed. Böhmer, no. 818, p. 549 (*Walchen*); for Italians as *Gallici*, *Königsaaler Geschichts-Quellen*, ed. Loserth, p. 348.
[115] Examples in Konrad von Megenberg, *Planctus*, ed. Scholz, pars I, cap. 33, p. 49.
[116] For a characteristic list, see Alexander von Roes, *Noticia seculi*, cap. 13, ed. Grundmann and Heimpel, p. 160.
[117] Thus, e.g., a letter of Count John of Hainault to Rudolf I, preserved in a formulary, perceiving behind the rebellion of the count of Flanders 'gallia garriens, aliarum insultatrix improba nacionum': printed in *Summa Curiae Regis*, ed. Stobbe, no. 255, p. 362; for the cowardice of *Welschen* in fifteenth-century German sources, see Sieber-Lehmann, *Spätmittelalterlicher Nationalismus*, pp. 291–3.

('Bishop Bedsheet', as Twinger calls him), who had been provided to the see of Strasbourg at the petition of Charles IV:

He was the proudest and – physically, and in appearance – most magnificent man you could find, and yet he was simple, soft, and unwise, and paid no regard to the state of the land, and cared only that he be brought plenty to eat, because he was a glutton, and would eat a whole goose or capon at a sitting … The bishopric lay more in the hands of his officials than his own.[118]

Twinger's portrait recalls Dietrich von Niem's characterisation of the papal *bon viveur* Clement VII (1378–94), whose 'Gallic urbanity' had availed him little in the Schism, and with whom 'our good old simple German emperors' offered for Dietrich such a wholesome contrast.[119] In the view of Alexander von Roes, French kings lived more like prelates, 'not in contemplation and prayer, but in softness and ease'.[120] It was not hard for German imperialists to point the moral, namely that supreme temporal power belonged not with such people but with their stern eastern neighbours.

In their representation by German polemicists and by some (though by no means all) chroniclers, the Romance peoples are therefore archetypically Other.[121] Their alleged identities are constructed and deployed in order to serve authorial ends of reaffirming German claims to domination in Italy and discrediting the dangerous rival imperialism of the French. Far from being mere random abuse, the denigration of neighbours in which some literate Germans were engaged drew upon well-established literary tropes in the service of coherent claims and arguments. Not only that, however, since the Other itself has a more ambivalent role here than might be supposed. The derogatory motifs which are deployed need to be viewed, at least in some of these portrayals, not in isolation but as elements within more complex patterns of assumption and argument.

In the view of Alexander von Roes, the Germans' western and southern neighbours did not possess faults alone – nor the Germans themselves only virtues. Rather, they had complementary and interlocking talents and shortcomings, which qualified each for a particular role within the divinely willed order, while debarring it from others. To the Romans or Italians (as *seniores*) pertained spiritual authority (*sacerdotium*): from

---

[118] *Chronik des Jacob Twinger*, ed. Hegel, pp. 675–6.
[119] Heimpel, *Dietrich*, p. 157. The contrast was drawn in Dietrich's treatise *On the Schism* (1409).
[120] Alexander von Roes, *Noticia seculi*, cap. 11, ed. Grundmann and Heimpel, p. 158.
[121] For a different judgement on German treatments of the French, see Jostkleigrewe, *Das Bild*, pp. 205–9 (though concentrating on selected vernacular chronicles more than polemical writings).

among them should be chosen the pope.[122] Higher learning belonged to
the French (*Gallici, Francigene*), for whom Alexander, beside his barbs,
has high praise. Their admirable qualities, which include (among other
things) circumspection, vigilance, sharp-wittedness and eloquence, fitted them ideally for their allotted task of defending orthodoxy with the
pen – so long, at least, as their innate pride could be kept from leading
them, and the Christian community, to ruin.[123] They had a natural love
of knowledge (*amor sciendi*).[124] It was true that they also tended towards
frivolity, and lacked the Germans' seriousness of purpose; but that was
because they were *iuniores* – younger members of a common family of
peoples, in which they had their due place.[125] The pope, to whom the
Germans should be brothers and equals, should accordingly treat the
gens Gallica 'like an obedient son'.

To speak of a people's character was implicitly to invoke the contrasting traits of other peoples; but these were not merely opposed, as some
scholarly models of 'the Other' expect and require, but interconnected.
To trace and affirm hierarchies, as Alexander and the other treatise-
writers sought to do, was inevitably to discuss relationships. The nations
of western Europe eyed each other not across a gulf of insurmountable
difference but across a peopled landscape, familiar, shared and fought
over. To Alexander, the French even looked familiar. In physiognomy
they resembled other northern peoples, while they were paler than
Spaniards, Moors or Greeks.[126] Their external appearance was that of
the Germans, except for those adornments – specifically, fashionable
hairstyles – which juvenility led them to favour.[127] They were free of that
physical 'coarseness' which distinguished the Franconians unfavour-
ably from Alexander's own Trojan Rhinelanders.[128] Frankishness was
something the French naturally shared with western Germans. And
while, for Alexander, they had it in a delayed, diluted and less potent

---

[122] Alexander von Roes, *Memoriale*, cap. 25, ed. Grundmann and Heimpel, p. 126.
[123] The French were *perspicatiores* (ibid., p. 126). For French pride, see Alexander von
Roes, *Noticia seculi*, caps. 13, 14, pp. 160–1; for pride in medieval thought, Bloomfield,
The Seven Deadly Sins, pp. 75, 105.
[124] Alexander von Roes, *Noticia seculi*, cap. 14, ed. Grundmann and Heimpel, p. 160.
[125] Alexander von Roes, *Memoriale*, cap. 18, ed. Grundmann and Heimpel, pp. 114–15.
The German Franks, by contrast, *tamquam seniores*, attested their kinship with the
Romans.
[126] Alexander von Roes, *Memoriale*, cap. 15, ed. Grundmann and Heimpel, pp. 106–7,
with the claim that the French have their name, *Gallici*, from the Greek *galla* (milk),
on account of the whiteness of their skin.
[127] Ibid., cap. 18, pp. 114–15; and cf. cap. 26, p. 128, also insisting on the visible similarities between the French and the Germans, *in vestibus* (manuscript classes A–D)
or *in habitu exteriori* (manuscript classes E–G).
[128] Ibid., cap. 18, pp. 113–14.

form, they remained in this respect in advance even of those German peoples, such as the Swabians and Bavarians, who could not be said to share in it at all. The French, like the Germans, were *franci* – 'free', with full power to rule within their realm, by the grant of an emperor.[129] Lupold von Bebenburg explained that only a lack of sources had prevented him writing more about the kings of France and England, as he intended; for the kings of France were descended from Charlemagne, while the English kings down to the Conquest were 'of Saxon German descent' (*de genere Saxonum Germanorum*).[130] Italians, Germans and French, as the treatise-writers made plain, shared a long, if conflict-laden, history, with roots in the Carolingian period. Yet together they went back further still, to a Roman epoch in which each had a part, and beyond that – for Alexander, crucially – to the migration of Trojan bands. Still more remotely, they shared a common inheritance from Japheth. The kinship which Alexander perceived between his principal peoples of Latin Christendom was no mere metaphor: beneath their divisions, they were bound by common blood.

Not only in this respect, however, would it be wrong to view these interconnected accounts of national character as examples of straight-forward 'binary difference'.[131] The Germans' own auto-stereotype is likewise too complex, in its nature and functioning, to be adjudged a mere tool of rhetorical conquest.[132] It is true that it was strongly polit-ical, and that it was deployed by some writers to defend the Germans' traditional claim to the Empire. The context, however, was hardly one of bold self-assertion. Indeed, we have seen already how recurrent and pervasive in German sources is the belief that plans were afoot to strip the German people of its imperial titles. It is a view encountered in the immediate aftermath of the Staufer era and in the time of the Councils, in a vernacular chronicle from remote Lübeck as well as in chancery documents or treatises arguing the imperialist cause. Most often, the French were identified as pretenders. And, while German national character might certainly appear relevant to these contests, its role was not only to affirm German claims. If there was much agreement about the German people's defining qualities, their judgement and wider sig-nificance were more debatable.

Alexander von Roes lamented that there were people in his time who asked how the Germans were to govern all Christendom when they were a people too coarse and clumsy even to attend properly to their

[129] See Scales, 'France and the Empire', pp. 407–8, and above, Ch. 7, p. 335.

[130] Lupold von Bebenburg, *Libellus de Zelo*, cap. 1, ed. Miethke and Flüeler, p. 415.

[131] For this term, Gilman, *Difference*, p. 24.

[132] Its complexities are further examined in Scales, '*Germen militiae*', esp. pp. 66–9.

own dress and manners.[133] Alexander here recounts mutterings picked up at the Angevin-dominated Curia of the early 1280s. Konrad von Megenberg, who was also at the papal court, likewise has his allegorical Pope invoke the Germans' coarseness and lack of cultivation as grounds for depriving them of the Empire.[134] Konrad's response, like that of Alexander, and in the time of the Councils Dietrich von Niem, was to diminish these alleged German defects, and even transform them into covert virtues, evidence of a simple and honest nature. Rude directness and no-nonsense vigour were pitted against courtly knee-bending, ineffectual chatter and vicious scheming.[135] Alexander's *Pavo* contrasts the imperial birds of prey – taciturn, without beauty, but swift to act – with the French Cockerel and papal Peacock, vain, dazzling and loud.[136] But that was not the end of the matter.

For a writer anxious to belittle the military credentials of the French, Alexander makes a curious case. Despite dismissing as mere juvenility their leadership of aristocratic fashion, he lists among the Cockerel's 'good' attributes joviality, amiability, generosity and even physical splendour – all qualities more suggestive, in contemporary estimation, of the perfect knight than the born scholar.[137] The French virtues which he identifies in the later *Noticia seculi* – justice, temperance, urbanity – seem similarly more redolent of the court than the schoolroom.[138] Even their besetting sin, pride, was a notoriously aristocratic one.[139] Despite his best efforts, Alexander could not avoid implicitly awarding the palm of knighthood to the new-style rival *militia* which had arisen beyond the Empire's western frontier.[140] The insight was by the late Middle Ages a general one: it was not only Konrad Kyeser who discerned in France the

---

[133] Alexander von Roes, *Memoriale*, cap. 14, ed. Grundmann and Heimpel, p. 104.

[134] Konrad von Megenberg, *Planctus*, ed. Scholz, pars I, cap. 14, p. 34.

[135] Thus, ibid., pars I, caps. 18, 19, pp. 36–7.

[136] Alexander von Roes, *Pavo*, ed. Grundmann and Heimpel, *passim*. It is a recurrent theme in fifteenth-century German writings that the Germans have not sung their own praises sufficiently, being a people preferring deeds to words: see above, Ch. 7, p. 297.

[137] Alexander von Roes, *Memoriale*, cap. 15, ed. Grundmann and Heimpel, p. 107. For fashionable (pseudo-)knightly dress as characteristically French (and morally suspect), see *Helmbrecht*, ed. Speckenbach, pp. 1–4, vv. 26–106. The poet describes the splendid cap, decorated with heroic scenes, including the exploits of (the French) Charlemagne, which the poem's eponymous anti-hero, an upstart peasant's son, has taken to wearing.

[138] Alexander von Roes, *Noticia seculi*, cap. 13, ed. Grundmann and Heimpel, p. 160.

[139] See Little, 'Pride'. In Gothic art, pride was frequently represented by the figure of a mounted knight, while in homiletic literature pride was closely linked with vainglory, and thus with physical magnificence and display: Bloomfield, *The Seven Deadly Sins*, p. 105. Alexander identified physical splendour as a characteristic of the French.

[140] See Scales, 'France and the Empire', pp. 408–9.

home of 'nobility and all affability'.[141] The French model, and French texts, had long supplied a foundation for German aristocratic literature, just as a French technical vocabulary was absorbed into German for the accoutrements of chivalrous living. German knights participated (not always with happy results) at fashionable French tournaments.[142] The German warrior elite had to measure itself against standards dictated by the western neighbour – in which ferocity in battle was now but one element.

The task did not always seem hopeless. The *Styrian Rhyming Chronicle* recounts how, when Albert I and Philip IV met on the Franco-imperial border in 1299, the French king, determined to outshine the imperial party, had brought with him 'many courtly knights'. Despite this, it was the Germans (*die Tiutschen curtoisen*) who came more magnificently apparelled.[143] Nevertheless, to experienced observers the Germans seemed on the whole to stand at a clear disadvantage, to which their own outdated attitudes contributed. Konrad von Megenberg regretted what he claimed was the habit among his fellow countrymen, of mocking learned knights as 'book-eaters':

They do not know writings, and the truth deserts them. They raise up boys in physical arms and send them into battle unarmed with prudence, not knowing that prudence vanquishes physical strength.[144]

The failures of German arms were not to be dismissed as the result merely of foreign treachery: some causes lay disturbingly close to home.

The militarised character of German society drew much contemporary comment. Towns in this period were acquiring mighty circuits of fortifications, like the 8 kilometres of walls which ringed late medieval Cologne. Their ruling elites fought on horseback and imitated the military-chivalric mode of life of rural nobles. The bellicosity of German high churchmen was proverbial.[145] 'Behold what spirited and

---

[141] *Conrad Kyeser aus Eichstätt, Bellifortis*, ed. Quarg, vol. II, p. 3. For further German expressions of admiration for French chivalry, see Thomas, 'Nationale Elemente', p. 375.
[142] As an example, see Thomas, 'Nationale Elemente', pp. 366–70.
[143] *Ottokars österreichische Reimchronik*, ed. Seemüller, p. 988, vv. 74960–94.
[144] Konrad von Megenberg, *Ökonomik*, lib. 2.iv, cap. 3, ed. Krüger, vol. II, pp. 170–1; and see Krüger, 'Das Rittertum', p. 303.
[145] See generally Arnold, 'German bishops'. Albert von Stade preserves the story of Archbishop Christian of Mainz, on campaign in Italy with Barbarossa, laying low nine men with his three-headed cudgel: *Annales Stadenses*, ed. Lappenberg, p. 347 (for 1177); an illustration in the picture-chronicle of Henry VII's expedition to Rome shows the work's patron, Archbishop Balduin, in battle at Rome (discussed below, 'Conclusion', p. 536).

warlike archbishops and bishops we have in Germany', wrote Richard of Cornwall to his nephew, the Lord Edward.[146] The pervasiveness of warrior values was remarked by Alexander von Roes; and the prospects for German society hardly looked encouraging. In *Teutonia*, he explains, the *militia* rules, whom clergy and people resemble in their rapacity and love of quarrels.[147] Those qualities might be directed inward, against native society, as well as outward, in war with others. When Henry VII's followers called the Bohemians regicides, pointing to their kingdom's turbulent recent past, Henry had allegedly retorted that 'we all know that many of our ancestors as king of the Romans died by the sword – but their killers were *Germans*'.[148] The period preceding Henry's accession was remembered in Germany, as we have seen elsewhere, as one of violence and lawlessness.[149] A century later, war and disorder within Germany remained the recurrent subject of the monarch's public acts.[150] In face of such troubled times, the tag of Teutonic *furor* proved capable of application not only ideologically, to propose what should be, but sociologically, to analyse what manifestly *was*.

It was hardly a comfortable quality for a people to lay claim to, and it was therefore well suited to discussing what in Germany seemed uncomfortable times. In theory, German fury underpinned an imperial claim; but its expression in practice might urge a very different conclusion. Characteristic of the German style of warfare, as some Germans themselves saw it, was a kind of heedless savagery: they were, as Alexander von Roes expressed it, 'cruel and bellicose men'.[151] Germans were harsh soldiers, their behaviour on the battlefield untempered by chivalrous restraint.[152] Even in a sympathetic chronicler's portrayal, Henry VII's troops in Rome behave 'like ravening wolves among defenceless

---

[146] *Ex annalibus Burtonensibus*, ed. Pauli, p. 480.

[147] Alexander von Roes, *Noticia seculi*, cap. 14, ed. Grundmann and Heimpel, p. 160. Even the Germans' *amor dominandi*, in Alexander's view a trait which qualified them for imperial power (ibid., pp. 159–60), gains a more troubling complexion when it is noted that Augustine had identified *libido dominandi* with the harshness and injustice of Pharaoh: see Russell, *The Just War*, p. 16.

[148] *Königsaaler Geschichts-Quellen*, ed. Loserth, p. 267.

[149] Above, Ch. 3, pp. 123–4.

[150] As examples, see: *RTA* 2, no. 63, p. 150; *RTA* 3, no. 212, p. 272; *RTA* 5, no. 470, p. 682.

[151] Above, p. 373.

[152] Gottfried von Ensmingen claims that the German custom of not taking prisoners made Rudolf I's French-speaking opponents unwilling to surrender: *Ellenhardi chronicon*, ed. Jaffé, pp. 185–6. According to Jansen Enikel, any Italian (*Wallich*) taken captive by Frederick II's German forces 'was bound to suffer': *Jansen Enikels Weltchronik*, ed. Strauch, p. 554, vv. 27911–15.

sheep'.[153] Germans, it seemed to some, displayed a want of discrimination in their use of arms. Konrad von Megenberg accused those who joined professional companies of waging unjust wars, since they provided military sustenance for the tyrants of Lombardy.[154] For Isidore of Seville, it might be noted, the essence of unjust war was *furor*.[155] Together with fury went an impulsiveness and unreason which likewise seemed to mark out the German military classes.[156] War itself made men – in late medieval imagination, particularly German men – beastly.[157] German armies in action might be undermined by a headlong rush for booty, which some judged to be characteristic of their people: that, it was believed, was how the fateful battle of Tagliocozzo had been lost.[158] The German *militia* on home turf was no different: for Lupold von Bebenburg, the princes were thieves and *raptores*, whose short-sighted egotism even threatened German control of the Empire.[159] They plundered not only others, but themselves. In Lupold Hornburg's dream-vision polemic, a personified *Rych* bewails the manner in which the poet's German fellow-countrymen (*lantfolk*) have 'with robberies, with murder and with arson' brought her to ruin.[160] It was therefore no wonder that, as Konrad von Megenberg observed, the French and English

---

[153] *Königsaaler Geschichts-Quellen*, ed. Loserth, p. 347. Heinrich von Herford describes Henry VII's troops as 'sparing neither sex nor age' as they 'raged' through Milan: *Liber de rebus memorabilioribus*, ed. Potthast, p. 228. Such comments provide a context for Alexander von Roes' determination to present the Germans as custodians, not ravagers, of the Christian sheepfold: St Peter's pastoral staff represented the Empire, by which the 'ravening wolf' was driven off: Alexander von Roes, *Memoriale*, cap. 36, ed. Grundmann and Heimpel, p. 146.

[154] Konrad von Megenberg, *Ökonomik*, lib. 2.i, cap. 3, ed. Krüger, vol. II, p. 22. See also Krüger, 'Das Rittertum', p. 314; and for German companies in Italy, Selzer, *Deutsche Söldner*.

[155] Russell, *The Just War*, p. 27.

[156] The chronicler Peter von Dusburg, writing in the Prussia of the Teutonic Order, tells of how German crusaders inadvertently butchered the kin and wasted the property of a Prussian ally, who had been too slow to indicate his friendly status, not realising 'how impetuous are the Germans [*Teutonici*] in war': *Cronica terre Prussie*, ed. Töppen, p. 91. For the *topos* of the Germans' want of prudence, recurrent in late medieval sources, see Sieber-Lehmann, *Spätmittelalterlicher Nationalismus*, p. 192.

[157] Hale, *Artists*, pp. 53, 67, for German soldiers as wild men in art from the end of the Middle Ages.

[158] *Ottokars österreichische Reimchronik*, ed. Seemüller, p. 41, vv. 3060–74. For an army to scatter in pursuit of booty was, the chronicler regretfully observed, typically German: 'wand leider solhes sinnes / sint die Tiutschen meisteil alle'.

[159] Lupold von Bebenburg, 'Ritmaticum querulosum', in *Politische Lyrik*, ed. Müller, vol. I, p. 176. For Germans as robbers, see Schönbach, 'Bartholomaeus Anglicus', pp. 74, 75: the people of Holland and the Rhine are less disposed to robbery than *alie Germanice nationes*.

[160] Lupold Hornburg, 'Dyse rede ist von des Ryches clage', in *Politische Lyrik*, ed. Müller, vol. I, p. 197, vv. 392–5.

monarchies were in better shape than the German. The fault lay not only with abuses engendered by the elective crown but, more fundamentally, with 'the fury [*furor*] and impatience of the Teutonic people, through which quarrels are sown among them every day'.[161]

For Konrad, drawing on the revived ethnographic lore of the ancient Mediterranean, the chances of any improvement in the Germans' condition looked bleak. Their fatal flaw, just like the happy distinction of the French, as celebrated by Pierre Dubois, was embedded in the implacable facts of climate and physiognomy. What made German knights such *furibundi* was 'the speed and quantity of blood in them', for Aristotle had shown that people living far from the sun lack prudence, and triumph through valour alone.[162] For those who took their lessons from history instead, the prospects for positive change were hardly better. Literate Germans, as we have seen already, traced their descent directly to those ancient northern peoples whose rude barbarian vigour had once driven the Romans from their lands. Proud etymologies froze and cherished the memory: Thuringians were 'tough' (*dura*), while late medieval Franks remained 'ferocious' as well as free.[163] Stories recounting bloody pasts affirmed the aptness of their militant titles.[164] Here and there, at best, manners and customs were softened. Bartholomaeus Anglicus meant to praise the natives of Meißen when he made of them 'a benign and pacific people, having by nature in all things less fierceness than the [other] Germans'.[165]

If improvement of a general kind were to come, it was more likely to come from outside. It took the Schism and upheaval in Paris, as well as the foundation of new universities on German soil, to move the philosopher Heinrich von Langenstein (d. 1397) exultantly to tear up the old map of national character, as traced more than a century before by Alexander von Roes. Scholarship (*studia*) in France was dissipated, he announced, the sun of wisdom eclipsed: learning had departed to illuminate a different people (*gens*). 'Certainly', concluded Heinrich, 'the

---

[161] Konrad von Megenberg, *Ökonomik*, lib. 2.i, cap. 6, ed. Krüger, vol. II, p. 14.

[162] Ibid., pp. 201–2. For ancient climatic theory and its medieval legacy, see: Glacken, *Traces on the Rhodian Shore*, esp. Ch. 2; Friedman, *The Monstrous Races*, Ch. 3; Murray, *Reason*, pp. 254–7.

[163] For this etymology of the Franks (which originated with Fredegar), see Lupold von Bebenburg, *Tractatus*, cap. 1, ed. Miethke and Flüeler, p. 243; for further examples: Meyvaert, '"Rainaldus"', p. 747; Borchardt, *German Antiquity*, p. 67; *Alexander von Roes: Schriften*, ed. Grundmann and Heimpel, p. 113 n. 1. For Thuringians, see Schönbach, 'Bartholomaeus Anglicus', p. 79 (cap. 166).

[164] See, e.g., the Saxon origin legend: *Sächsische Weltchronik*, ed. Weiland, pp. 259–65; and for its Germanisation, above, Ch. 7, p. 319.

[165] Schönbach, 'Bartholomaeus Anglicus', p. 74.

mouth of the chattering ones is now shut up, who claimed that there is no splendour of truth among the Germans, but rather the impetuous fury of monstrous men.'[166] His sentiments anticipate the humanists, who would mix admonitions to their fellow Germans to cast off their barbarous ways with pleasing reflections that they had already begun to do so.[167] On the whole, however, it was far from clear that Germans of Heinrich's day wholly wished to expel the monstrous man, and dispense with his formidable native powers.

The categories in which literate Germans thought about themselves and about their southern and western neighbours were literate categories, resting on the authority of long tradition. Yet the signs are that despite (or because of) their learned roots, the interwoven ethnic stereotypes which they deployed possessed for them considerable emotive power. This came in part from their venerable authority, which authenticated their claims for timeless national character, but also from their inner complexity. The image of the warrior-Germans seemed both to show why they alone should have the Empire and why they particularly should be denied it.[168] Such arguments mattered a good deal, not only to a tiny learned elite but to a more extensive and diffuse (if still not, in absolute terms, large) political public. Many of those same people cared also about the perceived shortcomings of government and good order in Germany – and found that the same models of national behaviour offered insights into these problems too. They showed them both why the manners and values of their (over-)sophisticated neighbours ought to be derided and shunned *and* why and how they might fruitfully be emulated or annexed. These were models of nationhood for a learned and complex western world, and their complexity nourished, and did not undermine, their compelling explanatory power. The same period, however, saw German-speakers moving in other, seemingly different worlds, and engaging in dealings with other, neighbouring peoples. It remains to be seen how – and how articulately – these relationships were understood.

---

[166] *Epistola Heinrici de Hassia informativa super scismate*, printed in Sommerfeldt, 'Die Stellung Ruprechts III', pp. 310–11: 'Certe iam obstructum est os loquencium iniqua: non est apud Germanos veritatis splendor, set preceps immanitatis furor!'

[167] As an example, Konrad Celtis's 'Ingolstadt address': in *Selections from Conrad Celtis*, ed. and trans. Forster, pp. 36–65.

[168] For some of the paradoxes contained in the image of the warrior-German, see Scales, 'Germen militiae', esp. pp. 79–82.

9 East: applying identities

Under the Virgin's mantle

There survives from the territories under the Teutonic Order a group of singular works of devotional art. Dating from around the end of the fourteenth century, they consist of wooden carvings of the Virgin Mary, whose mantle is hinged to reveal upon opening a central image of the Trinity, flanked by groups of human figures who huddle together in the wings.[1] Although distinctive, the Prussian *Schreinmadonna* was not without sources, or counterparts elsewhere.[2] The motif of the Virgin spreading her protective cloak had come to Latin Europe from Byzantium, where the relic itself was preserved. In the West, by the late Middle Ages, it had become conjoined with a more general principle, that Christ's mother extended her support to *communities*, particularly at times of peril. Major political formations, including entire peoples under their rulers, might thus call on her protection, no less than did more intimate gatherings of votaries.[3]

So what sorts of community came together under the sheltering cloak of these Teutonic Madonnas? The answer cannot be simple. Officers and knight-brethren of the Order are seen enjoying the company of identifiable kings – Wenceslas, Rupert of the Palatinate, Sigismund – and Roman cardinals. In another exemplar it is representatives of the Prussian estates who assemble beneath the Madonna's outstretched arms, with their overlords conspicuously absent. Noteworthy here are not only the links visibly affirmed, between the knights and the

---

[1] Surviving examples are described in Arnold (ed.), *800 Jahre*, pp. 119–20, with plates between pp. xvi and 1. For analysis, including identification of the figures, see Dygo, 'The political role', pp. 71–5.

[2] For the Virgin's depiction as protectress of human groups, see Belting, *Likeness*, pp. 356–7; for the *Schreinmadonna* as genre, Radler, *Die Schreinmadonna*.

[3] For the Virgin's political role, see Schreiner, '*Maria patrona*'. Béla IV of Hungary (r. 1235–70) referred to her as 'patrona et domina regni Hungarie gloriosissima' (ibid., p. 147). For her political importance within the German-speaking lands, see pp. 135–6 (Livonia, Dithmarschen), 138 (Strasbourg).

traditional great powers of the West, whence came their titles to rule, but also those which might have been traced, but seemingly are not – between the Order's brethren and the local communities of Prussians and Germans (and Poles, and others) over whom they ruled. Such a contrast invites questions, about the self-perception of the migrant warrior-lords within whose domains these images were made, about their apartness – and perhaps their Germanness. But it provokes also the recollection that the black-cross knights were in their day just one particular formation among the many communities of migrant Germans to which comparable reflections might be addressed.

How new communities took shape, how they conceived of a shared existence, whom they shut out and why, are matters of inescapable importance for the lands, lying mainly to the north and east of the Empire's historic northern core, which were settled with German-speakers in the central and later Middle Ages. These were regions which in modern times were to give unparalleled demonstration of the power of national sentiment violently to reorder human landscapes. The forced migration of several million Germans out of the lands of east-central Europe at the end of World War II was impelled by sentiments which went beyond a mere thirst for collective retribution. To some of their proponents at least, the expulsions were a wholesome remaking of ethnic patterns fatally disordered many centuries before, and the restoration of a primal, natural order of peoples.[4] In the view of Czechoslovak Communist leader Klement Gottwald, the eviction of the Sudeten Germans had set to rights 'the mistakes of our Czech kings, the Přemyslids, who invited the German colonists here'.[5]

The ethnic upheavals to which much of east-central Europe was subjected in the twentieth century are a stark reminder of the factors which, since their origins in the Middle Ages, set German communities in these wide regions apart from their co-linguists in the west. In the settlement lands, Germans were but one element – and in some regions, numerically a small one – within multi-ethnic communities and polities. Managing relations with neighbours of different ethnicity, while by no means necessarily a source of conflict, was here everywhere a fact of life. In all of these lands, Germans had intruded themselves, or been introduced, during the central Middle Ages, into the midst of

---

[4] For the ideological foundations of the expulsions, see Mazower, *Dark Continent*, Ch. 7.

[5] Quoted in Sayer, 'The language', p. 210.

existing, if often sparse, human populations. Only in a minority of the regions of east-central Europe had they arrived as conquerors, or settled in the wake of conquests made by other German-speakers. But virtually everywhere they enjoyed legal grants or other social advantages which, initially at least, distinguished their situation favourably from that of most of their non-German neighbours. Yet in most cases their privileges were the specific privileges of small groups, often granted and guaranteed by protector-lords who were not themselves German. Very few among the settlers or their descendants had anything to gain from invoking, let alone identifying emotionally with, the Reich, as institution or idea. Many of them in any case dwelt outside its territorial bounds. But even those who stood in principle under its rule were mindful of other, far more immediate and tangible, allegiances and identities. After the twelfth century, the Empire and its rulers had relatively little to do with the expanding eastern marchlands of German speech. Yet the Reich, as we have by now seen repeatedly, was a prime locus of late medieval German identity. In what sense, then, were the settler communities which established themselves within and beyond the Empire's eastern margins German at all?

The Germans who form the subject of the present chapter are therefore somewhat different in character from those with whom this book has so far mainly been concerned and, in order to gain a view of their identity, it will be necessary to adjust our angle of approach accordingly. The difference is not absolute, however. In part, we will still need to concentrate, as we have done up till now, upon ideas and ideologies, on regnal polities and extended political structures, and on the imagining, and textual construction, of large, historically grounded, ethno-political groups. Here as elsewhere, then, we are concerned with a German nation, and with other nations. Yet this chapter is also in part an account of many small groups and of the fashioning of group identities, through law and social action, in localised settings. It is on a comparatively intimate stage that the establishment and application of group boundaries and of principles of inclusion and exclusion must often be observed.[6] We are therefore also concerned here with something more multifarious, protean and situationally variable, and less articulately theorised, than a fully formed concept of nation:[7] with

---

[6] On this, see generally Barth, 'Introduction', pp. 9–19.
[7] For situationality in medieval collective identities, see Geary, 'Ethnic identity', esp. pp. 18, 21.

constructions, we might say, of German *ethnicity* – and of the non-German ethnic Other.[8]

In order to trace these, it will be necessary to establish the character and observe something of the variety of German-speaking settlement in medieval east-central Europe. Since ethnic formation is always a relational process, understanding how settlers and their descendants conceived of themselves and their neighbours requires some examination of what their neighbours had to say about them. An attempt must be made to take the temperature of the inter-ethnic discourse, while accepting that this varied sharply between places, times and social groups, and while also recognising that it is often impossible to recapture it at all. Indeed, much of the time there likely *was* no inter-ethnic discourse: other, local or familial, identities must normally have predominated. It will therefore be important here not to give undue weight to the more extreme constructions of inter-ethnic relations which certain eastern writings disclose, but which offer no reliable guide to day-to-day experience. Nevertheless, even extreme views merit some consideration, for what they reveal about the limits of the thinkable on problems of medieval inter-ethnic relations, and on appropriate solutions. For regions of Europe where the bounds of tolerable thought and action have in modern times proved so tragically broad, establishing the character and extent of ethnic radicalism in the medieval past has a particular interest and value.

Attention must also be given to the political frameworks into which the German migrants were incorporated, to the official identities attached to these and to their capacity to absorb the newcomers. No less important, however, were the many local and occupational groupings to which Germans and others belonged. Rarely, by contrast, do we find large, trans-regional associations having an identification – still less, an explicit self-identification – with German groups in the east. Special interest therefore attaches to two such formations which did arise, and which demand specific scrutiny: the Teutonic Order and the Hansa. German identity in the eastern lands was complex and varied, by turns socially assertive, muted and – in the source categories which have come down to us – all but inaudible. Its study requires a multi-track approach. It makes sense, however, to begin where the settlement movement itself began, in the heartlands of German speech, where literate commentators passed judgements on the eastern lands reflecting well-established patterns of ethnographic thought.

---

[8] Valuable here is Eriksen's definition of ethnicity as 'the enduring and systematic communication of cultural differences between groups considering themselves to be distinct': Eriksen, *Ethnicity*, p. 58.

Germans and the eastern Other

Such patterns can be observed with particular clarity in the accounts offered by German writers of the variety of small Slav peoples inhabiting northern continental Europe, between the Holstein peninsula and the Oder, and known collectively as Wends. The history of their dealings with German-speakers and of their wider fate is recounted by only a handful of authors, mostly living or originating in the Saxon marchlands where Wends remained, or had been until fairly recently, close neighbours. The stories which they tell are contradictory and confused in their chronologies, but thematically similar: the Wends had in times past been crushed, humiliated and evicted, by military forces from the west and south, which was why only scattered traces of them remained. According to Dietrich von Niem, they were driven from their lands and virtually annihilated in the tenth century by the Saxons, among whom a surviving remnant now dwelt, inhabiting marshy and wooded places and eking out a living by fishing and bird-catching.[9] The compiler of the *Saxon World Chronicle* told of the subjection of 'all Wendland' to Christianity under the Ottonians, of the Wends' apostasy and their conquest and re-Christianisation in the twelfth century.[10] Yet in his account, the Wends had also suffered an earlier expulsion, bringing them westward, when Charlemagne resettled in dispersed groups ten thousand people from beyond the Elbe, 'which is why Wendish villages are still found throughout the German lands'.[11] The *Sachsenspiegel*-glossator Johannes von Buch consigned the Wends' expropriation to a still remoter past. Those 'Thuringian nobles' whom, in the Saxon settlement legend, the émigré soldiers of Alexander the Great had slaughtered and expelled, were not, he insisted, 'real Thuringians' at all, but Wends.[12] Here was the tale of a centuries-long descent into abjection. 'And all the survivors of those [Wends] living in Saxony are serfs of the Saxons.'[13]

German observers continued, in a time when the social and cultural distinctions between these westernmost Slavs and their German

---

[9] Dietrich von Nieheim, *Viridarium*, ed. Lhotsky and Pivec, p. 100.

[10] The account was enriched by being able to draw upon the chronicle of the twelfth-century missionary priest Helmold von Bosau, whence were taken a number of lively, ethnically coloured anecdotes.

[11] *Sächsische Weltchronik*, ed. Weiland, p. 147. For a similar account (explaining the 'mennich wendisch dorp' still to be found in *Sassenland*), see *Magdeburger Schöppenchronik*, ed. Janicke, p. 45.

[12] *Glossen zum Sachsenspiegel-Landrecht: Buch'sche Glosse*, ed. Kaufmann, p. 1219 (to *Landrecht* III 44 § 3).

[13] Dietrich von Nieheim, *Viridarium*, ed. Lhotsky and Pivec, p. 101.

neighbours were in many places sharply diminishing or vanishing altogether, to insist upon their absoluteness and immutability. Their language, remarked Dietrich von Niem, was unknown to Germans, though the Wends claimed that Czechs, Poles and Pomeranians understood it.[14] Their customs, manners and dress were also quite distinct. An illustrated *Sachsenspiegel* manuscript shows Wends with their heads shaven below the crown, sporting distinctive striped leggings.[15] The memory of past wrongs, moreover, had left its own lasting rifts. Wends and Saxons do not sit in judgement on each other, explained Johannes von Buch, 'because they are ancient enemies'.[16] Dietrich von Niem put the matter more generally: Wends 'hate all foreign nations', and rob and kill strangers whenever they can.[17] The form of life of the natives of these northern marchlands was not only different, moreover, but less advanced – as some writers sought to suggest through their use of archaic ethnographic terms, evocative of a mood of timeless backwardness. Wends, for Dietrich von Niem, were 'Vandals' (the *gens Wandalorum*), whose homeland stretched for 14 days' journey from Saxony as far as Denmark and the 'kingdom of the Goths' (Sweden).[18] Heinrich von Herford depicted Ludwig IV's son, Margrave Ludwig of Brandenburg, speaking dismissively of his 'marshy' north-eastern patrimony, home to 'rude *Marchomanni*'.[19] For Dietrich (who insisted that, having dwelt since boyhood as their neighbour, he knew well their customs and character), Wends were distinguished by their coarse and rustic clothing.[20] They gained their sustenance more from pastoralism than arable agriculture – which they still conducted with 'a plough in the Roman fashion'. The raw predominated over the cooked in their diet. They were lawless without discrimination. It was their habit to

---

[14] Ibid.

[15] Heidelberg, Cod. Pal. germ. 164, from the beginning of the fourteenth century. For Wends, see Schmidt-Wiegand, 'Die Bilderhandschriften', pp. 244–7, 476, 478, 479, 495.

[16] *Glossen zum Sachsenspiegel-Landrecht: Buch'sche Glosse*, ed. Kaufmann, p. 1397 (to *Landrecht* III 70 § 1).

[17] Dietrich von Nieheim, *Viridarium*, ed. Lhotsky and Pivec, p. 101.

[18] Ibid., p. 100. 'Wendish' was also, however, employed in the late Middle Ages as a value-neutral geographical term for the south-western Baltic region, particularly in sources from the Hansa, where it designates Lübeck and other towns in those parts, which formed a constitutionally distinct group within the Hansa. See thus, e.g.: *HUB* 4, no. 243, p. 98 (13 February 1368): '… mit den steden van der Wendeschen siden' (here Lübeck, Rostock, Stralsund and Wismar); ibid., no. 311, p. 125 (3 August 1369): '… pro aliis civitatibus Slavici lateris'. For the 'Wendish towns' within the Hansa, see Dollinger, *Hansa*, p. 51.

[19] *Liber de rebus memorabilioribus*, ed. Potthast, p. 272.

[20] For what follows, see Dietrich von Nieheim, *Viridarium*, ed. Lhotsky and Pivec, pp. 100–1.

visit the Saxons' market towns (having no urban life of their own), but only in order to frequent taverns and get vomiting drunk. An evolutionary social scale is thus being applied, reflecting those rejuvenated values of ancient Mediterranean civilisation which we have encountered already.[21] Not Germans, however, but their neighbours are here assigned to its lowest rungs.

That this was not the only view which literate Germans might take of the western Slavs is demonstrated by the verses which late medieval German poets composed, in praise of particular Wendish princes.[22] Stereotypical accounts of the Wends as history's well-deserved losers and victims were only sustainable by ignoring the growing power and prestige of the western Baltic principalities, notably Pomerania and Mecklenburg. These enjoyed a golden age in the fourteenth century, under Wendish ruling dynasties whose sponsorship of urbanisation and of German settlement and culture did not lead them in the least to repudiate their Slavic roots. In Mecklenburg, the language of the immigrants was put to work in celebrating those roots, in the *Mecklenburg Rhyming Chronicle*, composed in honour of Prince Albert II (1318–79) by a German member of his chancery, Ernst von Kirchberg.[23] The chronicle, which exists in just a single, de luxe manuscript, was clearly conceived as a prestige artefact, with the purpose of positioning the Mecklenburg rulers and their dynasty within the highest princely circles of the Germano-Slavic east. The sumptuous miniatures with which it is adorned show the influence of illuminators' workshops in the Prague of Charles IV.[24] It was Charles who in 1348 had raised both Mecklenburg and neighbouring Pomerania to the status of principalities directly under the Reich. The cultural template which the Luxemburger had established at his Bohemian court, harnessing German and other western artists and writers to the celebration of an indigenous, Slavic regnal history and identity, was clearly attractive to his princely clients in the north. It was thus from a perspective of political centrality, not marginality, that Ernst set about recounting, in courtly German verse, the history 'von alden und von jungen Wentlanden' under the dukes. Here

---

[21] See above, Ch. 8, esp. pp. 357–60; and for their medieval application, including by writers in the Baltic zone, Bartlett, *Gerald*, Ch. 6.

[22] For Prince Wizlaw of Rügen, see below, n. 118. Albert II's predecessor in Mecklenburg, Henry II (d. 1319) was praised by the poet Frauenlob: *Politische Lyrik*, ed. Müller, vol I, p. 150.

[23] *Die Mecklenburgische Reimchronik*, ed. Cordshagen and Schmidt. For what follows, see: Scheibe, 'Dynastisch orientiertes Geschichtsbild'; J. Petersohn, 'Ernst von Kirchberg', in *VL* 2, cols. 618–20.

[24] Baier-Schröcke, *Die Buchmalerei*.

was triumphant Slavic dynastic history, tracing Mecklenburg's rulers from the legendary Obodrite king Billug to Prince Albert himself.[25] The chronicler's subjects were Wends with much to celebrate and little to excuse: even their land's Christianisation was portrayed as no act of German dominion, but the native princes' own achievement.[26]

Other eastern realms could point to still longer histories of association with the cultural mainstream of Latin Europe. Among these was the Empire's neighbour in the south-east, the kingdom of Hungary. The lands of the Hungarian crown constituted no zone of German conquest like the western Baltic, but a venerable sovereign realm. By the thirteenth century, Germans had long been entering Hungary in peace, under the protection of native kings who were themselves closely bound in blood to the German high nobility. High medieval German epic adorned such contacts with a penumbra of myth and heroic violence: Dietrich von Bern had once gone east, to Etzel's Hungarian court, as also, fatally, did the widowed Kriemhild.[27] Since 1308, moreover, the crown of St Stephen rested on Angevin heads, before passing in 1387 to the scarcely less westernised Sigismund of Luxemburg. Viewed from German soil, therefore, Hungary could hardly be painted as abject, primitive or obscure.

That did not, however, prevent Hungarians from themselves being repeatedly portrayed as barbarous: as a people inhabiting the uncertain margins of Latin Christendom, and sometimes of humanity itself.[28] In part, this image was constructed historically. Memories of the ravages of the Magyars, before their suppression in the tenth century by the Ottonians, were thus linked, in German report, to names invoking a more ancient and terrible past. In *Lohengrin* it is 'the Huns' (*die Híunèn*) whose victory, Henry I warns his princes, would be the undoing of all.[29] Into the fifteenth century, the behaviour of the Magyars was remembered by some as monstrous. According to Twinger, the Hungarians had spread terror by killing without distinction and drinking the blood of the dead.[30] They continued in the late Middle Ages to rate in some reports as cruel

---

[25] For Billug, see *Die Mecklenburgische Reimchronik*, ed. Cordshagen and Schmidt, pp. 22–3, and Scheibe, 'Geschichtsbild', pp. 50–1; and for the chronicle's view of Mecklenburg's history more generally, Schmidt, 'Mecklenburg und Pommern'.

[26] *Die Mecklenburgische Reimchronik*, ed. Cordshagen and Schmidt, pp. 48–50.

[27] See Sager, 'Hungarians'.

[28] See generally Andritsch, 'Das Ungarnbild'.

[29] *Lohengrin*, ed. Cramer, p. 286, vv. 1944–8. In recounting this period, the *Saxon World Chronicle* makes reference to 'the Huns, who are now Hungarians': *Sächsische Weltchronik*, ed. Weiland, p. 147.

[30] *Chronik des Jacob Twinger*, ed. Hegel, p. 415. Cf. Dietrich von Nieheim, *Viridarium*, ed. Lhotsky and Pivec, p. 92, comparing the Hungarians with the monstrous Phalangi, who dwell beyond Russia. By this date, the charge of blood-drinking was a

soldiers. According to the Styrian rhyming chronicle, Otakar II's defeated troops at the Marchfeld counted themselves lucky to fall as prisoners into German, not Hungarian, hands.[31] Just like the Germans themselves in western caricature, it was their very wildness that allowed Hungarians to excel in arms.[32] In the late thirteenth century, their religious affiliation still rated (not, it is true, wholly without contemporary justification) as uncertain.[33] To one Austrian annalist, it was a source of wonder that the Christian chants of Rudolf I's army were taken up even by the 'unbelieving Cumans' and 'semi-Christian Hungarians' who were fighting alongside the king against Otakar of Bohemia.[34] German writers thus continued in the late Middle Ages repeatedly to rank the Hungarians below their own people on the neo-classical scale of European civilisation.

Again, however, while tropes of ethnic backwardness were clearly available to literate Germans, not all saw fit to apply them. The signs are that the chivalrous classes inside the German frontier had come by the fourteenth century to regard Hungary and its elite as part of their own cultural landscape. The Austrian herald Peter Suchenwirt (d. 1395) lauded King Louis the Great (r. 1342–82) as a brilliant chivalric paragon: he was known to cherish Germans especially, and his battle cry ('Hurta, hurta, Ungerlant!') was proverbial in the best German knightly circles.[35] And while the cliché of the barbarous Hun enjoyed wide currency among the literate, closer and more contemporary characterisations of Hungarians are found repeatedly only in writings from the Austrian lands.[36] Even among Austrians, moreover, their occurrence is distinctly uneven. Hostile views of the near neighbour are found particularly in Latin annals from the second half of the thirteenth century, a time when the Danubian lands were exposed to the

---

long-repeated one. For the cliché of Hungarian cannibalism, traceable back to Regino of Prüm, see Sager, 'Hungarians', p. 29.

[31] *Ottokars österreichische Reimchronik*, ed. Seemüller, p. 277, vv. 17168–79.

[32] For the fighting abilities of Hungarians in Germanophone stereotype, Andritsch, 'Das Ungarnbild', pp. 24–9.

[33] The period was one in which the king, Ladislas IV (r. 1272–90), had drawn close to non-Christian elements in his lands. However, Ladislas's pagan reputation was also the result of hostile myth-making, provoked by the king's political difficulties: Berend, *Christendom*, pp. 171–83.

[34] *Continuatio Vindobonensis*, ed. Wattenbach, p. 709.

[35] *Politische Lyrik*, ed. Müller, vol. II, pp. 14–18 ('Von Chuonik Ludwig von Ungerlant'); and for Louis's esteeming of Germans (within Hungary) as a source of his fame: ibid., p. 33, vv. 225–8: 'Die weil er hat di Dautschen wert / So chlingt seins hohen lobs swert / Durich alle lant den maisten tail, / Er hat gelukch und siges hail.' Elsewhere, Suchenwirt recounts the murder of Charles of Durazzo at Visegrád in 1385, but without any recourse to anti-Hungarian stereotypes: ibid., pp. 40–1, vv. 69–120.

[36] Approximately 25 per cent of the *c.* 100,000 verses of the Styrian Rhyming Chronicle are concerned with Hungarian affairs: Andritsch, 'Das Ungarnbild', p. 25.

ravages of Hungarian armies.[37] The depiction by some Austrian writers of Hungarians as wild despoilers and faithless oath-breakers thus
had particular material stimuli. While they certainly drew upon more
deep-rooted patterns of ethnographic stereotype, these might also be
set aside. Context and authorial motive were all-important.

The variable presence of an eastern Other in German writings is particularly evident in accounts of the Bohemians. The lands under the
Přemyslid monarchs, in contrast to Hungary and most of Poland, historically lay within the frontiers of the Empire. The kings themselves
were therefore imperial vassals, performing the ceremonial office of
cupbearer and owing military service and a limited duty to travel to
assemblies on German soil.[38] By the end of the thirteenth century, their
membership of the (German) college of electors had been confirmed.[39]
The royal title itself was an imperial creation, and down to the time
of Charles IV the kings were crowned by the archbishop of Mainz.
The thirteenth-century Přemyslids had basked in the praise of German
poets, while after 1310 the crown of St Wenceslas lay with a western
dynasty. After 1347, for half a century the king of Bohemia also wore
the imperial diadem. Under Charles and Wenceslas, the Reich itself was
for much of the time ruled from Bohemia, and offices of government
entrusted to its inhabitants. Bohemia thus displayed the lineaments of
a developed – and with its vast silver reserves, immensely rich – western
kingdom.

In German portrayals of the Bohemians, a diverse range of authorial perspectives, attitudes and purposes was combined with the effects
of changing times and circumstances, and with a widespread recognition of underlying historical affinities, to produce a fluctuating picture. If familiar patterns of collective stereotype played a part in that
picture, their application tended to have particular explanations. The
violent anti-Czech tirade of which Dietrich von Niem delivered himself
(a 'people unworthy of the Christian name', a 'wretched people, who
should be tortured in the perpetual fires of Hell') was ostensibly a comment upon the brutal and sacrilegious style of war purportedly once
practised by the Bohemian allies of Lothar III (d. 1137).[40] However,
it probably also reflects deteriorating Czech–German relations at a

---

[37] As examples of such views, see: *Continuatio Claustroneuburgensis IV.*, ed. Wattenbach,
    p. 648; *Historia annorum 1264–1279*, ed. Wattenbach, p. 651, for the view that 'no
    Christian king ever committed such horrors' as did Hungarian forces in Austria; and
    for the political context, Hoensch, *Přemysl Otakar II.*, pp. 154–73.
[38] For their constitutional position, see: Richter, 'Die böhmischen Länder', pp. 269–70;
    Behr, *Literatur*, pp. 30–2.
[39] Above, Ch. 6, pp. 275–6.
[40] Dietrich von Nieheim, *Viridarium*, ed. Lhotsky and Pivec, pp. 92–3.

time of mounting religious tensions in the early fifteenth century, when Dietrich was writing. Before the Hussite era, however, only the struggle between Rudolf I and Otakar II drew widespread German attention.

On the whole, it is noteworthy how seldom that conflict was written up as a clash of peoples. Some German sources do admittedly disclose a taste for perfunctory outbursts of ethnically flavoured rhetoric, as in Engelbert von Admont's praise of Rudolf, 'who broke the pride of the Slavic sceptre'.[41] But not until a generation after Otakar's death did a handful of writers come to interpret the clash in explicitly ethnic terms, claiming that the Bohemian king (whose army at the Marchfeld had included contingents under German magnates) was an enemy to Germans as such.[42] Only now were the Czechs collectively ascribed a central place, most conspicuously by the Styrian rhyming chronicler, Otakar uz der Geul, who thus makes repeated, derogatory reference to a people from whom only 'deception, envy and hatred' are to be expected.[43]

Contemporary narratives, by contrast, preferred to concentrate on the figure of the magnificent Přemysl Otakar himself, presenting his struggle with the Habsburg as a dispute between vassal and lord, as a contest of chivalric warriors, or as a morality tale about the fall of Pride.[44] Such accounts are remarkable in three respects particularly. First, nearly all of the many Latin annals recounting Otakar's downfall are of Austrian provenance, as also are most of the principal later narratives. Here was primarily a frontier incident, interpreted for a frontier public by writers who themselves lived close to the scene of events. Secondly, opinion on Bohemia's 'golden king' was split, with many annalists from the 'German' side championing the Bohemian's

---

[41] Quoted in Graus, 'Přemysl Otakar II.', p. 81; and see Lhotsky, *Quellenkunde*, p. 282. Verses dating from 1276 revile the pro-Otakar burghers of Vienna for handing over the keys of their city to Slavs (Graus, 'Přemysl Otakar II.', p. 80 n. 106): 'Winna tui Sclavis est muri tradita clavis. / Hoc tibi culpa gravis, quod stare recondite mavis, / Quam quod eas ut avis in terra libera quavis / Complicibus pravis timor Bohemica suavis.'

[42] Thus *Chronicon Colmariense*, ed. Jaffé, p. 245; and see the comments of Graus, 'Přemysl Otakar II.', pp. 81–2. Their views are to be contrasted with those of the fourteenth-century German 'Dalimil' translator, working in Prague, for whom Otakar was a special friend to Bohemia's own German population: see below, p. 423.

[43] *Ottokars österreichische Reimchronik*, ed. Seemüller, p. 298, vv. 22440–3.

[44] For what follows, see generally Seibt, 'Die böhmische Nachbarschaft'. The fragmentary Middle High German verses, 'Böhmenschlacht', personalise Otakar's contest with Rudolf as a military encounter between two outstanding individuals, represented by their armorials; and it is as a 'Roman', not a German, that Rudolf overcomes the Bohemian king: *Politische Lyrik*, ed. Müller, vol. I, pp. 97–101; and see the *Cantilena de rege Bohemiae* (ibid., p. 101) for a German-vernacular lament on the death of Otakar, a chivalric paragon.

cause, at least up until his submission to Rudolf in 1276, and a handful sticking by him to the bitter end. Otakar's lordship in the Austrian duchies was by no means universally reviled; and to many Austrians, the Habsburgs and their Swabian henchmen who came after were just as much foreign intruders as were the Bohemians.[45] Furthermore, it is instructive to observe something of the variety of specific factors which might influence the judgements of individual writers. The annalist Heinrich von Heimburg, one of Otakar's staunchest defenders, was an Austrian, a priest at Gmünd an der Thaya; yet he had also spent time in a Moravian monastery and been consecrated deacon by the bishop of Prague.[46] The frontier thus acted not only to polarise but to complicate identities. Communities, like individuals, might feel the competing pull of affinities from both sides, overwriting and nullifying any imagined ethnic difference. Cistercians linked to the Austrian monastery of Heiligenkreuz thus wrote resolutely in favour of Otakar, a generous patron to their order.[47] His foundation at Goldenkron (Zlatá Koruna) in southern Bohemia (1263) had been populated with Heiligenkreuz monks.

Rarely, then, did German writers seek to reduce the affairs of Bohemia and its neighbours to a bipolar confrontation of Germans and Slavs. In most cases, events were portrayed as the outcome of regnal and dynastic politics, and were not viewed through an explicitly ethnic lens at all. Nevertheless, Czechs too were periodically depicted as stereotypically Other. Significant here is not the frequency of their portrayal, but its manner. This was not arbitrary, but drew upon templates widely familiar among literate medieval Europeans, with their origins in Graeco-Roman ethnography, designating peoples outside the civilised fold. Emphasis was thus placed upon allegedly primitive social habits, turbulent political arrangements, and brutal and predatory styles of war. Bohemian warfare, it was alleged, blighted the land, while the politics of the realm were hardly less disorderly.[48] In the same tradition, the Austrian Enikel drew attention to what he claimed was the Czech habit of heavy drinking: one Bohemian could see four Germans

---

[45] For Austrian views of Habsburg lordship, see below, Ch. 11, p. 515.

[46] *Heinrici de Heimburg annales*, ed. Wattenbach, pp. 711–18; Seibt, 'Die böhmische Nachbarschaft', p. 185.

[47] *Historia annorum 1264–1279*, ed. Wattenbach, pp. 652–4; and see Seibt, 'Die böhmische Nachbarschaft', pp. 174–5.

[48] For German portrayals of the Bohemians at war, see Görlich, *Zur Frage*, pp. 146–7, as well as *Königsaaler Geschichts-Quellen*, ed. Loserth, p. 50; *Ottokars österreichische Reimchronik*, ed. Seemüller, p. 237, vv. 17916–19; and for Dietrich von Niem's lurid view, above, p. 392.

under the table.[49] Broadly, these were the same lineaments of alterity which German writers applied to other peoples dwelling to their east and north-east, just as observers in the west and south of Latin Europe – and indeed, some Germans – applied them to the Germans themselves. What part, if any, they may have played in constructions of identity among the German settler communities in the east will need to be considered in due course.

By the late Middle Ages, literate Germans had more than just stereotypes to go on, and little reason to view the lands to their north and east as alien or unknown worlds, without relation to their own. On the contrary, awareness of these regions, and consciousness of what bound them to the German-speaking west, grew substantially between the thirteenth and fifteenth centuries.[50] A number of learned Latinate writers now gave account of the lands beyond the Elbe and of their peoples. An early, detailed instance of this is the Franciscan encyclopaedist Bartholomaeus Anglicus, who wrote at Magdeburg in the 1230s or 1240s. The Ebstorf map represented north-eastern Europe with a level of detail and accuracy unprecedented in its genre.[51] Dating from the same broad period, the *Saxon World Chronicle* displays comparable levels of close knowledge, recording with dates the founding of Riga (*de stat to Rige to Liflande*) by Bishop Albrecht von Buxtehude and Reval (*Revele to Estlande*) by the king of Denmark.[52] A Magdeburg town chronicler in the fourteenth century marvelled, on the basis of some knowledge, at the sheer extent of the Slav-speaking regions to his east.[53] The rhetorical formulation 'German – Romance – Slavic' (*Tiutsch – Welsch – Wint*), which is found recurrently in German verses, and which served for poetical purposes to invoke a sense of 'everyone', indicates an imagined conjoining of the Slavs with the other main European language groups.[54]

---

[49] *Jansen Enikels Weltchronik*, ed. Strauch, p. 537, vv. 27583–6.
[50] One specific illustration of this trend is the growing prominence of Scandinavian kings as the subject of German political verse in this period: Schöndorf, 'Danische Herrschergestalten'.
[51] For this and the growth of geographical knowledge more generally, see: Strzelczyk, 'Der Prozeß', esp. pp. 155–8; Friedland, 'Ostsee', p. 19.
[52] *Sächsische Weltchronik*, ed. Weiland, pp. 236, 242.
[53] *Magdeburger Schöppenchronik*, ed. Janicke, p. 41.
[54] Thus *Kaiserchronik: zweite (Schwäbische) Fortsetzung*, ed. Schröder, pp. 411, 412, vv. 21, 136. Among the 12 Christian languages of the 72 which came from Babel, Jansen Enikel lists first *Walsch*, *Windisch* and *Diutsch*: *Jansen Enikels Weltchronik*, ed. Strauch, pp. 533–4, vv. 27400, 27409, 27419. Occasionally, the community was extended to include Hungarians. See thus the opening of a verse by Meister Boppe: 'Des merke unt vröu dich, hoher, werder, wiser mensch, / du sist Tiutsch, Welsch, Windisch, Ungersch oder Tensch...' Printed in *Minnesinger*, ed. von der Hagen, vol. III, p. 381.

The prevailing impression is not, however, only of imagined bonds. Vernacular versifiers just as often chose to construct their rhetorical unities from the German and Romance tongues alone.[55] Alexander von Roes had no role to offer the eastern peoples within his programme for an inter-ethnic division of labour in universal governance, and he did not therefore trouble to enumerate their common qualities or position them in relation to the Germans. They dwelt not only beyond the forest, but also beyond the scope of his westward-directed vision.[56] The common heritage of Frankia, Rome and Troy was what counted for him, and the peoples of the east and north had little part in it. Although Alexander listed the king of Bohemia among the electors, he had no historical scheme to explain his accession, as he did for the German princes. The Bavarian popes-and-emperors chronicle traced a fundamental division between the Slav peoples (among them Czechs, Poles and Russians), descendants of Noah's son Ham, and the Germans and French, who were from Japheth. The distinction was supported by a sophisticated phonetic analysis, contrasting the palatal speech of Slavs with the dental vocalisation of western languages.[57] If connections there were with the east, it was still the lines of division which tended to stand out more clearly, and to appear more absolute than those which separated different western peoples.

Knowledge, although generally increasing, remained partial, and the opportunities for its acquisition subject to much social and regional variation. The campaigns of the Teutonic Order, in which visiting crusaders from the west participated alongside the regular knight-brethren, were the subject of recurrent, if seldom detailed, report in western German chronicles.[58] The more venturesome among the German nobility would have had ample opportunity to form impressions of the eastern and northern lands, as the itineraries of their chivalrous wanderings, recorded by the herald-poets of the fourteenth century, make plain.[59] The itinerant singers themselves, some of whom sought their bread at princely courts on the margins of German speech, might carry

[55] As an example, *Rymkronyk van Jan van Heelu*, ed. Willems, p. 304, vv. 8337–8 (*dietsch – walsch*).

[56] Alexander von Roes, *Noticia seculi*, cap. 9, ed. Grundmann and Heimpel, p. 156, for the forests separating the *regnum Francorum* 'a Sclavis, Boemis et Ungaris'.

[57] *Chronicon Imperatorum et Pontificum Bavaricum*, ed. Waitz, p. 221; and see Borst, *Der Turmbau*, vol. II.ii, pp. 826–8. The idea of Slav descent from Ham also featured in the Luxemburger genealogy painted at Karlstein, which thus traced Charles IV himself back to Noah's ill-favoured son: Suckale, 'Die Hofkunst im 14. Jahrhundert', p. 330.

[58] Examples: *Die Chronik Johanns von Winterthur*, ed. Baethgen, pp. 279–80; *Die Chronik des Mathias von Neuenburg*, ed. Hofmeister, p. 474.

[59] Thus, e.g., Gelre Herald (on Herr Claes Oem), Peter Suchenwirt (on Herr Friedrich von Kreusspeck): *Politische Lyrik*, ed. Müller, vol. II, pp. 7–13, 18–25.

home aphoristic portraits of the political habits of others. 'The Danish murderers have the prize; in murdering, no one is so wise', rhymed Master Rumelant, referring to the death of King Erik Klipping in 1286.[60] The southern Baltic coastlands, to whose urban life the Hansa lent at least a vestigial unity, tended to be the subject of more detailed and informed coverage than were other parts of east-central Europe. It was also within this zone that the advance of German-speakers during the central Middle Ages attained at least limited visibility for some westerners. To the chronicler Detmar, Thorn (Torún) on the Vistula was a 'German' town.[61]

Yet, as a Lübecker, Detmar's perspective on the Hanseatic east was a privileged one. More remarkable is how *little* awareness most German writings reveal of the infiltration of German and other western migrants into the eastern and northern lands, and of the gradual transformative impact which that process was exerting upon the ethno-cultural landscape. Their silence indicates a difficulty beyond mere ignorance: their fundamental lack of a conceptual vocabulary suitable for describing ethnically mixed political communities, or capturing the reality and consequences of linguistic and cultural interaction and change. Breslau, despite its mainly German inhabitants and hinterland of settlement zones, still, for German observers, lay squarely 'in Poland'.[62] Even Austrian writers, who must have known that neighbouring Bohemia had a significant German-speaking population, give little hint of the fact. Although the contemporary map of European peoples was believed to reflect the results of many ancient migrations and displacements, there was seemingly little notion of how that map might still be undergoing transformation, or might change further in the future. Only a king appeared capable of bringing about such change peacefully, and even he would likely require supernatural aid. Such was Jakob Twinger's (exaggerated) judgement on the transformative reign of Charles IV:

He was ... well educated in all branches of knowledge, and knew the black arts, as some claim. And he knew six languages, among which he loved the German

---

[60] *Politische Lyrik*, ed. Müller, vol. I, p. 84; and see Schöndorf, 'Dänische Herrschergestalten', esp. pp. 43–7. Rumelant (or 'Rumzlant') was active at a number of northern princely courts, including those of Mecklenburg and Pomerania; a direct relationship with Denmark is also likely: Schöndorf, 'Dänische Herrschergestalten', pp. 43, 69.

[61] *Detmar-Chronik*, ed. Koppmann, i.565.

[62] Thus *Die Chronik des Mathias von Neuenburg*, ed. Hofmeister, p. 58 (*in Presla Polonie*). Peter von Dusburg, writing in Prussia in the 1320s, similarly offers a definition of 'Poland' which includes Silesia, listing 'Polish' princes and nobles who came on crusade, from the lands between the Oder and the Vistula: *Cronica terre Prussie*, ed. Töppen, pp. 57–8.

language best of all. For that reason he greatly extended the German tongue. Thus, in Prague and throughout all Bohemia German is spoken most, where previously there was nothing but Czech [*behemesch*].[63]

But Charles IV was no ordinary king, and common expectations were of a different kind. Kingdoms, or even the shades of a decayed kingdom like Poland in the thirteenth century, seemed naturally to suppose the existence of just a single historical and cultural community within the regnal bounds.[64] Imagining a multi-ethnic polity – or at least, imagining it as more than a source of inevitable conflict – mostly defeated writers of the period.

Swords and ploughshares: Germans in the east

The process frequently, though inadequately, termed the German settlement of the east was both protracted and complex. Extending from the ninth to the fifteenth century (though with high points in the twelfth and thirteenth), it encompassed a bewildering variety of landscapes and human populations, and was driven forward by a diverse and shifting amalgam of factors. The settlement zone itself can be imagined as a deep, mobile and broken arc, extending across the continental land mass from Jutland to the Carpathians and from the Gulf of Finland to the Dolomites and the Istrian coast. Significant unifying elements are hard to discern. Topography and climate ranged from temperate lowlands under arable crops to alpine meadow and sub-Arctic tundra, from densely peopled coasts and river valleys to empty forest and trackless bog. By the late Middle Ages, some settlement regions already had large and numerous towns, while in others urban life was still almost unknown. The native populations of these lands spoke languages and dialects encompassing nearly all European linguistic families: Slavic, Baltic, Finno-Ugrian, Germanic and Romance. Some had been Latin Christians since the ninth century; others, in the far north-east, still adhered to paganism at the start of the fifteenth. Some inhabited institutionalised kingdoms with close similarities and ties to the realms of western Europe, or smaller, but likewise westward-facing, principalities. Others dwelt within more localised political worlds, were subject to a monastic or episcopal lord, to crusader-knights or to the vast empire of Lithuania. Some acknowledged rulers who spoke their own or some other eastern tongue, while others had German-speaking masters.

---

[63] *Chronik des Jacob Twinger*, ed. Hegel, pp. 484–5.
[64] For some of the means available to contemporaries to conceptualise new ('settler') communities in this period, see Frame, '"Les Engleys"'.

Across these immensely varied locales, the chronology and impulses of German advance and the character and density of infiltration varied sharply, as did the nature of the late medieval legacy.

In its earliest stages, the eastward extension of Germanic culture and lordship was closely bound up with imperial expansion – first under Charlemagne, then under the Ottonians – and with the closely linked propagation of the Christian faith. Magdeburg, founded in 968, was both military outpost and missionary see. The extension of Saxon power against the Wends was checked by the great revolt of 983 and the mass apostasy which followed, forcing the abandonment of Ottonian bishoprics east of the Elbe. By the early twelfth century, however, the twin processes of military expansion and Christianisation had resumed, now spearheaded by a number of powerful German dynasties, entrusted with the strengthening of the Empire's northern and eastern marches: the counts of Holstein, the dukes of Saxony and the margraves of Meißen and Brandenburg. Bishoprics were founded and refounded, and monastic communities planted in the newly won lands. The Wendish crusade of 1147 was only the most prominent manifestation of the Church's sustained backing for military ventures by the Christian powers of the region. Not all of these were under German leadership. The Danish monarchy was a significant military presence in the Baltic zone, and early in the thirteenth century embarked upon the conquest of Estonia in the far north-east. By this time, however, Christian-military expansionism was gaining an increasingly institutionalised character. The Teutonic Order, invited to the lower Vistula by the duke of Masovia in the 1220s, was the most successful and long-lived among a number of Christian knightly brotherhoods active on the north-east pagan frontier, with the declared aim of protecting missionary work. By the century's close, the whole of Prussia had been subjected militarily to the Order's rule.

Christian holy war and outright conquest, however, had only ever been an aspect of the spread of Germanic presence and influence in eastern societies; and by the thirteenth century, away from the military frontier in the eastern Baltic, these factors no longer played any part at all. The Middle Ages witnessed no unified Teutonic *Drang nach Osten*, as polemicists once contended. From an early date, Germans were entering the lands to their east by peaceful (though not for that reason necessarily always uncontroversial) means. The conversion to Catholic Christianity of the native rulers of Bohemia, Poland and Hungary in the tenth and eleventh centuries (and of the Baltic principalities of Mecklenburg and Pomerania in the twelfth) was followed by the recruitment of high-status Germans to their courts, and to staff the upper ranks of their churches.[65] Economic development was another significant motor of advance, particularly when it enjoyed the encouragement of native princes. A German merchant settlement is attested to in Prague as early as the eleventh century; in the late twelfth, its status and immunities were guaranteed by Bohemian ducal charter.[66] The conjunction of commercial growth with other factors, including territorial lordship and Christian holy war, was demonstrated to particularly striking effect in the twelfth- and thirteenth-century Baltic, where the emergent Hansa acted as a powerful catalyst to coastal urbanisation. The town of Riga, founded in 1201, with its access to the western-Russian river network, functioned from the start as missionary see and military garrison *and* as German merchant base.[67]

German modes of living moved eastwards at variable speeds and in diverse ways. Those which ultimately travelled furthest – forms of town law originating in Lübeck or Magdeburg, for example, or village layouts exported from Germany – reached their remotest destinations without the need for any accompanying German settlement.[68] Where people came too, they came in varying numbers, at different times and for different reasons. In the early thirteenth century, when the German settlement of Lusatia was already all but complete, migration to the Vistula basin under the Teutonic Order had yet to begin.[69] The progressive eastward spread of German-speakers displayed no simple geographical or chronological pattern. On the one hand, settler communities were already established in Transylvania by the late twelfth century, and by the fourteenth had penetrated remote Ruthenia; on the other, the westward-facing flatlands of Greater Poland, the central Hungarian plain and much of Bohemia were left relatively untouched (see Map 4). In certain regions, such as Livonia, the German element in the population was limited to knights, townspeople and clergy. Elsewhere, the migrants were specialist workers. On the south-eastern slopes of the Tatras in Upper Hungary, the German-speaking settlements which proliferated between the twelfth and fourteenth centuries housed miners, recruited to tap the rich local deposits of precious metals.

---

[65] For Poland, see Rogall, 'Polen', pp. 48–9; for Bohemia, Schwinges, ' "Primäre" und "sekundäre" Nation', pp. 507–8.

[66] Higounet, *Die deutsche Ostsiedlung*, p. 163; *Urkunden und erzählende Quellen*, ed. Helbig and Weinrich, vol. II, no. 93, pp. 352–7 (1176 × 1178). Comparable merchant settlements are attested to in Poland from the same period: Rogall, 'Polen', p. 48.

[67] See Christiansen, *The Northern Crusades*, pp. 92–7; Fletcher, *The Conversion*, pp. 493–5.

[68] For the spread of German town law, see Engel (ed.), *Großer historischer Weltatlas*, Map 41a.

[69] For the chronology of rural settlement, see Aubin, 'The lands', pp. 455–6.

What sets the twelfth and thirteenth centuries apart from earlier phases in the eastward movement of Germans is the number of those who were now drawn in. Walter Kuhn estimated that around 200,000 mainly German-speaking westerners may have settled in the lands between Elbe and Oder during the twelfth century, with perhaps a roughly equivalent number going east in the thirteenth.[70] Such figures inevitably rest upon much conjecture, and must be received with corresponding scepticism; but they do at least serve to highlight a crucial change: the settlement of the east had become a mass movement. In addition to the high-status individuals and relatively small specialist groups who had gone before, there now came large numbers of agriculturalists. Their advent brought the transformation of entire landscapes, the massive extension of cultivation (in which growing native populations were also now intensively engaged), and the establishment of very many new settlements.[71] By 1400, some 93 new towns and 1,400 new villages had been planted in the Teutonic Order's Prussian territories alone, while around 1,200 villages were founded in Silesia between 1200 and 1350.[72]

The factors impelling the migrations were several. Partly they are to be sought in the settlers' homelands, where rising population levels had often already stimulated widespread domestic land clearance and reclamation.[73] That was far from being the whole story, however, as substantial land grants, on generous terms, were generally still deemed necessary in order to induce settlers to come east.[74] The willingness of princes and landlords in the settlement zones to make such offers (and increasingly also to extend comparable benefits to native peasants) reflected a growing drive towards territorial improvement. It was not only Christian rulers who were alert to the potential advantages. In 1323, the Lithuanian prince Gediminas sent letters to the cities of the Baltic coast, including Lübeck, Stralsund and Rostock, and to the Franciscans and Dominicans of Saxony, seeking to induce German manpower to settle his territories.[75] The motivation for such campaigns lay not only in a desire for increased revenues, but in considerations

---

[70] Cited in Higounet, *Die deutsche Ostsiedlung*, p. 99.
[71] For the application of the new techniques to native peasant colonisation, see Górecki, *Economy*, esp. pp. 275–82.
[72] Moraw, *Von offener Verfassung*, p. 196; Aubin, 'The lands', p. 485.
[73] Higounet, *Die deutsche Ostsiedlung*, pp. 39–50.
[74] At the new village of Mährisch-Hermersdorf in Moravia in the 1260s, for example, settlers were to have 13 initial rent-free years on their plots, with 20 rent-free years for any additional lands which they cleared and cultivated: Higounet, *Die deutsche Ostsiedlung*, pp. 166–7.
[75] Rowell, *Lithuania Ascending*, pp. 205–7.

of defence (through the establishment of fortress-towns) and in perceived political and ideological opportunities. Augmenting the population of the land was deemed to add to the prestige of its ruler, while the presence of alien groups dependent upon his protection could serve to strengthen the prince against indigenous elites. Decisions to invite in German-speaking settlers therefore went beyond mere economic rationalism: they were inescapably political decisions, capable of inviting political judgement and controversy.

The impact of the settlers upon regional ethnic and cultural landscapes naturally also showed much variety. Long-term change was generally greatest where the migrants came earliest and in greatest strength, and where German-speaking core-lands lay close at hand. In Brandenburg, it is estimated that as early as the 1220s Slav-speaking Wends comprised only a third of the population.[76] By the fifteenth century, Germans and Wends had mostly merged, as they had also in many (though not all) parts of Mecklenburg, Pomerania and Saxony, to form largely undifferentiated German-speaking societies.[77] The Wendish tongue, still ascribed by the *Sachsenspiegel* an equal judicial status with German, occupied a more restricted position in later redactions of the code. In a growing number of locations, as at Magdeburg around the year 1290, or at Altenburg, Zwickau and Leipzig in 1327, Wendish ceased to have validity before the courts.[78] Such developments probably indicate above all a sharp regional decline in the number of monoglot Slavic-speakers, rather than the disenfranchisement of remaining Wends. Elsewhere the Germans' predominance was less great and their migration less sustained, and the course of cultural fusion thus more protracted. In Carinthia, if the *Styrian Rhyming Chronicle* is to be believed, the duke himself retained into the fourteenth century the right to answer accusers before the king 'in the Slavic language'.[79] In the commandery of Christburg in the *Ordenstaat* in the late fourteenth century, 1,421 German were living alongside 1,435 Prussian families. By the early fifteenth, Germans still comprised only around 40 per cent of

---

[76] Higounet, *Die deutsche Ostsiedlung*, p. 327.

[77] For evidence of the extent of Germanisation in Pomerania, see Benl, 'Pommern', pp. 49, 62. Pockets of Slav-speakers of varying size nevertheless long remained in some localities. Wends were thus still to be found, e.g., at Spandau near Berlin at the start of the sixteenth century: Vogel, *Der Verbleib*, p. 74.

[78] Hugelmann, 'Die Rechtsstellung', p. 237. For Wends in the *Sachsenspiegel*, see generally Willoweit, 'Gericht und Urteil'.

[79] *Ottokars österreichische Reimchronik*, ed. Seemüller, p. 267, vv. 20146–52. For the Carinthian ducal installation ceremony, during which the new duke had to answer a series of questions posed by a peasant in the Slav tongue, see below, Ch. 11, p. 512.

the population of the Order's Prussian territories as a whole.[80] Although wealthier Prussians assimilated to the incomers, further down society barriers remained more solid.[81] Not until the seventeenth century did the Prussian tongue die out.

How, within what settings, on whose terms and with what consequences native and settler populations came together depended upon a host of individual factors. There was no general template, and no certainty that German speech and manners would ultimately prevail. In the Bohemian lands, where Germans made up no more than a sixth of the total population by 1400, only in a limited number of locales, mainly along the frontiers facing Germany, did Germanisation of the Czech population gradually take place.[82] Elsewhere, it was the descendants of the migrants who were eventually absorbed, by weight of surrounding population numbers, into their Czech-speaking neighbourhoods. In some territories, the infiltration of Germans was confined to isolated groups and scattered settlements. In the bishopric of Freising in 1291, just a quarter of the villages were German.[83] In Pomerelia, the westernmost province of the *Ordensstaat*, Slav-speakers still comprised four-fifths of the population as late as *c.* 1410.[84] At Zagreb in the late fourteenth century, membership of the town council was divided between four different ethnic groups, among which Germans were not the most important.[85]

---

[80] For Christburg, see Wenskus, 'Der deutsche Orden', p. 423; for early fifteenth-century population distribution, Biskup, 'Das Problem', p. 13.

[81] For the survival of the Prussian language among the native freeholder-class, see Boockmann, 'Die neue Besiedlung', pp. 125–6. A similarly socially graded picture of assimilation is observable elsewhere. Thus, for Pomerania there is evidence that the native aristocracy had adopted the German language by the beginning of the fourteenth century, whereas Slavic speech proved more tenacious among the fishing communities of the coast and on the islands of Usedom and Wollin: Benl, 'Pommern', p. 63.

[82] Moraw, 'Das Mittelalter', p. 91; Richter, 'Die böhmischen Länder', p. 342. For the distribution of German settlement in Bohemia, see E. Schwarz, 'Die deutsche Siedelgebiete in Böhmen und Mähren-Schlesien in vorhussitischer Zeit', in Meynen (ed.), *Sudetendeutscher Atlas*, pp. 13–14. The pattern was the same in Silesia: in the south and west, where Germans predominated, native Poles were gradually assimilated, while in Upper Silesia, where Poles remained in the majority, Germans were by the fifteenth century adopting the Polish language: Moraw, 'Das Mittelalter (bis 1469)', p. 98. For the variable speed of Polonisation in the German-settled regions of Poland, see Rogall, 'Polen', p. 96.

[83] Higounet, *Die deutsche Ostsiedlung*, p. 159. In Carniola and Lower Styria, Slovenes are estimated to have made up around 80 per cent of the population: Wakounig, 'Von Přemysl Otakar II.', p. 66.

[84] Biskup, 'Das Problem', p. 12.

[85] Krahwinkler, 'Der Raum', pp. 51–2. The other groups were *Sclavi*, *Hungari* and *Latini* (*Gallici*).

It was in the towns, and particularly the larger towns, that the greatest concentrations of German-speakers were to be found. This was starkly true of Livonia, where the surrounding countryside was almost empty of German peasant settlers.[86] Already at the time of the Mongol invasion of Hungary, Pest (Ofen) was being described as 'a large and very rich German town' (*theutonica villa*).[87] Of 1,403 identifiable personal names from Silesian towns down to 1326, only 21 (1.4 per cent) are Slav, the rest German.[88] Names (often the only indicator we have for the population make-up of towns) are admittedly uncertain ethnic identifiers.[89] Nevertheless, other evidence repeatedly confirms the long-lasting dominance of Germanophone culture, at least within the elites. It was in German that a town book (*stat register*) was commenced in Bratislava (Pressburg) around the year 1370.[90] In Kraków in 1373, the spiritual needs of leading burghers were being met by one 'Nikolaus, preacher to the Germans', at St Mary's Church.[91] Where this German predominance was underpinned by law, it might prove tenacious. The Slovakian mining town of Neusohl (Banská Bistrica), established as a 'Saxons'-only settlement by Hungarian royal charter in 1255, retained to the end of the Middle Ages a solidly German character.[92] On the whole, however, in towns which could not depend upon a steady stream of incomers from a Germanophone rural hinterland, the native element tended naturally to rise, in numbers and social prominence, as German

[86] Johansen and von zur Mühlen, *Deutsch*, pp. 5, 19–20; Moraw, *Von offener Verfassung*, p. 200. There was, however, a rural German landlord class.

[87] Zimmermann, 'Südostsiedlung', p. 54.

[88] Moraw, 'Das Mittelalter (bis 1469)', p. 111.

[89] Surviving names tend mainly to offer insights into the composition of the elite. Older German scholarship was thus prone to underestimate the non-German component particularly among lower urban groups. For the difficulty of drawing conclusions from personal names, see: Benl, 'Pommern', p. 72, noting the growing popularity of biblical and Christian forenames among the Slav as well as German inhabitants of Pomerania; Johansen and von zur Mühlen, *Deutsch*, p. 7, observing that (hereditary) surnames such as 'Slavus' and 'Wend' cannot be treated as a reliable guide to the ethnic self-conception of their bearers. Boockmann, 'Die neue Besiedlung', pp. 131–2, highlights the multiple possible meanings of a range of seemingly unambiguous ethnic identifiers.

[90] Zimmermann, 'Südostsiedlung', p. 58. Polish town books were likewise often written in German in the thirteenth and fourteenthth centuries, although a subsequent shift towards Latin indicates the growing importance of Poles: Rogall, 'Polen', p. 69. German also long remained the language of government in Bohemian towns. Of the privileges which Wenceslas IV (r. 1378–1419) issued as king of Bohemia for the Prague communes, 13 were in German and only 1 in Czech (though a further 17 were in Latin); of his privileges for other Bohemian towns, 193 were in Latin, 104 in German and 10 in Czech: Bittner, *Deutsche*, p. 110.

[91] Rogall, 'Polen', p. 69.

[92] Zorn, 'Deutsche', p. 185.

eastward migration slackened in the fourteenth century. Lists of burghers admitted to the Old Town of Prague in the period 1324–93 suggest that an average of 24 per cent were Czechs.[93] In Kraków, even the bar upon Polish migrants imposed by Duke Bolesław the Chaste for his new foundation of 1257 was able only to delay, not defeat, this trend: already by 1392–9, Poles comprised more than a quarter of new burghers.[94]

Unsettled identities

Who, then, were the settlers? This question can be answered in a number of ways. A short and valid response would be that their origins, and their identities, were many and varied, and that – certain tiny, literate minorities apart, perhaps – on their arrival in the east they were not Germans in any meaningful sense at all. Of some significant groups, the latter is obviously true. Flemings had been prominent among the migrants into the western Baltic in the twelfth century, Walloons settled in Silesia, while Poles were among those to put down roots in the Prussian domains of the Teutonic Order.[95] But even those who used forms of the German language were scarcely unified by it. By and large, the speech and prior identity of the newcomers were of no concern whatever to those who induced them to settle.[96] The migrants did not come east as a coherent group, or even a plurality of such groups, but in innumerable obscure bands, variable but always small in size, and in most regions over the course of a long, discontinuous period.

---

[93] Ibid., p. 185. The thirteenth- and early fourteenth-century evidence shows Prague still to be in that period a solidly German city: see Moraw, 'Das Mittelalter', pp. 70–2; however, a study of house-owners in the Old Town in the period 1360–1410 reveals a sharp increase in the Czech element at all social levels: Šmahel, 'The idea of "nation"' (1969), p. 160. Other Bohemian towns show a similar pattern. In Königgrätz (Hradec Králové), Germans were by the end of the fourteenth century already a minority among the burghers, though they continued to dominate the council. In Mies (Stříbro), despite a general diminution, Germans remained predominant among the smiths, furriers and, particularly, miners. E. Schwarz, 'Die nationale Zusammensetzung verschiedener Städte in Böhmen und Mähren in vorhussitischer Zeit', in Meynen (ed.), Sudetendeutscher Atlas, p. 15.

[94] Zorn, 'Deutsche', p. 186. An estimate of the ethnic make-up of the population of fourteenth-century Kraków as a whole has proposed around 5,000 Poles, as against just 3,500 Germans, 800 Jews and 700 foreigners: Janeczek, 'Ethnische Gruppenbildungen', p. 411. For Duke Bolesław's 1257 settlement charter, see Rogall, 'Polen', p. 61.

[95] For Flemings, see Bartlett, Making of Europe, pp. 113–16; for non-German settlers in the Ordensstaat, Rowell, Lithuania Ascending, p. 11; for Romance-speaking immigrants in Silesia, Zientara, 'Walloons in Silesia'; for French-speaking Latini in the towns of western Hungary, Johansen and von zur Mühlen, Deutsch, p. 16.

[96] A fact underlined, e.g., by a diploma of Duke Przemisl of Poland (c. 1251), granting Bishop Bogufal of Poznań the right to settle in the castellany of Ciążyń 'Theutonicos

Their places of origin were many and varied. They seldom travelled far, and they tended, understandably, to choose new homes which resembled those which they had left behind. The new German burghers of Danzig in the thirteenth century thus came predominantly from other, established centres around the southern Baltic.[97] The movements which eventually scattered German-speakers to the furthest reaches of east-central Europe were multi-generational, and those who attained the remotest points were the children and grandchildren of migrants.[98] Seldom, then, were the settlers exposed to the identity-forging shock of an utterly alien world. Taken as a whole, moreover, they differed as much from each other as from their new neighbours. Different settler groups spoke dialects of German which varied to the point of mutual incomprehensibility.[99] Even within a single zone of lordship there was typically a plurality of dialect groups, whose speech reflected diverse places of origin, strung out beyond a long frontier.[100] The settlers' laws and customs had usually been adopted from a German region or centre, or some other settlement zone, lying relatively close at hand. Sometimes, at important locations, the process of legal accretion was more complex, but not more unified.[101] Other types of difference were directly visible on the ground, such as village forms and building styles, which again linked different settlement regions not to each other but to diverse, adjacent or more distant, German landscapes.[102]

There was little to favour the formation of extended communities of *any* kind among most of the migrants. Even between those who could trace roots to the same region, there were few natural bonds. Most were

---

sive quoslibet hominos extraneos': *Urkunden und erzählende Quellen*, ed. Helbig and Weinrich, vol. II, no. 65, p. 254.

[97] Keyser, 'Die deutsche Bevölkerung', p. 240. Keyser estimated that in Danzig in the period 1364–99, only 27 per cent of new burghers came from the lands of 'old' Germany, west of the Elbe, with fewer than 1 per cent from south Germany. Many of the Germans who settled in Silesia were from Thuringia and Upper Saxony: Moraw, 'Das Mittelalter (bis 1469)', p. 125. Occasionally migrant groups did undertake longer journeys, as did the Hollanders who settled in Prussia: Keyser, 'Die deutsche Bevölkerung', pp. 233–4.

[98] Boockmann, 'Die neue Besiedlung', p. 119. In most of Poland, the immigrants came from already established settlement regions, such as Brandenburg, Pomerania and Silesia: Rogall, 'Polen', pp. 62–3.

[99] For the dialectology of the settlement regions, see Higounet, *Die deutsche Ostsiedlung*, pp. 327–30. For Peter von Zittau's remarks on the mutual incomprehensibility of Bavarian and Saxon speech (doubtless in Bohemia), see below, Ch. 11, p. 502.

[100] For this pattern in Bohemia, see E. Schwarz, 'Die deutschen Mundarten in Böhmen und Mähren-Schlesien', in Meynen (ed.), *Sudetendeutscher Atlas*, pp. 9–10.

[101] For the plurality of laws applied in the Prague 'towns', see W. Weizsäcker, 'Die Verbreitung der deutschen Stadtrechte in Böhmen und Mähren-Schlesien', in Meynen (ed.), *Sudetendeutscher Atlas*, p. 25.

[102] See Higounet, *Die deutsche Ostsiedlung*, p. 170.

agriculturalists: a social group among whose members, in pre-modern societies, traces of common sentiment of a more-than-local kind are notoriously hard to discern.[103] Many German peasants were settled in their own distinct villages, as was common, for example, in Pomerania or in the Prussian *Ordensland*, whereas elsewhere, as in much of regnal Poland, they were intermixed with native villagers.[104] Yet whatever the form of their settlement, indications that it exerted any ethnogenetic effect whatever upon the mass of rural migrants are all but non-existent. Nobles and knights, across much of Europe the most significant link between regnal and local communities, were by no means always to be found among local German immigrants.[105] And where they did come, it was generally not as leaders – as a *Traditionskern* for incipient political communities – but as individual seekers after social betterment, for themselves and their kin.[106] Far from acting as anchormen for self-consciously distinct settler bands, nobles were therefore often especially keen (all too keen, on some indigenous judgements) to assimilate themselves through marriage to native elites.[107] In some regions, succeeding generations testify, in their personal names and choice of language, to a gradual, progressively fuller identification with native society.[108]

If we adopt the viewpoint of its initiators, the princes, prelates and improving landlords of the eastern territories, conceiving of the German settlement as a process of ethnic differentiation seems to make still less sense. Instead, they pursued policies of cultural and even ethnic syncretism with their western neighbours, in whose prestige and material benefits they wished to share. The tendency was old-established, as is evident from the marriage strategies of the Latin Christian dynasties of the east. So common had the practice become among such families of choosing German marriage partners for their offspring that by the late

---

[103] The classic model of pre-modern rural segmentation is that of Gellner, *Nations*, p. 9.
[104] Benl, 'Pommern', p. 62; Aubin, 'The lands', p. 457; Rogall, 'Polen', p. 62.
[105] They were thus relatively rare in Greater and Little Poland: Janeczek, 'Ethnische Gruppenbildung', p. 414.
[106] For the knights from Lower Saxony who were settled in Moravia by Bishop Bruno of Olmütz, see Higounet, *Die deutsche Ostsiedlung*, p. 167; for the immigration of German nobles, mostly *ministeriales*, into Silesia, Moraw, 'Das Mittelalter (bis 1469)', p. 124; for German knights in the Egerland, Moraw, 'Das Mittelalter', p. 111.
[107] For native hostility to elite settler groups, see below, pp. 410–14. Some urban patricians also wished to join themselves through marriage to native aristocracies – thus, those of Prague, who in the early fourteenth century exerted pressure to that effect: Demetz, *Prague*, p. 69.
[108] For this process in Poland, see: Janeczek, 'Ethnische Gruppenbildungen', pp. 414–16; Zientara, 'Die deutschen Einwanderer', p. 341.

Middle Ages their rightful ethnic ascription seems far from clear – and indeed, rather beside the point. Marriages with no fewer than nineteen German princesses can be counted in the history of the Bohemian Přemyslids.[109] The Piast duke Henry II of Silesia, who died in 1241 fighting the Mongols, had more German than Polish ancestors, among them his mother, St Hedwig (Jadwiga, d. 1243), of the Bavarian house of Andechs-Meran.[110] Another princess of the Andechs dynasty was married to King Andrew II of Hungary (r. 1205–35). From that union too was to come a female saint, destined this time for a German cult site: Elizabeth (d. 1231), bride to Landgrave Ludwig of Thuringia.[111] And in a manner akin to princely dynasties, monastic communities established their own cross-border family trees, binding the settlement territories to the German heartlands, and facilitating easy and frequent movement in both directions. This was true particularly of the new, hierarchically structured orders founded in the twelfth and thirteenth centuries. Cistercian and Premonstratensian communities in Austria, Bavaria or Thuringia were able in this way to propagate themselves in numerous daughter-houses beyond the Bohemian forest.[112] Bonds, not borders, as it seems, were what counted at the topmost levels in eastern society.

Among kings and princes, bishops and abbots, grand dukes and grand masters, the main principle fuelling the hunger for western manpower was *melioratio terrae*. Settlement of migrants was but one aspect: the most widely felt transformative force was not incoming German men and women, but German law, and the economic techniques and practices associated with it.[113] The settlers' law, with its more advanced principles and favourable terms, was easily and often willingly extended to native peasantries too, by rulers whose minds were set on material advantage and hardly ever on maintaining ethnic boundaries as such.[114] Soon enough, therefore, there was precious little that remained German, at least in any exclusionary sense, about *ius Teutonicum*. And it was not only modes of organisation and property ownership or new technologies that were traded freely across the open frontier, but also

---

[109] Mayer, 'Aufgaben', p. 140; Higounet, *Die deutsche Ostsiedlung*, p. 162; and see the genealogies in Bosl (ed.), *Handbuch*, vol. I, pp. 570–2.
[110] Conrads, 'Silesiographia', pp. 78–9.
[111] See generally Werner, 'Mater Hassiae'.
[112] Moraw, 'Das Mittelalter', pp. 102–9; Richter, 'Die böhmischen Länder', pp. 293–300.
[113] See generally Cordes, 'Deutsches Recht' (with bibliography).
[114] Even where such distinctions were apparently enforced, as famously in the 1257 'German' settlement of Kraków, the motive was economic – to prevent rural

social identities. Not only did Czechs, Poles, Wends and Hungarians learn to lay out their towns and plough their fields in the German manner; their rulers aspired to look, act, marry, live and speak like Germans. The Bohemian high nobility built German-type castles with Germanised names, which then became the ancestral names of their families: Riesenburg, Rosenberg, Hasenburg, Sternberg.[115] Přemysl Otakar II (r. 1253–78), the 'golden king' of Prague himself, had a castle at Klingenberg (Zvikov) adorned with glazed, heraldic floor-tiles bearing German-language inscriptions.[116] Western-style chivalric entertainments became fashionable at the eastern courts.[117] By the thirteenth century, the language of high-aristocratic self-fashioning was German. German poets and singers proclaimed the open-handedness of the courts of Breslau and Prague, and the brilliance and cultivation of their princes.[118] Some native lords went further. The Přemyslid Wenceslas II (d. 1305) earned through his own poetical feats a full-page spread in the great Heidelberg *Liederhandschrift*, where he is shown holding court in magnificent style, set above a throng of menials and entertainers. He was not the only eastern prince to try his hand at German verse.[119] The Silesian duke Bolesław the Bald (d. 1278) was famed for his fondness for the German tongue, although he reportedly spoke it so badly as to provoke amusement among his hearers.[120]

And not only did German-speaking westerners move east: in a complementary process, powerful German-speaking easterners were now going west. At the height of his powers around the year 1270, Otakar II had become the most formidable Latin-Christian prince east of the

---

manpower from migrating to the town – rather than cultural: Rogall, 'Polen', pp. 61–2; Menzel, 'Die Akzeptanz', pp. 212–13.

[115] Moraw, 'Das Mittelalter', p. 110; Behr, *Literatur*, p. 50 with n. 95.

[116] Hoensch, *Přemysl Otakar II.*, p. 185.

[117] Thus, for the tournament in Bohemia, see Moraw, 'Das Mittelalter', p. 98.

[118] For German literature at eastern courts, including those of Meißen, Brandenburg and Rügen, see Higounet, *Die deutsche Ostsiedlung*, pp. 334–5. The singer 'Goldener' lauded the Wendish prince Wizlaw of Rügen (d. 1325) – 'der junge helt in Rügenlande' – for his possession of a whole catalogue of chivalric virtues: *Politische Lyrik*, ed. Müller, vol. I, pp. 132–3 (and cf. p. 150, for similar verses from another singer, Frauenlob). For German poets' praise of the court of Breslau, see Moraw, 'Das Mittelalter (bis 1469)', p 85; for German speech and letters in Přemyslid Prague: Moraw, 'Das Mittelalter', pp. 100–1; Hoensch, *Přemysl Otakar II.*, pp. 192–4; Behr, *Literatur*.

[119] *Codex Manesse*, ed. Walther, pp. 8–9. The Manesse codex also contains two *Minnelieder* by a 'Duke Henry of Breslau', probably Henry IV (r. 1266–90): ibid., pp. 10–11. One of these discloses the influence of a song by Margrave Henry of Meißen. (The nobility of the Meißen region had close links with the court of Breslau.) Moraw, 'Das Mittelalter (bis 1469)', pp. 84–5.

[120] Rogall, 'Polen', p. 50.

Meuse, his direct rule and influence spanning the continent from the Baltic to the Adriatic.[121] Little wonder that those pre-eminent social-climbing westerners, the Habsburgs and Luxemburgs, should at this time have discovered at the eastern courts resources for dynastic ascent such as the imperial title itself was no longer able to offer. The eastern realms themselves tended to have – or with time increasingly to take on – the form of extensive, composite, multi-ethnic and even multi-faith polities. By the fourteenth century, these qualities were more pronounced than ever, under the rule of expansionist monarchs and quasi-monarchs with wide horizons: Casimir the Great of Poland (r. 1333–70), Louis the Great of Hungary (r. 1342–82), Charles IV of Bohemia (r. 1347–78), the grand princes of Lithuania, and the presiding officers of the Teutonic Order. Within their complex polyglot empires German settlers were just one element, of variable – if, in some locales, very considerable – significance. To draw a straight distinction between 'Germans' and 'natives' is always and everywhere to oversimplify.

Yet that is precisely what a handful of native commentators did; and some painted the distinction in the most lurid of colours, making of Germans an absolute Other, an irredeemably harmful foreign body in their host societies. Like the twentieth century's champions of ethnic purity in the east, they imagined and looked forward to the unpicking and remaking of an ethnically mixed society which they depicted as both unnatural and vicious. 'Ha, ha, Germans, ha, ha – out, out!', exults a marginal gloss in a volume of John Wycliffe's writings from late fourteenth-century Prague.[122] And within a decade of the century's ending, the German university masters and scholars were duly gone, as religious and national tensions rose in the Bohemian capital.[123] The construction of the Germans themselves in eastern writings displays recurrent features. According to a fourteenth-century pamphlet of Czech origin, they were a naturally 'servile people', whose fate since the earliest times had been to wander in the world.[124] As the itinerants went on their way, 'other peoples, who did not understand [their] language, because they barked like dogs, adjudged the Germans to be dumb', and

---

[121] See: Hoensch, *Přemysl Otakar II.*, pp. 38–48; Behr, *Literatur*, pp. 40–3.

[122] Šmahel, 'The idea of "nation"' (1969), p. 165. For the context of Wycliffe's reception in Prague, see Kaminsky, *Hussite Revolution*, pp. 23–35.

[123] Schmidt, 'Universitäts-Nationen', pp. 62–3. It has been proposed that up to 800 may have left, though even approximate figures are unattainable, and the actual number was probably considerably lower.

[124] 'Ein deutschfeindliches Pamphlet', ed. and trans. Wostry, p. 226. For this work (*De Theutunicis bonum dictamen*), see also Schwinges, ' "Primäre" und "sekundäre" Nation', esp. pp. 521–4.

thus 'the Slavs call every Teuton "Niemecz", that is to say, dumb'.[125] The de-humanising element is conspicuous here, and the canine metaphor recurrent. The Germans, who rule in pride like lions, 'will eventually be driven out like dogs'.[126] Jakub Świnka, the notoriously anti-German archbishop of Gniezno (1283–1314), was reputedly in the habit of calling Germans 'dog heads' – recalling the fabled, monstrous cynocephali of Graeco-Roman ethnography and contemporary encyclopaedias and *mappae mundi*.[127]

These Germans were not the hapless barbarians of familiar western stereotype, therefore, but figures of subtle malevolence.[128] They were arrogant mockers of native dress and manners.[129] Rather than conquering by force, the incomers typically insinuated themselves by fraud and cunning into positions of power in native society.[130] Their corrosive presence was ubiquitous. 'All because of you, treacherous tribe, many a land has been laid waste', alleges a fragmentary Old Czech Judas legend from the early fourteenth century.[131] (The comparison with Judas is itself revealing – and recurrent.) Their ambition knew no bounds. 'Wherever they go, / they always want to be first / and subject to no one at all', claimed a political song about the revolt of the German-speaking burghers of Kraków in 1310–11.[132]

In the eyes of the Germans' literate adversaries, history was filled with warnings about the effects upon the land of an alien infiltration which the record showed was unwelcome from the first. The twelfth-century Bohemian chronicler Cosmas, manuscripts of whose history were collected at the court of Charles IV, had already put into the

---

[125] 'Ein deutschfeindliches Pamphlet', ed. and trans. Wostry, p. 227. The chronicler Francis of Prague, writing in the mid-fourteenth century, tells the story of a German artisan in Prague who was struck *dumb* for speaking dismissively of St Wenceslas: *Chronicon Francisci Pragensis*, ed. Zachová, p. 168. For lack of recognisable speech as a mark of the monstrous, see Friedman, *The Monstrous Races*, pp. 29–30.

[126] 'Ein deutschfeindliches Pamphlet', ed. and trans. Wostry, p. 232. The (probably German) author of the *Chronica Polonorum* states that the battle of Hundesfeld (1109) was so called because the Poles called the Germans dogs: *Chronica Polonorum*, ed. Stenzel, p. 14. For this work and its author, see Görlich, *Zur Frage*, p. 31; for further such references, Zientara, 'Foreigners in Poland', p. 21.

[127] *Königsaaler Geschichts-Quellen*, ed. Loserth, p. 164: 'Ille autem ... tam acer Teutonicorum aemulus erat, quod ipsos solum canina capita nominare solebat.' For cynocephali, see Friedman, *The Monstrous Races*, p. 15.

[128] For this image, see above, Ch. 8, pp. 357–9.

[129] For an example, see Strzelczyk, 'Die Wahrnehmung', pp. 210–11.

[130] This is the main charge laid by *De Theutunicis bonum dictamen*: ibid., esp. pp. 228, 230–1.

[131] Thomas, 'Czech-German relations', pp. 201–2.

[132] *De quodam advocate Cracoviensi Alberto*, printed in Długopolski, 'Bunt Wójta Alberta' (here pp. 184–6); and see the comments of Strzelczyk, 'Die Wahrnehmung', p. 213.

mouth of a ducal courtier the opinion that a dog's tail or donkey turd would be preferable to a German on the bishop's throne of Prague.[133] Insular and xenophobic views of the indigenous past appear in some quarters to gather strength during the period in which German immigration reached its height. For the Czech rhyming chronicler 'Dalimil', who early in the fourteenth century set down a fiercely ethnocentric vision of Bohemian history, the entire national past could be recounted as a struggle against harmful foreign, specifically German, intrusion. Addressing himself to a middling Czech noble audience, the chronicler told of how groups of courtly parasites were repeatedly chased back to Germany by patriotic Bohemian princes in times past.[134] Princely policies of regnal improvement, which appear rational and moderate enough to modern eyes, were quickly recast in literate, late medieval memory as fully fledged programmes of ethnic replacement. One fourteenth-century Bohemian chronicler thus portrayed the immigrant-friendly Otakar II as wanting to hand all of Bohemia over to Meißners and Thuringians.[135] Occasionally, such fancies might be expanded into a more general historical vision. A Hussite manifesto of 1420 was able to warn that 'just as [the Germans] did to our tongue on the Rhine, in Misnia, in Prussia, and drove it out, the same they intend to do to us and occupy the places of the banished'.[136]

But, as some now sought to insist, injuries done in times past would be as nothing beside future ones, if prompt action were not taken. The sons of the Silesian duke Henry III of Glogau (Głogów) were charged with so inordinately favouring their German adherents that these were even able eventually to persuade them 'that they should exterminate the entire Polish people, both ecclesiastics and secular knights'.[137] The notoriously Germanophile bishop of Kraków, Jan Muskata, was similarly accused by members of his own cathedral chapter, in a legal process of 1307, of harbouring plans for outright genocide of Poles.[138]

---

[133] *Die Chronik der Böhmen*, ed. Bretholz, p. 116. The speaker proceeded to invoke the salutary example of Duke Spitihněv, 'who evicted all the Germans from this land in a single day'.

[134] For Dalimil's audience and vision of history, see: Graus, 'Die Ausformung', pp. 12–13; Graus, *Nationenbildung*, pp. 91–5; Schwinges, '"Primäre" und "sekundäre" Nation', pp. 514–20; and for the older literature, Kersken, *Geschichtsschreibung*, pp. 583–7. 'Dalimil' relied heavily upon Cosmas of Prague, but embroidered Cosmas's narrative with much pseudo-historical material of his own: see Graus, *Lebendige Vergangenheit*, pp. 91–8.

[135] The chronicle of Abbot Neplach. For the relevant passage, see *Quellen zur Geschichte der ostdeutschen Kolonisation*, ed. Kötzschke, p. 74.

[136] Šmahel, 'The idea of "nation"' (1969), p. 222.

[137] According to the *Annales capituli Posnaniensis*, quoted in Strzelczyk, 'Die Wahrnehmung', p. 210. On this, see also Zientara, 'Foreigners', pp. 20–1.

[138] *Monumenta Poloniae Vaticana*, ed. Ptásnik, p. 88: '... et quod eliminare nititur principem scilicet Wladislaum de terra et exterminare gentem Polonicam...'

Such charges were surely never intended to be taken literally: imminent disenfranchisement of native elites, not actual mass murder, is the spectre that their authors doubtless intended primarily to conjure up.[139] Nevertheless, these were no idle tales. Extreme danger called for extreme counter-measures: to purge or be purged. Here too, history offered precedents, sometimes with the highest authority. In the Old Czech *Life of St Procopius* (*c.* 1350), Germans are portrayed driving the monks from the saint's monastery following his death, only themselves to be ejected when Procopius miraculously returns, beating the interlopers about their heads with his crozier.[140] Wild talk of mass destruction lay at the extreme, rhetorical end of a spectrum of thinking which regarded the presence of immigrant groups as contingent and amenable to change.

From time to time, such thinking yielded tangible results. In Kuyavya and Masovia in the 1270s, pressure from native elites induced the ruling princes to withdraw privileges from their German followers and expel them from the land.[141] Some decades later, King John of Bohemia felt obliged to dismiss his German courtiers and replace them with Czechs.[142] Behind the overwrought rhetoric of impending doom, behind the literary *topoi* of the malevolent foreigner, can be discerned the shades of contending material interests. The coming of Germans to the eastern lands was never a process with winners alone.[143] Even peaceful immigration, into locations far remote from the pagan frontier, might bring hardship and resentment. Otakar II's settlement of Germans at the foot of the Prague Burg (1257) was achieved by evicting the native population.[144] In the countryside too, the establishment of new villages sometimes meant the displacement of existing ones, and the dislocation of their inhabitants.[145] Open violence involving settler

---

On these allegations, recurrent in the testimony of Kraków and Sandomir clergy against Muskata, see: Zientara, 'Die deutschen Einwanderer', p. 345; Zientara, 'Foreigners', pp. 14–15; Knoll, 'Economic and political institutions', pp. 168–9.

[139] For such language in medieval sources, see Scales, 'Bread', esp. pp. 298–9.

[140] Thomas, 'Czech-German relations', p. 208; and see Thomas, *Anne's Bohemia*, Ch. 5.

[141] Zientara, 'Foreigners', p. 15; Rogall, 'Polen', pp. 52–3.

[142] *Königsaaler Geschichts-Quellen*, ed. Loserth, pp. 371–2. The chronicler adds, however, that 'these things being done, the hoped-for peace still did not come'. For the flavour of Dalimil's accounts of comparable princely actions in times past, see *Rýmovaná Kronika Česká*, ed. Jiriček, pp. 94–5, ll. 1–38.

[143] The view presented in Menzel, 'Die Akzeptanz' (esp. p. 212), is altogether too sanguine about this.

[144] Hoensch, *Přemysl Otakar II.*, p. 103.

[145] Thus Benl, 'Pommern', p. 62.

groups, if hardly widespread, was certainly not unknown, particularly when political or commercial rivalries were in play. The resistance rendered to the Polish pretender Władisław Łokietek by certain towns, and their support for John of Bohemia's bid for the Polish throne, brought down terrible reprisals upon their German elites (1311–12). A later source claimed that in Kraków all were killed who could not pronounce certain familiar Polish words.[146] In 1332 at Skania, economic rivalries reportedly led to several hundred Germans, including many merchants, losing their lives.[147]

The anti-German diatribes to which native chroniclers, poets and pamphleteers occasionally give voice doubtless reflect above all the jealousies and anxieties of fairly small and privileged insider groups – at court, in the towns and in the Church. Seen in relation to the extent of the eastern lands and the length of the settlement process, such voices are not numerous. But to dismiss them for that reason as eccentric or irrelevant would be rash. If literate Germans, as we have seen, constructed the east as Other, writers in the settlement lands proved just as adept at casting a web of baleful explanatory stereotype around the incoming Germans. Treachery, subversion, pride, unwarranted ambition: the repertoire of hostile *topoi* encountered in eastern sources has much in common with German charges against their own putative competitor peoples in the south and west.[148] Yet the divisions traced by eastern writers appear more radical: there is little hint here of kindred peoples contending over an ultimately common heritage, as the Germans and French disputed the Frankish title, or as westerners more generally scrambled for a share of the Trojan name.

Moreover, their bleak view of the prospects for inter-ethnic harmony finds affirmation in shorter, more aphoristic remarks to be met with in other writings from the time. A *Description of Eastern Europe*, of French mendicant provenance from the fourteenth century, recorded the 'natural hatred' which the author claimed existed between Germans and Poles.[149] Some German observers reached a similar view. An account of the miracles of the emperor Henry II tells of an old and blind Wend

---

[146] For source and background, see: Rogall, 'Polen', pp. 76–8; Strzelczyk, 'Die Wahrnehmung', pp. 213–14.
[147] Dollinger, *Hansa*, p. 54.   [148] Above, Ch. 8, pp. 371–4.
[149] Quoted in Knoll, 'Economic and political institutions', p. 152: *odium naturale*. Contemporary opinion was admittedly not unanimous on the matter. A fourteenth-century interpolation in the *Chronicle of Great Poland* claimed that no two peoples were on such close and amicable terms as were Germans and Slavs.

who, urged to touch Henry's relics as they were borne past him in Merseburg, declined on the grounds that he could expect no help from a German saint.[150] Ludolf von Sagan, who had studied at Prague in the 1370s, equated the mutual antipathy of the German and Czech 'tongues' to that between Jews and Samaritans.[151] That articulate figures in native society portrayed the presence of Germans in their lands as an existential threat, and that outsiders claimed to discern deep animosities between settlers and natives, cannot have been unknown among the immigrant Germans. How, in the face of such views, they accounted for themselves and for their presence in the eastern lands is thus an important question for historians.

Addressing it seems, however, to have mattered rather less to the migrants themselves – at least if surviving writings are any guide. The settlers and their offspring are almost as dumb to the historian as Slavic caricature said they were. The number of historical works to emerge from the settler communities across the vast, diverse migration zones of the east is remarkably small, and even the few which do exist display a highly uneven distribution, geographically and socially. Most come from Bohemia and south-western Poland, and from the lands under the Teutonic Order. Their authors were drawn mainly from the post-Gregorian religious orders, including the Teutonic Order itself, and from the orbits of the eastern princely courts. Theirs, then, are predominantly institutional histories, written mainly in Latin and mostly looking out upon relatively self-contained worlds. The fewness of urban voices, in regions where German-speakers were typically concentrated above all in towns, is a particular anomaly. There are no vernacular town chronicles, a genre which after the mid-thirteenth century quickly took root in the German lands to the west. Prague, by the mid-fourteenth century the largest urban settlement in central Europe, produced no known historical writing demonstrably reflecting the perspectives of its rich German burgher elite.

---

[150] *Ex aliis miraculis S. Heinrici*, ed. Waitz, pp. 815–16. The author offers by way of explanation: 'Erat autem hic de terra et de genere Sclavorum; quibus simplicitas vel irrationalitas pravitate quadam ingenii naturalis est.'

[151] 'Antiquitatum nempe odium et nimis radicatum est inter hec due ydeomata Teutonicorum et Bohemorum, ut sicut Judei non contuntur Samaritis, sic ipsi Bohemo Teutonicus ad videndum est gravis': *Der Tractatus de Longevo Schismate*, ed. Loserth, p. 426. Ludolf claims here that non-heretical Czechs joined with the Wycliffites in forcing the German masters out of Prague in 1409 in order that, with their expulsion, they could govern the *terra Bohemorum* alone, as well as dominate the university. Ludolf also regarded it as remarkable that the martyred Jan Nepomucký was *Theutonicis et Bohemis amabilem*: *Catalogus abbatum Saganensium*, ed. Stenzel, p. 213.

Occasionally, German monastic writers in the settlement lands invoked a stereotyped indigenous Other as a foil for the achievements of their own communities. In so doing, they deployed essentially the same body of literate motifs which we have already seen other Germans applying when writing about the eastern peoples. The superiority of the monastic brethren allegedly found expression particularly in their facility for reshaping and improving their physical environment – achievements which were presented as being beyond the capabilities of the indigenous populations. Monastic authors, who could draw upon a body of institutional memory, felt themselves qualified to trace and judge the changes discernible in their material environment. Latin verses from the early fourteenth century, composed in the Silesian Cistercian monastery of Leubus (Lubiąż), thus present a vision of a wasteland made fertile. Yet it was never, as the poet makes plain, an empty wasteland. The monks' new home lay under forest because 'the Polish people' of the region, who 'were poor and idle', had left it that way.[152] The point is driven home by means of a dense and all too familiar repertoire of images of native underdevelopment: primitive agricultural techniques, poor clothing, absence of towns.

Another vision of monastic renewal, with a similar stock of derogatory judgements on indigenous ways, was set down by Ludolf, a native of Saxony who became abbot of the house of Augustinian canons at Sagan (Żagań), in western Silesia. Ludolf tells of how his reforming predecessor, Abbot Trudwin (1331–47), had relocated the community from its previous, remote setting ('a place of horror and empty wilderness') to a more populous spot: 'from the forest into the midst of humanity'.[153] Ludolf links the primitiveness of the brethren's spiritual and material life at their first home with their habitation there 'in the midst of a perverse nation', namely the native Poles.[154] And it was onto the convent's own Polish brethren ('who are more given to drinking than praying') that he put much of the blame for alleged earlier laxity.[155] But with human society had come civilisation and, adapting to a monastic setting the trope of the monstrous, a fuller humanity for the brethren themselves: from 'beasts' were thus made men.[156]

These accounts must, however, be read with an awareness of genre: the institutional history of religious communities which, particularly among the Cistercians, also entailed a mission to make the desert bloom. Bleak and barren landscapes – if here read also with an eye for

---

[152] *Rocznik lubiąski*, ed. Bielowski, pp. 709–10.
[153] *Catalogus abbatum Saganensium*, ed. Stenzel, p. 241.
[154] Ibid., p. 181.   [155] Ibid., p. 184.   [156] Ibid., p. 242.

ethnic difference – were an essential part of the common stock of origin myths.[157] Among German communities in the east more broadly, the perspective of their authors is a highly untypical one, in that they were able to write as masters over broad lands and their local populations: their voice is the voice of lordship. And it was as monastic lords – and not as 'Germans' – that they primarily wrote: their criticisms of native society were not matched by any explicit self-identification in ethnic terms. The number of such comments to survive, moreover, is vanishingly small when seen in relation to the very large number of German-dominated religious houses spread throughout the eastern realms.

Other writers from the same German monastic world, moreover, adopted a wholly different tone. During the thirteenth and early fourteenth centuries, an extensive chronicle was compiled by the Cistercians of Heinrichau (Henryków) in southern Silesia, recounting the house's origins and enumerating its landholdings.[158] Its two compilers also spoke with the voice of monastic lordship – but with voices attuned also to the fine nuances of local society, topography and history, in light of which their community's patchwork of properties was described. Although Heinrichau belonged to the self-same monastic milieu as Leubus, whose daughter-foundation it was, its chroniclers – concerned not with literary elegance but with the careful recording of legal titles – offered a vision of a community in a landscape altogether more down-to-earth. In place of rhetorical *topoi*, the reader encounters three-dimensional people, the complexity of whose identities is paid proper regard. Among these is an individual by the name of Albert, described as German in the paternal line and with a mother from among the Walloons of Breslau, who is further identified by a Polish nickname.[159] While German colonisation in the forests around the abbey is the subject of repeated reference, its consequences are not presented as solely beneficial. The chronicle records the anguish into which the abbot was put by one such local settlement, which resulted in women and girls dancing in the abbey's orchard on holy days, threatening 'a most dangerous loss of many souls' among the monks.[160]

Although some monastic writers found their purposes to be served by constructing their host society as Other (and some did not), none found much discernible use for self-identifying notions of Germanness. Such ideas are, if anything, still less conspicuous among those who wrote,

[157] See Guenée, *Histoire*, pp. 46–58.
[158] The fullest modern analysis is *A Local Society*, ed. and trans. Górecki.
[159] *Księga Henrykowska*, ed. Grodecki, p. 260.
[160] Ibid., p. 273.

in Latin or the German vernacular, in the service of a native prince. Once again – as Ernst von Kirchberg's celebration of the Slavic past of the princes of Mecklenburg has already made plain – genre and context were all. So fully did most such writers dedicate themselves to their masters' literary ends that their own ethnic identity is no longer always even ascertainable with any confidence. This is true of Peter Bitschen, a secular canon serving the duke of Brzeg (Brieg), who in the 1380s is believed to have written a *Chronicle of the Princes of Poland*.[161] While it is thought that Peter was probably a German-speaker by background, there is little in his history, which is well informed and mostly sympathetic about the Polish past, and not invariably flattering towards Germans, to confirm such a view. His writing reflects the objectives of his prince, not – or at least, not in ways which can now be confidently determined – his own self-consciousness.[162] In these respects he is fairly typical of the handful of Germans in the settlement lands to leave behind a substantive written record.

Their orientation is strongly illuminated by the courtier-poets who sought places within the followings of fashion-conscious eastern rulers. Reinmar von Zweter, who sang in praise of Wenceslas I (r. 1230–53), declared that, although born by the Rhine and raised in Austria, he had chosen Bohemia as a home – but that this was 'more on account of the lord than the land' (though the land too was 'good').[163] Such men, in their writings, naturally looked upward, to acknowledge a generous patron and strong protector, like the 'white lion' Charles IV, lauded by his resident (Saxon) poet Heinrich von Mügeln, rather than sideways, to affirm common ties.[164] Their habitual vocabulary was genealogical and heraldic, concerned with the blood of great families, not with their own.

---

[161] *Chronica principum Poloniae*, ed. Stenzel. The debate over Bitschen's identity in the older literature is summarised in Görlich, *Zur Frage*, pp. 36–7. For the difficulty of ascribing with confidence a definite ethnic identity to the authors of Silesian chronicles in this period, see also Jurek, 'Die Entwicklung', pp. 27–9, 34–5; and for this same problem in relation to the Prussian chronicler Nikolaus von Jeroschin, below, n. 250.

[162] For Bitschen's chronicle and its purpose (though without discussion of his ethnicity), see now A. Classen and W. Mrozowicz, 'Bitschen, Peter', in *EMC*, vol. I, pp. 182–4.

[163] *Politische Lyrik*, ed. Müller, vol. I, p. 8; and see Behr, *Literatur*, pp. 68–9. For Germanophone court poets and their praise for the Přemyslid kings (with Otakar II as the new Alexander), see generally: Bittner, *Deutsche*, pp. 52–5; Demetz, *Prague*, pp. 57–60.

[164] *Politische Lyrik*, ed. Müller, vol. II, p. 1 (Sta 18). As Bohemian and Roman king, Charles possessed for Heinrich the ideal qualities of both the lion and the eagle. See also K. Stackmann, 'Heinrich von Mügeln', in *VL* 3, cols. 815–27.

And it was not only his paid champions who thus made the prince their object. The same outlook characterised the German-speaking nobles and burgher communities, like those of Breslau, whom Peter Bitschen describes stoutly defending their city in turbulent times after the Mongol disaster of 1241.[165] The Silesian Piast dukes proved able to inspire strong loyalties among prominent immigrant groups in the divided Poland of the late thirteenth and early fourteenth centuries.[166] Much of that loyalty was naturally well calculated, strengthened by an awareness of the resentful voices being raised against the foreigner within native elite circles. The uncertain situation which seemed to confront high-ranking immigrant groups goes far to explain the general absence of openly ethnocentric notes from the recorded utterances of their members. It was not in their interest to stoke inter-ethnic tensions, but rather to give their loyal backing to princes capable of holding them in check. It was no doubt rivalries between native and incoming elite groups which Peter von Zittau, abbot of the Cistercian monastery of Königsaal, mainly had in mind in lamenting the 'ancient quarrels' which the Czechs maintained against their German neighbours.[167] Rulers capable of calming such inveterate troubles were thus to be given special honour. According to Ludolf von Sagan, Charles IV so loved peace and justice that, within his Bohemian kingdom, 'one people [*gens*] did not raise ... the sword against the other' in his time.[168] The implication is that, without the king's efforts, his ethnically divided subjects would naturally have done exactly that. For the Königsaal chronicler, the role of inter-ethnic healer belonged to Wenceslas II's consort, Guta von Habsburg.[169] But the nervous assumption underlying such images

---

[165] *Chronica principum Poloniae*, ed. Stenzel, p. 107.

[166] Zientara, 'Die deutschen Einwanderer', p. 343. Not only nobles and burghers looked to the dukes: they were also called upon to safeguard the properties of (German) religious communities against their neighbours: *A Local Society*, ed. and trans. Górecki, p. 21.

[167] *Königsaaler Geschichts-Quellen*, ed. Loserth, p. 69. Again, their mutual hostility was natural: they were *gentes discordes* (ibid., p. 72).

[168] *Catalogus abbatum Saganensium*, ed. Stenzel, p. 210. Charles intervened in his kingdom in an attempt to hold the balance between Czechs and Germans, stipulating (1356) that the town council in Beraun (Beroun) was to comprise equal numbers of each nationality: *Regesta Diplomatica*, vol. VI, ed. Mendl, no. 417, pp. 229–30; Seibt, 'Die Zeit der Luxemburger', p. 429. (By 1349, Czechs appear to have outnumbered Germans on the council 7:5: Schwarz, *Volkstumsgeschichte*, p. 55.) Charles was not the only ruler to act in this fashion for the sake of inter-ethnic peace. Louis the Great of Hungary twice intervened in the mixed German-Slovak town of Sillein (Zilina) in favour of equal representation for the two groups among the town's jurors and to rule both languages admissible in the town's court: Zimmermann, 'Südostsiedlung', p. 78.

[169] *Königsaaler Geschichts-Quellen*, ed. Loserth, p. 69.

is that royal peace-weavers were working against a tide of division and aversion that naturally threatened the incomers.

However, the courtier-poets also provide indication that Germans born within the settlement lands were starting to develop political sympathies broader than those newly arrived from beyond the frontier. Ulrich von Etzenbach, perhaps a native of Leitmeritz (Litoměřice) in northern Bohemia, mixed his praise of Otakar II and Wenceslas II with warm words for 'the *land* of the lion', in which he was born, extending the familiar heraldic motif to embrace a territorial community.[170] An etymological gloss on the German *Bêheim* made of his homeland a 'blessed house' or 'blessed land'.[171] There are indications of the idea of territory as a source of identity as well as constitutional status attaining particular importance in the political vocabulary of these regions. A territorial-constitutional allegiance, embracing land and lordship, may even have been deliberately fostered by some princes, aware of the dangers which a climate of ethnic polarisation could nurture within their composite realms.[172] In this spirit, the great confirmation of privileges which John of Luxemburg issued to his new Bohemian subjects in 1310 was careful to frame its definition of political community wholly in terms of birth or residence within the kingdom: there were no Czechs or Germans, only the king's native subjects (who were to be favoured with office) and foreigners (who were not).[173]

The same perspective finds expression in the chronicle from the royal monastery of Königsaal, whose abbot had played a central part in bringing John to Bohemia.[174] Its main author, Peter von Zittau, a German-speaker, had himself been born within the kingdom's

---

[170] Ulrich von Eschenbach, *Alexander*, ed. Toischer, p. 734, vv. 27625–8.

[171] Ulrich von Etzenbach, *Wilhelm von Wenden*, ed. Rosenfeld, p. 94, vv. 4696–4707. For the identity problem among Germans in Bohemia, see Scales, 'At the margin of community'.

[172] It is in this spirit that Bohemian royal charters celebrate the settlement of migrants, who glorify the king by increasing the number of his subjects: thus *Regesta Diplomatica*, vol. II, ed. Emler, no. 499, p. 191 (Otakar II for the new town of Polička, 1265).

[173] *Regesta Diplomatica*, vol. II, ed. Emler, no. 2245, pp. 973–5. The charter speaks of *regnicolae, terrigenae, Boemi vel Moravi* and *alienigenae, extranei*. Even under Wenceslas IV, despite the increasingly evident Czech–German tensions within the kingdom, the Bohemian royal chancery continued to use an ethnically blind documentary language, pitting 'natives' against 'aliens': see Seibt, *Hussitica*, p. 69. For the employment of the same terminology in Silesia in this period, see Jurek, 'Die Entwicklung', p. 21.

[174] For this monastery, founded by Wenceslas II on the site of a royal hunting lodge as a dynastic mausoleum, see P. Hilsch, 'Königsaal', in *LMA* 5, col. 1325; for the role of Bohemian Cistercian abbots, including Konrad of Königsaal, in John's accession, Seibt, 'Die Zeit der Luxemburger', p. 359.

frontiers.[175] Constitutional bonds seem for Peter to have spoken more compellingly than did any sense of being 'German'. He wrote sympathetically of Bohemian resistance to the harsh regency regime which the margrave of Brandenburg had sought to impose after Otakar II's death: no one willingly submits to the rule of strangers.[176] Peter thus appears at times to make of Bohemia a constitutional homeland within which ethnic categories are politically redundant. Yet closer scrutiny of his writings discloses a more complex, not to say contradictory, sense of identity – and one indicative of the tensions facing other Germans in the eastern realms also.[177]

In fact, though, Peter does seem to have felt his political identity to imply an ethnic one. Not only was he a loyal adherent of the kingdom: he belonged to the Bohemian people. He reported with approval Henry VII's supposed rebuff to his German followers, who had used derogatory stereotypes to characterise the state of Bohemian political life.[178] Peter also lamented what he claimed were the Bohemians' characteristic faults, but he presented them as those of his own *gens*.[179] Ethnic solidarity was, it seems, a necessary counterpart to his political allegiance; and yet, troublingly, it also presupposed an identity that was more than merely political. The conviction was already growing in his day that being 'Bohemian' implied a command of the Czech language.[180] Charles IV himself recounted in his autobiography how, returning to Bohemia as a young man, he had relearned the language of his childhood until he spoke it 'like another Bohemian'.[181] Charles's own *Majestas Carolina* (1350), codifying the kingdom's laws, insisted that no one might have a part in governing Bohemia who was ignorant of the Czech tongue.[182]

Whether Peter von Zittau understood Czech, he does not disclose; but he does write with insight about the German language as a source of identity: an identity in which he evidently felt he had some share.[183] And

---

[175] See J. Loserth, 'Peter von Zittau', in *ADB* 25, pp. 476–8.
[176] *Königsaaler Geschichts-Quellen*, ed. Loserth, pp. 53–4. And see p. 123 for Austrian resentment at the rule of the Habsburgs' Swabians.
[177] Discussed in Scales, 'At the margin of community', pp. 335–41.
[178] *Königsaaler Geschichts-Quellen*, ed. Loserth, p. 266. Peter proceeded to argue against ethnic stereotypes as such: no entire people should be blamed for the crimes of particular persons: ibid., p. 247.
[179] *Königsaaler Geschichts-Quellen*, ed. Loserth, p. 50.
[180] For the development of this view, see: Graus, 'Die Ausformung', p. 13; Graus, *Nationenbildung*, pp. 174, 177, 179.
[181] *Karoli IV Imperatoris Romanorum Vita*, ed. Nagy and Schaer, pp. 68–9 (*ut alter Boemus*).
[182] Šmahel, 'The idea of "nation"' (1969), p. 217.
[183] *Konigsaaler Geschichts-Quellen*, ed. Loserth, p. 52; and see below, Ch. 11, p. 502.

his condemnation of the failings of 'his' people (partly, in arms) contrasts sharply with his glorification, in familiar, strident fashion, of the feats of German soldiery north and south of the Alps. Peter praised Bohemia's rulers not because they were blind to their subjects' ethnic differences, but because they acknowledged them, and even mirrored them in their own persons. It was as a pious *Theutonica virgo* that Queen Guta had acted in judicial affairs. She did so, moreover, in order to provide her German subjects with recourse against the injustices of their Czech neighbours.[184] Peter undoubtedly felt himself to be, in a sense, both 'Bohemian' and 'German'. However, he lacked the requisite conceptual vocabulary, and perhaps even imaginative processes, to enable him in any stable fashion to be these things simultaneously. To write of *Bohemi* was, for Peter, to invoke at once both 'us' and 'them': his own community and one apart from (or even opposed to) it. *Theutonici*, within the kingdom and without, were also ultimately all one: the chronicler might glimpse distinctions, but he could not fix them with stable words. 'Bohemian' and 'German' were for Peter fully formed ethno-political entities, each with its own established webs of associations and signifiers. Each already drew a part of its meaning from not being the other.

Among the small and untypical handful of settlers whose own utterances and (more uncertainly) attitudes it is possible to study, Germanness was no badge of identity, to be openly and proudly displayed. For some it was a practical irrelevance, to be set aside when literary or political ends demanded, as they mostly did, that the accents be placed elsewhere. For some, who found it less easy to evade, it was a source of troublesome complications: Abbot Peter of Königsaal was German largely in spite of himself. For others again, if it could not be altogether shaken off, it might at least be qualified or diluted, in the cause of social integration and harmony. In the *Life* of St Hedwig of Silesia, it has been observed, only newcomers, not settled German-speakers, are called *Theutonici*.[185] The members of the Sandomir (Sandomierz) cathedral chapter who gave evidence at the trial of Bishop Muskata, and some of whom were themselves of German descent, may have chosen their words carefully when they spoke of '*foreign* Germans' whom their bishop had introduced, to the detriment of native Poles.[186]

---

[184] *Königsaaler Geschichts-Quellen*, ed. Loserth, p. 69.
[185] Zientara, 'Die deutschen Einwanderer', p. 342 with n. 32. Duke Henry the Bearded of Silesia designated his military campaign of 1229 against Archbishop Albert of Magdeburg an *expeditio contra Teutonicos*; yet his army included contingents of German burghers from Breslau and Neumarkt (Środa).
[186] Thus *Monumenta Poloniae Vaticana*, ed. Ptásnik, pp. 80–1 (Herbord, dean of Sandomir); Rogall, 'Polen', pp. 53–4; Zientara, 'Die deutschen Einwanderer', p. 342 n. 32. The distinction may also have had some currency within native society. Thus,

A more radical approach was adopted by the author of perhaps the strangest work to come out of the eastern realms: a German translation of the bitterly Germanophobic *Dalimil* chronicle, created for unknown reasons in Prague in the 1340s.[187] The translator, who was sympathetic to Bohemia's German population, combined amendments to the vocabulary of his source with a limited rewriting of its picture of the recent past, and also added some new material. The 'Germans', who in the Czech chronicle had at various points in Bohemian history wrongfully intruded themselves into the realm, became at the hands of the translator, commonly though not invariably, mere 'foreigners'.[188] Otakar II, meanwhile, blamed by *Dalimil* for his great favour to Germans, was lauded for that same reason by the translator, who added further verses of his own describing how the German population had wept and lamented at his death.[189] The *Dalimil* translation is unique among German writings from the settlement lands of its time, in presenting a historically broad, strongly mythologised, view of the territory and of the historical role of German-speakers within it. It is the closest thing we have to an origin legend for a German community in the east.

That it nevertheless fails to attain the ideological qualities normally associated with such legends is revealing. Even as the translator recounts the entry of Germans into Bohemia in times past, he softens and obscures the fact. Just like other ethnic myth-makers, his historical currency comprises bands of migrants, but migrants whose place in the land remained contested, and who were portrayed by the translator's own guiding authority as aliens and parasites. Faced with such a judgement, the translator was lost for words. He had no terms with which to denote a community of 'Germans' distinct from those who lurked beyond the frontier, and none for a historical community of the realm, except for that represented by the *Bemin* – who were Czechs.[190] The

---

even the virulently Germanophobic author of *De Theutunicis bonum dictamen* is careful to insist that the evil-doing Germans of whom he writes are outsiders, and that he does not seek to target German-speaking Bohemians: 'Ein deutschfeindliches Pamphlet', ed. and trans. Wostry, p. 232.

[187] *Di tutsch kronik von Behem lant*, ed. Jiriček; and see Hilsch, 'Di tutsch kronik'. For dating and authorship, see ibid., pp. 107, 110–11. There are indications that the translator may have been a cleric, perhaps a member of the Bohemian Hospitaller order of the Cross with the Red Star. The German chronicle's intended audience is uncertain, but its survival in just a single manuscript indicates a limited reception: ibid., p. 115. For the translator's treatment of German identity, see Scales, 'At the margin of community', pp. 342–5.

[188] *Di tutsch kronik von Behem lant*, ed. Jiriček, p. 83, ll. 24, 26, 28, as examples.

[189] Ibid., p. 196, ll. 139–43. For the translator's treatment of Otakar, see Hilsch, 'Di tutsch kronik', p. 108.

[190] Thus, *Di tutsch kronik von Behem lant*, ed. Jiriček, pp. 192–6.

welfare of his fellow Germans, therefore, continued to depend upon the hazards of succession to the throne producing from time to time one of those benevolent protector-princes of whom the *Dalimil*-author himself so fiercely disapproved. The German settlers lacked the assertive sense of agency and hard-won title fundamental to myths of origin: they had come, but they had not conquered.

Ethnic groups and boundaries

Come they nevertheless had. And the facts of their coming, and of their continued habitation in the eastern realms, in a host of mainly mundane ways made Germans of them. Hardly any of the original migrants had gone east as Germans. Their Germanness was a product of the new legal, social and cultural relationships which their arrival created, and which resulted in the formation of new groups and boundaries and led to their naming. Their ethnonym was inscribed in the terms of the settlement itself.[191] The property law of the immigrants, which at first set them apart as privileged groups, was routinely generalised, despite its regional varieties, as a 'law of the Germans' (*ius Theutonicorum*). Even where it was extended to indigenous communities, it remained a 'German law' (*ius Theutonicum, ius Theutonicale*).[192] The settlers' presence *as* Germans entered the routine documentary vocabularies of the east, where it was perpetuated through repetition. They were labelled with ethnic labels, which, in mostly quotidian and unremarkable ways, assumed and asserted large, general unities and divisions. Sometimes, legal change seemed to demand a more extensive remaking of cultural identities: a diploma of Duke Henry IV of Breslau insists that settlements brought under German law should exchange their Polish for German names.[193] A vocabulary of 'banal Germanness', dense and pervasive, was woven around the settler communities, in documents delineating their rights or recording the facts of their material existence.[194] There they are to be found enjoying their 'German liberty' (*libertas Teutonica*) and following 'German custom' (*mos Theutonicus*), measuring out their

---

[191] A more complex terminology obtained in the lands of the Hungarian crown, where the settlers were widely referred to as 'Saxons' as well as *Teutonici*: see Zimmermann, 'Südostsiedlung', esp. pp. 31–2.

[192] Thus, e.g., a diploma of 1250, in which Duke Henry III of Silesia charges *locatores* with settling the town of Brzeg, stipulating that 'Polonus vel cuiusconque ydiomatis homo liber, domum ibi habens, ius Theutonicum paciatur': *Urkunden und erzählende Quellen*, ed. Helbig and Weinrich, vol. I, no. 25, p. 154.

[193] Ibid., vol. II, no. 39, pp. 188–9 (1283).

[194] For the role of the everyday and the taken-for-granted in underpinning nationhood in modern societies, see Billig, *Banal Nationalism*, esp. Ch. 1.

'German tenements' (*mansi Theutonicales*) by the 'German rood' (*virga Teutonicalis*) – or, in a more domestic mood, living on 'the street of the Germans' (*in vico Theutonicorum*) or giving one of their womenfolk as a 'German wife' (*uxor Thetonica*) to a Polish neighbour.[195]

Local settler communities in town and country were therefore widely designated, by others but also in their own charters, privileges and administrative acts, as forming part of a larger, named whole. Their naming necessarily had identity-forming effects – although the German identities which resulted were often highly fluid and situationally dependent. German identity in the east was, for most of its nominal subjects, a notably narrow thing, tied particularly to ideas of legal status. For some at least, it was easily set aside when circumstances dictated. German merchants in late medieval Stockholm, with an eye to commercial advantage, were thus quite prepared to accept Swedish law and be considered *Swevi*.[196] Some, as we have seen already, found it prudent to suppress or qualify their Germanness, particularly in times of tension. Within certain locales at least, there was considerable intermarriage and cultural syncretism between settler and host communities.[197] Elsewhere, over time, settler groups assimilated fully to their host societies. Among many of the settlers, moreover, and in most daily situations, German identity, we can be confident, had little relevance, and was given scant consideration, or none at all.

Some immigrant groups, however, in particular those enjoying an advantageous social location, and above all groups within the towns, perceived a strong interest in differentiating themselves from native society. Such groups were able to invoke Germanness as a unifying identity, articulating it through an array of cultural and even topographical markers, as well as anchoring it in law and everyday social practice. Seldom did these Germans feel the need to make their common identity the object of articulate reflection or delineation. More important – and certainly more readily discerned by the modern eye – are its dichotomising and boundary-drawing functions. Ethnicity was here constructed within narrow and insular worlds, in order to repel

---

[195] *Urkunden und erzählende Quellen*, ed. Helbig and Weinrich, vol. I, no. 13, p. 102; ibid., no. 24, p. 150; ibid., no. 27, pp. 158–9; ibid., vol. II, no. 104, p. 394; *Urkunden zur Geschichte des Bisthums Breslau*, ed. Stenzel, no. 26, p. 32; Hindin, 'Ethnische Bedeutungen', p. 14.

[196] Wubs-Mrozewicz, 'Interplay', p. 56.

[197] Thus for Stockholm, where linguistic affinities between (Low) German and Swedish facilitated at least a measure of everyday intercourse between Germans and natives, see ibid., esp. p. 67.

rivals and to safeguard the cohesion of small, privileged groups united by day-to-day sociability, common values and common interests.

Ethnicity in the eastern towns usually showed a close correlation with social status, wealth and occupation. Social and economic distinctions overlay ethnic ones, rendering them visible and tangible. In Reval the Germans, as the wealthiest group, were naturally concentrated in the best streets with the biggest houses, while in Zagreb was to be found a 'street of the German shoemakers'.[198] Hardly anywhere was complete segregation enforced. Thus in Budweis (České Budějovice), although Germans and Czechs each tended to gravitate to particular trades, the *vicus Boemicalis* mentioned in fourteenth-century sources had German as well as Czech inhabitants.[199] Elsewhere, however, there are signs of the deliberate segregation of elements of urban sociability along ethnic lines, as in Königgrätz (Hradec Králové), where Germans and Czechs frequented separate bathhouses.[200] To the distinctions which had emerged more or less organically might therefore be added other, more purposeful marks of difference. There are strong indications from towns in the Bohemian lands, not only that the German and Czech communities often attended different places of worship, but also that the distinction was encapsulated in consciously contrasting churchbuilding styles.[201] There is even reason to think that completion of the most magnificent of the churches of the Prague Germans, Our Lady on the Týn, may have been linked to the commemoration of their urban privileges.

Privileges, constitutional and economic, formed a crux of local identity politics. Where Germans controlled the town council, attempts might be made to give their ascendancy lasting legal form. At Ofen, an urban statute maintained into the early fifteenth century that the municipal judge must be able to show descent from four German ancestors.[202] In towns where no single group predominated, questions of access to municipal office commonly became a focus for ethnic division and rivalry, with princes repeatedly feeling obliged to intervene to set quotas.[203] Economic affairs might be regulated along ethnic lines to the smallest detail. At Königgrätz, a charter of Charles IV's widow,

[198] Johansen and von zur Mühlen, *Deutsch*, pp. 109–10; Krahwinkler, 'Der Raum', p. 52. In Prague, too, the concentration of Germans in certain trades was reflected in their settlement in distinct quarters: Šmahel, 'The idea of "nation"' (1969), p. 160.
[199] Schwarz, *Volkstumsgeschichte*, p. 433.
[200] Ibid., p. 332.
[201] Hindin, 'Ethnische Bedeutungen' (p. 33 for the Týn church).
[202] Zorn, 'Deutsche', p. 186.
[203] For examples of this, see above, n. 168.

Elizabeth of Pomerania (1382), even spelt out which products were reserved to German bakers (*die dewczen peken*), and which might be baked by Czech *Golatczer*.[204] A notable aspect of such rulings is the recurrent identification of Germans and of other peoples: if the matters at issue were specific and local, they were nevertheless expressed not in terms of purely local relationships, but of large ethnic groups – 'imagined communities', extending far beyond daily experience.

During the course of the late Middle Ages, local elites in various ethnically mixed regions took increasingly systematic steps to entrench German identity as a criterion for access to social and economic power. There is no doubt that such access had always been dependent upon cultural assimilation to the dominant group; but there are also indications from earlier times that assimilation by natives was sometimes possible.[205] During the fourteenth century, however, ethnic boundaries in many places were more firmly drawn and their exclusionary potential exploited. The earliest known guild statutes which limit access to Germans only are those of the tailors and blanket-makers of Braunschweig (1323).[206] Around the year 1350, Wends were excluded from the grocers' guild in Lüneburg, while by 1353 the statute of the shoemakers of Beeskow in Lusatia forbade the engagement of Wendish apprentices.[207] In 1409 the town council in Lüneburg resolved 'no longer' to grant burgher rights to Wends.[208] Such prohibitions now became more widespread, although still far from universal.[209] From the early fifteenth century, German ancestry began increasingly to be recorded on birth certificates and letters of apprenticeship, and in other municipal documents.[210] In the towns of the far north-east, where the victory of Latin Christianity was recent and long remained incomplete, German dominance came to be particularly rigorously enforced. In 1375, non-Germans were excluded from the coopers' guild in Riga,

---

[204] Schwarz, *Volkstumsgeschichte*, p. 330.
[205] A celebrated early instance of such assimilation is 'Henniko Pruthenus', evidently a Prussian by birth, who appears among the councillors of Königsberg in 1285: see Boockmann, 'Die neue Besiedlung', p. 133. For another familiar case, the thirteen Lübeck councilmen with Wendish names listed in thirteenth-century records, see Johansen and von zur Mühlen, *Deutsch*, p. 7.
[206] Hopp, *Die Zunft*, p. 71.
[207] Johansen and von zur Mühlen, *Deutsch*, pp. 9–10.
[208] Ibid., p. 9. This, they stated, was in order to save the town from 'destruction'.
[209] Of forty-one sets of guild statutes surviving from the Brandenburg towns down to 1414, only three contain exclusionary clauses. Denial of burgher rights to Wends, which became the practice in some other regions, did not occur in the Mark: Vogel, *Der Verbleib*, pp. 122–3, 144.
[210] Johansen and von zur Mühlen, *Deutsch*, pp. 8–9.

while in 1399 their brewing rights were withdrawn. At Reval, the merchants' guild forbade its members to marry native Ests.[211]

Why these changes occurred when they did is not altogether clear. Throughout central Europe the late medieval period was marked by heightened competition between urban groups for access to power and by determined attempts by established elites to reinforce their dominance.[212] In those regions where different ethnic communities coexisted in the towns, these more general currents may well have lent impetus to ongoing processes of local ethnic polarisation, and to the creation of ethnically homogeneous social spaces.[213] Such practices, which were accompanied by an increasing stress upon blood and descent, did not everywhere favour German hegemony: where other groups were strong, policies of ethnic exclusion were sometimes directed against Germans.[214] However, the tenacity of the hold which German elites exercised over positions of social power in many eastern localities also reflected the circumstances of their settlement, as discrete, privileged communities enjoying autonomies guaranteed by princely charter. Not only urban institutions but also many religious houses thus long remained closed to non-Germans.[215]

Only in the eastern lands, where people of different ethnicity lived side by side, were constructions of German identity applied extensively

---

[211] Ibid., pp. 23–4. Nevertheless, the trend towards exclusion advanced more rapidly in some spheres than others: at Reval, Ests were still being admitted as burghers in the first third of the fifteenth century. Among some urban groups, the policing of the ethnic frontier doubtless had specific explanations: it has thus proved impossible to identify with confidence a single Est among the clergy of late medieval Reval. See ibid., pp. 288, 342.

[212] For these developments and their economic context, see generally Moraw, *Von offener Verfassung*, pp. 274–308. The importance of viewing clauses excluding non-Germans as part of a broader trend towards restricting guild access is emphasised by Vogel, *Der Verbleib*, pp. 128–9.

[213] For the growth of ethnocentrism and racism in late medieval Europe, see Bartlett, *The Making of Europe*, pp. 236–42.

[214] An early instance is the establishment in 1334 of an Augustinian convent at Roudnice by Bishop Jan IV of Prague, postulants to which were required to be of Czech descent from both parents: *Regesta Diplomatica*, vol. III, ed. Emler, no. 2008, pp. 781–2; Seibt, *Hussitica*, p. 63. Discrimination was admittedly not invariable, even at a relatively late date: the foundation charter for a hospital at Neuhaus (Jindřichův Hradec) in 1399 required its sworn council 'to receive Czech and German women on equal terms, not giving one group priority over the other, but receiving persons of each language without distinction'. Cited in Šmahel, 'The idea of "nation"' (1969), p. 152 n. 23. A celebrated subsequent case of ethnic homogenisation is the effective barring of Germans from the University of Prague in 1409: see above, n. 123.

[215] That Silesian Franciscan houses admitted 'hardly a single Polish brother, or none at all' was one of the long list of complaints against the German settlers submitted to the Curia by Archbishop Świnka of Gniezno (1285): *Urkunden und erzählende Quellen*, ed. Helbig and Weinrich, vol. II, no. 72, p. 274.

in this period to control and restrict local access to social and economic advantage. In regions where the settlers' language not only differed from those of their host societies but also mostly belonged to a quite different linguistic family, speech offered a natural means for identifying and confining the Other. In Prague in 1399 the parish priest at the Týn specifically forbade the singing of the Czech hymn *Buoh všemohúcí* (*God Almighty*).[216] No less important was the pervading of daily life by the criteria of linguistic exclusion. In the fifteenth century the Danzig joiners' guild deemed it necessary to prohibit not only speaking but even singing in Polish in its workshops: the rhythms of daily toil were to be measured out in German alone.[217] The language barrier attained its purest expression in the poly-ethnic world of the north-eastern Baltic, where the boundary between social spheres was reducible to a bare polarity: *dutsch–undutsch*.[218] Among those thereby united in what they lacked – the broad community of Not-Germans – were Slavs and Scandinavians as well as Balts and Finns. What these groups also lacked was the access to social power which German speech conferred.[219]

Group boundaries were especially stoutly defended, from both sides, when they were believed to enclose sacred spheres of life. This they did in various ways in the eastern lands, and not only on frontiers against pagans or purported schismatics: religion repeatedly set Germans apart from their neighbours within the Latin Christian east also. Divisions between settlers and natives did not therefore *only* reflect group strategies for self-assertion, crucial though these were:[220] they also signalled real, troubling and inescapable cultural differences. These are seen reflected, for example, in the decision of the synod of Leçzyca (1285), under Archbishop Świnka, that no benefices with cure of souls should henceforth be granted to priests without knowledge of Polish.[221] The foreigners and their foreign ways threatened the welfare of native souls – and not only through material problems of communication. A Polish memorandum to the papal Curia thus fulminated against the

---

[216] Šmahel, 'The idea of "nation"' (1969), p. 151 n. 21.
[217] Keyser, 'Die deutsche Bevölkerung', p. 241.
[218] Thus, e.g., *HUB* 4, no. 1118, p. 582 ('beyde Dutschen und Undutschen').
[219] Thus, e.g., Wenskus, 'Der deutsche Orden', p. 426 n. 5, for an ordinance of 1398 from Gerdauen (Zheleznodorozhny), Prussia, excluding natives from urban justice: 'Wir wellen ouch das der Scholtze der Stadt keinen preussen noch undewtschen sall richten.'
[220] The approach taken by some extreme models of ethnic-group formation, which dismiss as irrelevant the 'cultural stuff' which ethnic groups enclose, concentrating solely on their role in advancing their members' material interests: discussed in Eriksen, *Ethnicity*, esp. p. 53.
[221] Strzelczyk, 'Die Wahrnehmung', p. 212.

'*German* knights and *German* peasants' settled on Polish soil, who with-held the Peter's pence payments due in Poland and flouted native cus-tom in the payment of tithe.[222] Germans were 'schismatics'.[223] Religious difference, in the eyes of Polish churchmen, endowed the settlers with a unity as unmistakable as it was lamentable – as Germans. It is likely that the general character, and generalising tone, of Polish admonitions and demands, which cannot have failed to reach the settlers' ears, in their turn helped to nurture among them a perception of forming part of a single, more-than-local, whole.

Religious difference did not, therefore, only constitute a map of eth-nic boundaries but, through the power of its emotive appeal, also gave stimulus to their further reinforcement. Local disagreements flared particularly fiercely when they had a religious element. In Neuhaus (Jindřichův Hradec) in 1405, the regional commander of the Teutonic Order had to step in to resolve a quarrel (*zweytracht*) which had arisen between 'the Czech and German preachers' in the town.[224] Added to this was the capacity of the Church, through its organisational struc-tures, to fashion large, coherent communities of identification and action, in a manner otherwise rare in the eastern lands. It was this that enabled German-dominated Franciscan convents in Silesia to relocate en masse, in the face of much high-ranking Polish displeasure, into their Order's Saxon province.[225] And only religion – and sense of reli-gious difference, and even election – could have provided a unifying impulse sufficiently strong and pervasive to sustain the markedly eth-nocentric (and anti-German) Hussite movement in early fifteenth-cen-tury Bohemia.[226] Only when larger, unifying frameworks were present, and when those who dwelt within them were moved to act, did the potential exist for the local, ethnic solidarities so characteristic of the eastern lands to cohere into a more articulate sense of nation. If such frameworks are sought among the Germans, however, two alone sug-gest themselves.

---

[222] *Urkunden und erzählende Quellen*, ed. Helbig and Weinrich, vol. II, no. 72, p. 272.

[223] See Archbishop Świnka's indictment of the 'gentes exteras et schismaticas' – i.e. Germans – who had intruded themselves into the Polish Church under the tutelage of Bishop Muskata: *Monumenta Poloniae Vaticana*, ed. Ptásnik, p. 78.

[224] 'Ken Newenhawse sunderlichen vmb dy zweytracht der behemischen vnd der dewt-schen prediger.' Cited in Schwarz, *Volkstumsgeschichte*, p. 448.

[225] See Freed, *The Friars*, pp. 74–5. The Silesian convents had previously been in the Order's Bohemian province. Their relocation, in the 1260s and 1270s, was linked by Polish critics with anti-Polish measures by the Franciscans and with the advance of German settlement.

[226] For the background, see, in addition to Šmahel, 'The idea of "nation"' (1969) and (1970), Kaminsky, *Hussite Revolution*, esp. Chs. 1, 2.

Wider horizons: Teutonic Order and Hansa

Among the many privileged German communities to proliferate in the eastern lands during the central Middle Ages, the Teutonic Order occupies a unique status. Its officers came eventually to exercise sovereign rule over a vast, multi-ethnic territorial empire in the eastern Baltic. The Order's lands grew rapidly from an early core in the Vistula basin until they extended, by the mid-fourteenth century, from Danzig to Reval, Dorpat (Tartu) and beyond, sharing frontiers with the principalities of the Reich in the west and with Lithuania and the Rus in the north-east. The imperial monarchy had been closely involved in establishing the Order in northern Europe during the first half of the thirteenth century, and thereafter the German knights' relationship with the Reich retained a significance which had no parallel among other eastern settler communities.[227] The Grand Master bore on his banner the imperial eagle.[228] The Order was unusual in maintaining institutional ties between the regions which it conquered and colonised and properties and convents located in the German heartlands in the west. The German-speaking peasants and burghers who during the fourteenth century made their homes within the Order's domains subjected themselves to German lords as their fellow-migrants elsewhere in east-central Europe mostly did not. The knights, moreover, were crusader-lords, whose common way of life took as its defining ideal that heroic Christian warfare which, as we have seen already, also contributed so much to the self-perception of German elites within the Reich. Although their own appellation and their naming by others were far from standard, an ethnic ascription was almost invariable in their titles.[229] They were brethren of 'the German order', 'the German house', or 'the hospital of Our Lady, St Mary, of the order of the German house', or simply the 'German brethren' or 'German lords'.[230] Like almost no other late medieval institution – and quite unlike the Reich itself – the Teutonic Order faced the world in its own official writings as an avowedly German foundation.

---

[227] For the role of Frederick II, as well as that of the pope, in the Order's early history, see *Cronica terre Prussie*, ed. Töppen, pp. 31–2. In a letter of 1412, Sigismund praised the Order as 'ein vester schilt der cristenheite an den Prussischen orten': *RTA* 7, no. 126, p. 186.

[228] Illustrated from a fifteenth-century manuscript in Arnold (ed.), *800 Jahre*, p. 125. For the grant of this right by Frederick II, see *Cronica terre Prussie*, ed. Töppen, p. 32. For the Order's constitutional status, see above, Ch. 5, pp. 217–18.

[229] Almost, but not absolutely; for the Lübeck chronicler Detmar, for example, they were *godesriddere*: *Detmar-Chronik*, ed. Koppmann, i.496.

[230] Examples: *Originalurkunden*, vol. I, no. 182, p. 201; ibid., no. 337, p. 320; ibid., no. 463, p. 400; *Originalurkunden*, vol. II, no. 1601, p. 739; *Originalurkunden*, vol. IV,

It was also unusual among communities in the German settlement zone in developing a mature, institutionalised consciousness of its own existence and collective character. This found expression not only in the Order's own statutes and vast archives, but in a number of histories, written during its heyday between the late thirteenth and fifteenth centuries, recounting its origins and achievements. These were of varied and sometimes obscure authorship.[231] Yet, while they cannot be considered the product of an official or co-ordinated programme of collective memory-keeping, they do broadly concur in glorifying the crusader-knights and portraying their bloody deeds as praiseworthy and their objectives as worthwhile. Moreover, they were clearly written for an audience, with the object of reaffirming the warrior values of the knights and, through illustrious past example, encouraging their emulation. The majority were in German verse, an indication that they were directed at a non-learned, and perhaps substantially non-literate, public. One at least, the lengthy *Prussian Chronicle* of Nikolaus von Jeroschin, seems to have been written for reading to the brethren at mealtimes, and others may have served the same purpose.[232] What they have to say about the Order's own identity and its relationship with the Germans and their lands, as well as with the non-German peoples over whom the brethren ruled, is therefore of much interest.

The chroniclers are conspicuous in emphasising the Order's links with the German heartlands and in drawing attention to the contribution made by crusading forces from the German-speaking west

---

no. 3304, p. 453; *Cronica terre Prussie*, ed. Töppen, p. 39; *Di Kronike von Pruzinlant*, ed. Strehlke, p. 306, v. 263; *Livländische Reimchronik*, ed. Pfeiffer, p. 59, v. 2160.

[231] The earliest to survive is the *Livonian Rhyming Chronicle*, completed before 1290, perhaps by a knight-brother of the Order, recounting the holy war in Livonia from the late twelfth century to the author's own day: U. Arnold, 'Livländische Reimchronik', *VL* 5, cols. 855–62. It found a continuation in the (lost) *Younger Livonian Rhyming Chronicle* of Bartholomäus Höneke, chaplain to the *Landmeister* of Livonia, covering the period 1315–48: U. Arnold, 'Bartholomäus Höneke', *VL* 4, cols. 120–1. The earliest surviving chronicle dealing with Prussia (from the Order's arrival there) is the *Chronica terrae Prussiae*, completed in 1326 by Peter von Dusburg, a native of the Lower Rhine who may have become a canon and dean of Königsberg: J. Wenta, 'Peter von Dusburg', in *VL* 11, cols. 1188–92. Peter's Latin chronicle was turned into German verse and extended by the chaplain Nikolaus von Jeroschin (d. *c.* 1345): U. Arnold, 'Nikolaus von Jeroschin OT', in *VL* 6, cols. 1081–9. Towards the end of the fourteenth century, a largely military (and now mostly lost) account of the brethren's Lithuanian wars was composed by Wigand von Marburg, a herald with the Order: G. Vollmann-Profe, 'Wigand von Marburg', in *VL* 11, cols. 1658–62; and see generally: Boockmann, 'Die Geschichtsschreibung'; G. Dunphy, 'Teutonic Order chronicle tradition', in *EMC*, vol. II, pp. 1412–14.

[232] Arnold, 'Nikolaus von Jeroschin OT', in *VL* 6, col. 1086. The same function has been proposed for the *Livonian Rhyming Chronicle*, though this view is not unchallenged: Murray, 'The structure', esp. p. 241.

to the brethren's military campaigns. God had stirred the heart of 'many a noble hero' in 'the far-flung German Reich', to come to Prussia: it was above all *bellatores Alemannie* who made the journey east.[233] All this appears understandable enough: viewed objectively, the Baltic crusades were indeed a largely German venture, just as the Holy Land crusade had been dominated by French-speakers and the *Reconquista* by Spaniards. Noteworthy nonetheless is the tendency sometimes discernible to celebrate the prowess of German arms and their bloody feats against the heathen. Germans (*die diutschen*), the chroniclers repeatedly assure their audience, are 'dauntless heroes' (*helde unverzaget*) on crusade.[234] They 'cut gaping wounds', in battle, fighting against enemies routinely identified by ethnic labels.[235] 'Here comes in force the Germans' might!', cry out their opponents, disquieted at the 'clatter' of 'German swords'.[236] In Nikolaus von Jeroschin's chronicle, a Polish prisoner explains to the Prussians the nature of their opponents in the Order's brethren: they are 'heroes in battle' (*zu strîte helde*), 'outstanding knights' (*rittere ûzirwelde*), whom the pope has summoned against them, *von dûtschin landen*.[237] Here is a lexicon of superhuman violence and a joyful celebration of bloodshed borrowed directly from Germanic martial epic.[238] In the *Livonian Rhyming Chronicle*, when some of the native Courlanders flee the field, the knights of the Order and German 'pilgrims' fighting alongside them naturally stand firm.[239]

Collective identity also presupposes a contrasting and defining Other, and this too the Order's chroniclers supply. The brethren's enemies and subjects, particularly pagans and the newly baptised, are presented not merely as wayward but as fully formed barbarians, following the by now familiar literary model. They have the classical barbarian's unreliability. As the *Livonian Rhyming Chronicle* remarks of the Oeselians, 'deceitfulness was in their nature'.[240] For Peter von Dusburg, who supplies a fairly detailed ethnography for the several Prussian *nationes* which he lists, their natural simplicity showed itself in

---

[233] *Di Kronike von Pruzinlant*, ed. Strehlke, p. 353, vv. 4411–12; *Cronica terre Prussie*, ed. Töppen, p. 56.

[234] *Livländische Reimchronik*, ed. Pfeiffer, p. 139, vv. 5137–41.

[235] Ibid., p. 58, vv. 2115–18 (here *die Riuzen*).

[236] Ibid., p. 31, vv. 1130–2; p. 72, vv. 2651–3 ('der diutschen macht mit kreften kumt!').

[237] *Di Kronike von Pruzinlant*, ed. Strehlke, p. 343, vv. 3592–3605.

[238] For an analysis, from this perspective, of the *Livonian Rhyming Chronicle*, see Murray, 'The structure', pp. 244–8.

[239] *Livländische Reimchronik*, ed. Pfeiffer, p. 131, vv. 4852–7: 'dâ sach man Kûren vliehen / und von dem strîte ziehen / alenzeln alsô lange, / daz in grôzem twange / die bruoder beliben stân. / die diutschen wolden ouch nicht lân.'

[240] Ibid., p. 38, v. 1624.

qualities not wholly reprehensible.[241] They are content with plain food, take no care of their dress, and are unthinkingly hospitable, although also given to hard drinking; and, of course, they show in their paganism their unreason.[242] It has been said of the chroniclers writing on the Christian–pagan frontier that they apply to friend and foe primarily religious, not ethnic distinctions: between those who do God's work and those who oppose it.[243] Yet both sides seem also to have understood their battling deities as the champions of contending *peoples*: apostate Livs are to be found washing off the taint of baptism in the waters of the Dvina, and sending it back to Germany.[244] And the pagan peoples in their turn were described in a manner which served the familiar argument of the medieval colonist: that some races are fit only for subjection to others.[245] Prussians had forfeited the power of self-rule, and it was rightly so. Religion was thus itself made an attribute of peoplehood: in the failure of the gods was laid bare the inborn inadequacy of their votaries. There are remarkably few signs of the Germans on the Baltic frontier assimilating themselves to native ways, in the manner familiar from other medieval crusading frontiers, and indeed from other zones of German settlement.[246] Dichotomisation, not syncretism, remained the order of the day.

In light of all this, it is therefore surprising to note how modest was the part played by concepts of German identity in the Order's own self-definition and among chroniclers writing in praise of its wars. Away from titles and formulae, the Germanness of the knights was relatively

---

[241] *Cronica terre Prussie*, ed. Töppen, pp. 50–4. This takes the form of a *Descriptio terre Prussie* – a form of geographic-ethnographic essay recurrently found in Latin writings from marginal regions of medieval Europe, such as the Baltic and North Sea zones and the British Isles. For a discussion of the Prussians' presentation by Peter, see Matuzova, 'Mental frontiers'.

[242] *Cronica terre Prussie*, ed. Töppen, p. 53: 'Prutheni noticiam Dei non habuerunt. Quia simplices fuerunt, cum ratione comprehendere non potuerunt, et quia literas non habuerunt, ymmo in scripturis ipsum speculari non poterant.' Peter goes on to recount the Prussians' naive astonishment when shown the communicative power of letters.

[243] Thus Görlich, *Zur Frage*, pp. 121–34.

[244] *Heinrichs Livländische Chronik*, ed. Arbusow and Bauer, p. 4: 'baptismum, quem in aqua susceperant, in Duna se lavando removere putant, remittendo in Theuthoniam'. On this chronicle, written 1225–7 by the priest Heinrich 'of Livonia', see D. Berg, 'Heinrich von Lettland', in *VL* 3, cols. 776–8.

[245] For references, see above, Ch. 8, p. 358 n. 35.

[246] For the historiography of frontier syncretism, see Berend, 'Frontiers', pp. 159–60. The modest evidence for a meeting of minds across the Baltic frontier is collected in Mažeika, 'Granting power'. None of this, however, negates the prevailing impression that 'generally, there was not much shared between Christian and pagan on the warfront of the Baltic crusade': ibid., p. 158.

seldom remarked upon, at least in ways which have left a lasting record. As a cause for celebration, or as a basis for claims and arguments of the kind encountered in relation to the Empire, the subject is almost entirely absent from the sources. Rarely was any attempt made to link the knights' achievements with those of the Germans as bearers of the Empire. Indeed, writings from and about the Order mostly show little interest in or awareness of the Reich or its history.[247] The chroniclers' concerns were with Prussia, Livonia and their neighbours: Germany was elsewhere altogether, and far away.[248]

Yet when the Order's character and declared objectives are considered more closely, the elusiveness of its German components appears less remarkable. The Germanness of the Teutonic Knights, for all their titles, can be overstated. The Order never, for example (in contrast to other privileged migrant groups), explicitly stipulated that its brethren were to be of German birth. While most undoubtedly were, this was not invariable: Prussians are to be found among the knight-brethren in the fourteenth century.[249] Uncertainty even surrounds the identity of Nikolaus von Jeroschin, a chaplain with the Order and the author of its most substantial surviving chronicle, to whom German, Slavic and Prussian origins have all been imputed.[250] It is significant that his account of the Order's history allows no certain judgement on the matter. The warrior-monks were an elite, self-consciously set apart. They were, moreover, a small elite, with just a few hundred knights in Prussia in the thirteenth and fourteenth centuries.[251]

Such men were not well placed to propagate any – 'German' – culture of their own as the basis for a unifying territorial identity and, despite the slow assimilation of the native population to German speech and customs, there is little sign that the brethren even tried. On the

---

[247] Although Peter von Dusburg did append to his history of the Order brief notes on the popes and emperors who reigned between its foundation and his own time: see *Cronica terre Prussie*, ed. Töppen, p. 24 and pars IV.

[248] Thus *Di Kronike von Pruzinlant*, ed. Strehlke, p. 374, vv. 6200–6: 'slûc des tûvils wîgant / in gar mertirlîchir nôt / al dî aldin cristnen tôt, / dî ê von dûtschin landin / durch beschirmlîch andin / des geloubin und durch vrumin / hin zu Prûzin wâren kumin.'

[249] Wenskus, 'Der deutsche Orden', pp. 422–3.

[250] Arnold, 'Nikolaus von Jeroschin OT', in *VL* 6, cols. 1081–2. One factor which has led to doubt being cast upon Nikolaus's identity is his own protestation that (despite composing a lengthy German verse-chronicle) he knows little German. 'Und want ich tummer sinne bin, / meisterlîcher kunste wan, / darzû lutzil dûtschis kan, / ôt alse mich dî larte, / der spune mich ê narte': *Di Kronike von Pruzinlant*, ed. Strehlke, p. 306, vv. 302–6.

[251] The Order may have had around 600 knight-brethren in Prussia in the first half of the fourteenth century: Rowell, *Lithuania Ascending*, p. 296.

contrary, their lack of interest in the culture of their native subjects, beyond enforcing the most perfunctory Christianisation, was notorious: 'let Prussians remain Prussian' was said to be their watchword.[252] Indeed, the Order, fearful of lingering ill-will among the recent converts over whom it ruled, acted on occasion to widen the gulf with native society. In 1309, Grand Master Siegfried von Feuchtwangen, in response to rural disturbances, prohibited Prussians from holding burgher offices, joining guilds or engaging in trade.[253] Bonds with the Order's German-speaking subjects were hardly closer, however. The brethren mostly originated in regions of Germany different from the peasants and burghers who settled their lands, while their commitment to celibacy precluded the marriage ties through which incoming elites put down cultural roots elsewhere.[254] Even the bonds forged through companionship in arms were gradually lessened, as the Order from the later fourteenth century turned increasingly to mercenaries rather than its own tenants for auxiliary manpower.[255]

In the Order's own official doctrines, moreover, being German *explained* little of importance, in the way that it did for the Empire's German apologists. It furnished the brethren with no necessary common identity, for they found all the identity they required in their monastic Rule. And it supplied no charter. The Virgin Mary, whose lordship the Order fought to defend and extend, demanded the service not of Teutonic but biblical heroes, and such did the brethren aspire to be. The *imperium* may once have been transferred to the Germans, but the Order's castles and towns – Marienburg, Marienwerder, Frauenburg – inscribed upon the land the founding authority not of Caesar but of God's own mother.[256] And the mantle in which the Virgin enfolded her militant champions was not of German stuff. In spirit, the brethren had never left the Holy Land. German prowess in arms might provide their chroniclers with material for the occasional self-glorifying flourish, but it did not explain why the Knights had come to their chilly

---

[252] 'Lasset Preussen Preussen bleyben' (attributed to a Carthusian at a synod at Elbing, 1427): Górski, 'The Teutonic Order', p. 27.

[253] Johansen and von zur Mühlen, *Deutsch*, p. 11.

[254] For the knights' geographical origins, see: Christiansen, *The Northern Crusades*, p. 81; Burleigh, *Prussian Society*, p. 37. Recruitment regions included Westphalia, the Middle Rhine, Franconia and Thuringia. The Order's Livonian province, by contrast, was mostly in the hands of brethren of similar north-German origin to the settlers.

[255] Wenskus, 'Der deutsche Orden', p. 427.

[256] The various ways in which the Virgin's lordship in Prussia was given concrete expression are traced in Dygo, 'The political role', as well as Fischer, *Di himels rote*, Ch. 4. It is true that Peter von Dusburg imagined that Caesar had campaigned in Prussia

northern home or what it was they were doing there. The feats of war in which they rejoiced were those not of furious Teutons but reborn Maccabees.[257]

Yet official doctrine cannot be the whole story. The Franciscan ethnographer Bartholomaeus Anglicus, looking east from Magdeburg, noted how strange had been the religious observances of the Livs, 'before they were compelled by the Germans to abandon the cult of demons for the faith and cult of the one God'.[258] His words are a reminder that, to a sympathetic outside eye, the crusades in the eastern Baltic were indeed *gesta Dei per Teutonicos*. The Lübeck chronicler Detmar was in no doubt that the campaign of slaughter on which the Ests of Livonia embarked in 1343, after throwing off their Christianity, followed ethnic lines: they destroyed 'everything that was German'. It was in turn 'the Germans from the lands' who massacred the rebels on the island of Ösel (Saaremaa), to which they had withdrawn.[259] If the Germanness of the *Ordensritter* found no encapsulation in explicit ideology, it remained nonetheless a central element in the web of perception in which they were caught up. The brethren themselves cannot have been immune to this, any more than were the populations under their rule. As a concept, their ethnicity was under-articulated in the Order's own writings, despite its ubiquity in their titular self-designations. Nevertheless, it would be wrong to underestimate the Order's importance in forming – and polarising – perceptions of a specifically German presence in the east.

Rather different was the case of the Hansa. Like the Teutonic Order, the great trading confederation came to link the old imperial heartlands in the west with the much younger zones of German settlement which developed around the Baltic. Yet it joined them in a union more equal and more secular, and with an incomparably greater geographic scope. The Hansa's relationship with the Reich was, at least imaginatively, through rhetoric and imagery, more intimate than the Order's. Its members were the 'common merchants of the Roman Empire of Germany', the 'men and merchants of Germany, and particularly those belonging to the Roman Empire', or the 'merchants of the Roman Empire of the

---

(see above, Ch. 7, p. 315); but his supposed presence was obscure, while the Virgin's was everywhere celebrated.

[257] The Maccabees were a particular focus of the rich vernacular religious literature produced for the brethren: Fischer, *Di himels rote*, esp. Ch. 3.

[258] Schönbach, 'Bartholomaeus Anglicus', p. 73 (cap. 88).

[259] *Detmar-Chronik*, ed. Koppmann, i.496. See also Christiansen, *The Northern Crusades*, pp. 204–5. One of the leaders, when questioned about the rebels' motivation, reportedly declared that 'any German deserved to be killed, even if he were only two feet tall': *Die jüngere Livländische Reimchronik*, cited ibid., p. 265 n. 158.

German tongue'.[260] Such a linking of German identities with Roman titles, two full centuries before this became established in the diplomatic styles of the Reich itself, seems already to suggest the Hansa's identity-forming potential. The Hansa, like the Teutonic Order but even more insistently and multifariously, named itself as German. It was the 'German Hansa', 'the Hansa of the house of merchants from Germany', 'the common merchant of Germany' or of 'the German towns', its members 'German merchants', 'German shipmen' or, more specifically, 'Germans visiting Skania' or residents at 'the Germans' court' in Novgorod.[261]

The Hansa's Germanness, however, was more in the nature of a broad descriptive label applied to its constituent merchants and, from the fourteenth century, member-towns, than an entrance qualification devised to exclude others. It is true that almost all the Hansa towns had dominant elites speaking forms of German (with Dinant an isolated exception); but there is no indication that this was ever a formal membership requirement.[262] And in other respects it is their heterogeneity – constitutionally, politically and economically – that catches the eye. Despite the Hansa's titular invocations of the Reich, only some of its towns lay within the Empire's frontiers.[263] Others were located in the territories of the Teutonic Order; Stockholm was a member, as may also have been other Swedish towns, and so too was Kraków, under the Polish kings.[264] Visby on Gotland, another Swedish dependency, was central to the Hansa from its earliest days.

That is not to suggest that the confederation's self-declared Germanness was nebulous enough to admit of infinite extension.

---

[260] Examples: *HUB* 3, no. 115, p. 56 ('den ghemeynen coopluden van den Romeschen rike van Almanien'); *HUB* 2, no. 527, p. 232 ('homines et mercatores Almanie et specialiter sacro Romano imperio pertinentes'); ibid., no. 160, p. 71 ('die coepmanne van den Roemschen rike van der Duutscher tonghe').

[261] Examples: *HUB* 3, no. 160, p. 73 (*der Duschen henze*); *HUB* 2, no. 40, p. 20 (*hansa Alemannie*); ibid., no. 358, p. 150 ('hansa domus mercatorum Alemannie'); *HUB* 5, no. 369, p. 189 ('des gemeynen koufmans van Almanien'); *HUB* 4, no. 740, p. 303 ('de gemeyne kopman uth den Dudesschen steden'); *HUB* 2, no. 628, p. 276 (*de Dudesche kopman*); ibid., no. 476, p. 203 (*alle Dudische sciplude*); ibid., no. 486, pp. 208–9 ('Theutonic[i] terram Schone visitare solentes'); *HUB* 5, no. 745, p. 391 (*der Duoschen hove*). It is true that 'German' titles were not invariable, and particularly among the Hansa's neighbours more indefinite appellations were often favoured, such as *Esterlinges* in England and *Osterlingen* in Flanders: see Behrmann, '"Hansekaufmann"', pp. 162–4.

[262] Dollinger, *Hansa*, p. 124.

[263] Appeal to the Empire as a justification for Hansa membership was rare, but not unknown. In 1387, representatives of Nijmegen argued for their town's admission on the grounds that they 'van alden tyden to dem keiserryke horden': *Hanserecesse*, vol. I.ii, no. 342, cited in Hoen, *Eigenbewußtsein*, p. 181.

[264] Dollinger, *Hansa*, p. 128.

A demand by the English that their merchants be allowed to enjoy Hansa privileges was rejected on the grounds that foreign merchants' nations, from outside *Almanien*, were ineligible for admission.[265] On the whole, however, precisely what was believed to constitute the league's German identity is unclear, and was not stated explicitly at the time. What endowed the Hansa with unity, transcending its internal divisions, were the privileges, or 'law', which its members enjoyed. It was these above all that rendered meaningful the shared 'German' character of its constituent communities and their inhabitants. They were 'the common merchants of Germany belonging to the German law'. In 1303, the alderman and brethren of the Hansa in England wrote to Rostock, urging that those towns which had infringed the prohibition on trade with Lynn be placed 'outside the justice and liberty of the Germans'.[266] In May 1397, Johan Swarte, alderman of the Hansa, came to 'the Germans' guildhall' (*der Duotschen gylthalle*) in London and renounced 'the law that the merchant of Germany [*de kopman van Almaningen*] had in England', since he had chosen to become 'a free Englishman'.[267] From a law of merchants there developed a law to bind towns. A resolution of an assembly at Lübeck in 1358 decreed that any 'town of the German Hansa' failing to join the common blockade of Bruges was to suffer the loss of *Dudeschen rechtes*.[268] If the 'German law' of the new communities in the north and east anywhere exerted upon its beneficiaries a discernibly unifying – and Germanising – influence, then it was within the privileged legal framework of the Hansa.

How far, then, can the great mercantile confederation be said to have made Germans of the far-flung communities and civic elites which it came to embrace? The league has certainly been viewed as acting in this way. The retreat of the imperial monarchy from the northerly parts of the German *regnum* in the thirteenth century coincided with the rise of the Hansa, which, as a force for regional political as well as economic integration, to some degree filled the monarchy's role. It drew together regions, in the north and north-west, where the king no longer went, with the burgeoning zones of German speech and manners in the coastal north-east, where he had never aspired to go. The nature of the Hansa and of its members appears in some ways well suited to nurturing a far-reaching sense of shared belonging. Here, after all, was an association of trading towns, linked to each other and to the wider world by intensive networks of communications. The secular urban

---

[265] Hoen, *Eigenbewußtsein*, pp. 135–6.
[266] *HUB* 2, no. 40, p. 20.   [267] *HUB* 5, no. 260, pp. 137–8.
[268] *Hanserecesse*, vol. I.i, no. 212, cited in Hoen, *Eigenbewußtsein*, p. 132.

elites for which it supplied a common frame were well acquainted with pragmatic literacy and personally highly mobile.[269] Not uncommonly, merchant families had members in different, perhaps far distant, towns simultaneously, maintaining regular contact by letter.[270] In contrast to the embattled, introverted world of the Teutonic Order, Hanseatic traders faced outward, meeting the foreigner routinely in settings more varied, and culturally more interactive, than the field of war alone. The view from beyond the frontier was a familiar one for adherents of an institution which maintained residential trading bases in London and Bergen, Bruges and Novgorod.

It is not hard, therefore, to see how the Hansa *might* have encouraged perceptions of a common Germanness among its members. Yet indications that it did so are notably few. Part of the problem here lies with the nature, and therefore role, of the league itself. The Hansa was never more than a loose association of disparate, at times mutually antagonistic, urban communities and regional groups. It had no common core of self-declared doctrines or principles, and no official narrative of its own past. There were no 'Hanseatic' chronicles, although history was written within a number of member-towns. Among these, one alone stands out as sustaining for a time what could, with some qualification, be called a Germanocentric view of the past.

In Lübeck, the chief city (even 'capital') of the league, there was a tradition of historical writing unusually well informed and wide in its field of vision.[271] The chronicler Detmar, writing there in the vernacular in the late fourteenth century at the council's behest, presented a view of the past locating the city in relation to the politics of the western Baltic, but also embracing the history of the Reich. Detmar's world, for all its cosmopolitanism, and its regional and municipal concerns, remained a recurrently German one – even to a degree and in ways uncommon among writers from the Empire's northern core. German armies, in Detmar's account, not only perform their accustomed deeds of *manheit* south of the Alps, but are also to be seen riding out against their northern neighbours. 'German lords and princes' make their way to Prussia, to serve with the Teutonic Order.[272] It is 'Germans' who

---

[269] For pragmatic literacy among the Lübeck merchant elite, see Noodt, *Religion*, pp. 36–40. In the second half of the fourteenth century, Lübeck had two schools offering instruction in Latin to burghers' sons; by the early fifteenth, there were four schools, with evidence that reading and writing in German were being taught.

[270] For Hansa merchant families, see Dollinger, *Hansa*, Ch. 8.

[271] For Lübeck chronicles, see above, Ch. 3, p. 115; for the city as a Hansa 'capital', Jenks, 'A capital'.

[272] *Detmar-Chronik*, ed. Koppmann, i.510.

in 1343 go with 'the knights of God' across the ice against the rebellious Ests, and are even found invading Russia.[273] It is not just that Detmar knew something of the affairs of such far-off communities of German speech; he ascribed them an identity which was also his own.[274] 'The German lands', along with the Latin-derived *Almanien*, repeatedly supply his geographic frame.[275] Detmar was apt to introduce a vocabulary of Germanness even where it is absent from his own sources.[276] 'Germans' excel and are singled out, stepping forward, for example, in disproportionate numbers for the crusade.[277] Among the cardinals created in 1384 by Urban VI, Detmar makes a point of noting, were several *van Dudescher tungen*.[278] The German identity which he presents is one rich in meaning and purpose, particularly in relation to the Empire. The Reich, and the deeds of its rulers, form a strong element in Detmar's history, and provide one of the main occasions for naming 'the Germans', their princes and lands as such. His picture of recent imperial history, particularly in relation to the papacy, is openly partisan, and underlain by a repeated insistence that the German people's title to the Empire is under threat.[279] That he believed the title to be well merited is evident from his recurrent stress upon German prowess in arms.[280]

It has been proposed that Detmar's view of the past, with its strong German colouring and interest in the Reich, may have been familiar to members of Lübeck's mercantile elite, who sponsored his chronicle and among whom works of civic history may conceivably have circulated.[281] Yet to regard this as a 'Hanseatic' vision of history, reflecting a common self-consciousness stimulated by Hanseatic ties, would be a step too far. Lübeck, the commercial metropolis of northern Germany and its largest city, was hardly typical of Hansa towns, and nor was its rich, outward-looking chronicle tradition. Lübeck was also unusual in being an imperial city, maintaining a relationship with the monarchy which, if

---

[273] Ibid., pp. 488, 496.
[274] Hoen, *Eigenbewußtsein*, p. 124.
[275] As when recounting the ravages of the plague: *Detmar-Chronik*, ed. Koppmann, i.521.
[276] Hoen, *Eigenbewußtsein*, p. 179.
[277] *Detmar-Chronik*, ed. Koppmann, i.407.
[278] Ibid., p. 582. [279] See above, Ch. 7, p. 350.
[280] He thus recounts (under 1389) how the island fortress of Örebro, east of Stockholm, held out against Queen Margaret of Norway, since its castellan 'was a German, and knew more about the business of war than anyone else': *Detmar-Chronik*, ed. Koppmann, ii.26. For the attention which he gives to German contingents and their achievements in the Hundred Years War, see Hoen, *Eigenbewußtsein*, pp. 118–19.
[281] Hoen, *Eigenbewußtsein*, pp. 76–8. For the council elite's interest in history, see also Hoffmann, 'Geschichtsschreibung', pp. 300–1.

far from intensive, was nevertheless more substantial than that enjoyed by almost any other of the league's members. It is the relationship with the Empire, rather than his city's trading ties, which explains some of Detmar's choices of subject matter – such as his inclusion, among otherwise scanty notes on the reign of Charles IV, of more detailed accounts of the emperor's visit to the city, and of the revolt against him of the Swabian towns.[282]

In fact the signs are that, beyond small, well-placed circles in the Hansa's first city, the confederation was too remote, institutionally too spectral, and too much riven by inner rivalries to encourage in its members any strong conviction of belonging to a larger, supra-regional whole. Local and particular viewpoints won the day, just as they often did in the Hansa's own ill-attended general assemblies.[283] Kin, home-town, perhaps a regional hinterland, and the face-to-face community of fellow merchants: these were the bonds which spoke most insistent-ly.[284] The survival of large numbers of official documents can lead us to assume too readily that the vocabulary of common identity which these employ accurately reflects the routine mental categories of the league's burghers and traders. Thus, the rich private correspondence of the merchant Hildebrand Veckinchusen, from the late fourteenth and early fifteenth centuries, makes scant reference to Germany or the Germans – or even, indeed, to the Hansa itself.[285] Hildebrand's world (at least as we glimpse it through one inevitably narrow window, the business letter) is a highly concrete one, of kin-groups, cities, cargoes and contracts: it is not a world of peoples.

Others may, of course, have had different perspectives (as, in other contexts or idioms, may Hildebrand himself). Occasionally at least, Hansa sources do indeed convey an impression of ethnic modes of thought intruding themselves into commercial affairs at a level deeper than mere documentary formulae. In particular, the periodic conflicts between 'Germans' and 'Russians' in far-off, inhospitable Novgorod are sometimes recounted in official documents, and may well have been experienced by those involved, as clashes of rival peoples.[286] Moreover, the capacity of the league, through its common structures, weak though these mostly were, to affirm at least a vestigial sense of

[282] *Detmar-Chronik*, ed. Koppmann, i.551–3, 563.
[283] For these, see Dollinger, *Hansa*, pp. 92–7.
[284] Thus Behrmann, ' "Hansekaufmann" ', pp. 164–5.
[285] *Hildebrand Veckinchusen: Briefwechsel*, ed. Stieda.
[286] Thus *HUB* 2, no. 505, pp. 222–7 (10 November 1331): Hanseatic merchants in Novgorod write to Riga recounting details of 'de schelinghe tuschen den Dutschen unde den Ruscen to Naugarden', in which a number of people had lost their lives.

German identity among communities on the margins of the German world, and remote from the monarchy, should not be dismissed. How it might have worked is indicated by a letter from the town of Groningen in north Holland to Lübeck, declaring the town's willingness to participate in a common blockade of Flanders, 'like other German towns' (*als anders Duske stede*).[287] For some, the Hansa may thus have supplied in the late Middle Ages at least the vestiges of a structure within which to conceive of a shared German identity, independent of the shrinking rule of the Reich. Detmar felt able still to write of the *königsfern* northern magnates as 'German princes of Brabant, Guelders, Jülich, and Westphalia'.[288]

How German, therefore, were the German-speakers who inhabited the lands of east-central Europe? A range of factors conspire to make this a peculiarly difficult question to answer. What is clear is that no single answer will do. There is no doubt that the identities of the settlers themselves were complex and multi-layered, and subject to change over time. Germanness was only ever one element. Its content, and its importance relative to other elements, will have varied sharply between different regional communities; different local, social and occupational groups within the same region; and different times. Only very rarely, for small numbers of people, within specific, often conflict-laden settings can it have attained overriding importance. Even among those untypical minorities, its importance will have been situationally dependent, and will thus have fluctuated sharply. Even the most embattled patrician or courtier felt more German in some places and at some times than others.[289] For most of the settler communities, particularly in the countryside, a German identity can have mattered little, when they were conscious of one at all. For those to whom it did mean something, Germanness is best understood as a relational identity, constructed through social practice and legal privilege, against neighbours and rivals of different identity. It was, in short, an ethnic category, which attained its meaning from the proximity of other ethnic groups.[290] It was this proximity that had made Germans in the eastern territories what they were: hardly anyone would have

---

[287] *Codex Diplomaticus Lubecensis*, vol. III, no. 313, cited in Hoen, *Eigenbewußtsein*, p. 133.

[288] *Detmar-Chronik*, ed. Koppmann, i.487.

[289] For the potential for fluctuating levels and kinds of ethnicity within an individual over the course of a single day, see Eriksen, *Ethnicity*, p. 43.

[290] For 'ethnic categories', and for a scheme for classifying different levels of ethnic consciousness, see ibid., pp. 41–2. Locally, particularly in the towns, some German groups correspond to Eriksen's (more intensive) level of 'ethnic associations'.

come east as 'German'. Over the course of time, some settler communities and some individuals became progressively more German, others less so, while some ceased to be German at all. Those groups for whom Germanness mattered most urgently, and who thus took steps to police its bounds with tests of language and blood, lived overwhelmingly in the towns.

One reason why German identity in the east remains so obscure to us is that it was hardly ever made the subject of extended or systematic writings. When Germans in the east, *as* Germans, were subjected to close textual scrutiny, this almost always came from local non-German observers, who often took a hostile tone. There is, we might say, no 'ideology' of Germanness, no worked-out conception of a German nation (or even of a plurality of such nations) to be discovered in the writings of the settlers themselves. While some indigenous critics thought they knew only too well what Germans were like, and what they were doing in lands not their own, the immigrants had no comparably eloquent account to offer. The contrast must be understood above all in terms of their social locations. Apart from the untypical case of the *Ordensstaat*, there were no extensive political formations in the east over which German groups exercised control and with which they could straightforwardly identify. The multiethnic character of the eastern lands, and the imagined roots of their political communities in older, pre-settlement pasts, ensured that it was never possible for the immigrants directly to map *natio* onto *regnum*.[291] The more reflectively and articulately an eastern-German writer engaged with his political identity, therefore, the more likely he was, like Abbot Peter of Königsaal, to tie himself in knots. Most writings by German-speakers, however, were not of this kind: they were produced in the service of an eastern lord, to articulate his self-consciousness or political goals, or to acknowledge his munificence. Our problem, therefore, is partly one of sources; but we have the sources which we have (and do not have) for good reasons. In the eastern lands literate Germans only relatively seldom felt empowered to speak for – and of – themselves.

The result is to make it especially hard to take the temperature of German identity in the settlement regions. Once again, there can be no one answer to this question. However, it is also important to emphasise how much is simply unknowable. Filling the silence with assumptions

---

[291] For kingdoms as the forms for national communities, see: Reynolds, *Kingdoms and Communities*, esp. p. 250; Hoppenbrouwers, *Medieval Peoples*, pp. 18–20.

of a general harmony in which ethnicity had little part to play is hardly
more warranted than would be a face-value acceptance of the depictions
of general and implacable division offered by certain native writers. It
is true that the Heinrichau foundation book, perhaps our clearest window on everyday life, within one rural society at least, suggests a world
in which ethnic differences, while certainly kept in mind, were seldom
the main friction points.[292] Elsewhere, however, things are likely to have
been different. What was seen and heard, what words were exchanged
and in what tone, in the street, in the tavern, in the workplace or on the
way to church, it is impossible to recapture. Occasional remarks confirm
that there were sometimes hard words, and that they were remembered.
An anonymous tract from Prague accuses Germans of boasting that
they had single-handedly brought learning to Bohemia.[293] The charge
has a ring of truth. We should not too readily assume that the semi-
learned (though hardly intellectually taxing) stereotypes of eastern bar-
barity and German mastery that are so repetitiously present in writings
from the German side of the frontier never found a way into everyday
discourse in the east. Where Christians confronted pagans, but also at
moments of religious tension within the Latin Christian realms, ethnic
identity and alterity were especially starkly perceived. And we can be
sure that among socially prominent immigrant groups, at times of crisis
touching their social power and status, their Germanness would have
mattered greatly.

German identity in the eastern lands was less articulated and less
theorised than was the case in certain western writings. The two major,
trans-regional frameworks linked to German immigrant groups, the
Teutonic Order and the Hansa, while they certainly encouraged the
identification and naming of Germans, do not appear to have stimulated systematic thinking about Germanness, as for some did the
Reich. But it is not necessarily the most eloquent conceptions of identity that are the most keenly or widely felt, or have the most significant
consequences. German identity in the east was grounded in locality,
and anchored by grants of law and privilege. These were the focus
of tenacious group memory, and may sometimes even have been the
subject of formal acts of commemoration. For some – though surely
very few – a sense of identity must have been sharpened by the awareness that, as Germans, their continued presence in the east remained
far from secure – an awareness which opponents and rivals in native

---

[292] The best analysis of its content is *A Local Society*, ed. and trans. Górecki.
[293] Šmahel, 'The idea of "nation"' (1969), p. 164.

society were sometimes at pains to promote. For others, German identity offered a basis for social action to keep members of native society
down, and out. The period between the thirteenth and fifteenth centuries, so important in the development of a German political identity in the heartlands of the Reich, witnessed in the eastern territories
processes of identity-formation whose long-term significance was to be
scarcely less great.

10   Being German (I): place and name

Identifying landscapes

Abbot Peter, first of the Cistercian chroniclers of Heinrichau in Silesia, paints a vivid, at times almost a lyrical, picture of the material environment of his community. It was a world of mountains, streams, paths and, framing all, 'the beautiful forest'. Yet the chronicler's landscape was in the process of transformation, as new people and new settlements pushed forward into the sylvan scene. 'Perhaps', he mused 'our successors will wonder' at some of the things he recounted. 'To which we say that in the old days ... the land over there by the mountains was densely wooded, and almost completely deserted.'[1] Those 'old days' lay only a few decades in the past, yet so much had changed. The dense primeval forests which ringed Silesia, and which the native dukes had long preserved for the land's defence, reinforcing them with man-made obstacles (the *przesieka*, or in German *hach*), were being cleared away. Frontiers of a new kind were becoming necessary, and attainable. Abbot Peter's description of the process in action is characteristically graphic. In the course of a dispute about the abbey's properties, the contestants had climbed a mountain, the Ziegenrücken, from whose summit they gazed eastwards, towards the mountain ridge which marked the Bohemian frontier. A member of the party, one Albert the Bearded, a councillor of the duke, pointed out a cairn of stones on a distant mountain-top, with the words:

My friends and companions! If this seems right to you and pleases you, let us fix the boundaries of the abbey from this place through to that hillock beyond the valley. In the sign of truth, let us send two men, who should make for us a richly smoking fire in the valley in between, so that by observing the smoke from this place ... we may indirectly fix the abbey's boundary through the valley, up to that hillock beyond.[2]

[1] *Księga Henrykowska*, ed. Grodecki, p. 294. My translations here follow, with minor changes, those given in *A Local Society*, ed. and trans. Górecki, pp. 136, 139.
[2] *Księga Henrykowska*, ed. Grodecki, p. 298.

So it was done. The fire was lit and men went through the forest and, as they watched for the smoke, cut marks on the trees. The boundary which was thereby established for the Heinrichau monks, the chronicler remarks with satisfaction, long endured unchallenged.

Power and community were by the late Middle Ages coming to be inscribed with a new intensity upon the face of the land itself. As settlement advanced and claims to lordship clashed, the loosely framed frontiers of old, with their vague appeals to forests, watersheds and mountain ranges, yielded in some places to boundaries deliberately marked out with stakes, ditches, heaps of stones or earth, or other purpose-made landmarks.[3] Power in the landscape, and its limits, became closely describable.[4] A delineation of the frontier between Bohemia and the bishop of Meißen's lands in Upper Lusatia, made in 1241, has reference to nearly a hundred different landmarks, such as streams, fords, paths and burial sites.[5] Nowhere were dividing lines sharper and more purposefully drawn than in the territories under the Teutonic Order.[6] In Ermland, for example, the frontier was driven through the wilderness in a dead-straight line for fully 78 kilometres.[7] In the fourteenth century, the Order was able to have recourse to surveyors' instruments and technical manuals in laying hold of the land. And with the new precision came a new terminology, adapting into Latin and German (as *greniz*) the Slavic *granica*, to describe a boundary more precise, and more directly the work of human hands, than were the broad marches of times past.[8] These were the frontiers which now became discernible, directly and at close quarters – often incomplete and relatively short in their courses – holding a line between expansionist lordships in regions where the extensive marginal lands of old had been eaten up.[9]

Viewed as a whole, Germany formed no such zone of solidifying government and power, and only locally did its frontiers attain similarly visible and definite forms. The new vocabulary of territory did not arise in order to mark out a German sphere. In spite of that, at the close of the Middle Ages, a material, topographic 'Germany' was to emerge as the subject of close, evocative description. In the eyes of some Germans,

---

[3] Schich, 'Die "Grenze"', p. 139; Nicklis, 'Von der "Grenitze"'.

[4] Not only in the east. For the establishment of a staked-out, linear frontier to the duchy of Brabant, see Hirschmann, 'Landesbewußtsein?', pp. 227–8.

[5] Karp, *Grenzen*, pp. 107–10.

[6] For the stimulus to these developments, see Schich, 'Die "Grenze"', p. 146.

[7] Karp, *Grenzen*, p. 13.

[8] For this development, see: Schich, 'Die "Grenze"', pp. 151–4; Nicklis, 'Von der "Grenitze"', pp. 21–2.

[9] For an example of the process in action, on the Austro-Bohemian frontier, see Karp, *Grenzen*, p. 101.

the task had by then come to appear a necessity and a patriotic duty. At the end of the fifteenth century, Konrad Celtis laid plans for a vast, multi-author project to produce a full historical geography and topographic survey of the German lands. In the 1520s, Sebastian Münster sought to give fresh life to the by-then moribund venture. 'Let everyone lend a helping hand', he urged, 'to complete a work in which shall be reflected, as in a mirror, the entire land of Germany with all its peoples, its cities, its customs.'[10] Germany and the Germans had become visible, at a time when some cultured Germans were forming an increasingly vivid (though selective, and even fantastic) mental picture of what their native land looked like. Painters now gave these imaginings tangible expression, in landscapes which ascribed a prominent place to the brooding Teutonic forest of the recently rediscovered Tacitus.[11] There even emerged at this time, it has been suggested, distinctively (south-) German ways of seeing and responding to the seen.[12] With all this came a keen eye for the wonders of the homeland, natural and man-made.

The humanists' Germany was an illustrated Germany. The printed map created around 1500 by the Nuremberg compass-maker Erhard Etzlaub was replete with a road-system marked on a scale of German miles, and rendered the northern and eastern German regions with the same detail as the ancient heartlands.[13] In writing, too, the composition and limits of the German lands were described with a new-found ambition and sense of purpose. Celtis's *Four Books of Love According to the Four Corners of Germany* (1502) fixed the easternmost point of the author's self-professed amatory exploits – and thus, of 'Germany' itself – at Kraków. Bohemia lay at the centre of the land.[14] Of the *Germania* which formed the subject of his short geography of 1512, Johannes Cochlaeus wrote, 'in the south it is enclosed by Italy and Dalmatia, in the east by Hungary and Poland, in the north by the Baltic and the Great Ocean, and in the west by France and the British Sea'.[15] Yet his vision extended also to encompass an ethnically mixed Silesia, as well as Prussia, Pomerania and even Livonia, tendentiously described as 'the furthermost German and also Christian province'.[16]

Nobody shone a comparable light upon post-Hohenstaufen Germany. Writings from the two centuries after Frederick II giving account of

[10] Strauss, *Sixteenth-Century Germany*, p. 27.
[11] Wood, *Albrecht Altdorfer*, Ch. 3.
[12] Baxandall, *The Limewood Sculptors*, Ch. 6.
[13] Harvey, *Medieval Maps*, pp. 80–1; Brincken, 'Descriptio terrarum', pp. 644–6.
[14] Silver, 'Germanic patriotism', pp. 40–7; and see also Helmrath, 'Probleme', pp. 334–5.
[15] Johannes Cochlaeus, *Brevis Germanie Descriptio*, cap. 3 § 7, ed. Langosch, p. 66.
[16] Ibid., cap. 6 § 19, § 26, cap. 7 § 16, pp. 118, 122, 130.

the German lands and their inhabitants are characteristically terse, opaque and contradictory. Before the reception from Italy of patriotic humanist genres in the fifteenth century, and the confection of a sylvan Germanic antiquity which the new models encouraged, there seems to have been little stimulus to locate or celebrate the characteristically German as such. Accounts of the German lands themselves can seem to lack conviction, and before Etzlaub we do not even have a self-contained map.[17] It was not everywhere so. The British Isles were fairly convincingly mapped as early as the thirteenth century.[18] In the fourteenth, the Wilton Diptych appears to anticipate Shakespeare in setting a miniaturised England as a jewel in a silver sea.[19] Germany had nothing to compare.

That is not to say that horizons were not expanding in Germany too. In some respects, indeed, Germans in particular had their eyes opened. Already by the early fourteenth century, the Ebstorf map, with its closely packed towns and full, if not always accurate, delineation of the waterways of central Europe, indicates a growth in knowledge.[20] The same period saw the compilation of a number of geographies of the German lands, which did not limit themselves to heaping up ancient authorities. Even Bartholomaeus Anglicus, a non-native, wrote with warm directness about the pleasures of the Rheingau between Mainz and Bingen – a landscape 'of such beauty and such incredible fertility that it delights and reinvigorates, like a garden of inestimable luxuriousness, both inhabitants and even those journeying along the riverbank'.[21] Between the thirteenth and fifteenth centuries German-speakers took to the roads and waterways in unprecedented numbers, as merchants, friars, pilgrims, soldiers, students and masters, and to a host of other ends.[22] Long-distance travel helped to instil an awareness of the character and diversities of the German landscape itself, and of larger worlds beyond within which to comprehend it. Already in the mid-thirteenth century, the north-German friar Albert von Stade was able to discuss knowledgeably the Septimer route over the Alps (ideal, as he explained,

---

[17] Nikolaus von Kues appears to have produced a map of central Europe during the 1450s, but this is long since lost: Brincken, 'Descriptio terrarum', pp. 642–4.

[18] The British Isles were admittedly unusual in this respect: no other European region was repeatedly mapped in the Middle Ages. See Brincken, 'Descriptio terrarum', pp. 632–4, and for the maps themselves, Harvey, *Medieval Maps*, pp. 74–8.

[19] Gordon, *Making and Meaning*, pp. 57–8.

[20] See Friedland, 'Ostsee', p. 19. The dating is that of Kugler, *Die Ebstorfer Weltkarte*, ed. Kugler, vol. II, p. 69, arguing against previous views which placed the map in the early–mid-thirteenth century.

[21] Schönbach, 'Bartholomaeus Anglicus', pp. 75–6.

[22] For more on these developments, see above, Ch. 3, esp. pp. 105–7.

for travellers making for Swabia; less suitable for journeys further north).[23]

But landscapes might be appreciated without any need that they be called 'German'. Writers in the thirteenth and fourteenth centuries were quite capable of expressing a sense of locality, and sentiments of local attachment, all without recourse to any larger geographic frame.[24] And when landscape features *were* seen as indicating a more extended space, they were rarely for that reason made an object of sentiment.[25] That the German lands were ringed by mountains and forests, particularly on their southern and eastern flanks, was recognised as plain fact. It was in this prosaic spirit that a Magdeburg chronicler traced the progress of King Rupert and his forces across 'the German mountains' (*dat dudesche gebergete*) into Lombardy. Johann von Winterthur deemed noteworthy a great battle between birds which had reportedly been fought in the air 'in certain mountainous regions, where lie the bounds of Germany'; but the mountains themselves he took for granted.[26] In the same way, the vast woodlands which were held to separate the Germans from their eastern neighbours merely marked the tides of events. It was 'while passing through the Bohemian forest [*silva Bohemorum*] with his retinue' that Charles IV learned of the death of Ludwig the Bavarian.[27] Only rarely did the frontier forests become emblematic of divisions with a clear emotional charge. The German 'Dalimil' translator recounts how Duke Spitihněv II (r. 1055–61), after quarrelling with the German abbess of St George on the Prague Burg, had her loaded onto a cart and dumped beyond the frontier, 'in the Bavarian forest'.[28] The self-knowledge which the medieval forest famously granted to those who walked in its shade was not, for late medieval Germans (as it would be for their successors in the Renaissance), knowledge of themselves *as* Germans.[29] The crowned lady whom Otto Baldemann encounters as he wanders in

---

[23] *Annales Stadenses auctore Alberto*, ed. Lappenberg, pp. 338–40.
[24] As an example, see the praise of the Austrian lands around Vienna in the late thirteenth-century *Translatio sanctae Delicianae* by the Cistercian Gutolf von Heiligenkreuz: Schönbach and Redlich, 'Des Gutolf von Heiligenkreuz Translatio sanctae Delicianae', pp. 8–20.
[25] For the historical relationship between landscape and national sentiment in Germany, see Schama, *Landscape*, esp. pp. 92–9.
[26] *Die Chronik Johanns von Winterthur*, ed. Baethgen, pp. 217–18.
[27] *Heinricus Dapifer de Diessenhoven*, ed. Huber, p. 61.
[28] *Di tutsch kronik*, ed. Jiriček, p. 94, vv. 1–8. The translator here faithfully follows his Czech exemplar, which in turn was based on Cosmas: *Die Chronik der Böhmen des Cosmas von Prag*, ed. Bretholz, pp. 103–5. The anti-German accent, including the Bavarian-forest anecdote, was the work of 'Dalimil'.
[29] For the forest as a place of truth and revelation, see Jacques Le Goff, 'Le désert-forêt'.

a dream vision through a forest wilderness stands not for Germany but in traditional style for *daz romisch riche*.[30]

On German soil

The belief that particular human groups were bound to specific pieces of land came to assume a substantial part in medieval ideas about the nation.[31] This is hardly surprising. Medieval Christians had before their eyes God's covenant with the people of Israel, which had found expression in territorially highly specific terms.[32] When some European peoples in their turn laid claim to the Israelites' mantle of divine election, their lands too became holy. The revival of Roman political doctrines during the twelfth and thirteenth centuries and their application in favour of the consolidating territorial realms had given new emphasis to the notion of the *patria*, for which each man should be ready to die by virtue of birth within its bounds.[33] The myths recounting the origins of European peoples, which proliferated in the central Middle Ages, in keeping with their character as collective political charters, recounted how the forefathers had in a remote past come to the land which was to be their home, and how they had laid claim to it and made it their own. In some of these accounts, the idea of creating a relationship with the earth itself is vividly conveyed.[34] It is therefore noteworthy that the tale which has been described as the Germans' collective *origo*, recounting Caesar's victorious alliance with the northern peoples, told not of new lands found and won, but of the *titles* and *status* which Julius granted to his warriors.[35] The geographic destination which, by its attainment, made the Germans what they were was Rome. Nor do we find German soil depicted as the sacred earth of a domestic Holy Land. Few spoke of a German *patria*. Little wonder, then, that observers have perceived an uncertain – for some, *ominously* uncertain – relationship with territory and its limits as a peculiarity of medieval German identity.[36]

---

[30] *Politische Lyrik*, ed. Müller, vol. I, pp. 178–81. The same conceit was taken up by Lupold Hornburg (ibid., pp. 190–2).

[31] For the importance of territoriality for medieval nations, see: Davies, 'Names', p. 16; Reynolds, *Kingdoms and Communities*, pp. 258–9; and more generally, Smith, *Ethnic Origins*, p. 28 (*'Ethnie* [i.e. the precursors of nations] always possess ties to a particular locus or territory, which they call their "own" ').

[32] Grosby, 'Religion', p. 10.

[33] For *patria*, see below, p. 480.

[34] For the story of how the Saxons (through trickery) 'bought' the earth upon which they founded their settlements, see *Sächsische Weltchronik*, ed. Weiland, p. 260.

[35] For this, see above, Ch. 7, pp. 309–12.

[36] For the primacy of ethnic over geographic thought in Germany, see Schnell, 'Deutsche Literatur', p. 260.

It is not that accounts of the composition and extent of the German lands are lacking. Indeed, there survive quite a number, of varying detail and precision, preserved within a range of different genres, and dating particularly from the thirteenth and early fourteenth centuries. Writing in the 1230s, the poet Reinbot von Durne expressed the hope that his Middle High German legend of St George might find an audience throughout 'all the German lands', from Tirol to Bremen, from Pressburg to Metz.[37] The poet's measure of German geography is clearly, in keeping with his medium, the (very approximate) extent of German speech. Rather similar are the limits mapped by the Latin *Description of Germany* (*Descriptio Theutoniae*) compiled by a Dominican at Colmar in Alsace early in the fourteenth century. Here, Germany's bounds are somewhat more systematically defined: in the north, Utrecht and Lübeck, in the south, the Alps ('which are between *Italia* and *Germania*'), with Fribourg marking the western and Vienna the eastern extremity.[38] No late medieval writer provides a complete delineation of Germany's frontiers. It is consequently difficult to extend the mostly terse accounts which we have (and to judge whether their authors would have been capable of doing so) to attain a fuller view of what constituted the German lands, and why.

Different commentators adopted differing shades of emphasis, took different points of reference, or interpreted the same points in different ways. Alexander von Roes identified broad topographic markers: the North Sea and the Alps as northern and southern boundaries, with forests separating *Teutonia* from the Slav peoples and Hungarians in the east.[39] Rudolf von Ems, in his world chronicle, followed Honorius Augustodunensis in making the Elbe a northern limit of *obir Germanie* (with *nidir Germania* beyond), while for Bartholomaeus Anglicus, citing Isidore, the (Upper) Rhine was Germany's southern boundary.[40]

[37] *Der heilige Georg*, ed. Kraus, p. 3, vv. 59–64.
[38] *Descriptio Theutoniae*, ed. Jaffé, p. 238. However, the sole surviving manuscript of this work dates from the sixteenth century, and its terminology must thus be read with corresponding caution: see generally Brincken, 'Descriptio terrarum', pp. 635–6. The view of the Alps as a point of division was not confined to clerical writers, and probably represents a widespread view. It found pointed expression in an agreement of 1330 between Count John of Habsburg and Duke Otto of Austria, in which Septimer ('den Seteme den perg') is declared to separate 'Lamparten und Dutsche land': *Quellenwerk zur Entstehung der Schweizerischen Eidgenossenschaft*, ed. Schieß and Meyer, no. 1543, p. 748.
[39] Alexander von Roes, *Noticia seculi*, cap. 9, ed. Grundmann and Heimpel, p. 156.
[40] Rudolf von Ems, *Weltchronik*, ed. Ehrismann, pp. 31, 34, vv. 2220–4, 2423–5; and cf. Honorius Augustodunensis, *Imago Mundi*, I.23, ed. Flint, p. 59; Schönbach, 'Bartholomaeus Anglicus', p. 69 (cap. 13); and cf. *Etymologiarum sive Originum libri XX*, ed. Lindsay, II.14.4.4.

According to Bartholomaeus, *Germania superior*, although bounded by the Alps, also reached beyond them, meeting the Adriatic in the region of Aquileia.[41] Rudolf von Ems, who likewise depicted Germany as extending south of the ridge of the Alps, also emphasised the frontier role of Styria and Austria, at whose borders *tútschú lant* marched with the lands of Slavs and Hungarians.[42] The German geography which Jansen Enikel included in his world chronicle, although avowedly guided by linguistic criteria, in fact concentrated disproportionately on the south-east, his own native region. *Oesterrîch* and its neighbouring lands lie at Germany's heart, while the north is more thinly depicted and German-speaking regions west of the Rhine entirely ignored.[43] To other writers, by contrast, Austria seems scarcely to have belonged to the German lands at all. More than one chronicler distinguishes between 'Austrian' and 'German' nobles with the king, while a late thirteenth-century source tells of things gleaned 'in Bohemia, in Moravia, in Austria and in all Germany' (*tota Alamania*).[44] Whether such distinctions reflect awareness of the medieval duchy's strongly independent character and history, the influence of ancient geographic traditions identifying the Danube as Germany's eastern limit, or yet other factors, is seldom clear. For the *Saxon World Chronicle*, Austria had once been a marshy and waterlogged 'land of the Huns', which was subjugated by Charlemagne.[45]

Germans tended nevertheless to agree, at least broadly, on the extent of the German lands in the north, south and east. Their frame of reference was provided by political frontiers, topographic features and perceived cultural (particularly linguistic) differences, as well as, importantly, by the authority of earlier writers.[46] No single criterion invariably out-trumped others, and much depended on authorial intent and perspective. Lurking behind many accounts

---

[41] Schönbach, 'Bartholomaeus Anglicus', p. 69 (cap. 13).

[42] Rudolf von Ems, *Weltchronik*, ed. Ehrismann, p. 35, vv. 2567–72.

[43] *Jansen Enikels Weltchronik*, ed. Strauch, pp. 534–7, vv. 27419–558. Enikel names groups and lands on the middle and upper Rhine (*di Franken, Swâben*), and in central Germany (*die Sahsen, Mîchsner, Dürgen*), but most references relate to the far south and south-east (*Beiern, Oesterrîch, Tyrol, Görz, die Stîrer, die Kerndner*).

[44] *Annales breves Wormatienses*, ed. Pertz, p. 77; *Cronica S. Petri Erfordensis Moderna*, ed. Holder-Egger, pp. 320–1; *Sächsische Weltchronik: Thüringische Fortsetzung*, ed. Weiland, p. 308; *Regesta Diplomatica Bohemiae*, vol. II, no. 2674, p. 1170.

[45] *Sächsische Weltchronik*, ed. Weiland, p. 147. The chronicler was here following *Ekkehardi chronicon universale*, ed. Waitz, p. 162; but the reference to Austria (*Osterrik*) is his own.

[46] An agreement made by Charles IV, securing military service *in Duetschen landen,* thus set as its bounds the Alps and the (Bohemian) forest: *MGC* 9, no. 336, p. 254 (6 June 1349).

was a geographically hazier sense of Germany as defined by the lands of its four historic peoples, the Franks, Saxons, Swabians and Bavarians, together with eastern marchlands of often indeterminate extent (though there was general agreement that Bohemia, although an imperial principality, was *not* included).[47] That commentators did not find it easy to adjust their mental maps to take account of the progressive eastward movement of German settlement, even when they were aware of its effects, we have observed already (though the author of the *Descriptio Theutoniae* did include the see of Riga in a list of German metropolitans).[48] But when they came to give account of Germany's western limits, their picture frequently dissolves in confusion and contradictions – a problem of which late medieval writers were themselves often aware and with which a handful grappled, though with generally modest success.

The *Descriptio Theutoniae* seems at first to leave no room for doubt on the matter. Not only did Germany's westernmost markerpoint, Fribourg, lie well to the left of the Rhine, in the shadow of the Bernese Alps, but also the river itself 'passes through the land' (of Germany). Indeed, according to the accompanying *Description of Alsace*, the Rhine flows 'through the midst of Germany' (*per mediam Alamaniam*).[49] It is therefore with surprise that the reader learns from the same Colmar geographer that *Theutonia* is in fact located between Rhine and Elbe. On this point, the compiler makes appeal to the authority of a *mappa mundi*.[50] While nothing is known about this source, the reference is credible: the possibly near-contemporary Ebstorf map appears to have borne a label identifying 'the river Rhine, which divides Germany [*Germania*] from the parts of Gaul' (*Galliae*).[51] Evidently the *Descriptio*-author confronted divergent, indeed flatly contradictory, sources on the matter, none of which he felt able to dismiss or refute.

He was not alone in this. Rudolf von Ems set the Rhine as a western boundary, though he also noted that 'the German lands' extend beyond

---

[47] For the formative presence of these four peoples in medieval German thinking, see Thomas, 'Sprache und Nation', pp. 48–9. For Bohemia's exclusion see, e.g., its juxtaposition to 'Germany' in Charles IV's public documents: Müller-Mertens, 'Imperium und Regnum', pp. 585–6.

[48] Above, Ch. 9, pp. 396–7; *Descriptio Theutoniae*, ed. Jaffé, p. 238.

[49] *Descriptio Alsatiae*, ed. Jaffé, p. 237.

[50] *Descriptio Theutoniae*, ed. Jaffé, p. 238: 'Sita est Theutonia … inter Rhenum et Albam fluvios, ut in mappa mundi depingitur.'

[51] Illustrated in *Die Ebstorfer Weltkarte*, ed. Kugler, vol. I, pp. 128–9; and cf. Harvey, *Medieval Maps*, p. 30. However, the label bearing this wording is a modern reconstruction, by Konrad Miller, of a badly fragmentary text: *Die Ebstorfer Weltkarte*, ed. Kugler, vol. II, p. 282.

it.[52] Dietrich von Niem, who, like many others, identified Aachen as a German town, also placed Lotharingia, within which Aachen historically lay, in Gaul.[53] For Albertus Magnus, the Rhine marked the eastward limit of *Gallia Belgica*.[54] Yet Albert also remarks that the testimony of experience in some degree contradicts the authorities, and that the river in fact 'passes through Germany' (*Germania*). Basel, Strasbourg, Worms, Mainz and Utrecht, all to the left of the river, were located, he states, *in Alemannia et Germania*.[55] Bartholomaeus invoked the support of Orosius for the termination of Belgic Gaul at the Rhine, while also stretching the limits of Germany far to the west: Alsace was a German land, and Brabant and Lotharingia respectively the 'furthermost' and the 'ultimate and final' provinces of *Germania*.[56]

The accumulated weight of late antique and medieval texts did much to encourage the idea, traceable back to Caesar, that Germany (for earlier authorities, always *Germania*) and Gaul met at the Rhine.[57] The twelfth-century *Imago Mundi* of Honorius Augustodunensis proved particularly influential on the matter.[58] Its effects are probably visible in the seeming ascription of a Rhine frontier to the German lands by the highly patriotic Walther von der Vogelweide.[59] Common experience, however, reaffirmed the divisive quality of the great river, on whose course there stood no fixed crossing point between Basel and the sea,

---

[52] Rudolf von Ems, *Weltchronik*, ed. Ehrismann, p. 34, vv. 2410–17. Rudolf's account in turn influenced the German geographies of those works which relied upon him, notably the *Christherre Chronicle* and the world chronicle of Heinrich von München: Schnell, 'Deutsche Literatur', p. 266 n. 76.

[53] Dietrich von Nieheim, *Viridarium*, ed. Lhotsky and Pivec, p. 10.

[54] Albertus Magnus, *De Natura Loci*, cap. 7, ed. Hossfeld, p. 41.

[55] Ibid., cap. 2, p. 34.

[56] Schönbach, 'Bartholomaeus Anglicus', pp. 69, 70, 73 (caps. 13, 25, 26, 92); and see the comments of Schnell, 'Deutsche Literatur', p. 267.

[57] For the tradition, see: R. Wolters, 'Rhein: historisches', in *RGA* 24, pp. 525–9 (here p. 526); Scardigli, 'Germania (Provinzname) – Germania Magna', in *RGA* 11, esp. p. 245; Lugge, '*Gallia*', esp. p. 94. Caesar's division was influential already in antiquity, despite the fact that, even in Caesar's day, the Rhine was not the clear ethnic frontier which he implied. The idea of a division along the river's course remained important in spite of the subsequent establishment of the Roman provinces of Germania Superior and Germania Inferior (later Germania I and II) within Gaul to the left of the Rhine: Scardigli, 'Germania', esp. pp. 249, 253.

[58] Honorius Augustodunensis, *Imago Mundi*, I.23, I.27, ed. Flint, pp. 59, 62. Honorius, a canon and monk of Regensburg, compiled and revised his cosmological work, of which over a hundred manuscripts are known, between 1110 and 1139. It was a staple item in ecclesiastical libraries in late medieval Germany. See Flint, 'Honorius Augustodunensis', pp. 165–7, for manuscripts.

[59] Thus Walther's lyric, *Ir sult sprechen willekomen*: 'Von der Elbe unz an den Rin / und her wider unz an Ungerlant / mugen wol die besten sin, / die ich in der werlte han erkant.' Walther von der Vogelweide, *Die Lieder*, ed. Maurer, no. 21, p. 82; and for his Rhine frontier, Schnell, 'Deutsche Literatur', p. 266.

until the late fourteenth century when the *lange brück* was built somewhat further downstream, at Strasbourg. The Rhine functioned recurrently as local and regional boundary in the establishment of leagues and *Landfrieden*.[60] The perception, found among well-informed outsiders, that the lands west of the river displayed different (broadly, more advanced) cultural traits from the east, may have been shared by some Germans.[61] Among the nobility, ties with western dynasties, courts and court culture were closer there. The ancient Gaul–Germany division remained current in the late Middle Ages in the vocabulary and practice of ecclesiastical administration.[62] The crusading taxes which the French clergy paid to the papacy to fund the campaigns of Louis IX and his successors were also levied on some of the imperial dioceses west of the Rhine, despite explicit papal recognition that these lay 'outside the kingdom of France'.[63] In 1247, the churches of Cambrai, Liège, Utrecht, Metz, Toul and Verdun were all taxed, but no attempt was made to extend liability east of the river.[64] The *Gallia–Germania* river frontier retained its prominence in the minds of Latinate clerical writers. It was invoked repeatedly in the biographies of the archbishops of Trier.[65] 'Throughout Gaul and Germany' remained a chronicler's habit and cliché.[66]

Not everything that late medieval Germans knew of the Rhine or experienced at its margin spoke of division, however. The river itself was artery as well as barrier, its commerce binding together the settlements on both banks in a shared economy of news and rumour. Nor did the ancient overland trade routes which crossed northern Germany,

---

[60] Thus, e.g., in the agreement between Archbishop Siegfried of Cologne and Duke John I of Brabant, for mutual aid and support between the Meuse and the Rhine: *Die Regesten der Erzbischöfe von Köln*, ed. Knipping, no. 2971, p. 133 (17 December 1282).

[61] See Hirschmann, 'Landesbewußtsein?', pp. 238, 263; and cf. Schönbach, 'Bartholomaeus Anglicus', pp. 74, 75 (caps. 90, 125) on the comparatively civilised ways of Hollanders and Rhinelanders.

[62] For ecclesiastical vocabulary, see: Lugge, '*Gallia*', pp. 184–90 (also noting complexities and contradictions in the Church's usage); Schnell, 'Deutsche Literatur', p. 263; Kern, *Ausdehnungspolitik*, p. 19.

[63] *Extra regnum Francie*. For the use of this term, see *Les Registres de Gregoire X*, ed. Cadier and Guirard, fasc. I, nos. 323, 369, pp. 125, 140; and also Kern, *Ausdehnungspolitik*, pp. 83–4. Taxes on the western imperial churches became settled at a twentieth, in contrast to the tenth customarily paid by the French clergy. They nevertheless produced intense resentment, and drew protests, largely fruitless, from Rudolf I: *Die Regesten des Kaiserreiches unter Rudolf*, ed. Redlich, no. 1930, pp. 422–3.

[64] Redlich, *Rudolf von Habsburg*, p. 617.

[65] Thus, e.g.: *Vita Henrici archiepiscopi altera*, ed. Waitz, p. 458; *Gesta Boemundi archiepiscopi Treverensis*, ed. Waitz, p. 466. The Franciscan Albert von Stade also pointedly remarked that Trier did not belong to *Alemannia*: see above, Ch. 6, p. 277.

[66] Lugge, '*Gallia*', p. 98.

bound for the markets of Flanders, make any pause at the river. The regional great powers knitted together both banks: most spectacularly, the vast, composite lordship of the church of Cologne, which spanned the north-west from the Meuse to the Weser. The systems into which lesser territories fell likewise straddled the river. The Rhenish League of 1254 had from the beginning drawn its members from both sides. Chroniclers traced the political networks of the *partes Reni*, whose participants came from 'all around, both beyond [the river] and on this side'.[67] Cultural ties also leapt the Rhine. Regional language forms were common to both banks, as the schoolmaster Hugo von Trimburg acknowledged, identifying the *Rinliute* as a distinct dialect group within the German linguistic family.[68]

The administration of the Reich, which in a more closely governed realm might have decided matters definitively, did no such thing. Instead, political events nourished a mood of doubt. The rumours current around 1300, that the Empire's lands west of the Rhine were about to be surrendered to France, drew attention to the river's historically divisive quality.[69] The spread of the notion, popularised by Martin of Troppau, that the archbishops of Trier exercised an archchancellorship for Gaul, gave new impetus to an old idea, namely that *Germania* and *Gallia* denoted parts of the Empire to either side of the Rhine.[70] For the Strasbourg chronicler Closener, striving to render an opaque constitutional doctrine into the vernacular, imperial Gaul was German too – but, necessarily, in a different way from the eastern lands. Over the Rhine was the *Germania* of Mainz's archchancellorship, while Trier presided *in Gallia*, which was to say *in tutschen landen*, on Closener's own side of the river.[71] But that was not a settled view, and chancery documents in the vernacular rendered the *Gallia* of Trier's title as *Welsche lant*.[72] Writings issued in the ruler's name conveyed mixed messages. Frederick of Habsburg in 1315 invoked an imperial Germany embracing both banks, of which Swabia and Alsace together comprised the principal element and heart (*cor Alemanie*).[73] Privileges issued by Charles IV for his uncle, Archbishop Balduin, located Trier among

[67] *Die Kölner Weltchronik*, ed. Sprandel, p. 113 (1371).
[68] *Der Renner*, ed. Ehrismann, vol. III, p. 220, v. 22270.
[69] For this, see above, Ch. 4, pp. 170–1.
[70] Hugelmann, *Stämme*, p. 386; and for the Trier archchancellorship, see above, Ch. 4, pp. 183–4.
[71] *Fritsche (Friedrich) Closener's Chronik*, ed. Hegel, p. 35.
[72] Thus *RTA* 1, no. 3. p. 12 (Charles IV to Archbishop Kuno of Trier, 11 November 1374); and see ibid., no. 4, p. 21, for the archbishop's response, invoking his archchancellorship over *Welschlant*.
[73] *MGC* 5, no. 281, p. 241 (13 May 1315).

'the churches of *Germania*'.[74] The viceregal powers which Charles in 1377 bestowed on his son Wenceslas *in allen Tewtschen landen* for the event of Charles's absence listed among these lands Alsace, as well as regions around the Rhine.[75] Yet the perpetual vicariate which in 1396 Wenceslas felt impelled to grant to his half-brother Sigismund named the duchies of Brabant and Lorraine separately from the princely territories of *Germania* and *Alemania*.[76]

On the whole, it seems, the more empirical the observer, the less learned and consciously indebted to venerable authorities, and the more incidental or unthinking his reference, the more likely he was to treat the Rhine as a river within, not at the margin of, Germany. For Jansen Enikel, the Germans 'sit around the Rhine' while, according to a Bavarian universal chronicle, the populations of Hesbaye, Brabant, Flanders and Holland all lay historically within *Teutonia*.[77] In verses by the Viennese poet Peter Suchenwirt, a character tells how he made his way *tzu dautschen landen* – 'Metz and Trier, Cologne, Mainz'.[78] The *Saxon World Chronicle* recounts how Otto I's enemies had led the western Frankish king 'into the German lands, as far as the Rhine'.[79] Among the towns *in dütsche lant* which were attacked by the Northmen, according to Jakob Twinger, were Cologne, Trier, Liège, Strasbourg and even Tongeren, west of Maastricht.[80] A fragmentary popes-and-emperors chronicle from the Lower Rhine, datable to the early fourteenth century, portrays the Rhine as an axis, and no frontier, of *tota Germania*, with the great cities clustered to one side, and the lands facing 'towards Saxony' lying on the other.[81] The Lübeck chronicler Detmar reported how Edward III of England was aided at the siege of Tournai (1340) by 'the German princes of Brabant, Holland, Guelders, Jülich, from Westphalia, from the Rhine, and many other great lords'.[82] The countship of Luxembourg, according to the Königsaal chronicler, lay *in partibus Germaniae*.[83]

It was those writers who considered the western frontier most closely, who knew the region at first hand, and those who approached it

[74] *MGC* 8, no. 110, p. 180 (25 November 1346).
[75] *RTA* 1, no. 101, p. 185.
[76] *RTA* 2, no. 247, p. 429.
[77] *Jansen Enikels Weltchronik*, ed. Strauch, p. 534, v. 27422; *Chronicon Imperatorum et Pontificum Bavaricum*, ed. Waitz, p. 220.
[78] *Politische Lyrik*, ed. Müller, vol. II, p. 129, vv. 42–3.
[79] *Sächsische Weltchronik*, ed. Weiland, p. 161.
[80] *Chronik des Jacob Twinger*, ed. Hegel, pp. 413–14.
[81] 'Fragment einer niederrheinischen Papst- und Kaiserchronik', ed. Weiland, p. 382.
[82] *Detmar-Chronik*, ed. Koppmann, vol. I, p. 487.
[83] *Königsaaler Geschichts-Quellen*, ed. Loserth, p. 331.

historically, who usually saw the contradictions most starkly. Alexander von Roes, a native of Cologne, was one who attempted a resolution. He concurred that Germany (*Germania, Teutonia*) was divided from Gaul by the Rhine, and like others he made appeal to remote authority on the matter, citing Ambrose's *Hexameron* on the river's function as 'the celebrated wall of the Roman empire against wild peoples'.[84] Alsace was therefore situated in Belgic Gaul, as was the city of Trier.[85] And yet, Alexander insisted, Trier's inhabitants, like those of Cologne and Mainz, were *Germani* – despite the fact that all three churches, and much of the land which they governed, lay west of the river.[86] This, he argued, should surprise no one, since in ancient times the first *Germani* and Franks had driven the Gauls out of those parts.[87] 'Germany', and the extent of settlement of the 'Germans', Alexander explains, do not coincide: for historical reasons, the latter is greater. Neat as this seems, however, it did not entirely save him from contradictions of his own, with the Rhineland archbishops appearing at one point in his treatise not as German princes (as his model would have permitted) but 'princes of Germany' (*principes Germanie*).[88] In the end, a fully consistent account of Germany's western limits eluded Alexander as it did others.

History, which piled up memory like layers of sediment, repeatedly made a mockery of the mapmaker's firm lines. Albertus Magnus, another sometime denizen of Cologne, told a tale similar to Alexander's, though more briefly and in more general terms. Old names were not to be relied upon, as the relationship between peoples and lands had changed over time as a result of migrations and the expulsions that followed in their wake. Just as the Saxons once drove Thuringians and Slavs from their homelands, just as they colonised the British Isles, so also 'certain Romans, along with Germans' (*quidam Romani cum Alemannis*) had burst forth to occupy parts of Gaul beyond the Rhine, where they raised up cities. Thence came the people of Flanders and Brabant.[89] Complex migrations, ancient military ventures, the fruitful intermingling of north and south: here was yet a further variation on familiar themes, such as were presented, in diverse narrative guises, by the *Annolied*-poet, Alexander von Roes, and others besides. The Empire's

[84] Alexander von Roes, *Memoriale*, cap. 15, *Noticia seculi*, cap. 9: ed. Grundmann and Heimpel, pp. 105–6, 156.
[85] Alexander von Roes, *Memoriale*, caps. 16, 35, ed. Grundmann and Heimpel, pp. 110, 143.
[86] Ibid., cap. 11, p. 101; and see Lugge, '*Gallia*', pp. 131–2.
[87] Alexander von Roes, *Noticia seculi*, cap. 9, ed. Grundmann and Heimpel, p. 156.
[88] Alexander von Roes, *Memoriale*, cap. 24, ed. Grundmann and Heimpel, p. 124.
[89] Albertus Magnus, *De Natura Loci*, cap. 2, ed. Hossfeld, pp. 34, 36.

multi-lingual western marchlands retained the marks of the frontier-defying interplay of peoples within which they were first formed.

It was not, therefore, mere slavish adherence to obsolete authorities which induced Germans to offer their complex, internally inconsistent, accounts of the westward extent of their lands, for those authorities encapsulated certain enduring truths, even as they obscured others. German identity had from the earliest times been made at, as well as beyond, the fringes of the German territories, and was most fully formed when most interpenetrated by other identities: Roman, Frankish and Trojan. The Magdeburg *Schöppenchronik* recounts how Caesar had conquered *Germanienland*, 'that is to say the land by the Rhine, where Cologne, Trier and Mainz are located'.[90] It was at the uncertain western edge that, according to Alexander von Roes, Priam's migrant *Germani*, had made their home. Belgic or 'long-haired' Gaul (*Gallia comata*) was at one and the same time *prima Germania*.[91] It therefore made perfect sense that St Peter, in sending his pastoral staff into Belgic Gaul, to raise up the dead apostle Maternus, should have prefigured the Empire's translation to the Germans.[92] To travel to the heart of Germany was to go to its margin. The historical development and political geography of the Reich helped to ensure that this remained the case in the late Middle Ages. Charles IV announced in 1356 that not only would he shortly enter the German lands, but that he would proceed 'further', to the Rhine.[93] The Empire's lands west of the river, culturally and historically, were both bound to *and* distinct from those to the east. In paying regard to this tension, late medieval writers, far from disclosing an impoverished sense of territorial identity, articulated what in the German case was one of its formative elements.

The disquiet which the ambivalence of the German frontier could induce is indicated by the relief evidently felt when the several available criteria all appeared for once to point to a single conclusion. Bartholomaeus Anglicus felt able to declare firmly that Holland 'belongs to *Germania* in respect of situation, customs and lordship, and also language'.[94] Particularly revealing is his appeal to the political frontiers of the Empire's northern *regnum*, to which Holland pertained. Political

---

[90] *Magdeburger Schöppenchronik*, ed. Janicke, p. 7. For the centrality of the Rhine in late-medieval German imagination, see also Classen, 'Der Mythos', esp. pp. 714–15.
[91] See Alexander von Roes, *Memoriale*, cap. 17, ed. Grundmann and Heimpel, p. 112.
[92] Ibid., cap. 35, pp. 143–6. In the *Saxon World Chronicle*, by contrast, Maternus and his companions are sent into 'Germany' (*to Dudischeme lande*) in order to preach in Cologne: *Sächsische Weltchronik*, ed. Weiland, p. 95.
[93] *Strassburg UB* 5, no. 389, p. 336.
[94] Schönbach, 'Bartholomaeus Anglicus', p. 74 (cap. 90).

boundaries were the work of human hands, and ought therefore to have been amenable to precise definition – particularly in an age in which such precision was becoming increasingly attainable and desired. Political frontiers, moreover, seem to have had a particular importance for German identity, in light of the centrality of the imperial monarchy, and the changing ambit of imperial rule, to its definition. It was the course of the frontier that confirmed for Bartholomaeus that Holland lay within *Germania*. (By contrast, he assigns Flanders, which had a large population of Germanic speech but was mainly under the suzerainty of the French crown, to Belgic Gaul.)[95] Indeed, further south on the western frontier, the mere fact of habitation within imperial territory was sometimes enough, in contemporary eyes, to make *Allemands* of French-speaking populations.[96]

The Empire's German kingdom offers salutary indication of why the fabled nebulousness of Germany's medieval frontiers is easily overstated. While the limits of the *regnum* were not at all points clear, were in some places disputed, and were subject to change over time, they were no more debatable than were most medieval frontiers. Historians have been able with some precision to reconstruct the course of a boundary which, despite its great extent, was by the late Middle Ages continuous and effectively linear.[97] There were, it is true, points of ambiguity: the patriarchs of Aquileia were numbered among both the German and Italian imperial princes.[98] And the line was not everywhere equally sharp. Particularly on the eastern margins, the frontier continued into the fourteenth and fifteenth centuries to pass through empty forest and upland and in many places to elude precise definition.[99] Yet even in the east there were well-established dividing points, such as the Leitha where, as Johann von Viktring remarked, lay 'the frontier of the German and Hungarian kingdoms' (*limes regni Theutonici et Ungarici*).[100] Moreover, the growth of population and the advance of settlement ensured that by the later Middle Ages, in innumerable separate local processes, the open marchlands of old were giving way to clear and often visible lines in the landscape. In the west, meanwhile, relatively dense habitation, combined with the presence of an ambitious and much-governed

---

[95] Ibid., p. 71 (cap. 58). For the relationship of the imperial frontier to the German–Romance linguistic border in the west, see Kirn, *Politische Geschichte*, pp. 18–19.

[96] Schnell, 'Deutsche Literatur', pp. 270–1.

[97] See Moraw, *Von offener Verfassung*, pp. 44–5.

[98] Riedmann, 'Deutschlands Südgrenze', pp. 168–9. Uncertainty also surrounded, e.g., the allocation of the countship of Chiavenna: ibid., p. 173.

[99] For its course in the east, see Zernack, 'Deutschlands Ostgrenze', pp. 139–40; for the long persistence of indeterminate zones, Karp, *Grenzen*, pp. 101–2.

[100] *Liber certarum historiarum*, ed. Schneider, i.149.

neighbour, had produced a closely defined, if not always agreed, regnal border.[101] Rights over particular settlements and properties were here the subject of protracted competition between the French and imperial monarchies and their local dependants, with inquests employed on both sides to determine their proper belonging.[102]

Yet neither should the linearity of the German kingdom's frontiers, even in the west, be stressed unduly. Like most medieval boundaries, they had a strongly relative character, and coexisted with and were cut across by numerous other borders. Among these were the administrative divisions of the Church: metropolitan and diocesan boundaries repeatedly straddled the frontiers of the realm. Powers of lordship in particular locations were multiple and overlapping.[103] Feudal allegiances likewise ignored the frontier. Along the western edge of the *regnum*, a majority among the higher nobility, spiritual as well as secular, held fiefs from the French crown as well as the Reich.[104] The dukes of Brabant had been Capetian vassals since the twelfth century.[105] Henry of Luxemburg, long before his election to the Empire, had already done liege homage to the French king, while his younger brother Balduin, as archbishop of Trier, swore fealty to Philip IV in 1308.[106] Only long after the end of the Middle Ages did European 'state' borders in general attain anything approaching their modern, absolute quality.[107] The development of the frontiers of the *regnum*, however, had been especially protracted, complex and piecemeal, and took place relatively free of the urgent military imperatives which underlay frontier-making elsewhere in Europe – as in the closely defined lands under the Teutonic Order. There had been no systematic fortress-building and no networks of local military institutions. Over much of the frontier's course, the monarchy itself was remote, in the late Middle Ages often increasingly so, and its influence on developments vestigial or non-existent.

---

[101] Mieck, 'Deutschlands Westgrenze', esp. pp. 198–9. Among older studies, see: Kern, *Ausdehnungspolitik*; Kern, 'Die "Abtretung"', esp. pp. 558–61; Kirn, *Politische Geschichte*, pp. 41–2.

[102] For the inquests, see Jones, *Eclipse?*, pp. 266–7, 269, 281.

[103] For some of the problems with attempting to discern linear frontiers in the Middle Ages, see: Standen, 'Nine case studies', pp. 16, 27; Power, 'French and Norman frontiers', pp. 114–16; Berend, *Christendom*, esp. p. 14; Gerlich, *Geschichtliche Landeskunde*, pp. 294–5; and for the character of late medieval German frontiers, Birken, 'Deutschland', pp. 288–90.

[104] Surveyed in Jäschke, 'Reichsgrenzen und Vasallitäten'.

[105] Ibid., pp. 140–1.

[106] Pauly, 'Der historische Hintergrund', p. 11.

[107] Evans, 'Frontiers', esp. pp. 486–7, emphasising the importance of the eighteenth century.

None of this prevented late medieval people from regarding the course of the regnal frontier as important. It was at a border-point on the Meuse, at Quatrevaux, that Albert of Habsburg met with Philip IV in December 1299, partly to resolve just such questions of political geography.[108] Local traditions about what had taken place were still lively almost ninety years later, at a time beyond eye-witness recall.[109] A boundary stone had been laid. Local people had gathered to watch and coins were thrown, fixing the event in memory. Elsewhere in the region, copper boundary-markers were reportedly set up, some of them sunk into the bed of the Meuse.[110] These were said to have once been visible in the town of Verdun, though all were long gone by the late fourteenth century, when French royal inquisitors sought for them in vain. The existence of frontier markers was certainly no popular fancy. Albert von Stade, describing a journey from northern Germany to Rome, notes that at La Rouillée, west of the Meuse, 'a stone is located in the centre of the village beside the road, which divides the Empire from the kingdom of France'.[111] Another report mentions a stone carved on one face with the imperial eagle and on the other with the French lily.[112]

The frontier history of the *regnum* was everywhere primarily local history, and the frontier's visibility, and popular consciousness of its course, must have varied sharply between places and times. It is not therefore surprising that in the late Middle Ages political borders seem often to have played only a secondary part in defining a German territorial zone. The vast extent of the kingdom's frontiers, and their nebulousness even for the well informed, beyond the limits of their own local horizons, are the main reasons for this. Moreover, not everyone regarded the multi-lingual northern *regnum* as capable of standing for Germany and of overriding other bonds and divisions, such as those made by language. This must explain why a document of 1282 ascribes the church of Trent, since the high Middle Ages constitutionally part of the German realm, *ad Ytaliam*.[113] After burning a number of settlements around the town, Charles IV, according to Heinrich von Diessenhofen,

---

[108] For this meeting, particularly in its ritual and frontier-defining aspects, see Schwedler, *Herrschertreffen*, pp. 93–108.

[109] For the inquests, *Acta*, ed. Kern, nos. 278, 278a (1387, 1390), pp. 207–20; and see: Schwedler, *Herrschertreffen*, pp. 96–7; Mieck, 'Deutschlands Westgrenze', p. 205.

[110] Thomas, *Zwischen Regnum*, pp. 251–2. The late fourteenth-century witness statements regarding boundary markers are examined by Kern, 'Die "Abtretung"', pp. 562–7.

[111] *Annales Stadenses*, ed. Lappenberg, p. 336.

[112] Thomas, *Zwischen Regnum*, p. 252 n. 61.

[113] *MGC* 3, no. 304, p. 300. For the frontier of the *regnum* towards Italy, see: Riedmann, 'Deutschlands Südgrenze', p. 167; Kirn, *Politische Geschichte*, pp. 21–2.

made his way north towards Brixen (Bressanone), 'which' (in implied contrast to Trent) 'is situated in Germany' (*Alamania*).[114] The divisions which linguistic and cultural differences opened up at the edges of the German realm were mirrored and reinforced in the later Middle Ages by the administrative geography of the religious orders.[115] In the fourteenth century, the Carmelites' province of *Alemania inferioris* encompassed the northern Netherlands while the Francophone south was ascribed to *Picardia remotioris*. Liège, as well as Flanders, belonged to the Dominicans' French province, whereas the remainder of the Low Countries was allotted to *Saxonia*.

It was not, however, only the size of the *regnum* and its lack of institutional substance that hampered its ability to sustain a sense of German identity at its westerly extremities. This needs also to be understood in terms of the internal development of these regions and the growth within them of other, competing bonds of community and allegiance. Texts from the episcopal lordship of Liège, among whose inhabitants can be discerned a significant sense of common belonging, tend to limit the term *Alemannia* almost entirely to their eastern neighbours.[116] A late thirteenth-century genealogy of the dukes of Brabant likewise placed their consolidating territory outside a Germany presented as bounded by Danube and Rhine.[117] Alongside cultural and linguistic factors, equally important was the geographical remoteness particularly of the north-western lands from the heart of the Reich, and the growing strength of other, more immediate and tangible, identities.

Facing the North Sea, Frisia was a region of Germanic speech, which appeared (though not always to its own elites) to lie within the German *regnum*.[118] Yet its populations were nevertheless portrayed, by themselves and others, as a distinct people (*Frisones, Vresen*).[119] 'Germany' proper was elsewhere, and whether the Frisians themselves counted as Germans was far from clear.[120] In the late thirteenth and early fourteenth

---

[114] *Heinricus Dapifer de Diessenhoven*, ed. Huber, p. 56.
[115] For what follows, see Hirschmann, 'Landesbewußtsein?', pp. 244–5.
[116] Ibid., pp. 231–2.
[117] *Genealogia ducum Brabantiae ampliata*, ed. Heller, p. 394.
[118] It was located in the *regnum Teutonicum* (along with Bavaria, Swabia, Saxony and Thuringia) by Otto von Freising: *Chronica sive Historia de Duabus Civitatibus*, ed. Hofmeister, p. 272.
[119] *Ostfriesisches Urkundenbuch*, ed. Friedlaender, no. 59, p. 62 (1346): *wy Vresen*. For the counterposing of *Frisones* and *Theutonici*, *Vrese* and *Dudesche* (1278, 1400), see Müller, 'Nationaler Name', pp. 8, 73. Bartholomaeus Anglicus states that the inhabitants 'are called by the Germans [*a Germanicis*] *Frisones*': Schönbach, 'Bartholomaeus Anglicus', p. 72 (cap. 59).
[120] In their own estimation evidently not, though Twinger included them in a list of component 'German' peoples: *Chronik des Jacob Twinger*, ed. Hegel, 9.623–4.

centuries, Frisians maintained closer and more amicable dealings with the French kings than with the Reich.[121] Imagined ethnic distinctness was thus grounded in traditions of political independence, nourished by the daily experience of strong local communities and sustained by myths and memories of past achievements and of privileges won.[122] Frisian autonomy made particular appeal to the name of Charlemagne and to valiant ancestral deeds done in his service.[123] In face of such claims, and of lives lived out remote from kings and their mandates, the identity-forming power of the northern *regnum* proved small indeed.

Similar processes of fragmentation are also observable in the opposite direction, however. The northern, German-speaking, portion of the Burgundian kingdom not only lay close to one of the old-established monarchical heartlands of the German realm, but also had strong cultural affinities and links with the neighbouring German lands to the east and north-east. Diessenhofen identifies Solothurn, well within the Burgundian realm, as the first place in Germany (*Alamannia*) to destroy its Jews in 1348, as had already occurred 'throughout the kingdom of Arles'.[124] The disintegration of the Burgundian kingdom in the second half of the fourteenth century was prefigured by the gradual softening of its frontier towards Germany, where cultural and political bonds increasingly spoke louder than constitutional geography. Closener's account of the cross-border conflicts of German- and Romance-speaking imperial vassals defines the territorial frontier in linguistic-cultural, not constitutional terms: against 'the honour of Germany' (*dütsches landes ere*) was pitted 'all the Romance lands' (*allez daz welsche lant*).[125] In the late thirteenth century, two vernacular poems

Bartholomaeus located Frisia within 'the lower parts of Germany': Schönbach, 'Bartholomaeus Anglicus', p. 72 (cap. 59).

[121] Schneidmüller, 'Friesen', pp. 312–13; and see above, Ch. 4, p. 164; and for Frisia and the late medieval Reich more generally, Schubert, *Einführung*, pp. 35–6.

[122] Bartholomaeus, who identifies the Frisians as a *gens*, singles out their freedom (along with distinctive hairstyles, social habits and warlike manners) as an ethnic characteristic: Schönbach, 'Bartholomaeus Anglicus', p. 72 (cap. 59). For Frisians as *gens*, see also *HUB* 3, no. 647, p. 441 (*c.* 1337); and for the invocation of Frisian freedom *Ostfriesisches Urkundenbuch*, ed. Friedlaender, nos. 94, 212, pp. 85–6, 176 (1361, 1408). See also H. van Lengen, 'Friesische Freiheit', in *LMA* 4, col. 977.

[123] For this tradition, see Schneidmüller, 'Friesen', pp. 307–10. The tale was widely known. Thus, the Carinthian abbot Johann von Viktring could explain how Charles had granted the Frisians that liberty 'which they enjoy today', namely 'that they should have no foreign prince over them', but should govern their own *res publica* as they saw fit: *Liber certarum historiarum*, ed. Schneider, i.13.

[124] *Heinricus Dapifer de Diessenhoven*, ed. Huber, pp. 68–9.

[125] *Fritsche (Friedrich) Closener's Chronik*, ed. Hegel, p. 51. Closener was following the late thirteenth-century Latin account of Gottfried von Ensmingen: *Ellenhardi chronicon*, ed. Jaffé, p. 130.

by Konrad von Würzburg, *Das Turnier von Nantes* and *Partonopier und Meliur*, both derived dramatic effect from the theme of rivalry between the German and Romance tongues. At the time, Konrad was working at the episcopal court of Basel, in imperial Burgundy.[126]

If the limits of Germany remained disputable, its internal geography nevertheless became during the late Middle Ages a matter for increasingly close report. It was the habit of some chroniclers and poets to decorate their narratives with lists of individual German regions, conveying a vivid sense of multiple distinct landscapes comprising a larger whole.[127] One inner division in particular was taken over from earlier sources and elaborated upon: that between Upper and Lower Germany, *Oberlant* and *Niderlant*, *Alemannia* or *Germania* (or simply *partes*) *superior(es)* and *inferior(es)*.[128] Characteristically, different writers tended to agree in broad terms but rarely in detail about their respective limits. Lower Germany lay to the north and west, and in some reports specifically embraced the lower reaches of the Rhine. On one view, Emmerich marked its southern limit while, for another, this was set by the confluence of the Ahr.[129] Much depended upon individual perspectives.[130] Some conceptions of *Niderlant* were very broad, while others roughly equated with the modern Low Countries.[131] Ludwig IV's chancery wrote of Edward III's vicariate '*in partibus inferioribus*, namely in Brabant, Flanders and Holland'.[132] When seen from the south, however, even the Middle Rhine sometimes appeared to lie within Lower

[126] Thomas, 'Sprache und Nation', pp. 67–8. For the context of these works, see Ritscher, *Literatur und Politik*, pp. 59–64, 76–86.

[127] Thus, e.g., *Chronica de gestis principum*, ed. Leidinger, pp. 31–2; and see also 'Hirzelin' in *Politische Lyrik*, ed. Müller, vol. I, p. 124, vv. 120–3, enumerating the forces in Albert I's army at Göllheim (1298), 'von Beheim und von Ungerlant, / von Chärnden und von Osterrich, / von Swaben und von Westrich, / von Elsaz und von Oberlant'.

[128] The division originated in Roman administrative geography, and was conveyed to the Middle Ages in garbled form via late antique writings. Thus Isidore: *Etymologiarum sive Originum libri XX*, ed. Lindsay, II.14.4.4 ('Duae sunt autem Germaniae: superior iuxta septentrionalem Oceanum, inferior circa Rhenum'). The content of these concepts shifted with time. The division was affirmed by its incorporation into high medieval handbooks, notably that of Honorius Augustodunensis: *Imago Mundi*, I.23, I.24, ed. Flint, pp. 59–60. For Roman Germania, see *Die Ebstorfer Weltkarte*, ed. Kugler, vol. II, p. 284 (*Superior Germania*); and for Roman administrative divisions, Scardigli, 'Germania (Provinzname) – Germania Magna', in *RGA* 11, esp. pp. 249–53.

[129] For Emmerich (and other significant points), see Hirschmann, 'Landesbewußtsein?', pp. 233–5; for the Ahr, Möller, 'Köln', p. 222.

[130] See the references collected in Meisen, 'Niederland', esp. pp. 421–50.

[131] Bartholomaeus allotted Westphalia, between Weser and Rhine, to *Germania inferior*: Schönbach, 'Bartholomaeus Anglicus', p. 79 (cap. 170).

[132] Cited in *Heinricus Dapifer de Diessenhoven*, ed. Huber, p. 35.

Germany.[133] A letter of Ludwig IV made reference to 'the bishop of Trier and other nobles from *Niderland*'.[134] To a poet in the utmost southwest, indeed, the Habsburg army which rode against the Swiss on the ill-starred Sempach campaign (1386) was made up of 'Netherlanders'.[135] From a standpoint in Holland, by contrast, even Cologne pertained to 'the higher parts' of the realm, though in the judgement of southerners the merchants of that city were clearly Netherlanders.[136] Pomerania was 'Netherlandish' from a Brandenburg viewpoint, while a count of Holland might enter *Niderlant* by attacking Frisia.[137]

The view that late medieval Germans were peculiarly devoid of a sense of territorial identity is hard to maintain. On the contrary, the conviction that there existed a land – or, more characteristically, a plurality of lands – properly called 'German' was widely held among the literate. Their extent was regarded as finite and settled, and they were believed to have well-established, identifiable limits. If medieval writers found these difficult to fix with precision, the same was widely true elsewhere in late medieval Europe. That there was no single and continuous, sharp and agreed, German *greniz* is scarcely cause for surprise. Hardly anywhere did political identities rest upon conceptions of territory delineated with anything approaching the precision of modern state borders. Rare in any case is the patriot, medieval or modern, who carries at all times a detailed mental map of the homeland. In this as in other things, German exceptionality is easily overstated. More unusual are the confusions and contradictions which the sources reveal regarding the extent of the German lands, and even their internal composition. This hardly indicates an impoverished territorial consciousness, though it may suggest a troubled one. Far from inducing resignation, however, disagreements between the authorities, or between the authorities and live experience, repeatedly moved Germans to rethink the bounds of their lands and to seek solutions, although rarely with complete success. Complexity and uncertainty once again acted more as spurs than obstacles to identity.

There is no doubt that, for several reasons, the sources and co-ordinates for locating 'Germany' were unusually many and intractable. Part

[133] Thus *Die Chronik Johanns von Winterthur*, ed. Baethgen, p. 43.
[134] *MGC* 5, no. 232, p. 204 (17 March 1315). Perhaps significantly, the letter is directed at the Swiss.
[135] *Volkslieder*, ed. Liliencron, no. 33, p. 119: 'Die niderlenschen herren / die zugent ins oberland...'
[136] *MGC* 4.i, no. 135, p. 110 (1300), for Cologne.
[137] *HUB* 5, no. 586, p. 295; *Sächsische Weltchronik: erste Bairische Fortsetzung*, ed. Weiland, p. 326.

of the problem lay with the sheer extent of the German lands, and with the long and varied histories and traditions which their frontiers encoded. Lacking, moreover, were mature institutions of German regnal government and clear lines of power to affirm the realm's limits. Instead, the imperial monarchy was mostly but a further spectre, with its own peculiar and shifting shapes, to project indeterminately upon the others. With few centrally drawn co-ordinates to go on, writers fell back upon their own resources of knowledge and experience. As a result, their accounts of Germany were strongly coloured by their diverse regional perspectives. Each of these observations can also be fruitfully applied to another matter, intimately connected with how people defined their homelands: how they named them, and named their inhabitants.

Naming land and people

Literate people in the Middle Ages paid much attention to names and invested them with deep meanings, to which they believed the names themselves granted access. Modern scholarship has followed them in this, viewing the names which were given to medieval populations and their lands, and which they claimed for themselves, as offering special insights into their sense of who they were and why it mattered.[138] 'Nothing', as Rees Davies observed, 'touches our individual or collective identity more closely than the name or names with which we are associated. Our very essence seems to rest in them; to lose them is to be threatened with oblivion.'[139] As peoples and nations moved towards a deeper and more stable sense of their own existence, the argument goes, so their common names became clearer and more regular, and were more confidently invoked.[140]

Here, it seems, is another measure of medieval nation-making on which the Germans in special and revealing ways fell short. Yet it was hardly that late medieval Germans lacked common names for themselves and their lands. Instead, critical attention has been directed at what are judged to be the relatively late dates when these came into being, at the nature and origins of the names themselves and the processes in which they were formed, and at their slowness to attain

---

[138] See Smith, *Ethnic Origins*, pp. 22–4. Even Smith's pre-national *ethnie*, his simplest forms of common identity, were, he insists, inconceivable without names. For the centrality of naming to medieval nation-making, see Guenée, *States*, pp. 50–2.

[139] Davies, 'Names', p. 3.

[140] Ibid., pp. 8–9.

full development and wide acceptance.[141] By the late Middle Ages, the unchecked profusion of ways in which populations and territories might be named as 'German' has also been thought to reveal the peculiarly inchoate and ultimately thwarted character of nation-making in the German lands.[142] Here again, therefore, recent scholarship has favoured the order, standardisation and recurrent chancery formulae of the more centralised western monarchies over the chaotic variety and absence of directing purpose which appear to mark the German scene. Whether this familiar pessimism supplies the only lens through which the German evidence can appropriately be read remains, however, to be considered.

A common name for the peoples inhabiting the Empire's northern lands arose, it has often been pointed out, from what was at first a purely linguistic term: *Theodiscus*, a Latinised form of the Old High German *theod-isk* ('of the people'), first attested towards the close of the eighth century.[143] During the course of the ninth, *Theodisci* was joined by the classically derived *Teutonici*.[144] The new terminology developed south of the Alps, in Italy, where the military involvement of the Ottonians did much to transform what were at first rather indeterminate linguistic labels for the northern peoples into firmer political concepts.[145] Although the *Teutonici* are already to be encountered in Ottonian diplomas soon after the middle of the tenth century, these early applications appear to have been made under southern influence.[146] The concept of a single 'German' people, a compound of perceived linguistic difference and political unity, was therefore an Italian invention and export. However, it was one which by the early eleventh century northerners were themselves starting to adopt.[147] Thangmar's *Life* of Bishop Bernward of Hildesheim had depicted Otto III, in 1001, informing the rebellious Romans that for their sakes he had abandoned 'my Saxons and all Germans [*Theotisci*], my flesh and blood'.[148] Thietmar von Merseburg still made only sparing, Italian-derived use of *Teutonici*.[149] By the later eleventh century, however, the concept was

[141] The lateness of the Germans' naming as a people is emphasised, e.g., by Ehlers, 'Imperium', p. 102.
[142] For terminological multiplicity as a sign of weakness, see Schnell, 'Deutsche Literatur', pp. 261–2.
[143] Haubrichs, '*Theodiscus*', pp. 199–203.
[144] For these early developments, see: Thomas, 'Die Deutschen', esp. pp. 24–5; Reuter, *Germany*, pp. 51–3; Fried, *Der Weg*, pp. 17–18.
[145] Thomas, 'Das Identitätsproblem', pp. 138–9.
[146] Thomas, 'Die Deutschen', pp. 32–3.
[147] Vigener, *Bezeichnungen*, pp. 59–81.
[148] Cited in Thomas, 'Die Deutschen', p. 36.
[149] Ibid., p. 38.

sufficiently established among literate northerners for Abbot Norbert of Iburg, in his *Life* of Benno of Osnabrück, to present Charlemagne as founding the future political unity of 'the whole German people' (*universa gens Teutonica*).[150] By this time, the vocabulary of German identity had received a further boost from south of the Alps, through its widely noted polemical application by Gregory VII in his struggle with Henry IV.

Other, older terms, continued to be used, often in new and extended ways. The classically derived *Germani* was periodically employed by high medieval writers, particularly in rhetorically charged contexts.[151] Its currency was stimulated by its well-known use to designate the beneficiaries of the Empire's translation in Innocent III's *Venerabilem*. In the later Middle Ages, its learned pedigree would help to establish *Germani* as the favoured ethnic self-designation of the treatise-writers.[152] The Ottonian idea that 'the Franks' (*Franci*) might be invoked to designate all the emperor's northern followers was never wholly forgotten. It was reiterated in the twelfth century by the likes of Otto von Freising and Gottfried von Viterbo.[153] Late medieval polemicists such as Alexander von Roes and Lupold von Bebenburg mined the tradition to construct a German out of a Frankish identity.

Alongside the language of German peoplehood, there arose a matching vocabulary of territory. By the later twelfth and thirteenth centuries, *Teutonia* had become a ubiquitous term.[154] During this period, however, its hegemony was already being challenged by the extension of *Alemannia*, from its original meaning, indicating the Alemannic southwest, to embrace all the northern lands under the Empire.[155] The rise of *Alemannia* (along with, less commonly, the ethnonym *Alemanni*) was a result partly of the rule of the Alemannic Staufer, and partly of influences from the Germans' French-speaking neighbours, felt particularly in the Rhineland and the south-west, where the new usage found its earliest popularity.[156] Its reception was speeded by its early incorporation into the administrative terminology of the Church.[157] The antique

---

[150] Cited in Fried, *Der Weg*, pp. 20–1.
[151] Vigener, *Bezeichnungen*, pp. 3–7; Hugelmann, *Stämme*, pp. 276–7, 284.
[152] For its late medieval use, see Müller, 'Nationaler Name', pp. 38–49.
[153] For the tradition and its continuation: Thomas, 'Sprache und Nation', pp. 51–2; Hugelmann, *Stämme*, p. 278.
[154] Vigener, *Bezeichnungen*, pp. 159–65; Hugelmann, *Stämme*, p. 387. For its fate in the later Middle Ages, see Müller, 'Nationaler Name', pp. 93–6.
[155] Vigener, *Bezeichnungen*, pp. 179–91.
[156] Müller, 'Nationaler Name', pp. 84, 91–3; and for *Alemanni*, see: ibid., pp. 23–37; Hugelmann, *Stämme*, pp. 279–80, 285.
[157] See, e.g., Rudolf I's confirmation of the privileges of the Hospitalers *per Alemanniam*: *Acta*, ed. Böhmer, no. 401, p. 322. For the term's adoption by the mendicants, see

Germania, which had hitherto functioned as a narrowly geographic term for the lands east of the Rhine, also acquired a wider range of applications.[158] Its continued currency found endorsement in the title of the Mainz archchancellors. Together with the array of names for a German *regnum*, whose rise was considered elsewhere, these names represented the establishment, in the course of a comparatively short period, of an extensive and widely used Latin vocabulary of German identity and habitation.[159]

The formation of a comparable body of terms and concepts in the vernacular took place within roughly the same time-scale. The earliest use of 'German' (*diutisk*) with a clearly political-historical, rather than purely linguistic, meaning occurred in the *Annolied* (*c.* 1080), a further product of the age of Gregory VII.[160] Yet it has been judged significant of the faltering early development of a vernacular vocabulary of Germanness that the *Annolied*-poet was evidently unable to form a substantive for the 'German men' whose deeds he recounted, as he was able easily to do for the component peoples: Franks, Saxons, Swabians and Bavarians.[161] Not until the *Kaiserchronik* (*c.* 1150) do we encounter 'Germans' in the vernacular – and even then, only four times in a text of more than 17,000 verses.[162] Vernacular reference to a German people long remained rare – although invocations of 'German' men, lords, knights and the like now quickly multiplied in lyrics, romances and epics.[163] Also revealing, as it has often seemed, is the strong tendency of vernacular authors to favour the plural form 'German lands': *tiutschiu lant* – or sometimes, with equivalent meaning, *tiutschiu rîche*.[164] (The same idea was also capable of expression in Latin, through relatively common forms such as *partes Alemannie*.)[165] Mainz's archchancellorship for *Germania*, in imperial documents in the vernacular, was exercised *in Duschen landen*. While the singular, 'German land', was at

---

Schubert, *König und Reich*, p. 227. A twofold administrative division into *Alemannia superior* and *Alemannia inferior* was also employed by religious orders: see Müller, 'Deutsches Volk', p. 464.

[158] Vigener, *Bezeichnungen*, pp. 119–29. For late medieval use, see Müller, 'Nationaler Name', pp. 96–101.

[159] For *regnum*, see above, Ch. 4, pp. 177–81.

[160] Thomas, 'Sur l'histoire', pp. 30–1; Haubrichs, '*Theodiscus*', p. 208.

[161] Thomas, 'Die Deutschen', p. 39.

[162] *Kaiserchronik*, ed. Schröder, pp. 89, 371, 386, vv. 497, 16039, 16063, 16899; and see Thomas, 'Das Identitätsproblem', p. 144.

[163] Thomas, 'Sur l'histoire', p. 32.

[164] Thomas, 'Sprache und Nation', pp. 69–70. For the latter term, see, e.g., *Lohengrin*, ed. Cramer, pp. 317, 320, vv. 2571, 2633.

[165] For the use of *partes*, see Müller, 'Nationaler Name', p. 108.

no time wholly absent, the established habit of vernacular authors was to emphasise regional multiplicity over regnal unity.[166]

With the thirteenth century, the Germans took on a more settled vernacular existence. Walther von der Vogelweide had lamented the Church's impositions upon 'us Germans', while the much-read *Sachsenspiegel* (*c.* 1220–35) explained that 'the Germans [*de dudeschen*] shall rightfully elect the king'.[167] The same claim was trenchantly repeated in the south-German *Schwabenspiegel*, some decades later.[168] The *Saxon World Chronicle* invoked a German people repeatedly, although it was only towards the century's close that this form became established among south-German writers.[169] The second continuator of the *Kaiserchronik*, probably writing in the mid-1280s, thus recorded the indignation that 'many Germans' (*manec Tiutscher*) felt at the fiscal chicanery surrounding Richard of Cornwall's election.[170] The thirteenth century also saw the singular territorial designation gain some ground: it was employed repeatedly in the *Saxon World Chronicle*. Indeed, it is not in every case easy to tell whether a plural or singular sense was intended.[171] This occasional grammatical ambivalence would also have confronted late medieval readers, and was perhaps even welcomed by some writers, who may have valued the opportunity to infuse their words with ideas of multiplicity and unity simultaneously. Nevertheless, into the fifteenth century the vernacular continued to lack an established single-word term for 'Germany' (despite occasional scribal contractions, to produce *Tvtschemelande*, *Thutschlant* and similar). Instead, vernacular writers seeking a handy label had recourse to adaption or direct borrowing from the Latin: *Almanien*, *Almaengen* or *Almania* (favoured particularly in works from the north-west and north), *Germanien* or – recurrently in the *Styrian Rhyming Chronicle*, for example – simply *Germania*.[172]

---

[166] Kathryn Smits argued convincingly that, between the eleventh and thirteenth centuries, singular invocations of 'German land' – which characteristically appear as datives, in company with nominative and accusative plural forms, were in fact intended as plurals. After the mid-thirteenth century, however, 'genuine' singular forms are encountered in growing number: Smits, 'Tiutsch', esp. pp. 68–72.

[167] 'Sagt an, her Stoc, hat iuch der babest her gesendet, / dazr in richet und uns Tiutschen ermet unde pfendet?': Walther von der Vogelweide, *Die Lieder*, ed. Maurer, no. 73, p. 222; *Sachsenspiegel Landrecht* III, cap. 52 § 1, ed. Eckhardt, p. 237: 'De dudeschen scolen dorch recht den koning kesen.'

[168] *Schwabenspiegel*, ed. Eckhardt, *Landrecht*, cap. 120/124, p. 182.

[169] Thomas, 'Sur l'histoire', pp. 31–3.

[170] *Kaiserchronik, zweite (Schwäbische) Fortsetzung*, ed. Schröder, p. 412, vv. 110–14. For the establishment of the substantive form in south Germany, see Thomas, 'Sprache und Nation', p. 67.

[171] See Hoen, *Eigenbewußtsein*, p. 81.

[172] Müller, 'Nationaler Name', pp. 116–20.

By the end of the Staufer period, German writers therefore had available to them a rich, not to say bewildering, array of Latin and vernacular terms for their people and its homelands. A range of accompanying adjectives identified the Germans' qualities and characteristics and the paraphernalia of their external lives. By 1330, infringement of the statutes of the mercantile Confraternity of the Virgin in Greifswald was being punished by fines in tuns of 'German beer'.[173] The vocabulary of German identity had by this time lost much of its earlier tentativeness: by the fourteenth century, naming the Germans as such in the vernacular, as well as Latin, was widespread, even routine.[174] Meanwhile, developments continued. *Alemannia* completed its conquest of Germany, spreading outward from the south and west to become by the fourteenth century the most common Latin term for the German lands in their totality.[175] The process, admittedly, was not clear-cut, and the shades of earlier, more geographically restricted meanings lingered for a time, producing ambiguities.[176] How, for example, to understand the short verses, celebrating the election of a scion of the Alemannic Habsburgs as bishop of Constance in 1274, which urge all to praise God, 'but especially the *Alemanni*'?[177] Indeed, as late as the mid-fourteenth century Johann von Viktring was still employing *Alemannia* to signify both the south-west *and* the whole of Germany.[178]

Nevertheless, the term's rising popularity in the later Middle Ages as a geographic signifier (sometimes with the addition of *tota*, to underline its larger meaning) is unmistakable.[179] No other name seems to have been felt to express so effectively ideas – of growing significance for German identities – of material, finite, territorial space. The older

---

[173] *HUB* 2, no. 493, p. 213 ('eine tunne Dudesches bieres'); and see also *HUB* 4, no. 740, p. 303.

[174] For forms of 'the Germans' in the vernacular in the late Middle Ages, see Müller, 'Nationaler Name', pp. 69–75.

[175] Ibid., pp. 91–3.

[176] For changing usage, see Mertens, 'Spätmittelalterliches Landesbewußtsein', p. 119; for the continued application into the fifteenth century of the double formula *Germania et Alemania*, Schnell, 'Deutsche Literatur', p. 262 n. 58.

[177] Printed in full in Lhotsky, 'Apis Colonna', p. 13 n. 17. For similar ambivalence, see the poem by Konrad von Mure, celebrating Rudolf I's victory over Otakar of Bohemia, observing that king and queen alike 'trahunt genus ex Alemannis': Konrad von Mure, *De victoria regis Rudolfi*, p. 319.

[178] For examples of both forms, see *Liber certarum historiarum*, ed. Schneider, i.29, 37, ii.52, 57.

[179] Thus, e.g., *Continuatio Vindobonensis*, ed. Wattenbach, p. 714, for the summoning of 'omnes archiepiscopos et episcopos ac alios prelatos tocius Alemannie' to the Würzburg ecclesiastical council of March 1287. Alexander von Roes glossed the archbishop of Mainz's archchancellorship for *Germania* with *totius Alemanie*: *Memoriale*, cap. 24, ed. Grundmann and Heimpel, p. 125.

Teutonici, by contrast, continued to be widely employed as ethnic identifier, and also still supplied the main basis for adjectival and adverbial naming of the Germans.[180] It was a common designation for Hansa merchants and was used almost exclusively to identify settlers in the east. The German language remained for most Latin writers the *lingua Teutonica*. As written use of the vernacular grew, moreover, so also did the relative importance of vernacular terms in naming land and people.

Complexity and variety characterise the use of these various terms. Tracking their application is not wholly straightforward, since some writings from the period are known only through later manuscripts, which cannot always be relied upon to reproduce the terminology current at the time of composition.[181] Nevertheless, much of the riotous profusion which we encounter clearly has contemporary explanations. A writer's region of origin often went far to determine choice of names. But why Heinrich von Herford should have made near-exclusive use of *Teutonici*, why his contemporary Heinrich Taube employed only *Alamanni*, or why Bernhard von Kremsmünster adhered predominantly to *Germani*, must also be explained partly by personal preference.[182] Some writers completely changed their favoured terminology between works.[183] One reason for this freedom of choice lies in the absence of a binding royal chancery style for naming land and people, such as is found in other realms. While it is true that, from the later thirteenth century onward, imperial documents often employ the increasingly ubiquitous *Alemannia*, there were, as was remarked elsewhere, no standard formulae taking a German, rather than Roman, frame of reference.

One result of this absence of authoritative terms was the remarkable discrimination which some literate Germans were able to apply in their choice of names. A number of writers employed *Germania* and *Germani* in a historicising fashion, to identify a remote past, linked to, but also distinct from, more recent times – Germanic rather than German, we might almost say. In this spirit, Johann von Viktring employs *Germania* mainly for periods before the ninth century, thereafter generally using *Alemannia*, or more rarely *Teutonia*. The chronicle of the

---

[180] For the late medieval career of *Teutonici* in German sources, see Müller, 'Nationaler Name', pp. 3–19.

[181] A circumstance affecting the interpretation, for example, of the important Colmar group of histories, now mostly accessible only through the sixteenth-century manuscript on which the *MGH* editions (in *MGS* 17) relied, see Kleinschmidt, 'Dominikaner-Geschichtsschreibung'.

[182] See Müller, 'Nationaler Name', pp. 12, 26, 40–1.

[183] Thus, e.g., Alexander von Roes changed from predominant use of *Germania* in his *Memoriale* of 1281 to *Teutonia* in the *Noticia seculi* of 1288.

Erfurt Franciscans deploys *Germania* only when telling of the land's Christianisation.[184] Heinrich von Langenstein distinguished between the Empire's translation *in Germanos* in the person of Charlemagne and its passage *ad Theutonicos* under Otto the Great.[185] Comparable distinctions are sometimes found in vernacular works. Jansen Enikel wrote of how 'Ludwig, the emperor Charles's son, possessed the land of *Germania*'.[186] The vocabulary of German identity was not only an extensive but a flexible and expressive one.

It was also increasingly pervasive. Although precise quantification is impossible, not least on account of the subsequent loss of material, there is no doubt that the frequency of references to the Germans, their lands, qualities, institutions and way of life, increased significantly between the mid-thirteenth and the fifteenth century. Within this long period we can identify shorter ones, during which people and land were named with particular intensity. One of these lies in the later thirteenth century, centred on the eventful reign of Rudolf I; another coincides with Ludwig the Bavarian's protracted conflict with the Curia, between the early 1320s and the 1340s. Further stimulus was to come from the debates over the reform of Church and Reich in the fifteenth century. All the signs are, therefore, that the crises of the post-Staufer era, far from thwarting the development of a German identity, were a forcing-house – most visibly when the strains were at their most acute.

Even setting aside these particular periods of stimulus, however, the long-term trend was towards a growing density of reference. The eastward migration of German-speakers, as we have seen already, was accompanied by the multiplication of routine reference to the *Teutonici*, their communities and laws, in the documents which the settlement process called forth.[187] Anyone reaching the end of Jakob Twinger's chronicle (written, as the author himself states, for Strasbourg's 'astute laymen', lacking Latin) would have encountered the German people, their lands, rulers and language, in over 200 separate places. While it is true that few readers would have experienced Twinger's chronicle as the complete text enshrined in its nineteenth-century edition, even a shorter section is enough to convey a strongly Germanising flavour.[188] A study of late medieval Lübeck chroniclers has shown how these were apt to add new 'German' identifiers of their own, or convert specifically

[184] *Cronica minor*, ed. Holder-Egger, p. 604.
[185] Sommerfeldt, 'Zwei Schismatraktate', pp. 446–7.
[186] *Jansen Enikels Weltchronik*, ed. Strauch, p. 539.
[187] Above, Ch. 9, pp. 424–5.
[188] For the manuscripts, see Klein and Melville, 'Twinger', col. 1183.

regional terms into references to 'the German lands', when adapting their Latin sources to the vernacular.[189]

Not only did some writers now name the Germans more frequently; works making prominent reference to land and people also gained a wider dissemination. Good illustration of this is provided by the *Sachsenspiegel*, which, although compiled in the first half of the thirteenth century, only in the fourteenth began to be copied and received on a significant scale, at least if the numerous manuscript survivals are a reliable guide. By the fifteenth century, the law-book had become ubiquitous in the household libraries of German princely and noble families, and its southern counterpart, the *Schwabenspiegel*, was hardly less widely received.[190] While 'German' references in the *Sachsenspiegel* are not especially numerous (with thirteen in the *Landrecht* and four in the shorter *Lehnrecht*), they tend to occur at points of particular significance for readers.[191] *Lehnrecht*, for example, identified the 'land of the German tongue', subject to the Empire, as the sphere within which vassal-service was due.[192]

When the late medieval evidence is examined, the view that German writers were constrained by an impoverished or merely mechanical vocabulary of common identity is therefore hard to sustain. Indeed, it is rather the richness of their terminological resources, and the sense of purpose, and even passion, with which some now deployed them, which command attention. Some writers evidently valued the varied shades and resonances which the multiple names for the Germans enabled them to introduce into their works. These allowed Heinrich von Langenstein, for example, to heap comprehensive praise upon '*Almania*, noble and refined, *Theutonia*, strong and spirited, *Germania*, powerful, and renowned for her might, her riches and her warlike peoples'.[193] One element in the continued appeal of *Germani* and *Germania*, at least among the more self-consciously learned writers, was the basis which these terms offered for erudite puns, when brought together with words such as *germen*, *germinare*, *germanus* and *germanitas*.[194] The vocabulary of German identity appeared to constitute fitting material for such literary ornamentation.

---

[189] Hoen, *Eigenbewußtsein*, pp. 82, 92–3.
[190] For German families with *Sachsenspiegel*-manuscripts, see Nijsten, *In the Shadow*, pp. 246–52.
[191] See Hugelmann, *Stämme*, pp. 267–8.
[192] *Sachsenspiegel Lehnrecht*, cap. 4 § 1, ed. Eckhardt, p. 22.
[193] Sommerfeldt, 'Zwei Schismatraktate', p. 453.
[194] Thus, e.g., *Annales SS. Udalrici et Afrae Augustenses*, ed. Jaffé, p. 435, on dissensions among the electors 'quos nobilis Germania germinavit'. For further examples, see above, Ch. 8, pp. 365–8.

The possibilities opened up by different names went beyond the rhetorical, however, as they appeared each to promise access to different aspects of German identity. This is most obviously seen in the etymologies traced from them, and the histories and meanings which these were held to disclose. The Colmar *Descriptio Theutoniae* offered an unusually full range. The land was called *Theutonia* from the giant Theuto, *Alamannia* from 'the Alemannic Lake, on which lies the city of Constance', and *Germania* 'because it is said to bring forth many people; for it is claimed that no land of comparable size contains so many'.[195] The two latter explanations had behind them the authority of traditions extending back to late antiquity.[196] German etymologies are to be found in late medieval writings in colourful and contradictory variety.[197] And the more polemical an author's intent, the more likely he was to make appeal to them to support his case. Alexander von Roes offered three different ones, for *Germani*, *Franci* and *Teutonici*.[198] Moreover, he was quite prepared to argue for his favoured versions against rivals, taking specific exception to the idea that *Germania* was named from its fecundity in people, which, he claimed, appeared to 'contradict reality'.[199] (His own explanation was in terms of the land's gradual settlement by descendants of the Romans' Trojan kinsmen (*Germani*), the earliest Franks.) Alexander's partisan insistence on the matter is characteristic of his time.

To literate Germans, names mattered: to fight for their proper use was to defend against erosion the identities and communities to which they gave voice. Lupold von Bebenburg took up arms against those foolish noblemen who settled for calling themselves mere 'Rhinelanders' (*Renenses*), thereby negating their Trojan origins as Franks.[200] As for the Germans' several names, some writers treated these as simply interchangeable, and stated as much.[201] Others, however, were anxious to maintain distinctions. Alexander von Roes polemicised tirelessly against what he saw as French bids to usurp the proud Frankish title rightfully

---

[195] *Descriptio Theutoniae*, ed. Jaffé, p. 238.
[196] Thus Isidore: *Etymologiarum sive Originum libri XX*, ed. Lindsay, I.9.2.94 ('populi habitantes iuxta Lemannum fluvium'), II.14.4.4.
[197] See, e.g., that deriving the *Teutonici* from the idols Theuto and Thon: above, Ch. 7. p. 304.
[198] Alexander von Roes, *Memoriale*, caps. 16, 17, ed. Grundmann and Heimpel, pp. 109, 111, 113.
[199] Ibid., cap. 16, p. 112.
[200] Lupold von Bebenburg, *Tractatus*, cap. 3, ed. Miethke and Flüeler, p. 265.
[201] Thus *Descriptio Theutoniae*, ed. Jaffé, p. 238: 'Est locus ... qui Theutonia, seu Alemania, seu Germania nuncupatur.'

pertaining to their eastern neighbour.[202] The lazy use of *Alemannia*, to denote the whole of Germany, was for some a particular bugbear. Otto von Freising had raised objection already in the mid-twelfth century.[203] For Alexander it was a malevolent symptom of the attempted Swabian takeover, which the Staufer and their henchmen had staged, of the Reich itself.[204] It was not only treatise-writers who held opinions on such matters. According to the chronicler Bernhard von Kremsmünster, a people (he means the Bavarians) which might 'broadly' be called *Germani* was also 'inappropriately' named *Alemanni*.[205] If identity is honed and articulated through reflection and argument, the multiplicity of names which prevailed in the late Middle Ages for land and people undoubtedly provided Germans with much to argue about, and for.

Together they amounted to a language not merely of classification, but of identification. Much has traditionally been made of the allegedly late development of a specific terminology of German nationhood. It is true that systematic invocation of a *Germanica natio* only begins with the fifteenth century, reflecting the formative role of the Church councils and debates about the reform of the Reich.[206] Regular vernacular reference to a single *deutsches Volk* begins even later.[207] In spite of all this, the idea of a single German people is recurrently found much earlier, in writings from the post-Staufer period.[208] The Latin term most often applied is *gens*, which occurs in combinations with *Theutonica*, *Theutonie*, *Germana*, *Germanorum* and similar names.[209] Archbishop Balduin of Trier felt it necessary to remind Benedict XII of the proven loyalty of the *gens Germanica* to the Church.[210] Comparable use was sometimes made of *natio*, with Johann von Viktring, for example, writing of 'a certain poor man *Theutonice nacionis*'.[211] This term, however,

---

[202] Alexander von Roes, *Memoriale*, caps. 18, 26, ed. Grundmann and Heimpel, pp. 114, 128. The same objection was raised by Lupold von Bebenburg: *Tractatus*, cap. 3, ed. Miethke and Flüeler, p. 262. For the equation of *Francia* with France, see Lugge, '*Gallia*', esp. p. 168.

[203] *Ottonis et Rahewini Gesta Friderici I. Imperatoris*, ed. Waitz, p. 20.

[204] See above, Ch. 7, p. 348.

[205] *Bernardi, ut videtur, Liber de Origine et Ruina*, ed. Waitz, p. 639.

[206] For the development of this idea, see Müller, 'Nationaler Name', pp. 57–68.

[207] Ibid., p. 54. For rare medieval instances, with the more specific, medieval meaning of *Volk* as arms-bearers, see: *Kaiserchronik*, ed. Schröder, p. 84, vv. 245–6 (the revolt of *daz Dûtisc volch* against Roman rule); *Chronik des Jacob Twinger*, ed. Hegel, p. 332 (the entire *dütsche volg* marches with Caesar on Rome); and cf. *Mittelhochdeutsches Handwörterbuch*, ed. Lexer, vol. III, p. 437.

[208] For numerous examples, see Müller, 'Nationaler Name', esp. pp. 54–60.

[209] The use of *gens* is explored in Görlich, *Zur Frage*, pp. 89–95.

[210] *Nova Alamanniae*, vol. I, no. 547, p. 366.

[211] *Liber certarum historiarum*, ed. Schneider, ii.59.

bore a broad penumbra of meanings, including the purely local and even familial (quite apart from its technical application, to divide up bodies of university students and Church council participants), and is only ever with caution translatable as 'nation'.[212] The complexities of the word's use mirrored those of German identity itself, with Heinrich von Herford telling of a man who came to Rome in the time of Boniface VIII, a *Theutonicus* of Bavarian *natio*.[213] A further roughly cognate term sometimes employed was *populus*: it was the *Alemanicus populus*, whose rage, for one chronicler, the legate John of Tusculum had stirred up.[214]

There seems little reason to doubt the means available to late medieval Germans to express identification with a community extending beyond locality, region and lordship – and defined in ethnic terms. Despite this, it is notable that the word *patria*, although widespread in German writings, was rarely applied to Germany itself, as it was to other late medieval realms.[215] Instead, patriotism found its main focus at regional and territorial levels. It was in ducal Austria, not Germany at large, that in chronicle report Rudolf I was hailed as *patriae salvator* following his victory over Otakar.[216] Ludolf von Sagan's (adoptive) 'fatherland' was Silesia.[217] Even among imperialist treatise-writers, always the loudest champions of a German cause, it was seldom used with explicitly national intent. Lupold von Bebenburg is a rare exception, on one occasion invoking a *patria Germanie* as the object of his 'fervid zeal'; but he characteristically undercuts this at once by declaring his native Franconia (*Francia Germanica*) to be the true focus of his affections.[218] The fewness of self-declared German patriots in the late medieval record doubtless has complex explanations. However, a major element must lie with the absence from Germany of a political

---

[212] For some of its range of applications, see: Kahl, 'Einige Beobachtungen'; Hugelmann, *Stämme*, pp. 288–9; Görlich, *Zur Frage*, pp. 106–10.

[213] *Liber de rebus memorabilioribus*, ed. Potthast, p. 218. The order was also reversible, with Johann von Viktring making reference to 'quidam nobilis Theutonice nacionis ex Karinthia': *Liber certarum historiarum*, ed. Schneider, ii.140.

[214] Above, Ch. 6, p. 267; and, for *populus*, Görlich, *Zur Frage*, pp. 75–83.

[215] Fried, *Der Weg*, p. 22; Monnet, 'La patria', p. 95. For medieval usage, see generally Eichelberger, *Patria*. Heinrich von Herford identified *Theutonia* as Charlemagne's *patria*: *Liber de rebus memorabilioribus*, ed. Potthast, p. 78. For isolated late medieval application to Germany, see also Müller, 'Nationaler Name', p. 110.

[216] *Liber certarum historiarum*, ed. Schneider, i.236. As a further example of the term's use within a princely territory, see Nikolay, *Die Ausbildung*, p. 56: in 1286 the nobility of Guelders promise to collaborate with their count according to the customs of the *patria Geldrensis*.

[217] *Catalogus abbatum Saganensium*, ed. Stenzel, pp. 234–5.

[218] For this passage, see above, Ch. 6, p. 269; another isolated use of *patria* for Germany occurs in Lupold's *Ritmaticum Querulosum*: quoted above, Ch. 6, p. 268.

theology, of the kind found particularly in France, linking crown, dynasty and people, and thereby fusing polity and ethnicity in common exaltation.[219]

A word which in German usage sometimes came close to late medieval applications of *patria*, however, is the vernacular *zunge* – 'tongue', as synonym for 'people'. Like *patria*, it was capable simultaneously of expressing concepts of ethno-cultural community and rightful political order.[220] Both ideas were implicit in Walther von der Vogelweide's famous complaint at the lack of *ordenunge* into which *tiuschiu zunge* had fallen.[221] The widespread use of 'tongue', before the fifteenth century, as the main vernacular term denoting a German people, sets the Germans apart from their neighbours – a matter to which it will be necessary to return. Often, *zunge* was employed straightforwardly to distinguish 'Germans' as a group, as, for example, in *Lohengrin*, where it denotes the German contingent in Henry I's army.[222] Traders from the Hansa towns were identified as 'merchants of the Roman Empire of the German tongue'.[223] But *zunge* could also serve as a powerfully affective term, expressing a writer's own identification. In particular, in the troubled climate of the thirteenth and fourteenth centuries, it was employed for expressions of distress at the state of the people's political affairs.[224]

It has sometimes been suggested that there was less warmth in the Germans' manner of talking about themselves and their lands than is found among their medieval neighbours.[225] The contrast may conceivably have some validity for the twelfth century, where the 'fair France' of the *Chanson de Roland* lacks an obvious counterpart in German literature.[226] By the later Middle Ages, however, the language of German identity too was at times one of warm identification and praise. Here

---

[219] See Kantorowicz, *Two Bodies*, pp. 232–72; and, for French use of *patria*, Schneidmüller, *Nomen Patriae*, pp. 262–74

[220] For the political use of 'tongue' in Germany, see Thomas, 'Sprache und Nation', pp. 76–80.

[221] In his lyric *Ich saz uf eime steine* (1198 × 1201): Walther von der Vogelweide, *Die Lieder*, ed. Maurer, no. 12, p. 60.

[222] *Lohengrin*, ed. Cramer, p. 439, v. 4397. As a further military example, see *Rymkronyk van Jan van Heelu*, ed. Willems, p. 241, vv. 6525–6.

[223] As an example, *HUB* 2, no. 160, p. 71 (1309): '… die coepmanne van den Roemschen rike van der Duutscher tonghe'.

[224] See the poet 'Meißner', cited above, Ch. 6. The poet also castigates the 'greed' of *Diutsche zunge*, clearly meaning the princes. For this, see Schnell, 'Deutsche Literatur', p. 309.

[225] Thus, e.g., Thomas, 'Sprache und Nation', p. 70 (referring specifically to vernacular sources).

[226] The contrast is drawn by Fried, *Der Weg*, p. 22.

Walther von der Vogelweide was characteristically eloquent and precocious.[227] After the fall of the Staufer, in seemingly unpropitious times,
partisan voices multiply. *Germania* was 'noble' to one Latin annalist,
'illustrious' to another.[228] The importance, for some writers, of surrounding the German name with honour and preserving it from shame
has been encountered repeatedly already.[229] It was 'for the sake of the
German tongue' that the *Lohengrin*-poet refrained from naming those
who had failed to take up arms against the Hungarians.[230] Here were
no mere labels, but names which summoned hearers and readers to feel,
and to act.

They were names which had been formed within particular historical
processes, to which in their late medieval applications they continued
to attest. Above all, they had been made and shaped by others, and
adapted in the course of centuries of interaction between Germans and
a wider, particularly Romance-speaking, world. It was in recounting
engagements with that wider world that they found their most natural
application. Of the twenty-two 'German' references to be found in the
twelfth-century *Kaiserchronik* (a major source for late medieval chroniclers), twenty-one relate to Italian affairs.[231] Literate Germans had
learned to view their common existence through outside eyes, and they
remained into the late Middle Ages, in a sense, aliens to themselves. It
has been pointed out that the vernacular *Book of Kings of the New Law*
speaks of Germany with a singular voice only in relation to the pre-
Carolingian period, perceiving the territory from the viewpoint of its
Roman conquerors.[232] But when later periods are recounted, in which
Germans are history's makers, rather than merely its object, Germany
once again dissolved for the author into the familiar plurality of 'lands'.
This ability to adopt more than one perspective is characteristic of
German writers, and reflects the flexibility and subtlety of their vocab-
ulary of identity. Heinrich von Diessenhofen distinguished consistently

---

[227] Most famously, in *Ir sult sprechen willekomen* ('Tiusche man sint wol gezogen, / rehte
als engel sint diu wip getan...'): Walther von der Vogelweide, *Die Lieder*, ed. Maurer,
no. 21, p. 82.

[228] *Annales SS. Udalrici et Afrae Augustenses*, ed. Jaffé, p. 435 (*nobilis*); *Annales Sancti
Rudberti Salisburgenses*, ed. Wattenbach, p. 803 (*clara*); and see also the invocation of
'noble' *Germania* by Ludwig IV: *Nova Alamanniae*, vol. I, no. 175, p. 98 (1327).

[229] Above, Ch. 6, pp. 269–70.

[230] *Lohengrin*, ed. Cramer, p. 323, v. 2682.

[231] Thomas, 'Sur l'histoire', pp. 28–9.

[232] Smits, '*Tiutsch*', p. 82. Smits points out that, in vernacular sources of the thirteentth
century generally, the singular *tiutschez lant* is only consistently encountered when
the German lands and their component peoples are being imagined from without,
from the standpoint of Rome: ibid., pp. 85–6.

between Germans in Italy, where they were *Teutonici*, and on home soil, where he names them *Alamanni*.[233] A tendency can be seen in other late medieval chronicles to reserve invocations of 'the Germans' in general for recounting contacts with their neighbours.[234]

The consequences of a vocabulary of identity substantially shaped by others, beyond the Germans' southern and western frontiers, were not all of one kind. While its complex and undirected growth had by the late Middle Ages lent it an uncommon richness and flexibility, the same evolutionary course had also brought constraints. Some of the key terms and concepts had, after all, been formulated and applied historically with the object of keeping the turbulent northerners politically and culturally in their place. We have seen already how intimately medieval German identity was bound up with ideas of social and cultural underdevelopment. The *Theutonicus*, for German writers, never wholly shook off his etymological ties with a language distinct from and incompatible with Latin speech and culture. But the language of late medieval German identity did not only reflect external perceptions and judgements; also it charted the internal development and character of the German lands themselves. It therefore often seems, particularly in vernacular forms, to disclose an uncertain relationship between people and territory. The people may, in a sense, have been one, but its places of habitation and identification were historically plural. Although reference was sometimes made (famously, in the *Sachsenspiegel*) to 'German soil', it is rare to find the relationship between people and land so directly expressed.[235] Terminology, like contemporary notions of German geography, evoked multiple, never fully congruent, maps. It disclosed the underlying centrifugal forces of region and regional tradition. The theme of unity, by contrast, was expressed particularly in the idea of common speech.

---

[233] Müller, 'Nationaler Name', p. 27.
[234] Thus, e.g., the *Styrian Rhyming Chronicle*: see Schnell, 'Deutsche Literatur', pp. 295–6.
[235] *Sachsenspiegel Landrecht* III, cap. 64 § 1, ed. Eckhardt, p. 249. Another prominent invocation of *dutisker erde* is in the twelfth-century *Rolandslied* (vv. 1770–5): see Smits, '*Tiutsch*', pp. 65, 82–3.

11   Being German (II): language and locality

Kulturnation

Late in the fifteenth century, while returning from pilgrimage to Mount Sinai, Felix Fabri, Dominican friar of Ulm, came at last to an inn high in the Dolomites. There, with the relief of a homecoming, 'we found the whole family, along with the children, speaking our language, ignorant of the Italian tongue'.[1] Fabri recalled how he 'spoke with the children with great joy, because I delighted to hear them speaking German'. The memory was enough to prompt an instant outpouring of linguistic Germanophilia. Surely the German tongue was 'the noblest, most famous, most rational' of all. Indeed, it was wrongfully slighted by foreigners on account of its very potency, 'because our language is the tersest ... so that with a few words and syllables much is expressed, and those pregnant and brief words are difficult for the unaccustomed to ... pronounce'. Since the age of the Romantics, Fabri's sentiments have appeared quintessentially and timelessly German. Where else, after all, to seek the soul of a stateless people, but in its language? And what stirred the hearts of the literary patriots of *Vormärz* had surely roused their remote forebears also.[2] The idea that late medieval Germans found unity as a community of speech and letters is authentically Romantic, rooted in the literary studies of patriotic philologists like the Grimms. Once established in educated discourse, however, it proved remarkably resilient.[3]

---

[1] See: Prescott, *Once to Sinai*, pp. 270–1; for relevant Latin passages, Müller, 'Nationaler Name', pp. 79–80; and for Fabri himself, G. Gieraths, 'Fabri (Schmid), Felix', in *NDB* 4, pp. 726–7.

[2] For the significance of language in German Romantic nation-making, see Walser Smith, *The Continuities*, Ch. 2.

[3] Thus, for the Austrian medievalist Hugelmann, language remained 'the strongest lever for the forming of the [medieval] German nation': Hugelmann, 'Studien', p. 296. He was still repeating this view as late as the 1950s: *Stämme*, pp. 269–70, 506.

By the late twentieth century, it is true, students of the medieval period in general had grown more cautious: the role of language in forming and defining peoples, it now seemed, was complex, and other factors often mattered more.[4] German medievalists shared in this scepticism, and applied it to their studies of early German nationhood.[5] Outside Germany, however, the Romantic notion that the Germans – and the Germans specifically – underwent in the Middle Ages a primarily linguistic process of nation-making has remained tenacious. In this the German lands are still often contrasted with more centralised kingdoms, such as England and France, where taxes rather than texts made peoples.[6] 'It is probably best to begin with language in the search for German identity', recommends one well-informed observer.[7] On this view, the more complex and interconnected world of the later Middle Ages allowed a German *Kulturnation* to emerge and to assume a place, palely, alongside the more substantial *Staatsnationen* to its west.[8]

From these contrasting medieval paths to nationhood it is then, in the eyes of some, but a further short step to tracing divergent long-term historical courses, with an all-too-familiar destination, in the 'toxic waste dump' of the twentieth century:

The German predicament – consciousness of nationhood, absence of a state, strength of German as a literary language – made the particular form which German nationalism would take almost inevitable, the nationalism of *ius sanguinis*, the most dangerous of all nationalism's forms. A combination of high prestige and ineffectiveness in the medieval Empire held the German political nation in thrall, leaving the task of national identification to language and literature.[9]

---

[4] Davies, 'Language', pp. 2–3; and for pre-modern societies generally, Armstrong, *Nations*, pp. 241, 279, 282.

[5] Thus Ehlers, 'Die deutsche Nation', pp. 24, 56.

[6] Thus Guenée, *States*, p. 218: 'In the birth of French national identity ... a political fact – the existence of a king and a kingdom – was of primordial importance. Language [by contrast] certainly played a vital role in the development of German national consciousness.' For the same contrast, see Beaune, *The Birth*, p. 6.

[7] Du Boulay, *Germany*, p. 1. The same conclusion – that '"tongue" ... comes closest to marking a German identity in this period' – is reached in another modern English-language survey of late medieval Germany: Scott, 'Germany', p. 340.

[8] Thus Nicholas, *The Northern Lands*, p. 203: 'In Germany ideas of nationality were less political and more cultural than elsewhere, given that it was more a federation of territories than a national monarchy.' The cultural, particularly linguistic ties, binding together the German lands despite their political fragmentation are the subject of Du Boulay, 'The forming'. See also Black, *Political Thought*, pp. 109–10: 'In the later Middle Ages there were trends towards a more articulate self-consciousness of nationhood. This might be based upon language; Germans, Italians and Spaniards, despite their lack of political integration, expressed sentiments of nationhood.' For the idea of the *Kulturnation*, see Meinecke, *Cosmopolitanism*, p. 234.

[9] Hastings, *The Construction*, pp. 108–9; 'toxic waste dump' is the phrase of Geary, *The Myth*, p. 15.

Whether language and letters really did in late medieval Germany play the role which in better-ordered realms was taken by government is thus, it would appear, a matter of some importance.

Whatever modern scholars might think, moreover, there is no doubt that medieval people themselves often ascribed to language high importance in defining collective ties. In doing so, they were following venerable and compelling authorities. Isidore had famously declared that peoples originated with languages, and not the reverse.[10] More fundamentally, there was the Tower of Babel.[11] For Jansen Enikel, German was one of the seventy-two tongues which originated with its fall, and the Germans thus a people with Old Testament roots. Language was fundamental. After body and soul, it was God's greatest gift to humankind.[12] For Engelbert von Admont, a people (*gens*) was defined by having a single tongue, as well as its own homeland, customs and laws.[13] Kingdoms were also distinguished by their different languages.[14] These ideas were no mere learned abstractions. For the vernacular moralist Hugo von Trimburg, it was common speech, as well as the dress of the speakers (and differing weights and measures), which distinguished 'land from land'.[15]

The significance of such claims is heightened by the evidence which exists for the growing prominence of language, linguistic divisions and linguistically driven conflicts in European life between the thirteenth and fifteenth centuries. We have seen already how in the eastern and north-eastern zones of German speech primarily linguistic categories, *Deutsch* and *Undeutsch*, came in this period to form a basis for inclusion and exclusion within privileged local communities.[16] The mobile world of the central and late Middle Ages inspired among settled elites the fear of marginalisation by prestigious and well-connected newcomers.

---

[10] *Etymologiarum sive Originum libri XX*, ed. Lindsay, I.9.1.4: '... ex linguis gentes, non ex gentibus linguae exortae sunt'.

[11] For language and nation in the Old Testament, see Roshwald, *The Endurance*, p. 15.

[12] *Der Renner*, ed. Ehrismann, vol. III, p. 216, vv. 22167–9.

[13] Engelbert von Admont, *Vom Ursprung und Ende des Reiches*, ed. and trans. Baum, pp. 56–7 (cap. 12); and see Borst, *Der Turmbau*, vol. II.ii, p. 828. Engelbert believed that the diversity of languages, as well as peoples, antedated the building of the Tower of Babel: it was not a punishment for sin, but a law of nature.

[14] Engelbert von Admont, *Vom Ursprung und Ende des Reiches*, ed. and trans. Baum, pp. 76–7 (Ch. 15); and see also *Regesta Diplomatica Bohemiae*, vol. II, ed. Emler, no. 797, pp. 320–1, giving the terms of a composition between two religious communities, in the course of which it is explained that Bohemia lies outside the *regnum Alemanie*, since it is itself a kingdom (*cum sit regnum per se*) and speaks a different language.

[15] *Der Renner*, ed. Ehrismann, vol. III, p. 220, vv. 22261–2: 'An sprâche, an mâze und an gewande / Ist underscheiden lant von lande.'

[16] Above, Ch. 9, p. 429.

Where princes maintained cosmopolitan, outward-looking courts, this fear found expression in vocal resentment at the intrusion of alien tongues into the realm. 'Dalimil' recounts the story of the Bohemian duke Udalrich, who, to the consternation of his nobles, chose a Czech peasant girl for his wife over a German princess. In reply to their objections, he explained that a German would teach his children her own language and thereby imperil the survival of the realm itself.[17] If the story is eye-catching, the underlying assumption was commonplace (though perhaps more pervasive in some lands than others).

In diverse spheres of late medieval life, language supplied a prism for struggles and rivalries. Language tests were applied to distinguish friend from foe at life-or-death moments of popular unrest.[18] Rumoured plans for linguistic genocide served as a rallying cry to the political community. The ascent of new social groups, particularly in the towns, speeded the entry of the common tongue into high politics and government. The use of vernacular languages, in many parts of Europe, within a growing range of written genres extended their expressive power and the horizons of their users. Late medieval religious movements, orthodox and heretical, took their stand upon access to divine truth in the common tongue. In Hussite Bohemia, a full-scale social and religious uprising took as its focus a Czech nation explicitly conceived of as a community of shared speech (*jazyk*).[19] The power of language became during the late Middle Ages, in specific contexts and locations, a formative social element. What, then, of Germany, where other over-all shaping elements have been found so notoriously wanting?

Language and people

There is no doubt that the troubled decades which followed the end of the Staufer saw significant developments in the character and application of the German tongue. The emergence of a written German language – albeit one which for a long time would continue to be marked by major regional differences – was already under way in the twelfth and early thirteenth centuries. In the early stages, a crucial part had been taken by the princely courts, which had acted as centres of patronage for chivalric epics, romances and lyric poetry. The result was an expanded vocabulary, enriched particularly by the absorption of many French loan-words, and the development of a supra-regional elite

---

[17] *Di tutsch kronik*, ed. Jiriček, pp. 82–4.
[18] See Scales, 'Bread', pp. 286–7.
[19] See Seibt, *Hussitica*, Ch. 3.

form of German, comprehensible to courtly audiences from Austria to Thuringia and beyond.[20] After the mid-thirteenth century, the expressive power of the vernacular continued to expand and its written use to become more widespread. The proliferation of urban schools, some of whose masters were also employed in chanceries and involved in urban literary circles, did much to accelerate the process.[21] Some authors now wrote both in Latin and in their native tongue.[22] Hugo von Trimburg praised the poet Marner for his 'lively German and fair Latin, like cooling fountains, heady wine'.[23] The rise of religious mysticism, rooted in the Dominican convents of the south and west, extended the capacity of the language to express sophisticated and abstract ideas.[24] Its widespread adoption during the same period as a medium for preaching did much to raise the social visibility of the vernacular as a vehicle for structured argument and persuasion.[25]

The thirteenth and early fourteenth centuries were the time in which written German gradually infiltrated the fields of government and law. The change reflected above all the adoption of literate modes by newly prominent social elements, the lower nobility and, in particular, ruling elites in the growing towns.[26] These groups lacked the means easily to produce, or often even comprehend, Latin documents, and therefore led the way in applying the vernacular to pragmatic ends. The nature of the earliest texts – urban law-books, land registers and manorial documents, as well as charters – reflects their interests and concerns.[27] The vernacular was used, for example, in the financial accounts for the construction of the walls of Koblenz in the years 1276–89.[28] The geographical distribution of writings in German is also significant. They cluster at first particularly around the great communications arteries of the Rhine and the Danube. The Alemannic south-west showed particular advance.[29] Here, isolated vernacular documents are encountered even before mid-century, such

---

[20] Polenz, *Geschichte*, pp. 46–51. By the fourteenth century around 2,000 French words had entered German.
[21] Ibid., pp. 57–8.
[22] See Schnell, 'Deutsche Literatur', p. 300.
[23] *Der Renner*, ed. Ehrismann, vol. I, p. 49, v. 1199–1200: 'lustic tiutsch und schoene latîn / Alsam frischen brunnen und starken wîn'.
[24] Polenz, *Geschichte*, pp. 52–3; Bumke, *Geschichte*, pp. 414–22; Wells, *German*, p. 108.
[25] Bumke, *Geschichte*, pp. 422–6.
[26] Bentzinger, 'Die Kanzleisprachen', p. 1667; Schmidt-Wiegand, 'Deutsche Sprachgeschichte', p. 81; Wolff, *Les origines*, pp. 140–1; Schnell, 'Deutsche Literatur', pp. 300–1; Guchmann, *Der Weg*, Ch. 5.
[27] Vancsa, *Auftreten*, pp. 8–16; Wells, *German*, pp. 103–5.
[28] Britnell, 'Pragmatic literacy', p. 21.
[29] See Polenz, *Geschichte*, p. 57.

as a charter dividing properties within the Habsburg family, from the late 1230s.[30] During the 1250s, *Landfrieden* for Austria and Bavaria were issued in German.[31] From around the same time, writings in the native tongue are also encountered in growing numbers on the Lower Rhine, as far downstream as Holland.[32] Brabant also saw the early application of Middle Netherlandish (though Old French was adopted even earlier).[33] Not until the 1290s, by contrast, do vernacular documents appear in Brandenburg and Thuringia.[34] Only around the middle of the fourteenth century did a written Low German start to be widely employed in the Hanseatic north.[35] The *Corpus der altdeutschen Originalurkunden bis zum Jahr 1300*, compiled by Friedrich Wilhelm, offers a vivid impression of the pace of change in the first century of German documentary prose. The thirty-six items printed from the 1250s are in stark contrast to the *nearly three thousand* datable between 1283 and 1300, filling three of Wilhelm's four volumes.[36]

The advance of the vernacular as a documentary medium did not find universal favour. The more established chanceries were slow to adopt it, and members of Latinate elites looked on with suspicion.[37] Among these was the Zurich canon and schoolmaster Konrad von Mure, who stood close to the Habsburg king Rudolf I. Noting the growing popularity of the native language, Konrad warned that, while less formal communications might indeed be written in 'barbaric, that is Teutonic' form, this should be avoided for the weightiest legal instruments.[38] For the chronicler Jakob Twinger, we will recall, the fact of their survival in the vernacular alone was enough to render historically inadmissible the purported feats of Hildebrand and Dietrich von Bern.[39] Eike von Repgow, in a rhymed prologue to the *Sachsenspiegel*, explained that he had first compiled his work in Latin, only turning it into German at the behest of his patron, Hoyer von

---

[30] Vancsa, *Auftreten*, pp. 26, 32–3.
[31] Ibid., p. 5.   [32] Ibid., pp. 29–30.
[33] Croenen, 'Latin', pp. 110–12, 116.
[34] Vancsa, *Auftreten*, pp. 36–9.
[35] Ibid., p. 41.   [36] See Wells, *German*, p. 105.
[37] For the survival of Latin, see also Borst, *Der Turmbau*, vol. II.ii.
[38] *Barbarice et theutonice*. Konrad was referring particularly to the forms appropriate in pursuing a case at the papal Curia. Quoted in Vancsa, *Auftreten*, p. 104. As late as the 1380s, the Viennese scholar Leopold Stainreuter (writing in the vernacular) could declare the German language (*Teusche zunge*) as 'the least and, in comparison to Latin, the wildest that we know: hence it is called *barbara*, meaning "wild"'. Quoted in Werbow, '"Die gemeine Teutsch"', p. 48. For contemporary views on the unsuitability of German for capturing the subtleties of Latin, see Reiffenstein, 'Metasprachliche Äußerungen', pp. 2212–13.
[39] Above, Ch. 7, pp. 304–5.

Falkenstein.[40] (That the impetus should have come from a secular nobleman is characteristic.)

The emergence of more settled regional forms of written German was slow and uncertain. Nevertheless, between the thirteenth and fifteenth centuries significant change in this direction did take place.[41] Consolidation was especially geographically wide-ranging in the north, where the Hansa and its far-flung network of trading towns generated a busy traffic of commercial and legal texts. The result was the evolution of a written Low German, with substantially common features across the entire Hansa zone, from Westphalia and the North Sea coast to the eastern Baltic, yet clearly distinct from the forms of German in use to the south.[42] Within central and southern Germany, the vernacular displayed greater local variety; but here too, more stable and homogeneous regional forms were taking root. In the fourteenth and fifteenth centuries, one stimulus came from the gradual adoption of written German in the government of the princes. The vernacular was already employed in around half of the documents issued between 1294 and 1314 by the dukes of Upper Bavaria.[43] Of particular importance was the Trier chancery of Archbishop Balduin, as the first to evolve more standard documentary forms in German.[44]

By the end of the fourteenth century, there are signs that some writers were able to navigate across the regional textual landscapes of the German lands with much assurance. Scribes in the city of Cologne systematically introduced Upper German linguistic features into their correspondence with important southern centres like Nuremberg.[45] At the court of the Wittelsbach counts of Holland in the late fourteenth century there developed a hybrid Bavaro-Netherlandish literary language, comprehensible alike in Straubing and The Hague.[46] Historical works, fundamental to defining common identities among their audiences,

---

[40] *Sachsenspiegel Landrecht*, 'Vorrede in Reimpaaren', ed. Eckhardt, p. 49: 'Nu danket al gemene / deme van Valkenstene, / De greve Hoier is genant, / dat an dudisch is gewant / Dit buk dorch sine bede: / Eike van Repchowe it dede.'

[41] Wiesinger, 'Sprachausformung', pp. 336–9.

[42] Polenz, *Geschichte*, p. 60. In the north and north-east, only Prussia remained outside this Low-German sphere, largely on account of the central- and south-German origin of many of the Order's knights.

[43] Schubert, *Fürstliche Herrschaft*, p. 31. By the period 1351–5, Middle Netherlandish accounted for approximately two-thirds of Brabant's ducal charters, with roughly a third in Latin and 5 per cent in French: Croenen, 'Latin', p. 112.

[44] Vancsa, *Auftreten*, p. 45.

[45] Möller, 'Köln', pp. 226–7. Cologne's correspondence in the same period with Low-German recipients also shows some comparable linguistic accommodation, though less pronounced: ibid., p. 230.

[46] Van Oostrom, *Court*, p. 10.

were in Germany being composed in the vernacular from comparatively early dates: in verse, from the mid-twelfth century (if not before); in prose, probably from the early thirteenth – a century which witnessed a remarkable blossoming of German-language chronicles.[47] By the eve of the Reformation, histories were being written in German and in Latin in roughly equal numbers (though in the mid-fourteenth century Latin works still predominated, in a ratio of almost four to one).[48] By the late Middle Ages, written application of the vernacular and the facility of literate Germans in its manipulation were well in advance of what is found, for example, in England – a land traditionally judged as precocious in developing the characteristics of nationhood.[49] The situation encountered in certain other parts of late medieval Europe, of social and political elites employing languages quite alien to those over whom they ruled (which for Gellner disclosed the impossibility of pre-modern nations), does not generally characterise the German lands.[50] At most, nobles, and those who aspired to pass for such, might decorate their speech with fashionable Low-German affectations, a habit known as *vlaemen* ('to speak like a Fleming').[51] Language in Germany therefore, at least within local and regional limits and away from linguistic frontiers, did not fragment society in the fundamental ways it sometimes did elsewhere.

The role of the imperial monarchy in the slow extension of the vernacular was remarkably small, however. The late medieval efflorescence of the various forms of the German language was impelled primarily by processes of social, cultural and religious change; and where politics did play a part, it was mainly the politics of locality and region. There was no question of German monarchs deliberately promoting the language of their people, as kings and princes occasionally did elsewhere, in a conscious attempt to strengthen regnal bonds.[52] What, in any case, would that language have been? While the kings themselves were mostly (though in varying degrees) German-speakers, many of their subjects clearly were not.[53] If language in Germany was an agent

[47] Green, *Medieval Listening*, p. 265.
[48] Sprandel, 'Geschichtsschreiber', pp. 300–1.
[49] For the lateness of the development of a written vernacular in England, see Catto, 'Written English'.
[50] For his celebrated diagram of 'power and culture in the agro-literate polity', see Gellner, *Nations*, p. 9. For Burgundian and French examples, see Armstrong, 'The language question', esp. pp. 408–9.
[51] *Mittelhochdeutsches Handwörterbuch*, ed. Lexer, vol. III, p. 385.
[52] For an English example of this, see Allmand, *Henry V*, Ch. 19.
[53] An exception is the absentee Alfonso of Castile. Of Richard of Cornwall's command of German little is known, though it is unlikely to have been extensive. For Henry VII, see above, Ch. 4, p. 196.

of nation-making, then it must, it seems, have been of the free-floating, cultural kind: it was certainly not promoted for political ends by the only conceivable leaders of a 'German' political community, the rulers of the Reich.

There are, it is true, isolated contemporary portrayals of the king defending or even advancing the use of German in imperial affairs, and some limited ways in which kings actually did so. The *Styrian Rhyming Chronicle* depicts Rudolf I as upbraiding Bishop Wernhard of Seckau, while the latter was representing Otakar of Bohemia before an assembly of German princes, for delivering in Latin his attack upon the legitimacy of Rudolf's royal title.[54] The bishop should keep his Latin for the choir 'at Mainz or at Trier', since monarch and secular nobles could not understand it. The princes, as the chronicler recounts it, thereupon joined in, loudly supporting the king and urging him to affirm their 'old custom', of using German at assemblies. If Rudolf's response, as depicted here, was essentially conservative (and believable), Johann von Viktring, perhaps inspired by this report, credited the same king with more radical intentions. Because of the errors and uncertainties to which Latin led, and its capacity to mislead the laity, Rudolf decreed in assembly with the princes that privileges were henceforth to be written *vulgariter.*[55] The claim is almost certainly incorrect; but the fact that Abbot Johann, writing at a time when the imperial chancery was making growing use of the vernacular, should have made it reveals much about what an educated churchman by that date regarded as an appropriate and likely royal act.

And in some ways the Reich really was among the pioneers. The great imperial peace ordinance promulgated at Mainz during Frederick II's northern sojourn in 1235 attracted contemporary notice as the earliest *Landfriede* in German (though it is likely that the peace was first drawn up in Latin).[56] The Mainz text then became a basis for peace ordinances issued by post-Staufer kings, which were thus also mainly, and after Rudolf I invariably, in the vernacular. Although the first Habsburg king did not promote the general adoption of German for diplomas, the vernacular did become the norm for documents issued by his curial court (*Hofgericht*), which even employed a seal with a vernacular inscription.[57]

---

[54] *Ottokars österreichische Reimchronik*, ed. Seemüller, pp. 173–4, vv. 13067–13143.
[55] *Liber certarum historiarum*, ed. Schneider, i.221.
[56] *MGC* 2, no. 196a, pp. 248–63 (with Latin text ibid., no. 196, pp. 241–7). A Cologne chronicler noted its issue 'Teutonico sermone in membrane scripta omnibus': *Chronica regia Coloniensis*, ed. Waitz, Continuatio IV, p. 267; and see Bergmann, 'Deutsche Sprache', p. 170.
[57] Vancsa, *Auftreten*, p. 18.

In the acts of monarchs, as in other spheres of government, the German language made its earliest advances in judicial matters, where general comprehensibility was of prime importance. A document in Rudolf's name concerning his 1281 Bavarian *Landfriede* instructed that 'no judge shall preside in any court except that he have by him the peace-text, written in German' (*daevtsch geschriben*).[58]

The kings who followed Frederick II and his son in Germany were peculiarly well suited to oversee the extension of the native tongue, as the regional, comital nobility from which they hailed was a group already turning to it for its own written acts. William of Holland had already made a grant of town law in the vernacular in 1246, as count; he would issue another under the royal seal some years later.[59] Nor is there any denying the spectacular advance of the German language in imperial documents during the century-and-a-half which followed William's reign. If fewer than 6 per cent of known writings in Albert I's name were in the vernacular, the fourteenth century would bring a sharp quickening of the pace.[60] Documents in German already comprised 56 per cent of the output of Ludwig IV's chancery in the period between 1315 and the king's departure for Italy in 1327.[61] The vernacular also accounted for around half of the documents sealed in the name of Charles IV, even in spite of the vast international scope of that monarch's affairs.[62] Under Wenceslas, German then attained a clear predominance, establishing itself as the norm for writings addressed to non-clerical recipients in the northern lands.[63]

There are signs, moreover, that the kings themselves understood the communicative power of the native tongue, and occasionally exploited it directly. Some of them were credited by contemporaries with considerable linguistic capabilities. Even the Rhineland count Adolf of Nassau, according to the Colmar chronicler, knew Latin and French as well as German.[64] We have seen already how Ludwig IV was accused by his enemies of arranging for simultaneous German translation of his public denunciations of the Avignon Curia.[65] But no late medieval ruler

---

[58] *Originalurkunden*, vol. I, no. 475, p. 415. The stipulation had been taken over from earlier Bavarian *Landfrieden*: Vancsa, *Auftreten*, p. 5.

[59] See Vancsa, *Auftreten*, p. 10.

[60] Figures for Albert and for other post-Interregnum kings are given by Lawo, 'Sprachen der Macht', pp. 523–5.

[61] Bansa, *Studien*, p. 89. In the later years of Ludwig's reign, the proportion of his documents issued in German was even greater: Lawo, 'Sprachen der Macht', pp. 528–9.

[62] Schmitt, *Urkundensprache*, pp. 3–4.

[63] Hlaváček, *Urkunden- und Kanzleiwesen*, p. 88.

[64] *Chronicon Colmariense*, ed. Jaffé, p. 257.

[65] Above, Ch. 3, p. 145.

rivalled Charles IV in reputed linguistic skills and interest in language problems. These were the subject of outside comment at the time of his accession and after his death.[66] Charles boasted in his autobiography that he spoke, wrote, and read Czech, French, Italian and Latin, as well as German, with equal facility.[67] In chronicle report, his linguistic powers attained mythic heights.[68] The provision for acquainting the electors' sons in boyhood with the main languages in use within the Empire was probably the emperor's own distinctive contribution to the Golden Bull.[69]

However, the seeming prominence of kings and their acts in extending the application of the German language is largely illusory. There is no solid reason to suppose that Charles IV especially favoured or promoted German among the several languages of the Reich. On the contrary, all the signs are that he regarded himself as called upon, in the Empire just as in his dynastic lands, to rule even-handedly over realms defined by their multiplicity of tongues.[70] An anecdote preserved in the Magdeburg *Schöppenchronik* even presents Charles as capable on occasion, for political ends, of feigning ignorance of the German spoken by those coming before his court, and evidently expecting to be believed in this.[71] While other evidence makes clear that Charles in fact knew the language well (as his own – *proprie* – according to Ludolf von Sagan), on the whole his part, and that of his government, in the extension and standardisation of written German has been much exaggerated.[72] An influential older view, associated with Konrad Burdach, according to which Charles's Prague chancery was instrumental in developing a composite, trans-regional *Schreibsprache*, the foundation of early modern New High German, has been shown to be unsustainable.[73] In fact, there was little discernible standardisation in Caroline chancery forms,

---

[66] In 1346 Clement VI spoke in consistory in praise of a prince who knew Latin, Italian, French, 'Slavonic', Hungarian and German: *MGC* 8, no. 100, p. 148. For Ludolf von Sagan, who credited Charles with a command of Czech, Italian and Latin, as well as German, see below. Further references are collected by Lawo, 'Sprachen der Macht', p. 535.

[67] *Karoli IV Imperatoris Romanorum Vita*, ed. Nagy and Schaer, pp. 68–9.

[68] Above, Ch. 9, pp. 397–8.

[69] *Die Goldene Bulle*, cap. 31, ed. Fritz, p. 90.

[70] For Charles's attitude to languages, see: Schneider, 'Herrscheramt', pp. 134–5, 144; Macek, 'Die Hofkultur Karls IV.', pp. 239–40.

[71] *Magdeburger Schöppenchronik*, ed. Janicke, p. 228 (1358).

[72] *Catalogus abbatum Saganensium*, ed. Stenzel, p. 211.

[73] Burdach developed his thesis in his eleven-volume *Vom Mittelalter zur Reformation*, publication of which began in 1893. He based his claims on earlier work by K. Müllenhoff: Schmitt, *Die deutsche Urkundensprache*, pp. 5–6, 15; Polenz, *Geschichte*, pp. 65–6; Wells, *German*, pp. 134–5. See also Guchmann, *Der Weg*, Ch. 6.

which reflected rather than drove the advancing consolidation of the language across parts of central and southern Germany. Here again, it was the commercial and cultural life of the towns, and the quickening pulse of communications between them, together with the extended influence of princely chanceries, that helped to fashion new linguistic unities where royal government could not.[74]

It would be rash, by contrast, to suppose that imperial documents, given their relatively modest numbers, could have exercised a major influence on the course of developments. From the start, royal scribes typically had not led but followed. Vernacular documents in the names of the early post-Staufer kings tended to be written in the dialects of their beneficiaries, who, even if they did not in every case take responsibility for producing the finished document, were clearly a decisive influence upon its form.[75] Even the issue of imperial *Landfriede*-texts might reflect local initiative. The several surviving manuscripts of Rudolf I's general peace of 1287 all display different forms, and none appears to have originated in the royal chancery.[76] Kings therefore issued vernacular documents because this was what growing numbers of their subjects wanted and found convenient. Occasionally this is stated directly. When Adolf of Nassau renewed Frederick Barbarossa's grant of town law to Hagenau, he explained that he was acceding to the burghers' request, that the twelfth-century privilege *in latîne* be written out afresh and confirmed, *in thvtsch*.[77] In the development of the German language in the late Middle Ages, the role of the imperial monarchy was largely passive.

In spite of this, shared language, for literate late medieval Germans, was more than just a communications medium; it was a basis for common identity. The Germans were, unusually in Europe, a people named from language (a circumstance noted already by the fifteenth-century treatise-writer Gobelinus Persona); and language played a significant part in narratives of who they were.[78] Such accounts tended to acknowledge the different regional traditions and forms of speech in the German lands while simultaneously pointing, via language, to larger – German – unities. In twelfth-century Bavarian report it was the ancient *Norici*, settlers of Bavaria, who had sown among the German

---

[74] Polenz, *Geschichte*, pp. 68–9.
[75] Vancsa, *Auftreten*, pp. 63, 71.
[76] Ibid., p. 67.   [77] *Originalurkunden*, vol. II, no. 1653, pp. 777–8.
[78] Gobelinus remarked in his *Cosmidromius* (completed 1418), 'notandum est, quod Teutonici a proprio eorum ydiomate, quod in superiori Alemania Teutzsch et in inferiori Alemania secundum diversitatem regionum dudesch nominant, appellati sunt'. Quoted in Müller, 'Nationaler Name und nationales Bewußtsein', pp. 17–18.

peoples the language of their homeland in the East.[79] For Alexander von Roes, as the descendants of the original Trojan *Germani* had migrated east of the Rhine, so their language had spread, in coarsened form, to Franconia and Thuringia. Ultimately, language is for Alexander the test of the German, ruling Bavarians and Swabians *in*, despite his inability to link them to the Franks, and ruling the French, who did share in Frankish blood, *out*.[80] Alexander appealed to Charlemagne's *lingua materna* as definitive proof of his Germanness.[81]

If the histories of the German lands and their peoples were several, their language was imagined as one, a common bond. According to Jakob Twinger, it was deliberately adopted to this end, in ancient times, by Trebata the Assyrian, looking for a means to bind together his army, which was drawn from different lands and spoke different tongues.[82] Here was a fundamentally political vision of the origins of the Germans, recalling the one recounted in the *Annolied*, in which language had supplied the common element among the several peoples which came together in arms under Caesar. But as Twinger told it, the story also drew attention to the question of whence the German language itself had come. On one view, it came from the ancient Orient, brought north with migrant warrior bands of Franks, Bavarians or *Treveri*. To those who believed with Enikel that the German tongue originated at Babel, such a view made sense. Some discerned deeper and more substantial roots in the north, however. Its ancient prevalence is suggested by the startling claim advanced in a Bavarian popes-and-emperors chronicle, that German was used throughout western Europe until Charlemagne imposed Romance speech, from France through Spain and Burgundy to Lombardy.[83] For Alexander von Roes, the Teutonic tongue was once spoken by the daughters of the giant Theutona, who taught it to their husbands, the incoming Trojan Franks.[84] From this perspective, the German language was aboriginal. But where the tales agreed was in regarding language as possessing, above and beyond all divisions, an essential unity.[85]

[79] Borst, *Der Turmbau*, vol. II.ii, pp. 670–1.
[80] Alexander von Roes, *Memoriale*, cap. 19, ed. Grundmann and Heimpel, p. 114: 'Francigene ... a Germanis sive Francis ydeomate discordantes...'
[81] Alexander von Roes, *Noticia seculi*, cap. 18, ed. Grundmann and Heimpel, p. 165. Dietrich von Niem, in his *Nemus unionis*, wrote of Charles as *natione et lingua Theutonicus*: Dietrich von Niem, *Nemus unionis*, tractatus vi, cap. 33, p. 483.
[82] *Chronik des Jacob Twingers*, ed. Hegel, p. 700.
[83] *Chronicon Imperatorum et Pontificum Bavaricum*, ed. Waitz, p. 223.
[84] Above, Ch. 7, p. 296.
[85] An early thirteenth-century manuscript with writings attributable to the circle of Hildegard of Bingen included the startling, and at this date unusual, claim that Adam

Although the communications barriers between different regional forms of German in the late Middle Ages were formidable, a major emphasis in writings from the time fell instead upon divisions between German-speakers and others. It was not only in the east that the linguistic category of 'Not-German' (*untütsch*) was invoked to label the outsider.[86] To their Slav neighbours, Germans themselves were speechless.[87] The limits of the German tongue, as we have seen, supplied a principal measure for the extent of the German lands. For some, the idea of an overarching German linguistic unity was nourished by the fact that the amalgam of German dialect-regions was bordered on most sides by populations speaking quite different tongues. Only towards the Scandinavian lands, whose languages had by the late Middle Ages been heavily infused with Low-German elements, was the distinction less stark, and less often remarked upon.[88] We have seen already how readily German poets reached for the encompassing rhetorical trope *tütsch – welsch – wint*.[89]

Language frontiers had undeniable reality, and spoke of difference. In certain spheres at least, they might function actively to make and enclose communities. Pilgrimage sites located at the western edge of the German-language zone, although they drew pilgrims from far and wide within the German lands, exerted no attraction in neighbouring French-speaking territories.[90] Crossing linguistic frontiers was experienced by travellers with special immediacy, as Albert von Stade signals in his Roman itinerary, noting of the western border settlement of Landene that 'this village speaks a mixture of French and German'.[91] A vividly sensory experience of difference is conjured up by the chronicler Jan van Heelu, describing the clamour of German and French voices among the knights joining battle at Worringen in 1288.[92] Alexander von Roes infuses with the contending colours of Romance and Teutonic speech the parliament of squabbling fowls in his allegorical *Pavo*.[93] Language might be invoked not only to signal conflict but even seemingly to account for it, as it was by Gottfried von Ensmingen, who sought to reduce the

---

and Eve spoke German, 'which is not divided into diverse tongues, as is Romance': Schnell, 'Deutsche Literatur', p. 306.

[86] Thus see the example cited in Thomas, 'Sprache und Nation', p. 79.

[87] See above, Ch. 9, pp. 410–11.

[88] See Nicholas, *The Northern Lands*, p. 190.

[89] Above, Ch. 9, p. 395.

[90] Hirschmann, 'Landesbewußtsein?', p. 255, referring specifically to Trier and to Thann in Alsace.

[91] *Annales Stadenses auctore Alberto*, ed. Lappenberg, p. 336.

[92] *Rymkronyk van Jan van Heelu*, ed. Willems, pp. 225, 292–3, vv. 6044–5, 7975–8.

[93] Heimpel, 'Über den "Pavo"', pp. 203–6. The poem's strong onomatopoeia led Heimpel to the view that it was written to be 'performed', with the speaker modulating his voice to give an impression of the sounds of the birds portrayed.

territorial rivalries around the Upper Rhine in the 1280s to a straight fight between 'Germans' and 'Gauls'.[94] Matthias von Neuenburg gives a vivid account of the actual ill-feeling which might flow across a linguistic divide, telling of how the French-speaking Odo de Grandison came before an unwilling Albert I for investiture as bishop of Basel.[95] As the two men, each ignorant of the other's language, talked past one another, Odo grew visibly and audibly increasingly agitated, until a quick-thinking translator intervened to diffuse the escalating crisis.

As the Grandison case shows, frontier divisions did not exist only in the mind, but found expression in material communications problems. For the fourteenth-century mystic Heinrich Seuse, the hurdle of language offered a suitably strong metaphor. 'An unloving heart can no more understand a love-filled speaker than a German one of Romance tongue.'[96] Strasbourg's dealings with its French-speaking neighbours in Alsace attest to the slow pace and the potential for misunderstanding which limited linguistic skills on both sides occasioned. In February 1398 the nobleman Henri de Blâmont wrote to the city, whose authorities had declared themselves unable to read his communications in French. 'You ought to know', Henri cautioned, 'that I cannot easily understand your German letters either, because I am a *walch*; but I assure you that if I had a scribe who knew German, and I could write to you my thoughts and my wishes, I would gladly write to you in German' (*tútsch*).[97] Even Germans whom we might suppose to have been well equipped to cope with foreign tongues sometimes appear to have commanded surprisingly modest resources. Some, it is true, were apparently capable of prodigious linguistic feats. In the fifteenth century, a German merchant in Reval congratulated himself on having mastered Estish (*Undutsch*) in just seventeen weeks.[98] But on the whole it is the obstacles to communication which loom largest. For Hansa merchants, Russian in particular represented a hurdle, and gaining a mastery of it was evidently regarded as no easy matter, despite some provisions for instruction in youth.[99] The need for translators to produce Russian texts of German business

[94] Above, Ch. 8, pp. 367–8.
[95] *Die Chronik des Mathias von Neuenburg*, ed. Hofmeister, p. 68.
[96] '... als wenig verstan, als ein tiutscher einen walhen': Heinrich Seuse, *Das Büchlein der Ewigen Wahrheit*, quoted in Byrn, 'National stereotypes', pp. 146, 152.
[97] *Strassburg UB* 6, no. 1341, p. 710 (1 February 1398); and see also ibid., no. 382, p. 203 (Bishop Frederick to the town of Strasbourg, 6 August 1387).
[98] Johansen and von zur Mühlen, *Deutsch*, pp. 374–5.
[99] In the by-laws of the German merchants at Novgorod it was ruled in 1346 that only persons under 20 years of age were to learn Russian. Evidently this was regarded as a challenge to which not all were equal: Stieda, 'Zur Sprachkenntnis', p. 159. There is more detail on merchant communications in the north-east in Glück, *Deutsch*, pp. 263–90.

documents, and the periodic difficulty, even in a town like Reval, of locating one, hampered commerce on the north-eastern frontier.[100] The encompassing presence on most frontiers of fundamental linguistic divisions thus helped to nurture a substantial measure of agreement among literate Germans regarding the extent and limits of their own language. Exceptionally, its bounds might be stretched to encompass geographically remote peoples, notably, in a handful of cases, the English, whose Germanisation, for poetic ends, may have drawn some inspiration from the kingship of Richard of Cornwall.[101] On the whole, however, there was a settled view that 'German' denoted those several related idioms employed by the (by the late Middle Ages, widely scattered) descendants of the historic northern peoples of the Reich. It thus drew together under a common name a remarkable diversity of regional forms. Jan van Heelu explained how he had composed his rhyming chronicle as a teaching aid for the daughter of Edward I of England ('Vrouwe Margriete van Inghelant'), bride to the duke of Brabant's son, who lacked knowledge of *dietsch*.[102] While modern scholars, both within Germany and beyond, mostly prefer to translate such a term as 'Netherlandish' or 'Dutch', rather than 'German', it is likely that cultural sensitivities here lead them into anachronism.[103] Although there are indeed indications that some Netherlanders thought of their region as a place apart from 'Germany', there is little sign that they yet regarded their language as distinct, or that it was so regarded by others.[104] It is true that Jakob van Maerlant, in his translated *Life of St Francis* (c. 1273), made a distinction between the vernacular,

---

[100] *HUB* 5, no. 686, p. 352 (Dorpat to Reval, 23 September 1405). The limitations of Hansa merchants' own command of Russian are underlined by their routine dependence on the professional translator (*Tolke*), who appears in Hanseatic sources at an early date: Stieda, 'Zur Sprachkenntnis', pp. 157–8.

[101] For Konrad von Würzburg's *Turnier von Nantes*, with its tournament team of princes of Germanic speech under 'King Richard of England', see above, Ch. 4, p. 198. In Johann von Würzburg's early fourteenth-century epic *Wilhelm von Österreich*, it is stated, in the context of an account of the organisation of an army, that 'the Englishmen all want to be [regarded as] German': Johann von Würzburg, *Wilhelm von Österreich*, ed. Regel, p. 237, vv. 16791–2. The English chronicler Matthew Paris claimed that the German princes chose Richard of Cornwall both on account of his English speech, which sounded like German, and because of his ancient and more recent blood ties with them, including kinship with the Welf emperor Otto IV: *Matthaei Parisiensis, Chronica Majora*, ed. Luard, p. 603.

[102] *Rymkronyk van Jan van Heelu*, ed. Willems, p. 1, vv. 1–4.

[103] It is, of course, quite appropriate to speak of 'Middle Netherlandish' if this is understood as a distinctive regional form of German among others: for its development, see Polenz, *Geschichte*, p. 62.

[104] The evidence for Netherlanders' sense of belonging in this period is complex: see Hirschmann, 'Landesbewußtsein?', pp. 237–9.

Dietsch, and a local dialect form, *Duuts*. However, references to a distinct Netherlandish tongue are otherwise unknown before the later fifteenth century.[105] Johann de Beke, in a fourteenth-century description of Holland, followed Bartholomaeus Anglicus in citing language as one reason for ascribing that land to *Germania*.[106] The Netherlandish mystic Gerhard Zerbolt of Zutphen (d. 1398), one of the first Brethren of the Common Life, defended the use of his native tongue in religious devotions in a treatise *On German Books* (*De libris teutonicalibus*).[107]

That some Germans should have drawn the limits of their purported common tongue so widely becomes the more startling in light of the deep divisions which the concept subsumed.[108] Hugo von Trimburg captured the paradox precisely: 'whoever wants to write German [*tiutsch*] must give his attention to various different languages' (*sprâche*).[109] There was no 'common German' in the late Middle Ages.[110] Hugo himself characterised in richly (though not necessarily reliably) onomatopoeic style the different regional forms. Ludolf von Sagan recalled the difficulties with which, after his arrival as an outsider (*alienigena*), the 'Silesian language' (*ligwa Sleziana*), meaning the German dialect used in the region around his new monastery, had presented him.[111] While forms of trans-regional written communication did gradually gain in strength, the impediments long remained formidable. Under Ludwig IV, the proportion of documents issued in the vernacular to German-speaking recipients declined sharply with increasing distance from the Bavarian dialect-zone of Ludwig's chancery.[112] In 1358, details of Hanseatic policy had to be translated out of Lübeck Low German for the benefit of the Nurembergers.[113] A devotional treatise in the Brabant idiom by Jan Ruusbroec of Groenendael (d. 1381) was only with difficulty comprehensible even in neighbouring Flanders.[114] In Lüneburg around 1400 it was still deemed necessary to translate Jan van Boendale's *Dietsche Doctrinale* out of its original 'Brabantine German' (as Jan had termed it) into 'Saxon'.[115]

[105] Ibid., pp. 239–40.
[106] Cited ibid., p. 237; and cf. Schönbach, 'Bartholomaeus Anglicus', p. 74 (cap. 90).
[107] Suntrup, 'Der Gebrauch', pp. 264–5.
[108] See Wiesinger, 'Sprachausformung', pp. 335–6.
[109] *Der Renner*, ed. Ehrismann, vol. III, p. 220, vv. 22253–5.
[110] As Werbow has shown, early references to such a 'common' tongue refer simply to everyday, in contrast to elevated, speech, not to a language shared by all: Werbow, '"Die gemeine Teutsch"', pp. 47, 53.
[111] *Catalogus abbatum Saganensium*, ed. Stenzel, p. 231.
[112] Bansa, *Studien*, p. 92, for figures. Documents issued to the Low-German zone were still almost entirely in Latin.
[113] Schubert, *Einführung*, p. 28.
[114] Armstrong, 'The language question in the Low Countries', pp. 387–8.
[115] Nicholas, *The Northern Lands*, p. 186.

Nor were such linguistic fissures matters only of mundane practicality: they touched upon perception and affection. Germans knew well enough that the forms of language used within their lands were various, and they invested these differences with meaning. For the preacher Berthold von Regensburg (mid-thirteenth-century), *Oberlant* and *Niderlant* stood, as moral symbols, respectively for heaven and hell; but Berthold reflects something of the same stark polarity onto their everyday usage, explaining that 'people from *Oberlant*, from below Zurich, speak quite differently from the Netherlanders, those from Saxony'.[116] Even within the German lands, language differences traced the vestiges of ethnic distinction. For Berthold, not only the speech but the customs and dress of Upper and Low Germans told them apart.[117] Speaking and being were one. The satirist known as 'Seifried Helbling' expressed the wish that the Austrian who apes foreign fashions should lose his *Ostersprach*, and he who dons Saxon attire be reduced to gibbering in Low German.[118]

Geographically remote versions of German were not homely, but foreign-seeming. When Konrad von Megenberg wrote of 'my maternal German', he meant specifically Franconian, in contrast to other idioms.[119] As Hugo von Trimburg remarks, 'everyone likes speaking the language with which he was brought up'.[120] In *Helmbrecht*, a tale of doomed social climbing from the late thirteenth-century south-east, the eponymous anti-hero, a young would-be knight of peasant stock, returns home to regale his kinsfolk with (among other linguistic exotica) snippets of pseudo-courtly Low German. The family farmhand, baffled at this, concludes that the familiar-looking stranger must have been raised 'in Saxony or in Brabant'.[121] Helmbrecht's father, however, while declaring that he has no wish to share the family board with one from such distant parts, urges the young man, should he really be the returning son, to 'honour your mother and me', and 'speak just one word of German' (*ein wort tiutischen*).[122] While the poet is not necessarily depicting the northern speech as strictly a foreign tongue, he does

---

[116] Berthold von Regensburg, *Vollständige Ausgabe seiner Predigten*, ed. Pfeiffer, vol. I, pp. 250–1.

[117] Ibid., p. 251.

[118] Quoted in Bruckmüller, *Nation Österreich*, p. 155.

[119] He is referring here to the juniper bush. 'Der kranwitpaum haizt in meiner müeterleichen däutsch ain wechalter': *Das Buch der Natur von Konrad von Megenberg*, ed. Pfeiffer, p. 325; and see the comments of Wiesinger, 'Sprachausformung', p. 335.

[120] *Der Renner*, ed. Ehrismann, vol. III, p. 222, vv. 22306–7.

[121] Wernher der Gartenaere, *Helmbrecht*, ed. Speckenbach, pp. 21–2, vv. 717–18, 743–8, 764–8.

[122] Ibid., p. 22, vv. 757–9.

make quite clear that, to an Austrian or Bavarian, it is not the German that counts: the German of hearth and home.

It is not hard, therefore, to share in the bewilderment of Abbot Peter of Königsaal (who from his vantage point in Bohemia could speak with knowledge) at the fact that the Bavarian and the Saxon, neither of whom understands the other's speech, are nevertheless each properly called German.[123] Far from being an organic reflection of some primordial 'national' culture, even the concept of a single 'German' language was highly artificial, problematic and apparently arbitrary in its scope. That the concept had arisen, and that some late medieval people invested it with significance, was the outcome above all of political and historical processes. In these, the imperial monarchy had been centrally involved – and, though mainly as idea, remained central in the late Middle Ages. What commands attention about the medieval 'German' language is not, therefore, its particular remoteness from the political, but rather its old-established and habitual application to identify political formations. Most fundamentally, it had given a name to the German people itself – those speakers of the 'vulgar tongue'. The same idea underlay the routine and habitual metaphors deployed by late medieval writers: 'tongue' was people, body-politic. 'German' was a linguistic fiction (or, if we prefer, a construct) which, historically, had labelled, and thereby derived reality from, political facts.

In the historical past, just as in the origin-legends, language had bracketed armies which otherwise shared little in common beyond service to an imperial lord. It was Italians, ignorant of the varieties of 'German' speech, but all too well aware of its otherness, who had cast a common linguistic mantle over the northern troops who had come south under the Ottonians and their successors.[124] Into the late Middle Ages, in Italy, a body of German-speaking soldiers might on occasion stand proxy for imperial authority itself.[125] The German tongue had a special, imperial status. It was the only language widely used within the Reich which the Golden Bull did not require that the sons of the temporal electors be taught, since it was axiomatic that all (including the Bohemian) would master it without instruction.[126] Its association with imperial rule went deeper than that, however. The aural qualities of the German language were held to be heroically martial (or, to Italian

[123] *Königsaaler Geschichts-Quellen*, ed. Loserth, p. 52.
[124] Thomas, 'Das Identitätsproblem', pp. 154–5; Fried, *Der Weg*, p. 19.
[125] Thus *MGC* 3, no. 608, p. 570 (21 September 1282). For this document, see above, Ch. 6, p. 268.
[126] *Die Goldene Bulle*, cap. 31, ed. Fritz, p. 90 ('cum verisimiliter Theutonicum ydioma sibi naturaliter inditum scire presumantur et ab infancia didicisse').

and French detractors, chaotically bellicose).[127] Its tones are heard in the hard voices of the birds of prey in the *Pavo* of Alexander von Roes. Germanic speech was embedded at the heart of the Frankish-imperial monarchy from the start. The personal names of Frankish warrior-kings of old make perfect sense to speakers of a Germanic tongue, remarks Alexander, whereas this deeper understanding is closed to Romance-speakers.[128]

The Empire's relationship with the German tongue appears para-doxical. On the one hand, the multi-lingual nature of the *imperium* was fundamental to its universal claims, and was explicitly invoked in major public documents, and in the rituals of the monarchy itself.[129] On the other, the German language was closely associated with imperial rule and indeed, both for champions and critics, was fused with the very character of the Reich. In light of this, the advancing use of German in the acts of the Empire's rulers between the thirteenth and the fifteenth centuries cannot have failed to play some part, particularly within Germany, in shaping perceptions of the monarchy itself. Here as elsewhere, a German political identity was nourished and strengthened after 1250 by processes of change within which the role of the monarchy was at once materially peripheral and culturally central.

'German' language therefore did indeed have a part in 'making' the Germans in the late Middle Ages; but its importance should not be overstated. It was a rather abstract notion, whose application was largely passive and descriptive. Felix Fabri's effusive warmth towards his native tongue finds no real counterpart among writers from the two centuries after the end of the Staufer. Language attained relevance in recounting certain specific forms of conflict: those which occurred across linguistic boundaries, between German-speakers and their neighbours. But it supplied no mystical key to the German soul, as it would come to do in the time of Herder and Fichte. The 'German' tongue itself was hardly less a historical-political than a linguistic artefact: it was far from being the badge of a *Kulturnation*. Only at the frontier, particularly within the extended, linguistically mixed settlement zones of the east, did language (along with kinship, law, occupation and manners) come to act

---

[127] Above, Ch. 8, p. 354.
[128] Alexander von Roes, *Noticia seculi*, cap. 18, ed. Grundmann and Heimpel, p. 165.
[129] A coronation *ordo* from the reign of Frederick III stipulated that the king-elect on his way to his coronation should sit on the throne at Rhens, and there have it proclaimed 'in dreien zungen ... latein, welisch und teutsch' that he wished to proceed to Aachen and receive the crown: Volk, 'Von Grenzen', p. 293; and see above, Ch. 5, p. 229. The Empire's multi-lingual character was also enshrined in the Golden Bull: *Die Goldene Bulle*, cap. 31, ed. Fritz, p. 90.

directly in making, affirming and policing the limits of common identities and shaping the daily experience of collective life.[130] There alone does it make at least some sense to *begin* with language in looking for the Germans. The contrast also serves as a reminder that collective bonds were experienced by most late medieval Europeans within local and regional spheres, which also provided a starting point for imagining broader identities. Of nowhere was this truer than Germany.

Homelands

The German lands in the late Middle Ages, it was widely agreed, remained, as they had always been, home not to one people but several.[131] It was axiomatic for a thirteenth-century Bavarian chronicler, when recounting events of the Roman period, to write of 'all the nations of upper and lower Germany'.[132] And as things once were, so they remained. Archbishop Siegfried of Cologne in 1288 assembled against his regional enemies an army 'drawn from diverse regions and nations of Germany'.[133] Albertus Magnus saw no reason to modify his late antique source, Pseudo-Aethicus, on the fact that *multae gentes* inhabited *Germania et Alemania*.[134] Chroniclers of the high Middle Ages had likewise discerned a plurality of *Germaniae nationes*, and their works continued to be read, copied and cited.[135] On the whole, it was no common fatherland but the multiple, more intimate *patriae* that made the more direct appeal to the sympathies (and material interests) of late medieval Germans.[136] The several 'German' peoples antedated the one. Their heritage, often appropriated and adapted by local and regional powers, was usually more pervasively present in the local landscape and in memory, and in many ways had more to offer those who identified with it. The *Sachsenspiegel* famously explained how each individual German land (*iewelk dudisch lant*) – meaning those of the Saxons, Bavarians, Franks and Swabians – was once a separate kingdom, before

---

[130] See above, Ch. 9, pp. 424–30.
[131] For the relationship between regional identities and 'nation' in Germany, and for comparisons with France, see generally: Monnet, 'La patria', esp. pp. 89–93; Moeglin, 'Nation et nationalisme'.
[132] *Chronicon Imperatorum et Pontificum Bavaricum*, ed. Waitz, p. 221: 'omnes Germanie naciones superioris et inferioris'.
[133] *Chronica de origine ducum Brabantiae*, ed. Heller, p. 412.
[134] Albertus Magnus, *De Natura Loci*, cap. 7, ed. Hossfeld, p. 41. For his source on this, see Mertens, 'Spätmittelalterliches Landesbewußtsein', p. 122.
[135] Thus *Ekkehardi chronicon universale*, ed. Waitz, p. 161.
[136] For the regional use of *patria*, see above, Ch. 10, p. 480.

their subjugation by Caesar.[137] The much-repeated story of German nation-making which originated with the *Annolied* likewise began with ancient, pre-Roman plurality, including multiple mythical accounts of the origins of the northern peoples. The idea that there had once been several realms in Germany went deep, even if there was no consensus as to when and how that state of affairs had ceased. For a late fourteenth-century Thuringian chronicler, it was a jealous Charles the Fat who had finally and definitively 'destroyed all the kingdoms in Germany, and reduced them to duchies'.[138]

By the thirteenth century, moreover, the number of distinct, self-conscious political communities had grown, reflecting high medieval social and constitutional changes in the German lands. From Austria to Mecklenburg, Bavaria to Brabant, clerks, poets and chroniclers now spoke a language of solidarity and prestige which often seems to lack few elements of full-blooded peoplehood. The German territories, whether long-existing or of more recent origin, were able to become during the later Middle Ages objects of affective identification, laying claim to their own separate, illustrious and obligatory common pasts. This in large part reflected their development as communities of political action and also often of law. That, by contrast, there existed no overarching, all-'German' sphere of shared political experience will by now be abundantly clear. But neither did the German lands, in any sense beyond the most spectral, constitute a single legal community. In identifying themselves with a common law, the inhabitants of individual German regions were therefore laying claim to a significant mark of medieval nationhood that the Germans as a whole could not.

The idea that the German lands *together* made up a distinctive legal sphere was admittedly not entirely absent. Caesar, it was alleged, had freed his German followers from Roman statute law, allowing them to be judged by their co-linguists alone. In the late Middle Ages there was much recognition of the strong similarities in legal customs and practices between different German regions, reflected in the wide dissemination of *Sachsenspiegel* manuscripts, far beyond the sphere of validity of Saxon law.[139] The extent of inter-regional legal correspondence was demonstrated by the relative ease with which the Saxon code was adapted to south-German use, as the *Schwabenspiegel* (which in its turn was drawn

---

[137] *Sachsenspiegel Landrecht* III, cap. 53 § 1, ed. Eckhardt, p. 238.
[138] *Historia Erphesfordensis Anonymi Scriptoris*, p. 912; and see Moeglin, 'Sentiment', p. 348.
[139] The general authority which it quickly attained is emphasised by Schmidt-Wiegand, 'Deutsche Sprachgeschichte', p. 80.

upon far outside Swabia). Indeed, another codification, produced in Augsburg at around the same time, the so-called *Deutschenspiegel*, may have been intended to enjoy more general applicability – though, as the work's survival in just a single manuscript discloses, if this was the aim it was not fulfilled.[140] The compiler felt able to make reference to principles of inheritance law common to 'all German people' (*alle tiutsche liute*).[141] The view was clearly current that certain legal practices were distinctively German.[142] Frederick II's Mainz *Landfriede* had invoked the emperor's peace-keeping duties *per totam Germaniam*; and, as we have seen already, late medieval monarchs periodically issued laws with applicability throughout, but not beyond, the German territories of the Reich.[143] 'German law', moreover, was a routine point of reference for settler-communities and their hosts throughout the eastern marchlands; and the Hansa too was an avowedly German legal community to its members.[144]

Yet these latter references were obviously to the privileges of specific (albeit large and important) groups, and not to a law for all Germans. And appeals to any such general law are remarkably rare. Provisions made in 1276 for royal arbitration in a dispute between Count Meinhard of Tirol and Bishop Henry of Trent stipulated that in settling the matter the king was to follow his own judgement and not 'the custom of Germany' (*consuetudo Alemanie*).[145] But the reference is exceptional, and is probably best understood in terms of the location of both parties, within the furthest frontiers of the German lands. Viewed from such a perspective the Germans, always more distinctly visible from outside, could be ascribed a unity of law less discernible from within. At any rate, it remains hard to view the Germans in the late Middle Ages as constituting in any substantial sense a single legal community.[146] The general absence of contemporary invocations of such a community only strengthens this view.

---

[140] Hugelmann, 'Die Rechtsstellung', p. 231.
[141] *Deutschenspiegel und Augsburger Sachsenspiegel*, ed. Eckhardt and Hübner, cap. 32 § 2, p. 110.
[142] An agreement between Ludwig IV and King Frederick of Trinacria thus made reference to the practice of swearing with right hand on chest, 'quod loco iuramenti et pro iuramento habetur per omnes Alamannos secundum consuetudinem Alamannorum regum Romanorum': *MGC* 6, no. 320, p. 232 (25 July 1327).
[143] *MGC* 2, no. 196, p. 241; and for other imperial enactments, see above, Ch. 4, pp. 186–8.
[144] See above, Ch. 9, pp. 438–9.
[145] *Urkundenregesten*, ed. Diestelkamp and Rödel, no. 85, pp. 67–8 (25 May 1276).
[146] For the relative weakness of this idea in the sources, see Hugelmann, *Stämme*, p. 233.

In the German territories and regions it was otherwise. Law and justice, as late medieval Germans experienced and imagined them, were rooted in a soil that was tangible and particular. 'Every land [*lant*] has its custom', remarks Hugo von Trimburg.[147] The *Sachsenspiegel* still insisted upon the right of Germans, in most matters, to enjoy before the king the laws of their several ancient peoples.[148] The regional vicariates enshrined in the Golden Bull reflected the same assumption, that the monarch was set over a plurality of old-established legal communities.[149] The *lant*, it is often contended, possessed for its inhabitants (*lantvolk*) an intimate and compelling reality which grander and more remote conceptions – notably, the Reich – lacked.[150] It is easy to see the force of this view. The word itself was an old one.[151] As much a body of persons as an area of territory (though a territorial basis was never absent, and in the late Middle Ages grew increasingly prominent), the *lant* – with its Latin cognates, such as *terra*, *territorium* or *provincia* – was particularly the sphere of a common law and custom (*lantreht*, *lantsite*).[152] That law did not need to differ much from the laws of other, neighbouring lands: its association with a distinct community was what mattered.[153] Fundamentally, such law was customary, and was transmitted through memory and traditional practices; but by the thirteenth century the law of the land was also beginning to be written down, typically in the vernacular, with the Austrian code of 1237 among the earliest such compilations.[154]

This was but one reflection of a broader trend towards the development of more intensive and intrusive forms of government in the German territories. The process had drawn stimulus from the extensive privileges conceded to the princes by Frederick II in the 1230s, and had been further accelerated by the centrifugal currents in German political life, as well as by new economic opportunities, urbanisation and social change, in the decades which followed. It found expression in the establishment of new forms of administrative office under the prince's control, in the growth of writing and record-keeping, and in

---

[147] *Der Renner*, ed. Ehrismann, vol. III, p. 220, vv. 22259–60: 'Ein ieglich lant hât sînen site, / Der sînem lantvolke volget mite.'

[148] *Sachsenspiegel Landrecht* III, cap. 33 § 1, ed. Eckhardt, p. 214: 'Iewelk man hevet sin recht vor deme koninge.'

[149] *Die Goldene Bulle*, cap. 5, ed. Fritz, p. 59.; and see Stoob, *Kaiser Karl IV.*, p. 108.

[150] A view trenchantly argued by Bosl, 'Staat', § 242, p. 786.

[151] See Bünz, 'Das Land', pp. 54–5.

[152] The classic account is Brunner, *Land und Herrschaft*, esp. pp. 180–7, 194–5. See also: Bünz, 'Das Land', pp. 64–5; Smits, '*Tiutsch*', pp. 51–3; Stelzer, 'Landesbewußtsein', pp. 163–5; Droege, *Landrecht*, esp. pp. 54–5.

[153] Stelzer, 'Landesbewußtsein', pp. 209–10, for the material indistinguishability of Carinthian and Styrian law.

[154] For these developments, see G. Köbler, 'Landrecht', in *LMA* 5, cols. 1672–3.

the gradual emergence of settled residential and administrative cen-tres.[155] Hitherto-independent enclaves were being broken down, and their lords compelled or, more typically, induced to acknowledge the prince's supremacy. In some regions, notably Bavaria, the *Landfriede* developed as an instrument of nascent judicial sovereignty.[156] In paral-lel with this, the territory itself attained clearer and more durable con-tours, its frontiers defended and defined by princely fortresses, its limits realised with a new precision and detail, on parchment but also on the ground.[157] The *Landbook of the Mark Brandenburg* (1375), compiled at Charles IV's behest as a survey of his family's new north-eastern lord-ships, set out lands and frontiers with a precision which no contempor-ary description of Germany came close to matching.[158]

The *lant* attained its most substantial form, however, when its mem-bers, who at first were nobles and *ministeriales*, came together with their lord in counsel, law-speaking and judgement.[159] The high medieval *terra Coloniensis*, for example, was the community formed by the archbishops of Cologne and the military *familia* of their Lotharingian duchy to the left of the Rhine.[160] Admittedly, not every German lordship, as it devel-oped, related to the populations under its dominion in this way (and not every German land acknowledged just one lord, or even any lord at all).[161] But by the later thirteenth century, in widely scattered regions, the *lant* was providing a framework for the development of increasingly complex and mutually demanding relationships between princes and enlarged political communities. By the fourteenth century, established bonds between lords and their noble followers were being extended to encompass urban elites and even, exceptionally, peasant communities. By the century's close, these interactions were in some regions starting to take on institutional forms, in the periodic meetings of princes with the political classes of the land in assemblies of estates.[162]

[155] See generally: Schubert, *Fürstliche Herrschaft*, esp. pp. 27–33; Willoweit, 'Die Entwicklung'; Patze, 'Die Herrschaftspraxis'.
[156] See Bosl, 'Landfriede'.
[157] Janssen, 'Burg', p. 296. For territories defined by fortified frontiers, see Petri, 'Territorienbildung', pp. 405–6.
[158] *Das Landbuch der Mark Brandenburg*, ed. Schultze: for the frontiers of the Mark, pp. 2–4; and see Patze, 'Die Herrschaftspraxis', p. 365.
[159] Brunner, *Land und Herrschaft*, pp. 198–203; Bruckmüller, *Nation Österreich*, pp. 169–71.
[160] Ewig, 'Zum lothringischen Dukat', esp. pp. 224–5.
[161] See Nikolay-Panter, 'Terra', pp. 112–13, contrasting the lordship of the archbishops of Cologne, where a *terra*, comprised of the archbishops' military followers, devel-oped during the high Middle Ages, and that of the church of Trier, where there was no such development.
[162] See: Bosl, 'Staat', § 254, pp. 827–8; and for the eastern Habsburg lands: Bruckmüller, *Nation Österreich*, pp. 172–4, 180–1; Zöllner, 'Perioden', pp. 65–6.

Stimulus came both from the heightened demands which some lords were now imposing, particularly in the form of taxation, and from specific crises, such as succession failures, minorities and dynastic plans for territorial divisions.[163] Perceived threats to the integrity of the *lant* acted as a particular spur to aristocratic and urban elites, which came increasingly to regard themselves as its guardians. Such crises had a special capacity to nurture among leading groups sentiments of common purpose and belonging. Already in the second half of the thirteenth century, the Brabantine towns, no less than the ducal chancery, were writing of *terra nostra*.[164] Following the death of Duke Rainald of Guelders in 1343, the towns of Guelders and Zutphen came together in a peace-keeping league, in recognition of the 'dire necessity' facing 'the common land' (*tghemeynne lant*).[165] Meanwhile, within more fragmented political landscapes, traditions of regional peace-keeping alliances, along with urban merchants' associations, and particular judicial formations such as the Westphalian *Veme*, were all capable of fulfilling an identity-forming role.[166]

It was under these circumstances that various groups and individuals were now moved to give account of their own relationships with the land and its history. Prominent among them were the princes themselves and their literate champions, at court and in religious institutions close to the court. A powerful motive here was the fabrication of legitimising historical continuities, particularly at moments when fractures and disruptions had become disturbingly apparent.[167] To soften the effect of these, various means were available. It was hardly coincidence that Albert I, the first Habsburg duke of Austria, and to native Austrian elites a Swabian interloper, gave at least three of his sons names evoking the preceding Babenberger dynasty.[168] In the fourteenth century, the Habsburgs visibly associated themselves with Austria and its past, in their patronage of religious houses and in the extension and decoration of St Stephen's Church in Vienna, as well as attempting to gain the canonisation of the Babenberger Leopold III (1095–1163).[169] Historical writings now emphasised the long continuities of Austrian

---

[163] For taxation and the rise of the estates, see Isenmann, 'The Holy Roman Empire', pp. 248–9.
[164] Nikolay, *Die Ausbildung*, pp. 115–16.
[165] Henn, 'Städtebünde', p. 56.
[166] Examined for Westphalia by Johanek, 'Landesbewußtsein', pp. 280–4, 292; and for the role of leagues in the north more broadly, see Henn, 'Städtebünde'.
[167] See Moeglin, 'Sentiment', p. 326.
[168] Fichtenau, 'Herkunft', pp. 15–17. Indeed, of Albert's six sons, only one, Rudolf, bore a name entirely without Babenberger connections.
[169] Stelzer, 'Landesbewußtsein', pp. 187–8. For St Stephen's, see: Feuchtmüller, 'Die "Imitatio" Karls IV.'; Kovács, 'Die Heiligen', pp. 97–8; and for the Habsburgs' relationship with the Babenberger, Fichtenau, 'Herkunft', pp. 14–17.

history and of margravial and ducal rulership.[170] The merging of dynasty and historic *lant* was most likely to succeed when it was also promoted by the writings of sympathetic religious communities. Such was the case in the duchy of Braunschweig, established as late as 1235. There, a series of works emanating from the collegiate house of St Blasius and the Benedictine abbey of St Michael in Lüneburg trimmed and moulded the memory of the Welf dynasty (whose ties to Saxony were in fact no older than the twelfth century) to fit an ancient, wholly Saxon past.[171] Prince, land and people were gradually made one, as the dukes became followers in the footsteps of Widukind and the Ottonian emperors.[172]

Constructions of a common past might be employed not only to cement imaginary links between dynasty and people but also to endow princes and lands alike with illustrious pedigrees, capable of withstanding comparison with the claims of neighbours and rivals. Here, the emphasis often fell upon blood. According to their late thirteenth-century genealogists, the dukes of Brabant were of not only Carolingian but also Trojan descent, and true heirs to the Frankish royal line.[173] Mecklenburg's Niklotid dynasty became in the fourteenth century descendants of dark-age monarchs, rulers over a vast southern-Baltic empire extending from Hamburg to the Vistula.[174] A more encompassing approach raised up the land itself in myth. In the wake of the Golden Bull, which had left them so conspicuously empty-handed, the Habsburgs felt a particular need for rhetorical compensation.[175] One means of attaining it was through forgery. The so-called *Privilegium maius* (1358–9), fabricated under the auspices of Duke Rudolf IV, thus furnished Austria with an existence already in Roman times.[176] A couple of decades later, the *Chronicle of Ninety-Five Lordships* of Leopold von Wien pushed the history of the land, and the continuous succession of its rulers, back even further, into remote

---

[170] See Moeglin, 'Dynastisches Bewußtsein', pp. 618–19.
[171] See Schneidmüller, 'Landesherrschaft', esp. pp. 82–3, 86–8.
[172] Schneidmüller thinks this exemplifies a trend also observable in other parts of Germany in the late Middle Ages: simultaneously a 'genealogisation' and a 'territorialisation' of historical writing: ibid., p. 89. See also Schneidmüller, 'Friesen', pp. 315–18.
[173] *Genealogia ducum Brabantiae heredum Franciae*, ed. Heller, pp. 387–91; and see Ridder, 'Gefühl', pp. 197–9.
[174] Scheibe, 'Geschichtsbild', pp. 50–1.
[175] See Niederstätter, *Die Herrschaft Österreich*, pp. 149–50.
[176] Lhotsky, *Privilegium Maius*, pp. 18–19, for *plaga orientalis terrae*, *terra orientalis* in forged diplomas of Caesar and Nero.

Jewish and pagan antiquity.[177] By such means were the standing of rulers and people alike reimagined, from the top downward.

That was not, however, the only perspective attainable. Religious communities might also seek by recounting the history of the land to reach the prince (but perhaps also a more extended circle) with messages of their own. Characteristically, these concentrated on promoting the antiquity and significance of the chronicler's own institution, and emphasising the historic closeness of its ties to the land's rulers.[178] Such projects gained urgency from the circumstance that princely dynasties often had a number of historic mausolea and other prestigious foundations within a particular land, any one of which they might choose to favour with their patronage. Added to this, when the ruling house changed, the incoming family would generally have its own old-established sites of memory, often in regions far remote from the new territory.[179] For the construction of territorial no less than broader ethnic identities, therefore, particular stimulus came from moments of perceived crisis and abrupt and troubling change.

Commentators from varied backgrounds, with diverse interests to represent, were moved to respond; and the history and contemporary affairs of a *lant*, particularly when it was politically close-knit, found a number of interested audiences. The anti-Habsburg verses of 'Seifried Helbling' were directed at a Lower-Austrian noble public.[180] There were also chroniclers who addressed themselves to groups among the established nobility. One such was Otakar uz der Geul, whose extended histories in vernacular rhyme, which included accounts of affairs in his native Styria, were evidently composed for audiences of listeners as well as readers.[181] The interest in the native past and the imperative to endow it with meaning were felt particularly keenly from within the political community of the *lant*, which in the late Middle Ages was far from organic and seldom harmonious. While a town such as Braunschweig

---

[177] *Österreichische Chronik von den 95. Herrschaften*, cap. 42, ed. Seemüller, p. 26, telling how one Abraham von Temonaria, a pagan, came 859 years after the Flood to a 'land by the Danube', which a Jew had named Judeisapta, the future Austria; and see: Moeglin, 'Dynastisches Bewußtsein', p. 619; Niederstätter, *Die Herrschaft Österreich*, pp. 373–4.

[178] Monastic writings and cults might also provide local urban elites with access to a broader territorial identity, as was the case in late medieval Flanders: Moeglin, 'Land', p. 52.

[179] Thus, e.g., the fourteenth-century chronicle from the Thuringian monastery of Reinhardsbrunn may have sought to encourage the new Wettiner dynasty to emulate the favour shown to Reinhardsbrunn by earlier Thuringian landgraves: Moeglin, 'Sentiment', p. 336.

[180] See Liebertz-Grün, *Das andere Mittelalter*, pp. 24–6.

[181] For the evidence, see Green, *Medieval Listening*, p. 206.

might invoke historical figures in order to advertise its allegiance to its Welf lords, others sought in common history justifications for more independent claims.[182] It was as 'towns of the land of Saxony' that Goslar, Lüneburg and several other centres made appeal to King Wenceslas, with the aim of evading subjection to the peace-keeping pretensions of the Welf duke Otto.[183] The idea of belonging to an ancient community of law could prove on such occasions a powerful resource. In 1358 the burghers of Magdeburg cited (admittedly, without success) the *Sachsenspiegel* – whose authority in the matter they traced back to Constantine and Sylvester – in support of their claim not to be legally answerable outside Saxony (*buten Sassenlande*).[184] In the past lay the roots of common privilege. The Frankish legacy appeared on occasion no less rich in local opportunity. Strasbourg thus appealed to Wenceslas against the bann which, without troubling to leave Bohemia, the king had imposed on the town: such a sentence, he was informed, might be delivered only 'on Frankish soil' (*uffe frenckschem ertriche*).[185]

It was within the comparatively intimate bounds of the land, and not on a wider stage, that the traditions which might nourish such a sense of collective entitlement were most readily cultivated and experienced. Nowhere did these receive more memorable enactment than in Carinthia.[186] There, a new duke was required to undergo investiture in an old-established public ritual which the duchy's late medieval lords, the Habsburgs, despite evident objections, were only in the fifteenth century able to abolish. Reports differ regarding the details of the ceremony, but the broad picture is clear.[187] The new duke made his way to the traditional Carinthian investiture-stone, where he was met by a free peasant, in whose family the right descended, seated upon the stone. The duke himself donned peasant dress and was subjected by the stone's occupant to a series of questions 'in the Slavic tongue', to

---

For the Welfs and the Saxon past in Braunschweig's public art, see above, Ch. 3, p. 137.

[183] Henn, 'Städtebünde', p. 59.

[184] *Magdeburger Schöppenchronik*, ed. Janicke, p. 227. The view of Constantine, alongside Charlemagne, as a founder of Saxon law was already advanced in the Magdeburg *Weichbildchronik* (*c*. 1235–*c*. 1250): Funke, *Cronecken*, p. 66 n. 291.

[185] *Strassburg UB* 6, no. 687, pp. 364–5 (1 October 1392).

[186] For what follows, see Fräss-Ehrfeld, *Geschichte Kärntens*, pp. 343–8.

[187] The two main accounts are by Otakar uz der Geul and by Johann von Viktring, who knew Otakar but also introduced material of his own (drawing on his presence at Otto of Habsburg's investiture as duke in 1335), some of which contradicts Otakar's version. See: *Ottokars österreichische Reimchronik*, ed. Seemüller, pp. 264–6, vv. 19973–20132; *Liber certarum historiarum*, ed. Schneider, i.251–2, 290–2.

test his suitability. Upon receiving appropriate answers, and also being given various gifts, the peasant vacated the stone, though not before bestowing a light blow to the cheek of its new claimant. Thereupon the duke, on one account, mounted the stone himself and swung his sword to the earth's four corners, thereby assuming lordship over the duchy.[188] The ritual was enacted before an audience of considerable though uncertain size, representing the political community of Carinthia. It underlines the capacity of the land to serve as the object of conceptions of community at once abstract – indeed, 'imagined' – and visibly real.

Not only traditions, but the familiar words and things in which traditions were embodied, and through which they were sown and renewed in popular memory, worked most powerfully where they were most readily to hand. The battle cries of regional and local levies, under noble or communal headship, though capable, exceptionally, of extension to invoke even the name of Rome, characteristically made appeal to more tangible homelands. 'Osterriche!', 'hei Costinz!', shout the Habsburg companies ranged against King Adolf at Göllheim in 1298.[189] The visual language of heraldry, which spread so rapidly in the course of the thirteenth century, quickly came to speak not only of dynasty but community. In chronicle report, 'the panther of Styria' and 'the white band of Austria' become animate symbols of the land itself under arms.[190] The medlar flowers which stood for the legendary origins of the house of Guelders propagated themselves as early as 1273 to the town seal of Goch.[191] Within the comparatively intimate bounds of region and locality, the numinous power of sacred objects and the ritual acts surrounding them – shrines, relics, processions and pilgrimages – was readily unlocked to sanctify the community at large.[192] While the Reich may have entitled itself holy, many towns were visibly so, guarded by

[188] *Liber certarum historiarum*, ed. Schneider, i.251.
[189] 'Hirzelin', in *Politische Lyrik*, ed. Müller, vol. I, p. 124. For the incorporation of Rome into the battle cry of the count of Berg, see above, Ch. 5, p. 234.
[190] *Ottokars österreichische Reimchronik*, ed. Seemüller, p. 159, vv. 12031–3. At the battle of Groissenbrunn (1260), Ulrich von Wildon, landmarshal of Styria, bears the arms of the land, 'ein banier grüene als ein gras / darinn ein pantel swebte / blanc, als ob ez lebte': ibid., 5.i.96, vv. 7297–9.
[191] Nijsten, *In the Shadow*, p. 411.
[192] A striking example of a community-affirming relic is the Cologne fragment of St Peter's pastoral staff, borne each year during Rogation Week through the streets of the city, from the cathedral to the convent of St Maria on the Capitol. In his account and interpretation of this ritual, Alexander von Roes causes the relic to glorify both the city and (particularly) church of Cologne *and* the Germans as bearers of the Empire: *Memoriale*, caps. 35, 36, ed. Grundmann and Heimpel, pp. 143–7.

saints whose images gazed down from their gates or out from their great seals, just as their remains might be visited within the walls.[193] Local landmarks – trees, springs, hills, ancient earthworks and monuments – became the object of word-of-mouth tales, to which even the learned might prove susceptible.[194] If some of these also looked outward to larger mythical pasts, as did the many Westphalian sites linked in local report with Widukind or Charlemagne, they nevertheless cast their aura upon finite, regional landscapes. Literate myths of power attained wider audiences through embodiment in visible and remarkable local objects. A griffin's claw, linked in late medieval legend with the fantastic oriental exploits of Henry the Lion, was hung up for all to see in the town of Braunschweig.[195] The imaginative resources available to the community of the *lant* might prove substantial indeed.

The language of *lant*, moreover, was at times scarcely distinguishable from that of people, and where we glimpse the assumptions underlying its use, these too suggest at times a proto-ethnic community.[196] Johann von Viktring tells how the Habsburg duke Albert II demanded to know of his Carinthian subjects, prior to the compilation of a vernacular written code, by what laws they wished to live, 'that they might be a single people' (*ut esset populus unus*).[197] In the *Schwabenspiegel*, the Swabians even implicitly constitute a 'tongue', in the ethnic sense.[198] The name of the homeland was to be invoked with warmth.[199] Its 'benefit and honour' were to be pursued, as Strasbourg urged, in favour of

---

[193] For the numerous saints (*godis ritter*) who guarded Cologne, see Gotfrid Hagen, *Boich*, ed. Schröder, p. 188, vv. 5853–90. The twelfth-century walls of Cologne were deliberately contrived to have twelve gates, evoking the heavenly Jerusalem. The Frankentor, facing the Rhine, bore images of the Magi, who were prominent among the city's holy protectors. The tomb of the Roman senator Arimaspes, credited with granting Trier its laws, was believed in the Middle Ages to be located within the Porta Nigra, the city's great late-Roman gate. See Haverkamp, ' "Heilige Städte" ', pp. 130–1, 137.

[194] For some of those relating to Saxony recorded by Dietrich von Niem, see Heimpel, *Dietrich*, pp. 231, 237–8.

[195] Metzger, 'Greifen', p 15; and for the literary tradition, Behr, 'Das Nachleben', p. 10. For Henry's late medieval *memoria*, see also Graus, *Lebendige Vergangenheit*, pp. 359–62.

[196] For Austria, see the comments of Bruckmüller, *Nation Österreich*, pp. 155–7.

[197] *Liber certarum historiarum*, ed. Schneider, ii.213; and see Stelzer, 'Landesbewußtsein', p. 195.

[198] *Schwabenspiegel*, ed. Eckhardt, *Landrecht*, cap. 30/34, p. 80, for their entitlement to a place in battle 'vor aller sprache'.

[199] Thus, Ulrich von Liechtenstein, scion of a Styrian ministerial family and one of the land's most important nobles, in his *Frauendienst* (probably completed 1255), invokes 'worthy Styria' (*daz werde Stirelant*): Ulrich von Liechtenstein, *Frauendienst*, ed. Spechtler, str. 650.5, p. 135. For Ulrich's career in Styria, see J.-D. Müller, 'Ulrich von Liechtenstein', in *VL* 9, cols. 1274–82.

the land of Alsace.[200] The *lant* invited identification of an immediacy
rarely extended to the 'German people' as a whole: its polemicists spoke
insistently a language of 'we' and 'us'.[201] It could be made rhetorically
to lament its own misfortune: 'I, poor land of Austria'.[202] Its people
might show themselves unworthy: 'Seifried Helbling' searched in vain
for just 'seven true Austrians'.[203] Yet ultimately there was no doubting
where their first concern should lie. Jansen Enikel portrays a follower
of the Babenberger Frederick the Quarrelsome in 1246 urging the duke
against personally leading an army to meet Bohemian invaders, with the
argument that, were he to die, 'people and land' (*liut und lant*) would
also be lost, falling into 'foreign hands'.[204]

It was only natural, therefore, that Albert, the new Habsburg duke
of Austria, should have wished to surround himself with men 'of his
own Swabian people' (*nationis suae Suevica*). But the resentment of his
Austrian and Styrian subjects was just as understandable: 'the rule of
an alien nation' (*alienae nationis dominium*) was the curse of a land.[205]
There were good material reasons why this seemed so. In Austria, native
elites found their access to the prince's favour barred by a cadre of foreign intruders, who aided their Habsburg master in enforcing a stern
regime which challenging established noble privileges.[206] Meanwhile,
the land's riches were seen to flow abroad. In 1295–6 the Austrian
nobility rose against Duke Albert, who (like John of Bohemia a decade later) had to agree to dismiss the foreigners – 'his Swabians' – from
court.[207] And 'please God', wrote a contemporary Latin annalist, 'that
they never return. Amen.'[208]

As the Habsburg case makes plain, foreign servitude was hardly less
resented when its enforcers spoke a form of German. Indeed, the enemy
which threatened hearth and home during this period most often spoke
German, as the songs and verses preserving the memory of local ravages remind us. He was no less alien for that. It was as foreign despoilers that an army of 'nobles from the Rhine' had invaded Thuringia

---

[200] *Strassburg UB* 6, no. 79, p. 51 (6 June 1382): 'des landes nutz und ere zu Elsasz'.
[201] As an example, see 'Seifried Helbling', no. 14, in *Politische Lyrik*, ed. Müller, vol. I,
pp. 115–17. A 'German' language of 'we' and 'us' was famously spoken by Walther
von der Vogelweide (above, Ch. 10, p. 473), but it remained very rare.
[202] 'Seifried Helbling', no. 5, in ibid., p. 105.
[203] In his second satire, cited in Liebertz-Grün, *Seifried Helbling*, p. 50: 'siben tehte
Ôsterman'.
[204] Jansen Enikel, *Fürstenbuch*, in *Enikels Werke*, ed. Strauch, p. 657, vv. 2996–8.
[205] *Königsaaler Geschichts-Quellen*, ed. Loserth, p. 123.
[206] For early Habsburg rule, see Niederstätter, *Die Herrschaft Österreich*, pp. 96–104.
[207] Stelzer, 'Landesbewußtsein', pp. 172–4. For context, see also Liebertz-Grün, *Das
andere Mittelalter*, pp. 27–8.
[208] *Continuatio Vindobonensis*, ed. Wattenbach, p. 719.

under Adolf of Nassau, leaving a trail of destruction; and it was with the grim satisfaction of the native contemplating hated foreigners that a singer recounted the dreadful mutilations inflicted on those who fell into local hands.[209]

Some late medieval German lands, of course, overlay the settlement-zones of imagined ancient peoples, peoples with origin legends older than those of the Germans themselves, staking claims to pasts far more remote. There was no doubt at all that the populations of those regions remained in the late Middle Ages members of distinct *gentes* and *nationes*. In addition to the four great, habitually named 'German', peoples, there were other imagined ethnic groups of various sizes, claiming comparable (and historically linked) pasts: the Saxons' ancient adversaries the Thuringians, for example, or the men of Trier. How widely these myths of settlement and solidarity were remembered in the late Middle Ages has been the subject of debate; but in written texts at least, they now circulated more extensively than ever.[210] Much-copied vernacular chronicles – the *Saxon World Chronicle*, for example, or Twinger's histories of Franks and *Treveri* – retold them at length within the more spacious interpretative frames of Christendom and the Reich. The peoples which formed their subject had occupied territories extensive enough to allow a rich diversity of late medieval communities to appropriate a share, in explanation and justification of their own existence. Hence we find the Saxon settlement myth recounted at length in Magdeburg town chronicles, or that of the Franks by a learned protagonist of the archbishops of Cologne.

The legends on which the German lands drew were relentlessly military in character, often deploying the twin themes of doughty service to imperial conquerors and stubborn resistance when those conquerors withheld from their servants the merited prize of freedom.[211] In their militarism, they resembled accounts of the origins of the German people itself – and they were, indeed, as more than one writer showed, capable of enlargement beyond their original subject people to accommodate

---

[209] *Volkslieder*, ed. Liliencron, no. 3, pp. 9–10.
[210] Graus, *Lebendige Vergangenheit*, pp. 126–7, emphasised their literary-antiquarian character; for views suggesting a wider dissemination, see Funke, *Cronecken*, p. 104.
[211] Thus, e.g., the legend of the Bavarian duke Adelgar (in some versions Theodo), his humiliation at Roman hands and subsequent successful revolt, which gained wide dissemination through the *Kaiserchronik* (of Bavarian origin): *Kaiserchronik*, ed. Schröder, pp. 202–12, vv. 6622–7135; and see Graus, *Lebendige Vergangenheit*, pp. 110–11, and, for a thirteenth-century version, *Der kunige buoch*, ed. Massmann, p. cxxxvi.

other German-speaking communities.[212] And it was not only the more
developed legends that dwelt on the martial qualities of the populations
which they praised. Brabanters were 'bold by nature', Saxons 'intractable and rock-hard'.[213] Styrians abhorred cowardice, while Swabians
in their fierceness were prototypes of the Turk.[214] And just as the historical image of the bellicose German was held by some to explain that
people's possession of the Empire, so the warlike claims of various component peoples and communities were called on to justify their self-rule
and account for their privileges. The title of the Swabians to the front
rank in battle was just the most widely known of these.[215]

In common with the depiction of larger 'nations', moreover, such self-
images did not stand in isolation, but were linked into more extended,
if often crude and largely unreflective, webs of stereotype, applicable to
German no less than non-German neighbours.[216] Although these con-
sisted much of the time merely of stock, interchangeable insults, they
nevertheless facilitated the construction of rhetorical hierarchies, within
which late medieval people might favourably position their own communities, their honours and claims, in relation to others. Sometimes
they were more regionally specific. Bavaria, for Jansen Enikel, had rich
merchants.[217] Frisia, declared the Eichstätt canon Heinrich Taube, was
the 'cess-pool of the world', whose inhabitants fired their hearths with
cow-dung.[218] More interesting are those remarks which ascribe to the
populations themselves common character traits. Sometimes these were
simply unflattering glosses upon another's proud self-image. Swabians,
dauntless fighters in their own estimation, were thus rash and boastful
(as well as grasping, clannish and treacherous) when viewed through
Styrian eyes.[219] It speaks for the wide currency of some of these abu-
sive tags that they were generally deemed to require little elucidation.
Cryptic reference to herring-eating Thuringians was thus probably a

[212] For examples of this, see above, Ch. 7, pp. 318–24.
[213] For Brabant, see Ridder, 'Gefühl', pp. 204–5; for Saxons, Schönbach, 'Bartholomaeus
    Anglicus', p. 66 (cap. 13). For further warrior-stereotypes, see above, Ch. 8, pp.
    364–70.
[214] *Ottokars österreichische Reimchronik*, ed. Seemüller, p. 765, vv. 57434–6; *Die Chronik
    Johanns von Winterthur*, ed. Baethgen, p. 212.
[215] For this, see above, Ch. 8, p. 365.
[216] For a range of regional stereotypes, see Wackernagel, 'Die Spottnamen', as well as
    Walther, 'Scherz'.
[217] *Jansen Enikels Weltchronik*, ed. Strauch, p. 536, vv. 27517–22.
[218] *Die Chronik Heinrichs Taube*, ed. Bresslau, p. 59.
[219] *Ottokars österreichische Reimchronik*, ed. Seemüller, p. 333, vv. 25251–64 (boastful-
    ness); and cf. pp. 1075, vv. 82050–9 (conspiracies), 1186, vv. 91215–21 (greed). See
    also the comments of Liebertz-Grün, *Das andere Mittelalter*, p. 138.

dig at their supposed meanness.[220] In the south-German *Helmbrecht*, the wayward peasant's son spurns his father's wise advice with the retort that it would be easier teaching a Saxon.[221]

The *lant* was not a community of law and political action only; it was also a sphere of common culture and values. To be happy, it needed to be under the rule of native lords. Its population might be distinguished externally by speech, dress, hairstyles and manners, no less than by its legal order. Native culture and habitus reflected the inner qualities of the people, affirmed by conceptions of an empowering common past. Just like the law itself, familiar ways of doing and being were venerable and therefore binding. They merited 'all honour', and their neglect was the breach of a sacred trust.[222] To abandon inherited norms for fashionable foreign ways (as, according to 'Seifried Helbling', the Austrians were all too prone to do) was to go to the devil.[223] For the *Helmbrecht*-poet, too, firm roots, in familiar homeland no less than social estate, were essential for the good life. To sever the bonds to either was to erase the natural marker-points for moral behaviour. And it mattered not whether the objects of such misplaced desire were Hungarians, Poles or Bohemians, or Thuringians, Westphalians, Hessians or any other Germans.[224] Helmbrecht is as fatally lost to himself when he imitates the courtly Brabanter as when he is mis-speaking Czech or regaling his sister with cod-Latin.[225] From *lant* came identity – an identity which appears often to meet (in some ways more fully than did the German) the criteria of medieval nationhood. Its baleful antithesis was not the non-German but, more immediately, the non-native.

Late medieval Germany appears as if set apart by the extent of its regionalism, and by the clear importance of the territorial community, the *lant*, as an object of affective identification. This perception has

---

[220] Walther, 'Scherz', p. 294. For further examples, see Byrn, 'National stereotypes', pp. 143, 150.

[221] *Helmbrecht*, ed. Speckenbach, p. 12, vv. 422–3.

[222] Thus, in 'Seifried Helbling''s second satire, personified Virtues declare that there is no greater disgrace than 'daz ein lantsit wirt verkêrt, / der wol ist aller êren wert': Liebertz-Grün, *Seifried Helbling*, p. 51. In *Helmbrecht*, it is significant that the rightful native form of speech to which the father begs his son revert is that of 'our forebears': *Helmbrecht*, ed. Speckenbach, p. 22, vv. 752–3: 'sprich ein wort nâch unserm site, / als unser vordern tâten'.

[223] See 'Seifried Helbling', no. 14, in *Politische Lyrik*, ed. Müller, vol. I, pp. 115–17; and Liebertz-Grün, *Das andere Mittelalter*, pp. 46–7; and cf. Helbling's third satire, cited in Liebertz-Grün, *Seifried Helbling*, pp. 51–2: for an Austrian to adopt the ways of other lands was to reveal 'daz hât der tiuvel im erkorn'.

[224] Thus the long list of 'unnatural' Austrians, German- and non-German-speaking alike, listed by 'Seifried Helbling': Liebertz-Grün, *Seifried Helbling*, p. 51.

[225] *Helmbrecht*, ed. Speckenbach, p. 21, vv. 721–2, 727–8.

gathered strength since the first publication of Otto Brunner's seminal delineation of its character, *Land und Herrschaft*, in 1939.[226] By the early twenty-first century medieval German 'land-consciousness' (*Landesbewußtsein*) had become a distinct phenomenon for study, alongside (though also for some roughly synonymous with) medieval national consciousness. The trend reflected in part the perceived withering away of the nation in late twentieth-century Europe, and the rise in its place of a (to some eyes more wholesome) politics of region.[227] For German medievalists, moreover, *lant* has offered a safe access route to otherwise troublesome identities and sentiments: a means of exploring the historic lineaments of Germanness without too much mention of the Germans.[228] Studies in regional identity, like their *vaterländisch* forebears, are unmistakably about 'us, now' as well as 'them (or rather, us again), then'.

The community of the land has therefore in recent times suffered on occasion from a comparable readiness on the part of historians to strain limited evidence in order to locate the object of warm-hearted desire. In certain accounts, the leading figures and groups within the territorial community are now to be discerned acting with a mix of provincial patriotism, cool rationality and enlightened self-interest evocative of a well-run, late twentieth-century *Bundesland*.[229] Yet real though it unquestionably was, the importance of the *lant* as an object of common identification is also more debatable, complex and variable, and less exclusive, than it is sometimes made to appear. The term itself identified – and in modern scholarly usage identifies still – a disconcertingly wide range of political and cultural formations: territories united by little beyond shared dynastic allegiance; ancient (and less ancient) realms of memory, law and tradition; horizontally defined unities of familiar common action; and even mere neutral geographic locales.[230] As such, it labelled (and labels) very diverse kinds and levels of solidarity and identification, without in itself disclosing those diversities. Politically, it could mean much, but also little or nothing. Taking the emotional

---

[226] For the significance of Brunner's work, see: Kaminsky and Melton, 'Translators' introduction'; Melton, 'From folk history', pp. 272–80; Bünz, 'Das Land', pp. 58–68.

[227] See the reflections of Schneidmüller, 'Spätmittelalterliches Landesbewußtsein', p. 394.

[228] For the 'ideologically compromised' character of elements of post-World War II *Landesgeschichte*, see Rexroth, 'Geschichte erforschen?', pp. 139–40.

[229] This seems to me fairly to characterise, e.g., the picture painted by Nikolay, *Die Ausbildung*, esp. pp. 149–50.

[230] Bünz, 'Das Land', pp. 54–5.

temperature of the *lant*, or indeed a locality within it, is scarcely less problematic than gauging that of the nation.[231] The strong, articulate solidarities which Brunner and others found in late medieval Austria or Styria cannot be regarded as characteristic, or perhaps even particularly widespread. Yet it is not always made clear just who would have been stirred by the 'land-consciousness' which scholars have in recent times invoked so readily, how widely it was diffused, and at what levels of concentration. Often, it is simply impossible to say.

Many of the arguments commonly deployed to question the substance of a late medieval 'German nation' apply equally, or more strongly, to smaller territorial communities. They too, conceptually, often had remarkably shallow roots. 'Austria', as a political identity (or rather, plurality of identities) emerged during the twelfth and thirteenth centuries, even if the name itself, in one form at least, was somewhat older.[232] Some territories into the late Middle Ages had no explicit name at all.[233] Brabant down to the 1260s lacked a single, settled form of identification, and elsewhere too, as in Swabia, terminological variety long prevailed.[234] Nor were only names multiple. The Saxons, for all their proud history, possessed in the Middle Ages no agreed common origin, but at least three competing ones, of which that which traced them back to Alexander's Macedonians was but the most illustrious.[235]

While the various claimants to the Saxon heritage may therefore have had more *memoria* than they could readily cope with, other lands seem to have made do with surprisingly little. Some regions had well-established holy protectors; others did not.[236] Moreover, if common pasts really were fabricated in the German territories, as historians have sometimes supposed, as resources of princely ('state-building') propaganda, then the project seems often to have been pursued with an odd lack of conviction. In Guelders, where historical writing flourished in

---

[231] For the fundamental problems in the way of accessing (and assessing) late medieval *Landesbewußtsein*, see Schneidmüller, 'Spätmittelalterliches Landesbewußtsein', pp. 404–5.

[232] Dienst, 'Ostarrîchi – Oriens – Austria'; Zöllner, '1000 Jahre Österreich?', p. 45; Bruckmüller, *Nation Österreich*, pp. 157–8. For Austria's long-lasting cultural and conceptual links with Bavaria, see Moeglin, 'Dynastisches Bewußtsein', pp. 616–17.

[233] Thus the territory of the archbishops of Cologne in Westphalia: Janssen, 'Die Erzbischöfe', p. 90.

[234] See Mertens, 'Spätmittelalterliches Landesbewußtsein', esp. p. 119.

[235] For the varieties and their development, see Graus, *Lebendige Vergangenheit*, pp. 112–30.

[236] For Swabia's lack of strongly defined patron saints, see Mertens, 'Spätmittelalterliches Landesbewußtsein', p. 131; for the cult of St Elizabeth in Hesse, Werner, 'Mater Hassiae', esp. pp. 500–19.

the land at large in the fifteenth century, it struck no roots at court.[237] In Bavaria, work undertaken in monastic scriptoria in the twelfth and early thirteenth centuries, to gather materials for a history tracing the Wittelsbach dukes back to the Carolingians, was subsequently abandoned, not to be resumed until the end of the Middle Ages.[238] Creating a past for the Bavarian people as a whole likewise made only halting progress, after a substantial high medieval start.[239] Little was done to forge dynastic and ethnic histories into one. Nor is it in every case clear who would have supplied the audience for territorial myth-making. If a handful of such works circulated fairly widely (with over fifty surviving or known copies of the Austrian *Chronicle of Ninety-Five Lordships*, for example), many others had a highly limited or inaccessible manuscript tradition, and can never have reached more than a tiny, select audience.[240]

The cultivation of common histories and myths, but also their neglect or abandonment, or their failure to grow in the first place, had multiple, complex explanations.[241] The *lant* was not an identity that could be conjured into being at the will of a prince. And it is not in any case likely that most princes consciously or consistently willed such a process. The Habsburgs' engagement with the Babenberger legacy, for example, sporadic actions notwithstanding, was distinctly fitful and half-hearted overall. The richest and most prestigious dynasties mostly did not wish to be associated too closely with just one of their territories.[242] As the estates came to recognise all too well, the familial priorities and strategies of their rulers were not to be constrained within territorial bounds, and often threatened, rather than nourished, the identity and integrity of the *lant*.[243]

---

[237] Nijsten, *In the Shadow*, pp. 413–14.
[238] Moeglin, 'Die Genealogie', pp. 35–7.
[239] Ibid., pp. 39–41. For the earliest legendary histories of the Bavarians, see: Graus, *Lebendige Vergangenheit*, pp. 109–10; Borst, *Der Turmbau*, vol. II.ii, pp. 669–71.
[240] The *Mecklenburg Rhyming Chronicle*, e.g., survives in just a single de luxe manuscript: see above, Ch. 9, p. 389; the Thuringian historiographical tradition, although quite extensive, was exclusively Latinate and largely monastic before the fifteenth century: Moeglin, 'Sentiment', pp. 328–31. For manuscripts of the *Chronicle of Ninety-Five Lordships*, see Moeglin, 'Dynastisches Bewußtsein', p. 619 n. 87.
[241] The array of factors which, in combination, might stimulate territorial historical writing is analysed by Moeglin, 'Sentiment', pp. 325–6. And see also Moeglin, 'Die Genealogie', pp. 40–1, for the decline of historical writing at old-established Bavarian monastic houses in the late Middle Ages, and the fracturing of memory which resulted.
[242] For the ambivalence of even the Habsburgs' relationship with Austria, see Moeglin, 'Dynastisches Bewußtsein', pp. 626–8.
[243] See the reflections of Moraw, 'Landesgeschichte', pp. 181–2.

If regional and territorial identities were not in every case demonstrably more potent than German ones, neither should it be assumed that they inevitably developed in place of, or at the expense of, a broader sense of political nation. Klaus Graf found that in Swabia in the late Middle Ages, just as in the eighteenth century, these were mutually reinforcing (as they would again prove to be for patriotic Prussians in the nineteenth).[244] Likewise in the imperial towns, a proud sense of locality was underpinned by the consciousness of belonging to the larger, legitimising, historical community of the Reich.[245] Invocations of both regional *and* 'German' affinities multiplied within the same chronological frame, between the twelfth and fifteenth centuries. References to both alike clustered increasingly thickly in writings from the post-Staufer period. At the end of the Middle Ages, the grand geographical schemes of the humanists were to be founded upon a conviction that the nation was best discerned through study of the region.[246]

The mythical pasts of the four ancient German peoples and of the single community in which under Caesar they were united were recounted together in the much-copied and much-repeated tale popularised in the *Kaiserchronik*. Region often represented less an alternative to larger identities – 'the Germans', the Reich – than a standpoint from which to inspect and interpret them. Austria was, according to the *Privilegium Maius*, far from being a place apart, the 'shield and heart of the Holy Roman Empire'.[247] The duke of Brabant, titular margrave of the Empire, was 'Caesar's gladiator', to a genealogist.[248] If the Rhineland represented, for Alexander von Roes, a uniquely prestigious landscape within Germany, that was on account of its privileged historical relationships both with (Roman and Frankish) emperorship and with German identity itself. To be a Rhinelander, or Westphalian or Franconian, was, to reflective minds, to be most fully German. Indeed, so readily might the part be made to stand for the whole that some perceived a danger of it *swallowing* the whole. Just as Alexander shuddered at the prospect of a general Swabian takeover, so the German princes had reportedly chided Ludwig IV in 1344 with the vow that never again would they permit the Reich to be 'transferred to the Bavarians'.[249]

[244] Graf, 'Souabe', p. 297. A comparable case is made more broadly by Applegate, 'A Europe', p. 1177.
[245] Thus Monnet, 'Particularismes', p. 390.
[246] Illustrated by Helmrath, 'Probleme', esp. p. 337.
[247] Lhotsky, *Privilegium Maius*, p. 21.
[248] *Genealogia ducum Brabantiae metrica*, ed. Heller, p. 404.
[249] *Die Chronik Johanns von Winterthur*, ed. Baethgen, p. 246.

The strong forces of regional tradition and sentiment go far to explain why late medieval Germans so often disagreed about the meaning of the past. Saxon polemicists and chroniclers praised the deeds of Saxon emperors, while Rhinelanders and Franconians glorified Pippin and Charlemagne. For Dietrich von Niem, not the Christian Frank but his pagan adversary, the Saxon Widukind, was a heroic figure.[250] 'Oh, what a *Bavarian* he was!', enthuses the Lohengrin-poet, who moved in circles close to Ludwig IV, speaking of the holy Salian Henry II.[251] Yet, as these and numerous other instances disclose, the prevailing diversity of regional standpoints did not result only in multiple, isolated accounts of separate imagined pasts, but also in variant readings of a perceived common heritage of more than regional scope. The Swabian compiler of the vernacular *Gmünder Chronicle* (*c*. 1400) declared it his intention to recount 'something of the Roman kings, particularly those who came to the Roman Empire since the great King Charles, and above all, those who came to the Roman Empire from the duchy of Swabia'.[252] By the later Middle Ages there was an increasingly rich diversity of ways of being German.

Germany was different. Such has been the judgement of historians, and it is not hard, in surveying the main components of medieval peoplehood – territoriality, terminology, language, law – to find justification for such a view. More difficult, however, is to say how we should name this difference, and what significance we ought to ascribe to it. There is no doubt that the role of monarchy and royal government in defining a German people was different from, and mostly less than, that commonly ascribed to rulers and the institutions through which they acted elsewhere in late medieval Europe. Royal government was only one element, and not generally the most important, in establishing the extent of the German lands. Royal documents in Germany did not teach their recipients a standardised vocabulary of identification and allegiance. Monarchs and their servants did not play a prominent part in shaping the German language and extending its written use. Nor

---

[250] Thus Dietrich von Nieheim, *Gesta Karoli Magni Imperatoris*, in *Dietrich von Nieheim: Historie de Gestis Romanorum Principum, Cronica, Gesta Karoli Magni Imperatoris*, ed. Colberg and Leuschner, p. 307. Widukind (whom Dietrich calls both 'king' and 'duke') was 'vir mire fortitudinis, statura communis hominis longitudine magna precellens, decorus facie ac plurimum bellicosus, ita quod de genere gygantum processisse credebatur'. It is true that the curialist and bishop Dietrich emphasised Widukind's conversion as proof of his virtue. Nevertheless, he wrote within a pro-Widukind tradition well established in his native Westphalia. See: Johanek, 'Landesbewußtsein', pp. 289–90; Heimpel, *Dietrich*, p. 230.

[251] *Lohengrin*, ed. Cramer, p. 567, v. 7559.

[252] Quoted in Johanek, 'Weltchronistik', pp. 321–2.

did they establish a single, all-German sphere of law. They were in no position to override the plethora of local and regional identities through which political life was constructed and experienced. Mostly they did not even try.

It is therefore easy to see why a distinguished recent essay on the subject should have reached the conclusion that before the eighteenth century 'Germany was a cultural not a political nation'.[253] Nevertheless, I cannot agree with this view. Knowledgeable Germans cared about the extent of the German lands, despite their inability to reach a consensus on the matter. And they regarded the problem as at least broadly political – even though the imagined legacy of long-past politics, regional partisanships and the politics of linguistic frontier zones were often more important than the deeds of contemporary kings in shaping their judgements. What the Germans and their lands ought rightly to be called was likewise a political question, since names afforded – or, if chosen wrongly, impeded – access to empowering and legitimising common pasts. That was why the matter was capable of stirring such passions. The German language as a concept was itself a creation of past imperial politics, and it remained in the late Middle Ages linked, in the minds both of Germans and their neighbours, with ideas of imperial rule.[254] Moreover, linguistic criteria were recurrently drawn upon, even misleadingly, to label the parties to conflicts and even to explain those conflicts themselves. The German language constructed 'us' against 'them'. Local and regional solidarities did not so much drain the political substance from ideas of 'the German' as, in many ways, enrich and complicate them, and afford standpoints from which to invest them with meaning.

Late medieval Germans, we might almost say, suffered less from a poverty than a surfeit of identity. The selves within their breasts, including their German selves, were too many for comfort, and few authoritative criteria were available to facilitate their ordering or to inform choices between them. The result was much confusion and contradiction, but also reflection and discrimination in the ways in which thoughtful Germans identified land and people. While not all its elements were equally developed, the number of writings touching upon German identity, and the conviction and even passion with which some at least were imbued, sit ill with its familiar depiction as peculiarly weak and insubstantial. Even the inconsistencies observable within and

[253] Walser Smith, *The Continuities*, p. 44.
[254] For the primacy of imperial politics over language in making a German identity in the high Middle Ages, see Thomas, 'Sprache und Nation', pp. 49, 60.

between different texts speak above all of the richness and complexity of the ideas with which they engaged. The sources of Germanness were many, and reconciling them was not straightforward, or even necessarily desirable. In the period after the fall of the Staufer, however, they were exposed to scrutiny and elucidation as never before.

Conclusion: endings and beginnings

Becoming visible

When the international exhibition on the Holy Roman Empire, which had formed an edifying cultural coda to Germany's summer of sporting patriotism, closed its doors in December 2006, it was widely judged to have been an outstanding success.[1] In the space of just three-and-a-half months nearly 300,000 visitors had packed Magdeburg's Kunsthistorisches Museum to gaze at the glittering array of treasures heaped up by medieval emperors and their followers between the reigns of Otto the Great and Maximilian I of Habsburg. Without question, then, an event rich in meanings; but just what *did* it mean? A sumptuously produced two-volume catalogue had sought to provide answers. Much emphasis was given to the exhibition's role in fostering local and regional ties in the Ottonian metropolis and its modern *Land* of Sachsen-Anhalt.[2] What, though, of other, larger identities? Here, the editors explained, twin developments in contemporary history, the unification of Germany and the advancing political consolidation of Europe itself had opened the way to new conceptions of a shared past. The Magdeburg exhibition too, therefore, bore witness to the ending of the German *Sonderweg*, and the European termination of Germany's long westward journey.

In the study of the Reich, 'a new European breadth' had replaced the old 'national constraint'.[3] Such a change was especially to be welcomed since it was above all 'the nationalistic and national-patriotic

---

[1] The exhibition, occasioned by the 200th anniversary of the end of the Reich, was held in two parts, between late August and mid-December 2006, with the medieval section housed in Magdeburg while the Deutsches Historisches Museum in Berlin covered the period between the sixteenth century and 1806. The exhibition was staged under the auspices of the Council of Europe.

[2] For the instrumentalisation of medieval art exhibitions in Germany since the 1970s, particularly to underpin the self-consciousness of the German regional *Länder*, see Johanek, 'Zu neuen Ufern', p. 142; for their harnessing to the cause of European unity, Müller-Mertens, 'Römisches Reich', pp. 3–4.

[3] Hasse and Puhle, 'Von Otto dem Grossen', p. 19.

526

viewpoint of the nineteenth and twentieth centuries' that had long barred the way to 'a clear view of the history and culture of the Holy Roman Empire'. Instead, it was as a union of many European peoples with a polycentric constitutional structure and no single *Staatsvolk* at its heart that the Empire was rightly to be understood. Only at the close of the Middle Ages, under the Habsburgs, had a narrower *Reich deutscher Nation* started to become discernible. 'Art for (or even explicitly about) Germany' was therefore not on offer to the visitor to Magdeburg.[4] That was despite most of the display objects having originated within the Empire's German lands, and despite the exhibition itself standing under the patronage of the German *Bundespräsident*.

Nor was there any good reason why it should have been: medieval art objects are generally too multiple and elusive in their meanings to be read as simple badges of identity, 'national' or other. Nevertheless, to the outside eye, the absence of a German dimension to the Empire's presentation at Magdeburg was conspicuous.[5] Not one among the nearly forty scholarly essays published in the accompanying catalogue found anything of substance to say about the Empire's contribution to the development of pre-modern German identity.[6] Yet for its sponsors and organisers, the Magdeburg exhibition was far from representing merely a display of treasures from a remote past, for viewers to invest with such significance as they chose: it had everything to do with community and identity, but of a particular – above all, European – kind. Europe had cleansed the medieval Reich, stripping away the accumulated dark layers of German-national varnish, to reveal – to the 'impartial' viewer – a pristine Empire: an early prototype for contemporary regional and federal political structures.[7] The general omission of an explicitly German layer of signification was therefore in keeping with the exhibition's

---

[4] An illuminating comparison can be made with an exhibition of late medieval art staged three years earlier in London. Here the organisers had no inhibitions about claiming that the artefacts on show represented 'Art for England'. This was in spite of the fact that the Plantagenets, like the rulers of the Empire, were monarchs over a plurality of lands and peoples, and that few, particularly among the finer pieces on display, were of English manufacture. See Marks and Williamson (eds.), *Gothic*; and, for the matter of identity, Keene, 'National and regional identities'.

[5] Not *only* to the outside eye, however. The contemporary political messages discernible in the exhibition and the absence of German points of reference also attracted domestic comment: thus, A. Kilb, 'Als wir Barbaren Kaiser waren', *Frankfurter Allgemeine Zeitung*, 27 August 2006.

[6] A companion volume, the product of an exhibition-linked colloquium, contained one essay addressing the German nation in comparison with medieval France and England: Ehlers, 'Imperium'. Ehlers emphasises the retardation of German nation-making relative to the western neighbours, quoting Pleßner approvingly on the matter (p. 101), and offering an overall vision similar to that of Winkler.

[7] Hasse and Puhle, 'Von Otto dem Grossen', p. 19.

overarching vision and purpose. It reflected the same priorities and susceptibilities which, this book has suggested, have resulted in a relative under-articulation of medieval German identity as a theme in recent scholarship, particularly when viewed in light of the ongoing boom in the study of medieval ethnicity and nation-making in general.

It has therefore been this book's aim, by viewing the medieval evidence from a vantage point relatively detached from contemporary German political culture and historiography, to propose a reassessment. Attention has focused on the period between the thirteenth and fifteenth centuries as the earliest moment in the German past to yield a significant quantity and variety of evidence invoking the idea of a German people and a German political community. Moreover, the weakness in Germany during this same period of the political forms and institutions which are commonly associated with early European nation-making renders the German case an especially fruitful one. Explaining the proliferation of references invoking the Germans and their lands, despite (and perhaps even partly as a result of) the frailty of German political structures, promises to illuminate – and invite reassessment of – the dynamics of European nation-making more broadly.

Yet the briefest consideration of the character of late medieval German society appears to urge scepticism in reading the evidence, and to caution against overrating its significance. Although the social penetration of concepts of German identity can seldom be gauged even approximately, they clearly did not – any more than did other medieval national affinities – form an object of a mass allegiance comparable with the political nations of modernity. Nor did they constitute an overriding bond, naturally taking precedence over other ties. In very few instances indeed – and even then, only locally, in the fragmented societies on and beyond the Empire's eastern margins – did Germanness provide a basis for common social action. Taking the temperature of late medieval German identity is far from easy; but we can be sure that for most of those subscribing to it, most of the time, it remained distinctly mild. Moreover, even to speak as if there were a single German identity, common to learned polemicists, urban and monastic chroniclers, Hansa merchants, itinerant soldiers and friars, and the settler populations of the eastern marchlands, is misleading. There existed not one but many ways of being German in the late Middle Ages; and only rarely did different modes of Germanness come into contact and dialogue.

Away from the broad frontier zones of the German lands, and a handful of centres where relatively learned clerics gathered to discuss the state of Church and Empire, invocations of a conception of common German selfhood in late medieval writings can seem fairly modest in quantity and scope. The German nation is conspicuously absent, for example, from the more mundane registers of late medieval German verse, even when political themes are addressed.[8] The imperialist treatise-writers, whatever the historical significance of their emergence at this time, were not a large group, and their writings generally attained little dissemination until long after their deaths. And while a number were conspicuously engaged by the question of the Empire's German character, this is not true of all.[9] Everything that we can discern about the nature of German society in the period, moreover, appears to indicate the strong predominance of local and regional ties over more extensive affinities.

The German lands constituted a political community of a distinctive character. Its distinguishing features generally appear highly unfavourable to nurturing imagined ethnic bonds among the scattered populations. Monarchical institutions were limited and the hand of royal rule was lightly and unevenly felt, leaving substantial portions of the Empire's northern territories effectively untouched from year to year. On the whole, imperial government grew weaker between the thirteenth and fifteenth centuries. The court of the kings and emperors was generally modest, lacked a stable geographic location, and was for most of the period situated towards, or even beyond, the margins of the German lands. Constitutional notions of subject-hood under the king were spectral in the extreme, and the means of granting and policing such status in any case lacking.[10] The absence of durable structures of monarchical government also goes far to explain the invisibility, except in the vaguest terms, of any conception of the Empire's German populations as a single community of law. Materially at least, the imperial monarchy both demanded of its ostensible subjects and offered them relatively little. Under these circumstances, it is easy to explain why the circle around the ruler did not become a base for the dissemination of official doctrines and patriotic motifs, such as occurred elsewhere in late medieval Europe, notably in France.

Germany itself, moreover, was understood as merely one element – albeit an especially important one – within a larger, composite

---

[8] 'Germany' and 'the Germans' are thus all but invisible as such in the verses printed in *Die historischen Volkslieder*, ed. Liliencron, which are mostly about wars and other incidents *between* German-speakers. Only when relations with foreigners were the theme, or the state of the Reich itself was being discussed (and lamented), was an ethnic frame of reference more likely to be chosen.

[9] The most salient exception is Engelbert von Admont: see above, Ch. 5.

[10] For the importance of such ideas for the late medieval English monarchy, see Ruddick, 'Ethnic identity', pp. 25–6.

and multi-ethnic Empire. Consequently, although references to the Germans and their lands were certainly not rare in writings from the imperial chancery, there existed no coherent and stable constitutional vocabulary, framed to articulate the idea of a distinct German territorial polity. Instead, a political language of imperial universalism continued to hold widespread sway, and even to gain in prominence, both in the official acts of the Empire's rulers and in an array of other writings produced within the German realm. And whereas the Reich merged its German populations into a larger, supra-national political community, the many German-speaking groups which settled within the broad eastern marchlands generally lacked unifying, trans-regional political structures of any kind.

Nor does what is known about the concept of German identity itself, and about the circumstances which nurtured its emergence, appear to suggest vitality. Some of its main elements, including the names for land and people, were not of native origin, but had been taken over from neighbouring lands – above all, from Italy. What united the original authors of conceptions of 'the German' – from Roman ethnographers and encyclopaedists down to medieval Italian and French churchmen – was a view of the northerners as their cultural, and often also moral, inferiors. Names, labels and judgements originating beyond Germany's frontiers found expression from time to time in circumstances of conflict with the Empire and its rulers. The Investiture Contest offers an early instance of trans-Alpine controversy and strife acting as a crucible of German identity. The pattern was to recur repeatedly, down to and beyond the turbulent reign of Ludwig the Bavarian in the fourteenth century. If medieval Germans constituted an imagined community, much of the formative work of imagining had been done to serve the ends of others.

It is a reflection of these troublesome roots, but also of the troubled times in which they wrote, that so much of what late medieval Germans had to say about themselves appears self-contradictory, anxious, uncertain and incomplete. Among the more articulate and reflective voices, a somewhat defensive celebration of collective deeds and entitlements mingled with elements of introspection and warning. Did those qualities which allegedly made the Germans what they were in fact underpin, or rather call into question, their claims to the highest titles and honours? The questioning mood and recurrent disagreements between different writers which characterise the more extended and thoughtful works of the period hardly suggest the confident collective pride which it is often claimed lies at the heart of national identity in any age. Disagreements, indeed unresolved contradictions, are also repeatedly evident on more apparently prosaic matters, such as the origins of the Germans' common names, or the geographic extent of their lands, reflecting a chaotic abundance of available sources and an absence of authoritative criteria for judging between them. Elements of collective identity familiar from elsewhere in Europe, such as a single, unifying settlement myth, are notably lacking.

Yet, to suggest that conceptions of German identity were troubled or diffuse, or that they had peculiar and distinctive characteristics, is quite different from arguing that they were especially weak or historically insignificant. Indeed, there is some reason to regard identities which, like the German, were the subject of contention, as *more* substantial, placing more strains and demands upon their adherents, than those which could be invoked without challenge. In debate and controversy, and not in bland consensus, lay (and lies) the troubled heart of the nation. The German nation became in the late Middle Ages to an unusual degree debatable.

Much of the evidence commonly adduced to argue for the relative weakness of German identity appears on closer inspection either to have been overstated or to be capable of other, contrasting interpretations. Such arguments, moreover, tend to disregard other categories of evidence, inviting different conclusions. Conceptions of a native territory, and the vocabulary of common Germanness itself, each emerges from late medieval writings more as intractably complex than as deficient as such. These complexities were in their turn a matter for reflection among literate Germans, who sought, although seldom wholly successfully, to reach resolutions of their own. The idea of a common German language, while hardly less problematic, was far from being merely the expression of a pale *Kulturnation*, but was a construct of firmly political character, bound up with ideas about the imperial monarchy and its history. The mythical common pasts which late medieval writers linked with the name of the Germans may have possessed different coordinates and celebrated different heroes than those characteristically found among their neighbours. Yet none of this in itself necessarily rendered the Germans' collective myths less compelling for their audiences or their ethnic basis less substantial. Regional and local identities, while certainly strongly (if variably) present in late medieval writings, did not necessarily develop at the expense of a larger sense of common German peoplehood. Instead, at least among the more articulate observers, they often supplied a standpoint from which to recount notions of a more extended collective existence, and to infuse these with meaning.

The resources of German identity were more extensively and richly present and more widely (and contentiously) invoked in the later

Middle Ages than is commonly acknowledged. A major reason why they tend to be overlooked or underrated is that they do not generally take the forms, or appear in the places, or relate to structures of power in the manner that we have come to expect, based on what we think we know about early nation-making elsewhere in Europe. Yet, in certain respects, constructions of common ethnicity and constitutional arguments derived from them, occupied a more substantial place in late medieval German political culture than was the case in realms where the crown descended within a single dynasty. The divine favour which in neighbouring France was claimed to have alighted upon a particular royal bloodline was believed by the Empire's German adherents to have fixed upon a specific *people* – their own – as imperial heir to the Romans. It was in part the fact that, after the Staufer, the fundamental fitness of the Germans to bear that imperial mandate was in certain circles called into question that spurred some German imperialists to formulate their people's qualifications with a new explicitness. This was most readily achieved through tendentious comparisons with the alleged collective qualities of other, rival peoples. Interlinked *topoi* of common selfhood and alterity performed, in late medieval German discourse, functions more substantial and serious than the mere exchange of unconsidered abuse, often held to characterise the application of such motifs.[11]

The expression of ethnic difference, and its embodiment in group stereotypes, is encountered with particular starkness in some German writings from this period. This has a number of explanations, in addition to the role played by the doctrine of *translatio imperii* in encouraging an ethnic mode of constitutional argument. The antique legacy of learned ethnography appeared to offer German writers particularly suggestive (if also disturbingly ambivalent) models, since these had already been applied to the ancient Germanic peoples by classical writers. The Germans tended to be imagined as a distinct ethnic group, surrounded on their several borders by other, sharply different and equally distinct, ethno-linguistic communities. The nature of the linguistic map of continental Europe, which confronted the Empire's German-speaking populations on most sides with members of quite different language communities, seemed to encourage such polarisation. This may have been further reinforced by the comparatively limited ethno-linguistic mixing which characterised the German heartlands themselves, where was to be found no poly-ethnic metropolis to compare with Bruges, London or Rome – or even with Prague, Pressburg or Zagreb. Although the imperial monarchy ruled over a plurality of peoples, it

---

[11] A point argued in Scales, '*Germen militiae*', esp. pp. 79–80.

never developed the intrusive governmental processes which elsewhere sometimes served to undercut ethnic differences with ties of political allegiance or to promote assimilation to a common high culture. Nor did structures of princely government always prove strong enough to subsume ethnic differences in the eastern realms, where both German and non-German groups at times reached readily for vocabularies of ethnic Otherness, and formulated principles of ethnic exclusion, in framing and pursuing their rival claims.

Studies stressing the particular obstacles to identity-formation across the German lands seldom mention the comparatively favourable elements which these regions also contained. In the late Middle Ages, some of these lay in the field of political communications. Despite the strength of regional identities and divisions, Germany was relatively free from some of the characteristically medieval cultural fractures which are to be found elsewhere in Europe – notably, that between elite and popular languages. The rapid economic development of many German regions, which gathered pace during the thirteenth century, helped to ensure that communicative channels within and between the German lands had never been as varied or substantial as they became in the decades after 1250. The proliferation of towns, and the emergence of networks of important urban centres, stimulated the movement of people, news and ideas. The use of writing was applied with a new intensity, flexibility and (with the rise of a written vernacular) accessibility. An array of non-textual communications media, from carved and painted images to pageants and ceremonies, attained heightened public visibility, particularly within the towns. During this same late medieval period, the new urban religious orders established their own networks of information, edification and persuasion, striking deep roots among the common people.

Considered within these varied frames of social and cultural dynamism, the role of the imperial monarchy itself in identity-formation attains a complexity which familiar viewpoints stressing only its limitations tend to obscure. The evidence of late medieval report bears this out. 'Germany' was widely understood as a significant geographic space, within which to recount events of contemporary importance and concern. Prominent among these were the doings of kings and emperors. Reference to imperial affairs is surprisingly widespread in thirteenth- and fourteenth-century writings, including works produced in regions remote from the peregrinations of the monarchs themselves. Some of their authors reveal themselves as unexpectedly well informed. Even when they do not, they often betray significant levels of emotional engagement, and a willingness to pass judgement. Late medieval

Germans may not always have commanded a full and precise knowledge of the acts of their rulers, but they nevertheless felt moved to explain why they mattered. Not uncommonly, their significance was as a cause for disquiet, sometimes even condemnation.

Why monarchy was kept in mind in late medieval Germany has several explanations. One lies in its very limitations. Its crises and inadequacies attracted notice because they were regarded as endangering public order, with widely detrimental consequences. Because the ways of imperial government were uncertain, they demanded careful scrutiny from anyone hoping to enjoy the benefits or evade the burdens which still lay within the monarch's power. But it was not only material dangers that made the Empire's weakness seem alarming. The imperial monarchy continued in the late Middle Ages to be widely viewed as distinguished and illustrious and, in the eyes of some, integral to larger schemes of general Christian well-being. The Reich continued to matter, holding out to late medieval Germans the memory and the promise of power, while rarely revealing to them its (perhaps unwelcome) substance. Here lies one explanation for the large crowds which gathered for occasions of imperial spectacle, and for the attentive reporting of such events by chroniclers and others.

Despite its institutional weakness, monarchy enjoyed considerable visibility in Germany. This took several forms. The substantially itinerant character of royal rule ensured a succession of memorable public appearances, in a multiplicity of locations within the German lands. By the late Middle Ages, the growing towns were providing a more extensive and diverse audience for the acts of kings than these had enjoyed in earlier times. And even in those broad and growing regions of Germany where they did not come in person, the Empire's rulers retained a degree of presence – and never as visibly as in the decades after 1250. Not only did they come to be represented, and their authority symbolised, in a growing range and quantity of artefacts, fixed and portable, costly and commonplace, monumental and miniaturised, in a rich diversity of media and materials. The long imperial past recounted by the chroniclers was recalled by numerous surviving traces scattered far and wide in the landscapes north of the Alps. These diverse monuments to bygone emperors and dynasties were added to, and their visibility augmented and renewed, in the decades after the end of the Staufer.

To be reminded of the imperial monarchy was to be reminded of an institution which was widely viewed, despite its far-reaching doctrinal claims, as fundamentally and definingly German. The *imperium*, in its territorial aspect, was understood historically as the extension of a German regnal core. Both the contraction of the Empire's non-German territories and the increasing rarity and brevity of its rulers' sojourns south of the Alps lent the post-Staufer Reich a more distinctly German aspect. The German lands formed its rulers' main material base and, in the eyes of their northern partisans, the principal theatre of their actions and responsibilities. Germany came first. The monarchs' affairs, including their conflicts with the papacy, were understood particularly in terms of their impact upon Germany. The kings and emperors themselves, along with the electors and other princes, were identified as German, sometimes even in the face of apparently strong evidence to the contrary. Their triumphs or failures were understood as reflecting honour or shame upon the German people – a viewpoint which was applied particularly to deeds done beyond Germany's frontiers or in conflict with non-German neighbours.

It is true, of course, that the monarchy's imperial character was expressed in a political vocabulary emphasising universal, Christian-Roman, tasks and titles: one which, particularly in its most elevated forms, had very little to say about the Germans. It is also the case that the language of *imperium* grew even more grandiloquent, and was more insistently and pervasively applied, in the decades between the Staufer and the Councils. The imperial mission of their rulers was widely embraced by German chroniclers and treatise-writers in the late Middle Ages, who readily recounted the service of past monarchs for Church and Faith, and emphasised the geographic breadth of the stage upon which they had rendered it. Far from hankering after a more narrowly German pattern of rule, their complaint tended to be that the kings and emperors of their own time were not Christian-Roman enough.

But imperialism was itself, in the eyes of many late medieval Germans, a German pattern of rule – indeed, *the* defining German form. It was the most gloriously imperial of past monarchs who were most often celebrated as giving proof, through their achievements, of ideal, purportedly German qualities. During the thirteenth century, some Germans came to view the conflicts of the imperial monarchy with the papacy and its western allies as the clashes not only of powers or principles, but of peoples, embodying different and incompatible collective qualities. And imperial doctrine, in insisting upon a uniquely close relationship with the universal Church, served also to shape German identity more indirectly, by drawing Germans into especially close, though by no means always harmonious, relationships with the Church itself. It was the intrusive structures of ecclesiastical administration and law which, in times of crisis between the Two Powers, proved capable of providing the German populations of the Reich with an abrupt reminder that they were subject not only to popes but also to kings and emperors. For the

Germans – even those of socially obscure or geographically *königsfern* origins – who made their way up its career ladder, the Church offered an education, contacts and experiences particularly conducive to reflection upon the Reich and its relationship with their people. We glimpse these influences unmistakably in the writings of the small handful, such as Alexander von Roes or Dietrich von Niem, whose encounters stimulated systematic tracts on the subject.

Departures

At some time around the year 1340, Archbishop Balduin of Trier commissioned a magnificent picture-chronicle to commemorate the deeds of his brother, the emperor Henry VII, south of the Alps. This remarkable manuscript, which came to be bound together with the archbishop's administrative *acta*, has been encountered in these pages already. It tells a vivid tale. Events first gather pace in the north, as the electors assemble and Henry is shown being raised on the altar at Frankfurt, crowned at Aachen, and on his knees before the Three Kings of Cologne. Supplies arrive by the wagonload, and the German *militia* trudges south, banners aloft. Beyond the Alps, cities fall to the imperial conqueror, towers are toppled and justice done in violent scenes of almost comic-book animation. The army marches on, with an impetus altogether more irresistible than Henry's own under-resourced slog south had proved to be. A climax comes with the battles for Rome, where Balduin himself assumes centre-stage. High on horse, bedecked in the red-cross mantle of *Kurtrier*, he is seen splitting the skull of an adversary, identified as a member of the Roman Orsini, with a terrible sword-blow.[12]

The Luxemburg picture-chronicle brings together a number of themes which have emerged from the preceding chapters. The imperial might of the Roman-German monarchy after the Staufer lived more visibly in imagination than in hard reality. But live it did, since the imaginative impulse in some quarters remained strong. Germans became visible as such, to themselves and others, when they served the Empire. Indeed, it was precisely his status as an elector and the emperor's companion-in-arms that led Balduin, scion of the French-speaking Luxemburger, to identify himself as German at all.[13] It was in the course of imperial expeditions that German identity, to German eyes, attained particular visibility, in heroic feats performed against non-German adversaries and subject populations. In Balduin's manuscript, the scenes of stylised

[12] Margue, Pauly and Schmid (eds.), *Der Weg zur Kaiserkrone*, pp. 76–7.
[13] See above, Ch. 6, p. 278.

violence which herald the appearance of imperial forces before town
after town attain to the quality of an ethnically charged *adventus* ritual.
The image of the fearsome German warrior, like other recurrent elements of German identity, was of southern origin. But it was an image
which was appropriated and reimagined in the north, just as it surely
was within the tranquillity of Balduin's private apartments, to suit
northern needs. Germans were at their most visible, to others and thus
also themselves, when they departed their native soil. The late Middle
Ages were a time of many such departures – and not only on parchment. If kings and their armies now set out less frequently, many other
Germans made their lives at or beyond the frontier, particularly in the
east. Merchants took up quarters in Bruges, Venice or Novgorod, and
scholars and churchmen made their way to Paris or Prague, Rome or
Avignon. These many and varied journeys proved rich in materials for
identity-forming reflections and debates about Germans and others.

The ways of nation-making in medieval Europe were multifarious,
and in the late Middle Ages increasingly so. Its course in the German
lands has much to reveal, and merits closer attention than it has in
recent times received. It indicates that it was not only within emergent
structures of centralising government that conceptions of ethno-political community could gain in strength. Monarchy mattered a good deal,
but its recollection might matter almost as much as its contemporary
substance – and a perceived lack of substance could matter too. Not
only confident self-assertion but also crisis, and currents of doubt and
anxiety, could be powerful motors of common identity. The raw materials of that identity might appear troublingly ambivalent in character:
names and motifs fashioned or promoted not by native patriots but by
hostile or fearful neighbours, or embedded in intractable ancient texts.
Nowhere in late medieval Europe did conceptions of nationhood and
sentiments of ethno-political solidarity attain levels of social penetration or a mobilising potential comparable to the modern period. It is
probable that the Middle Ages have in recent times been ascribed by
some of their students rather more importance than they deserve in the
history of nation-making in Europe as a whole.[14] There is no doubt that
the significance of ethnic bonds and ideas in late medieval Germany
needs to be assessed with a sceptical eye, and viewed within longer
perspectives. Nevertheless, there seem few good grounds for thinking
that such notions mattered less among Germans than among others at
the time.

---

[14] For some cogent criticisms of medievalist positions, see Breuilly, 'Changes', pp.
69–84.

Not only for wider European developments, but also for the course of nation-making in Germany the late Middle Ages have much to disclose. While the Reich did not thwart the development of a sense of German nationhood, it certainly did much to endow it with distinctive qualities. In writings from the decades after the Staufer, ideas and attitudes are sometimes to be encountered which are more commonly associated with the Reformation era or even the age of Romanticism. By the fifteenth century it is possible to discern, at least in a handful of tracts and chronicles, the spectral forms of a German history – in which early glory is followed by decline, controversy and rumoured betrayal – whose shapes were to recur in the nationalist narratives of a much later age. If the road ahead appears a long one, its signposting in German began in the late Middle Ages.

Sources and bibliography

UNPUBLISHED PRIMARY SOURCES

Düsseldorf, Hauptstaatsarchiv Nordrhein-Westfalen, Urk. Kurköln 179
Universitätsbibliothek Erlangen, ms. 533, ff. 19v–21v

PUBLISHED PRIMARY SOURCES

Acta Imperii Angliae et Franciae ab a. 1267 ad a. 1313: Dokumente vornehmlich zur Geschichte der auswärtigen Beziehungen Deutschlands, ed. F. Kern (Tübingen: Mohr, 1911)

Acta Imperii Inedita, Saeculi 13 et 14: Urkunden und Briefe zur Geschichte des Kaiserreiches und des Königreichs Sizilien, ed. E. Winkelmann, 2 vols. (Innsbruck, 1880, repr. Aalen: Scientia, 1964)

Acta Imperii Selecta: Urkunden deutscher Könige und Kaiser 928–1398 mit einem Anhang von Reichssachen, ed. J.F. Böhmer (Innsbruck, 1870, repr. Aalen: Scientia, 1967)

Albertus Magnus, *De Natura Loci*, in *Alberti Magni Opera Omnia*, vol. V.ii, ed. P. Hossfeld (Münster: Aschendorff, 1980)

Alexander von Roes, *Memoriale de Prerogativa Imperii Romani*, in *Alexander von Roes: Schriften*, ed. H. Grundmann and H. Heimpel (*MG Staatsschriften* 1.i, Stuttgart: Hiersemann, 1958)

Noticia seculi, in *Alexander von Roes: Schriften*, ed. H. Grundmann and H. Heimpel (*MG Staatsschriften* 1.i, Stuttgart: Hiersemann, 1958)

Pavo, in *Alexander von Roes: Schriften*, ed. H. Grundmann and H. Heimpel (*MG Staatsschriften* 1.i, Stuttgart: Hiersemann, 1958)

Annales Blandinienses, ed. L. Bethmann, in *MGS* 5 (Hannover: Hahn, 1844)

Annales breves Wormatienses (873–1356), ed. G.H. Pertz, *MGS* 17 (Hannover: Hahn, 1861)

Annales breves Wormatienses (1165–1295), ed. G.H. Pertz, in *MGS* 17 (Hannover: Hahn, 1861)

Ex annalibus Burtonensibus, ed. R. Pauli, in *MGS* 27 (Hannover: Hahn, 1885)

Annales Colmarienses maiores, ed. P. Jaffé, in *MGS* 17 (Hannover: Hahn, 1861)

Annales Erphordenses Fratrum Praedicatorum, ed. O. Holder-Egger, in *Monumenta Erphesfurtensia saec. XII. XIII. XIV.*, *MGSrG* 35 (Hannover and Leipzig: Hahn, 1899)

Annales Halesbrunnenses maiores (1126–1313), ed. G. Waitz, in *MGS* 24 (Hannover: Hahn, 1879)

Annales Hamburgenses (1–1265), ed. J.M. Lappenberg, in *MGS* 16 (Hannover: Hahn, 1859)

Annales Lubicenses a. 1264–1324, ed. J.M. Lappenberg, in *MGS* 16 (Hannover: Hahn, 1859)

Annales Sancti Rudberti Salisburgenses, ed. W. Wattenbach, in *MGS* 9 (Hannover: Hahn, 1851)

Annales Sindelfingenses, ed. G.H. Pertz, in *MGS* 17 (Hannover: Hahn, 1861)

Annales SS. Udalrici et Afrae Augustenses, ed. P. Jaffé, in *MGS* 17 (Hannover: Hahn, 1861)

Annales Stadenses auctore Alberto, ed. J.M. Lappenberg, in *MGS* 16 (Hannover: Hahn, 1859)

Das Anno-Lied, ed. M. Opitz (1639, repr. Heidelberg: Winter, 1946)

Bernardi, ut videtur, Liber de Origine et Ruina Monasterii Cremifanensis, ed. G. Waitz, in MGS 25 (Hannover: Hahn, 1880)

Berthold von Regensburg, *Vollständige Ausgabe seiner Predigten*, ed. F. Pfeiffer, 2 vols. (Vienna, 1862, 1880, repr. Berlin: De Gruyter, 1965)

Braunschweigische Reimchronik, ed. L. Weiland, *MGDtChron* 2 (Hannover: Hahn, 1877)

Catalogus abbatum Saganensium, in *Scriptores rerum Silesiacarum oder Sammlung schlesischer Geschichtsschreiber*, ed. G.A.H. Stenzel, vol. I (Breslau: Max, 1835)

Catalogi archiepiscoporum Coloniensium: Continuatio postrema, ed. H. Cardauns, in *MGS* 24 (Hannover: Hahn, 1879)

Kronika Beneše z Weitmile, ed. J. Emler, in *Fontes rerum Bohemicarum* 4 (Prague: Nakl. Musea Království českého, 1884)

Die Chronik der Böhmen des Cosmas von Prag, ed. B. Bretholz, *MGSrG*, NS 2 (Berlin: Weidmann, 1923)

Chronicon Colmariense, ed. P. Jaffé, in *MGS* 17 (Hannover: Hahn, 1861)

Chronica de ducibus Bavariae, in *Bayerische Chroniken des XIV. Jahrhunderts*, ed. G. Leidinger, *MGSrG* 19 (Hannover and Leipzig: Hahn, 1919)

Chronicon Francisci Pragensis / Kronika Františka Pražského, ed. J. Zachová (Dějin Českých, Nová řada 1, Prague: Nadace Patriae, 1997)

Chronica Fratris Salimbene de Adam Ordinis Minorum, ed. O. Holder-Egger, in *MGS* 32 (Hannover: Hahn, 1913)

Chronica de gestis principum, in *Bayerische Chroniken des XIV. Jahrhunderts*, ed. G. Leidinger, *MGSrG* 19 (Hannover and Leipzig: Hahn, 1919)

Die Chronik der Grafen von der Mark von Levold von Northof, ed. F. Zschaeck, *MGSrG*, NS 6 (Berlin: Weidmann, 1929)

Die Chronik Heinrichs Taube von Selbach, ed. H. Bresslau, *MGSrG*, NS 1 (Berlin: Weidmann, 1922)

Chronicon Imperatorum et Pontificum Bavaricum, ed. G. Waitz, in *MGS* 24 (Hannover: Hahn, 1879)

Chronik des Jacob Twinger von Königshofen, ed. C. Hegel, in *CdtS* 8 and 9 (Leipzig: Hirzel, 1870–1)

Die Chronik Johanns von Winterthur, ed. F. Baethgen, *MGSrG*, NS 3 (Berlin: Weidmann, 1924)

Chronicon Magni Presbyteri Continuatio, a. 1195–1355, ed. W. Wattenbach, in *MGS* 9 (Hannover: Hahn, 1851)

Die Chronik des Mathias von Neuenburg, ed. A. Hofmeister, *MGSrG*, NS 4 (Berlin: Weidmann, 1924)

Cronica minor minoritae Erphordensis, ed. O. Holder-Egger, in *Monumenta Erphesfurtensia saec. XII. XIII. XIV.*, *MGSrG* 35 (Hannover and Leipzig: Hahn, 1899)

Chronicon Moguntinum 1347–1406 und Fortsetzung bis 1478, ed. C. Hegel, in *CdtS* 18 (Leipzig: Hirzel, 1882)

Chronica de origine ducum Brabantiae, ed. J. Heller, *MGS* 25 (Hannover: Hahn, 1880)

Chronica Polonorum, in *Scriptores rerum Silesiacarum oder Sammlung schlesischer Geschichtsschreiber*, vol. I, ed. G.A.H. Stenzel (Breslau: Max, 1835)

Chronica principum Poloniae, in *Scriptores rerum Silesiacarum oder Sammlung schlesischer Geschichtsschreiber*, vol. I, ed. G.A.H. Stenzel (Breslau: Max, 1835)

Di Kronike von Pruzinlant des Nicolaus von Jeroschin, ed. E. Strehlke, in Th. Hirsch, M. Töppen and E. Strehlke (eds.), *Scriptores rerum Prussicarum* 1 (Leipzig: Hirzel, 1861)

Chronica regia Coloniensis (Annales Maximi Colonienses), ed. G. Waitz, *MGSrG* 18 (Hannover: Hahn, 1880)

Cronica S. Petri Erfordensis Moderna, ed. O. Holder-Egger, in *Monumenta Erphesfurtensia saec. XII. XIII. XIV.*, *MGSrG* 35 (Hannover and Leipzig: Hahn, 1899)

Cronica terre Prussie, ed. M. Töppen, in *Scriptores rerum Prussicarum* 1, ed. Th. Hirsch, M. Töppen and E. Strehlke (Leipzig: Hirzel, 1861)

Chronicon vulgo dictum Chronicon Thomae Wykes, ed. H.R. Luard, *RS* 36.iv (London: Longman, 1869)

Chronik von 1368 bis 1406 mit Fortsetzung bis 1447, ed. F. Frensdorff, in *CdtS* 4 (Leipzig: Hirzel, 1865)

Codex Epistolaris Rudolfi I Rom. Regis, epistolas CCXXX anecdotas continens, ed. F.J. Bodmann (Leipzig: Weidmann, 1806)

Codex Manesse: Die Miniaturen der Großen Heidelberger Liederhandschrift, ed. I.F. Walther (Frankfurt am Main: Insel, 1988)

Cölner Jahrbücher des 14. und 15. Jahrhunderts, ed. H. Cardauns, in *CdtS* 13 (Leipzig: Hirzel, 1876)

Conrad Kyeser aus Eichstätt, Bellifortis: Umschrift und Übersetzung, ed. G. Quarg, 2 vols. (Düsseldorf: VDI, 1967)

Continuatio Claustroneuburgensis IV., ed. W. Wattenbach, in *MGS* 9 (Hannover: Hahn, 1851)

Continuatio Claustroneuburgensis sexta, ed. W. Wattenbach, in *MGS* 9 (Hannover: Hahn, 1851)

Continuatio Garstensis, ed. W. Wattenbach, in *MGS* 9 (Hannover: Hahn, 1851)

Continuatio praedicatorum Vindobonensium a. 1025–1283, ed. W. Wattenbach, in *MGS* 9 (Hannover: Hahn, 1851)

Continuatio Ratisbonensis, ed. P. Jaffé, in *MGS* 17 (Hannover: Hahn, 1861)

Continuatio Vindobonensis, a. 1267–1283, ed. W. Wattenbach, in *MGS* 9 (Hannover: Hahn, 1851)

Corpus der altdeutschen Originalurkunden bis zum Jahr 1300 1 (*1200–1282*), ed. F. Wilhelm (Lahr (Baden): Schauenburg, 1932)

Corpus der altdeutschen Originalurkunden bis zum Jahr 1300 2 (*1283–1292*), ed.
F. Wilhelm and R. Newald (Lahr (Schwarzwald): Schauenburg, 1943)
Corpus der altdeutschen Originalurkunden bis zum Jahr 1300 3 (*1293–1296*), ed.
H. de Boor and D. Haacke (Lahr (Baden): Schauenburg, 1957)
Corpus der altdeutschen Originalurkunden bis zum Jahr 1300 4 (*1297-Ende 13.*
Jh.), ed. H. de Boor and D. Haacke (Lahr (Schwarzwald): Schauenburg,
1963)
Corpus Iuris Canonici, ed. A. Friedberg, 2 vols. (Leipzig: Tauchnitz, 1879–81)
Descriptio Alsatiae, in *Chronicon Colmariense*, ed. P. Jaffé, in *MGS* 17 (Hannover:
Hahn, 1861)
Descriptio Theutoniae, in *Chronicon Colmariense*, ed. P. Jaffé, in *MGS* 17
(Hannover: Hahn, 1861)
Detmar-Chronik von 1101–1395 mit der Fortsetzung von 1395–1450, ed.
K. Koppmann in *CdtS* 19 and 26 (Leipzig: Hirzel, 1884, 1899)
Deutsche Reichstagsakten 1 (*Deutsche Reichstagsakten unter König Wenzel, erste*
Abth., 1376–1387), ed. J. Weizsäcker (Munich: Cotta, 1867)
Deutsche Reichstagsakten 2 (*Deutsche Reichstagsakten unter König Wenzel, zweite*
Abth., 1388–1397), ed. J. Weizsäcker (Munich: Oldenbourg, 1874)
Deutsche Reichstagsakten 3 (*Deutsche Reichstagsakten unter König Wenzel, dritte*
Abth., 1397–1400), ed. J. Weizsäcker (Munich: Oldenbourg, 1877)
Deutsche Reichstagsakten, 4 (*Deutsche Reichstagsakten unter König Ruprecht, erste*
Abth., 1400–1401), ed. J. Weizsäcker (Gotha: Perthes, 1882)
Deutsche Reichstagsakten 5 (*Deutsche Reichstagsakten unter König Ruprecht, zweite*
Abth., 1401–1405), ed. J. Weizsäcker (Gotha: Perthes, 1885)
Deutsche Reichstagsakten 6 (*Deutsche Reichstagsakten unter König Ruprecht, dritte*
Abth., 1406–1410), ed. J. Weizsäcker (Gotha: Perthes, 1888)
Deutsche Reichstagsakten 7 (*Deutsche Reichstagsakten unter Kaiser Sigmund, erste*
Abth., 1410–1420), ed. D. Kerler (Munich: Oldenbourg, 1878)
Deutschenspiegel und Augsburger Sachsenspiegel, ed. Karl August Eckhardt and
Alfred Hübner, *MGFiGa* NS 3 (Hannover: Hahn, 1933)
'Ein deutschfeindliches Pamphlet aus Böhmen aus dem 14. Jahrhundert', ed.
and trans. W. Wostry, *Mitteilungen des Vereins für Geschichte der Deutschen*
in Böhmen 53 (1915), 193–238
Dietrich von Nieheim, *Historie de Gestis Romanorum Principum, Cronica,*
Gesta Karoli Magni Imperatoris, ed. K. Colberg and J. Leuschner (*MG*
Staatsschriften 5.ii, Stuttgart: Hiersemann, 1980)
Viridarium Imperatorum et Regum Romanorum, ed. A. Lhotsky and K. Pivec
(*MG Staatsschriften* 5, Stuttgart: Hiersemann, 1956)
Dietrich von Niem, *Nemus unionis*, in *Thedorici a Niem pontificii quondam scribae,*
deinde episcopi Verdensis Historiarum sui temporis Libri IIII (Strasbourg:
Lazari Zetzneri, 1609)
Dispatches with Related Documents of Milanese Ambassadors in France and
Burgundy, 1450–1483, ed. P.M. Kendall and V. Ilardi, 3 vols. (Athens,
OH: Ohio University Press, 1970–81)
Długopolski, E., 'Bunt Wójta Alberta', *Rocznik Krakowski* 7 (1905), 135–86
Die Ebstorfer Weltkarte, ed. H. Kugler, 2 vols. (*Atlas, Untersuchungen und*
Kommentar) (Berlin: Akademie, 2007)
Ekkehardi chronicon universale, ed. G. Waitz, in *MGS* 6 (Hannover: Hahn, 1844)

Ellenhardi chronicon, ed. P. Jaffé, in *MGS* 17 (Hannover: Hahn, 1861)

Engelbert von Admont, *Vom Ursprung und Ende des Reiches und andere Schriften*, ed. and trans. W. Baum (Graz: Leykam, 1998)

Ex aliis miraculis S. Heinrici I., ed. G. Waitz, in *MGS* 4 (Hannover: Hahn, 1841)

Flores Temporum, ed. O. Holder-Egger, in *MGS* 24 (Hannover: Hahn, 1879)

'Fragment einer niederrheinischen Papst- und Kaiserchronik aus dem Anfange des 14. Jahrhunderts', ed. L. Weiland, *Nachrichten der königlichen Gesellschaft der Wissenschaften zu Göttingen, Philologische-historische Klasse* 40 (1894), 375–83

Fritsche (Friedrich) Closener's Chronik, ed. C. Hegel, in *CdtS* 8 (Leipzig: Hirzel, 1870)

The Gelasian Sacramentary: Liber Sacramentorum Romanae Ecclesiae, ed. H.A. Wilson (Oxford: Clarendon Press, 1894)

Genealogia ducum Brabantiae ampliata, ed. J. Heller, *MGS* 25 (Hannover: Hahn, 1880)

Genealogia ducum Brabantiae heredum Franciae, ed. J. Heller, *MGS* 25 (Hannover: Hahn, 1880)

Genealogia ducum Brabantiae metrica, ed. J. Heller, *MGS* 25 (Hannover: Hahn, 1880)

Gesta Arnoldi, ed. G. Waitz, in *MGS* 24 (Hannover: Hahn, 1879)

Gesta Bertholdi Episcopi Argentinensis, in *Die Chronik des Mathias von Neuenburg*, ed. A. Hofmeister, *MGSrG*, NS 4 (Berlin: Weidmann, 1924)

Gesta Boemundi archiepiscopi Treverensis, ed. G. Waitz, in *MGS* 24 (Hannover: Hahn, 1879)

Gesta Treverorum, ed. G. Waitz, in *MGS* 8 (Hannover: Hahn, 1848)

Glossen zum Sachsenspiegel-Landrecht: Buch'sche Glosse, ed. F.-M. Kaufmann, *MGFiGa* NS 7, 3 vols. (Hannover: Hahn, 2002)

Die Goldene Bulle Kaiser Karls IV. vom Jahre 1356, ed. W.D. Fritz, *MGFiGa* 11 (Weimar: Böhlaus Nachf., 1972)

Gotfrid Hagen, *Dit is dat boich van der stede Colne*, ed. R. Schröder, in *CdtS* 12 (Leipzig: Hirzel, 1875)

Hansisches Urkundenbuch 2, ed. K. Höhlbaum (Halle (Saale): Waisenhaus, 1879)

Hansisches Urkundenbuch 3, ed. K. Höhlbaum (Halle (Saale): Waisenhaus, 1882–6)

Hansisches Urkundenbuch 4, ed. K. Kunze (Halle (Saale): Waisenhaus, 1896)

Hansisches Urkundenbuch, 5, ed. K. Kunze (Leipzig: Duncker & Humblot, 1899)

Heinrici de Heimburg annales, a. 861–1300, ed. W. Wattenbach, in *MGS* 18 (Hannover: Hahn, 1861)

Heinrichs Livländische Chronik, 2nd edn, ed. L. Arbusow and A. Bauer, *MGSrG* 2 (Hannover: Hahn, 1955)

Heinricus Dapifer de Diessenhoven 1316–1361, in *Fontes rerum Germanicarum: Geschichtsquellen Deutschlands*, vol. IV, ed. A. Huber (Stuttgart: Cotta, 1868)

Hermanni Altahensis annales (1137–1273), ed. P. Jaffé, in *MGS* 17 (Hannover: Hahn, 1861)

Hermanni Altahensis Continuatio, ed. P. Jaffé, in *MGS* 17 (Hannover: Hahn, 1861)

Hildebrand Veckinchusen: Briefwechsel eines deutschen Kaufmanns im 15. Jahrhundert, ed. W. Stieda (Leipzig: Hirzel, 1921)

Historia Annorum 1264–1279, ed. W. Wattenbach, in *MGS* 9 (Hannover: Hahn, 1851)

Historia Diplomatica Friderici Secundi, ed. J.-L.-A. Huillard-Bréholles, 7 vols. (Paris: Plon, 1852–61)

Historia Erphesfordensis Anonymi Scriptoris de Landgraviis Thuringiae, in *Illustrium Veterum Scriptorum, Qui Rerum a Germanis per Multas Aetates Gestarum Historias vel Annales Posteris Reliquerunt, ex bibliotheca Joannis Pistorii*, vol. I (Frankfurt: Claudii Marnii haeredum, 1613)

Die historischen Volkslieder der Deutschen vom 13. bis 16. Jahrhundert, ed. R. von Liliencron, vol. I (Leipzig, 1865, repr. Hildesheim: Olms, 1966)

Honorius Augustodunensis, *Imago Mundi*, ed. V.I.J. Flint, *Archives d'histoire doctrinale et littéraire du moyen âge* 49 (1982)

Excerpta ex Expositione Hugonis de Rutlingen in Chronicam Metricam, 1218–1348, in *Fontes rerum Germanicarum: Geschichtsquellen Deutschlands*, vol. IV, ed. A. Huber (Stuttgart: Cotta, 1868)

Der Renner von Hugo von Trimburg, ed. G. Ehrismann, 4 vols. (Berlin: De Gruyter, 1970)

Iohannis abbatis Victoriensis Liber certarum historiarum, ed. F. Schneider, *MGSrG* 36.i and 36.ii (Hannover and Leipzig: Hahn, 1909–10)

Isidori Hispalensis Episcopi Etymologiarum sive Originum libri XX, ed. W.M. Lindsay, 2 vols (Oxford: Clarendon Press, 1911)

Jahrbücher des zittauischen Stadtsschreibers Johannes von Guben, ed. E.F. Haupt, *Scriptores rerum Lusaticarum* 1 (Görlitz: Heinze, 1837)

Jansen Enikel, *Fürstenbuch*, in *Jansen Enikels Werke*, ed. P. Strauch, *MGDtChron* 3.i (Hannover: Hahn, 1891)

Jansen Enikels *Weltchronik*, in *Jansen Enikels Werke*, ed. P. Strauch, *MGDtChron* 3.i (Hannover: Hahn, 1891)

Jäschke, K.-U., 'Zu den Gesta Adolfi Regis von 1299/1316', in D. Berg and H.-W. Goetz (eds.), *Historiographia Mediaevalis: Fs für Franz-Josef Schmale* (Darmstadt: Wissenschaftliche Buchgesellschaft, 1988), pp. 221–45

Johann von Würzburg, *Wilhelm von Österreich*, ed. E. Regel (Dublin and Zürich: Weidmann, 1970)

Johannes Cochlaeus, *Brevis Germanie Descriptio (1512)*, ed. K. Langosch (Darmstadt: Wissenschaftliche Buchgesellschaft, 1969)

Kaiserchronik eines Regensburger Geistlichen, ed. E. Schröder, *MGdtChron* 1 (Berlin: Weidmann, 1895)

Kaiserchronik, erste (Bairische) Fortsetzung, ed. E. Schröder, *MGdtChron* 1 (Berlin: Weidmann, 1895)

Kaiserchronik, zweite (Schwäbische) Fortsetzung, ed. E. Schröder, *MGdtChron* 1 (Berlin: Weidmann, 1895)

Karl Meinet, ed. A. von Keller (Stuttgart: Literarischer Verein, 1858)

Karoli IV Imperatoris Romanorum Vita ab eo ipso conscripta et Hystoria Nova de Sancto Wenceslao Martyre; Autobiography of Emperor Charles IV and his Legend of St Wenceslas, ed. B. Nagy and F. Schaer (Budapest: CEU Press, 2001)

Knighton's Chronicle 1337–1396, ed. and trans. G.H. Martin (Oxford: Clarendon Press, 1995)

Die Kölner Weltchronik 1273/88–1376, ed. R. Sprandel, *MGSrG*, NS 15 (Munich: MGH, 1991)

Die Königsaaler Geschichts-Quellen mit den Zusätzen und der Fortsetzung des Domherrn Franz von Prag, ed. J. Loserth, *Fontes rerum Austriacarum: Oesterreichische Geschichtsquellen* 1 (Abtheilung 8) (Vienna: Karl Gerold's Sohn, 1875)

Der kunige buoch, ed. H.F. Massmann, in A. von Daniels (ed.), *Rechtsdenkmäler des deutschen Mittelalters: Land- und Lehensrechtbücher*, vol. 2 (Berlin: Gustav Hempel, 1863)

Konrad von Megenberg, *Ökonomik*, ed. S. Krüger, 3 vols. (*MG Staatsschriften* 3.v, Stuttgart: Hiersemann, 1973–84)

Planctus Ecclesiae in Germaniam, ed. R. Scholz, in *Die Werke des Konrad von Megenberg*, vol. I (*MG Staatsschriften* 2, 1941, repr. Stuttgart: Hiersemann, 1977)

Tractatus contra Wilhelmum Occam, in *Unbekannte kirchenpolitische Streitschriften aus der Zeit Ludwigs des Bayern (1327–1354): Analysen und Texte*, ed. R. Scholz, pt. II (Texte) (Rome: Loescher, 1914)

De translacione Romani imperii, in *Unbekannte kirchenpolitische Streitschriften aus der Zeit Ludwigs des Bayern (1327–1354): Analysen und Texte*, ed. R. Scholz, pt. II (Texte) (Rome: Loescher, 1914)

Das Buch der Natur von Konrad von Megenberg: Die erste Naturgeschichte in deutscher Sprache, ed. F. Pfeiffer (1861, repr. Hildesheim: Olms, 1962)

Konrad von Mure, *De victoria regis Rudolfi contra Odoacrum regem Bohemorum*, printed in Kleinschmidt, *Herrscherdarstellung*, Appendix I

Konrad von Würzburg, *Heinrich von Kempten*, in Konrad von Würzburg, *Heinrich von Kempten, Der Welt Lohn, Das Herzmaere*, ed. and trans. H. Röllecke (Stuttgart: Reclam, 1968)

Partonopier und Meliur, ed. K. Bartsch (Berlin: De Gruyter, 1970)

Das Turnier von Nantes, in *Kleinere Dichtungen Konrads von Würzburg*, ed. E. Schröder (Berlin: Weidmann, 1959)

Księga Henrykowska, ed. R. Grodecki (Poznań and Wrocław: Instytut Zachodni, 1949)

Das Landbuch der Mark Brandenburg, ed. J. Schultze (Berlin: Gsellius, 1940)

Das Leben der Heiligen Elisabeth vom Verfasser der Erlösung, ed. M. Rieger (Stuttgart: Literarischer Verein, 1868)

Liber chronicarum (Nuremberg: Anton Koberger, 1493)

Liber de rebus memorabilioribus sive Chronicon Henrici de Hervordia, ed. A. Potthast (Göttingen: Dieterich, 1859)

Die Limburger Chronik des Tilemann Elhen von Wolfhagen, ed. A. Wyss, *MGDtChron* 4.i (Hannover: Hahn, 1883)

Livländische Reimchronik, ed. F. Pfeiffer (Stuttgart, 1844, repr. Amsterdam: Rodopi, 1969)

A Local Society in Transition: The Henryków Book and Related Documents, ed. and trans. P. Górecki (Toronto: Pontifical Institute of Mediaeval Studies, 2007)

Lohengrin: Edition und Untersuchung, ed. T. Cramer (Munich: Fink, 1971)

Lupold von Bebenburg, *Libellus de Zelo Christiane Religionis Veterum Principum Germanorum*, in *Politische Schriften Lupolds von Bebenburg*, ed. J. Miethke and C. Flüeler (*MG Staatsschriften* 4, Hannover: Hahn, 2004)

Tractatus de Iuribus Regni et Imperii, in *Politische Schriften Lupolds von Bebenburg*, ed. J. Miethke and C. Flüeler (*MG Staatsschriften* 4, Hannover: Hahn, 2004)

Die Magdeburger Schöppenchronik, ed. K. Janicke, *CdtS* 7 (Leipzig: Hirzel, 1869)

Margue, M., Pauly, M. and Schmid, W. (eds.), *Der Weg zur Kaiserkrone: der Romzug Heinrichs VII. in der Darstellung Erzbischof Balduins von Trier* (Trier: Kliomedia, 2009)

Martini continuatio Coloniensis, in *Chronica regia Coloniensis (Annales Maximi Colonienses)*, ed. G. Waitz, *MGSrG* 18 (Hannover: Hahn, 1880)

Martini Minoritae Flores Temporum ab Hermanno Januensi continuati usque ad Carolum IV. Imp., in *Corpus Historicum Medii Aevi*, ed. J.G. Eccard, vol. I (Leipzig: Gleditschii, 1723)

Martini Oppaviensis Chronicon Pontificum et Imperatorum, ed. L. Weiland, in *MGS* 22 (Hannover: Hahn, 1872)

Matthaei Parisiensis, Monachi Sancti Albani, Chronica Majora, ed. H.R. Luard, *RS* 57.iv (London: Longman, 1877)

Mecklenburgische Reimchronik des Ernst von Kirchberg, ed. C. Cordshagen and R. Schmidt (Cologne, Weimar and Vienna: Böhlau, 1997)

MGC 2 (1198–1272), ed. L. Weiland (Hannover: Hahn, 1896)

MGC 3 (1273–1298), ed. J. Schwalm (Hannover and Leipzig: Hahn, 1904–6)

MGC 4.i (1298–1313), ed. J. Schwalm (Hannover and Leipzig: Hahn, 1906)

MGC 4.ii (1298–1313), ed. J. Schwalm (Hannover and Leipzig: Hahn, 1909–11)

MGC 5 (1313–1324), ed. J. Schwalm (Hannover and Leipzig: Hahn, 1909–13)

MGC 6.i (1325–1330), ed. J. Schwalm (Hannover and Leipzig: Hahn, 1914–27)

MGC 8 (1345–1348), ed. K. Zeumer and R. Salomon (Hannover: Hahn, 1910–26)

MGC 9 (1349), ed. M. Kühn (Weimar: H. Böhlaus Nachf., 1974–83)

MGC 10 (1350–1353), ed. E. Müller-Mertens (Weimar: H. Böhlaus Nachf., 1979–91)

MGC 11 (1354–1356), ed. W.D. Fritz (Weimar: H. Böhlaus Nachf., 1978–92)

MGH Leges 2, ed. G.H. Pertz (Hannover: Hahn, 1837)

Minnesinger: Deutsche Liederdichter des zwölften, dreizehnten und vierzehnten Jahrhunderts, ed. F.H. von der Hagen, 4 vols. (Leipzig: Barth, 1838)

Monumenta Poloniae Vaticana, vol. III, ed. J. Ptásnik (Kraków: Academia Litterarum Cracoviensis, 1914)

Der Nibelunge Nôt, mit den Abweichungen von der Nibelunge Liet, den Lesarten sämmtlicher Handschriften und einem Wörterbuch, ed. K. Bartsch, 2 vols. (Leipzig: Brockhaus, 1870–80)

Notae Weingartenses, ed. G. Waitz, in *MGS* 24 (Hannover: Hahn, 1879)

Nova Alamanniae: Urkunden, Briefe und andere Quellen besonders zur deutschen Geschichte des 14. Jahrhunderts, vornehmlich aus den Sammlungen des Trierer Notars und Offizials, Domdekans von Mainz Rudolf Losse aus Eisenach in der Ständischen Landesbibliothek zu Kassel und im Staatsarchiv zu Darmstadt, ed. E.E. Stengel, 2 vols. (Berlin: Weidmann, 1921, 1930)

Die Oberrrheinische Chronik, in *Deutsche Chroniken*, ed. H. Maschek (Leipzig: Reclam, 1936)

Oeuvres de Froissart, ed. K. de Lettenhove, vol. XVIII (*Pièces justificatives 1319–1399*) (1867–77, repr. Osnabrück: Biblio, 1967)

Österreichische Chronik von den 95. Herrschaften, ed. J. Seemüller, *MGDtChron* 6 (Hannover: Hahn, 1906–9)

Ostfriesisches Urkundenbuch, ed. E. Friedlaender, vol. I (787–1470) (Emden: Haynel, 1878)

Ottokars österreichische Reimchronik, ed. J. Seemüller, *MGDtChron* 5.i and 5.ii (Hannover: Hahn, 1890, 1893)

Ottonis Episcopi Frisingensis Chronica sive Historia de Duabus Civitatibus, ed. A. Hofmeister, *MGSrG* 45 (Hannover and Leipzig: Hahn, 1912)

Ottonis et Rahewini Gesta Friderici I. Imperatoris, ed. G. Waitz, *MGSrG* 46 (Hannover: Hahn, 1884)

Pius II, *Commentaries*, vol. I (Books I–II), ed. M. Meserve and M. Simonetta (Cambridge, MA and London: Harvard University Press, 2003)

The Poems of Lupold Hornburg, ed. C.H. Bell and E.G. Gudde (Berkeley and Los Angeles, CA: University of California Press, 1945)

Prescott, H.F.M., *Once to Sinai: The Further Pilgrimage of Friar Felix Fabri* (London: Eyre & Spottiswoode, 1957)

Quellen zur Geschichte der ostdeutschen Kolonisation im 12. bis 14. Jahrhundert, ed. R. Kötzschke (Leipzig and Berlin: Teubner, 1912)

Quellensammlung zur Geschichte der deutschen Reichsverfassung im Mittelalter und Neuzeit, ed. K. Zeumer (Leipzig: Hirschfeld, 1904)

Quellenwerk zur Entstehung der Schweizerischen Eidgenossenschaft (Abteilung I: Urkunden), vol. II, ed. T. Schieß and B. Meyer (Aarau: Sauerländer, 1937)

De Recuperatione Terre Sancte: Traité de politique générale par Pierre Dubois, ed. Ch.-V. Langlois (Paris: Picard, 1891)

Regesta Diplomatica nec non Epistolaria Bohemiae et Moraviae, vol. II (1253–1310), ed. J. Emler (Prague: Československá akademie ved., 1882)

Regesta Diplomatica nec non Epistolaria Bohemiae et Moraviae, vol. III (1311–33), ed. J. Emler (Prague: Československá akademie ved., 1890)

Regesta Diplomatica nec non Epistolaria Bohemiae et Moraviae, vol. VI (1355–63), ed. B. Mendl (Prague: Academia Scientiarum Bohemoslovenicae, 1929)

Die Regesten der Erzbischöfe von Köln im Mittelalter, vol. III (1205–1304), ed. R. Knipping (Bonn: Gesellschaft für Rheinische Geschichtskunde, 1909–13)

Les Registres de Gregoire X (1272–1276) et de Jean XXI (1276–1277), ed. L. Cadier and J. Guirard, 4 fascs. (Paris: Thorin, 1892–1906)

Die Regesten des Kaiserreiches unter Rudolf, Adolf, Albrecht, Heinrich VII. 1273–1313, ed. O. Redlich (Regesta Imperii 6.i, 1898, repr. with appendix by C. Brühl, Hildesheim: Olms, 1969)

Die Regesten des Kaiserreiches unter Kaiser Karl IV. (1346–1378), ed. A. Huber (Regesta Imperii 8, Innsbruck: Wagner, 1877)

Regesten der Pfalzgrafen am Rhein 1214–1508, ed. L. von Oberndorff, vol. II.i (Innsbruck: Wagner, 1912)

Der heilige Georg Reinbots von Durne, ed. C. von Kraus (Heidelberg: Winter, 1907)

Rocznik lubiąski 1241–1281, oraz wierz o pierwotnych zakonniach Lubiąża, ed. A. Bielowski, in *Monumenta Poloniae Historica* 3 (Lwów: W Komisie księgarni Gubrynowicza I Schmidta, 1878)

Rudolf von Ems, *Weltchronik*, ed. G. Ehrismann, 2nd edn (Dublin and Zurich: Weidmann, 1967)

Rymkronyk van Jan van Heelu betreffende den Slag van Woeringen, van het Jaer 1288, ed. J.F. Willems (Brussels: Hayez, 1836)

Rýmovaná Kronika Česká / Di tutsch kronik von Behem lant, ed. J. Jiriček, in *Fontes rerum Bohemicarum* 3 (Prague: Nakl. Musea Království českého, 1882)

Sachsenspiegel Landrecht, ed. K.A. Eckhardt, *MGFiGa* NS 1.i, 3rd edn (Göttingen: Musterschmidt, 1973)

Sachsenspiegel Lehnrecht, ed. K.A. Eckhardt, *MGFiGa* NS 1.ii, 3rd edn (Göttingen: Musterschmidt, 1973)

Sächsische Weltchronik, ed. L. Weiland, in *MGDtChron* 2 (Hannover: Hahn, 1877)

Sächsische Weltchronik: erste Bairische Fortsetzung, ed. L. Weiland, in *MGDtChron* 2 (Hannover: Hahn, 1877)

Sächsische Weltchronik: zweite Bairische Fortsetzung, ed. L. Weiland, in *MGDtChron* 2 (Hannover: Hahn, 1877)

Sächsische Weltchronik: Sächsische Fortsetzung, ed. L. Weiland, in *MGDtChron* 2 (Hannover: Hahn, 1877)

Sächsische Weltchronik: Thüringische Fortsetzung, ed. L. Weiland, in *MGDtChron* 2 (Hannover: Hahn, 1877)

Schönbach, A.E., 'Des Bartholomaeus Anglicus Beschreibung Deutschlands gegen 1240', *MIöG* 27 (1906), 54–90

Schönbach, A.E. and Redlich, O., 'Des Gutolf von Heiligenkreuz Translatio sanctae Delicianae', *Sitzungsberichte der k.k. Akademie der Wissenschaften in Wien, philosophisch-historische Klasse* 159 (1908), 1–38

Schwabenspiegel Kurzform, ed. K.A. Eckhardt, *MGFiGa* NS 4, 2nd edn (Hannover: Hahn, 1974)

Selections from Conrad Celtis 1459–1508, ed. and trans. L. Forster (Cambridge University Press, 1948)

Die Siegel der Deutschen Kaiser und Könige von Pippin bis Ludwig den Bayern, ed. O. Posse (Dresden: Baensch, 1909)

Sifridi presbyteri de Balnhusin historia universalis et compendium historiarum, ed. O. Holder-Egger, *MGS* 25 (Hannover: Hahn, 1880)

Sommerfeldt, G., 'Die Stellung Ruprechts III. von der Pfalz zur deutschen Publizistik bis zum Jahre 1400', *ZGORh* NF, 22 (1907), 291–319

'Zwei Schismatraktate Heinrichs von Langenstein', *MIöG* Ergbd 7 (1907), 436–69

Strauss, G. (ed. and trans.), *Manifestations of Discontent in Germany on the Eve of the Reformation* (Bloomington, IN and London: Indiana University Press, 1971)

Summa Curiae Regis: Ein Formelbuch aus der Zeit König Rudolfs I. und Albrechts I. (Aus einer Erlanger Handschrift des XIV. Jahrhunderts), ed. O. Stobbe (Vienna: Oesterreichische Akademie der Wissenschaften, 1855)

Der Tractatus de Longevo Schismate des Abtes Ludolf von Sagan, ed. J. Loserth, in *Beiträge zur Geschichte der husitischen Bewegung*, vol. III (Archiv für österreichische Geschichte 59, Vienna: Karl Gerold's Sohn, 1880)

Ulman Stromers *'Puechel von meim geslechet und von abentewr' 1349 bis 1407*, ed. K. Hegel, in *CdtS* 1 (Leipzig: Hirzel, 1862)

Ulrich von Eschenbach, *Alexander*, ed. W. Toischer (Tübingen: Litterarischer Verein in Stuttgart, 1888)

Ulrich von Etzenbach, *Wilhelm von Wenden*, ed. H.-F. Rosenfeld (Berlin: Akademie, 1957)

Ulrich von Liechtenstein, *Frauendienst*, ed. F.V. Spechtler, 2nd edn (Göppingen: Kümmerle, 2003)

Urkunden und erzählende Quellen zur deutschen Ostsiedlung im Mittelalter, ed. H. Helbig and L. Weinrich, 2 vols. (Darmstadt: Wissenschaftliche Buchgesellschaft, 1975)

Urkunden zur Geschichte des Bisthums Breslau im Mittelalter, ed. G.A. Stenzel (Breslau: Max, 1845)

Die Urkunden Heinrich Raspes und Wilhelms von Holland, ed. D. Hägermann and J.G. Kruisheer, *MG Dip.* 18 (Hannover: Hahn, 1989, 2006)

Die Urkunden Kaiser Sigmunds (1410–1437), vol. I (1410–1424), ed. W. Altmann (Regesta Imperii 11, Innsbruck: Wagner, 1896–7)

Urkundenbuch der Stadt Strassburg 5 (*Politische Urkunden von 1332 bis 1380*), ed. H. Witte and G. Wolfram (Strassburg: Trübner, 1896)

Urkundenbuch der Stadt Strassburg 6 (*Politische Urkunden von 1381 bis 1400*), ed. J. Fritz (Strassburg: Trübner, 1899)

Urkundenregesten zur Tätigkeit des deutschen Königs- und Hofgerichts bis 1451, vol. III, ed. B. Diestelkamp and U. Rödel (Quellen und Forschungen zur höchsten Gerichtsbarkeit im alten Reich: Sonderreihe, Cologne and Vienna: Böhlau, 1986)

Vita Henrici archiepiscopi altera, ed. G. Waitz, in *MGS* 24 (Hannover: Hahn, 1879)

Walther von der Vogelweide, *Die Lieder*, ed. Friedrich Maurer (Munich: Fink, 1972)

Die Weltchronik Heinrichs von München: Neue Ee, ed. F. Shaw, J. Fournier and K. Gärtner (Berlin: Akademie, 2008)

Wernher der Gartenaere, *Helmbrecht*, ed. K. Speckenbach (Darmstadt: Wissenschaftliche Buchgesellschaft, 1974)

Eine Wiener Briefsammlung zur Geschichte des deutschen Reiches und der österreichischen Länder in der zweiten Hälfte des XIII. Jahrhunderts, ed. O. Redlich (Mitteilungen aus dem vatikanischen Archive 2, Vienna: Tempsky, 1894)

SECONDARY WORKS

Abulafia, D., *Frederick II: A Medieval Emperor* (London: Allen Lane, 1988)

'Kantorowicz and Frederick II', *History* 62 (1977), 193–210

Abulafia, D. and Berend, N. (eds.), *Medieval Frontiers: Concepts and Practices* (Aldershot: Ashgate, 2002)

Allmand, C., *Henry V* (London: Methuen, 1992)

The Hundred Years War: England and France at War c.1300–c.1450 (Cambridge University Press, 1988)

Althoff, G., 'Die Beurteilung der mittelalterlichen Ostpolitik als Paradigma für zeitgebundene Geschichtsbewertung', in G. Althoff (ed.), *Die Deutschen und ihr Mittelalter: Themen und Funktionen moderner Geschichtsbilder vom Mittelalter* (Darmstadt: Wissenschaftliche Buchgesellschaft, 1992), pp. 147–64

Die Macht der Rituale: Symbolik und Herrschaft im Mittelalter (Darmstadt: Primus, 2003)

'Das Mittelalterbild der Deutschen vor und nach 1945', in P.-J. Heinig, S. Jahns *et al.* (eds.), *Reich, Regionen und Europa im Mittelalter und Neuzeit: Fs für Peter Moraw* (Berlin: Duncker & Humblot, 2000), pp. 731–49

'Die Rezeption des Reiches seit dem Ende des Mittelalters', in Puhle and Hasse (eds.), *Heiliges Römisches Reich: Essays*, pp. 477–85

Amelung, P., *Das Bild des Deutschen in der Literatur der italienischen Renaissance, 1400–1559* (Munich: Huebner, 1964)

Amory, P., *People and Identity in Ostrogothic Italy, 489–554* (Cambridge University Press, 1997)

Anderson, B., *Imagined Communities: Reflections on the Origin and Spread of Nationalism* (London: Verso, 1983)

Andritsch, J., 'Das Ungarnbild in der österreichischen Historiographie im Mittelalter', in W. Höflechner, H.J. Mezler-Angelberg and O. Pickl (eds.), *Domus Austriae: eine Festgabe Hermann Wiesflecker zum 70. Geburtstag* (Graz: Akademische Druck- und Verlagsanstalt, 1983), pp. 19–35

Angermeier, H., *Königtum und Landfriede im deutschen Spätmittelalter* (Munich: Beck, 1966)

Annas, G., *Hoftag – Gemeiner Tag – Reichstag: Studien zur strukturellen Entwicklung deutscher Reichsversammlungen des späten Mittelalters (1349–1471)*, 2 vols. (Göttingen: Vandenhoeck & Ruprecht, 2004)

Appelt, H., 'Die Kaiseridee Friedrich Barbarossas', *Österreichische Akademie der Wissenschaften, philosophisch-historische Klasse: Sitzungsbericht* 253 (1967), 1–32

Applegate, C., 'A Europe of regions: reflections on the historiography of sub-national places in modern times', *AHR* 104 (1999), 1157–82

Armstrong, C.A.J., 'The language question in the Low Countries: the use of French and Dutch by the dukes of Burgundy and their administration', in J.R. Hale, J.R.L. Highfield and B. Smalley (eds.), *Europe in the Late Middle Ages* (London: Faber and Faber, 1965), pp. 386–409

Armstrong, J.A., *Nations Before Nationalism* (Chapel Hill, NC: University of North Carolina Press, 1982)

Arnold, B., *Medieval Germany, 500–1300: A Political Interpretation* (Basingstoke: Macmillan, 1997)

Princes and Territories in Medieval Germany (Cambridge University Press, 1991)

Arnold, K., 'Im Ringen um die bürgerliche Freiheit: die Stadt Würzburg im späten Mittelalter (ca. 1250–1400)', in U. Wagner (ed.), *Geschichte der Stadt Würzburg*, vol. I (*Von den Anfängen bis zum Ausbruch des Bauernkriegs*) (Stuttgart: Theiss, 2001), pp. 94–109

Arnold, U. (ed.), *800 Jahre Deutscher Orden* (Gütersloh and Munich: Bertelsmann, 1990)

Aubin, H., 'The lands east of the Elbe and German colonization eastwards', in M.M. Postan (ed.), *The Cambridge Economic History of Europe*, vol. I, new edn (Cambridge University Press, 1966), pp. 449–86

Babel, R. and Moeglin, J.-M. (eds.), *Identité régionale et conscience nationale en France et en Allemagne du Moyen Âge à l'époque moderne* (Sigmaringen: Thorbecke, 1997)

Bachmann, E., 'Karolinische Reichsarchitektur', in Seibt (ed.), *Kaiser Karl IV.*, pp. 334–9

Baethgen, F., 'Zur Geschichte der Weltherrschaftsidee im späteren Mittelalter', in P. Classen and P. Scheibert (eds.), *Fs Percy Ernst Schramm*, vol. I (Wiesbaden: Steiner, 1964), pp. 189–203

Bagge, S., 'Nationalism in Norway in the Middle Ages', *Scandinavian Journal of History* 20 (1995), 1–18

Baier-Schröcke, H., *Die Buchmalerei in der Chronik des Ernst von Kirchberg im Landeshauptarchiv Schwerin* (Schwerin: Landeshauptarchiv, 2007)

Baldamus, A., Schwabe, E. and Ambrosius, E. (eds.), *F.W. Putzgers Historischer Schul-Atlas: große Ausgabe* (Bielefeld and Leipzig: Velhagen & Klasing, 1926)

Balduin von Luxemburg: Erzbischof von Trier, Kurfürst des Reiches 1285–1354 (Katalog zur Landesausstellung in Trier, 1. Juni bis 1. September 1985, no editor, Koblenz: Landesarchivverwaltung Rheinland-Pfalz, 1985)

Baldwin, J.W., *The Government of Philip Augustus: Foundations of French Royal Power in the Middle Ages* (Berkeley, CA: University of California Press, 1986)

Bansa, H., *Studien zur Kanzlei Kaiser Ludwigs des Bayern vom Tag der Wahl bis zur Rückkehr aus Italien (1314–1329)* (Kallmünz: Lassleben, 1968)

Barraclough, G., *The Origins of Modern Germany*, 2nd edn (Oxford: Blackwell, 1947)

Barth, F., 'Introduction', in F. Barth, *Ethnic Groups and Boundaries: The Social Organisation of Cultural Difference* (London: Allen & Unwin, 1969), pp. 9–38

Barthes, R., 'Myth today', in S. Sontag (ed.), *A Barthes Reader* (London: Jonathan Cape, 1982), pp. 93–149

Bartlett, R., *Gerald of Wales, 1146–1223* (Oxford: Clarendon Press, 1982)

  The Making of Europe: Conquest, Colonization, and Cultural Change, 950–1350 (Harmondsworth: Penguin, 1993)

  'Medieval and modern concepts of race and ethnicity', *Journal of Medieval and Early Modern Studies*, 31 (2001), 39–56

Bartlett, R. and MacKay, A. (eds.), *Medieval Frontier Societies* (Oxford: Clarendon Press, 1986)

Bastert, B., '"der Cristenheyt als nücz als kein czelffbott": Karl der Große in der deutschen erzählenden Literatur des Mittelalters', in B. Bastert (ed.), *Karl der Große in den europäischen Literaturen des Mittelalters* (Tübingen: Niemeyer, 2004), pp. 127–47

Bauer, R., 'München als Landeshauptstadt', *ZblLg* 60 (1997), 115–26

Baxandall, M., *The Limewood Sculptors of Renaissance Germany* (New Haven, CT and London: Yale University Press, 1980)

Beaune, C., *The Birth of an Ideology: Myths and Symbols of Nation in Late-Medieval France*, trans. S.R. Huston (Berkeley and Los Angeles, CA: University of California Press, 1991)

Bedos-Rezak, M., 'Medieval identity: a sign and a concept', *AHR* 105 (2000), 1489–1533

Begert, A., *Böhmen, die böhmische Kur und das Reich vom Hochmittelalter bis zum Ende des Alten Reiches* (Husum: Matthiesen, 2003)

Literatur als Machtlegitimation: Studien zur Funktion der deutschsprachigen Dichtung am böhmischen Königshof im 13. Jahrhundert (Munich: Fink, 1989)

Behr, H.-J., 'Das Nachleben Heinrichs des Löwen in der Literatur des Spätmittelalters', in J. Luckhardt and F. Niehoff (eds.), *Heinrich der Löwe und seine Zeit: Herrschaft und Repräsentation der Welfen 1125–1235*, vol. III (Munich: Hirmer, 1995), pp. 9–14

Behrmann, T., ' "Hansekaufmann", "Hansestadt", "Deutsche Hanse"? Über hansische Terminologie und hansisches Selbstverständnis im späten Mittelalter', in T. Scharff and T. Behrmann (eds.), *Bene vivere in communitate: Beiträge zum italienischen und deutschen Mittelalter – Hagen Keller zum 60. Geburtstag* (Münster: Waxmann, 1997), pp. 155–76

Below, G. von, *Der deutsche Staat des Mittelalters: ein Grundriß der deutschen Verfassungsgeschichte*, vol. I (Leipzig: Quelle & Meyer, 1914)

Belting, H., *Likeness and Presence: A History of the Image Before the Era of Art*, trans. E. Jephcott (Chicago and London: University of Chicago Press, 1994)

Benedictow, O.J., *The Black Death 1346–1353: The Complete History* (Woodbridge: Boydell & Brewer, 2004)

Benl, R., 'Pommern bis zur Teilung von 1368/72', in W. Buchholz (ed.), *Pommern* (DGOE, Berlin: Siedler, 1999), pp. 48–86

Benson, R.L., 'Political *renovatio*: two models from Roman antiquity', in R.L. Benson and G. Constable (eds.), *Renaissance and Renewal in the Twelfth Century* (Oxford: Clarendon Press, 1982), pp. 339–86

Bentzinger, R., 'Die Kanzleisprachen', in W. Bensch, A. Betten, O. Reichmann and S. Sonderegger (eds.), *Sprachgeschichte: ein Handbuch zur Geschichte der deutschen Sprache und ihre Erforschung*, 2nd edn, vol. II.ii (Berlin and New York: De Gruyter, 2000), pp. 1665–73

Berend, N., *At the Gate of Christendom: Jews, Muslims and 'Pagans' in Medieval Hungary, c.1000–c.1300* (Cambridge University Press, 2001)

'Frontiers', in H. Nicholson (ed.), *Palgrave Advances in the Crusades* (Basingstoke: Palgrave Macmillan, 2005), pp. 148–71

Berg, D., *Deutschland und seine Nachbarn 1200–1500* (Munich: Oldenbourg, 1997)

Berger, S., *The Search for Normality: National Identity and Historical Consciousness in Germany Since 1800* (Oxford and New York: Berghahn, 1997)

Berges, W., *Die Fürstenspiegel des hohen und späten Mittelalters* (Leipzig: Hiersemann, 1938)

Bergmann, R., 'Deutsche Sprache und römisches Reich im Mittelalter', in Schneidmüller and Weinfurter (eds.), *Heilig – Römisch – Deutsch*, pp. 162–84

Bernhardt, J.W., *Itinerant Kingship and Royal Monasteries in Early Medieval Germany, c. 936–1075* (Cambridge University Press, 1993)

Bernheimer, R., *Wild Men in the Middle Ages: A Study in Art, Sentiment, and Demonology* (New York: Octagon, 1970)

Beumann, H., 'Die Bedeutung des Kaisertums für die Entstehung der deutschen Nation im Spiegel der Bezeichnungen von Reich und Herrscher', in Beumann and Schröder (eds.), *Aspekte der Nationenbildung*, pp. 317–65

'Zur Nationenbildung im Mittelalter', in O. Dann (ed.), *Nationalismus in vorindustrieller Zeit* (Munich: Oldenbourg, 1986), pp. 21–33

Beumann, H. and Schröder, W. (eds.), *Aspekte der Nationenbildung im Mittelalter* (Nationes 1, Sigmaringen: Thorbecke, 1978)

Billig, M., *Banal Nationalism* (London: Sage, 1995)

Binski, P., *Westminster Abbey and the Plantagenets: Kingship and the Representation of Power 1200–1400* (New Haven, CT and London: Yale University Press, 1995)

Birken, A., 'Deutschland zur Zeit Karls IV. (1378)', in E.W. Zeeden (ed.), *Großer historischer Weltatlas*, vol. II *(Mittelalter: Erläuterungen)* (Munich: Bayerischer Schulbuch-Verlag, 1983), pp. 288–90

Biskup, M., 'Das Problem der ethnischen Zugehörigkeit im mittelalterlichen Landesausbau in Preußen: zum Stand der Forschung', *Jahrbuch für die Geschichte Mittel- und Ostdeutschlands* 40 (1991), 3–25

Bittner, K., *Deutsche und Tschechen: zur Geistesgeschichte des böhmischen Raumes*, vol. I *(Von den Anfängen zur hussitischen Kirchenerneuerung)* (Brünn: Röhrer, 1936)

Black, A., *Political Thought in Europe 1250–1400* (Cambridge University Press, 1992)

Black, I., 'An accidental tourist in the Hundred Years War: images of the foreign world in Eustache Deschamps', in Forde, Johnson and Murray (eds.), *Concepts of National Identity*, pp. 171–87

Blackbourn, D., *The Long Nineteenth Century* (Fontana History of Germany 1780–1918, London: Fontana, 1997)

Bleisteiner, C.D., 'Der Doppeladler von Kaiser und Reich im Mittelalter: Imagination und Realität', *MIöG* 109 (2001), 4–52

Bloch, M., *Feudal Society*, vol. II, trans. L.A. Manyon (London: Routledge & Kegan Paul, 1965)

The Royal Touch: Sacred Monarchy and Scrofula in England and France, trans. J.E. Anderson (London: Routledge & Kegan Paul, 1973)

Blockmans, W.P., 'A typology of representative institutions in late medieval Europe', *Journal of Medieval History* 4 (1978), 189–215

Blockmans, W.P., Holenstein, A. and Mathieu, J. (eds.), *Empowering Interactions: Political Cultures and the Emergence of the State in Europe, 1300–1900* (Farnham: Ashgate, 2009)

Bloomfield, M.W., *The Seven Deadly Sins: An Introduction to the History of a Religious Concept, with Special Reference to Medieval English Literature* (East Lansing, MI: Michigan State College Press, 1952)

Boase, T.S.R., *Boniface VIII* (London: Constable, 1933)

Boehm, B.D. and Fajt, J. (eds.), *Prague: the Crown of Bohemia 1347–1437* (New Haven, CT: Yale University Press, 2005)

Boockmann, H., 'Die Eroberung Preußens durch den Deutschen Orden', in H. Boockmann, *Ostpreußen und Westpreußen* (DGOE, Berlin: Siedler, 1992), pp. 75–115

'Die Geschichtsschreibung des Deutschen Ordens: Gattungsfragen und "Gebrauchssituation"', in Patze (ed.), *Geschichtsschreibung*, pp. 447–81

Der Historiker Hermann Heimpel (Göttingen: Vandenhoeck & Ruprecht, 1990)

'Die neue Besiedlung Preußens', in H. Boockmann, *Der Deutsche Orden: Zwölf Kapitel aus seiner Geschichte*, 3rd revd edn (Munich: Beck, 1989), pp. 115–37

Die Stadt im späten Mittelalter (Munich: Beck, 1986)

Borchardt, F.L., *German Antiquity in Renaissance Myth* (Baltimore, MD: Johns Hopkins University Press, 1971)

Borgolte, M., 'Anfänge deutscher Geschichte? Die Mittelalterforschung der zweiten Nachkriegszeit', *Tel Aviver Jahrbuch für deutsche Geschichte* 25 (1996)

'Vom Sacrum Imperium zum Heiligen Römischen Reich Deutscher Nation: mittelalterliche Reichsgeschichte und deutsche Wiedervereinigung', in B. Martin (ed.), *Deutschland in Europa: ein historischer Rückblick* (Munich: dtv, 1992)

'Vor dem Ende der Nationalgeschichten? Chancen und Hindernisse für eine Geschichte Europas im Mittelalter', *HZ* 272 (2001)

Borgolte, M., Schiel, J., Schneidmüller, B. and Seitz, A. (eds.), *Mittelalter im Labor: die Mediävistik testet Wege zu einer transkulturellen Europawissenschaft* (Berlin: Akademie, 2008)

Borst, A., *Der Turmbau von Babel: Geschichte der Meinungen über Ursprung und Vielfalt der Sprachen und Völker*, vol. II.ii (Stuttgart: Hiersemann, 1959)

Bosl, K., 'Landfriede', in H. Rössler and G. Franz (eds.), *Sachwörterbuch zur deutschen Geschichte*, vol. I (Munich: Oldenbourg, 1958), pp. 604–6

'Staat, Gesellschaft, Wirtschaft im deutschen Mittelalter', in H. Grundmann (ed.), *Gebhardts Handbuch der deutschen Geschichte*, 9th edn, vol. I (Stuttgart: Union Verlag, 1970), § 242, 254

Boswell, J., *Christianity, Social Tolerance and Homosexuality: Gay People in Western Europe from the Beginning of the Christian Era to the Fourteenth Century* (University of Chicago Press, 1980)

Bowlus, C.R., 'The early *Kaiserreich* in recent German historiography', *Central European History* 23 (1990), 349–67

'Ethnogenesis models and the age of migrations: a critique', *Austrian History Yearbook* 26 (1995), 147–64

Bowsky, W.M., *Henry VII in Italy: The Conflict of Empire and City-State 1310–1313* (Lincoln, NE: University of Nebraska Press, 1960)

Braunfels, W. and Schramm, P.E. (eds.), *Karl der Große*, vol. IV (*Das Nachleben*) (Düsseldorf: Schwann, 1967)

Bräutigam, G., 'Nürnberg als Kaiserstadt', in Seibt (ed.), *Kaiser Karl IV.*, pp. 339–43

Brentano, R., *Rome Before Avignon: A Social History of Thirteenth-Century Rome* (London: Longman, 1974)

Bresslau, H., *Geschichte der Monumenta Germaniae Historica* (Hannover: Hahn, 1921)

Handbuch der Urkundenlehre für Deutschland und Italien, 3 vols., 2nd edn
(Leipzig: De Gruyter, 1912–1931)
Breuilly, J., 'Changes in the political uses of the nation: continuity or discontinuity?', in Scales and Zimmer (eds.), *Power and the Nation*, pp. 67–101
The Formation of the First German Nation-State, 1800–1871 (Basingstoke: Macmillan, 1996)
Briggs, C.F., *Giles of Rome's De Regimine Principum: Reading and Writing Politics at Court and University, c.1275–c.1525* (Cambridge University Press, 1999)
Brincken, A.-D. von den, 'Descriptio terrarum: zur Repräsentation von bewohntem Raum im späteren deutschen Mittelalter', in A.-D. von den Brincken, *Studien zur Universalkartographie des Mittelalters*, ed. T. Szabó (Göttingen: Vandenhoeck & Ruprecht, 2008), pp. 623–46
'Geschichtsschreibung', in U. Liebertz-Grün (ed.), *Aus der Mündlichkeit in die Schriftlichkeit: höfische und andere Literatur, 750–1320* (Hamburg: Rohwolt, 1988), pp. 304–13
'Martin von Troppau', in Patze (ed.), *Geschichtsschreibung*, pp. 155–93
Britnell, R., 'Pragmatic literacy in Latin Christendom', in R. Britnell (ed.), *Pragmatic Literacy, East and West 1200–1330* (Woodbridge: Boydell, 1997), pp. 3–24
Brockmann, S., *Nuremberg: The Imaginary Capital* (Rochester, NY: Camden House, 2006)
Brown, E.A.R., 'Persona et Gesta: the image and deeds of the thirteenth-century Capetians – the case of Philip the Fair', *Viator* 19 (1988), 219–46
Bruckmüller, E., *Nation Österreich: kulturelles Bewußtsein und gesellschaftlich-politische Prozesse*, 2nd edn (Vienna, Cologne and Graz: Böhlau, 1996)
Brühl, C., *Deutschland – Frankreich: die Geburt zweier Völker* (Cologne and Vienna: Böhlau, 1990)
Brühl, C. and Schneidmüller, B. (eds.), *Beiträge zur mittelalterlichen Reichs- und Nationsbildung in Deutschland und Frankreich* (Historische Zeitschrift Beiheft 24, Munich: Oldenbourg, 1997)
Brunner, H., 'Das Turnier von Nantes: Konrad von Würzburg, Richard von Cornwall und die deutschen Fürsten', in J. Kühnel, H.-D. Mück and U. Müller (eds.), *De Poeticis Medii Aevi Quaestiones: Kate Hamburger zum 85. Geburtstag* (Göppingen: Kümmerle, 1981), pp. 105–27
Brunner, O., *Land und Herrschaft: Grundfragen der territorialen Verfassungsgeschichte Österreichs im Mittelalter*, 5th edn (Darmstadt: Wissenschaftliche Buchgesellschaft, 1965)
Bryce, J. (Viscount), *The Holy Roman Empire* (Oxford: Shrimpton, 1864; revd edn, London: Macmillan, 1928)
Bryce, J., 'Die Entstehung des trierischen Erzkanzleramtes in Theorie und Wirklichkeit', *HJb* 32 (1911), 1–48
Buchner, M., 'Die Entstehung und Ausbildung der Kurfürstenfabel: Eine historiographische Studie', *HJb* 33 (1912), 255–322
Bumke, J., *Geschichte der deutschen Literatur im hohen Mittelalter* (Munich: dtv, 1990)
Höfische Kultur: Literatur und Gesellschaft im hohen Mittelalter (Munich: dtv, 1986)

Bünz, E., 'Das Land als Bezugsrahmen von Herrschaft, Rechtsordnung und Identitätsbildung: Überlegungen zum spätmittelalterlichen Landesbegriff', in Werner (ed.), *Spätmittelalterliches Landesbewußtsein*, pp. 53–92

Burdach, K., *Vom Mittelalter zur Reformation: Forschung zur Geschichte der deutschen Bildung*, 11 vols. (Berlin: Weidmann, 1893–1937)

Burgard, F., 'Rudolf Losse (um 1310–1364)', in *Rheinische Lebensbilder* 14 (Cologne: Rheinland, 1994), pp. 47–70

Burke, P., 'Frontiers of the monstrous: perceiving national characters in early modern Europe', in L.L. Knoppers and J.B. Landes (eds.), *Monstrous Bodies / Political Monstrosities in Early Modern Europe* (Ithaca, NY and London: Cornell University Press, 2004), pp. 25–39

The Italian Renaissance: Society and Culture in Italy, revised edn (Princeton University Press, 1987)

The Renaissance Sense of the Past (London: Arnold, 1969)

Burleigh, M., *Germany Turns Eastwards: A Study of Ostforschung in the Third Reich* (Cambridge University Press, 1988)

'The knights, nationalists and the historians: images of medieval Prussia from the Enlightenment to 1945', *European History Quarterly* 17 (1987)

Prussian Society and the German Order: An Aristocratic Corporation in Crisis c.1410–1466 (Cambridge University Press, 1984)

Burns, J.H., *Lordship, Kingship, and Empire: The Idea of Monarchy, 1400–1525* (Oxford: Clarendon Press, 1992)

Busch, J.W., 'Mathias von Neuenburg, Italien und die Herkunftssage der Habsburger', *ZGORh* 142 (1994), 103–16

Busson, A., *Die Idee des deutschen Erbreichs und die ersten Habsburger* (Vienna: Karl Gerold's Sohn, 1878)

Bynum, C.W., *Wonderful Blood: Theology and Practice in Late Medieval Northern Germany and Beyond* (Philadelphia: University of Pennsylvania Press, 2007)

Byrn, R.F.M., 'National stereotypes reflected in German literature', in Forde, Johnson and Murray (eds.), *Concepts of National Identity*, pp. 137–53

Campbell, J., 'The late Anglo-Saxon state: a maximalist view', in J. Campbell, *The Anglo-Saxon State* (London: Hambledon, 2000), pp. 1–30

Canning, J., *A History of Medieval Political Thought 300–1450* (London and New York: Routledge, 1996)

'Ideas of the state in thirteenth and fourteenth-century commentators on the Roman law', *TRHS* 5th ser., 33 (1983), 1–27

Cantor, N.F., *Inventing the Middle Ages* (Cambridge: Lutterworth Press, 1991)

Carpenter, D.A., 'The English royal chancery in the thirteenth century', in *Écrit et pouvoir dans les chancelleries médiévales: espace français, espace anglais* (Textes et Études du Moyen Âge, Turnout: Brepols, 1997), pp. 25–53

The Struggle for Mastery: Britain 1066–1284 (London: Penguin, 2003)

Carter, G., 'Bruno von Rappoltstein: Power Relations in Late Medieval Alsace', unpublished MA thesis, University of Durham (2007)

Catto, J., 'Written English: the making of the language 1370–1400', *P&P* 179 (2003), 24–59

Chadraba, R., 'Kaiser Karls IV. devotio antiqua', *Mediaevalia Bohemica* 1 (1969), 51–68

'Der "zweite Konstantin": zum Verhältnis von Staat und Kirche in der karo-linischen Kunst Böhmens', *Umeni* 26 (1978), 505–20

Chaytor, H.J., *From Script to Print: An Introduction to Medieval Literature* (Cambridge University Press, 1945)

Christiansen, E., *The Northern Crusades: The Baltic and the Catholic Frontier 1100–1525* (Basingstoke: Macmillan, 1980)

Clanchy, M.T., *England and Its Rulers 1066–1272* (London: Fontana, 1983)

From Memory to Written Record: England 1066–1307 (London: Arnold, 1979)

Classen, A., 'Introduction: the self, the other, and everything in between: xeno-logical phenomenology of the Middle Ages', in A. Classen (ed.), *Meeting the Foreign in the Middle Ages* (London and New York: Routledge, 2002), pp. xi–lxxiii

'Der Mythos von Rhein: Geschichte, Kultur, Literatur und Ideologie', in Ulrich Müller and Werner Wunderlich (eds.), *Burgen, Länder, Orte* (Constance: UVK, 2008), pp. 711–25

Clemens, L., *Tempore Romanorum constructa: zur Nutzung und Wahrnehmung antiker Überreste nördlich der Alpen während des Mittelalters* (Stuttgart: Hiersemann, 2003)

Cohen, J.J., *Of Giants: Sex, Monsters, and the Middle Ages* (Minneapolis, MN: University of Minnesota Press, 1999)

Cohn, N., *The Pursuit of the Millennium: Revolutionary Millenarians and Mystical Anarchists of the Middle Ages* (London: Secker & Warburg, 1957)

Colberg, K., and Leuschner, J., 'Einleitung', in Dietrich von Nieheim, *Historie de Gestis Romanorum Principum, Cronica, Gesta Karoli Magni Imperatoris*, ed. Katharina Colberg and Joachim Leuschner (*MG Staatsschriften* 5.ii, Stuttgart: Hiersemann, 1980), pp. vii–lvii

Colley, L., *Britons: Forging the Nation 1707–1837* (New Haven, CT and London: Yale University Press, 1992)

Connor, W., 'A nation is a nation, is a state, is an ethnic group, is a ...', in W. Connor (ed.), *Ethnonationalism: The Quest for Understanding* (Princeton University Press, 1994), pp. 90–117

Conrads, N., 'Silesiographia oder Landesbeschreibung', in N. Conrads (ed.), *Schlesien* (DGOE, Berlin: Sielder, 1994), pp. 13–36

Contamine, P., *War in the Middle Ages*, trans. M. Jones (Oxford: Blackwell, 1984)

Cordes, A., 'Deutsches Recht', in A. Cordes *et al.* (eds.), *Handwörterbuch zur deutschen Rechtsgeschichte*, vol. II (Berlin: Schmidt, 2008), cols. 1003–7

Croenen, G., 'Latin and the vernaculars in the charters of the Low Countries: the case of Brabant', in M. Goyens and W. Verbeke (eds.), *The Dawn of the Written Vernacular in Western Europe* (Leuven University Press, 2003), pp. 107–25

Crossley, P., 'The politics of presentation: the architecture of Charles IV in Bohemia', in S. Rees Jones, R. Marks and A.J. Minnis (eds.), *Courts and Regions in Medieval Europe* (Woodbridge: York Medieval Press, 2000), pp. 99–172

Crossley, P. and Opačić, Z., 'Prague as a new capital', in Boehm and Fajt (eds.), *Prague: The Crown of Bohemia*, pp. 59–73

Matthew, D.J.A., 'Reflections on the medieval Roman Empire', *History* 77 (1992), 363–90

Matuzova, V.I., 'Mental frontiers: Prussians as seen by Peter von Dusburg', in A. V. Murray (ed.), *Crusade and Conversion on the Baltic Frontier 1150–1500* (Aldershot: Ashgate, 2001), pp. 253–9

Maué, H., 'Nuremberg's cityscape and architecture', in *Gothic and Renaissance Art in Nuremberg 1300–1550* (Munich: Prestel, 1986), pp. 27–50

Maurer, H., 'Theodor Mayer (1883–1972): sein Wirken vornehmlich während der Zeit des Nationalsozialismus', in K. Hruza (ed.), *Österreichische Historiker 1900–1945* (Vienna, Cologne and Weimar: Böhlau, 2008), pp. 493–530

Mayer, T., 'Aufgaben der Siedlungsgeschichte in den Sudetenländern', *Deutsche Hefte für Volks- und Kulturbodenforschung* 1 (1931), 129–51

'Das deutsche Königtum und sein Wirkungsbereich', in Th. Mayer, *Mittelalterliche Studien: Gesammelte Aufsätze* (Lindau and Constance: Thorbecke, 1959), pp. 28–44

Mažeika, R., 'Granting power to enemy gods in the chronicles of the Baltic crusades', in Abulafia and Berend (eds.), *Medieval Frontiers*, pp. 153–71

Mazower, M., *Dark Continent: Europe's Twentieth Century* (Harmondsworth: Penguin, 1999)

McDonald, M., 'The construction of difference: an anthropological approach to stereotypes', in S. Macdonald (ed.), *Inside European Identities: Ethnography in Western Europe* (Providence, RI and Oxford: Berg, 1993), pp. 219–36

McHardy, A.K., 'Liturgy and propaganda in the diocese of Lincoln during the Hundred Years War', in S. Mews (ed.), *Religion and National Identity* (Studies in Church History 18, Oxford: Blackwell, 1982), pp. 215–27

McKenna, J.W., 'How God became an Englishman', in D.J. Guth and J.W. McKenna (eds.), *Tudor Rule and Revolution: Essays for G.R. Elton from His American Friends* (Cambridge University Press, 1982), pp. 25–43

Mediae Latinitatis Lexicon Minus, ed. J.F. Niermeyer and C. van de Kieft, revised by J.W.J. Burgers (Leiden and Boston: Brill, 2002)

Meier, T., 'Königs- und Kaiserbegräbnisse im Spätmittelalter', *ZhF* 29 (2002), 323–38

Meinecke, F., *Cosmopolitanism and the National State*, English trans. by R.B. Kimber (Princeton University Press, 1970)

Meisen, K., 'Niederland und Oberland', *RhVjbl* 15/16 (1950/51), 417–64

Melton, J. van Horn, 'From folk history to structural history: Otto Brunner (1898–1982) and the radical-conservative roots of German social history', in H. Lehmann and J. van Horn Melton (eds.), *Paths of Continuity: Central European Historiography from the 1930s to the 1950s* (Cambridge University Press, 1994), pp. 263–97

Melve, L., *Inventing the Public Sphere: The Public Debate During the Investiture Contest (c. 1030–1122)*, 2 vols. (Leiden and Boston: Brill, 2007)

Menache, S., 'Symbols and national stereotypes in the Hundred Years War', in S. Menache, *The Vox Dei: Communications in the Middle Ages* (Oxford University Press, 1990), pp. 191–209

Mentgen, G., 'Die Pest-Pandemie und die Judenpogrome der Jahre 1348–1350/1351', in Puhle and Hasse (eds.), *Heiliges Römisches Reich: Essays*, pp. 299–309

Davies, R.R., *The First English Empire: Power and Identities in the British Isles 1093–1343* (Oxford University Press, 2000)

'The medieval state: the tyranny of a concept?', *Journal of Historical Sociology* 16 (2003), 280–300

'The peoples of Britain and Ireland 1100–1400 (I): identities', *TRHS* 6th ser., 4 (1994), 1–20

'The peoples of Britain and Ireland 1100–1400 (II): names, boundaries and regnal solidarities', *TRHS* 6th ser., 5 (1995), 1–20

'The peoples of Britain and Ireland 1100–1400 (III): laws and customs', *TRHS* 6th ser., 6 (1996), 1–23

'The peoples of Britain and Ireland 1100–1400 (IV): language and historical mythology', *TRHS* 6th ser., 7 (1997), 1–24

De Boer, D.E.H., 'Ludwig the Bavarian and the scholars', in J.W. Drijvers and A.A. MacDonald (eds.), *Centres of Learning: Learning and Location in Pre-Modern Europe and the Near East* (Leiden: Brill, 1995), pp. 229–44

Demandt, A. (ed.), *Deutschlands Grenzen in der Geschichte* (Munich: Beck, 1990)

Demandt, K.E., 'Der Endkampf des staufischen Kaiserhauses im Rhein-Maingebiet', *Hessisches Jahrbuch für Landesgeschichte* 7 (1957), 102–64

Demetz, P., *Prague in Black and Gold: The History of a City* (London: Allen Lane, 1997)

Dempf, A., *Sacrum Imperium: Geschichts- und Staatsphilosophie des Mittelalters und der politischen Renaissance* (Munich: Oldenbourg, 1929)

Denton, J.H., *Philip the Fair and the Ecclesiastical Assemblies of 1294–1295* (Transactions of the American Philosophical Society 81, Philadelphia: American Philosophical Society, 1991)

Dictionary of Medieval Latin from British Sources, ed. R.E. Latham (London: British Academy, 1975–)

Dienst, H., 'Ostarrîchi – Oriens – Austria: Probleme "österreichischer" Identität im Hochmittelalter', in R.G. Plaska, G. Stourzh and J.P. Niederkorn (eds.), *Was heißt Österreich? Inhalt und Umfang des Österreichbegriffs vom 10. Jahrhundert bis heute* (Vienna: Österreichische Akademie der Wissenschaften, 1995), pp. 35–50

Dollinger, P., *The German Hansa*, trans. and ed. D.S. Ault and S.H. Steinberg (Stanford, CA: Stanford University Press, 1964)

Dove, A., *Der Wiedereintritt des nationalen Prinzips in die Weltgeschichte* (Akademische Festrede zur Stiftungsfeier und Preisvertheilung in der Aula der Universität Bonn, gehalten am 3. August 1890, Bonn: Emil Strauß, 1890)

Drabek, A.M., *Reisen und Reisezeremoniell der römisch-deutschen Herrscher im Spätmittelalter* (Vienna: Geyer, 1964)

Droege, G., *Landrecht und Lehnrecht im hohen Mittelalter* (Bonn: Röhrscheid, 1969)

Drossbach, G., 'Neue Forschungen zur spätmittelalterlichen Rezeptions-geschichte Konrads von Megenberg', *ZbLg* 72 (2009), 1–17

Du Boulay, F.R.H., 'The forming of German identity', *History Today* 40 (1990), 14–21

'The German town chroniclers', in R.H.C. Davis and J.M. Wallace-Hadrill (eds.), *The Writing of History in the Middle Ages: Essays Presented*

to Richard William Southern (Oxford: Clarendon Press, 1981), pp.
    445–69
Germany in the Later Middle Ages (London: Athlone, 1983)
Dümmler, E., 'Über den furor Teutonicus', Sitzungsberichte der Preussischen
    Akademie der Wissenschaften zu Berlin (phil.-hist. Klasse) 9 (1897),
    112–26
Dunbabin, J., 'Aristotle in the schools', in B. Smalley (ed.), Trends in Medieval
    Political Thought (Oxford: Blackwell, 1965), pp. 65–85
Duncan, A.A.M., The Nation of Scots and the Declaration of Arbroath (1320)
    (London: Historical Association, 1970)
Dunk, T.H. von der, Das Deutsche Denkmal: eine Geschichte in Bronze und Stein
    vom Hochmittelalter bis zum Barock (Cologne, Weimar and Vienna: Böhlau,
    1999)
Dygo, M., 'The political role of the cult of the Virgin Mary in Teutonic Prussia
    in the fourteenth and fifteenth centuries', Journal of Medieval History 15
    (1989), 63–80
Eberhard, W., 'Herrschaft und Raum – Zum Itinerar Karls IV.', in Seibt (ed.),
    Kaiser Karl IV., pp. 101–8
'Ost und West: Schwerpunkte der Königsherrschaft bei Karl IV.', ZhF 8
    (1981), 13–24
Ebner, A., Quellen und Forschungen zur Geschichte und Kunstgeschichte des Missale
    Romanum im Mittelalter (Freiburg im Breisgau: Herder, 1896)
Eckert, W.P., 'Die Juden im Zeitalter Karls IV.', in Seibt (ed.), Kaiser Karl IV.,
    pp. 123–30
Eggert, W., 'Bemerkungen zur Intitulatio in den Urkunden Karls IV.', in
    Lindner, Müller-Mertens and Rader (eds.), Kaiser, Reich und Region, pp.
    295–311
Ehlers, C., Metropolis Germaniae: Studien zur Bedeutung Speyers für das Königtum
    (751–1250) (Göttingen: Vandenhoeck & Ruprecht, 1996)
Ehlers, J. (ed.), Ansätze und Diskontinuität deutscher Nationsbildung im Mittelalter
    (Sigmaringen: Thorbecke, 1989)
'Die deutsche Nation des Mittelalters als Gegenstand der Forschung', in
    Ehlers (ed.), Ansätze, pp. 11–58
(ed.), Deutschland und der Westen Europas im Mittelalter (VuF 56, Stuttgart:
    Thorbecke, 2002)
'Elemente mittelalterlicher Nationsbildung in Frankreich (10.–13.
    Jahrhundert)', HZ 231 (1980), 565–87
Die Entstehung des deutschen Reiches (Munich: Oldenbourg, 1994)
'Imperium und Nationsbildung im europäischen Vergleich', in Schneidmüller
    and Weinfurter (eds.), Heilig – Römisch – Deutsch, pp. 101–18.
Die Kapetinger (Stuttgart: Kohlhammer, 2000)
'Methodische Überlegungen zur Entstehung des deutschen Reiches im
    Mittelalter und zur nachwanderzeitlichen Nationenbildung', in Brühl and
    Schneidmüller (eds.), Beiträge, pp. 3–13
'Nation und Geschichte: Anmerkungen zu einem Versuch', ZhF 11 (1984)
Eichelberger, T., Patria: Studien zur Bedeutung des Wortes im Mittelalter (6.–12.
    Jahrhundert) (Nationes 9, Sigmaringen: Thorbecke, 1991)

Eley, G., 'Nations, publics, and political cultures: placing Habermas in the nineteenth century', in C. Calhoun (ed.), *Habermas and the Public Sphere* (Cambridge, MA: MIT Press, 1992), pp. 289–339

Elias, N., *The Germans: Power Struggles and the Development of Habitus in the Nineteenth and Twentieth Centuries*, trans. and with preface by E. Dunning and S. Mennell (Cambridge: Polity, 1996)

Elze, R., 'Die "Eiserne Krone" in Monza', in Schramm, *Herrschaftszeichen und Staatssymbolik*, vol. II, pp. 450–79

Engel, J. (ed.), *Großer historischer Weltatlas: Zweiter Teil – Mittelalter*, 2nd edn (Munich: Bayerischer Schulbuch-Verlag, 1979)

Engels, O., 'Der Reichsgedanke auf dem Konstanzer Konzil', *HJb* 86 (1966), 80–106

Eriksen, T.H., *Ethnicity and Nationalism*, 2nd edn (London and New York: Pluto Press, 2002)

Erkens, F.-R., *Kurfürsten und Königswahl: zu neuen Theorien über den Königswahlparagraphen im Sachsenspiegel und die Entstehung des Kurfürsten-kollegiums* (MGH Studien und Texte 30, Hannover: Hahn, 2002)

Siegfried von Westerburg (1274–1297): die Reichs- und Territorialpolitik eines Kölner Erzbischofs im ausgehenden 13. Jahrhundert (Bonn: Röhrscheid, 1982)

'Zwischen staufischer Tradition und dynastischer Orientierung: Das Königtum Rudolfs von Habsburg', in E. Boshof and F.-R. Erkens (eds.), *Rudolf von Habsburg 1273–1291: eine Königsherrschaft zwischen Tradition und Wandel* (Cologne, Weimar and Vienna: Böhlau, 1993), pp. 33–58

Ertl, T., 'Alte Thesen und neue Theorien zur Entstehung des Kurfürstenkollegiums', *ZhF* 30 (2003), 619–42

Eubel, K., 'Die Minoriten Heinrich Knoderer und Konrad Probus', in *HJb* 9 (1888), 393–449

Evans, R.J.W., 'Frontiers and national identities in Central Europe', *International History Review* 14 (1992), 480–502

Ewig, E., 'Zum lothringischen Dukat der Kölner Erzbischöfe', in *Aus Geschichte und Landeskunde: Franz Steinbach zum 65. Geburtstag* (Bonn: Röhrscheid, 1960), pp. 210–46

Fahlbusch, M., 'Die "Südostdeutsche Forschungsgemeinschaft": Politische Beratung und NS-Volkstumspolitik', in W. Schulze and O.G. Oexle (eds.), *Deutsche Historiker im Nationalsozialismus* (Frankfurt am Main: Fischer, 1999), pp. 241–64

Fajt, J., 'Karl IV. – Herrscher zwischen Prag und Aachen', in Kramp (ed.), *Krönungen*, vol. II, pp. 489–500

Faulstich, W., *Medien und Öffentlichkeit im Mittelalter 800–1400* (Göttingen: Vandenhoeck & Ruprecht, 1996)

Feine, H.E., *Tausend Jahre deutscher Reichssehnsucht und Reichswirklichkeit* (Cologne: Schaffstein, 1935)

Ferguson, W.K., *The Renaissance in Historical Thought: Five Centuries of Interpretation* (Cambridge, MA: Houghton Mifflin, 1948)

Feuchtmüller, R., 'Die "Imitatio" Karls IV. in den Stiftungen der Habsburger', in Seibt (ed.), *Kaiser Karl IV.*, pp. 378–86

Fichtenau, H., 'Herkunft und Bedeutung der Babenberger im Denken späterer Generationen', *MIöG* 84 (1976), 1–30

Fillitz, H., 'Die Reichskleinodien', in Kramp (ed.), *Krönungen*, vol. I, pp. 141–9

Finke, H., *Weltimperialismus und nationale Regungen im späteren Mittelalter* (Rede gehalten bei der Jahresfeier der Freiburger Wissenschaftlichen Gesellschaft am 28. Okt. 1916, Freiburg im Breisgau and Leipzig: Speyer & Kaerner, 1916)

Fischer, M., *'Di Himels Rote': The Idea of Christian Chivalry in the Chronicles of the Teutonic Order* (Göppingen: Kümmerle, 1991)

Fleckenstein, J., *Early Medieval Germany*, trans. B.S. Smith (Amsterdam: North-Holland, 1978)

Fletcher, R., *The Conversion of Europe: From Paganism to Christianity 371–1386 AD* (London: HarperCollins, 1997)

Flint, V.I.J., 'Honorius Augustodunensis of Regensburg', in P.J. Geary (ed.), *Authors of the Middle Ages: Historical and Religious Writers of the Latin West*, vol. II (Aldershot: Variorum, 1995), pp. 95–183

Foester, T., *Vergleich und Identität: Selbst- und Fremddeutung im Norden des hochmittelalterlichen Europa* (Berlin: Akademie, 2009)

Fögen, M.T., 'Römisches Recht und Rombilder im östlichen und westlichen Mittelalter', in Schneidmüller and Weinfurter (eds.), *Heilig – Römisch – Deutsch*, pp. 57–83

Folz, R., *The Concept of Empire in Western Europe from the Fifth to the Fourteenth Century*, trans. S.A. Ogilvie (London: Arnold, 1969)

Le Souvenir et la légende de Charlemagne dans l'Empire germanique médiéval (Paris: Les Belles Lettres, 1950)

Foot, S., 'The historiography of the Anglo-Saxon "nation-state"', in Scales and Zimmer (eds.), *Power and the Nation*, pp. 125–42

'The making of Angelcyn: English identity before the Norman Conquest', *TRHS* 6th ser., 6 (1996), 25–50

Forde, S., Johnson, L. and Murray, A.V. (eds.), *Concepts of National Identity in the Middle Ages* (University of Leeds, 1995)

Fößel, A., 'Die deutsche Tradition von Imperium im späten Mittelalter', in F. Bosbach and H. Hiery (eds.), *Imperium / Empire / Reich: ein Konzept politischer Herrschaft im deutsch-britischen Vergleich* (Munich: Saur, 1999), pp. 17–30

Fournier, P., *Le Royaume d'Arles et de Vienne (1138–1378): Étude sur la formation territoriale de la France dans l'Est et le Sud-Est* (Paris: Picard, 1891)

Fowler, G.B., *Intellectual Interests of Engelbert of Admont* (New York: Columbia University Press, 1947)

Fraesdorff, D., *Der barbarische Norden: Vorstellungen und Fremdheitskategorien bei Rimbert, Thietmar von Merseburg, Adam von Bremen und Helmold von Bosau* (Berlin: Akademie, 2005)

Frame, R., '"Les Engleys néeys en Irlande": the English political identity in medieval Ireland', *TRHS*, 6th ser., 3 (1993), 83–103

Franke, M.E., *Kaiser Heinrich VII. im Spiegel der Historiographie* (Cologne, Weimar and Vienna: Böhlau, 1992)

Fräss-Ehrfeld, C., *Geschichte Kärntens*, vol. I (Klagenfurt: Heyn, 1984)

Freed, J.B., *The Friars and German Society in the Thirteenth Century* (Cambridge, MA: Medieval Academy of America, 1977)

Frey, B., 'Karl IV. in der älteren Historiographie', in Seibt (ed.), *Kaiser Karl IV.*, pp. 399–404

Pater Bohemiae – Vitricus Imperii; Böhmens Vater, Stiefvater des Reichs: Kaiser Karl IV. in der Geschichtsschreibung (Bern: Lang, 1978)

Fricke, E., *Die westfälische Veme im Bild: Geschichte, Verbreitung und Einfluss der westfälischen Vemegerichtsbarkeit* (Münster: Aschendorff, 2002)

Fried, J., *Der Weg in die Geschichte: die Ursprünge Deutschlands bis 1024* (Berlin: Propyläen, 1994)

Fried, T., 'Schnöder Mammon oder Repräsentationsobjekt? Kaiserliche und kurfürstliche Münzen zu Zeiten der Goldenen Bulle', in Hohensee, Lawo, Lindner *et al.* (eds.), *Die Goldene Bulle*, vol. I, pp. 465–91

Friedland, K., 'Ostsee und Osteuropa im Weltbild des 13. Jahrhunderts', in E. Hübner, E. Klug and J. Kusber (eds.), *Zwischen Christianisierung und Europäisierung: Beiträge zur Geschichte Osteuropas im Mittelalter und früher Neuzeit. Fs für Peter Nitsche zum 65. Geburtstag* (Stuttgart: Steiner, 1998), pp. 17–21

Friedman, J.B., *The Monstrous Races in Medieval Art and Thought* (Cambridge, MA: Harvard University Press, 1981)

Fuhrmann, H., *Germany in the High Middle Ages c.1050–1200*, trans. T. Reuter (Cambridge University Press, 1986)

'"Quis constituit Teutonicos iudices nationum?": the trouble with Henry', *Speculum* 69 (1994), 344–58

Fuhrmann, M., *Alexander von Roes: Ein Wegbereiter des Europagedankens?* (Sitzungsberichte der Heidelberger Akademie der Wissenschaften, Philosophisch-Historische Klasse, 1994, Bericht 4, Heidelberg: Winter, 1994)

Fulbrook, M., *German National Identity After the Holocaust* (Oxford: Polity, 1999)

Funder, A., *Reichsidee und Kirchenrecht: Dietrich von Nieheim als Beispiel spätmittelalterlicher Rechtsauffassung* (Freiburg, Basel and Vienna: Herder, 1993)

Funke, B., *Cronecken der Sassen: Entwurf und Erfolg einer sächsischen Geschichtskonzeption am Übergang vom Mittelalter zur Neuzeit* (Braunschweig: Stadtbibliothek Braunschweig, 2001)

Gabriele, M. and Stuckey, J. (eds.), *The Legend of Charlemagne in the Middle Ages: Power, Faith, and Crusade* (New York: Palgrave Macmillan, 2008)

Galbraith, V.H., 'Nationality and language in medieval England', *TRHS*, 4th ser. 23 (1941), 113–28

Garrison, M., 'Divine election for nations – a difficult rhetoric for medieval scholars?', in L.B. Mortensen (ed.), *The Making of Christian Myths in the Periphery of Latin Christendom (c. 1000–1300)* (Copenhagen: Museum Tusculanum Press, 2006), pp. 275–314

Geary, P.J., 'Ethnic identity as a situational construct in the early Middle Ages', *Mitteilungen der anthropologischen Gesellschaft in Wien* 113 (1983), 15–26

The Myth of Nations: The Medieval Origins of Europe (Princeton University Press, 2002)

Phantoms of Remembrance: Memory and Oblivion at the End of the First Millennium (Princeton University Press, 1994)

Geith, K.-E., *Carolus Magnus: Studien zur Darstellung Karls des Großen in der deutschen Literatur des 12. und 13. Jahrhunderts* (Bern: Francke, 1977)

Gellner, E., *Nations and Nationalism* (Oxford: Basil Blackwell, 1983)

Genet, J.-P., 'La typologie de l'État Moderne, le droit, l'espace', in N. Coulet and J.-P. Genet (eds.), *L'État Moderne: le droit, l'espace et les formes de l'État: Actes du colloque tenu à la Baume Les Aix 11–12 octobre 1984* (Paris: Centre National de la Recherche Scientifique, 1990), pp. 7–17

Gerlich, A., *Geschichtliche Landeskunde des Mittelalters: Genese und Probleme* (Darmstadt: Wissenschaftliche Buchgesellschaft, 1986)

Studien zur Landfriedenspolitik König Rudolfs von Habsburg (Mainz: Institut für geschichtliche Landeskunde, 1963)

Giesebrecht, W. von, 'Die Entwicklung des deutschen Volksbewußtseins', in W. von Giesebrecht, *Deutsche Reden* (Leipzig: Duncker & Humblot, 1871)

Geschichte der deutschen Kaiserzeit, 2 vols. (Braunschweig: Schwetschke, 1855–58)

Gillingham, J., 'The beginnings of English imperialism', *Journal of Historical Sociology* 5 (1992), 392–409 (reprinted in Gillingham, *The English in the Twelfth Century*)

'The context and purposes of Geoffrey of Monmouth's History of the Kings of Britain', *Anglo-Norman Studies* 13 (1990), pp. 99–118 (reprinted in Gillingham, *The English in the Twelfth Century*)

The English in the Twelfth Century: Imperialism, National Identity and Political Values (Woodbridge: Boydell, 2000)

The Kingdom of Germany in the High Middle Ages (900–1200) (London: Historical Association, 1971)

Gilman, S.L., *Difference and Pathology: Stereotypes of Sexuality, Race, and Madness* (Ithaca, NY: Cornell University Press, 1985)

Given, J., *State and Society in Medieval Europe: Gwynedd and Languedoc Under Outside Rule* (Ithaca, NY and London: Cornell University Press, 1990)

Given-Wilson, C., *Chronicles: The Writing of History in Medieval England* (London and New York: Hambledon, 2004)

Glacken, C.J., *Traces on the Rhodian Shore: Nature and Culture in Western Thought from Ancient Times to the End of the Eighteenth Century* (Berkeley, CA: University of California Press, 1967)

Gloger, B., *Kaiser, Gott und Teufel: Friedrich II. von Hohenstaufen in Geschichte und Sage* (Berlin: VEB, 1970)

Glück, H., *Deutsch als Fremdsprache in Europa vom Mittelalter bis zur Barockzeit* (Berlin and New York: De Gruyter, 2002)

Goebel, S., *The Great War and Medieval Memory: War, Remembrance and Medievalism in Britain and Germany, 1914–1940* (Cambridge University Press, 2007)

Goetz, H.-W., Jarnut, J. and Pohl, W. (eds.), *Regna and Gentes: The Relationship Between Late Antique and Early Medieval Peoples and Kingdoms in the Transformation of the Roman World* (Leiden: Brill, 2003)

Goez, W., *Translatio Imperii: ein Beitrag zur Geschichte des Geschichtsdenkens und der politischen Theorien im Mittelalter und in der frühen Neuzeit* (Tübingen: Mohr, 1958)

Gollwitzer, H., 'Zur Auffassung der mittelalterlichen Kaiserpolitik im 19. Jahrhundert', in R. Vierhaus and M. Botzenhart (eds.), *Dauer und Wandel der Geschichte: Aspekte Europäischer Vergangenheit. Festgabe für Kurt von Raumer zum 15. Dezember 1965* (Münster: Aschendorff, 1966), pp. 483–512

Goodman, A., *Margery Kempe and Her World* (London: Longman, 2002)

Gordon, D., *Making and Meaning: The Wilton Diptych* (London: National Gallery, 1993)

Górecki, P., *Economy, Society, and Lordship in Medieval Poland 1100–1250* (New York: Holmes & Meier, 1992)

Görich, K., 'Kaiser Otto III. und Aachen', in Kramp (ed.), *Krönungen*, vol. I, pp. 275–82

Görlich, P., *Zur Frage des Nationalbewußtseins in Ost-deutschen Quellen des 12. bis 14. Jahrhunderts* (Marburg/Lahn: Johann-Gottfried-Herder-Institut, 1964)

Górski, K., 'The Teutonic Order in Prussia', *Medievalia et Humanistica* 17 (1966), 20–37

Gorski, P.S., 'The mosaic moment: an early modernist critique of modernist theories of nationalism', *American Journal of Sociology* 105 (2000), 1428–68

Gouguenheim, S., 'Les Structures politiques', in M. Parisse (ed.), *De la Meuse à l'Oder: l'Allemagne au xiiie siècle* (Paris: Picard, 1994)

Graf, K., 'Souabe: identité régionale à la fin du Moyen Âge et à l'époque moderne', in Babel and Moeglin (eds.), *Identité régionale*, pp. 293–303

Grant, A., 'Aspects of national consciousness in medieval Scotland', in C. Bjørn, A. Grant and K.J. Stringer (eds.), *Nations, Nationalism and Patriotism in the European Past* (Copenhagen: Academic Press, 1994), pp. 68–95

Grau, A., *Der Gedanke der Herkunft in der deutschen Geschichtsschreibung des Mittelalters: Trojasage und Verwandtes* (Würzburg: Triltsch, 1938)

Graus, F., 'Die Ausformung mittelalterlicher Nationen im 13. Jahrhundert: Böhmen und Polen im Vergleich', *Jahrbuch für die Geschichte Mittel- und Ostdeutschlands* 41 (1993), 3–16

'Kaiser Karl IV.: Betrachtungen zur Literatur eines Jubiläumsjahres (1378/1978)', *Jahrbücher für die Geschichte Osteuropas* 28 (1980), 71–88

Lebendige Vergangenheit: Überlieferung im Mittelalter und in den Vorstellungen vom Mittelalter (Cologne and Vienna: Böhlau, 1975)

Die Nationenbildung der Westslawen im Mittelalter (Sigmaringen: Thorbecke, 1980)

Pest – Geissler – Judenmorde: das 14. Jahrhundert als Krisenzeit (Göttingen: Vandenhoeck & Ruprecht, 1987)

'Přemysl Otakar II.: Sein Ruhm und sein Nachleben', *MIöG* 79 (1971), 57–110

Green, A., *Fatherlands: State-Building and Nationhood in Nineteenth-Century Germany* (Cambridge University Press, 2001)

'Political institutions and nationhood in Germany: c.1750–c.1914', in Scales and Zimmer (eds.), *Power and the Nation*, pp. 315–32

Green, D.H., *Medieval Listening and Reading: The Primary Reception of German Literature 800–1300* (Cambridge University Press, 1994)

Greenfeld, L., *Nationalism: Five Roads to Modernity* (Cambridge, MA and London: Harvard University Press, 1992)

Grimm, J. and Grimm, W., *Deutsches Wörterbuch*, 16 vols. (Leipzig: Hirzel, 1854–1960)

Grimme, E.G., *Der Aachener Domschatz* (Düsseldorf: Schwann, 1972)

'Das gotische Rathaus der Stadt Aachen', in Kramp (ed.), *Krönungen*, vol. II, pp. 509–15

'Karl der Große in seiner Stadt', in Braunfels and Schramm (eds.), *Karl der Große*, vol. IV, pp. 229–73

Grosby, S., 'Religion and nationality in antiquity: the worship of Yahweh and ancient Israel', in A.S. Leoussi and S. Grosby (eds.), *Nationality and Nationalism*, vol. II (London and New York: Taurus, 2004), pp. 3–34

Groten, M., *Köln im 13. Jahrhundert: gesellschaftlicher Wandel und Verfassungsentwicklung* (Cologne, Weimar and Vienna: Böhlau, 1998)

'Richard von Cornwall (1257–1272)', in Kramp (ed.), *Krönungen*, vol. I, pp. 433–9

Grundmann, H., 'Das deutsche Nationalbewußtsein und Frankreich: vom Antichristspiel bis zu Alexander von Roes', *Jahrbuch der Arbeitsgemeinschaft des rheinischen Geschichtsvereins* 2 (1936), 51–60

Geschichtsschreibung im Mittelalter: Gattungen – Epochen – Eigenart, 4th edn (Göttingen: Vandenhoeck & Ruprecht, 1987)

'Politische Gedanken mittelalterlicher Westfalen', *Westfalen* 27 (1948), 5–20

'Sacerdotium – Regnum – Studium: zur Wertung der Wissenschaft im 13. Jahrhundert', *AKug* 34 (1951), 5–21

'Über die Schriften des Alexander von Roes', *DA* 8 (1950), 154–237

Wahlkönigtum, Territorialpolitik und Ostbewegung im 13. und 14. Jahrhundert (Gebhardts Handbuch der deutschen Geschichte, vol. V, Munich: dtv, 1973)

Grundmann, H. and Heimpel, H., 'Einleitung', in *Alexander von Roes: Schriften*, ed. H. Grundmann and H. Heimpel (*MG Staatsschriften* I.i, Stuttgart: Hiersemann, 1958), pp. 1–90

Guchmann, M.M., *Der Weg zur deutschen Nationalsprache*, vol. I (Berlin: Akademie, 1964)

Guenée, B., 'État et nation en France au Moyen Âge', *Rh* 237 (1967), 17–30

Histoire et culture historique dans l'occident médiéval (Paris: Aubier Montaigne, 1980)

States and Rulers in Later Medieval Europe, trans. J. Vale (Oxford: Blackwell, 1985)

The Structural Transformation of the Public Sphere: An Inquiry into a Category of Bourgeois Society, trans. T. Burger (Cambridge, MA: MIT Press, 1989)

Hageneder, O., 'Weltherrschaft im Mittelalter', *MIöG* 93 (1985), 257–78

Hale, J.R., *Artists and Warfare in the Renaissance* (London and New Haven, CT: Yale University Press, 1990)

Hallam, E.M., 'Philip the Fair and the cult of St Louis', in S. Mews (ed.), *Religion and National Identity* (Studies in Church History 18, Oxford: Blackwell, 1982), pp. 201–14

Hallam, E.M., and Everard, J., *Capetian France 987–1328*, 2nd edn (Harlow: Longman, 2001)

Haller, J., *Die Epochen der deutschen Geschichte*, rev. edn (Stuttgart: J.G. Cotta, 1935)

Hammer, W., 'The concept of the new or second Rome in the Middle Ages', *Speculum* 19 (1944), 50–62

Hampe, K. *et al.* (eds.), *Karl der Große oder Charlemagne? Acht Antworten deutscher Geschichtsforscher* (Berlin: Mittler, 1935)

Hardtwig, W., *Nationalismus und Bürgerkultur in Deutschland 1500–1914* (Göttingen: Vandenhoeck & Ruprecht, 1994)

Harvey, P.D.A., *Medieval Maps* (London: British Library, 1991)

Harvie, C., 'James Bryce', in *Oxford Dictionary of National Biography*, ed. H.C.G. Matthew and B. Harrison, vol. VIII (Oxford University Press, 2004), pp. 404–12

Haskins, C.H., 'The spread of ideas in the Middle Ages', *Speculum* 1 (1926), 19–30

Hasse, C.-P. and Puhle, M., 'Von Otto dem Grossen bis zum Ausgang des Mittelalters', in Puhle and Hasse (eds.), *Heiliges Römisches Reich: Essays*, pp. 18–31

Hastings, A., *The Construction of Nationhood: Ethnicity, Religion and Nationalism* (Cambridge University Press, 1997)

Haubrichs, W., '*Theodiscus*, deutsch und germanisch – drei Ethnonyme, drei Forschungsbegriffe', in H. Beck *et al.* (eds.), *Zur Geschichte der Gleichung "germanisch-deutsch"* (Berlin and New York: De Gruyter, 2004), pp. 199–227

Hauck, A., *Kirchengeschichte Deutschlands*, vol. V (Leipzig: Hinrichs, 1911)

Haverkamp, A., ' "… an die große Glocke hängen": Über Öffentlichkeit im Mittelalter', *Jahrbuch des Historischen Kollegs, 1995* (Munich: Oldenbourg, 1996), pp. 71–112

' "Heilige Städte" im hohen Mittelalter', in F. Graus (ed.), *Mentalitäten im Mittelalter: Methodische und inhaltliche Probleme* (VuF 35, Sigmaringen: Thorbecke, 1987), pp. 119–56

Heer, F., 'Zur Kontinuität des Reichsgedankens im Spätmittelalter', *MIöG* 58 (1950), 336–50

Hehl, E.-D., 'Die Erzbischöfe von Mainz bei Erhebung, Salbung und Krönung des Königs (10. bis 14. Jahrhundert)', in Kramp (ed.), *Krönungen*, vol. I, pp. 97–104

Heimpel, H., 'Alexander von Roes und das deutsche Selbstbewußtsein des 13. Jahrhunderts', *AKug* 26 (1935), 19–60

Deutsches Mittelalter (Leipzig: Koehler & Amelang, 1941)

Dietrich von Niem (c. 1340–1418) (Münster: Regensbergsche, 1932)

Die halbe Violine: eine Jugend in der Haupt- und Residenzstadt München (Wiesbaden: Insel, 1958)

'Königlicher Weihnachtsdienst im späteren Mittelalter', *DA* 39 (1983), 131–206

'Über den "Pavo" des Alexander von Roes', *DA* 18 (1957), 171–227

Helmrath, J., 'Probleme und Formen nationaler und regionaler Historiographie des deutschen und europäischen Humanismus um 1500', in Werner (ed.), *Spätmittelalterliches Landesbewußtsein*, pp. 333–92

Helzel, F., *Ein König, ein Reichsführer und der Wilde Osten: Heinrich I. (919–936) in der nationalen Selbstwahrnehmung der Deutschen* (Bielefeld: Transcript, 2004)

Henn, V., 'Städtebünde und regionale Identitäten im hansischen Raum', in P. Moraw (ed.), *Regionale Identität und soziale Gruppen im deutschen Mittelalter* (*ZhF* Beiheft 14, Berlin: Duncker & Humblot, 1992), pp. 41–64

Herb, G.H., *Under the Map of Germany: Nationalism and Propaganda 1918–1945* (London and New York: Routledge, 1997)

Herde, P., 'From Adolf of Nassau to Lewis of Bavaria, 1292–1347', in M. Jones (ed.), *NCMH*, vol. VI (*c. 1300–c. 1415*) (Cambridge University Press, 2000), pp. 515–50

Herkommer, H., 'Kritik und Panegyrik: zum literarischen Bild Karls IV. (1346–1378)', *RhVjbl* 44 (1980), 68–116

Herzberg-Fränkel, S., 'Geschichte des deutschen Reichskanzlei 1246–1308', *MIöG* Ergbd 1 (1885), 254–97

Herzogenberg, J. von, 'Die Bildnisse Kaiser Karls IV.', in Seibt (ed.), *Kaiser Karl IV.*, pp. 324–34

Hesse, C., 'Der Blick von außen: die Anziehungskraft der spätmittelalterlichen Universität Wien auf Studenten und Gelehrte', in K. Mühlberger and M. Niederkorn-Bruck (eds.), *Die Universität Wien im Konzert europäischer Bildungszentren, 14.–16. Jahrhundert* (Vienna and Munich: Böhlau-Oldenbourg, 2010), pp. 101–12

Higounet, C., *Die deutsche Ostsiedlung im Mittelalter*, trans. M. Vasold (Munich: dtv, 1990)

Hillenbrand, E., 'Der Geschichtsschreiber Johann von Viktring als politischer Erzieher', in H. Maurer and H. Patze (eds.), *Fs für Berent Schwineköper* (Sigmaringen: Thorbecke, 1982), pp. 437–54

Hilsch, P., 'Die Krönungen Karls IV.', in Seibt (ed.), *Kaiser Karl IV.*, pp. 108–11
'Di tutsch kronik von Behem lant: der Verfasser der Dalimilübertragung und die deutschböhmische Identität', in K. Hebers, H.H. Kortüm and C. Servatius (eds.), *Ex ipsis rerum documentis: Beiträge zur Mediävistik. Fs für Harald Zimmermann zum 65. Geburtstag* (Sigmaringen: Thorbecke, 1991), pp. 103–15

Hindin, S. A., 'Ethnische Bedeutungen der sakralen Baukunst: "deutsche" und "tschechische" Pfarrkirchen und Kapellen in Böhmen und Mähren (1150–1420)', in E. Schlotheuber and H. Seibert (eds.), *Böhmen und das Deutsche Reich: Ideen und Kulturtransfer im Vergleich (13.–16. Jahrhundert)* (Munich: Oldenbourg, 2009), pp. 1–33

Hirsch, B., 'Zur "Noticia saeculi" und zum "Pavo"; mit einem Exkurs über die Verbreitung des pseudojoachimitischen Büchleins "De semine scripturarum"', *MIöG* 38 (1920), 571–610

Hirsch, H., 'Der mittelalterliche Kaisergedanke in den liturgischen Gebeten', in H. Hirsch, *Aufsätze zur mittelalterlichen Urkundenforschung* (Cologne: Böhlau, 1965), pp. 1–20

Hirsch-Reich, B., 'Alexander von Roes Stellung zu den Prophetien', *MIöG* 67 (1959), 306–17

Hirschi, C., *Wettkampf der Nationen: Konstruktionen einer deutschen Ehrgemeinschaft an der Wende vom Mittelalter zur Neuzeit* (Göttingen: Wallstein, 2005)

Hirschmann, F.G., 'Landesbewußtsein im Westen des Reiches? Die Niederlande, die Rheinlande und Lothringen', in Werner (ed.), *Spätmittelalterliches Landesbewußtsein*, pp. 223–64

Hlaváček, I., 'The Luxemburgs and Rupert of the Palatinate, 1347–1410', in M. Jones (ed.), *NCMH*, vol. VI (*c. 1300–c. 1415*) (Cambridge University Press, 2000), pp. 551–69

Das Urkunden- und Kanzleiwesen des böhmischen und römischen Königs Wenzel (IV.) 1376–1419 (MGH Schriften 23, Stuttgart: Hiersemann, 1970)

Hlawitschka, E., 'Vom Ausklingen der fränkischen und Einsetzen der deutschen Geschichte: ein Abwägen von Kriterien', in Brühl and Schneidmüller (eds.), *Beiträge*, pp. 52–82

Hobsbawm, E.J., 'Mass-producing traditions: Europe, 1870–1914', in E. Hobsbawm and T. Ranger (eds.), *The Invention of Tradition* (Cambridge University Press, 1983), pp. 263–307

Nations and Nationalism Since 1780: Programme, Myth, Reality, 2nd edn (Cambridge University Press, 1992)

Hoen, B., *Deutsches Eigenbewußtsein in Lübeck: zu Fragen spätmittelalterlicher Nationsbildung* (Sigmaringen: Thorbecke, 1994)

Hoensch, J.K., *Die Luxemburger* (Stuttgart: Kohlhammer, 2000)

Kaiser Sigismund: Herrscher an der Schwelle zur Neuzeit, 1368–1437 (Munich: Beck, 1996)

Přemysl Otakar II. von Böhmen: der goldene König (Graz: Styria, 1989)

Hofacker, H.G., *Die schwäbischen Reichslandvogteien im späten Mittelalter* (Stuttgart: Klett-Cotta, 1980)

Hoffmann, E., 'Der Besuch Kaiser Karls IV. in Lübeck im Jahr 1375', in Paravicini (ed.), *Nord und Süd*, pp. 73–95

'Geschichtsschreibung', in E. Hoffmann, 'Lübeck im Hoch- und Spätmittelalter', in A. Graßmann, *Lübeckische Geschichte* (Lübeck: Schmidt-Römhild, 1988), pp. 298–301

Hoffmann, P., *Die bildlichen Darstellungen des Kurfürstenkollegiums von den Anfängen bis zum Ende des Hl. Römischen Reiches (13.–18. Jahrhundert)* (Bonn: Röhrscheid, 1982)

Hohensee, U., Lawo, M., Lindner, M. *et al.* (eds.), *Die Goldene Bulle: Politik – Wahrnehmung – Rezeption*, 2 vols. (Berlin: Akademie, 2009)

Hollegger, M., '"Erwachen vnd aufsten als ein starcker stryter": zu Formen und Inhalt der Propaganda Maximilians I.', in Hruza (ed.), *Propaganda*, pp. 223–34

Hopp, D.G., *Die Zunft und die Nichtdeutschen im Osten, insbesondere in der Mark Brandenburg* (Marburg/Lahn: Johann-Gottfried-Herder-Institut, 1954)

Hoppenbrouwers, P., *Medieval Peoples Imagined* (Universiteit van Amsterdam, 2005)

Hruza, K., 'Heinz Zatschek (1901–1965): "radikales Ordnungsdenken" und "gründliche, zielgesteuerte Forschungsarbeit"', in K. Hruza (ed.), *Österreichische Historiker 1900–1945* (Vienna, Cologne and Weimar: Böhlau, 2008), pp. 677–792

(ed.), *Propaganda, Kommunikation und Öffentlichkeit (11.–16. Jahrhundert)* (Vienna: Österreichische Akademie der Wissenschaften, 2002)

'Propaganda, Kommunikation und Öffentlichkeit im Mittelalter', in Hruza (ed.), *Propaganda*, pp. 9–25

Huffman, J.P., *Family, Commerce, and Religion in London and Cologne: Anglo-German Emigrants, c.1000–c.1300* (Cambridge University Press, 1998)

Hugelmann, K.G., 'Mittelalterliches und modernes Nationalitätenproblem', *Zeitschrift für Politik* 19 (1930), 734–42

'Die Rechtsstellung der Wenden im deutschen Mittelalter: ein Beitrag zum Recht der Fremdsprachigen im mittelalterlichen Deutschen Reich', *ZSSRg (GA)* 58 (1938), 214–56

Stämme, Nation und Nationalstaat im Deutschen Mittelalter (Stuttgart: Kohlhammer, 1955)

'Studien zum Recht der Nationalitäten im deutschen Mittelalter', *HJb* 47 (1927), 275–96 and 48 (1928), 565–85

Hughes, M., *Nationalism and Society: Germany 1800–1945* (London: Arnold, 1988)

Huizinga, J., 'Patriotism and nationalism in European history', in *Men and Ideas: History, the Middle Ages, the Renaissance. Essays by Johan Huizinga*, trans. J.S. Holmes and H. van Marle (London: Eyre & Spottiswoode, 1960), pp. 97–155

Husband, T., *The Wild Man: Medieval Myth and Symbolism* (New York: Metropolitan Museum of Art, 1980)

Irrgang, S., *Peregrinatio Academica: Wanderungen und Karrieren von Gelehrten der Universitäten Rostock, Greifswald, Trier und Mainz im 15. Jahrhundert* (Stuttgart: Franz Steiner, 2002)

Isenmann, E., *Die deutsche Stadt im Spätmittelalter* (Stuttgart: Ulmer, 1988)

'The Holy Roman Empire in the Middle Ages', in R. Bonney (ed.), *The Rise of the Fiscal State in Europe, c. 1200–1815* (Oxford University Press, 1999), pp. 243–80

'Kaiser, Reich und deutsche Nation am Ausgang des 15. Jahrhunderts', in Ehlers (ed.), *Ansätze*, pp. 145–246

Jackson, P., 'Christians, barbarians and monsters: the European discovery of the world beyond Islam', in P. Linehan and J.L. Nelson (eds.), *The Medieval World* (London and New York: Routledge, 2001), pp. 93–110

Jacobs, H.-J., 'Das Bild Karls des Großen in der Stadt Frankfurt im 14. Jahrhundert', in L. Saurma-Jeltsch (ed.), *Karl der Große als vielberufener Vorfahr: sein Bild in der Kunst der Fürsten, Kirchen und Städte* (Sigmaringen: Thorbecke, 1994), pp. 63–86

Janeczek, A., 'Ethnische Gruppenbildungen im spätmittelalterlichen Polen', in T. Wünsch (ed.), *Das Reich und Polen: Parallelen, Interaktionen und Formen der Akkulturation im hohen und späten Mittelalter* (VuF 59, Ostfildern: Thorbecke, 2003), pp. 401–76

Jank, D., 'Die Darstellung Ottos des Großen in der spätmittelalterlichen Historiographie', *AKuG* 61 (1979), 69–101

Janssen, W., 'Burg und Territorium am Niederrhein im späten Mittelalter', in H. Patze (ed.), *Die Burgen im deutschen Sprachraum* (VuF 19.i, Sigmaringen: Thorbecke, 1976), pp. 283–324

'Die Erzbischöfe von Köln und ihr "Land" Westfalen im Spätmittelalter', *Westfalen* 58 (1980), 82–95

'Reichsgrenzen und Vasallitäten – zur Einordnung des französisch-deutschen Grenzraums im Mittelalter', *JbwdLg* 22 (1996), 113–78

'Zu universalen und regionalen Reichskonzeptionen beim Tode Kaiser Heinrichs VII.', in H. Maurer and H. Patze (eds.), *Fs für Berent Schwineköper* (Sigmaringen: Thorbecke, 1982), pp. 415–35

Jenks, S., 'A capital without a state: Lübeck *caput tocius Hanze* (to 1474)', *Historical Research* 65 (1992), 134–49

Joachimsen, P., *Geschichtsauffassung und Geschichtsschreibung in Deutschland unter dem Einfluß der Humanismus* (Leipzig and Berlin: Teubner, 1910)

Vom deutschen Volk zum deutschen Staat: eine Geschichte des deutschen Nationalbewußtseins (Leipzig and Berlin: Teubner, 1916)

Johag, H., *Die Beziehungen zwischen Klerus und Bürgerschaft in Köln zwischen 1250 und 1350* (Bonn: Röhrscheid, 1977)

Johanek, P., 'Landesbewußtsein in Westfalen im Mittelalter', in Werner (ed.), *Spätmittelalterliches Landesbewußtsein*, pp. 265–92

'Weltchronistik und regionale Geschichtsschreibung im Spätmittelalter', in Patze (ed.), *Geschichtsschreibung*, pp. 287–330

'Zu neuen Ufern? Beobachtungen eines Zeitgenossen zur deutschen Mediävistik von 1975 bis heute', in Moraw and Schieffer (eds.), *Die deutschsprachige Mediävistik*, pp. 139–74

Johansen, P. and Mühlen, H. von zur, *Deutsch und Undeutsch im mittelalterlichen und frühneuzeitlichen Reval* (Cologne and Vienna: Böhlau, 1973)

Jones, C., *Eclipse of Empire? Perceptions of the Western Empire and Its Rulers in Late-Medieval France* (Turnhout: Brepols, 2007)

'Understanding political conceptions in the later Middle Ages: the French imperial candidatures and the idea of the nation-state', *Viator* 42.ii (2011), 1–32

Jones, W.R., 'The image of the barbarian in medieval Europe', *Comparative Studies in Society and History* 13 (1971), 376–407

Jostkleigrewe, G., *Das Bild des Anderen: Entstehung und Wirkung deutschfranzösischer Fremdbilder in der volkssprachlichen Literatur und Historiographie des 12. bis 14. Jahrhunderts* (Berlin: Akademie, 2008)

Jurek, T., 'Die Entwicklung eines schlesischen Regionalbewußtseins im Mittelalter', *Zeitschrift für Ostmitteleuropa-Forschung* 47 (1998), 21–48

Kahl, H.-D., 'Einige Beobachtungen zum Sprachgebrauch von natio im mittelalterlichen Latein mit Ausblicken auf das neuhochdeutsche Fremdwort "Nation"', in H. Beumann and W. Schröder (eds.), *Aspekte der Nationenbildung im Mittelalter: Ergebnisse der Marburger Rundgespräche 1972–1975* (Sigmaringen: Thorbecke, 1978), pp. 63–108

Kala, T., 'The incorporation of the northern Baltic lands into the western Christian world', in Murray (ed.), *Crusade and Conversion*, pp. 3–20

Kaminsky, H., *A History of the Hussite Revolution* (Berkeley and Los Angeles, CA: University of California Press, 1967)

Kaminsky, H. and Melton, J. Van Horn, 'Translators' introduction', in O. Brunner, *Land and Lordship: Structures of Governance in Medieval Austria*, English trans. (Philadelphia: University of Pennsylvania Press, 1992), pp. xiii–lxi

Kampers, F., *Die deutsche Kaiseridee in Prophetie und Sage* (Munich: Lüneburg, 1896)

'Zur "Notitia saeculi" des Alexander de Roes', in *Festgabe für Karl Theodor von Heigel* (Munich: Haushalter, 1903), pp. 105–24

Kämpf, H., *Pierre Dubois und die geistigen Grundlagen des französischen Nationalbewußtseins um 1300* (Berlin and Leipzig: Teubner, 1935)

Kannowski, B., *Die Umgestaltung des Sachsenspiegelrechts durch die Buch'sche Glosse* (MGH Schriften 56, Hannover: Hahn, 2007)

Kantorowicz, E.H., *Kaiser Friedrich der Zweite* (Berlin: Bondi, 1928)

The King's Two Bodies: A Study in Medieval Political Theology (Princeton University Press, 1957)

Karp, H.-J., *Grenzen in Ostmitteleuropa während des Mittelalters: ein Beitrag zur Entstehungsgeschichte der Grenzlinie aus dem Grenzsaum* (Cologne and Vienna: Böhlau, 1972)

Kästner, H., '"Der großmächtige Riese und Recke Theuton": etymologische Spurensuche nach dem Urvater der Deutschen am Ende des Mittelalters', *Zeitschrift für deutsche Philologie* 110 (1991), 68–97

Kaufhold, M., *Deutsches Interregnum und europäische Politik: Konfliktlösungen und Entscheidungsstrukturen 1230–1280* (MGH Schriften 49, Hannover: Hahn, 2000)

Gladius Spiritualis: das päpstliche Interdikt über Deutschland in der Regierungszeit Ludwigs des Bayern (1324–1347) (Heidelberg: Winter, 1994)

Kavka, F., 'Karl IV. (1349–1378) und Aachen', in Kramp (ed.), *Krönungen*, vol. II, pp. 477–84

Kedourie, E., *Nationalism*, 4th edn (Oxford: Blackwell, 1993)

Keen, M., *Chivalry* (New Haven, CT, and London: Yale University Press, 1984)

Keene, D., 'National and regional identities', in Marks and Williamson (eds.), *Gothic*, pp. 46–55

Keeney, B.C., 'Military service and the development of nationalism in England, 1272–1327', *Speculum* 22 (1947), 534–49

Keller, H., 'Die Einsetzung Ottos I. zum König (Aachen, 7. August 936) nach dem Bericht Widukinds von Corvey', in Kramp (ed.), *Krönungen*, vol. I, pp. 265–73

Zwischen regionaler Begrenzung und universalem Horizont: Deutschland im Imperium der Salier und Staufer 1024 bis 1250 (Berlin: Propyläen, 1986)

Kempf, F., *Papsttum und Kaisertum bei Innocenz III.: die geistigen und rechtlichen Grundlagen seiner Thronstreitpolitik* (Rome: Pontificia Università gregoriana, 1954)

Kern, F., 'Die "Abtretung" des linken Maasufers an Frankreich durch Albrecht I.', *MIöG* 31 (1910), 558–81

Die Anfänge der französischen Ausdehnungspolitik bis zum Jahr 1308 (Tübingen: Mohr, 1910)

'Die Reichsgewalt des deutschen Königs nach dem Interregnum', *HZ* 106 (1911), 39–96

Kershaw, I., *Hitler, 1889–1936: Hubris* (London: Penguin, 1998)

Kersken, N., *Geschichtsschreibung im Europa der "nationes": nationalgeschichtliche Gesamtdarstellungen im Mittelalter* (Cologne, Weimar and Vienna: Böhlau, 1995)

Kessel, V., 'Sepulkralpolitik: die Krönungsgrabsteine im Mainzer Dom und die Auseinandersetzung um die Führungsposition im Reich', *Geschichtliche Landeskunde* 45 (1997), 9–34

Keyser, E., 'Die deutsche Bevölkerung des Ordenslandes Preußen', in W. Volz (ed.), *Der Ostdeutsche Volksboden: Aufsätze zu den Fragen des Ostens*, revi. edn (Breslau: Hirt, 1926), pp. 232–43

Kienast, W., *Deutschland und Frankreich in der Kaiserzeit (900–1270): Weltkaiser und Einzelkönige*, 3 vols. (Stuttgart: Hiersemann, 1974–75)

Kiernan, V.G., 'State and nation in western Europe', *P&P* 31 (1965), 20–38

Kingsford, C.L., 'A legend of Sigismund's visit to England', *EHR* 26 (1911), 750

Kintzinger, M., *Die Erben Karls des Großen: Frankreich und Deutschland im Mittelalter* (Ostfildern: Thorbecke, 2005)

'Zeichen und Imaginationen des Reiches', in Schneidmüller and Weinfurter (eds.), *Heilig – Römisch – Deutsch*, pp. 345–71

Kirfel, H.J., *Weltherrschaftsidee und Bündnispolitik: Untersuchungen zur auswärtigen Politik der Staufer* (Bonn: Röhrscheid, 1959)

Kirn, P., *Aus der Frühzeit des Nationalgefühls: Studien zur deutschen und französischen Geschichte sowie zu den Nationalitätenkämpfen auf den Britischen Inseln* (Leipzig: Koehler & Amelang, 1943)

Politische Geschichte der deutschen Grenze, 3rd edn (Leipzig: Koehler & Amelang, 1944)

Klaniczay, G., *Holy Rulers and Blessed Princesses: Dynastic Cults in Medieval Central Europe*, trans. Éva Pálmai (Cambridge University Press, 2002)

Kleinschmidt, E., 'Die Colmarer Dominikaner-Geschichtsschreibung im 13. und 14. Jahrhundert: neue Handschriftenfunde und Forschungen zur Überlieferungsgeschichte', *DA* 28 (1972), 371–496

Herrscherdarstellung: Zur Disposition mittelalterlichen Aussageverhaltens untersucht an Texten über Rudolf I. von Habsburg (Bern and Munich: Francke, 1974)

Klemperer, V., *The Language of the Third Reich: LTI – Lingua Tertii Imperii, A Philologist's Notebook*, trans. M. Brady (London and New York: Continuum, 2006)

Kluge, B., 'Das Münzwesen des Mittelalters im Römisch-Deutschen Reich', in Puhle and Hasse (eds.), *Heiliges Römisches Reich: Essays*, pp. 373–82

Knoll, P., 'Economic and political institutions on the Polish-German frontier in the Middle Ages: action, reaction, interaction', in Bartlett and MacKay (eds.), *Medieval Frontier Societies*, pp. 151–74

Koch, G., *Auf dem Wege zum Sacrum Imperium: Studien zur ideologischen Herrschaftsbegründung der deutschen Zentralgewalt im 11. und 12. Jahrhundert* (Vienna, Cologne and Graz: Böhlau, 1972)

Koch, H., 'Jordanus von Osnabrück: Ein Beitrag zu seiner Biographie', *Osnabrücker Mitteilungen* 89 (1984), 11–24

Koht, H., 'The dawn of nationalism in Europe', *AHR* 52 (1946), 265–80

Kölmel, W., *Regimen Christianum: Weg und Ergebnisse des Gewaltenverhältnisses und des Gewaltenverständnisses (8. bis 14. Jahrhundert)* (Berlin: De Gruyter, 1970)

Kornrumpf, G., 'Heldenepik und Historie im 14. Jahrhundert: Dietrich und Etzel in der Weltchronik Heinrichs von München', in C. Gerhardt, N.F. Palmer and B. Wachinger (eds.), *Geschichtsbewußtsein in der deutschen Literatur des Mittelalters* (Tübingen: Niemeyer, 1985), pp. 88–109

Köster, G., 'Zwischen Grabmal und Denkmal: das Kaiserdenkmal für Speyer und andere Grabmonumente für mittelalterliche Könige und Kaiser im 15. und 16. Jahrhundert', in Puhle and Hasse (eds.), *Heiliges Römisches Reich: Essays*, pp. 399–409

Kötzsche, D., 'Darstellungen Karls des Großen in der lokalen Verehrung des Mittelalters', in Braunfels and Schramm (eds.), *Karl der Große*, vol. IV, pp. 157–214

Kovács, E., 'Die Heiligen und heiligen Könige der frühen Habsburger (1273–1519)', in K. Schreiner and E. Müller-Luckner (eds.), *Laienfrömmigkeit im späten Mittelalter: Formen, Funktionen, politisch-soziale Zusammenhänge* (Munich: Oldenbourg, 1992), pp. 93–126

Krahwinkler, H., 'Der Raum zwischen Adria und Drau im Früh- und Hochmittelalter', in A. Suppan (ed.), *Zwischen Adria und Karawanken* (DGOE, Berlin: Siedler, 1998), pp. 18–52

Kramp, M. (ed.), *Krönungen. Könige in Aachen – Geschichte und Mythos*, 2 vols. (Mainz: Zabern, 1999)

Krieger, K.-F., *Die Habsburger im Mittelalter: von Rudolf I. bis Friedrich III.* (Stuttgart: Kohlhammer, 1994)

König, Reich und Reichsreform im Spätmittelalter (Munich: Oldenbourg, 1992)

Die Lehnshoheit der deutschen Könige im Spätmittelalter (ca. 1200–1437) (Aalen: Scientia, 1979)

Krüger, K.H., *Die Universalchroniken* (Typologie des sources du moyen âge occidental 16, Turnhout: Brepols, 1976)

'Einleitung', in Konrad von Megenberg, *Ökonomik*, ed. S. Krüger (*MG Staatsschriften* 3.v, Stuttgart: Hiersemann, 1973–84), vol. I, pp. ix–xxxix

'Lupold von Bebenburg', in G. Pfeiffer (ed.), *Fränkische Lebensbilder*, vol. IV (Würzburg: Schöningh, 1971), pp. 49–86

'Das Rittertum in den Schriften des Konrad von Megenberg', in J. Fleckenstein (ed.), *Herrschaft und Stand: Untersuchungen zu Sozialgeschichte im 13. Jahrhundert* (Göttingen: Vandenhoeck & Ruprecht, 1977), pp. 302–28

Krynen, J., *L'Empire du roi: idées et croyances politiques en France xiiie–xve siècle* (Paris: Gallimard, 1993)

Kunze, H., 'Die Königsbilder im Strassburger Münster', *ZGORh* NF, 27 (1912), 612–39

Kurze, D., 'Nationale Regungen in der spätmittelalterlichen Prophetie', *HZ* 202 (1966), 1–23

Ladner, G., 'Formularbehelfe in der Kanzlei Kaiser Friedrichs II. und die "Briefe des Petrus de Vinea"', *MIöG* Ergbd 12 (1933), 92–198

Lamprecht, K., *Deutsche Geschichte*, 6th edn, vol. I (Berlin: Weidmann, 1920)

Larner, J., *Marco Polo and the Discovery of the World* (New Haven, CT and London: Yale University Press, 1999)

Lau, F., *Geschichte der Stadt Düsseldorf*, vol. I (*Von den Anfängen bis 1815*) (Düsseldorf: Bagel, 1921)

Lawo, M., 'Sprachen der Macht – Sprache als Macht: Urkundensprachen im Reich des 13. und 14. Jahrhunderts', in Hohensee, Lawo, Lindner et al. (eds.), *Die Goldene Bulle*, vol. I, pp. 517–50

Lawrence, C.H., *The Friars: The Impact of the Early Mendicant Movement on Western Society* (London: Longman, 1994)

Le Goff, J., 'Le désert-forêt dans l'Occident médiéval', in J. Le Goff, *L'imaginaire médiéval: Essais* (Paris: Gallimard, 1985), pp. 59–75

Le Roy Ladurie, E., *The Royal French State, 1460–1610*, trans. J. Vale (Oxford: Blackwell, 1994)

Leerhoff, G., ' "Des Reiches Herrlichkeit" – Das Mittelalterbild der deutschen Nationalgeschichtsschreibung im 19. Jahrhundert', in C. Carcenac-Lecomte (ed.), *Steinbruch: Deutsche Erinnerungsorte* (Frankfurt am Main: Lang, 2000), pp. 273–92

Legner, A. (ed.), *Die Parler und der schöne Stil 1350–1400: Europäische Kunst unter den Luxemburgern*, 3 vols. (Cologne: Museen der Stadt Köln, 1978)

Lehmann, P., 'Konstanz und Basel als Büchermärkte während der großen Kirchenversammlungen', in P. Lehmann, *Erforschung des Mittelalters: Ausgewählte Aufsätze*, vol. I (Stuttgart: Hiersemann, 1959), pp. 253–80

Leistikow, D., 'Die Aufbewahrungsorte der Reichskleinodien – vom Trifels bis Nürnberg', in *Die Reichskleinodien: Herrschaftszeichen des Heiligen Römischen Reiches* (Göppingen: Stadtarchiv, 1997), pp. 184–213

Leuschner, J., 'Karl Gottfried Hugelmann', *HZ* 191 (1960), 483–4

Levison, W., 'Zur Geschichte der Kanonissenstifter', in W. Levison, *Aus rheinischer und fränkischer Frühzeit: ausgewählte Aufsätze* (Düsseldorf: Schwann, 1948), pp. 489–516

Lhotsky, A., 'Apis Colonna: Fabeln und Theorien über die Abkunft der Habsburger: ein Exkurs zur Cronica Austrie des Thomas Ebendorfer', in H. Wagner and H. Koller (eds.), *Alphons Lhotsky, Aufsätze und Vorträge*, vol. II (Vienna: Verlag für Geschichte und Politik, 1971), pp. 6–105

Privilegium Maius: die Geschichte einer Urkunde (Munich: Oldenbourg, 1957)

Quellenkunde zur mittelalterlichen Geschichte Österreichs (*MIöG* Ergbd, 19, Graz: Böhlau, 1963)

Lhotsky, A. and Pivec, K., 'Einleitung', in Dietrich von Nieheim, *Viridarium Imperatorum et Regum Romanorum*, ed. A. Lhotsky and K. Pivec (*MG* Staatsschriften 5, Stuttgart: Hiersemann, 1956), pp. vii–xxv

Liebertz-Grün, U., *Das andere Mittelalter: erzählte Geschichte und Geschichtserkenntnis um 1300* (Munich: Fink, 1984)

'Erzählte Zeitgeschichte um 1300', in U. Liebertz-Grün (ed.), *Aus der Mündlichkeit in die Schriftlichkeit: höfische und andere Literatur, 750–1320* (Hamburg: Rohwolt, 1988), pp. 314–32

Seifried Helbling: Satiren kontra Habsburg (Munich: Beck, 1981)

Lindner, M., 'Es war an der Zeit: die Goldene Bulle in der politischen Praxis Kaiser Karls IV.', in Hohensee, Lawo, Lindner *et al.* (eds.), *Die Goldene Bulle*, vol. I, pp. 169–95

'Die Goldene Bulle Kaiser Karls IV. von 1356', in Puhle and Hasse (eds.), *Heiliges Römisches Reich: Essays*, pp. 311–21

'Kaiser Karl IV. und Mitteldeutschland', in Lindner, Müller-Mertens and Rader (eds.), *Kaiser, Reich und Region*, pp. 83–180

Lindner, M., Müller-Mertens, E. and Rader, O.B. (eds.), *Kaiser, Reich und Region: Studien und Texte aus der Arbeit an den Constitutiones des 14.*

Jahrhunderts und zur Geschichte der Monumenta Germaniae Historica (Berlin: Akademie, 1997)

Lindner, T., *Die Veme* (Paderborn: Schöningh, 1896)

Little, L.K., 'Pride goes before Avarice', *AHR* 76 (1971), 16–49

Llobera, J.R., 'State and nation in medieval France', *Journal of Historical Sociology* 7 (1994), 343–62

Lohse, G., 'Das Nachleben Karls des Großen in der deutschen Literatur des Mittelalters', in Braunfels and Schramm (eds.), *Karl der Große*, vol. IV, pp. 337–47

Loud, G.A., 'The *gens Normannorum* – myth or reality?', in *Proceedings of the Battle Conference on Anglo-Norman Studies*, vol. IV, ed. R. Allen Brown (Woodbridge: Boydell, 1982), pp. 104–16

Löwe, H., 'Karl der Große 742–814', in H. Heimpel, Th. Heuss and B. Reifenberg (eds.), *Die großen Deutschen: deutsche Biographie*, vol. I (Berlin: Propyläen, 1956), pp. 19–34

Lück, H., 'Der Sachsenspiegel als Kaiserrecht: vom universalen Geltungsanspruch eines partikularen Rechtsbuches', in Puhle and Hasse (eds.), *Heiliges Römisches Reich: Essays*, pp. 263–75

Luden, H., *Geschichte des Teutschen Volkes*, 12 vols. (Gotha: Perthes, 1825–37)

Lugge, M., *'Gallia' und 'Francia' im Mittelalter: Untersuchungen über den Zusammenhang zwischen geographisch-historischer Terminologie und politischem Denken vom 6.-15. Jahrhundert* (Bonn: Röhrscheid, 1960)

Lydon, J.F., 'Nation and race in medieval Ireland', in Forde, Johnson and Murray (eds.), *Concepts of National Identity*, pp. 103–24

Macek, J., 'Die Hofkultur Karls IV.', in Seibt (ed.), *Kaiser Karl IV.*, pp. 237–41

Machilek, F., 'Karl IV. und Karl der Große', *Zeitschrift des Aachener Geschichtsvereins* 104/5 (2002–3), 113–45

Ludolf von Sagan und seine Stellung in der Auseinandersetzung um Konziliarismus und Hussitismus (Munich: Lerche, 1967)

'Privatfrömmigkeit und Staatsfrömmigkeit', in Seibt (ed.), *Kaiser Karl IV.*, pp. 87–101

Maddicott, J.R., 'The county community and the making of public opinion in fourteenth-century England', *TRHS*, 5th ser. 28 (1978), 27–43

The Origins of the English Parliament, 924–1327 (Oxford University Press, 2010)

Mann, M., *The Sources of Social Power*, vol. I (*A History of Power from the Beginning to A.D. 1760*) (Cambridge University Press, 1986)

Marks, R. and Williamson, P. (eds.), *Gothic: Art for England 1400–1547* (London: V&A, 2003)

Markschies, A., 'Ludwig IV., der Bayer (1314–1347): Krone und Krönungen', in Kramp (ed.), *Krönungen*, vol. II, pp. 469–76

'Das Bild Rudolfs von Habsburg als "Bürgerkönig" in Chronistik, Dichtung und moderner Historiographie', *BdtLg* 112 (1976), 203–28

Die Städtepolitik Rudolfs von Habsburg (Göttingen: Vandenhoeck & Ruprecht, 1976)

Maschke, E., *Das Erwachen des Nationalbewußtseins im deutsch-slawischen Grenzraum* (Leipzig: Hinrichs, 1933)

Menzel, J.J., 'Die Akzeptanz des Fremden in der mittelalterlichen deutschen Ostsiedlung', in A. Patschovsky and H. Zimmermann (eds.), *Toleranz im Mittelalter* (VuF 45, Sigmaringen: Thorbecke, 1998), pp. 207–19

Mertens, D., 'Mittelalterbilder in der Frühen Neuzeit', in G. Althoff (ed.), *Die Deutschen und ihr Mittelalter: Themen und Funktionen moderner Geschichtsbilder vom Mittelalter* (Darmstadt: Wissenschaftliche Buchgesellschaft, 1992), pp. 29–54

'Spätmittelalterliches Landesbewußtsein im Gebiet des alten Schwaben', in Werner (ed.), *Spätmittelalterliches Landesbewußtsein*, pp. 93–156

Metzger, W., 'Greifen, Drachen, Schnabelmenschen: Heinrich der Löwe in erzählenden Darstellungen des Spätmittelalters', in J. Luckhardt and F. Niehoff (eds.), *Heinrich der Löwe und seine Zeit: Herrschaft und Repräsentation der Welfen 1125–1235*, vol. III (Munich: Hirmer, 1995), pp. 15–25

Meyer, C. and Dartmann, C., 'Einleitung', in C. Dartmann and C. Meyer (eds.), *Identität und Krise? Zur Deutung vormoderner Selbst-, Welt- und Fremderfahrungen* (Münster: Rhema, 2007), pp. 9–22

Meyer, R.J., *Königs- und Kaiserbegräbnisse im Spätmittelalter: von Rudolf von Habsburg bis zu Friedrich III.* (Cologne, Weimar and Vienna: Böhlau, 2000)

Meynen, E. (ed.), *Sudetendeutscher Atlas* (Munich: Arbeitsgemeinschaft zur Wahrung Sudetendeutscher Interessen, 1954)

Meyvaert, P., ' "Rainaldus est malus scriptor Francigenus": voicing national antipathy in the Middle Ages', *Speculum* 66 (1991), 743–63

Mieck, I., 'Deutschlands Westgrenze', in Demandt (ed.), *Deutschlands Grenzen*, pp. 197–239

Mierau, H.-J., Die Einheit des Imperium Romanum in den Papst-Kaiser-Chroniken des Spätmittelalters', *HZ* 282 (2006), 281–312

"Exkommunikation und Macht der Öffentlichkeit: Gerüchte im Kampf zwischen Friedrich II. und der Kurie', in Hruza (ed.), *Propaganda*, pp. 47–80

'Das Reich, politische Theorien und die Heilsgeschichte: Zur Ausbildung eines Reichsbewußtseins durch die Papst-Kaiser-Chroniken des Spätmittelalters', *ZhF* 32 (2005), 543–73

Mierau, H.-J., Sander-Berke, A. and Studt, B., *Studien zur Überlieferung der Flores Temporum* (MGH Studien und Texte 14, Hannover: Hahn, 1996)

Miethke, J., 'Konrads von Megenberg Kampf mit dem Drachen: der Tractatus contra Occam im Kontext', in C. Märtl, G. Drossbach and M. Kintzinger (eds.), *Konrad von Megenberg (1309–1374) und sein Werk: das Wissen der Zeit* (Munich: Beck, 2006), pp. 73–97

'Politisches Denken und monarchische Theorie: das Kaisertum als supra-nationale Institution im späteren Mittelalter', in Ehlers (ed.), *Ansätze*, pp. 121–44

'Das Publikum politischer Theorie im 14. Jahrhundert: Zur Einführung', in J. Miethke (ed.), *Das Publikum politischer Theorie im 14. Jahrhundert* (Munich: Oldenbourg, 1992), pp. 1–24

'Wirkungen politischer Theorie auf die Praxis der Politik im Römischen Reich des 14. Jahrhunderts: Gelehrte Politikberatung am Hofe Ludwigs des Bayern', in J. Canning and O.G. Oexle (eds.), *Political Thought and the Realities of Power in the Middle Ages / Politisches Denken und die Wirklichkeit der Macht im Mittelalter* (Göttingen: Vandenhoeck & Ruprecht, 1998), pp. 173–210

Miethke, J. and Flüeler, C., 'Einleitung', in *Politische Schriften Lupolds von Bebenburg*, ed. J. Miethke and C. Flüeler (*MG Staatsschriften* 4, Hannover: Hahn, 2004), pp. 1–231

Militzer, K., 'Der Erzbischof von Köln und die Krönungen der deutschen Könige (936–1531)', in Kramp (ed.), *Krönungen*, vol. I, pp. 105–11

Minkenberg, G., 'Der Aachener Domschatz und die sogenannten Krönungsgeschenke', in Kramp (ed.), *Krönungen*, vol. I, pp. 59–68

Mitteis, H., *Die deutsche Königswahl: ihre Rechtsgrundlagen bis zur Goldenen Bulle*, 2nd edn (Brünn, 1944, repr. Darmstadt: Wissenschaftliche Buchgesellschaft, 1987)

Der Staat des hohen Mittelalters: Grundlinien einer vergleichenden Verfassungsgeschichte des Lehnszeitalters, 3rd edn (Weimar: Hermann Böhlaus Nachf., 1948)

Mittelhochdeutsches Handwörterbuch, ed. Matthias Lexer, 4 vols. (1872–8, repr. Stuttgart: Hirzel, 1992)

Moeglin, J.-M., 'Dynastisches Bewußtsein und Geschichtsschreibung: zum Selbstverständnis der Wittelsbacher, Habsburger und Hohenzollern im Spätmittelalter', *HZ* 256 (1993), 593–635

'Die Genealogie der Wittelsbacher: Politische Propaganda und Entstehung der territorialen Geschichtsschreibung in Bayern im Mittelalter', *MIöG* 96 (1988), 33–54

'Die historiographische Konstruktion der Nation – "französische Nation" und "deutsche Nation" im Vergleich', in Ehlers (ed.), *Deutschland und der Westen Europas*, pp. 353–77

'Land, Territorium und Dynastie als Bezugsrahmen regionalen Bewußtseins am Beispiel Flanderns', in Werner (ed.), *Spätmittelalterliches Landesbewußtsein*, pp. 19–52

'Nation et nationalisme du Moyen Âge à l'Époque moderne (France-Allemagne)', *Rh* 301 (1999), 537–53

'Sentiment d'identité régionale et historiographie en Thuringe à la fin du Moyen Âge', in Babel and Moeglin (eds.), *Identité régionale*, pp. 325–63

Mohr, A., *Das Wissen über die Anderen: zur Darstellung fremder Völker in den fränkischen Quellen der Karolingerzeit* (Münster: Waxmann, 2005)

Mohr, W., 'Alexander von Roes: die Krise in der universalen Reichsauffassung nach dem Interregnum', in P. Wilpert (ed.), *Universalismus und Partikularismus im Mittelalter* (Berlin: De Gruyter, 1968), pp. 270–300

Möller, R., 'Köln und das "Oberländische" im Spätmittelalter', *RhVjbl* 65 (2001), 222–40

Monnet, P., 'Particularismes urbains et patriotisme local dans une ville allemande de la fin du Moyen Âge: Francfort et ses chroniques', in Babel and Moeglin (eds.), *Identité régionale*, pp. 389–400

'La Patria médiévale vue d'Allemagne, entre construction impériale et identités régionales', *Le Moyen Âge* 107 (2001), 71–99

Moore, R.I., *The Formation of a Persecuting Society: Power and Deviance in Western Europe, 950–1250* (Oxford: Blackwell, 1987)

Moraw, P., 'Bestehende, fehlende und heranwachsende Voraussetzungen des deutschen Nationalbewußtseins im späten Mittelalter', in Ehlers (ed.), *Ansätze*, pp. 99–120

'Gedanken zur politischen Kontinuität im deutschen Spätmittelalter', in Mitarbeiter des Max-Planck-Instituts für Geschichte (eds.), *Fs für Hermann Heimpel zum 70. Geburtstag am 19. September 1971* (Göttingen: Vandenhoeck & Ruprecht, 1972), vol. II, pp. 45–60

'Grundzüge der Kanzleigeschichte Kaiser Karls IV. (1346–1378)', *ZhF* 12 (1985), 11–42

'Kanzlei und Kanzleipersonal König Ruprechts', *Archiv für Diplomatik* 15 (1969), 428–531

'Kontinuität und später Wandel: Bemerkungen zur deutschen und deutschsprachigen Mediävistik 1945–1970/75', in Moraw and Schieffer (eds.), *Die deutschsprachige Mediävistik*, pp. 103–38

'Landesgeschichte und Reichsgeschichte im 14. Jahrhundert', *JbwdLg* 3 (1977), 175–91

'Das Mittelalter', in F. Prinz (ed.), *Böhmen und Mähren* (DGOE, Berlin: Siedler, 1993), pp. 24–178

'Das Mittelalter (bis 1469)', in N. Conrads (ed.), *Schlesien* (DGOE, Berlin: Siedler, 1994), pp. 38–176

'Nord und Süd in der Umgebung des deutschen Königtums im späten Mittelalter', in Paravicini (ed.), *Nord und Süd*, pp. 51–70

'Politische Sprache und Verfassungsdenken bei ausgewählten Geschichtsschreibern des deutschen 14. Jahrhunderts', in Patze (ed.), *Geschichtsschreibung*, pp. 695–726

'Reich (Das späte Mittelalter)', in O. Brunner, W. Conze and R. Koselleck (eds.), *Geschichtliche Grundbegriffe: Historisches Lexikon zur politisch-sozialen Sprache in Deutschland*, vol. V (Stuttgart: Klett Cotta, 1984), pp. 446–56

'Die Reichsregierung reist: die deutsche Kaiser von den Ottonen bis zu den Staufern ohne festen Regierungssitz', in Schultz (ed.), *Die Hauptstädte der Deutschen*, pp. 22–32

'Vom Raumgefüge einer spätmittelalterlichen Königsherrschaft: Karl IV. im nordalpinen Reich', in Lindner, Müller-Mertens and Rader (eds.), *Kaiser, Reich und Region*, pp. 61–81

Von offener Verfassung zu gestalteter Verdichtung: Das Reich im späten Mittelalter 1250 bis 1490 (Berlin: Propyläen, 1985)

'Wesenszüge der "Regierung" und "Verwaltung" des deutschen Königs im Reich (ca. 1350–1450)', in W. Paravicini and K.F. Werner (eds.), *Histoire compare de l'administration (IVe–XVIIIe siècles)* (Munich: Artemis, 1980), pp. 149–67

'Zur Mittelpunktsfunktion Prags im Zeitalter Karls IV.', in K.-D. Grothusen and K. Zernack (eds.), *Europa slavica, Europa orientalis: Fs für Herbert Ludat zum 70. Geburtstag* (Berlin: Duncker & Humblot, 1980), pp. 445–89

Moraw, P. and Schieffer, R. (eds.), *Die deutschsprachige Mediävistik im 20. Jahrhundert* (VuF 62, Ostfildern: Thorbecke, 2005)

Morrall, J.B., *Political Thought in Medieval Times*, 3rd edn (London: Hutchinson, 1971)

Morrissey, R., *L'empereur à la barbe fleurie: Charlemagne dans la mythologie et l'histoire de France* (Paris: Gallimard, 1997)

Most, R., 'Der Reichsgedanke des Lupold von Bebenburg', *Deutsches Archiv für Geschichte des Mittelalters* 4 (1941), 444–85

Motyl, A. (ed.), *Encyclopedia of Nationalism*, vol. II (*Leaders, Movements, and Concepts*) (San Diego, CA: Academic Press, 2001)

Muir, R. and Philip, G. (eds.), *Philip's Historical Atlas Mediaeval and Modern*, 6th edn (London: Philip, 1927)

Muldoon, J., *Empire and Order: The Concept of Empire, 800–1800* (Basingstoke: Macmillan, 1999)

Müller, H., 'Köln und das Reich um 1400: Anmerkungen zu einem Brief des französischen Frühhumanisten Jean de Montreuil', in H. Vollrath and S. Weinfurter (eds.), *Köln: Stadt und Bistum in Kirche und Reich des Mittelalters. Fs für Odillo Engels zum 65 Geburtstag* (Cologne, Weimar, Vienna: Böhlau, 1993), pp. 589–621

Müller, J.-D., 'Wandel von Geschichtserfahrung in spätmittelalterlicher Heldenepik', in C. Gerhardt, N.F. Palmer and B. Wachinger (eds.), *Geschichtsbewußtsein in der deutschen Literatur des Mittelalters* (Tübingen: Niemeyer, 1985), pp. 72–87

Müller, S., 'Die Königskrönungen in Aachen (936–1531): ein Überblick', in Kramp (ed.), *Krönungen*, vol. I, pp. 49–58

Müller, U., 'Sangspruchdichtung', in U. Liebertz-Grün (ed.), *Aus der Mündlichkeit in die Schriftlichkeit: Höfische und andere Literatur, 750–1320* (Deutsche Literatur: eine Sozialgeschichte, vol. I, Reinbek bei Hamburg: Rowohlt, 1988), pp. 185–92

Untersuchungen zur politischen Lyrik des deutschen Mittelalters (Göppingen: Kümmerle, 1974)

Müller, W., 'Deutsches Volk und deutsches Land im späteren Mittelalter', *HZ* 132 (1925), 450–65

'Nationaler Name und nationales Bewußtsein der Deutschen vom Ende des XIII. bis zum Ausgang des XV. Jahrhunderts', unpublished DPhil thesis, Universität Heidelberg (1923)

Müller-Mertens, E., 'Constitutiones et acta publica – Paradigmenwechsel und Gestaltungsfragen einer Monumenta-Reihe', in Lindner, Müller-Mertens and Rader (eds.), *Kaiser, Reich und Region*, pp. 1–59

'Frankenreich oder Nicht-Frankenreich? Überlegungen zum Reich der Ottonen anhand des Herrschertitels und der politischen Struktur des Reiches', in Brühl and Schneidmüller (eds.), *Beiträge*, pp. 45–52

'Imperium und Regnum im Verhältnis zwischen Wormser Konkordat und Goldener Bulle: Analyse und neue Sicht im Lichte der Konstitutionen', *HZ* 284 (2007), 561–95

Regnum Teutonicum: Aufkommen und Verbreitung der deutschen Reichs- und Königsauffassung im frühen Mittelalter (Vienna, Cologne and Graz: Böhlau, 1970)

'Römisches Reich im Besitz der Deutschen, der König an Stelle des Augustus: Recherche zur Frage: seit wann wird das mittelalterlich-frühneuzeitliche Reich von den Zeitgenossen als römisch und deutsch begriffen?', *HZ* 282 (2006), 1–58

'Vom Regnum Teutonicum zum Heiligen Römischen Reich Deutscher Nation: Reflexionen über die Entwicklung des deutschen Staates im Mittelalter', *Zeitschrift für Geschichtswissenschaft* 11 (1963), 319–46

Münkler, H. and Grünberger, H., 'Enea Silvio Piccolominis Anstösse zur Entdeckung der nationalen Identität der "Deutschen"', in Münkler, Grünberger and Mayer, *Nationenbildung*, pp. 163–233

'Origo et Vetustas: Herkunft und Alter als Topoi nationaler Identität', in Münkler, Grünberger and Mayer, *Nationenbildung*, pp. 235–61

Münkler, H., Grünberger, H. and Mayer, K., *Nationenbildung: die Nationalisierung Europas im Diskurs humanistischer Intellektueller. Italien und Deutschland* (Berlin: Akademie, 1998)

Murray, A., *Reason and Society in the Middle Ages* (Oxford: Clarendon Press, 1987)

Murray, A.V. (ed.), *Crusade and Conversion on the Baltic Frontier 1150–1500* (Aldershot: Ashgate, 2001)

Myers, A.R., *Parliaments and Estates in Europe to 1789* (London: Thames & Hudson, 1975)

Näf, W., 'Frühformen des "Modernen Staates" im Spätmittelalter', *HZ* 171 (1951), 225–43

Němec, R., 'Herrscher – Kunst – Metapher: das ikonografische Programm der Residenzburg Lauf an der Pegnitz als eine Quelle der Herrschaftsstrategie Karls IV.', in Hohensee, Lawo, Lindner *et al.* (eds.), *Die Goldene Bulle*, vol. I, pp. 369–401

Nicholas, D., *The Northern Lands: Germanic Europe, c. 1270–c. 1500* (Chichester: Wiley-Blackwell, 2009)

Niederstätter, A., *Die Herrschaft Österreich: Fürst und Land im Spätmittelalter* (Österreichische Geschichte 1278–1411, ed. Herwig Wolfram, Vienna: Ueberreuter, 2001)

Nijsten, G., *In the Shadow of Burgundy: The Court of Guelders in the Late Middle Ages*, trans. T. Guest (Cambridge University Press, 2004)

Niklis, H.-W., 'Von der "Grenitze" zur Grenze: die Grenzidee des lateinischen Mittelalters (6.–15. Jhdt.)', *BdtLg* 128 (1992), 1–27

Nikolay, W., *Die Ausbildung der ständischen Verfassung in Geldern und Brabant während des 13. und 14. Jahrhunderts: ein Beitrag zur Entstehung und Konsolidierung mittelalterlicher Territorien im Nordwesten des alten deutschen Reiches* (Bonn: Röhrscheid, 1985)

Nikolay-Panter, M., 'Terra und Territorium in Trier an der Wende vom Hoch- zum Spätmittelalter', *RhVjbl* 47 (1983), 67–123

Nilgen, U., 'Herrscherbild und Herrschergenealogie der Stauferzeit', in Kramp (ed.), *Krönungen*, vol. I, pp. 357–67

Nonn, U., 'Heiliges Römisches Reich Deutscher Nation: zum Nationen-Begriff im 15. Jahrhundert', *ZhF* 9 (1982), 129–42

Noodt, B., *Religion und Familie in der Hansestadt Lübeck anhand der Bürgertestamente des 14. Jahrhunderts* (Lübeck: Schmidt Römhild, 2000)

Nussbaum, N., *German Gothic Church Architecture*, trans. S. Kleager (New Haven, CT and London: Yale University Press, 2000)

Oberkrome, W., *Volksgeschichte: methodische Innovation und völkische Ideologisierung in der deutschen Geschichtswissenschaft 1918–1945* (Göttingen: Vandenhoeck & Ruprecht, 1993)

Oexle, O.G., 'German malaise of modernity: Ernst H. Kantorowicz and his "Kaiser Friedrich der Zweite"', in R.L. Benson and J. Fried (eds.), *Ernst Kantorowicz* (Stuttgart: Steiner, 1997), pp. 33–56

'The Middle Ages through modern eyes: a historical problem', *TRHS* 6th ser., 9 (1999), 121–42

'"Staat" – "Kultur" – "Volk": deutsche Mittelalterhistoriker auf der Suche nach der historischen Wirklichkeit 1918–1945', in Moraw and Schieffer (eds.), *Die deutschsprachige Mediävistik*, pp. 63–101

Offler, H.S., 'England and Germany at the beginning of the Hundred Years War', *EHR* 54 (1939), 608–31

'Empire and papacy: the last struggle', *TRHS* 5th ser., 6 (1956), 21–47

'The "influence" of Ockham's political thinking: the first century', in H.S. Offler, *Church and Crown in the Fourteenth Century: Studies in European History and Political Thought*, ed. A.I. Doyle (Aldershot: Ashgate, 2000), pp. 338–65

'The origins of Ockham's *Octo Quaestiones*', *EHR* 82 (1967), 323–32

Opll, F., *Das Itinerar Kaiser Friedrich Barbarossas (1152–1190)* (Vienna, Cologne, Graz: Böhlaus Nachf., 1978)

Orth, E., 'München und die Reichsstädte: Ludwig IV. im Kampf mit dem Papsttum', in Schultz (ed.), *Die Hauptstädte der Deutschen*, pp. 57–66

Page, G., *Being Byzantine: Greek Identity Before the Ottomans* (Cambridge University Press, 2008)

Paravicini, W., 'The court of the dukes of Burgundy: a model for Europe?', in R.G. Asch and A.M. Birke (eds.), *Princes, Patronage and the Nobility: The Court at the Beginning of the Modern Age c. 1450–1650* (Oxford University Press, 1991), pp. 69–102

(ed.), *Nord und Süd in der deutschen Geschichte des Mittelalters* (Sigmaringen: Thorbecke, 1990)

Partner, P., *The Lands of St Peter: The Papal State in the Middle Ages and the Early Renaissance* (London: Eyre Methuen, 1972)

Patschovsky, A., 'The holy emperor Henry "the First" as one of the dragon's heads of apocalypse: on the image of the Roman Empire under German rule in the tradition of Joachim of Fiore', *Viator* 29 (1998), 291–322

Patze, H. (ed.), *Geschichtsschreibung und Geschichtsbewußtsein im späten Mittelalter* (Sigmaringen: Thorbecke, 1987)

'Die Herrschaftspraxis der deutschen Landesherren während des späten Mittelalters', in W. Paravicini and K.F. Werner (eds.), *Histoire compare de l'administration (IVe–XVIIIe siècles)* (Munich: Artemis, 1980), pp. 363–91

'Mäzene der Landesgeschichtsschreibung im späten Mittelalter', in Patze (ed.), *Geschichtsschreibung*, pp. 331–70

Pauler, R., *Die deutschen Könige und Italien im 14. Jahrhundert: von Heinrich VII. bis Karl IV.* (Darmstadt: Wissenschaftliche Buchgesellschaft, 1997)

Pauly, M., 'Der historische Hintergrund von Romfahrt und Bilderchronik', in M. Margue, M. Pauly and W. Schmid (eds.), *Der Weg zur Kaiserkrone: der Romzug Heinrichs VII. in der Darstellung Erzbischof Balduins von Trier* (Trier: Kliomedia, 2009), pp. 9–16

Pennington, K., 'Henry VII and Robert of Naples', in J. Miethke (ed.), *Das Publikum politischer Theorie im 14. Jahrhundert* (Munich: Oldenbourg, 1992), pp. 81–92

The Prince and the Law 1200–1600: Sovereignty and Rights in the Western Legal Tradition (Berkeley, CA: University of California Press, 1993)

Peters, U., *Literatur in der Stadt: Studien zu den sozialen Voraussetzungen und kulturellen Organisationsformen städtischer Literatur im 13. und 14. Jahrhundert* (Tübingen: Niemeyer, 1983)

Petersohn, J., 'Über monarchische Insignien und ihre Funktion im mittelalterlichen Reich', *HZ* 266 (1998), 47–96

Petri, F., 'Territorienbildung und Territorialstaat des 14. Jahrhunderts im Nordwestraum', in E. Ennen, A.H. von Wallther, and M. van Rey (eds.), *Franz Petri: zur Geschichte und Landeskunde der Rheinlande, Westfalen und ihrer Nachbarländer* (Bonn: Röhrscheid, 1973), pp. 392–472

Peyer, H.C., 'Die Entstehung der Eidgenossenschaft', in *Handbuch der Schweizer Geschichte*, vol. I (Zürich: Berichthaus, 1972), pp. 161–238

'Das Reisekönigtum des Mittelalters', *Vierteljahresschrift für Sozial- und Wirtschaftsgeschichte*, 51 (1964), 1–21

Pfaff, C., 'Die Münchner Minoriten: Ratgeber Ludwigs des Bayern', in R. Imbach and E. Tremp (eds.), *Zur geistigen Welt der Franziskaner im 14. und 15. Jahrhundert* (Fribourg: Universitätsverlag, 1995), pp. 45–57

Pferschy-Maleczek, B., 'Der Nimbus des Doppeladlers: Mystik und Allegorie im Siegelbild Kaiser Sigmunds', *ZhF* 28 (1996), 433–71

Pivec, K. and Heimpel, H., *Neue Forschungen zu Dietrich von Niem* (Göttingen: Vandenhoeck & Ruprecht, 1951)

Plassmann, A., *Origo gentis: Identitäts- und Legitimitätsstiftung in früh- und hochmittelalterlichen Herkunftserzählungen* (Berlin: Akademie, 2006)

Pleßner, H., *Die verspätete Nation: über die politische Verführbarkeit bürgerlichen Geistes* (Frankfurt am Main: Suhrkamp, 1974)

Pohl, W. and Reimitz, H. (eds.), *Strategies of Distinction: The Construction of Ethnic Communities, 300–800* (Leiden: Brill, 1998)

Polenz, P. von, *Geschichte der deutschen Sprache*, 10th edn (Berlin: De Gruyter, 2009)

Post, G., *Studies in Medieval Legal Thought: Public Law and the State* (Princeton University Press, 1964)

Postan, M.M., 'The trade of medieval Europe: the north', in M.M. Postan and E.E. Rich (eds.), *The Cambridge Economic History of Europe from the Decline of the Roman Empire*, vol. II (Cambridge University Press, 1952), pp. 119–256

Pounds, N.J.G., *An Economic History of Medieval Europe*, 2nd edn (London: Longman, 1994)

Power, D., 'French and Norman frontiers in the central Middle Ages', in Power and Standen (eds.), *Frontiers in Question*, pp. 105–27

Power, D. and Standen, N. (eds.), *Frontiers in Question: Eurasian Borderlands, 700–1700* (Basingstoke: Macmillan, 1999)

Powicke, M., *The Thirteenth Century 1216–1307*, 2nd edn (Oxford: Clarendon Press, 1962)

Powitz, G. and Buck, H. (eds.), *Die Handschriften des Bartholomaeusstifts und des Karmeliterklosters in Frankfurt am Main* (Frankfurt am Main: Klostermann, 1974)

Prestwich, M., *Edward I* (London: Methuen, 1988)

Prochno, J., 'Terra Bohemiae, regnum Bohemiae, corona Bohemiae', in M. Hellmann (ed.), *Corona Regni: Studien über die Krone als Symbol des Staates im späteren Mittelalter* (Darmstadt: Wissenschaftliche Buchgesellschaft, 1961), pp. 190–224

Puhle, M. and Hasse, C.-P. (eds.), *Heiliges Römisches Reich Deutscher Nation 962 bis 1806: von Otto dem Grossen bis zum Ausgang des Mittelalters*, 2 vols. (*Essays, Katalog*) (Dresden: Sandstein, 2006)

Rader, O.B., 'Aufgeräumte Herkunft: zur Konstruktion dynastischer Ursprünge an königlichen Begräbnisstätten', in Hohensee, Lawo, Lindner *et al.* (eds.), *Die Goldene Bulle*, vol. I, pp. 403–30

Zwischen Friedberg und Eco: die Interpretation von Urkundentexten Karls IV. oder vom Gang durch die Säle der Erkenntnis', in Lindner, Müller-Mertens and Rader (eds.), *Kaiser, Reich und Region*, pp. 245–93

Radke, G.M., *Viterbo: Profile of a Thirteenth Century Papal Palace* (Cambridge University Press, 1996)

Radler, G., *Die Schreinmadonna, "Vierge ouvrante"* (Frankfurt am Main: Kunstgeschichtliches Institut der Johann Wolfgang Goethe-Universität, 1990)

Ranum, O., 'Introduction', in O. Ranum (ed.), *National Consciousness, History, and Political Culture in Early Modern Europe* (Baltimore, MD: Johns Hopkins University Press, 1975), pp. 1–19

Rashdall, H., *The Universities of Europe in the Middle Ages*, vol. II.i (Oxford: Clarendon Press, 1895)

Raumer, F. von, *Geschichte der Hohenstaufen und ihrer Zeit*, 6 vols. (Leipzig: Brockhaus, 1823–25)

Redlich, O., *Rudolf von Habsburg: das deutsche Reich nach dem Untergang des alten Kaisertums* (Innsbruck, 1903, repr. Aalen: Scientia, 1965)

Reeves, M., *The Influence of Prophecy in the Later Middle Ages: A Study in Joachimism* (Oxford: Clarendon Press, 1969)

Reiffenstein, I., 'Metasprachliche Äußerungen über das Deutsche und seine Subsysteme bis 1800 in historischer Sicht', in W. Bensch, A. Betten, O. Reichmann and S. Sonderegger (eds.), *Sprachgeschichte: ein Handbuch zur Geschichte der deutschen Sprache und ihre Erforschung*, 2nd edn, vol. II.iii (Berlin and New York: De Gruyter, 2003), pp. 2205–29

Remensnyder, A.G., *Remembering Kings Past: Monastic Foundation Legends in Medieval Southern France* (Ithaca, NY and London: Cornell University Press, 1995)

Remppis, M., *Die Vorstellungen von Deutschland im altfranzösischen Heldenepos* (Halle a. S.: Karras, 1911)

Resmini, B., *Das Arelat im Kräftefeld der französischen, englischen und angiovinischen Politik nach 1250 und das Einwirken Rudolfs von Habsburg* (Cologne and Vienna: Böhlau, 1980)

Reuter, T., 'Assembly politics in western Europe from the eighth century to the twelfth', in T. Reuter, *Medieval Polities and Modern Mentalities*, ed. J.L. Nelson (Cambridge University Press, 2006), pp. 193–216

Germany in the Early Middle Ages, c. 800–1056 (London: Longman, 1991)

'Introduction: reading the tenth century', in T. Reuter (ed.), *NCMH*, vol. III (*c. 900–c. 1024*) (Cambridge University Press, 1999), pp. 1–24

'John of Salisbury and the Germans', in M. Wilks (ed.), *The World of John of Salisbury* (Studies in Church History, Subsidia 3, Oxford: Blackwell, 1984), pp. 415–25

'The making of England and Germany, 850–1050: points of comparison and difference', in A.P. Smyth (ed.), *Medieval Europeans: Studies in Ethnic Identity and National Perspectives in Medieval Europe* (Basingstoke: Macmillan, 1998), pp. 53–70

'Mandate, privilege, court judgement: techniques of rulership in the age of Frederick Barbarossa', in T. Reuter, *Medieval Polities and Modern Mentalities*, ed. J.L. Nelson (Cambridge University Press, 2006), pp. 413–31

'The medieval German *Sonderweg*? The Empire and its rulers in the high Middle Ages', in A.J. Duggan (ed.), *Kings and Kingship in Medieval Europe* (London: Kings College London, 1993), pp. 179–221

'The Ottonians and Carolingian tradition', in T. Reuter, *Medieval Polities and Modern Mentalities*, ed. J.L. Nelson (Cambridge University Press, 2006), pp. 268–83

Rexroth, F., 'Geschichte erforschen oder Geschichte schreiben? Die deutschen Historiker und ihr Spätmittelalter 1859–2009', *HZ* 289 (2009), 109–47

Reynolds, S., 'The historiography of the medieval state', in M. Bentley (ed.), *Companion to Historiography* (London and New York: Routledge, 1997), pp. 117–39

Kingdoms and Communities in Western Europe, 900–1300, 2nd edn (Oxford: Clarendon Press, 1997)

'Medieval *origines gentium* and the community of the realm', *History* 68 (1983), 375–90

'Our forefathers? Tribes, peoples, and nations in the historiography of the age of migrations', in A.C. Murray (ed.), *After Rome's Fall: Narrators and Sources of Early Medieval History: Essays Presented to Walter Goffart* (University of Toronto Press, 1998), pp. 17–36

Richards, J., *Sex, Dissidence and Damnation: Minority Groups in the Middle Ages* (London: Routledge, 1990)

Richter, K., 'Die böhmischen Länder im Früh- und Hochmittelalter', in K. Bosl (ed.), *Handbuch der Geschichte der böhmischen Länder*, vol. I (Stuttgart: Hiersemann, 1967), pp. 163–347

Ridder, P. de, 'Dynastisches und nationales Gefühl in Brabant während der Regierungszeit Herzogs Jan I. (1267–1294), des Siegers der Schlacht von Worringen', *Jahrbuch des kölnischen Geschichtsvereins* 50 (1979), 193–220

Riedmann, J., 'Deutschlands Südgrenze', in Demandt (ed.), *Deutschlands Grenzen*, pp. 166–96

'Die leere Mitte: das erste Auftreten der Habsburger', in Schultz (ed.), *Die Hauptstädte der Deutschen*, pp. 44–56

Ritscher, A., *Literatur und Politik im Umkreis der ersten Habsburger: Dichtung, Historiographie und Briefe am Oberrhein* (Frankfurt am Main: Lang, 1992)

Roberg, B., *Das zweite Konzil von Lyon (1274)* (Paderborn: Schöningh, 1990)

Robinson, I.S., *Authority and Resistance in the Investiture Contest: The Polemical Literature of the Late Eleventh Century* (Manchester University Press, 1978)

'Church and papacy', in J.H. Burns (ed.), *The Cambridge History of Medieval Political Thought c.350–c.1450* (Cambridge University Press, 1988), pp. 252–305

Rodenberg, C., 'Zur Geschichte der Idee eines deutschen Erbreiches im 13. Jahrhundert', *MIöG* 16 (1895), 1–43

Roeck, B., 'Venice and Germany: commercial contacts and intellectual inspirations', in B. Aikema and B.L. Brown (eds.), *Renaissance Venice and the North: Crosscurrents in the Time of Bellini, Dürer and Titian* (London: Thames & Hudson, 1999), pp. 44–55

Rogall, J., 'Polen vom Mittelalter bis zu den Polnischen Teilungen', in Joachim Rogall (ed.), *Land der großen Ströme: Von Polen nach Litauen* (DGOE, Berlin: Sielder, 1996), pp. 48–99

Rosario, I., *Art and Propaganda: Charles IV of Bohemia, 1346–1378* (Woodbridge: Boydell, 2000)

Roscheck, P., 'Französische Kandidaturen für den römischen Kaiserthron in Spätmittelalter und Frühneuzeit (1272/73–1519)', unpublished DPhil thesis, University of Saarbrücken (1984)

Rösener, W., 'Zur Problematik des spätmittelalterlichen Raubrittertums', in H. Maurer and H. Patze (eds.), *Fs für Berent Schwineköper* (Sigmaringen: Thorbecke, 1982), pp. 469–88

Roshwald, A., *The Endurance of Nationalism: Ancient Roots and Modern Dilemmas* (Cambridge University Press, 2006)

Rowan, S.W., 'Imperial taxes and German politics in the fifteenth century: an outline', *Central European History* 13 (1980), 203–17

Rowell, S.C., *Lithuania Ascending: A Pagan Empire Within East-Central Europe, 1295–1345* (Cambridge University Press, 1994)

Ruddick, A., 'Ethnic identity and political language in the king of England's dominions: a fourteenth-century perspective', in L. Clark (ed.), *The Fifteenth Century VI: Identity and Insurgency in the Late Middle Ages* (Woodbridge: Boydell, 2006), pp. 15–31

'National sentiment and religious vocabulary in fourteenth-century England', *Journal of Ecclesiastical History* 60 (2009), 1–18

Ruehl, M.A., '"In this time without emperors": the politics of Ernst Kantorowicz's *Kaiser Friedrich der Zweite* reconsidered', *Journal of the Warburg and Courtauld Institutes* 63 (2000), 187–242

Runciman, S., *The Sicilian Vespers: A History of the Mediterranean World in the Later Thirteenth Century* (Harmondsworth: Penguin, 1960)

Runge, K., 'Die fränkisch-karolingische Tradition in der Geschichtsschreibung des späten Mittelalters', unpublished DPhil thesis, Universität Hamburg (1965)

Russell, F.H., *The Just War in the Middle Ages* (Cambridge University Press, 1975)

Sager, A., 'Hungarians as *vremde* in medieval Germany', in A. Classen (ed.), *Meeting the Foreign in the Middle Ages* (London and New York: Routledge, 2002), pp. 27–44

Said, E.W., *Orientalism: Western Conceptions of the Orient* (Harmondsworth: Penguin, 1991)

Sauerländer, W., 'Two glances from the north: the presence and absence of Frederick II in the art of the Empire; the court art of Frederick II and the opus francigenum', in W. Tronzo (ed.), *Intellectual Life at the Court of Frederick II Hohenstaufen* (Washington, DC: National Gallery of Art, 1994), pp. 189–209

Saurma-Jeltsch, L.E., 'Karl der Große im Spätmittelalter: zum Wandel einer politischen Ikone', *Zeitschrift des Aachener Geschichtsvereins* 104/105 (2003), 421–61

'Das mittelalterliche Reich in der Reichsstädt', in Schneidmüller and Weinfurter (eds.), *Heilig – Römisch – Deutsch*, pp. 399–439

'Zeichen des Reiches im 14. und frühen 15. Jahrhundert', in Puhle and Hasse (eds.), *Heiliges Römisches Reich: Essays*, pp. 337–47

Sayer, D., *The Coasts of Bohemia: A Czech History* (Princeton University Press, 1998)

'The language of nationality and the nationality of language: Prague 1780–1920', *P&P* 153 (1996), 164–210

Scales, L.E., 'Alexander of Roes: Empire and Community in Later Thirteenth-Century Germany', unpublished PhD thesis, University of Manchester (1993)

'At the margin of community: Germans in pre-Hussite Bohemia', *TRHS*, 6th ser., 9 (1999), 327–52

'Bread, cheese and genocide: imagining the destruction of peoples in medieval western Europe', *History* 92 (2007), 284–300

'The Cambridgeshire Ragman Rolls', *EHR* 113 (1998), 553–79

'Central and late medieval Europe', in D. Bloxham and D. Moses (eds.), *Genocide: Oxford Handbook* (Oxford University Press, 2010), pp. 280–303

'France and the Empire: the viewpoint of Alexander of Roes', *French History* 9 (1995), 394–416

'*Germen militiae*: war and German identity in the later Middle Ages', *P&P* 180 (2003), 41–82

'Identifying "France" and "Germany": medieval nation-making in some recent publications', *Bulletin of International Medieval Research* 6 (2000), 21–46

'The illuminated Reich: memory, crisis, and the visibility of monarchy in late medieval Germany', in J.P. Coy, B. Marschke and D.W. Sabean (eds.), *The Holy Roman Empire, Reconsidered* (New York and Oxford: Berghahn, 2010), pp. 73–92

'Rose without thorn, eagle without feathers: nation and power in late medieval England and Germany', *German Historical Institute London Bulletin* 31 (2009), 3–35

Scales, L.E. and Zimmer, O. (eds.), *Power and the Nation in European History* (Cambridge University Press, 2005)

Scattergood, V.J., *Politics and Poetry in the Fifteenth Century* (London: Blandford Press, 1971)

Schäfer, Dietrich, *Deutsches Nationalbewußtsein im Licht der Geschichte* (Jena: Fischer, 1884)

Schäfke, Werner, *Kölns romanische Kirchen* (Cologne: DuMont, 1984)

Schaller, H.M., 'Endzeiterwartungen und Antichrist Vorstellungen in der Politik des 13. Jahrhunderts', in M. Kerner (ed.), *Ideologie und Herrschaft im Mittelalter* (Wege der Forschung 530, Darmstadt: Wissenschaftliche Buchgesellschaft, 1982), pp. 305–24

'Die Kaiseridee Friedrichs II.', in J. Fleckenstein (ed.), *Probleme um Friedrich II.* (VuF 16, Sigmaringen: Thorbecke, 1974), pp. 109–34

Schama, S., *Landscape and Memory* (London: Fontana, 1996)

Scheibe, M., 'Dynastisch orientiertes Geschichtsbild und genealogische Fiktion in der Mecklenburgischen Reimchronik des Ernst von Kirchberg', in M. Thumser (ed.), *Schriftkultur und Landesgeschichte: Studien zum südlichen Ostseeraum vom 12. bis zum 16. Jahrhundert* (Cologne, Weimar, and Vienna: Böhlau, 1997), pp. 23–61

Schenk, G.J., *Zeremoniell und Politik: Herrschereinzüge im spätmittelalterlichen Reich* (Cologne, Weimar and Vienna: Böhlau, 2003)

Schenkluhn, Wolfgang, 'Monumentale Repräsentationen des Königtums in Frankreich und Deutschland', in Kramp (ed.), *Krönungen*, vol. I, pp. 369–78

Schich, W., 'Die "Grenze" im östlichen Mitteleuropa im hohen Mittelalter', *Siedlungsforschung: Archäologie – Geschichte – Geographie* 9 (1991), 135–46

Schieffer, R., 'Weltgeltung und nationaler Verführung: die deutschsprachige Mediävistik vom ausgehenden 19. Jahrhundert bis 1918', in Moraw and Schieffer (eds.), *Die deutschsprachige Mediävistik*, pp. 39–61

Schlesinger, W., 'Die Entstehung der Nationen: Gedanken zu einem Forschungsprogramm', in Beumann and Schröder (eds.), *Aspekte der Nationenbildung*, pp. 11–62

Schlötter, P., 'Marc Bloch as a critic of the historiographical nationalism of the interwar years', in S. Berger, M. Donovan and K. Passmore (eds.), *Writing National Histories: Western Europe Since 1800* (London and New York: Routledge, 1999), pp. 125–36

Schmid, A., 'Die Hoftage Kaiser Ludwigs des Bayern', in P. Moraw (ed.), *Deutscher Königshof, Hoftag und Reichstag im späteren Mittelalter* (VuF 48, Stuttgart: Thorbecke, 2002), pp. 417–49

Schmid, W., 'Vom Rheinland nach Böhmen: Studien zur Reliquienpolitik Kaiser Karls IV.', in Hohensee, Lawo, Lindner et al. (eds.), *Die Goldene Bulle*, vol. I, pp. 431–64

Schmidt, R., 'Die Prager Universitäts-Nationen bis zum Kuttenberger Dekret von 1409 und die Anfänge "nationaler" Gedanken im Königreich Böhmen', in H. Rothe (ed.), *Deutsche in den böhmischen Ländern* (Cologne: Böhlau, 1992), pp. 47–65

'Mecklenburg und Pommern in der Reimchronik des Ernst von Kirchberg (1378)', in H. Bei der Wieden and T. Schmidt (eds.), *Mecklenburg und seine Nachbarn* (Rostock: Schmidt Römhild, 1997), pp. 69–92

Schmidt-Wiegand, R., 'Die Bilderhandschriften des Sachsenspiegels als Quelle der Kulturgeschichte', in R. Schmidt-Wiegand and D. Hüpper (eds.), *Der Sachsenspiegel als Buch* (Frankfurt am Main: Peter Lang, 1991), pp. 219–60, 464–95

'Deutsche Sprachgeschichte und Rechtsgeschichte bis zum Ende des Mittelalters', in W. Bensch, A. Betten, O. Reichmann and S. Sonderegger (eds.), *Sprachgeschichte: ein Handbuch zur Geschichte der deutschen Sprache und ihre Erforschung*, 2nd edn, vol. II.ii (Berlin and New York: De Gruyter, 2000), pp. 72–87

Schmitt, L.E., *Die deutsche Urkundensprache in der Kanzlei Kaiser Karls IV. (1346–1378)* (Tübingen: Niemeyer, 1972)

Schmugge, L., 'Kurie und Kirche in der Politik Karls IV.', in Seibt (ed.), *Kaiser Karl IV.*, pp. 73–6

'Über "nationale" Vorurteile im Mittelalter', *DA* 38 (1982), 439–59

Schneider, B., 'Geschichtswissenschaft im Nationalsozialismus: das Wirken Erich Maschkes in Jena', in T. Kaiser, S. Kaudelka and M. Steinbach (eds.), *Historisches Denken und gesellschaftlicher Wandel: Studien zur Geschichtswissenschaft zwischen Kaiserreich und deutscher Zweistaatlichkeit* (Berlin: Metropol, 2004), pp. 91–114

Schneider, F. (ed.), *Universalstaat oder Nationalstaat: Macht und Ende des Ersten deutschen Reiches (Die Streitschriften von Heinrich v. Sybel und Julius Ficker zur deutschen Kaiserpolitik des Mittelalters)*, 2nd edn (Innsbruck: Wagner, 1943)

Schneider, J., 'Die Reichsstädte', in Puhle and Hasse (eds.), *Heiliges Römisches Reich: Essays*, pp. 411–23

Schneider, R., 'Karls IV. Auffassung vom Herrscheramt', in T. Schieder (ed.), *Beiträge zur Geschichte des mittelalterlichen deutschen Kaisertums* (*HZ* Beihefte 2, NF, Munich: Oldenbourg, 1973), pp. 122–50

'Karolus qui et Wenceslaus', in K.-U. Jäschke and R. Wenskus (eds.), *Fs für Helmut Beumann* (Sigmaringen: Thorbecke, 1977), pp. 365–87

Schneidmüller, B., 'Friesen – Welfen – Braunschweiger: Träger regionaler Identität im 13. Jahrhundert', in Babel and Moeglin (eds.), *Identité régionale*, pp. 305–24

Die Kaiser des Mittelalters: von Karl dem Großen bis Maximilian I. (Munich: Beck, 2006)

'Landesherrschaft, welfische Identität und sächsische Geschichte', in P. Moraw (ed.), *Regionale Identität und soziale Gruppen im deutschen Mittelalter* (*ZhF* Beiheft 14, Berlin: Duncker & Humblot, 1992), pp. 65–101

Nomen Patriae: die Entstehung Frankreichs in der politisch-geographischen Terminologie (10.–13. Jahrhundert) (Nationes 7, Sigmaringen: Thorbecke, 1987)

'Ordnung der Anfänge: die Entstehung Deutschlands und Frankreichs in historischen Konstruktionen des Hoch- und Spätmittelalters', in W. Pohl (ed.), *Die Suche nach den Ursprüngen: von der Bedeutung des frühen Mittelalters* (Vienna: Österreichische Akademie der Wissenschaften, 2004), pp. 291–306

'Reichsnähe-Königsferne: Goslar, Braunschweig und das Reich im späten Mittelalter', *Niedersächsisches Jahrbuch für Landesgeschichte* 64 (1992), 1–52

'Sehnsucht nach Karl dem Großen: vom Nutzen eines toten Kaisers für die Nachgeborenen', *GWU* 51 (2000), 284–301

'Spätmittelalterliches Landesbewußtsein – deutsche Sonderentwicklung oder europäische Forschungslücke? Eine Zusammenfassung', in Werner (ed.), *Spätmittelalterliches Landesbewußtsein*, pp. 393–409

'Widukind von Corvey, Richer von Reims und der Wandel politischen Bewußtseins im 10. Jahrhundert', in Brühl and Schneidmüller (eds.), *Beiträge*, pp. 83–102

Schneidmüller, B. and Weinfurter, S., *Heilig – Römisch – Deutsch: das Reich im mittelalterlichen Europa* (Dresden: Sandstein, 2006)

Schnell, R., 'Deutsche Literatur und deutsches Nationalbewußtsein in Spätmittelalter und Früher Neuzeit', in Ehlers (ed.), *Ansätze*, pp. 247–319

'Lateinische und volkssprachliche Vorstellungen: zwei Fallbeispiele (Nationalbewußtsein; Königswahl)', in N. Henkel and N.F. Palmer (eds.), *Latein und Volkssprache im deutschen Mittelalter 1100–1500* (Tübingen: Max Niemeyer, 1992), pp. 123–41

Scholz, R., *Unbekannte kirchenpolitische Streitschriften aus der Zeit Ludwigs des Bayern (1327–1354): Analysen und Texte*, pt. I (Analyse) (Rome: Loescher, 1911)

Schöndorf, K.E., 'Dänische Herrschergestalten in der politischen Lyrik des deutschen Mittelalters und der frühen Neuzeit', *Collegium Medievale* 6 (1993), 35–79

Schönwälder, K., *Historiker und Politik: Geschichtswissenschaft im Nationalsozialismus* (Frankfurt am Main and New York: Campus, 1992)

Schramm, P.E., *Herrschaftszeichen und Staatssymbolik: Beiträge zu ihrer Geschichte vom dritten bis zum sechzehnten Jahrhundert*, 3 vols. (MGH Schriften 13, Stuttgart: Hiersemann, 1954–56)

Schraub, W., *Jordan von Osnabrück und Alexander von Roes: ein Beitrag zur Geschichte der Publizistik im 13. Jahrhundert* (Heidelberg: Winter, 1910)

Schreiner, K., '*Maria patrona*: la sainte vierge comme figure symbolique des villes, territoires et nations à la fin du Moyen Age et au début des temps modernes', in Babel and Moeglin (eds.), *Identité régionale*, pp. 133–53

'Die Staufer in Sage, Legende und Prophetie', in *Die Zeit der Staufer* (Stuttgart: Württembergisches Landesmuseum, 1977), vol. III, pp. 249–62

Schubert, E., ' "bauerngeschrey": zum Problem der öffentlichen Meinung im spätmittelalterlichen Franken', *JbfL* 34/5 (1975), 883–907

Einführung in die Grundprobleme der deutschen Geschichte im Spätmittelalter (Darmstadt: Wissenschaftliche Buchgesellschaft, 1992)

Fahrendes Volk im Mittelalter (Bielefeld: Verlag für Regionalgeschichte, 1995)

Fürstliche Herrschaft und Territorium im späten Mittelalter (Munich: Oldenbourg, 1996)

König und Reich: Studien zur spätmittelalterlichen deutschen Verfassungsgeschichte (Göttingen: Vandenhoeck & Rupprecht, 1979)

'Königswahl und Königtum im spätmittelalterlichen Reich', *ZhF* 4 (1977), 257–338

'Ludwig der Bayer im Widerstreit der öffentlichen Meinung seiner Zeit', in H. Nehlsen and H.-G. Hermann (eds.), *Kaiser Ludwig der Bayer: Konflikte,*

Weichenstellungen und Wahrnehmung seiner Herrschaft (Paderborn: Schöningh, 2002), pp. 163–97

'Probleme der Königsherrschaft im spätmittelalterlichen Reich: das Beispiel Ruprechts von der Pfalz (1400–1410)', in R. Schneider (ed.), *Das spätmittelalterliche Königtum im europäischen Vergleich* (Sigmaringen: Thorbecke, 1987), pp. 135–84

'Zur Konzeption des kaiserlichen Landgerichts Nürnberg: eine unbeachtete Überlieferung des Memoriale des Alexander von Roes', *JbfL* 31 (1971), 335–42

Schulin, E., *Hermann Heimpel und die deutsche Nationalgeschichtsschreibung* (Heidelberg: Winter, 1998)

Schultheiß, F.G., *Geschichte des deutschen Nationalgefühles: eine historisch-psychologische Darstellung*, vol. I (Munich and Leipzig: G. Franzschen Verlag, 1893)

Schultz, U. (ed.), *Die Hauptstädte der Deutschen: von der Kaiserpfalz in Aachen zum Regierungssitz Berlin* (Munich: Beck, 1993)

Schulze, H., *The Course of German Nationalism: From Frederick the Great to Bismarck 1763–1867*, trans. S. Hanbury-Tenison (Cambridge University Press, 1991)

States, Nations and Nationalism from the Middle Ages to the Present, trans. W.E. Yuill (Oxford: Blackwell, 1996)

Schulze, H.K., *Grundstrukturen der Verfassung im Mittelalter*, vol. III (*Kaiser und Reich*) (Stuttgart: Kohlhammer, 1998)

Schulze, W., *Deutsche Geschichtswissenschaft nach 1945* (*HZ*, Beiheft, NF 10, Munich: Oldenbourg, 1989)

Schütte, S., 'Der Aachener Thron', in Kramp (ed.), *Krönungen*, vol. I, pp. 213–22

Schütz, A., 'Der Kampf Ludwigs des Bayern gegen Papst Johannes XXII. und die Rolle der Gelehrten am Münchner Hof', in H. Glaser (ed.), *Wittelsbach und Bayern: Die Zeit der frühen Herzöge – von Otto I. zu Ludwig dem Bayern* (Munich: Hirmer, 1980), pp. 388–97

Schwarz, E., *Volkstumsgeschichte der Sudetenländer*, vol. I (Munich: Lerche, 1965)

Schwarz, J., *Herrscher- und Reichstitel bei Kaisertum und Papsttum im 12. und 13. Jahrhundert* (Cologne, Weimar and Vienna: Böhlau, 2003)

Schwedler, G., *Herrschertreffen des Spätmittelalters: Formen – Rituale – Wirkungen* (Ostfildern: Thorbecke, 2008)

Schwind, F., *Die Landvogtei in der Wetterau: Studien zu Herrschaft und Politik der staufischen und spätmittelalterlichen Könige* (Marburg: Elwertsche, 1972)

Schwinges, R.C., 'Admission', in H. de Ridder-Symoens (ed.), *A History of the University in Europe*, vol. I (*Universities in the Middle Ages*), (Cambridge University Press, 1992), pp. 171–94

'On recruitment in German universities from the fourteenth to the sixteenth centuries', in W.J. Courtenay and J. Miethke (eds.), *Universities and Schooling in Medieval Society* (Leiden: Brill, 2000), pp. 32–48

'"Primäre" und "sekundäre" Nation: Nationalbewußtsein und sozialer Wandel im mittelalterlichen Böhmen', in K.-D. Grothusen and K. Zernack (eds.), *Europa slavica – Europa orientalis: Fs für Herbert Ludat zum 70. Geburtstag* (Berlin: Duncker & Humblot, 1980), pp. 490–532

'Verfassung und kollektives Verhalten: zur Mentalität des Erfolges falscher Herrscher im Reich des 13. und 14. Jahrhunderts', in F. Graus (ed.), *Mentalitäten im Mittelalter* (VuF 35, Sigmaringen, 1987), pp. 177–202

Scior, V., *Das Eigene und das Fremde: Identität und Fremdheit in den Chroniken Adams von Bremen, Helmolds von Bosau und Arnolds von Lübeck* (Berlin: Akademie, 2002)

Scott, J.A., *Dante's Political Purgatory* (Philadelphia: University of Pennsylvania Press, 1996)

Scott, T., 'Economic landscapes', in B. Scribner (ed.), *Germany: A New Social and Economic History*, vol. I *(1450–1630)* (London: Arnold, 1996), pp. 1–31

'Germany and the Empire', in C. Allmand (ed.), *NCMH*, vol. VII *(c.1415–c.1500)* (Cambridge University Press, 1998), pp. 337–66

Society and Economy in Germany, 1300–1600 (Basingstoke: Palgrave, 2002)

Scott, T. and Scribner, B., 'Urban networks', in B. Scribner (ed.), *Germany: A New Social and Economic History*, vol. I *(1450–1630)* (London: Arnold, 1996), pp. 113–43

See, K. von, *Deutsche Germanen-Ideologie vom Humanismus bis zur Gegenwart* (Frankfurt am Main: Athenäum, 1970)

Seeber, G., 'Von Barbarossa zu Barbablanca: Zu den Wandlungen des Bildes von der mittelalterlichen Kaiserpolitik im Deutschen Reich', in E. Engel and B. Töpfer (eds.), *Kaiser Friedrich Barbarossa: Landesausbau – Aspekte seiner Politik – Wirkung* (Weimar: Böhlau, 1994), pp. 205–20

Seeliger, G., 'Die Registerführung am deutschen Königshof bis 1493', *MIöG* Ergbd 3 (1890/94), 223–363

Segl, P., 'Die Feindbilder in der politischen Propaganda Friedrichs II. und seiner Gegner', in F. Bosbach (ed.), *Feindbilder: die Darstellung des Gegners in der politischen Publizistik des Mittelalters und der Neuzeit* (Cologne, Vienna and Weimar: Böhlau, 1992), pp. 41–71

Seibt, F., 'Die böhmische Nachbarschaft in der österreichischen Historiographie des 13. und 14. Jahrhunderts', in F. Seibt, *Mittelalter und Gegenwart: ausgewählte Aufsätze*, ed. W. Eberhard and H.-D. Heimann (Sigmaringen: Thorbecke, 1987), pp. 171–96

Hussitica: Zur Struktur einer Revolution (Cologne and Graz: Böhlau, 1965)

(ed.), *Kaiser Karl IV.: Staatsmann und Mäzen* (Munich: Prestel, 1978)

'Karl IV.', in J. Mötsch and F.-J. Heyen (eds.), *Balduin von Luxemburg, Erzbischof von Trier – Kurfürst des Reiches 1285–1354* (Mainz: Verlag der Gesellschaft für mittelrheinische Kirchengeschichte, 1985), pp. 89–102

Karl IV.: Ein Kaiser in Europa 1346 bis 1378 (Munich: Süddeutscher Verlag, 1978)

'Die Zeit der Luxemburger und der hussitischen Revolution', in K. Bosl (ed.), *Handbuch der Geschichte der böhmischen Länder*, vol. I (Stuttgart: Hiersemann, 1967), pp. 349–568

Selzer, S., *Deutsche Söldner im Italien des Trecento* (Tübingen: Niemeyer, 2001)

Seton-Watson, H., *Nations and States: An Enquiry into the Origins of Nations and the Politics of Nationalism* (London: Methuen, 1977)

Sherman, C.R., *The Portraits of Charles V of France (1338–1380)* (New York University Press, 1969)

Sherwin-White, A.N., *Racial Prejudice in Imperial Rome* (Cambridge University Press, 1970)

Sieber-Lehmann, C., *Spätmittelalterlicher Nationalismus: die Burgunderkriege am Oberrhein und in der Eidgenossenschaft* (Göttingen: Vandenhoeck & Ruprecht, 1995)

Silver, L., 'Forest primeval: Albrecht Altdorfer and the German wilderness landscape', *Simiolus* 13 (1983), 4–43

'Germanic patriotism in the age of Dürer', in D. Eichelberger and C. Zika (eds.), *Dürer and His Culture* (Cambridge University Press, 1998), pp. 38–68

Skinner, Q., 'Ambrogio Lorenzetti: the artist as political philosopher', *Proceedings of the British Academy* 72 (1986), 1–56

Šmahel, F., 'The idea of the "nation" in Hussite Bohemia', *Historica* 16 (1969), 143–247, and 17 (1970), 93–197

'Spectaculum et pompa funebris: das Leichenzeremoniell bei der Bestattung Kaiser Karls IV.', in F. Šmahel, *Zur politischen Präsentation und Allegorie im 14. und 15. Jahrhundert* (Munich: Oldenbourg, 1994), pp. 1–37

Smith, A.D., *Chosen Peoples: Sacred Sources of National Identity* (Oxford University Press, 2003)

The Ethnic Origins of Nations (Oxford: Blackwell, 1986)

'National identities: modern or medieval?', in Forde, Johnson and Murray (eds.), *Concepts of National Identity*, pp. 21–46

National Identity (Harmondsworth: Penguin, 1991)

Smits, K., '*Tiutsch* und *lant* in mittelhochdeutschen und mittelniederdeutschen Quellen vom Annolied bis in die zweite Hälfte des 13. Jahrhunderts', *Zeitschrift für deutsche Philologie* 96 (1977), 49–86

Sommer, K.P., 'Eine Frage der Perspektive? Hermann Heimpel und der Nationalsozialismus', in T. Kaiser, S. Kaudelka and M. Steinbach (eds.), *Historisches Denken und gesellschaftlicher Wandel: Studien zur Geschichtswissenschaft zwischen Kaiserreich und deutscher Zweistaatlichkeit* (Berlin: Metropol, 2004), pp. 199–223

Sommerlechner, A., *Stupor Mundi? Kaiser Friedrich II. und die mittelalterliche Geschichtsschreibung* (Vienna: Österreichische Akademie der Wissenschaften, 1999)

Southern, R.W., *Western Society and the Church in the Middle Ages* (Harmondsworth: Penguin, 1970)

Spiegel, G.M., *Romancing the Past: The Rise of Vernacular Prose Historiography in Thirteenth-Century France* (Berkeley, CA: University of California Press, 1993)

Spindler, M. (ed.), *Handbuch der bayerischen Geschichte*, vol. II (Munich: Beck, 1974)

Sprandel, R., 'Geschichtsschreiber in Deutschland 1347–1517', in F. Graus (ed.), *Mentalitäten im Mittelalter* (VuF 35, Sigmaringen, 1987), pp. 289–319

'Was wußte man im späten Mittelalter in Süddeutschland über Norddeutschland und umgekehrt? Studien zur Geschichtsschreibung 1347–1517', in Paravicini (ed.), *Nord und Süd*, pp. 219–30

Sproemberg, H., 'La naissance d'un État allemand au Moyen Âge', *Le Moyen Âge* 64 (1958), 213–48

Spufford, P., *Power and Profit: The Merchant in Medieval Europe* (London: Thames & Hudson, 2002)

Stadtwald, K., *Roman Popes and German Patriots: Antipapalism in the Politics of the German Humanist Movement from Gregor Heimburg to Martin Luther* (Geneva: Droz, 1996)

Standen, N., 'Nine case studies of premodern frontiers', in Power and Standen (eds.), *Frontiers in Question*, pp. 13–27

Steinbach, H., *Die Reichsgewalt und Niederdeutschland in nachstaufischer Zeit (1247–1308)* (Stuttgart: Klett, 1968)

Stelzer, W., 'Landesbewußtsein in den habsburgischen Ländern östlich des Arlbergs bis zum frühen 15. Jahrhundert', in Werner (ed.), *Spätmittelalterliches Landesbewußtsein*, pp. 157–222

Stengel, E.E., *Avignon und Rhens: Forschungen zur Geschichte des Kampfes um das Recht am Reich in der ersten Hälfte des 14. Jahrhunderts* (Weimar: Böhlau, 1930)

'Kaisertitel und Souveränitätsidee: Studien und Vorgeschichte des modernen Staatsbegriffs', in E.E. Stengel, *Abhandlungen und Untersuchungen zur Geschichte des Kaisergedankens im Mittelalter* (Cologne and Graz: Böhlau, 1965), pp. 250–301

'Regnum und Imperium: Engeres und weiteres Staatsgebiet im alten Reich', in E.E. Stengel, *Abhandlungen und Untersuchungen zur Geschichte des Kaisergedankens im Mittelalter* (Cologne and Graz: Böhlau, 1965), pp. 171–205

Stenzel, G.A.H., *Geschichte Deutschlands unter den Fränkischen Kaisern*, 2 vols. (Leipzig: Tauchnitz, 1827–28)

Stieda, W., 'Zur Sprachkenntnis der Hanseaten', *Hansische Geschichtsblätter* 11 (1885), 157–61

Stolleis, M., *Heiliges Römisches Reich deutscher Nation, Deutsches Reich, 'Drittes Reich'* – *Transformation und Destruktion einer politischen Idee* (Wetzlar: Gesellschaft für Reichskammergerichtsforschung, 2007)

Stoob, H., *Kaiser Karl IV. und seine Zeit* (Graz, Vienna and Cologne: Styria, 1990)

Strauss, G., 'The course of German history: the Lutheran interpretation', in G. Strauss, *Enacting the Reformation in Germany: Essays on Institution and Reception* (Aldershot: Variorum, 1993), pp. 665–86

Sixteenth-Century Germany: Its Topography and Topographers (Madison, WI: University of Wisconsin Press, 1959)

'The laicization of French and English society in the thirteenth century', *Speculum* 15 (1940), 76–86

Strayer, J.R., *The Albigensian Crusade* (New York: Dial Books, 1971)

'France: the Holy Land, the Chosen People, and the Most Christian King', in T.K. Rabb and J.E. Seigel (eds.), *Action and Conviction in Early Modern Europe: Essays in Memory of E.H. Harbison* (Princeton University Press, 1969), pp. 3–16

On the Medieval Origins of the Modern State (Princeton University Press, 1970)

The Reign of Philip the Fair (Princeton University Press, 1980)

Strickland, D.H., *Saracens, Demons and Jews: Making Monsters in Medieval Art* (Princeton, NJ and Oxford: Princeton University Press, 2003)

Stringer, K., 'Social and political communities in European history: some reflections on recent studies', in C. Bjørn, A. Grant and K.J. Stringer (eds.), *Nations, Nationalism and Patriotism in the European Past* (Copenhagen: Academic Press, 1994), pp. 9–34

Stromer, W. von, 'Nuremberg in the international economics of the Middle Ages', *Business History Review* 44 (1970), 210–21

Oberdeutsche Hochfinanz, 1350–1450, 3 vols. (Wiesbaden: Franz Steiner, 1970)

Struve, T., 'Die falschen Friedriche und die Friedenssehnsucht des Volkes im späten Mittelalter', in *Fälschungen im Mittelalter: internationaler Kongress der Monumenta Germaniae Historica, München, 16.–19. September 1986* (MGH Schriften 33.i, Hannover: Hahn, 1988), pp. 317–37

'Utopie und gesellschaftliche Wirklichkeit: zur Bedeutung des Friedenskaisers im späten Mittelalter', *HZ* 225 (1977), 65–95

Strzelczyk, J., 'Der Prozeß der Aktualisierung Polens und Osteuropas im Verständnis der gelehrten Kreise des 13. Jahrhunderts (mit besonderer Berücksichtigung der Otia imperialia des Gervasius von Tilbury und der Ebstorfer Weltkarte)', in H. Kugler (ed.), *Ein Weltbild vor Columbus: Die Ebstorfer Weltkarte: Interdisziplinäres Colloquium 1988* (Weinheim: VCH, 1991), pp. 146–66

'Die Wahrnehmung des Fremden im mittelalterlichen Polen', in O. Engels and P. Schreiner (eds.), *Die Begegnung des Westens mit dem Osten* (Sigmaringen: Thorbecke, 1993), pp. 203–20

Suchan, M., 'Die Hofkunst im 14. Jahrhundert', in Puhle and Hasse (eds.), *Heiliges Römisches Reich: Essays*, pp. 323–35

Die Hofkunst Kaiser Ludwigs des Bayern (Munich: Hirmer, 1993)

'Publizistik im Zeitalter Heinrichs IV. – Anfänge päpstlicher und kaiserlicher Propaganda im "Investiturstreit"?', in Hruza (ed.), *Propaganda*, pp. 29–45

'Zur Ikonografie der deutschen Herrscher des 14. Jahrhunderts: Rudolf I. – Ludwig IV. – Karl IV.', in Hohensee, Lawo, Lindner *et al.* (eds.), *Die Goldene Bulle*, vol. I, pp. 327–48

Suntrup, R., 'Der Gebrauch der Quellen in der Argumentation von "De libris teutonicalibus"', in N. Staubach (ed.), *Kirchenreform von unten: Gerhard Zerbolt von Zutphen und die Brüder vom gemeinsamen Leben* (Frankfurt am Main: Lang, 2004), pp. 264–76

Tersch, H., 'Die Darstellung der römischen Frühgeschichte in deutschsprachigen Chroniken des Spätmittelalters', *MIöG* 99 (1991), 23–68

Unruhe im Weltbild: Darstellung und Deutung des zeitgenössischen Lebens in deutschsprachigen Weltchroniken des Mittelalters (Vienna, Cologne and Weimar: Böhlau, 1996)

Thamer, H.-U., 'Mittelalterliche Reichs- und Königstraditionen in den Geschichtsbildern der NS-Zeit', in Kramp (ed.), *Krönungen*, vol. II, pp. 829–37

Thomas, A., *Anne's Bohemia: Czech Literature and Society, 1310–1420* (Minneapolis, MN: University of Minnesota Press, 1998)

'Czech-German relations as reflected in Old Czech literature', in Bartlett and MacKay (eds.), *Medieval Frontier Societies*, pp. 199–215

Thomas, H., 'Die Deutschen und die Rezeption ihres Volksnamens', in Paravicini (ed.), *Nord und Süd*, pp. 19–50

'Das Identitätsproblem der Deutschen im Mittelalter', *GWU* 43 (1992), 135–56

'Julius Caesar und die Deutschen: zu Ursprung und Gehalt eines deutschen Geschichtsbewußtseins in der Zeit Gregors VII. und Heinrichs IV.', in S. Weinfurter (ed.), *Die Salier und das Reich* (Sigmaringen: Thorbecke, 1992), vol. III, pp. 245–77

'Der Lohengrin: eine politische Dichtung der Zeit Ludwigs des Bayern', *RhVjbl* 37 (1973), 152–90

Ludwig der Bayer (1282–1347): Kaiser und Ketzer (Regensburg: Pustet, 1993)

'Nationale Elemente in der ritterlichen Welt des Mittelalters', in Ehlers (ed.), *Ansätze*, pp. 345–76

'Sprache und Nation: zur Geschichte des Wortes deutsch vom Ende des 11. bis zur Mitte des 15. Jahrhunderts', in A. Gardt (ed.), *Nation und Sprache: die Diskussion ihres Verhältnisses in Geschichte und Gegenwart* (Berlin and New York: De Gruyter, 2000), pp. 47–101

Studien zur Trierer Geschichtsschreibung des 11. Jahrhunderts, insbesonders zu den Gesta Treverorum (Bonn: Röhrscheid, 1968)

'Sur l'histoire du mot "Deutsch" depuis le milieu du XIIᵉ siècle jusq'à la fin du XIIIᵉ siècle', in Babel and Moeglin (eds.), *Identité régionale*, pp. 27–35

'Warum hat es im deutschen Mittelalter keine nationale Chroniken gegeben?', in D. Buschinger (ed.), *Chroniques nationales et chroniques universelles: actes du colloque d'Amiens 16–17 janvier 1988* (Göppingen: Kümmerle, 1990), pp. 165–82

Zwischen Regnum und Imperium: die Fürstentümer Bar und Lothringen zur Zeit Kaiser Karls IV. (Bonn: Röhrscheid, 1973)

Thomas, H.M., *The English and the Normans: Ethnic Hostility, Assimilation, and Identity 1066–c. 1220* (Oxford University Press, 2003)

Thompson, J.W., *Feudal Germany*, 2 vols. (University of Chicago Press, 1928)

Thum, B., 'Öffentlichkeit und Kommunikation im Mittelalter: zur Herstellung von Öffentlichkeit im Bezugsfeld elementarer Kommunikationsformen im 13. Jahrhundert', in H. Ragotzky and H. Wenzel (eds.), *Höfische Repräsentation: Das Zeremoniell und die Zeichen* (Tübingen: Niemeyer, 1990), pp. 65–87

'Öffentlich-Machen, Öffentlichkeit, Recht: zu den Grundlagen und Verfahren der politischen Publizistik im Spätmittelalter', *Zeitschrift für Literaturwissenschaft und Linguistik* 37 (1980), 12–69

Tilly, C., *Coercion, Capital and European States, AD 990–1990* (Cambridge, MA: Blackwell, 1990)

Tönnies, F., *Gemeinschaft und Gesellschaft* (Leipzig: Fues, 1887)

Töpfer, B., *Das kommende Reich des Friedens: zur Entwicklung chiliastischer Zukunftshoffnungen im Hochmittelalter* (Berlin: Akademie, 1964)

Trautz, F., 'Studien zur Geschichte und Würdigung König Adolfs von Nassau', *Geschichtliche Landeskunde* 2 (1965), 1–45

Treichler, W., *Mittelalterliche Erzählungen und Anekdoten um Rudolf von Habsburg* (Bern and Frankfurt am Main: Lang, 1971)

Treitschke, H. von, *Das deutsche Ordensland Preussen* (Leipzig: Insel, 1862)

Trusen, W., 'Rolandsäulen', in A. Erler and E. Kaufmann (eds.), *Handwörterbuch zur deutschen Rechtsgeschichte*, vol. IV (Berlin: Schmidt, 1990), cols. 1102–6

Tuck, A., 'Richard II and the house of Luxemburg', in A. Goodman and J. Gillespie (eds.), *Richard II: The Art of Kingship* (Oxford: Clarendon Press, 1999), pp. 205–29

Turville-Petre, T., *England the Nation: Language, Literature, and National Identity, 1290–1340* (Oxford: Clarendon Press, 1996)

Ubl, K., *Engelbert von Admont: ein Gelehrter im Spannungsfeld von Aristotelismus und christlicher Überlieferung* (Munich: Oldenbourg, 2000)

'Die Rechte des Kaisers in der Theorie deutscher Gelehrter des 14. Jahrhunderts (Engelbert von Admont, Lupold von Bebenburg, Konrad von Megenberg)', in C. Märtl, G. Drossbach and M. Kintzinger (eds.), *Konrad von Megenberg (1309–1374) und sein Werk: Das Wissen der Zeit* (Munich: Beck, 2006), pp. 353–87

Ullmann, W., 'The development of the medieval idea of sovereignty', *EHR* 64 (1949), 1–33

A History of Political Thought: The Middle Ages, rev. edn (Harmondsworth: Penguin, 1970)

Van Oostrom, F.P., *Court and Culture: Dutch Literature, 1350–1450*, trans. A.J. Pomerans (Berkeley, CA: University of California Press, 1992)

Vancsa, M., *Das erste Auftreten der deutschen Sprache in den Urkunden* (Leipzig: Hirzel, 1895)

Verbeek, A., 'Die architektonische Nachfolge der Aachener Pfalzkapelle', in Braunfels and Schramm (eds.), *Karl der Große*, vol. IV, pp. 113–56

Vick, B.E., *Defining Germany: The 1848 Frankfurt Parliamentarians and National Identity* (Cambridge, MA, and London: Harvard University Press, 2002)

Vigener, F., *Bezeichnungen für Volk und Land der Deutschen vom 10. bis zum 13. Jahrhundert* (Heidelberg: Winter, 1901)

Vogel, W., *Der Verbleib der wendischen Bevölkerung in der Mark Brandenburg* (Berlin: Duncker & Humblot, 1960)

Volk, O., 'Von Grenzen ungestört – auf dem Weg nach Aachen: die Krönungsfahrten der deutschen Könige im späten Mittelalter', in W. Haubrichs *et al.* (eds.), *Grenzen erkennen – Begrenzungen überwinden: Fs für Reinhard Schneider zur Vollendung seines 65. Lebensjahres* (Sigmaringen: Thorbecke, 1999), pp. 263–97

Voltmer, E., 'Der Rheinische Bund (1254–1256): eine neue Forschungsaufgabe?', in J. Mötsch and J. Dollwet (eds.), *Propter culturam pacis: der Rheinische Städtebund von 1254/56: Katalog zur Landesausstellung in Worms* (Koblenz: Landesarchivverwaltung Rheinland-Pfalz, 1986), pp. 117–43

Wackernagel, W., 'Die Spottnamen der Völker', *Zeitschrift für deutsches Altertum und deutsche Literatur* 6 (1848), 254–61

Wakounig, M., 'Von Přemysl Otakar II. bis zu Maximilian I. von Habsburg', in A. Suppan (ed.), *Zwischen Adria und Karawanken* (DGOE, Berlin: Siedler, 1998), pp. 65–86

Waley, D. and Denley, P., *Later Medieval Europe 1250–1520*, 3rd edn (Harlow: Longman, 2001)

Walser Smith, H., *The Continuities of German History: Nation, Religion, and Race Across the Long Nineteenth Century* (Cambridge University Press, 2008)

Walther, H., 'Scherz und Ernst in der Völker- und Stämme-Charakteristik mittellateinischer Verse', *AKuG* 41 (1959), 263–301

Walther, H.G., *Imperiales Königtum: Konziliarismus und Volkssouveränität* (Munich: Fink, 1976)

Warner, M., *Joan of Arc: The Image of Female Heroism* (London: Weidenfeld & Nicolson, 1981)

Waswo, R., 'Our ancestors, the Trojans: inventing cultural identity in the Middle Ages', *Exemplaria* 7 (1995), 269–90

Watt, J.A., 'Spiritual and temporal powers', in J.H. Burns (ed.), *The Cambridge History of Medieval Political Thought c.350–c.1450* (Cambridge University Press, 1988), pp. 367–423

The Theory of Papal Monarchy in the Thirteenth Century: The Contribution of the Canonists (London: Burns & Oates, 1965)

Watts, J., *The Making of Polities: Europe, 1300–1500* (Cambridge University Press, 2009)

Weiler, B., 'Image and reality in Richard of Cornwall's German career', *EHR* 113 (1998), 1111–42

'The *Negotium Terrae Sanctae* in the political discourse of Latin Christendom, 1215–1311', *International History Review* 25 (2003), 1–36

Weirich, H., 'Über das Königslager: ein Beitrag zur Verfassungsgeschichte des spätmittelalterlichen deutschen Reiches', *Deutsches Archiv für Geschichte des Mittelalters* 3 (1939), 211–35

Weisert, H., 'Der Reichstitel bis 1806', *Archiv für Diplomatik* 40 (1994), 441–513

Weiss, R., *The Renaissance Discovery of Classical Antiquity* (Oxford: Blackwell, 1969)

Weiß, S. (ed.), *Regnum et Imperium: die französisch-deutschen Beziehungen im 14. und 15. Jahrhundert / Les Relations franco-allemandes au XIVe et au XVe siècle* (Munich: Oldenbourg, 2008)

Wells, C.J., *German: A Linguistic History to 1945* (Oxford: Clarendon Press, 1985)

Wenskus, R., 'Der deutsche Orden und die nichtdeutsche Bevölkerung des Preußenlandes mit besonderer Berücksichtigung der Siedlung', in W. Schlesinger (ed.), *Die deutsche Ostsiedlung des Mittelalters als Problem der europäischen Geschichte* (VuF 18, Sigmaringen: Thorbecke, 1975), pp. 417–38

Stammesbildung und Verfassung: das Werden der frühmittelalterlichen Gentes (Cologne: Böhlau, 1961)

Wenzel, H., *Höfische Geschichte: literarische Tradition und Gegenwartsdeutung in den volkssprachigen Chroniken des hohen und späten Mittelalters* (Frankfurt am Main: Lang, 1980)

Werbow, S.N., '"Die gemeine Teutsch": Ausdruck und Begriff', *Zeitschrift für deutsche Philologie* 82 (1963), 44–63

Werminghoff, A., 'Zur Lehre von der Erbmonarchie im 14. Jahrhundert', *Historische Vierteljahrschrift* 20 (1920/21), 150–61

Werner, K.-F., 'Das hochmittelalterliche Imperium im politischen Bewußtsein Frankreichs (10.–12. Jahrhundert)', *HZ* 200 (1965), 2–60

'Les Nations et le sentiment national dans l'Europe médiévale', *Rh* 244 (1970), 285–304

'Völker und Regna', in Brühl and Schneidmüller (eds.), *Beiträge*, pp. 15–44

Werner, M., 'Mater Hassiae – flos Ungariae – gloria Teutoniae: Politik und Heiligenverehrung im Nachleben der hl. Elisabeth von Thüringen', in J. Petersohn (ed.), *Politik und Heiligenverehrung im Mittelalter* (VuF 42, Sigmaringen: Thorbecke, 1994), pp. 449–540

(ed.), *Spätmittelalterliches Landesbewußtsein in Deutschland* (VuF 61, Ostfildern: Thorbecke, 2005)

Werunsky, E., *Geschichte Kaiser Karls IV. und seiner Zeit*, 4 vols. (Innsbruck: Wagner, 1880–1892)

Wieruszowski, H., *Vom Imperium zum nationalen Königtum: vergleichende Studien über die publizistischen Kämpfe Kaiser Friedrichs II. und König Philipps des Schönen mit der Kurie* (Munich and Berlin: Oldenbourg, 1933)

Wiesinger, P., 'Regionale und überregionale Sprachausformung im Deutschen vom 12. bis 15. Jahrhundert unter dem Aspekt der Nationsbildung', in Ehlers (ed.), *Ansätze*, pp. 321–43

Wilhelm, F., 'Das Aufkommen der Idee eines deutschen Erbreiches', *MIöG Ergbd* 7 (1907), 1–19

Wilks, M., *The Problem of Sovereignty in the Later Middle Ages: The Papal Monarchy with Augustinus Triumphus and the Publicists* (Cambridge University Press, 1963)

Williamson, P., *Gothic Sculpture 1140–1300* (New Haven, CT and London: Yale University Press, 1995)

Willoweit, D., 'Die Entwicklung und Verwaltung der spätmittelalterlichen Landesherrschaft', in K.G.A. Jeserich, H. Pohl and G.-C. von Unruh (eds.), *Deutsche Verwaltungsgeschichte*, vol. I (Stuttgart: DVA, 1983), pp. 66–143

'Gericht und Urteil über den Wenden', in K. Kroeschell (ed.), *Fs für Hans Thieme zu seinem 80. Geburtstag* (Sigmaringen: Thorbecke, 1986), pp. 83–96

Winkler, H.A., *Der lange Weg nach Westen*, 2 vols. (Munich: Beck, 2000); English trans. as *Germany: The Long Road West*, trans. A.J. Sager, 2 vols. (Oxford University Press, 2006, 2007)

Wittneben, E.L., 'Lupold von Bebenburg und Wilhelm von Ockham im Dialog über die Rechte am Römischen Reich des Spätmittelalters', *DA* 53 (1997), 567–86

Wohlgemuth, H., *Das Urkundenwesen des deutschen Reichshofgerichts 1273–1378: eine kanzleigeschichtliche Studie* (Quellen und Forschungen zur höchsten Gerichtsbarkeit im alten Reich 1, Cologne and Graz: Böhlau, 1973)

Wolf, A., *Die Entstehung des Kurfürstenkollegs 1198–1298: zur 700-jährigen Wiederkehr der ersten Vereinigung der sieben Kurfürsten*, 2nd edn (Idstein: Schulz-Kirchner, 2000)

Litteris et Patriae: Das Janusgesicht der Historie (Stuttgart: Steiner, 1996)

'Seit wann spricht man von *Kurfürsten*? Eine begriffsgeschichtliche Untersuchung', in J. Dahlhaus and A. Kohnle (eds.), *Papstgeschichte und*

Landesgeschichte: Fs für Hermann Jakobs zum 65. Geburtstag (Cologne, Vienna and Weimar: Böhlau, 1995), pp. 401–35

Wolff, P., *Les origines linguistiques de l'Europe occidentale* (Paris: Hachette, 1970)

Wolfram, H., *History of the Goths*, 2nd edn (Berkeley, CA: University of California Press, 1988)

Wood, C.S., *Albrecht Altdorfer and the Origins of Landscape* (London: Reaktion, 1993)

Wood, C.T., 'Regnum Francie: a problem in Capetian administrative usage', *Traditio* 23 (1967), 117–47

Wood, D., *Clement VI: The Pontificate and Ideas of an Avignon Pope* (Cambridge University Press, 1989)

Wormald, P., '*Engla lond*: the making of an allegiance', *Journal of Historical Sociology* 7 (1994), 1–24

Wriedt, K., 'Die Annales Lubicenses und ihre Stellung in der Lübecker Geschichtsschreibung des 14. Jahrhunderts', *DA* 22 (1966), 556–86

Wubs-Mrozewicz, J., 'Interplay of identities: German settlers in late medieval Stockholm', *Scandinavian Journal of History* 29 (2004), 53–67

Wyss, R.L., 'Die neun Helden: eine ikonographische Studie', *Zeitschrift für Schweizerische Archäologie und Kunstgeschichte* 17 (1957), 73–106

Zatschek, H., *Das Volksbewußtsein: sein Werden im Spiegel der Geschichtsschreibung* (Brünn: Rohrer, 1936)

Zeller, G., 'Les rois de France candidats à l'Empire', *Rh* 173 (1934), 273–311

Zender, M., 'Die Verehrung des hl. Karl im Gebiet des mittelalterlichen Reiches', in Braunfels and Schramm (eds.), *Karl der Große*, vol. IV, pp. 100–12

Zernack, K., 'Deutschlands Ostgrenze', in A. Demandt (ed.), *Deutschlands Grenzen*, pp. 140–65

Zeumer, K., 'Die böhmische und die bayerische Kur im 13. Jahrhundert', *HZ* 94 (1905), 209–50

Heiliges römisches Reich deutscher Nation: eine Studie über den Reichstitel (Weimar: Hermann Böhlaus Nachfolger, 1910)

Zientara, B., 'Die deutschen Einwanderer in Polen vom 12. bis zum 14. Jahrhundert', in W. Schlesinger (ed.), *Die deutsche Ostsiedlung des Mittelalters als Problem der europäischen Geschichte* (VuF 18, Sigmaringen: Thorbecke, 1975), pp. 333–48

'Foreigners in Poland in the 10th–15th centuries: their role in the opinion of the Polish medieval community', *Acta Poloniae Historica* 29 (1974), 5–28

'Walloons in Silesia in the twelfth and thirteenth centuries', *Quaestiones Medii Aevi* 2 (1981), 127–50

Zimmer, O., *A Contested Nation: History, Memory and Nationalism in Switzerland, 1761–1891* (Cambridge University Press, 2003)

Zimmermann, H., 'Die deutsche Südostsiedlung im Mittelalter', in G. Schödl (ed.), *Deutsche Geschichte im Osten Europas: Land an der Donau* (Berlin: Siedler, 1995), pp. 21–88

Zimmermann, K.L., 'Die Beurteilung der Deutschen in der französischen Literatur des Mittelalters mit besonderer Berücksichtigung der chansons de geste', *Romanische Forschungen* 29 (1911), 222–316

Zmora, H., *State and Nobility in Early Modern Germany: The Knightly Feud in Franconia 1440–1567* (Cambridge University Press, 1997)

Zöllner, E., '1000 Jahre Österreich? Die Babenberger und ihre Epoche', in H. Dienst and G. Heiß (eds.), *Erich Zöllner, Probleme und Aufgaben der österreichischen Geschichtsforschung* (Munich: Oldenbourg, 1984), pp. 39–54

'Perioden der österreichischen Geschichte und Wandlungen des Österreichbegriffes bis zum Ende der Habsburgermonarchie', in H. Dienst and G. Heiß (eds.), *Erich Zöllner, Probleme und Aufgaben der österreichischen Geschichtsforschung* (Munich: Oldenbourg, 1984), pp. 55–86

Zorn, W., 'Deutsche und Undeutsche in der städtischen Rechtsordnung des Mittelalters in Ost-Mitteleuropa', *Zeitschrift für Ostforschung* 1 (1952), 182–94

Index

9 781107 460348